OXFORD WORLD'S CLASSICS

THE ANNALS

GAIUS (or Publius: the evidence is ambiguous) CORNELIUS TACITUS is widely regarded as the greatest of all Roman historians. We know relatively little about his life. He was born around AD 56, and is known to have engaged in the standard political career of a young Roman aristocrat, holding the offices of quaestor (in 81 or 82), praetor (in 88), and consul (in 97), along with a variety of other administrative and military posts, including (by 88) membership of the college of priests known as the *quindecimviri sacris faciundis*. He was governor of Asia (a province of the empire consisting of part of modern Turkey) 112–13. In a high-profile trial in 99–100 he and his friend Pliny the Younger successfully prosecuted Marius Priscus for corruption while governor of Africa. Tacitus probably lived beyond 117; but his precise date of death is unknown. He was betrothed in 77 to the daughter of Julius Agricola, later governor of Britain, and married her shortly afterwards: her name, however, is unknown.

Tacitus' writings include the *Agricola* and the *Germania*, both published in 98. The date of a third work, the *Dialogue on Orators*, is disputed; some have thought it his first work, but it may well post-date both the *Agricola* and the *Germania*. All three of these survive complete. His major works were the *Histories* (published around 109) and the *Annals* (published some time after 117); only about a third of the former and just over half of the latter survive.

J. C. YARDLEY has translated Livy's *The Dawn of the Roman Empire* (Books 31–40) and *Hannibal's War* (Books 21–30) for Oxford World's Classics, Justin for the American Philological Association's Classical Resources series, and Curtius Rufus for Penguin Classics. He is also the author of *Justin and Pompeius Trogus* (2003) and (with Waldemar Heckel) *Alexander the Great* (2004).

ANTHONY A. BARRETT was formerly Professor and Distinguished University Scholar at the University of British Columbia. He is currently studying Anglo-Saxon, Norse, and Celtic at Sidney Sussex College, Cambridge. His most recent books are *Livia: First Lady of Imperial Rome* (2002) and (as editor and contributor) *Lives of the Caesars* (2007).

OXFORD WORLD'S CLASSICS

*For over 100 years Oxford World's Classics have brought
readers closer to the world's great literature. Now with over 700
titles—from the 4,000-year-old myths of Mesopotamia to the
twentieth century's greatest novels—the series makes available
lesser-known as well as celebrated writing.*

*The pocket-sized hardbacks of the early years contained
introductions by Virginia Woolf, T. S. Eliot, Graham Greene,
and other literary figures which enriched the experience of reading.
Today the series is recognized for its fine scholarship and
reliability in texts that span world literature, drama and poetry,
religion, philosophy and politics. Each edition includes perceptive
commentary and essential background information to meet the
changing needs of readers.*

OXFORD WORLD'S CLASSICS

TACITUS

The Annals
The Reigns of Tiberius, Claudius, and Nero

Translated by
J. C. YARDLEY

With an Introduction and Notes by
ANTHONY A. BARRETT

OXFORD
UNIVERSITY PRESS

OXFORD
UNIVERSITY PRESS

Great Clarendon Street, Oxford ox2 6DP

Oxford University Press is a department of the University of Oxford.
It furthers the University's objective of excellence in research, scholarship,
and education by publishing worldwide in

Oxford New York

Auckland Cape Town Dar es Salaam Hong Kong Karachi
Kuala Lumpur Madrid Melbourne Mexico City Nairobi
New Delhi Shanghai Taipei Toronto

With offices in

Argentina Austria Brazil Chile Czech Republic France Greece
Guatemala Hungary Italy Japan Poland Portugal Singapore
South Korea Switzerland Thailand Turkey Ukraine Vietnam

Oxford is a registered trade mark of Oxford University Press
in the UK and in certain other countries

Published in the United States
by Oxford University Press Inc., New York

British Library Cataloguing in Publication Data

Data available

Library of Congress Cataloging in Publication Data

Data available

Typeset by Cepha Imaging Private Ltd., Bangalore, India
Printed in Great Britain
on acid-free paper by
Clays Ltd., St Ives plc.

ISBN 978-0-19-282421-9

CONTENTS

ABBREVIATIONS

CIL	*Corpus Inscriptionum Latinarum*
Josephus, *AJ*	Josephus, *Jewish Antiquities*
Livy, *Per.*	Livy, *Periochae*
Ovid, *Ex P.*	Ovid, *Epistulae ex Ponto*
Philo, *Leg.*	Philo, *Legatio ad Gaium*
Pliny, *NH*	Pliny the Elder, *Natural History*
Pliny, *Ep.*	Pliny the Younger, *Epistulae*
Plutarch, *Caes.*	Plutarch, *Caesar*
RG	*Res Gestae*
Seneca, *Contr.*	Seneca the Elder, *Controversiae*
Seneca, *Apoc.*	Seneca the Younger, *Apocolocyntosis*
Ep.	*Epistulae*
QN	*Quaestiones naturales*
Suetonius, *Aug.*	Suetonius, *Augustus*
Cal.	*Caligula*
Claud.	*Claudius*
Jul.	*The Deified Julius*
Tib.	*Tiberius*
Vesp.	*Vespasian*
Vit.	*Vitellius*
Tacitus, *Agr.*	Tacitus, *Agricola*
Ann.	*Annals*
Germ.	*Germania*
Hist.	*Histories*
Val. Max.	Valerius Maximus

INTRODUCTION

Tacitus' Life

THE life of ancient Rome's greatest historian, Publius Cornelius Tacitus, is known in broad outline, but many of the important details are either missing or contentious. Even his name is uncertain. The only surviving manuscript of the opening books of the *Annals*, the Medicean, dating to the ninth century AD and carrying considerable authority, calls him Publius, and that name has become more or less established by tradition. But Sidonius Apollonaris, a bishop and poet of considerable standing in the fifth century, creates an element of doubt, giving him the *praenomen* Gaius. A letter about Tacitus written by his good friend Pliny the Younger (*Ep.* 9.23) suggests very strongly that the two men came from the same general area. Pliny was a native of Como, in northern Italy. Tacitus may likewise have originated from the Gallic area of northern Italy or perhaps from the highly Romanized province of Gallia Narbonensis in what is now southern France. His forebears would at some point have received citizenship under the patronage of a now unknown Roman official with the distinguished *nomen* of 'Cornelius' who would have continued to be honoured in the names of the descendants of the newly enfranchised Italians (just as many 'Gallic' Italians bore Julius Caesar's *nomen* Julius). The final element of his name, the *cognomen* 'Tacitus', is not a common one, and it is very possible that the historian is the son of the Cornelius Tacitus, equestrian procurator (financial officer) of Gallia Belgica, mentioned by his friend's uncle, Pliny the Elder, in his encyclopaedic work, the *Historia Naturalis* (*NH* 7.76). If this identification is correct, it would make Tacitus a member of the equestrian class, in the rank below that of senator, and his entry into the Roman Senate would have marked him as a *novus homo*, a 'new man', who obtained access to that body despite having no senators in his family line.

A number of rules prescribed the age at which ambitious Romans could enter the various magistracies open to them. Since we know the dates when Tacitus assumed some of his offices (see below), we can be reasonably confident that he was born not long after AD 55 and would thus have come into the world just after Nero succeeded Claudius as emperor. Nero committed suicide in 68. Tacitus as a young boy could well have witnessed first-hand the crisis that then afflicted Italy and southern Gaul as a succession of military leaders vied to replace the last, discredited, member of the Julio-Claudian dynasty. The ultimate victory of Vespasian, emperor 69–79, brought a period of relative calm. It is during his reign that we have the first datable event of Tacitus' life. In 77 he married the daughter of Gnaeus Julius Agricola, soon to be appointed governor of Britain. We also know that he was able to go to Rome to begin a public career. We have some details of that career from his own writing. In a striking line of the *Histories*, he credits three emperors with his progress. He claims that his public life was 'begun by Vespasian, enhanced by Titus, and still further advanced by Domitian' (*Hist.* 1.1.3). Scholars supplement this statement with information derived from a marble funerary inscription that has long been known but only recently identified by the distinguished historian Géza Alföldy as almost certainly belonging to the tomb of Tacitus.[1] The inscription reveals that the deceased was a member of a board of ten, with responsibility for judging lawsuits. This was one of the standard minor magistracies, known as the 'vigintivirate', held by young men at the beginning of their public careers, presumably in Tacitus' case under Vespasian. The next office in the inscription is lost, but may well have been that of tribune (military officer) in a legion, a common form of service for young men ambitious for a public career. Tacitus says that his career was enhanced under Titus, which may mean that in about 81 he held the quaestorship. This office, open under Augustus to men in at least their twenty-fifth year and generally involving financial duties, was a key stage in a public career, since it gave the holder access to the Senate. The Rome inscription speaks of the deceased as having been 'quaestor of Augustus', a signal honour, since of the twenty quaestors elected only two had this special designation, being chosen personally by the emperor to represent him in the Senate during his absences. It would, in that case, have been very

---

[1] *CIL* VI.1574; see Géza Alföldy, 'Bricht der Schweigsame sein Schweigen? Eine Grabinschrift in Rom', *Mitteilungen des deutschen archäologischen Instituts, römische Abteilung*, 102 (1995), 251–68; A. R. Birley, 'The Life and Death of Cornelius Tacitus', *Historia*, 49 (2000), 230–47.

appropriate to acknowledge the special favour of Titus. The quaestorship was often followed by one of two offices, that of aedile, concerned mainly with municipal administration, or of tribune, appointed to protect the rights and interests of the plebeians. The inscription speaks of Tacitus having followed this second option. As the third element of imperial favour, Tacitus also says that he was advanced by Domitian. This is doubtless explained by a comment in the *Annals* that in 88 he obtained the praetorship (*Ann.* 11.11). Eighteen praetors were elected annually at this period, their duties relating to the administration of justice.

At the same time as he was praetor, Tacitus tells us, he was also a member of an important priestly college, the board of fifteen charged with supervising certain religious ceremonies (*quindecimvir sacris faciundis*), an important duty in 88, when Domitian chose to celebrate the Secular Games, one of the most important events in Rome's calendar. Between 89 and 93 Tacitus was absent from Rome, perhaps with some military responsibility or as governor of a minor province. His absence, at a time when Domitian's autocracy was at its most vicious, was propitious, since that period saw the execution of a number of important Romans. He seems to have returned to Rome by the autumn of 93, and was present there during the treason trials taking place in the city.[2] Whether he was absent for the next three years we have no way of telling, but in any case the situation was much improved for the senatorial order in general by the assassination in September 96 of Domitian, to be succeeded by Marcus Cocceius Nerva. Perhaps the elderly Nerva's most significant contribution to Roman history was his adoption in 97 of Marcus Ulpius Traianus, the future emperor Trajan, who would succeed Nerva in January 98 and usher in an era deemed by Gibbon, perhaps not totally without justification, as the happiest period of human history. The year 97 was also important for Tacitus personally, since towards the end of it he held the most senior administrative post available in Rome, the consulship, in accordance with the practice whereby the two consuls appointed initially in any year (*ordinarii*) would assume office on 1 January but often step down and be succeeded by 'suffect' consuls. The consulship was open to men aged 42 and older unless

---

[2] We know this from the *Agricola*, which contains useful incidental biographical information on Tacitus.

they had ex-consuls in their family line, which made it available from a much earlier age, possibly 32. As consul, Tacitus delivered the oration at the funeral of the highly regarded Lucius Verginius Rufus (Pliny, *Ep.* 2.1).

There would have been several options open for Tacitus after his consulship but we have no record of any immediate office. We do know that, along with Pliny the Younger, he represented the province of Africa against its former governor Marius Priscus on a charge of extortion in a case that began in early 99 and ended in January 100 (Pliny, *Ep.* 2.11). Pliny opened, speaking for five hours. Tacitus did the summing up, and Pliny testifies to his impressive and persuasive eloquence. They were successful, and Cornutus Tertullus, the consul-designate for the following year, spoke before the Senate of their commendable performance.

Pliny is our richest source of information on Tacitus' character and personality. He wrote eleven letters to Tacitus, and mentions him in three more. Their tone is intimate, and Pliny speaks warmly of their close friendship, expressing pleasure that their names will forever be linked through their writings (*Ep.* 9.14). He is especially taken by an anecdote that Tacitus told him, of how a stranger asked Tacitus his identity, and when the reply was, 'Surely you know me from my writing', the stranger wanted to know if he was Tacitus or Pliny (*Ep.* 9.23). Pliny also says he desires immortality by the inclusion of one of his cases in Tacitus' history, which he believes, presciently, will be eternal, although this proved not to be true of Pliny's case, if it was ever included (*Ep.* 7.33). He receives a speech sent to him by Tacitus for criticism (*Ep.* 8.7), but concedes his friend's superiority as an orator (*Ep.* 7.20). In one letter Pliny gives his view of the right length for speeches, long and full rather than brief, but he tellingly says that his mind could be changed by Tacitus (*Ep.* 1.20). Pliny seeks his friend's assistance in finding teachers for a school he is attempting to fund at Comum, his birthplace (*Ep.* 4.13). He agrees to support a young candidate for office as a favour to Tacitus (*Ep.* 6.9). There is also a good deal of light banter. Pliny laments that he cannot do serious work when relaxing in the country (*Ep.* 9.10), but he also reports that when he went on a hunting trip he took his writing materials with him, for which he expects to be teased (*Ep.* 1.6). Other letters show Pliny communicating with Tacitus as a historian. In two, he responds to requests for detailed accounts of the eruption of Vesuvius, during which his uncle, the Elder Pliny, lost his life (*Ep.* 6.16, 20).

Tacitus was absent from Rome in 104 and 105 (Pliny, *Ep.* 4.13). He may have held some administrative post in a province, but we have no way of knowing. Beyond his joint prosecution of Marius Priscus, there is only one further public service recorded after the consulship, in an inscription from the province of Asia when Tacitus was governor there, probably 112/13.[3] The proconsulship of Asia was generally regarded, with Africa, as one of the twin pinnacles of the senatorial career. It has been suggested that this tenure of office in Asia explains Tacitus' great interest in events in that province. No further office is known. Nor do we know the date of Tacitus' death. He almost certainly survived Trajan. But how long he survived into Hadrian's reign is far from certain. At best we can perhaps say that he died between 117 and 130.

Previous Historians

The earliest Roman history in any form approaching the modern concept of history can be dated to the end of the third century BC, when Quintus Fabius Pictor, a patrician member of the Senate, produced a history written in Greek, a work that foreshadowed successive histories by placing stress on Roman character as an important element in Rome's worldly success. Further histories were written in Greek, but by the second century the tradition was established of history written in Latin. The celebrated man of firmness, Marcus Porcius Cato, censor (magistrate in charge of public morality, among other things) in 184 BC, wrote a history of Rome in Latin in seven books. Its early part, to which the generic title of *Origines* most properly belongs, dealt with the origins of Rome and other cities of Italy. By Book 4 he had reached the First Punic War (264–241) and in the final book he included contemporary events, right down to the year of his death (149). His work has survived only in fragments, but their pervasive attitude is one of a deep conservatism, a trait that would be found in subsequent historians. There was much historical activity in the years following Cato's death, but Cicero could still write disparagingly in 55 BC in his work 'On the Orator' (*De Oratore* 2.52)

---

[3] *L'Année Epigraphique*, 180.110 (Mylasa).

that the earlier Roman histories were no more than an 'annalistic confection'. If Cicero's comment was justified at the time, however, the situation was very soon rectified by the publication of the first two works of Roman history written in Latin to have survived, Caesar's *Civil War (Bellum Civile)* and *Gallic War (Bellum Gallicum)*. These are composed in brilliant, uncluttered narrative, meant at least in part to serve a purpose beyond pure historical exposition, that of justifying Caesar in the action he took against not only his foreign enemies, but also his political foes. Moreover, as if further to counter the slur on Roman historiography, shortly after Caesar's death in 44 Sallust undertook his *Catilina*, a masterly account of the notorious conspiracy of 63 BC headed by a disaffected member of the nobility, Lucius Sergius Catilina. It is suffused by the notion of the role that *virtus* plays in human affairs, and particularly in the political decline that occurred in Rome in the decades down to Catiline. Sallust's descriptions of aristocratic behaviour show him to be deeply troubled by the moral decadence of Rome and of the old Roman aristocracy, whose degeneracy he paints in the blackest colours. Sallust's next work, the *Jugurtha*, focuses more on military narrative. But here, too, he dwells upon the feebleness of the Senate and of the aristocracy. He reverted to the themes of moral decline in his final work, the annalistic *Histories*, which has survived only in fragments. Sallust is considered to have had a considerable influence on Tacitus, in his Latin style and in his view of history as a demonstration of social disintegration.

Perhaps second only to Tacitus in stature as a Roman historian is Livy, who began his magisterial work on Roman history about AD 27. The work covered an enormous time-span, from the founding of Rome—hence its title *Ab Urbe Condita*—down to the death of Drusus, son of Livia, in 9 BC. Thirty-five books survive of the 142 Livy wrote. It could perhaps be argued that the very scale of Livy's history precluded any deep analysis of sources, and by and large he seems to have been satisfied simply to draw on previous authorities. Livy was undoubtedly a great stylist, praised for his 'milky richness' (*lactea ubertas*) as Quintilian described it in his great work on oratory, the *Institutio Oratoria*, but Livy cannot claim an important place in the development of historiography, and Quintilian concedes that Sallust was the greater historian.

In its structure, Livy's history was annalistic, meaning that its narrative was organized on a year-by-year basis. This method was by no means Livy's innovation. It is difficult to say when annalistic Roman history was first written. It may not have been before the mid-second century BC in a meaningful sense, but certainly an influential landmark seems to have been reached in that period with the composition of *annales maximi* by Publius Mucius Scaevola, the chief priest (*Pontifex Maximus*), in eighty books, from Rome's origins to his own day. In this work Scaevola set out formally on a year-by-year basis the chief business of the state, military, civil, and religious. In fact, an annalistic structure made much sense for republican history, since the change of consul would have major impact on the affairs of the state.

Of the historians between Livy and Tacitus, only Velleius Paterculus has survived in substance. Born in about 19 BC, of equestrian stock, Velleius pursued a military career, before moving through the senatorial ranks to the praetorship in AD 16. His *Historiae Romanae* is a compendium of Roman history from the legendary past, as far back as the Trojan War, down to AD 30. The earlier parts are missing and must have been summary indeed. He becomes more detailed as he reaches his own day, focusing very much on the figure of Tiberius. His esteem for his old commander has won him many detractors, but it is only fair to note that his coverage of Rome's second emperor, which contrasts with the darker picture given by Tacitus, is limited to Tiberius' successful period as a military commander and to the earlier part of his reign, before things started to go awry.

The Annals

On Nerva's accession, Tacitus pondered the idea of an account of the grim period of Domitian that had preceded it, but in 97–8, when he was in his early forties, he opted to write first a shorter piece, inspired by affection, the *Agricola*. This was intended to record the career of his father-in-law, Gnaeus Julius Agricola, who died in 93 (*Agr.* 3) and in keeping with the traditions of ancient biography it is something of a eulogy of its subject. Agricola's reputation was based largely on his governorship of Britain and much of the work is devoted to those seven years. But the book is also an attack on

Domitian, whose repressive regime may well have coloured Tacitus' general views on the principate. He records how Domitian spitefully held back Agricola, and at the beginning of the *Agricola* he speaks of the problems of recovering his voice after fifteen years of forced silence. But for all that, there is no evidence that Tacitus or his career suffered under Domitian; in fact, that career may have flourished. As noted above, Tacitus credits the emperor in the *Histories* for his personal advancement.

Already in the *Agricola* Tacitus was beginning to manifest his distinctive Latin style, and this would reach its fullest expression later, in the *Annals*. That style is in many ways remarkable, and perhaps no other ancient writer has imposed his mark so distinctively on the language. Tacitean Latin is always recognizable as such. Like Sallust, Tacitus rejected Ciceronian verbosity in favour of pointed concision and trenchant epigrams. Moreover, in both vocabulary and syntax, he showed a penchant for the unusual and the striking. He went out of his way to use words that were poetic and archaic. It might be argued that archaisms were intended to evoke an earlier, perhaps purer, age but much of the time it seems that he was intent on producing a startling effect. In this also he was perhaps a disciple of Sallust, who was reputed to have hired an assistant to scour Cato for archaisms that he could use.

The *Agricola* was followed soon after by the *Germania*, an ethnographic study of the peoples of Germany, contrasting their simple integrity with the decaying morals of Rome of Tacitus' own time. It is also seen by some scholars as a missive to Trajan about the enormous danger to Rome posed by the Germans, whom Domitian claimed to have subdued, with more triumphs than victories as Tacitus worded it (*Germ.* 37). If so, it missed its mark, since Trajan preferred to maintain the Domitianic myth, and placed his military focus on Dacia and the Danube frontier then turned to Parthia. The *Germania* may have been followed by the *Dialogus de Oratoribus* (*Dialogue on Orators*), on the familiar theme of the decline of the standards of oratory. This work pretends to reflect a discussion that Tacitus had heard in the year 75. It lacks much of the distinctiveness of Tacitus' style, and some have argued that it should be placed early in Tacitus' career or that it was not written by him at all. The broad consensus of modern scholars, however, is that the work is by Tacitus, probably written after the *Germania*.

If Tacitus did indeed write the *Dialogus* just after the turn of the century, he may already have been working on the great historical survey adumbrated in the *Agricola* (*Agr.* 3.3). At some point Pliny sent Tacitus an account (*Ep.* 6.16) of the eruption of Vesuvius in August 79, to assist in a historical work Tacitus was then writing. This work must clearly have been the *Histories*. It takes its beginning from the point when the consuls took up office, on 1 January 69, while the latter half of 68 after the death of Nero is covered in a brief retrospective. This arrangement is testimony to Tacitus' strong commitment to the 'annalistic' format of his great historical works, where events are generally followed in sequence through the course of the year. The exception is that in the *Annals* events on the frontiers, in areas like Britain and the Parthian empire, are grouped in small clusters of years, in violation of the annalistic scheme, a diversion that is sometimes, though not invariably, signalled by Tacitus himself (6.38, 12.40, 13.9). The *Histories* ended with the death of Domitian in 96. We know from Pliny that Tacitus was writing this work in 106/7 and that Pliny was convinced that it would be immortal (*Ep.* 7.33.1).

In the preface to the *Histories*, Tacitus declared it as his intention, when he had finished the task in hand, to go back to the happier times under Nerva and Trajan (*Hist.* 1.1.4). He seems, however, to have abandoned this plan and in his most celebrated work, the *Annals*, went back to the death of Augustus to write the history of the succeeding emperors to the death of Nero (AD 14–68). We do not know when he began this, but we do have an indication that he was already well into the work in 116, since his reference to the Euphrates at *Ann.* 4.5 suggests that he wrote this section after Trajan's final defeat of the Parthians, which belongs to that year. Together, the *Histories* and *Annals* made up thirty books, but there is no agreement on how they were divided.[4] Traditionally, sixteen are assigned to the *Annals*, fourteen to the *Histories*, although some scholars assign two more to the *Annals*, arguing for a hexadic structure, with six books allotted to Tiberius, six to Caligula and Claudius, and the same number to Nero. Of the thirty books referred to by St Jerome, some half have survived, the first five books of the *Histories* down to AD 70 (the last in a fragmentary state), Books 1–6 of the *Annals* (Book 5 being very

---

[4] St Jerome, the famous scholar and teacher of the late fourth and early fifth century, provides the information that there were thirty books.

fragmentary) covering the reign of Tiberius, and Books 11–16 (the first and last books in this final grouping are not complete) beginning midway through Claudius' reign and breaking off two years before the end of Nero's. We cannot even be sure that Tacitus had finished the *Annals* before his death.

Tacitus' method seems now to have undergone something of a modification. He discards the long Preface employed in the *Histories*, beginning the *Annals* with a very short prefatory comment on Rome's earlier history and with the briefest of programmatic statements, namely that he will say a few words about Augustus, then cover Tiberius and the rest (*Ann.* 1.1). Elsewhere, he reveals that it was his intention, should he have time later, to write the history of Augustus (see *Ann.* 3.24). He did not cover this reign in detail in the *Annals*, perhaps because he thought that the accession of Tiberius was of such great symbolic importance in marking the point where the personal autocracy of Augustus became the institutionalized autocracy of Rome. It is also noteworthy that in this later work he feels somewhat freed from the annalistic shadow, through not obliging himself to begin with the consuls of AD 15. The transition of power from Augustus to Tiberius is more crucial than blind adherence to strict annalistic procedure.

Tacitus' views as a historian are patent in the *Annals*. He was deeply opposed to the principate as a constitutional form, and committed to the republican system of senatorial government. This is not to say that he could not recognize the benefits brought to Rome by the relatively enlightened reigns of Nerva and Trajan, but it was a system that was bound to have a corrosive effect on the ruled, if not necessarily on the ruler. We should be careful of Tacitus' famous claim to write *sine ira et studio,* 'without rancour or bias' (*Ann.* 1.1), an echo of the claim made in the *Histories*, 'without partiality and without hatred' (*Hist.* 1.1). It is indeed the case that in only a very few instances do we need to feel that he has presented facts with deliberate dishonesty. But behind the 'facts' lurk his own prejudices. His ascription of motives, and his reporting of rumours and supposedly widely held beliefs, have an inevitable impact on the reader. Ironically, Tacitus seems to have flourished under the imperial system, even under the despised and despotic Domitian, and his consulship and his governorship of Asia show him in many ways to have been a 'company man'. The antipathy towards the system that emerges from the *Annals* is thus all the more surprising. It was a system under which he seems to have done so well.

There is general agreement that the great masterpiece of the *Annals* is the account of Tiberius, who is depicted as a deeply complex and fundamentally deceptive individual. His natural shyness is characterized as arrogance, his acts of generosity as hypocritical. To some degree the apparently unique fullness and complexity of Tiberius' portrait may be accidental. No reign has survived intact, but a smaller portion of Tiberius is missing than of any other emperor and, importantly, only in his case do we have both the beginning and the end (almost all of Book 5 and the beginning of Book 6 are lost, so we have a gap of about two years between AD 29 and 31). In a sense, it can be said that the tone is set in the preliminary chapters, when Augustus seductively and hypocritically strips the Romans of their political independence. Tacitus concedes that under Augustus there was 'no fear for the moment' (1.4) and in the reported discussions that attended his funeral many pointed to the great benefits of the Augustan age and the limited use that Augustus had made of force (1.9). But Augustus had established a system that was inherently corrupt, and Tacitus' great achievement was to trace the degradation of Roman politics through the course of Tiberius' reign, to show that his character and personality were unable to withstand this debasing force of the imperial system. Few rulers provide as powerful an object lesson of the truth of Lord Acton's much repeated sententia about the corrupting effect of absolute power.

In his obituary of the emperor at the end of Book 6, Tacitus divides Tiberius' life into various phases. He excelled as a private individual, and as a military commander, under Augustus. The first part of his reign, down to about AD 22, was in many respects positive. He at least put on a show of virtue while his natural and adopted sons, Drusus and Germanicus, were alive. He then went into a phase of mixed good and evil during the lifetime of his mother Livia. We thus see his character evolve in his relationship with other people who seemed to exercise some restraint over him.

This early phase is covered in the first three books, which form a triad, balancing the second triad, Books 4–6, which covers the disastrous second half of the reign, when Tiberius slips into an ever more despicable despotism. The division is distinctly marked at the beginning of Book 4, where we learn that in this year (AD 23) a change for the worse occurred, the cause being the evil effect of Sejanus. In 26 Sejanus persuaded Tiberius to leave Rome, ultimately for the island of Capri. The loss of much of Book 5 is most unfortunate, since it would have traced the growth of Sejanus' power, leading to the pinnacle of his success, when he joined Tiberius as a colleague in the consulship in January 31. We also lose the fall of Sejanus in October of that year. Under the influence of Sejanus, Tiberius lapsed into savagery, although he kept his lusts concealed. Finally, freed of him, Tiberius rushed headlong into crime and scandal, as he became increasingly bitter and distrustful. In this final phase we realize that, ironically, Sejanus had exercised a restraining influence of sorts.

After Book 6, the loss of Books 7–10, and the first part of 11, means that the entire account of Caligula (37–41) is missing. Scattered references to that emperor from elsewhere in the *Annals*, alluding to his 'monstrous personality' (6.20) or 'disturbed mind' (13.3), leave no doubt that Tacitus would have been hostile. In their broad structure, the books that treat the reigns of Claudius and of Nero after him follow the same pattern as those of the first half of the extant *Annals*. They exhibit the same mixture of military and domestic affairs, and within the latter domestic context the same blend of relations between the emperor and the Senate, and the emperor and his family (and close advisers). We are missing roughly half of Claudius' reign, down to mid-47. Whether the early lost books presented a more sympathetic Claudius we cannot, in their absence, know. When the narrative resumes, the emphasis has begun to fall on the efforts of those in the court to manipulate the emperor, namely his freedmen and his wives. In the Tiberian books, by contrast, while Livia is a powerful figure, her role is played out largely in the background. Women like Messalina and Agrippina the Younger take centre stage in the Claudian period. And while Tiberius was swayed by a Sallustius or a Sejanus, under Claudius it is freedmen like Narcissus and Pallas who seem to be shaping 'policy'. As a consequence, Claudius does not have the forceful and dominant role of Tiberius.

The last four extant books of the *Annals* cover all but the last two years of Nero's reign. At one level, the beginning of the reign seems promising, as Nero is guided by Seneca and Burrus, and seeks to rule prudently and generously, deferring to the Senate. But Nero, like

Tiberius, had come to power through a mother's machinations and, ominously, the beginning of his reign, like that of Tiberius', is marked by murder. Very soon the narrative changes to the theme of sexual indulgence, cruelty, and self-degradation on the stage. The extant *Annals* break off in the midst of a reign of terror against the senators. Thus, while we may discern the same theme of the corruption of power as we did during Tiberius' reign, Nero is in fact treated quite differently. Both Nero and Tiberius are amoral tyrants who cause fear and dread in their subjects. But Tiberius had once been a great man, and had he not become emperor that greatness would probably have survived intact. His flaws did not become apparent until he assumed power, when his character did not have the strength to resist the corrupting forces of the system devised by Augustus. Nero was merely despicable, lacking any redeeming qualities. There is also a subtle change in technique observable from the earlier to the later books. The focus moves somewhat from the personality of the emperor and his direct impact on events to colourful set-pieces that are recognized as superb examples of dramatic narrative: the marriage of Messalina and Silius, the murder of Agrippina, the fire of Rome. The Pisonian conspiracy is given an extended narrative treatment missing in any of the other treason accounts of Tiberius' reign. Thus there is in the latter part of the extant *Annals* a dramatic tension and literary art that is generally not found in the earlier books.

Tacitus' Use of Sources

There is no general agreement on the use that Tacitus made of documentary evidence. Although for the modern historian primary evidence is supreme, and the modern historian will feel obliged, wherever possible, to consult primary archives, there was no such zeal among ancient historians, who saw their role as much more that of improving on the work of their predecessors. Tacitus does on occasion use direct oral evidence. At *Ann.* 3.16, he reports being told by older men how Gnaeus Cornelius Piso was often seen carrying a document (it supposedly held secret instructions from Tiberius against Germanicus) and also hearing from his elders the otherwise incredible account of what happened at the wedding of Messalina and Gaius Silius (*Ann.* 11.27).

The evidence for Tacitus' use of archival as opposed to oral information is far from clear-cut. To a degree the problem is the shadowy nature of some of this archival evidence. That is certainly the case of the daily record, the *acta diurna*. Its contents are a matter of considerable speculation, but, usefully for the historians of the period, it would doubtless have contained much information on the activities of the imperial family. Tacitus refers to his use of it on a number of occasions (*Ann.* 3.3, 13.31, 16.22), commenting on one occasion (13.31) on the trivial nature of its contents. We are on somewhat surer ground with the deliberations of the Senate, recorded in the *acta senatus*. We know that when the actual senatorial decrees (*consulta*) had been passed copies of their texts were deposited in the treasury, and it is likely that the same happened to general proceedings, the *acta*, although we do not know how detailed the reports might have been. Scholars like Ronald Syme have argued that Tacitus' achievements as a historian can be attributed to a large degree to his extensive use of senatorial records. Many of the details preserved in the *Annals*, such as the motions and the counterproposals with names attached to them, suggest a familiarity with such material, but whether they come from direct personal consultation or through an intermediary cannot be determined. There is, however, only one instance of Tacitus' referring to his own direct consultation of the records, at *Ann.* 15.74, where he says that he finds in the records of the Senate (*commentarii senatus*) that the consul-designate Cerialis Anicius proposed a temple to the deified Nero.

Recently discovered decrees have allowed us to make a comparison between Tacitus and the primary evidence. The decree passed by the Senate on 10 December following the trial of Piso on the charge of murdering Germanicus (the *senatus consultum de Cn. Pisone Patre*) in AD 20 is now known to us from fragments discovered in Spain since the 1980s, arguably the most important Latin epigraphic discovery of the twentieth century. It has offered an excellent opportunity to test Tacitus' account of the trial and its aftermath. It does indicate that he had drawn considerably on the senatorial decree and in many respects represents it faithfully, for instance in the acknowledgement that the decision to stay proceedings against Plancina, Piso's wife, came about through the intervention of Livia. But while it is undisputed that his account does ultimately derive from the decree, we once again cannot be sure if he examined it in person. Of course, we know that in the case of this decree copies were made on bronze and posted throughout the empire, so even a close familiarity with the text does not mean that the original *acta* were consulted. A somewhat different story is told by another document known to us from Spanish discoveries, the *Tabula Siarensis*, recreated from bronze fragments found in 1982 in the Spanish town of Siara, supplementing an inscription already known since 1947 from the town of Heba in Etruria (the *Tabula Hebana*). These list the honours approved by the Senate for the late Germanicus towards the end of AD 19. Tacitus clearly had access to the decree, but because it suited his agenda to create the impression that Germanicus was wronged, even after death, he chooses to present the information in such a way as to create a distinctly negative impression of Tiberius (and his mother). He asserts that they were absent from the ceremonies that took place in Rome to mark the death, and that even Germanicus' mother Antonia did not take part (under pressure from Tiberius and Livia, he claims). But the extant record of the honours shows that Tiberius was actively involved in selecting tributes for Germanicus, and consulted Antonia and Livia among others. Tacitus comments on the public displeasure that Germanicus received only modest funerary ceremonies in Rome (*Ann.* 2.83, 3.3–5). But the *Tabula* records a mass of honours. To highlight only one example, Tacitus notes that there were complaints at the absence of eulogies. But the *Tabula* records that eulogies were in fact delivered in the Senate, and by none other than Tiberius himself (along with his son Drusus). Thus Tacitus' knowledge of primary evidence is no guarantee that he will faithfully replicate it.

When it came to recording the spoken word, we do know that Tacitus exercised the privilege claimed by Greek and Roman writers to rewrite speeches rather than reproduce the originals. This is nicely illustrated by Claudius' speech on the introduction of the Gauls into the Roman Senate, where we can compare Tacitus' version (*Ann.* 11.24) with the record of the actual speech, substantially preserved in bronze panels at Lyons,[5] to which Tacitus would almost certainly have had direct access, should he have chosen to avail himself of it. It is hard to conclude that he did not make use of the original speech since there are so many points in common. That said,

---

[5] H. Dessau, *Inscriptiones Latinae d Selectae* (1892–1916), 212.

his version is barely even a loose paraphrase of the original. Clearly the historian saw it as his role to capture the spirit of the occasion rather than to present a documentary record of it.

Similarly, it was not the general practice of ancient historians to identify their secondary sources. Tacitus rarely mentions his sources by name. He will more often refer vaguely to *scriptores* (writers) or even more vaguely to such groups as *quidam* ('certain people'; see 1.29, 2.40), and when he does on the rare occasion mention a source by name it is often on issues that are, surprisingly, not of great political or historical importance. His main motive seems not to be to establish the integrity of a statement on a weighty matter, but rather to engage in a form of one-upmanship with his predecessors. Sometimes he makes use of speeches and private memoirs. He cites the journals of the great commander Corbulo about the state of the Parthian and Roman forces when the latter were blockaded in Armenia (15.16). When he cites the memoirs of Agrippina the Younger for evidence that her mother sought permission from Tiberius to remarry (*Ann.* 4.53), he proudly asserts that the information had not been noted by the *scriptores annalium*. He refers to Tiberius' speeches on two occasions (1.81, 2.63), and once quotes one of his letters (6.6), accurately, we can surmise, since it reappears almost verbatim in Suetonius (*Tib.* 67.1).

For the later parts of the *Annals* Tacitus would have used writers close to his own period. One of these is familiar to modern readers. Pliny the Elder, uncle of Tacitus' friend Pliny the Younger, was a man of equestrian rank who held a number of procuratorships under Vespasian and ended up as commander of the fleet at Misenum in Campania. As noted earlier, he died during the eruption of Vesuvius in 79. The elder Pliny was a prolific writer, who wrote a history of the *Bella Germaniae* (*The German Wars*) in twenty books, to which Tacitus refers. In the story of Agrippina's famous stance at the surviving bridge over the Rhine as she welcomed the retreating Roman troops, Tacitus cites that work (*Ann.* 1.69). Pliny also wrote an annalistic history in thirty-one books, totally lost, which Tacitus would almost certainly have used, since we know he did draw on Pliny's encyclopedic *Historia Naturalis* for general historical information, for instance in the description of Agrippina presiding at the Fucine lake in a golden cloak (12.56; Pliny, *NH* 33.63; see also Dio 60.33.3).

Other Tacitean sources are little more than names. Cluvius Rufus is thought to have been a suffect consul under Caligula. He performed as the herald of Nero for his performances in Rome, and was assigned the same responsibility when Nero went on his Greek tour in 67 (Suetonius, *Nero* 21.2; Dio 63.14.3). His history may have covered the reigns of Claudius and Nero and some have seen him as Tacitus' main source for that section of the *Annals*. All Tacitus' references to him relate to the reign of Nero, although Syme argues that he might have been used in the lost Caligulan or Claudian chapters. Another historian mentioned by name is Fabius Rusticus, whom Tacitus describes as the most eloquent of the moderns, as Livy was of the ancients. Fabius published a history in AD 83/4, but we do not know where it began or ended. Some have suggested that he might have continued a history written by Seneca the Elder.

There is no general agreement on how widely Tacitus consulted these secondary sources. One school of thought is that he tends to rely on a single authority, the other, a view promoted by Syme, is that he would weigh up a number of different sources and then reach an independent opinion. They are rarely named. At *Ann.* 14.2 he balances the claims of Fabius Rusticus and Cluvius Rufus (supported by other unnamed authorities) about whether it was Nero or his mother Agrippina who initiated their incestuous relationship, and at *Ann.* 13.20 he cites these two along with the elder Pliny on the issue of whether Nero questioned Burrus' loyalty in AD 55. Fabius Rusticus is cited as the sole authority for the claim that Gavius Silvanus, the praetorian tribune charged with issuing the death writ to Seneca in 65, sought the clearance of the praetorian prefect before going ahead (*Ann.* 15.61), while Pliny's claim that Antonia, Claudius' daughter, lent her weight to the Pisonian conspiracy is treated with considerable scepticism (15.53). The relationship between Tacitus and our other two important sources for the Julio–Claudian period is far from settled. Tacitus and Suetonius are generally thought to be independent of each other, despite a number of similarities. The case that Dio made use of Tacitus is perhaps somewhat stronger, but it is also possible that all three writers drew on independent sources that are now lost.

Afterlife

For all the acclaim garnered by Tacitus' works in their day from an individual like Pliny, their survival owes as much to chance as to their perceived importance. There is in fact little evidence that Tacitus had much of an impact on immediately succeeding generations. His namesake, the emperor Tacitus of the third century, imagined himself to be descended from the historian and felt obliged to issue an order that copies of his works should be made to rescue him from the neglect (*incuria*) of readers.[6] Admittedly, in the fourth century Ammianus Marcellinus defined his own work as a continuation of Tacitus, which might point to a revival of interest, but Ammianus seems to have been an exception. Christian writers generally scorned Tacitus because of his anti-Christian bias, and while the fifth-century historian and theologian Orosius might quote liberally from him (from the *Histories*) he had little respect for him as a historian. In the sixth century the chronicler Cassiodorus' reference to 'a certain Cornelius' when citing the *Germania* (45.4–5) suggests that Tacitus had by then sunk into a considerable obscurity.[7]

During the Middle Ages copies of the *Annals* would certainly have been made, but there is no evidence that they were known outside the monasteries. Of these copies, remarkably, only two have survived, containing roughly the first and second halves of the work. The earliest is the first Medicean, written in the ninth century, possibly in Fulda, containing Books 1–6. The later Medicean, embracing Books 11–16 (and all of the extant *Histories*), was written in the Benedictine monastery of Monte Cassino in the eleventh century, and remained virtually unknown until it was brought to Florence by Boccaccio in the second half of the fourteenth century. These two manuscripts are the source of all we know of the text of both the *Annals* and the *Histories* (the 'minor' works of Tacitus were transmitted in a single manuscript of which only a small portion has survived, copied in Fulda or the neighbouring monastery at Hersfeld in the ninth century).

Printed editions of the *Annals* began in the latter part of the fifteenth century, and consisted of only the later books, those preserved in the second Medicean, the source for the editions. The first

---

[6] *Historia Augusta* (*Tacitus*) 10.3.
[7] Orosius, *Adversus Paganos* 1.5.1; Cassiodorus, *Variae* 5.2.

Medicean did not come to light for some six hundred years after it was copied, when it was purchased by Pope Leo X and brought to Rome. Under the auspices of the Pope, a text of *Annals* 1–6, based directly on the first Medicean, was published in 1515. It was not in fact until 1607 that a 'complete' text of the *Annals*, based on both primary manuscripts, was produced.

In the fifteenth century the morally uplifting works of Cicero and Livy were generally favoured, but already from the beginning of that century we see Tacitus making inroads. In 1404 the republican Leonardo Bruni cited him for evidence of how despotic emperors had crushed the virtues and inherent genius of the Roman people. In Italy, his impact began to be felt perhaps most strongly after the foreign invasions and the ruthless sack of Rome in 1527. The old ideals of Cicero and Livy now seemed out of vogue and Tacitus' dark political visions of the cruelty and hypocrisy of rulers resonated with writers like Francesco Guicciardini, who saw in Tacitus a disturbing double message, that he could teach decent people the prudence needed to live under tyrants, but could also teach tyrants how to impose their tyranny. The late sixteenth century saw a great surge of interest in Tacitus and in the early part of the next century more editions of him were produced than of any other ancient Greek or Roman historian. The spread of absolutism and of institutions like the Inquisition saw him as a champion of liberties. Alternatively, he could also be seen as a threat to the established order. Jesuit thinkers saw him as a menace and attacked him for his disloyalty and for his questioning of authority.

While a writer like Tacitus can capture the mood of the times and as a consequence be much cited and quoted by other writers to buttress their views, actual influence is more difficult to substantiate. It is perhaps only in Germany that Tacitus can be seen to have influenced history. In the fifteenth century Pope Pius II used the newly rediscovered *Germania* in a letter to the Chancellor of Mainz to counter charges of corruption of the papacy. While Pius did have his supporters, acquaintance with the *Germania* produced results opposite to what he had sought and stirred a nascent German nationalism. Anti-clerical writers contrasted the virtues of the Germans of old with the vices of both ancient and contemporary Rome. The publication in 1515 of the early books of the *Annals* created a German hero, Arminius, who became a symbol of German nationalism and leader of a people who were untainted both morally and racially. Renamed Hermann by Martin Luther, he became the symbol of German nationalism. The Hermann of the famous monumental Hermannsdenkmal, erected in the mid-nineteenth century, supposedly near the site of the Varian disaster in the Teutoburg Forest, and in our own time a sacred monument of veneration by white supremacists, is a phenomenon that descends in a direct line from Tacitus' Arminius.

Happily, Tacitus' effect has generally been much more benign. His name seems omnipresent from the Renaissance on. The scholarly James I of England alludes to him constantly in his 1603 *Precepts on the Arts of Governing*. Francis Bacon thought he could not be outranked for his moral stance or for his wisdom. Montaigne admired his political insights; Edward Gibbon was so indebted to him that his magnificent prose style, with its linguistic subtleties and sophisticated ironies, reads almost like a translated text of Tacitus. John Adams and Thomas Jefferson, opponents in many spheres, were united in admiring Tacitus more than any other ancient author. It is the case that in the nineteenth century, as the study of history became much more professional, more 'scientific', the reputation of Tacitus as a historian declined, given that his emotionalism and deep prejudices were seen to have coloured his judgement. In particular, he was subjected to criticism by the great German scholar Mommsen. This hostility has since waned. Tacitus' experience of the destructiveness of tyranny has made the *Annals* a work of special relevance to the contemporary reader in the light of our experience of the last century. The dark pessimism engendered by two world wars, and especially the deep cynicism that marked the second half of the twentieth century, when governments sought to hide reality under a veneer of hypocritical 'spin', is totally in tune with the dark message of the *Annals* and its grim picture of imperial duplicity. Moreover, our view of history is now more sophisticated. In an age when 'scientific' history has been unscrupulously exploited by authorities in the service of political agenda, Tacitus' claims to freedom from bias are still met with scepticism but also with the acknowledgement that no historical writing can possibly be untainted by the *ira* and *studium* that he forswore. As a consequence, since the Second World War Tacitus has enjoyed something of a renaissance, among both lay and scholarly readers. A digital survey of books in the British Library published on him since 1945 reveals no fewer than 261 items. This is admittedly a rough and ready statistic, but perhaps a good sign that Tacitus' work is indeed on course to acquire the immortality that his friend Pliny predicted.

NOTE ON THE TEXT AND TRANSLATION

THE translation is based on the Teubner text of H. Heubner (editio correctior, 1994). In a very few places I have accepted readings different from Heubner's, and the places where these affect the translation are to be found in the Appendix. There are also occasional divergences from Heubner's punctuation (e.g. at 2.37.2, 6.34.1, 12.68.2), but as punctuation reflects editorial interpretation rather than manuscript readings these are not indicated.

For the most part the ancient names have been retained for people (Pompey is an exception, to assist the reader to differentiate Julius Caesar's rival from his also-famous son, Sextus Pompeius) and for places, except where these are usually referred to by historians in their modern forms (Rome, of course, but also Naples, Rhodes, Britain, etc.). In the case of rivers, the ancient names are again retained, for the most part, except for the major ones of Germany and France that occur with some frequency in the text (Rhine, Elbe, Rhône) and England's Thames. Places and rivers, with their modern names, can be found in the Glossary. As for the emperors, who are often referred to as simply 'Caesar', I have generally tried to avoid confusion by supplying the commonly used name (Tiberius, Claudius, or Nero).

I have consulted numerous other translations, most of them to be found in the Select Bibliography, and the standard commentaries also listed there: the indispensable Furneaux on the entire œuvre; Miller, Goodyear, Woodman and Martin, Shotter, and Martin, on the individual books of the first Medicean; Woodcock and Miller on Books 14 and 15 respectively. The book I probably consulted more frequently than any other in the four years it has taken to bring this work to fruition is the translation of A. J. Woodman, a fascinating version of Tacitean Latin into an English equivalent. I hope my translation will be seen as a complement—and indeed a compliment—to Professor Woodman's, from which, replete as it is with new and interesting insights, I have learned much.

Although the preparation of the various components of this volume reflected a division of labour, the book as a whole is the result of very close collaboration, since each of the authors read through the other's chapters and improved the other's contributions with countless suggestions and observations. But it is also a collaborative venture in a broader sense, since the task of completing it was considerably lightened by the generous assistance of a number of individuals.

The authors express their gratitude first of all to Judith Luna, editor of the Oxford World's Classics series, for initially offering us the project, and for seeing it through with characteristic efficiency and courtesy, and to Elizabeth Stratford for her usual thorough copy-editing (now experienced for the third time by one of the authors). They also wish to thank Laura Gagné, currently a doctoral student at the University of Toronto, for her compilation of the index, and Chris Kelk, Doreen Barrett, and Laura Gagné for their generous offers, quickly snapped up, to proofread the entire work.

The translator has debts of gratitude to record. Chris Pelling and Dexter Hoyos both read parts of the translation and offered many valuable suggestions and much appreciated encouragement. John Jacobs (Yale University) also deserves special mention. Having generously offered his services as a proofreader, he provided me with a thorough critique of the translation and notes, pointing out many omissions and infelicities. Although I am sure that errors remain, thanks to him they are far fewer than they would otherwise have been.

J.C.Y.

SELECT BIBLIOGRAPHY

Tacitus' Life

Alföldy, G., 'Bricht der Schweigsame sein Schweigen? Eine Grabinschrift in Rom', *Mitteilungen des deutschen archäologischen Instituts, römische Abteilung*, 102 (1995), 251–68.

Birley, A. R., 'The Life and Death of Cornelius Tacitus', *Historia*, 49 (2000), 230–47.

Editions

Borzsák, I., *Cornelii Taciti libri qui supersunt*, vol. i (Leipzig, 1992).

Fisher, C. D., *Tacitus: Annales* (Oxford, 1906).

Heubner, H., *Cornelii Taciti libri qui supersunt* (Stuttgart, 1994).

Wellesley, K., *Cornelii Taciti libri qui supersunt*, vol. ii (Leipzig, 1986).

Commentaries

Benario, H. W. B., *Tacitus Annals 11 and 12* (Lanham, Md., 1983).

Furneaux, H., *The Annals of Tacitus* (Oxford, vol. i 1896², vol. ii 1907²).

Goodyear, F. R. D., *The Annals of Tacitus*, vol. i (Cambridge, 1972).

—— *The Annals of Tacitus*, vol. ii (Cambridge, 1981).

Koesterman, E., *Cornelius Tacitus: Annalen* (Heidelberg, 1963–7).

Martin, R., and Woodman, A. J., *Annals: Book IV. Tacitus* (Cambridge, 1989).

Martin, R., *Tacitus: Annals V and VI* (Warminster, 2001).

Miller, N., *Tacitus: Annals Book 1* (London, 1963).

—— *Tacitus: Annals 14* (Bristol, 1987).

—— *Annalium Liber XV* (London, 1963).

Shotter, D. C. A., *Cornelius Tacitus: Annals IV* (Warminster, 1989).

Woodcock, E. C., *The Annals of Tacitus, Book XIV* (London, 1939).

Woodman, A. J., and Martin, R., *The Annals of Tacitus, Book 3* (Cambridge, 1996).

Translations

The Works of Tacitus, translated by Alfred John Church and William Jackson Brodribb (London, 1864–77).

Tacitus: The Annals of Imperial Rome, translated by Michael Grant (Harmondsworth, revised edn. 1959).

Tacito: Annali, translated and edited by Lidia Pighetti, 2 vols. (Milan, 1984–94).

Tacite: Annales, translated and edited by Pierre Wuilleumier, revised and corrected by Joseph Hellegouarc'h, 4 vols. (Paris, 1990–6).

Tacitus: The Annals, translated with an Introduction and Notes by A. J. Woodman (Indianapolis and Cambridge, 2004).

General Books on Tacitus

Benario, H. W. B., *An Introduction to Tacitus* (Athens, Ga., 1975).

Luce, T. J., and Woodman, A. J. (eds.), *Tacitus and the Tacitean Tradition* (Princeton, 1993).

Martin, R., *Tacitus* (London, 1981).

Mellor, R., *Tacitus* (London, 1993).

——(ed.), *Tacitus: The Clasical Heritage* (New York, 1995).

Syme, R., *Tacitus* (Oxford, 1958).

Walker, B., *The Annals of Tacitus: A Study in the Writing of History* (Manchester, 1952).

Woodman, A. J., *Tacitus Reviewed* (Oxford, 1998).

General Books on the Period

Barrett, A. A., *Agrippina: Sex, Power and Politics in the Early Empire* (London and New Haven, 1996).

Champlin, E., *Nero* (Cambridge, Mass., and London, 2003).

Griffin, M. T., *Nero: The End of a Dynasty* (London, 2000²).

Levick, B., *Claudius* (New Haven and London, 1990).

—— *Tiberius the Politician* (London, 1976).

Matyszak, P., *The Sons of Caesar: Imperial Rome's First Dynasty* (New York and London, 2006).

Seager, R., *Tiberius* (London, 2005²).

Shotter, D., *Nero* (London, 2005).

—— *Tiberius Caesar* (London, 2004²).

Talbert, R., *The Senate of Imperial Rome* (Princeton, 1984).

Wiedemann, T., *The Julio-Claudian Emperors* (London, 1989).

Further Reading in Oxford World's Classics

Pliny the Younger, *Complete Letters,* translated and edited by P. G. Walsh.

Plutarch, *Roman Lives,* translated by R. Waterfield, edited by P. A. Stadter.

Suetonius, *Lives of the Caesars,* translated and edited by C. Edwards.

Tacitus, *The Histories,* translated by W. H. Fyfe, revised and edited by D. S. Levene.

—— *Agricola, Germany,* translated and edited by A. R. Birley.

CHRONOLOGY OF SIGNIFICANT EVENTS

Bold type indicates events covered in detail in the extant Annals.

BC:

63   Birth of Octavian (23 September).

44   Assassination of Julius Caesar (15 March).

43   Formation of the Triumvirate of Octavian, Antony, and Lepidus.

31   Battle of Actium and defeat of Antony and Cleopatra.

27   The Octavian settlement.

25   Marriage of Julia and Marcellus.

21   Marriage of Julia and Agrippa.

11   Marriage of Julia and Tiberius.

10   Birth of Claudius.

6   Tiberius' retirement to Rhodes.

AD:

2   Return of Tiberius. Death of Lucius Caesar.

4   Death of Gaius Caesar. Adoption of Tiberius by Augustus.

9   Disaster of Quinctilius Varus in Germany.

12   Birth of Caligula.

14   **Death of Augustus. Accession of Tiberius.**

16   **Trial of Libo Drusus.**

19   **Death of Germanicus (19 October).**

20   **Trial of Calpurnius Piso and Plancina.**

23   **Death of Drusus, son of Tiberius.**

26   **Departure of Tiberius for Capri.**

29   **Death of Livia.**

31   Downfall of Sejanus. Death of Nero, son of Germanicus.

33   **Death of Drusus, son of Germanicus. Death of Agrippina the Elder.**

37   **Death of Tiberius. Accession of Caligula.** Birth of Nero (15 December).

41   Assassination of Caligula. Accession of Claudius.

43   Claudian invasion of Britain.

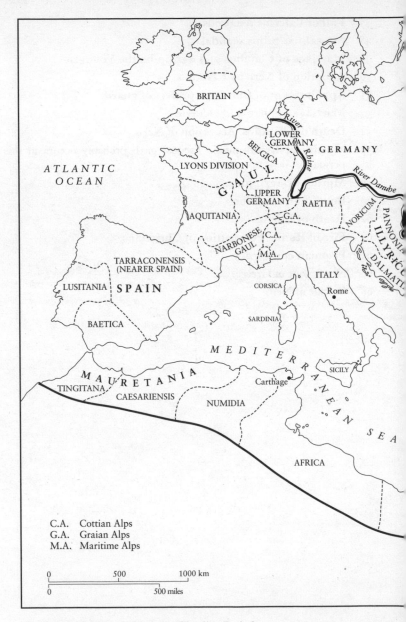

The Roman Empire in the Julio-Claudian Period

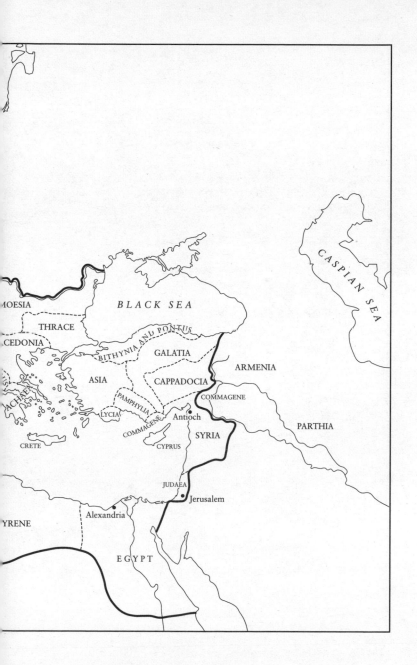

MOESIA

THRACE

CEDONIA

ACHAEA

CRETE

YRENE

BLACK SEA

BITHYNIA AND PONTUS

ASIA

GALATIA

CAPPADOCIA

ARMENIA

COMMAGENE

PAMPHYLIA

LYCIA

COMMAGENE

CYPRUS

Antioch

SYRIA

PARTHIA

JUDAEA

Jerusalem

Alexandria

E G Y P T

CASPIAN SEA

THE ANNALS

BOOK ONE

1. Kings first governed the city of Rome; liberty and the consulship were established by Lucius Brutus.* Dictatorships were employed to meet crises. The rule of the decemvirs* lasted no more than two years, and the consular authority of the military tribunes* was also short-lived. The ascendancy of Cinna* was not of long duration, nor that of Sulla; and the dominance of Pompey and Crassus* swiftly passed to Caesar, the armed might of Lepidus and Antonius to Augustus. Augustus then brought a world exhausted from civil dissension under his authority, with the title of 'First Citizen'.

The Roman people of old had their successes and their failures related by famous authors; and there was no shortage of fine minds for recording the Augustan period, until the groundswell of obsequiousness frightened them off. The histories of Tiberius, Gaius, Claudius, and Nero were distorted because of fear while they reigned, and, when they were gone, were composed with animosities still fresh. Hence my decision to deal only briefly with Augustus— and specifically with the final days—and then to move on to the principate of Tiberius and its aftermath, without rancour or bias,* far removed as I am from motives for these.

2. After Brutus and Cassius* were killed, there was no longer a state military force; and when Pompeius* had been vanquished in Sicily, Lepidus discarded, and Antonius killed, even the Julian party was left with no leader other than Caesar Octavian.* Dropping the title 'triumvir', Octavian presented himself as a consul, and as a man satisfied to hold tribunician authority in order to safeguard the people. Then, by seducing the military with donatives, the masses with grain allowances, and everybody with the pleasure of peace, he gradually increased his powers, drawing to himself the functions of Senate, magistrates, and laws. He met no resistance. The most dynamic men had fallen in battle or through the proscriptions; and the remaining nobles rose to wealth and offices in proportion to their appetite for servitude. Having benefited from the revolution, they preferred the security of the current regime to the dangers of the old. The provinces* were not averse to this arrangement, either. Rivalries between the powerful and the greed of magistrates had raised doubts

about the rule of the Senate and people, and there was little help to be had from the laws, which were constantly undermined by violence, political engineering and, most importantly, by graft.

3. To bolster his supremacy, Augustus* promoted his sister's son, Claudius Marcellus,* still just a boy, to the positions of pontiff and curule aedile. He also elevated Marcus Agrippa*—a man of low birth but a fine soldier, and his partner in victory—with repeated consulships, and later, when Marcellus died, took him as his son-in-law. His stepsons, Tiberius Nero and Claudius Drusus,* he honoured with the title *Imperator*, despite his own family being still intact. For he had brought into the house of the Caesars Agrippa's sons, Gaius and Lucius, and, despite feigning opposition to the idea, had passionately wished to see them styled 'Princes of the Youth' and made consuls-designate even before they had set aside the toga of boyhood. After Agrippa's demise, Lucius and Gaius Caesar were taken off by premature natural deaths, or else by the machinations of their step-mother, Livia,* Lucius en route for the Spanish armies, and Gaius as he was returning from Armenia incapacitated by a wound.* Drusus was long deceased; Tiberius was the only surviving stepson; everything shifted towards him. He was adopted as son, as colleague in power, as partner in tribunician authority, and put on display throughout the armed forces, his mother not acting surreptitiously as before, but with open encouragement.

In fact, Livia had got such a hold on the ageing Augustus that he banished to the island of Planasia his only surviving grandson, Agrippa Postumus.* It is true that the man was a stranger to all decent qualities and possessed of a block-headed pride in his physical strength, but he had been found guilty of no misconduct. In contrast to this treatment, Augustus put Drusus' son Germanicus* at the head of eight legions on the Rhine and ordered his adoption by Tiberius, despite there already being an adolescent son* in Tiberius' house. This was meant to increase the number of supports for his power.

At that time no war remained except that against the Germans, fought to erase the disgrace of the loss of the army under Quinctilius Varus* rather than from a desire to advance the bounds of empire or win some worthwhile prize. At home there was tranquillity, and officials bore the same titles as before. Younger people had been born after the victory at Actium and even the old, for the most part, had been born during the period of the civil wars, leaving only a minute fraction that had witnessed the republic.

4. Thus the nature of the state had changed, and no trace of the old integrity of character was anywhere to be found. Equality had been discarded, and everybody focused on the emperor's commands. There was no fear for the moment, as long as Augustus' age and strength could sustain the man himself, his house and the peace. When he grew weak with advanced age and attendant physical infirmity, when the end was near and hopes of change arose, a few chatted idly about the benefits of freedom; more feared war, others wanted it. The great majority disparaged their forthcoming masters with gossip of various kinds. Agrippa was a savage who had been incensed by insult, it was said; in age and experience he was unequal to such great responsibility. Tiberius Nero had maturity as far as years went, and a distinguished military record; but he also had that old, ingrained arrogance* of the Claudian family and, despite all efforts to suppress them, numerous hints of his viciousness broke through to the surface. He had also been brought up from his earliest years in a ruling house, it was noted. Consulships and triumphs had been heaped on him when he was young, and even in his years of exile on Rhodes* (passed off as 'retirement') resentment, hypocritical behaviour and covert depravity were the focus of his life. Then there was his mother with her female capriciousness. They would be slaves to a woman and two youngsters along with her; these would tyrannize the state for the time being, and later tear it to shreds.

5. As people made these and other such observations, Augustus' health took a turn for the worse, and some suspected foul play on his wife's part. In fact, the rumour had spread that, taking a select few into his confidence and accompanied only by Fabius Maximus,* Augustus had a few months earlier sailed to Planasia* to visit Agrippa. On the island there were, reportedly, floods of tears and gestures of affection from both parties, arousing expectations that the young man would be taken back into his grandfather's house. This, it was said, Maximus had divulged to his wife, Marcia, who in turn divulged it to Livia. The emperor came to know about it, and shortly afterwards, Maximus passed away—whether it was suicide or not is unclear—and Marcia was apparently heard sobbing at his funeral, blaming herself for causing her husband's death. Whatever the truth* of the matter, Tiberius was summoned home by an urgent

letter from his mother when he had barely set foot in Illyricum, and it is not known for sure whether he found Augustus still breathing or already lifeless when he reached him in the town of Nola.* For Livia had kept the house and surrounding streets strictly guarded, with encouraging bulletins issued periodically until all the measures that the crisis demanded were put in place. At that point notice was simultaneously given that Augustus had died and that Tiberius was in power.

6. The first criminal act* of the new principate was the murder of Postumus Agrippa. Agrippa was caught off-guard and unarmed, but a determined centurion still had trouble dispatching him. Tiberius said nothing of the matter in the Senate. He pretended that his father had left orders for the tribune in charge of guarding him not to put off killing Agrippa as soon as he himself had lived his last day.

There is no doubt that Augustus had made many bitter complaints about the young man's character and had secured ratification of Agrippa's exile by senatorial decree. But he never brought himself to murder one of his own, and that he would have killed a grandson to provide security for a stepson beggared belief. The more likely explanation* is that Tiberius and Livia hurriedly effected the assassination of a young man whom they eyed with suspicion and loathing, Tiberius out of fear, and Livia from a stepmother's hatred.

When the centurion followed standard military procedure and reported that his 'orders had been carried out', Tiberius replied that he had given no such orders and that what had been done had to be accounted for before the Senate. Sallustius Crispus* was party to the secret—it was he who had sent the written instructions to the tribune—and when he heard of this he feared that he might be made the scapegoat, and that lying or revealing the truth would be equally dangerous. He therefore cautioned Livia not to let word get out of the inner workings of the palace, of advice given by friends or of services performed by soldiers, and to see that Tiberius did not undermine the strength of the principate by bringing everything before the Senate. The rule of governing, he said, was that accounts balanced only when set before one person.

7. In Rome,* meanwhile, they all rushed into servitude—consuls, senators, and knights. The higher the rank, the greater the hypocrisy and haste. With expressions composed to show neither pleasure at the passing of one emperor nor too much gloom at another's inauguration,

they blended tears and joy, grief and sycophancy. The consuls Sextus Pompeius and Sextus Appuleius were the first to swear allegiance to Tiberius Caesar, and, in the consuls' presence, Seius Strabo* and Gaius Turranius* followed (Strabo was prefect of the praetorian cohorts, and Turranius prefect of the grain supply*). Next came the Senate, the military, and the people.

In fact, Tiberius used the consuls to initiate every action, as though he was acting under the old republic and in two minds about taking power. Even the proclamation with which he now summoned the Senate to the Curia he made only under the title of his tribunician authority, conferred on him under Augustus. The wording of the proclamation was brief and low-key. It stated that he would raise the question of honours to be paid to his father—and meanwhile he was not leaving Augustus' body—and that this was the only official duty that he was assuming.

However, on Augustus' death he had given the password to the praetorian cohorts as *Imperator*; he had sentries, armed guards, and the other trappings of the court; he had a military escort into the Forum, a military escort into the Curia. He sent dispatches to the armies as if he had succeeded to the principate, and there was no trace of indecision—except in his addresses in the Senate. The principal reason for this was his fear of Germanicus.* For Germanicus had at his disposal so many legions, innumerable allied auxiliaries, and awesome support amongst the people—and he might prefer to hold power rather than wait for it. Tiberius also made some concession to popular opinion, wishing to appear to have been summoned and chosen by the state rather than to have crept into it through a wife's scheming and a dodderer's adoption. Later on it was understood that he had feigned the indecisiveness in order to fathom out the inclinations of the leading men; he would distort their words and expressions to give them a criminal intent, and keep them in mental storage.

8. On the first day of the Senate Tiberius permitted no business other than Augustus' obsequies. The will of the deceased was brought in by the Vestal Virgins,* and it named Tiberius and Livia* as heirs. Livia was adopted into the Julian family and given the Augustan name. Augustus had entered his grandsons and great-grandsons as heirs in default, and third in line the highest-ranked men of the state (most of whom he loathed, but it was done for show,

and to boost his reputation with posterity). His bequests did not exceed the norm for a private citizen, apart from the gifts of 43,500,000 sesterces to the common people, a thousand each to soldiers of the praetorian cohorts, and three hundred per man to legionaries and members of the cohorts composed of Roman citizens.

Discussion of funeral honours followed, and the most impressive proposals were those of Asinius Gallus,* that the cortège be taken through the triumphal gate,* and Lucius Arruntius,* that it be preceded by the titles of laws Augustus had passed and the names of peoples he had conquered. A further proposal, from Messala Valerius,* was that the oath of allegiance to Tiberius be renewed each year. Asked by Tiberius if he had brought forth this suggestion on his instructions, Messalla replied that he had spoken of his own accord, and that where interests of state were involved he would rely solely on his own judgement, even at the risk of causing offence. That was the only form of obsequiousness still left to try.

The senators called out for the body to be carried to the pyre on the shoulders of members of their order. Tiberius spared them this responsibility with a condescending restraint, and issued a warning to the masses by official edict. They had once by their excess of enthusiasm disrupted the funeral of the deified Julius,* he said, and they must not now try to have Augustus cremated in the Forum instead of at the resting place reserved for him in the Campus Martius.

On the day of the funeral the soldiers virtually stood on guard. There was much mirth amongst those who had personally seen—or been told of it by their parents—that day when servitude was still new, and the attempt to regain liberty came to nothing, the day when the murder of the dictator Caesar was seen by some as the worst of deeds and by others as the finest. Now, they said, an aged emperor who had long ruled, and even provided his heirs with the means to repress the state, needed military protection so that his burial could proceed peacefully!

9. After that there was much chatter about Augustus himself. The majority expressed wonder over banalities: the day on which he once assumed power was the same date as the last day of his life, and he had ended that life at Nola in the same house and bedroom as his father Octavius. Much was said, too, about the number of his consulships*—equal to those of Valerius Corvus and Gaius Marius put together—and about his uninterrupted thirty-seven years of

tribunician authority, the twenty-one occasions on which he won the title *Imperator*, and other honours, held many times or newly conferred. In discriminating circles, however, his life variously received praise or criticism. Some saw him driven to a civil conflict—one that could not be planned for or fought by honourable means—by loyalty to his father and the plight of the state, in which the laws then had no place. Many were the concessions he had made to Antonius, they said, and many to Lepidus—just as long as he could exact vengeance from his father's killers. After Lepidus lapsed into indolent senility and Antonius' debauchery proved his undoing, the only remedy for the divided country was the rule of one man. And yet the political organization had not meant monarchy or a dictatorship, but merely accepting the title 'First Citizen'. Now the empire's bounds were the Ocean or far-off rivers. There was an integrated complex of legions, of provinces, of fleets—of everything. There was justice amongst the citizens, restraint towards the allies. The city itself had been marvellously embellished.* The use of force had been rare, and only to assure peace elsewhere.

10. The contrary view was that Augustus' loyalty to his father and the crises faced by the state had been just a façade. In fact, these people said, it was lust for supremacy that had led Augustus to mobilize veterans with largesse, to raise an army while he was still a boy and a private citizen, to bribe a consul's legions* and to feign support for the Pompeian party.* Soon he appropriated the insignia and authority of a praetor by a decree of the Senate. Then Hirtius and Pansa* were killed. Perhaps it was the enemy that saw them off, or perhaps it was a case of Pansa having poison applied to a wound, and Hirtius dying at the hands of his own soldiers in a plot masterminded by Octavian. In any case, Octavian then took over the troops of both, seized the consulship against the Senate's will, and turned against the state the arms he had been given to combat Antonius. The ensuing proscription of citizens and apportionment of lands did not find favour even with those who carried them out. It is true that the deaths of Cassius and the Brutuses were a concession to an inherited feud (though private animosities should be surrendered to the public good), but Pompeius* was hoodwinked with a bogus peace, Lepidus with an illusory friendship. Subsequently Antonius was lured on by the treaties of Tarentum and Brundisium* and by marriage to the sister, and with his death paid the price for that treacherous connection.

Certainly peace followed, but a bloody one—witness the defeats of Lollius* and Varus, the killings at Rome of men like Varro, Egnatius, and Iullus.*

Augustus' personal life did not escape criticism either. There was the stealing of Nero's wife* and the ridiculous consulting of the pontiffs on whether she could legitimately marry if she had conceived a child but not yet given birth; there was the extravagant lifestyle of Vedius Pollio;* and finally there was Livia, detrimental to the state as a mother, detrimental to the house of the Caesars as a stepmother. In wanting himself worshipped with temples* and godlike effigies, and with flamens and priests, they said, Augustus had left no room for honours to be paid to the gods. Even his adoption of Tiberius as his successor was not based on affection, or on regard for the state. No, they continued, he recognized Tiberius' arrogance and ruthlessness, and had sought renown from the worst of comparisons. For it is true that a few years earlier, when requesting of the Senate a second term of tribunician authority for Tiberius, Augustus had, in an otherwise complimentary address, thrown in certain observations about the man's demeanour, lifestyle, and habits. While apparently vindicating Tiberius, these were really meant as an affront.

At all events, the obsequies were duly performed, and Augustus was officially granted his temple and heavenly honours.

11. After that the prayers were addressed to Tiberius. He offered sundry comments on the greatness of the empire and his own lack of ambition. Only the deified Augustus had the mental qualities capable of shouldering such a burden, he observed, and when he himself had been invited by Augustus to share his responsibilities, he had learned from experience how arduous, and how subject to fortune, the task of worldwide rule actually was. In fact, their community relied on the support of many distinguished men, he said, and within it they should not make one individual responsible for everything—it would be easier for a number of people to work together to carry out the duties of state.

The address was more impressive than persuasive. Even on subjects where he was not trying to obfuscate, Tiberius' language was always, whether by nature or from practice, vague and obscure, but on that occasion he was trying to cover up completely his true feelings, and so it became all the more convoluted and equivocal. The senators, whose only fear was that they might appear to understand him, burst into tearful laments and appeals, holding out their hands to the gods, to the statue of Augustus, and to the knees of Tiberius himself. At that point he ordered a document* to be brought out and read aloud. In it were catalogued the resources of the state: the number of citizens and allies under arms; all the fleets, client kingdoms, and provinces; all taxes direct and indirect; and all necessary expenditures and gifts. Augustus had listed everything in his own handwriting, and had added the recommendation, through fear, perhaps, or from jealousy, that the empire be restricted to its existing frontiers.

12. Meanwhile, as the Senate lapsed into the most cringing entreaties, Tiberius casually remarked that, while he was not up to the task of the entire administration of the state, he would take responsibility for any part of it that he might be assigned. Then Asinius Gallus said: 'Please, Caesar, which area of government would you like to be assigned?'

Flustered by the unexpected question, Tiberius fell silent for a moment. Then, gathering his thoughts, he answered that his diffidence would not let him choose or refuse any area of something that he would prefer to be excused from altogether. Gallus, who had surmised Tiberius' displeasure from his expression, added that the point of his question was not to have him compartmentalize functions that should not be divided, but to get from Tiberius himself an admission that the state was one body, and that it should be directed by one man's mind. He added a eulogy of Augustus, and reminded Tiberius of his victories and his many years of fine service as a civilian. Not even with that did he assuage the man's anger, however. For Gallus had long been hated by him because of his marriage to Marcus Agrippa's daughter, Vipsania,* who had once been Tiberius' wife. This suggested that Gallus had ambitions beyond those of a private citizen, and that he retained the characteristic aggressiveness of his father, Asinius Pollio.

13. After this Lucius Arruntius, whose remarks differed little from those of Gallus, caused just as much offence. In fact, while Tiberius had no long-standing grudge against Arruntius, he suspected him because he was wealthy and enterprising, with outstanding qualities and a correspondingly high public profile. Now Augustus, in his final conversations, had discussed possible candidates for the principate, noting those who, though suitable, would refuse it, those who were

unfit but would want it, and those who were both capable and eager
to have it. He had named Marcus Lepidus* as competent but unin-
terested, Asinius Gallus as eager but inadequate, and Lucius
Arruntius as one who was not unqualified and who, given the opportunity, would venture to take it. On the identity of the first two there
is agreement, but some sources have Gnaeus Piso* instead of
Arruntius, and with the exception of Lepidus all of them were soon
unjustly convicted on various charges trumped up by Tiberius.

Quintus Haterius and Mamercus Scaurus* also provoked his suspicious nature, Haterius by saying 'How long, Caesar, are you going
to let the republic be without a head?' and Scaurus for remarking
that, since Tiberius had not vetoed the consuls' motion by using his
tribunician authority, there remained hope that the Senate's prayers
would not be ineffectual. Haterius received an immediate tongue-
lashing, but Scaurus, for whom Tiberius felt a more deep-seated
resentment, he simply passed by in silence. Then, worn down by the
general outcry and individual appeals, he gradually shifted his stance,
not going so far as to say he was accepting the power, but ending his
refusals and their petitioning.

It is a well-known fact that Haterius went into the Palatium to
apologize, threw himself down at the knees of Tiberius, who was
taking a walk, and only just missed being killed by the guards because
Tiberius fell over, either accidentally or because he was tripped by
Haterius' grasp on him. The emperor's attitude was not softened
by the danger that a man of such distinction had faced, until Haterius
made an appeal to Augusta and was protected by her anxious
intercession.

14. Much senatorial adulation* was focused on Augusta,* too,
some proposing that she be styled 'Parent', and others 'Mother', of
the nation, and several that the words 'Son of Julia' be added to the
emperor's name. Tiberius insisted that honours paid to women
should be circumscribed, and that he would show similar restraint
with regard to those paid to himself; but he was really tormented
with jealousy, and felt that the promotion of a woman was a slight to
himself. So he would not permit her even to be assigned a lictor,* and
vetoed an 'altar of adoption' and other such honours. On the other
hand he requested proconsular *imperium* for Germanicus Caesar, and
had a delegation sent to him to confer it, and also to console him in
his sorrow over the death of Augustus. The reason for the same

request not being made for Drusus was that Drusus was consul-
designate and then present in the city. Tiberius nominated* twelve
candidates for the praetorship, the number passed on to him by
Augustus, and though the Senate urged him to increase it he swore
an oath never to go beyond that figure.

15. It was at this time that elections* were first transferred from
the Campus to the Senate; for, up to that date, though the most
important elections reflected the emperor's choice, some were still
left to the partiality of the people voting in their tribes. The people,
apart from some idle chatter, did not protest against the removal of
this right, and the Senate, freed from having to offer bribes and from
humiliating canvassing, was happy to comply. Tiberius undertook to
recommend no more than four candidates whose appointment would
not be rejected or contested. The plebeian tribunes meanwhile made
a petition to put on games, at their own expense, which were to be
added to the calendar and called the Augustal Games,* after
Augustus. In fact, money from the treasury was authorized for the
event, and it was also decided that the tribunes should be entitled to
wear triumphal garb in the Circus, but they were not allowed to ride
in the chariot. Before long the celebration of the games was turned
over to that praetor allotted the jurisdiction between citizens and
foreigners.

16. Such was the state of civic affairs when a mutiny broke out
amongst the legions in Pannonia.* There were no fresh reasons for it;
it was simply that the change of emperors offered the prospect of
unrestricted rioting and hopes of deriving profit from civil war.

Three legions had been quartered together for the summer under
the command of Junius Blaesus,* and when he heard of Augustus'
passing and Tiberius' accession Blaesus had suspended routine
duties for mourning, or rejoicing. That was the start of the men's
unruly behaviour. They became fractious, lending an ear to what any
good-for-nothing had to say; and eventually they were hungry for
extravagant and easy living, and averse to discipline and hard work.

There was in the camp a certain Percennius who had once been a
leader of a claque in the theatres and had then become a common soldier. He had a ready tongue and, from rousing support in the theatre,
had learned how to stir up a crowd. Percennius worked gradually on
the men, who were naive and uncertain what the conditions of service would be like after Augustus. He held conversations with them

at night, or when the day turned towards evening, and gathered about him all the most undesirable elements, when better men had slipped away.

17. Eventually, after finding others who were ready to assist with the mutiny, he asked the men, as though in a public harangue, why they obeyed like slaves the few centurions they had, and the even fewer tribunes. When would they dare to demand a solution to their problems, he asked, if they would not approach a new emperor, still unsure of himself, with their appeals, or their swords. Their inertia over so many years* had been a big enough mistake—enduring thirty or forty campaign seasons that turned them into old men, most of them maimed from their wounds! Even discharge did not end their service, he continued; encamped next to their standard, they endured the very same hardships under a different name! And anyone surviving all the perils was still hauled off to remote lands where he would be given some boggy marsh or hilly desert as so-called 'farmland'. Indeed, a soldier's life was hard and unrewarding, he said. Body and soul, he was worth ten *asses* a day, and from that his clothing, weapons, and tents were to be purchased, and bribes found to avoid the brutality of the centurions and gain exemption from chores. But the lash and wounds, the harsh winters and exhausting summers, savage war and profitless peace—there was certainly no end to those! And there would be no relief unless terms were established for entering service, with a denarius a day as their pay, and the sixteenth year marking the end of their duty—and no being kept on under the standards after that, but a cash payment of their gratuity being made to them in the same camp. The praetorian cohorts* received pay of two denarii, and were sent home after sixteen years—could it be that they faced more dangers? He was not belittling the praetorians' guard-duty in the city, he said, but in their own case it was a matter of living amongst savage tribes and having the enemy in view from their tents!

18. There was noisy approval from the crowd as various grievances surfaced. Some indignantly pointed to stripes from the lash, others to their grey hair, and the majority to their threadbare clothing and unclad limbs. Finally they reached such a pitch of fury that they mooted the idea of merging the three legions into one. They were deterred by their rivalry, as each man wanted for his own legion the honour of providing the name; and so they changed tack, and

placed together the three eagles* and the standards of the cohorts. At the same time they proceeded to pile up clods of earth and build a platform, to make the spot more prominent. As they were forging ahead with this, Blaesus appeared. He began to reprimand them, and to pull them back one at a time, shouting: 'Stain your hands with my blood instead! It will be a lesser crime for you to kill a legate than to revolt against the emperor. Either I shall live and keep my legions loyal, or be killed and make you regret your actions all the sooner.'

19. The turf kept rising none the less, and it was only when it had reached the men's chests that Blaesus' determination paid off and they abandoned the undertaking. Blaesus then made an eloquent address, explaining that soldiers' petitions should not be communicated to the emperor by means of mutiny and civil disorder. Those serving in the past, he said, had not made such radical proposals to their commanders, nor had they themselves to the deified Augustus—and, besides, to burden an emperor with worries at the start of his reign was very bad timing. But even if they intended to claim in peacetime what even victors in civil wars had not demanded, why were they considering violent action, abandoning their customary obedience and the discipline that was rightly expected of them? He then recommended that they choose some representatives and give them their instructions in his presence.

The men cried out that Blaesus' son, a tribune, should take charge of the delegation and request military discharge for them after sixteen years—they would give him his other instructions once that met with success. There was a measure of peace after the young man's departure. The soldiers were very self-satisfied, however: that their commander's son was presenting their common cause showed that force had extorted what they would not have gained by good behaviour.

20. Before the mutiny began, some maniples had been sent off to Nauportus to work on roads, bridges, and other projects, and on hearing about the disorder in the camp they pulled up their standards and plundered the nearest villages, including Nauportus itself, which was the size of a town. When the centurions tried to stop them, they subjected them to derision and insults, and finally to beatings. The anger was particularly directed against the camp prefect,* Aufidienus Rufus. They pulled him from his wagon, loaded him with baggage, and drove him forward at the head of the column,

sneeringly asking him if he was enjoying such heavy packs and such long marches. Rufus, in fact, had spent a long time as a private before becoming a centurion and, shortly afterwards, camp prefect. He had been trying to reintroduce the stringent discipline of former days and, being an old hand at hard physical labour, he was all the more exacting because he had endured it himself.

21. The arrival of these troops revived the mutiny, and men wandered off to pillage the surrounding districts. To intimidate the others, Blaesus ordered a lashing and imprisonment for a few, particularly those loaded with plunder; for even at that stage the legate was still obeyed by his centurions and the best of the private soldiers. The men struggled with those dragging them off; they grabbed the knees of those around them; at one moment they called on individuals by name, and at the next on the century, the cohort, and the legion to which they variously belonged, crying out that they all faced the same danger. At the same time they heaped insults on their commander, appealed to the gods in heaven, and did everything possible to stir up resentment, pity, fear, and anger. All rushed to the spot. Breaking into the guardhouse, they released the prisoners and accepted into their ranks deserters and men convicted of capital crimes.

22. The violence now flared up even more, and the mutiny acquired additional leaders. A certain Vibulenus, a common soldier, was lifted onto the shoulders of bystanders before Blaesus' dais, and he addressed his disorderly colleagues, who were eagerly waiting to see what he had in mind. 'Yes, you have restored light and breath to these innocent unfortunates,' he said, 'but who can restore life to my brother, who can restore my brother to me? He was sent to you from the army in Germany* to discuss our collective interests, but last night *he* had him murdered by the gladiators* he maintains and keeps under arms to kill his soldiers. Answer me, Blaesus—where did you dispose of the body? Even enemies do not begrudge burial! When I have satisfied my grief with kisses and tears, tell them to butcher me, too. Only let these men here bury us—killed not for any crime, but because we were acting for the good of the legions!'

23. Vibulenus made his words all the more provocative by weeping and beating his breast and face with his hands. Then he flung aside the men on whose shoulders he was being carried, and threw himself on his face at the feet of one man after another. Such was the

distress and animosity that he aroused that some of the soldiers put
in irons the gladiators amongst Blaesus' slaves, and others the rest of
his servants. Another group poured out to look for the corpse. They
were close to killing the commander—but it quickly became known
that no corpse was to be found, that the slaves denied the murder
under torture, and that Vibulenus had never had a brother. Instead,
they drove off the tribunes and the camp prefect, plundering their
baggage when they fled, and the centurion Lucilius was murdered.
(With typical soldiers' wit, the men had nicknamed this man 'Give
me another' because, when he broke a vine-rod on a soldier's back,
he would, in a loud voice, call out for another and then a third.) The
others all found places to hide, apart from Julius Clemens, who alone
was held back: with his quick intelligence he was thought a good
choice for relaying the soldiers' demands. The Eighth and Fifteenth
legions were actually ready to fight each other, the one demanding
the execution of a man named Sirpicus, and the men of the Fifteenth
sheltering him; but the soldiers of the Ninth Legion intervened with
appeals, and threats when they were ignored.

24. Tiberius was a secretive man, and was especially prone to concealing bad news, but the report of these developments prompted
him to dispatch his son Drusus* to the scene with some leading men
of the city and two praetorian cohorts. Drusus had no specific
instructions, but was to take decisions as the situation required. His
cohorts, too, had been brought up beyond their usual strength with
some crack troops. They were further reinforced by a large contingent of the praetorian cavalry and by the strongest German* troops
then serving as the emperor's bodyguard. Along with them went the
prefect of the praetorian guard, Aelius Sejanus* (who had been
assigned to his father, Strabo, as his colleague, and who had great
influence with Tiberius). Sejanus was to give the young man guidance, and keep the soldiers focused on the dangers they faced, and on
their prospective rewards.

When Drusus approached, the legions, as a mark of respect, came
forth to meet him. They did not, however, have their usual welcoming demeanour and glittering insignia; they were offensively squalid,
and, though they tried to look downcast, their expression was closer
to defiance.

25. After Drusus entered the rampart, the men secured the gates
with sentries, and ordered companies of armed men to position

themselves at certain points in the camp. The others surrounded the dais in a large crowd. Drusus stood there, his hand raised calling for silence. When the men turned their eyes back on their assembled masses, there would be a burst of fractious shouts; but then they trembled at the sight of Drusus. Indistinct muttering was followed by a fierce outcry and, suddenly, silence; and their conflicting emotions made them both fearful and frightening.

Finally, when there was a break in the uproar, Drusus read out his father's letter. In it Tiberius had written that he felt a particular concern for the brave legions with which he had gone through many campaigns,* and that when his mind could find respite from grief he would discuss their demands with the Senate. Meanwhile he had sent his son to grant promptly what could be given on the spot; the rest must await consideration by the Senate which, he said, they should regard as lacking neither in generosity nor in severity.

26. The reply from the gathering was that the centurion Clemens had been given instructions to take to Rome. Clemens began to talk of discharge after sixteen years' service, of bonuses at the termination of service, of a denarius as a day's pay, and of veterans no longer being kept on duty. When, in response, Drusus pleaded that it was for the Senate and his father to decide, he was shouted down. Why had he bothered coming, they asked, if he had no intention of increasing the soldiers' pay or lightening their burdens—in fact with no power to help them whatsoever? No, but beatings and executions— everyone was allowed those! Tiberius, they continued, used to thwart the wishes of the legions by appealing to Augustus' name, and Drusus had now revived that same tactic. Were they never to have visits from anyone apart from minors of the ruling family? Clearly the emperor referring soldiers' benefits and nothing else to the Senate was an innovation—was the Senate also going to be consulted when punishments or battles were on the agenda? Or were rewards under the control of their masters but punishments subject to no authority?

27. Finally the men left the tribunal, shaking their fists at any members of the praetorian guard or Drusus' retinue that they came across, looking for a motive for a dispute and a way to start an armed confrontation. They were particularly incensed with Gnaeus Lentulus,* for it was thought that, being older than the others and having greater military distinction, he was stiffening Drusus' resolve and was, more

than anyone, scandalized at the soldiers' misbehaviour. Not much later they crowded around him as he was leaving (for he started heading back to the winter quarters when he saw danger looming). Where was he going, they asked—was it to the emperor or to the senators, so that he could oppose the legion's interests before them, as well? At the same time they advanced menacingly, and hurled stones at him. Already bloodied from a blow from one of these, and sure he was facing death, he was saved only when a large contingent that had come with Drusus rushed to the spot.

28. It was a night of foreboding that threatened to explode into villainy, but chance provided relief, for, in a suddenly clear sky, the moon* seemed to become dim. The soldiers, ignorant of the cause, took it as an omen of their present circumstances. They saw the failure of the heavenly body as representing their own efforts, and assumed that their undertakings would be successful if the goddess had her radiant splendour restored. Accordingly, they raised a clamour by beating on brass instruments and by blowing trumpets and horns together, and became happy or dejected according to whether she seemed brighter or dimmer. And when some clouds arose to obstruct their view, and they believed she was buried in darkness, they lamented that unending toil was predicted for them, and that the gods were appalled at their criminal acts—when the mind is thrown off balance, so easily inclined to superstition does it become.

Feeling he should capitalize on the turn of events and make prudent use of what chance had offered him, Drusus ordered the rounds made of the tents, and the centurion Clemens was summoned, along with any others whose qualities made them favourites of the mob. These men infiltrated the watches, the guard posts and the sentries at the gates, offering them hope and working on their fears. 'How long are we going to keep the emperor's son under siege?' they would say. 'How will our quarrels end? Are we going to take an oath of loyalty to Percennius and Vibulenus? Will Percennius and Vibulenus grant us pay as soldiers, land when retired? In short, will they assume authority over the Roman people in place of the Neros and Drususes?* No, why should not we, the last to offend, be the first to repent? Joint demands are slowly met; you can immediately earn, and immediately receive, a private favour.'

This caused excitement, and mutual suspicion, drawing new recruit away from veteran, and legion from legion. Then, gradually, their readiness to obey returned. They left the gates and replaced in their regular location the standards that they had brought together at the start of the mutiny.

29. At daybreak Drusus convened an assembly, and although he had little experience in public speaking he criticized their past behaviour and praised their present conduct with a natural dignity. He was not daunted by threats and menaces, he said, but if he perceived that they were reverting to reasonable behaviour, and if he heard them pleading for forgiveness, he would urge his father in a letter to lend a forgiving ear to the legions' appeals. When they begged him to do this, the same Blaesus was once again sent to Tiberius, along with Lucius Aponius, a Roman knight on Drusus' staff, and Iustus Catonius, a centurion of the first rank.

There followed a clash of opinions. Some advocated waiting for the representatives to return and in the meantime trying to pacify the soldiers with friendly overtures; others were for taking stronger measures. The crowd did not know moderation, they said—they would use terror unless they were intimidated, but once afraid they could be safely disregarded. While they were in the grip of superstition, their fear of the leader should be intensified by removing the ringleaders of the mutiny. Drusus was naturally inclined to more severe methods: he had Vibulenus and Percennius summoned and executed. Many authors relate that they were buried within the general's tent, but some that their corpses were thrown outside the earthwork for all to see.

30. After that all the major agitators were searched out. Some wandered out of the camp and were cut down by the centurions or soldiers of the praetorian cohorts; others the companies themselves surrendered to demonstrate their loyalty. To increase the anxieties of the rank and file, winter had arrived early, bringing relentless rainstorms that were so fierce that it was impossible for the men to leave their tents or gather together, and barely possible for them to save their standards that were being swept away by the high winds and rainwater. The fear of divine anger also persisted: it was no coincidence that stars faded and storms swooped down on them—sinners as they were! There was no other remedy for their ills but to leave that ill-starred and polluted camp, and return to their various winter quarters after purifying themselves of their guilt. First the Eighth Legion went back, then the Fifteenth. The Ninth had been

clamouring for them to wait for Tiberius' letter, but soon, left alone when the others departed, they pre-empted the necessity looming before them by taking action themselves. And seeing that calm had been restored for the moment, Drusus went back to the city without awaiting the return of the soldiers' representatives.

31. At about the same time there was unrest amongst the legions in Germany, and for the same reasons, and here it was all the more violent because of the greater numbers involved. They also had high hopes that Germanicus Caesar would be unable to tolerate another's rule, and would therefore put himself in the hands of his legions which, by their power, would sweep away everything before them.

There were two armies* on the banks of the Rhine. The one called the 'upper army' was under the legate Gaius Silius,* while Aulus Caecina* had charge of the 'lower'. Overall command lay with Germanicus, who was at that time busy conducting a census of the Gallic provinces. The troops in Silius' charge merely looked on with ambivalent feelings to see how the mutiny of the others turned out, but the men of the lower army slid into frenzy. It started with the Twenty-First and Fifth legions, and then the First and Twentieth were pulled into the troubles—they were quartered in the same summer camp in the lands of the Ubii, where they had nothing to do, or only light duties. There were present, after a recent levy in Rome,* a large number of city troops used to riotous living and averse to hard work, and on hearing of the death of Augustus these proceeded to fill the simple minds of the others with ideas. The time had come, they would say, for the veterans to demand their overdue discharge, and the younger men a higher pay—and all should demand an end to the wretched conditions and seek redress for the brutality of the centurions. This came not from a single individual, as was the case with Percennius amongst the Pannonian legions, and it did not fall on the frightened ears of soldiers who saw before them other armies stronger than their own—the mutiny had many faces, and many voices. The fate of Rome lay in their hands, they said. It was by their victories that the state grew, and it was their name* that commanders adopted.

32. The legate did not stand in their way, for the madness of the mob had broken his will. In a sudden rage the men drew their swords and advanced on the centurions, the primal source of the soldiers' resentment and the starting point of their ferocity. They knocked

them down and applied the lash, sixty strokes per man, to match the number of centurions,* and then flung them, maimed, mangled, and in some cases lifeless, before the rampart or into the River Rhine. Septimius fled to the dais and fell prostrate at Caecina's feet, but so vehement were the demands made for him that he was surrendered for execution. The man who would gain fame with later generations for the assassination of Gaius Caesar,* Cassius Chaerea,* was at that time a hot-headed young man, and he opened up a path with his sword through the armed men that stood in his way. No tribune and no camp commandant had authority any longer, and the men apportioned among themselves guard-duty, patrols, and any other functions deemed necessary in the circumstances. To those with a deeper interest in the mentality of soldiers the clearest sign of a serious and uncompromising rebellion was the fact that it was not a matter of scattered pockets of unrest, or a few people inspiring it. There was uniform anger, and uniform silence, so evenly spread and so determined that one could have believed the men were acting under orders.

33. Meanwhile, news of Augustus' demise was brought to Germanicus while he was conducting the census (which I mentioned earlier) throughout the Gallic provinces. Germanicus was married to Augustus' granddaughter, Agrippina, and had had several children by her and, being himself the son of Drusus, brother of Tiberius, he was the grandson of Augusta. He was, however, disquieted by the veiled hatred that his uncle and grandmother felt for him, a hatred all the more bitter for being unjustified. For the memory of Drusus still loomed large amongst the people of Rome, and it was believed that he would have restored their freedom had he come to power—hence their support for Germanicus, in whom they placed the same hopes. He was a young man of unassuming character and admirable courtesy, far different from Tiberius with his arrogant and inscrutable talk and looks. There were also the tiffs between the women. Livia had a stepmother's* resentment to set her against Agrippina, and Agrippina herself was somewhat irascible, but by her virtue and love for her husband she could turn her indomitable spirit to good effect.

34. In fact, the closer Germanicus came to the prospect of supreme power, the more he exerted himself on Tiberius' behalf, and he bound himself, his own circle and the Belgic communities

with an oath of allegiance to the emperor. Then, on hearing of the uprising of the legions, he left hurriedly and met them outside their camp, their eyes downcast as though from remorse. After he entered the earthwork, discordant complaints became audible. Some men took his hand and, pretending to plant kisses on it, put his fingers into their mouths so that he could feel their toothless gums; others drew his attention to their limbs bent with age. The assembly before him seemed a total muddle, and he ordered the men to form up in companies. They would hear better as they were, came the reply. The standards should be brought forward, then—that at least would distinguish the cohorts from each other. They obeyed, slowly.

Then, after commencing with some respectful remarks on Augustus, Germanicus turned to the victories and triumphs* of Tiberius, reserving his highest praise for the emperor's glorious achievements in the two Germanys with these legions now present. He went on to praise to the skies the consensus found in Italy, and the loyalty of the Gallic provinces—nowhere was unrest or discord to be found. The comments were received with silence, or low muttering.

35. When he touched on the mutiny, Germanicus asked where their soldierly conduct had gone, and their splendid discipline of old. Where had they driven their tribunes, where their centurions? All together they bared their bodies, reproachfully exhibiting the scars their wounds had left and the marks of the lash. Next, with confused shouts, they berated him for the prices payable for exemptions, the meagreness of their pay, and the gruelling nature of their tasks, mentioning specifically the construction of the earthwork and ditches, the gathering of forage, timber and firewood and all the other duties required of them from necessity or to avoid inactivity in the camp. The most ferocious cry arose from the veterans. They enumerated their thirty or more campaigns, and begged him to help them, for they were exhausted. He should not let them go to their deaths still working at the same oppressive tasks, but set a limit to their punishing service with a retirement that was not impoverished. There were even some who demanded the money left them by the deified Augustus in his will, adding words of good omen for Germanicus; and they indicated their support if he wanted supreme power.

With that, as if tainted with their crime, he leaped hastily from the dais. The men blocked his path with their weapons, threatening harm if he did not go back. Germanicus, however, crying aloud that he preferred to die rather than abandon his loyalty, grasped the sword at his side, raised it aloft and would have driven it into his breast had not those close by seized his sword hand and forcefully restrained it. The far edge of the crowd, which was also the most densely packed, urged him to carry through the stroke, and so, too— though it defies belief—did a number of individuals who came up to him. In fact, a soldier by the name of Calusidius drew his own sword and offered it to him, adding that it was sharper. Even in their fury the crowd found this heartless and uncivilized, and there was a long enough pause for Germanicus to be hurried to his tent by his staff.

36. In the tent there was discussion of remedying the situation. For there were reports that a delegation was being prepared to bring the upper army over to the same cause, that the chief town of the Ubii had been singled out for destruction, and that hands that had been steeped in loot would burst forth to plunder the Gallic provinces, too. Anxiety was increased because the enemy was aware of the Roman mutiny, and a pull-out from the banks of the Rhine would precipitate an invasion. On the other hand, arming auxiliary troops and allies against the defecting legions meant civil war. Severity spelled danger, bribery was unprincipled; if the soldiers were granted nothing or everything the state was likewise in jeopardy. Accordingly, when the arguments had been weighed up in their deliberations, it was decided that a letter be written in the emperor's name authorizing demobilization for all with twenty years' service, discharge for those with sixteen (these men being kept under the standard but with no duties save repelling the enemy), and payment, in double the amount, of the legacies the men had claimed.

37. The men realized that these were measures improvised to meet the emergency and demanded instant implementation. The discharges were hurriedly put into effect by the tribunes; the financial rewards were deferred until each man reached winter quarters. However, the Fifth and Twenty-First legions would not leave until payment was made right there in the summer camp, the money being raised out of the travelling allowances of Germanicus' staff and his own personal funds. The legate Caecina led the First and Twentieth legions back to the city of the Ubii, and it was a scandalous march, since the moneybags extorted from the commander were being carried along amidst the standards and the eagles. Germanicus left to join

the upper army, and found no reluctance to take the oath of allegiance among the Second, Thirteenth, and Sixteenth legions, though the Fourteenth hesitated somewhat. The cash and the discharges were delivered, even though the men did not demand them.

38. Meanwhile, amongst the Chauci the *vexillarii* of the rebellious legions that were on garrison duty began to spread disaffection, and were momentarily halted by the immediate execution of two soldiers. This order had been given by the camp prefect, Manius Ennius, who was setting a good example rather than acting with legitimate authority. Later, as the unrest increased, he fled, but was discovered. Concealment providing no safety, he then sought help in a stroke of boldness and declared that it was not against their prefect that their violence was being directed, but against Germanicus their commander, and Tiberius their emperor. At the same time, frightening those who stood in his way, he seized the standard and pointed it towards the river-bank. Then, crying out that anyone leaving the column would be treated as a deserter, he led the men back to their winter quarters, still fractious but not daring to take action.

39. Meanwhile the delegates from the Senate came to Germanicus, who had now returned, at the altar of the Ubii.* There were two legions wintering there, the First and the Twentieth, along with recently discharged veterans who were serving under the standard. These men were frightened and crazed with guilt, and they were overcome with fear that the men had come at the Senate's behest to annul the concessions they had extracted by the mutiny. A crowd always finds a scapegoat, no matter how groundless the charges, and the men picked on the ex-consul Munatius Plancus,* the head of the delegation, as being responsible for the Senate's decree. At bedtime they began to demand their standard, which was housed in Germanicus' quarters. Swiftly converging on the entrance, they proceeded to break down the doors, forced Germanicus from his bed and with threats of death made him hand over the standard.

Shortly afterwards, as they roamed the streets of the camp, they came across the delegates who, having heard the uproar, were heading for Germanicus. They plied them with insults, and made ready to kill them, especially Plancus, whose high office had precluded flight. And, in his hour of danger, Plancus had no sanctuary apart from the encampment of the First Legion. There, grasping the standards and the eagle, he sought the protection of religion, and, but for the eagle-bearer Calpurnius, who prevented the ultimate act of violence, a delegate of the Roman people would, in a Roman camp, have stained with his own blood the altars of the gods, a rare occurrence even in a struggle between enemies.

Finally, at daybreak, general, soldiers, and what had happened between them during the night began to be recognized for what they were. Germanicus entered the camp, ordered Plancus to be brought to him, and took him onto the dais. He then berated the men for the deadly outbreak of insanity—its reappearance a result of heaven's, rather than the soldiers', anger, he said—and explained why the delegates had come. He eloquently bemoaned the violation of the rights of the delegation, and the serious and undeserved incident involving Plancus, as well as the great disgrace the legion had incurred. The crowd were awestruck rather than calmed, and Germanicus sent the delegates off with an escort of auxiliary cavalry.

40. In this alarming situation there was general criticism of Germanicus for his failure to proceed to the upper army, where obedience and assistance against the rebels could be found. Enough, and more than enough, damage had been done, it was thought, by the granting of discharge and cash payments, and by easygoing policies. Even if Germanicus thought little of his own safety, why keep his little son and pregnant wife amid madmen who violated all the laws of humanity? Those, at least, he should send back to the boy's grandfather and the state. Germanicus vacillated a long time. His wife rejected the idea, declaring that she was a descendant* of the deified Augustus and not his inferior when facing danger, but finally, with copious tears, Germanicus embraced his wife's womb, and the son they shared, and made her leave.

The wretched column of women began to move out—the commander's wife, a refugee, clasping her tiny son* to her breast, and around her, uttering cries of grief, the wives of Germanicus' staff-members, who were being dragged along with her. And those who stayed behind were no less dejected.

41. It was not a picture of a Caesar at the height of success, and in his own camp, but what might be seen in a captured city; and the pitiful lamentations attracted the ears and eyes even of the soldiers. They came forth from their tents. What was this weeping, they asked. What was this sad procession? These were women of distinction, with no centurion, no common soldier to act as guard, and there was nothing appropriate to a commander's wife, no sign of her usual retinue. They were going to the Treveri, consigned to the protection of foreigners!

Then came shame and compassion, and recollections of Agrippina's father Agrippa, and Augustus her grandfather. They thought of her father-in-law Drusus, of the woman herself and her outstanding fertility* and renowned chastity. They thought of the infant, born in the camp* and brought up in the legions' barracks, the boy to whom they gave the soldiers' nickname 'Caligula' because (in order to win the support of the ordinary soldiers) he was usually shod with this sort of footwear.* But nothing affected them as greatly as the envy they felt for the Treveri. They resorted to appeals, and blocked the way, asking them to go back, and stay, some of them coming to intercept Agrippina, but most going back to Germanicus. And Germanicus, smarting with hurt and anger that was still fresh, addressed them as they milled round him:

42. 'My wife and son are not dearer to me than my father and country, but my father will be protected by his own majesty, and the Roman empire by its other armies. My wife and children I would gladly offer up to destruction for your glory, but now I am taking them far away from your frenzy. Thus whatever villainy lies ahead may receive expiation from my blood alone, and the murder of Augustus' great-grandson and the slaying of Tiberius' daughter-in-law will not add to your guilt. For what, in these past days, have you not attempted? What have you left inviolate? What name shall I give this gathering? Should I address you as "Soldiers", you who have laid siege to your emperor's son with your rampart and weapons? Or as "Citizens", you who have snubbed the Senate's authority? In addition, you have violated the rights due even to an enemy, as well as the sacrosanctity of an embassy and international convention.

'The deified Julius checked a mutiny in his army with a single word, addressing as "Quirites"* men who refused the oath of allegiance to him. The deified Augustus* petrified the legions at Actium with the look on his face. I am not yet in their company, but I am descended from them; if it were actually the soldiers of Spain and Syria that were flouting my authority, that would still be strange and outrageous. And is it really the First and Twentieth legions that are giving such splendid thanks to your leader—the First, which received its standards from Tiberius, and you here, who shared so many of his victories, and were enriched by him with so many prizes? Is this the message I am to take to my father, as he hears only good news from the other provinces? That his own recruits and veterans are not satisfied with discharge or money? That here alone are centurions murdered, tribunes driven out, legates kept in prison? That the camp and the rivers are sullied with blood, and that the breath that I draw remains at the mercy of men who hate me?

43. 'Ah, my improvident friends! Why did you take away that sword, which I was preparing to drive into my heart, on that first day we had a meeting? His was a better and warmer gesture—that man who offered me his sword. I should at least have fallen while not yet an accessory to my army's many crimes! And you might have chosen as leader a man who could have left my own death unpunished but avenged that of Varus and the three legions. For, despite their offers of assistance, god forbid that the Belgae gain the glory and fame of having helped the Roman people and subdued the tribes of Germany! I pray rather that your spirit, deified Augustus, now taken to heaven, and the vision and memory of you, father Drusus, wash away this stain, and direct the wrath of our internecine feuding towards the destruction of the enemy. I pray that you do so through these same soldiers of yours, already starting to feel shame and entertain thoughts of glory. And, yes, I see a change in your expressions, men, and in your hearts. If you are ready to restore the delegates to the Senate, your obedience to your emperor, and my wife and children to me, then stand back from the contagion and segregate the mutinous elements. That will be sure proof of your regret, and a guarantee of loyalty.'

44. This turned the men to entreaty,* and they admitted the truth of his reproaches, begging him to punish the truly guilty, pardon those who had made a mistake, and lead them against the enemy. His wife should be called back, and the legions' foster-child should return to them, and not be surrendered to the Gauls as a hostage.

Agrippina could not return, Germanicus explained, because the birth of their child was imminent, and so was winter; his son would return, and all else they must see to themselves. Changed men now, they ran off in different directions, clapped the prime troublemakers in irons, and dragged them before Gaius Caetronius, legate of the First Legion. Caetronius judged and punished them individually, in the following manner. The legions stood as in an assembly, with swords drawn, and the defendant was put on show by a tribune on a raised platform. If the legions shouted out that he was guilty, he would be hurled head first into them and butchered. And the soldiers relished the bloodshed, as if they were absolving themselves of guilt. Nor did Germanicus try to check them: it was not being done at *his* bidding, and the individuals responsible for the atrocity would also suffer the opprobrium for it.

The veterans followed their example, and were shortly afterwards sent into Raetia. This was ostensibly for the defence of the province against the threat of the Suebi, but in reality so they would be pulled away from a camp that still inspired horror, as much for the severity of the remedy applied as the memory of the original crime.

Germanicus then conducted the revision of the list of centurions. When called on by the commander, each man stated his name, rank, and country of origin; and he also gave the number of campaigns he had served in, his acts of valour in battle, and his military awards, if he had any. If the tribunes and the legion vouched for his industry and good character, he retained his rank; when they were in agreement in accusing him of greed or brutality, he was discharged.

45. The current predicament resolved, there remained a problem no less difficult—the intractability of the Fifth and Twenty-First legions, who were wintering sixty miles away, at a place called Vetera. They had been the first to start the mutiny, and had been responsible for all its most heinous crimes. They were neither deterred by the punishment of their comrades nor influenced by their remorse, and were still enraged. Germanicus therefore prepared to send armed forces, a fleet, and allied troops down the Rhine, intending to decide the matter militarily if his authority were snubbed.

46. In Rome, what had transpired in Illyricum was not yet known, and news had arrived of the uprising of the German legions. An alarmed community criticized Tiberius for toying with the senators and commons, both bodies weak and unarmed, with his feigned reluctance, while in the meantime the troops were in revolt and could not be restrained by a couple of boys not yet possessing the authority of an adult. He should have gone himself, they said, and set his majesty as emperor before men who were bound to yield when they set eyes on a ruler of long experience, a man who had supreme power to punish or reward them. Could it be that Augustus,* in the weakness of old age, had made so many visits to Germany, and yet Tiberius, in the prime of his years, was sitting in the Senate quibbling at the

words of its members? Enough care had been taken to secure the
servitude of Rome—now some medicine needed to be applied to the
soldiers' spirits, to make them ready to accept peace.

47. Unmoved in the face of such criticisms, Tiberius was determined not to leave the hub of the empire and put himself and the
state at risk. For he had many conflicting thoughts troubling him.
The army in Germany was stronger, the one in Pannonia closer. The
German army could count on the resources of the Gallic provinces;
the other threatened Italy. To which should he attend first? And
suppose those put second were incensed by the slight! By using his
sons, however, the two could be dealt with together, and without
compromising his imperial stature, which enjoyed greater respect at
a distance. At the same time it was pardonable for the young men to
refer some items to their father, and any resistance to Germanicus or
Drusus could be appeased or smashed by himself. But what was
there in reserve if the mutineers spurned the emperor? Nevertheless,
he selected a retinue, brought baggage together, and fitted out ships,
as though about to leave at any moment. Presently, offering variously
the onset of winter or the pressure of business as excuses, he fooled
first the most intelligent, then the public, and finally, and for the
longest time, the provinces.

48. Although Germanicus had put together an army and stood
ready to punish the rebels, he felt that they should still be given some
time in case the recent lesson made them cautious about their own
safety. He therefore sent a letter ahead to Caecina informing him that
he was coming in force, and that unless they punished the offenders
before his arrival he would resort to indiscriminate bloodshed.
This letter Caecina read out in private to his eagle- and standard-
bearers, and to the most reliable elements in camp, encouraging them
to rescue all the men from disgrace, and themselves from death. In
peace, he said, attention was paid to cases and their merits; when war
broke out, innocent and guilty went down together.

These individuals approached the men they considered suitable
and, observing that the legions were for the most part loyal, they
fixed a time, at the legate's suggestion, for an armed assault on the
most loathsome and seditious troublemakers. Then, giving a signal
to one another, they burst into the tents and slaughtered the unsuspecting soldiers, with no one, apart from the accomplices, knowing
how the massacre started, or where it would end.

49. This was a scene different from all the civil conflicts that have ever occurred. It was not a battle or a fight between soldiers from different camps, but one between men from the same sleeping-quarters, men whom the day had seen eating together, and the night resting together. They split into two factions and hurled their weapons. Shouts, wounds, blood—all this was evident, but the reason unknown. Everything else was determined by chance. Some loyal soldiers were cut down, too, when the troublemakers realized against whom the savagery was directed and also took up arms. And there was no legate and no tribune present to enforce restraint; the mob was granted a free hand, and vengeance to the point of saturation. Soon Germanicus came into the camp. Weeping profusely, he cried out that this was not a cure but a disaster, and he ordered the bodies to be burned.

They were still in a bloodthirsty mood, and the desire swept over them to march on the enemy as atonement for their insanity—only if they received honourable wounds to their impious breasts could their comrades' shades be appeased. Germanicus went along with his soldiers' enthusiasm. He bridged the river and sent over twelve thousand legionaries, twenty-six allied cohorts, and eight cavalry squadrons whose discipline had not suffered in that mutiny.

50. The Germans, who were not far off, were delighted that we were hindered first by the period of mourning for the late Augustus, and then by dissension. The Roman commander, however, marched swiftly, cutting through the Caesian Forest and the fortified boundary begun by Tiberius, and encamping on the boundary, protected by a rampart front and rear, and by a barricade on the sides. Then he made his way through dark woodlands and pondered which of the two paths to take, the usual route, which was short, or the one that was more difficult and less attempted, and for that reason not under enemy surveillance. The longer route was chosen, and the pace accelerated; for scouts had brought word that this was a festal night for the Germans and one joyously celebrated with a ceremonial feast.

Caecina was instructed to go ahead with some lightly equipped cohorts and clear away obstacles in the woods; the legions followed a short distance behind. They were helped by a starlit night. Reaching the villages of the Marsi, they surrounded the enemy with armed details, the villagers even at that point lying in their beds or hard by the tables, feeling no apprehension and with no sentinels posted.

Everything was in careless disarray; and there was no fear of war—but even their peace was merely the languorous torpor of the drunken.

51. So that the raid could cover more ground, Germanicus divided his eager legions into four divisions, and spread devastation over an area of fifty miles with fire and the sword. Neither sex nor age aroused pity. Places secular and holy alike were razed to the ground, including those tribes' most famous sanctuary, which they called the Sanctuary of Tanfana. The soldiers cut down men half-asleep, unarmed, or wandering aimlessly about, without receiving a wound.

The massacre brought forth the Bructeri, the Tubantes, and the Usipetes, and these proceeded to invest the woodlands through which lay the army's return route. The general learned of this and pressed forward, ready to march and to fight. Some cavalry and auxiliary cohorts took the lead; the First Legion followed; and, with the baggage in the centre, the legionaries of the Twenty-First closed up the left flank and those of the Fifth the right, while the Twentieth Legion strengthened the rear. After these came the rest of the allies.

The enemy, however, made no move until the column was stretched out through the forest; then, with only perfunctory assaults on the flanks and vanguard, they attacked the rear with all their might. The light-armed cohorts were being thrown into disarray by the closely ordered German companies when Germanicus rode up to the legionaries of the Twentieth and kept shouting in a loud voice that *this* was their opportunity to cancel out the mutiny. They should press on, he said, and swiftly turn their guilt into glory. Their spirits flared up, and with a single charge they broke through the enemy, drove them to open ground and cut them down. At the same time, the vanguard emerged from the woods and built a fortified camp. After that it was a trouble-free march, and the men, encouraged by their recent achievements and forgetting the past, were settled in their winter quarters.

52. The news brought joy and anxiety to Tiberius. He was pleased that the mutiny had been crushed, but what he saw as Germanicus' attempt to win the favour of his troops by doling out money and accelerating discharge—that was galling, as was the glory he had won in combat. Even so he made a report to the Senate on the man's achievements and spoke at length about his valour, but in language too ostentatiously ornate for it to be believed that it came from the heart. His praise for Drusus and the ending of the Illyrian revolt was

shorter, but he was more earnest, and his language carried conviction. He confirmed for the Pannonian legions, too, all the concessions
that Germanicus had made.

53. Julia* saw her final day that same year. Because of her sexual
misconduct she had earlier been imprisoned on the island of Pandateria
by her father Augustus, and subsequently in the town of Rhegium,
hard by the Sicilian strait. She had been married to Tiberius when
Gaius and Lucius Caesar were still alive, and had despised him as her
inferior; and this was the fundamental reason for Tiberius' withdrawal to Rhodes. After coming to power he brought about her end
by letting her waste away in protracted destitution, banished, disgraced, and, after the assassination of Postumus Agrippa, devoid of
all hope, for he thought that her killing would remain unnoticed
because of the length of her exile.

Tiberius' vicious treatment of Sempronius Gracchus* was similarly motivated. From a noble family, Gracchus had a nimble wit and
a misused eloquence, and he had debauched the same Julia while she
was married to Marcus Agrippa. That was not the limit of his lechery, either. When Julia was passed on to Tiberius, the determined
adulterer proceeded to inspire defiance in her, and hatred towards
her husband; and the letter she wrote to her father Augustus vilify-
ing Tiberius was thought to have been composed by Gracchus.
Gracchus was therefore shipped off to Cercina, an island in the
African sea, where he endured an exile lasting fourteen years. Soldiers
were then sent to assassinate him, and they found him on the
shore, on a projecting spit of land, expecting no happy outcome.
When they arrived, Gracchus asked for a few moments to relay his
final instructions to his wife Alliaria in a letter, and then stretched
out his neck for his killers. In the resolute manner of his death he was
not unworthy of the name Sempronius; it was in his life that he had
fallen short of it. Some have recorded that the soldiers in question
did not come from Rome but were sent by Lucius Asprenas,* the
proconsul of Africa, on Tiberius' orders, the emperor hoping—in
vain—that the murder could be blamed on Asprenas when word of
it got out.

54. That same year saw a ceremonial innovation with the addition
of a priesthood of Augustal brothers,* modelled on the college of
Titian brothers that Titus Tatius had once established to preserve
Sabine ritual. Twenty-one members were drawn by lot from the

foremost members of the community, and Tiberius, Drusus, Claudius, and Germanicus were added to that number. The Augustal Games were first established at that time, but they were disrupted by quarrelling that broke out because of rivalry amongst the actors. Augustus, humouring Maecenas,* who was passionately in love with Bathyllus,* had tolerated this form of entertainment, but he was not averse to such avocations himself, and thought participating in the pleasures of the common people a democratic gesture. Tiberius' character was rather different, but he did not as yet dare to put on a more austere course a people that had been indulged for so many years.

55. In the consulship of Drusus Caesar and Gaius Norbanus, a triumph* was decreed for Germanicus, although the war was still in progress. Germanicus had been engaged in full-scale preparations for the summer campaign, but at the start of spring he anticipated that with a sudden raid on the Chatti. For he had come to hope that the enemy's loyalties were divided between Arminius* and Segestes,* men noted respectively for treachery and fidelity towards us. Arminius was the troublemaker of Germany, while Segestes frequently gave Varus notice (especially at their last dinner before the hostilities broke out) that a rebellion was afoot, and urged him to put Segestes himself in irons—along with Arminius and the other chieftains. The ordinary people would not take any risk with their leaders removed, he said, and Varus would have the time to distinguish the guilty from the innocent. But Varus was fated to fall victim to Arminius' ferocity, and, though Segestes was drawn into the conflict because his people were all agreed on it, he remained in disagreement, his hatred intensified by a personal grudge. For Arminius had carried off his daughter, who had been betrothed to another man. Thus he became the hated son-in-law of a resentful father-in-law, and what creates bonds of affection in the case of friendly parties only served to stimulate rage in the case of enemies.

56. Germanicus put at Caecina's disposal four legions, five thousand auxiliaries, and a number of irregular companies of Germans living west of the Rhine, while he himself took the same number of legions, and twice as many allies. He established a fortress on the outlines of his father's fortifications on Mt. Taunus and hurriedly marched his lightly equipped force against the Chatti, leaving Lucius Apronius* behind to build roads and bridge rivers. For, because of

the dry weather (something rare in that climate) and the shallowness of the streams, he had made the journey speedily and without difficulty, but there was fear of rainstorms and swollen rivers for his return. In fact, his arrival so surprised the Chatti that all handi-capped by age or sex were immediately captured or put to the sword. The men of fighting age had swum across the River Adrana, and were trying to thwart the Romans' attempts to bridge it. When they were driven off by artillery and arrows, they sued for peace-terms, without success. A few then sought refuge with Germanicus, and the others abandoned their hamlets and villages, and scattered through-out the woodlands. Germanicus put the tribal capital, Mattium, to the torch and laid waste the open countryside, after which he turned towards the Rhine. The enemy did not now dare to harass the rear of the withdrawing Romans, their usual practice whenever their retreat has been a ploy rather than prompted by fear. It had been the inten-tion of the Cherusci to bring help to the Chatti, but Caecina deterred them by armed intervention at various points, and with a successful battle he also checked the Marsi when they dared to engage him.

57. Shortly afterwards a delegation arrived from Segestes pleading for Roman assistance against the aggression of his countrymen, by whom he was being blockaded. (By advocating war, Arminius now carried greater weight with these people—in the eyes of barbarians the more recklessly aggressive a man is, the more he is regarded as trustworthy and important in times of unrest.) Segestes had made his son, whose name was Segimundus, a member of the delegation, but a guilty conscience made the boy hesitate. For after being ordained as a priest* at the altar of the Ubii, he had, in the year of the German defection, torn off his priestly garlands and fled to the rebels. He was, however, led to hopes of Roman clemency, and he fulfilled his father's instructions. He was given a kind reception, and was sent over to the Gallic bank of the river with an armed escort. Germanicus thought it worth his while to turn his column round; he met the blockading force in a battle, and Segestes was rescued, along with a large band of his kinsfolk and retainers. Amongst these were some noblewomen, including the wife of Arminius, who was also the daughter of Segestes, but who had more of her husband's spirit than her father's—she was not reduced to tears and uttered not a word of entreaty. Her hands clasped in her lap, she merely stared down at her expectant abdomen. Spoils from Varus' debacle were

also brought in—they had been given as plunder to many of the men now surrendering—and there was also Segestes himself, a towering figure, and fearless in the recollection that he had honoured his alliance.

58. Segestes' address went much like this:

'This is not my first day of unswerving loyalty towards the Roman people. Ever since I was awarded citizenship by the deified Augustus I have chosen my friends and enemies with a view to your advantage. And that was not from hatred of my fatherland (for traitors are resented also by the side they promote), but because I felt the interests of the Romans and Germans to be the same, and that peace was preferable to war. That was why I brought a charge against Arminius before Varus, the former commander of your army—Arminius, kidnapper of my daughter and violator of your treaty. I was kept waiting by that commander's indolence, and as there was little protection in the laws I demanded that Varus put me in irons along with Arminius and his henchmen. That night is my witness—and I wish it had been my last! What followed can only be deplored, not defended, but I *did* put Arminius in irons and was myself put in them by his supporters. And now, on my first opportunity to address you, I favour the old situation over the new, peace over turmoil, and I do so not to win reward, but to clear myself of any charge of treachery, and also as an appropriate negotiator for the German people, should they prefer contrition to destruction. For my son's youthful indiscretion I beg forgiveness, and that my daughter was brought here under duress I do admit. It will be for you to consider which should take precedence, the fact that she is pregnant by Arminius, or that she is a child of mine.'

Responding with clemency, Germanicus promised safety for Segestes' children and kinsmen, and for him personally a home in the old province. He then led back his army and was, at Tiberius' suggestion, given the title *Imperator*. Arminius' wife bore a child of the male sex. His boyhood was spent in Ravenna, and the humiliation that was later inflicted on him I shall tell of at the appropriate point.*

59. The story of Segestes' surrender and kind welcome spread abroad, being received with optimism or melancholy according to whether people opposed war or wanted it. Arminius had a violent nature in any case, but the seizure of his wife and the condemnation

to servitude of his wife's foetus drove him to frenzy, and he passed swiftly through the Cherusci calling for war against Segestes, and war against Germanicus. Nor did he hold back his insults: a fine father, he declared, a great general, and a brave army—all those hands carrying off one little woman! In *his* case, three legions and as many legates had fallen before him, he said, for *his* way of waging war was not by dirty tricks or taking on pregnant women—it was in the open and against an armed foe. Still on view in the groves of the Germans were the Roman standards that he had hung up to honour their ancestral gods! Let Segestes live on his conquered river-bank, and let him restore to his son the priesthood he had relinquished! Germans would never feel at ease with having seen the rods and axes and the toga between the Elbe and the Rhine! Other tribes, ignorant of Roman rule, were unfamiliar with her punishments and unacquainted with her taxes. And since they had now shaken these off, and since Augustus, now set among the gods, and his chosen successor Tiberius had left there empty-handed, they should not tremble before an inexperienced youth* and a mutinous army. If they preferred their fatherland, parents, and ancient culture to masters and resettlement elsewhere, they should follow Arminius' lead to glory and liberty rather than Segestes' to ignominious servitude.

60. The bordering tribes were also roused to action by these words, not just the Cherusci; and Inguiomerus, Arminius' uncle, was brought on side as well, a man of long-standing influence with the Romans—hence greater fear on Germanicus' part. So that war should not descend on him in one fell swoop, he sent Caecina through the Bructeri to the River Amisia with forty Roman cohorts to divide the enemy, while the prefect Pedo* led the cavalry through the territory of the Frisians. Germanicus himself put four legions aboard some ships and sailed through the lakes, and then infantry, cavalry, and fleet rendezvoused at the river mentioned above. The Chauci promised auxiliary troops, and were accepted as brothers-in-arms. When the Bructeri proceeded to torch their own property, Lucius Stertinius, sent out by Germanicus, routed them with a light-armed unit, and during the carnage and the looting Stertinius came upon the eagle of the Nineteenth Legion that had been lost with Varus. From there, the column was marched to the furthest limits of the Bructeri, and all the land between the rivers Amisia and Lupia was devastated. This was not far from the Teutoburg Forest, in

which the remains of Varus and his legions were said to be lying unburied.

61. The desire therefore came over Germanicus to give those soldiers and their leader their last rites, and the whole army there with him was moved to pity for relatives and friends, and indeed for the vicissitudes of warfare and the human condition. Caecina was sent ahead to reconnoitre the hidden recesses of the woods, and lay down bridges and causeways over the soggy marshland and treacherous plains, and they advanced into the sombre area, a ghastly sight prompting ghastly memories. Varus' first camp,* with its wide circumference and with the headquarters marked out, revealed the handiwork of the three legions; then, from a half-demolished rampart and a shallow ditch, one could detect the point where an already shattered remnant of the force had taken a position. In the middle of the field were whitening bones, scattered or in piles, where men had fled or made a stand. Close by lay pieces of weapons and limbs of horses, and there were also skulls nailed to tree-trunks. In groves close by were barbarous altars where the enemy had sacrificed tribunes and first-rank centurions. And survivors of that catastrophe, who had managed to slip away from the battle or from captivity, would describe how the legates had fallen in this spot, how the eagles were taken in that; and show where Varus was dealt his first wound, and where he met his end by a blow from his own ill-starred hand. They indicated the dais from which Arminius had addressed his troops, enumerated the gibbets he used for the prisoners, and pointed out the live-burial pits, and told how he had arrogantly mocked the standards and the eagles.

62. So it was that, in the sixth year after the catastrophe, a Roman army was present to inter the bones of the three legions, with nobody knowing whether he was covering with earth the remains of strangers or of relatives, but all doing so as though they were kith and kin. Their anger with the enemy mounted, and they were at the same time sad and wrathful. Germanicus laid the first sod for the construction of the barrow, paying a welcome tribute to the dead and sharing the grief of all present.

Tiberius did not approve. Perhaps he looked at everything that Germanicus did in a negative light, or perhaps he believed that, after the sight of soldiers dead and unburied, the army would be reluctant to do battle and more fearful of the enemy. Also, he thought, a commander invested with an augurate* and its ancient ceremonial duties should have had no contact with funeral rites.

63. Germanicus gave chase as Arminius fell back into the wilderness, and at the first opportunity he ordered the cavalry to charge ahead and seize the level ground on which the enemy had positioned himself. Arminius, who had instructed his men to form up in close order and advance towards the woods, now suddenly turned them round, and soon afterwards gave men he had concealed in the woods the signal to rush out. The Roman cavalry was thrown into disarray by this new fighting line, and reserve cohorts were sent in, but as these ran into the crowd of men fleeing the fight they only served to increase the confusion. They were being pushed into a swamp well known to the victors, and treacherous for those unaware of it, but then Germanicus brought up his legions and deployed them for battle. From that came terror for the enemy, a surge of confidence for the Roman soldiers; and they parted on equal terms.

Shortly afterwards Germanicus led his army back to the Amisia, and then ferried back the other legions by ship, as he had brought them up. Some of the cavalry he ordered to head for the Rhine along the ocean shoreline. Caecina was leading back his own troops and, although his return was along well-known paths, he was told to cross the Long Bridges with all possible speed. These constituted a narrow pathway—it had been built some time earlier by Lucius Domitius*—through the bleak marshlands, and apart from that there was nothing but a bog of thick, heavy mud, intersected by streams that rendered it hazardous. Around about, on a gently rising gradient, were woods, which Arminius at that time filled with men. For, thanks to short cuts and the speed of his column, he had arrived ahead of the Roman troops that were encumbered with baggage and weapons.

Uncertain how to repair the bridges that were dilapidated with age, and at the same time ward off the enemy, Caecina decided to lay out a camp on the spot so that men could start on the work while others took on the fighting.

64. In an effort to break through the guard-emplacements and assault the working parties, the barbarians proceeded to harass, encircle, and charge the Romans, and the cries of the workers mingled with those of the fighters. Everything was against the Romans. The area with its deep marshes was both unstable for making a stand

and too slippery for an advance; their bodies were weighed down by their breastplates; they were unable to hurl their javelins amidst the waters. It was different for the Cherusci—they were used to marsh-land fighting, were long-limbed, and had huge pikes for inflicting wounds even at a distance.

It was night that finally delivered the already wavering legions from the uneven fight. Their success rendered the Germans tireless. Taking no rest even at that point, they set about diverting to the lower ground all the waters that had their source in the hills rising round about, and with the ground flooded, and such work as had been completed now submerged, the labour of the soldiers was doubled.

This was Caecina's fortieth season,* either under orders or in command; he had known successes and reverses,* and was therefore unperturbed. As he considered the options before him, the only solu-tion he could find was to keep the enemy shut in the woods until the wounded and the heavier-armed elements of his column went ahead—for between the mountains and the marshland stretched a piece of flat land that could accommodate a thin battle-line. The Fifth Legion was then chosen to serve on the right flank, and the Twenty-First for the left, while the men of the First were selected to lead off the column, and the Twentieth to face those who would be in pursuit.

65. It was a restless night for various reasons. From their joyful banquets the barbarians filled the low-lying valleys and echoing woods with their happy singing and savage cries; on the Roman side there were feeble campfires and fitful murmurings, and the men lay scattered along the rampart, or wandered amidst the tents, sleepless rather than alert. Their general was terrified by a frightful dream. He thought he saw a blood-covered Quinctilius Varus arise from the marsh and heard him calling, but he did not respond and pushed away his hand when Varus stretched it out to him.

When day broke, and the legions were sent to the flanks, they abandoned their posts, either from fear or defiance, and swiftly occu-pied some flat terrain beyond the swamp. Arminius, however, despite having an opportunity to attack, did not charge out immediately. It was only when the Roman baggage became stuck in the mud and the ditches, when the soldiers around it were in disarray, when the stan-dards lost their order and (as usually happens in such circumstances) every man was swift to help himself but his ears were slow to respond to commands—only then did he give the Germans the command to attack. 'Look,' he kept shouting, 'it's Varus and his legions caught up in the same fate once more!' And with that he took a hand-picked group and cut through the column, inflicting wounds mostly on the horses. The animals, slipping in their own blood and the mud of the marshland, threw their riders, scattered those in their way and trampled underfoot those who were down.

The greatest effort was expended around the eagles, which could not be carried forward in the face of spears raining down on them, but could not be planted in the soggy ground, either. While Caecina was attempting to hold his line together, his horse was run through beneath him, and he fell and was surrounded by the enemy—or would have been but for the intervention of the First Legion. The situation was helped by the greed of the enemy, who left the kill to chase after plunder, and as the day drew towards evening the legions clambered out on to open, solid ground.

But that was not the last of their tribulations. A rampart had to be raised and materials sought for the earthwork; and they had lost most of the implements for digging soil and cutting turf. They had no tents for the maniples, no dressings for the wounded. They shared food sullied with slime and blood, all the while bemoaning the deathly gloom and the fact that, for so many thousands of men, only a single day now remained.

66. It so happened that a horse broke its halter and, wandering about terrified by the shouting, knocked down some of the people who got in its way. Men thought the Germans had broken in, and such was the consternation that all rushed to the gates—and the back gate was the one particularly sought since it faced away from the enemy and was safer for flight. Caecina discovered it was a false alarm, but he was unable to stop or hold back his men either by his personal authority or pleas, or even by grabbing them. He then flung himself down in the gateway and finally blocked their path by appealing to their compassion, as they would have had to proceed over the commander's body. At the same time the tribunes and centurions convinced them that their panic was groundless.

67. Caecina then gathered the men together at his headquarters, told them to listen in silence to what he had to say and warned them of the dire situation facing them. Their only way to safety lay in their

weapons, he said, but these needed to be judiciously employed; and they had to remain within the rampart until the enemy closed in on them in hopes of storming the position. After that they had to charge out from all sides, and with that charge the Rhine would be reached. If they fled, he added, they had before them more woods, deeper bogs, and a brutal enemy, whereas victory meant honour and glory. He reminded them of what was dear to them at home, what redounded to their honour in the camp; about their reverses he said nothing. After that, starting with his own, he passed on the horses of the legates and tribunes to all the bravest fighters, and without partiality, so these could charge the enemy before the infantry attack.

68. The Germans, from anticipation, greed, and a clash of opinions amongst their leaders, were just as agitated. Arminius urged them to allow the Romans to come out and, when they came out, to surround them once more in the sodden and difficult terrain. Inguiomerus advocated a more impetuous course, which pleased the barbarians—an armed blockade of the rampart. Storming it would then be easy, he explained, there would be more prisoners and the booty would be intact.

And so, at daybreak, they filled in the ditches, threw hurdles over them, and tried to grasp the top of the rampart—there were few soldiers on it, and they were apparently rooted to the spot with fear. When the Germans had a handhold on the fortifications, the cohorts were given the signal, and horns and bugles rang out together. Then, shouting and charging, they poured around the German rear, derisively exclaiming that here there were no woods or marshes, only a fair field and fair gods. The enemy had been envisioning an easy kill, with opponents few and poorly equipped, but then the resounding bugles and flashing arms burst upon them—all the more stunning for being unexpected—and they fell, as helpless in defeat as they had been greedy in success. Arminius quit the field unhurt, Inguiomerus after a serious wound, and the slaughter of the rank and file lasted as long as Roman anger and daylight. Only at nightfall did the legions return and, though physically drained by increased wounds and the ongoing shortage of food, they found strength, health, provisions—everything, in fact—in victory.

69. A rumour had meanwhile spread that the army had been cut off, and that a column of Germans was on the offensive and heading for Gaul; and if Agrippina had not stopped a bridge over the Rhine

from being demolished, there were men ready to commit such an outrage out of fear. However, this great-hearted woman took upon herself the duties of a leader during those days, and dispensed clothing or dressings to all the needy or wounded amongst the soldiers. Gaius Plinius,* the author of *The German Wars*, records that Agrippina* stood at one end of the bridge praising and thanking the returning legions. This made a deep impression on Tiberius: her solicitude was no straightforward matter, and it was not against foreigners that the support of the soldiers was being sought! Commanders were left with nothing to do, he mused, when a woman* inspected the maniples, appeared before the standards, tried distributing largesse—as if she were not courting popularity enough by carrying her son around dressed as a common soldier and wanting him to be called 'Caesar Caligula'! And she already had greater influence with the armies than legates and generals did, and it was by her, a woman, that a mutiny had been quelled which the emperor's name could not stop. Such thoughts were inflamed and aggravated by Sejanus, who, through his acquaintance with Tiberius' character, would sow the seeds of hatreds for use much later—hatreds that Tiberius was intended to store up now and bring out when they had grown.

70. Germanicus transferred to Publius Vitellius* command of two of the legions—the Second and the Fourth—that he had brought by sea. Vitellius was to march them overland so that the fleet would be lighter when it was navigating shallow seas or ran aground at ebb tide. Vitellius initially had a smooth journey on dry soil or where the tide had a gentle flow. Soon his column was seized and buffeted by the blasts of a north wind—and it was also the season of the equinox,* the time at which the ocean has its greatest swell. The land was submerged, and sea, shoreline, and fields all looked the same, with treacherous areas indistinguishable from the solid, and shallow spots from the deep. They were bowled over by the waves, pulled under by the currents; pack-animals, their loads, and dead bodies floated amongst them and bumped into them. The companies became completely intermingled, standing in water sometimes up to their chests, sometimes up to their heads; and on occasion, when they lost their footing, they became separated or they sank. Shouts of mutual encouragement were of no use against the onset of the floodwaters. There was no difference between the active man and the idler,

between the prudent and the incautious, between calculated and random response. Everything was swept up in the same devastating force.

Finally Vitellius struggled out onto higher ground and brought his column up to the same spot. They passed the night without provisions and without fire, most of them naked or maimed, no less wretched than men under enemy blockade. For in that situation there was the added factor of an honourable death, whereas these men faced an end without glory.

Daylight brought back the land, and they made it to the river to which Germanicus had advanced with the fleet. The legions were then put on board, while rumour was spreading that they had been drowned; and their survival was not believed before men actually saw that Germanicus and his army had returned.

71. Stertinius had been sent ahead to accept the surrender of Segestes' brother, Segimerus, and by now he had brought Segimerus and his son to the community of the Ubii. Both were pardoned, Segimerus readily, the son with some hesitation because it was said that he had treated the corpse of Quinctilius Varus with disrespect. As for making good the losses sustained by the army, the Gallic provinces, the Spanish provinces, and Italy competed with each other with offers of weapons, horses, and gold, according to their various resources. Germanicus commended them for their enthusiastic support, but took for the campaign only the weapons and horses, assisting the men with cash of his own. To soften the memory of the disaster with an act of camaraderie, he made the rounds of the wounded and praised individuals for their exploits; and, inspecting their injuries, he used hope of victory in one case, prospects of glory in another, and encouragement and solicitude with them all, to confirm both their loyalty to himself and their spirit for battle.

72. That year triumphal insignia* were granted by decree to Aulus Caecina, Lucius Apronius, and Gaius Silius for their exploits with Germanicus. Tiberius refused the title of 'Father of the Nation', which had been pressed on him on numerous occasions by the people, and he would not allow an oath of obedience to his measures, although it was proposed by the Senate. Everything in the mortal realm was uncertain, he would say, and the more he acquired the more slippery the ground he trod. But he did not, for all that, convince people that he had liberal sympathies; for he had reintroduced the treason law.

This law bore the same name in earlier times, but the cases coming to trial were different then, focusing on any who had done harm to an army by treachery, or to the public by sedition—in short, anyone who had lessened the majesty of the Roman people by wrongdoing on an official level. Actions were prosecuted; words were not punishable. It was Augustus who, angered by Cassius Severus'* immoderate slander of distinguished men and women with his scandalous compositions, initiated judicial proceedings against defamatory writings under the specious cover of this law. Presently, when Tiberius' opinion was sought by the praetor Pompeius Macer on whether cases of treason should go to trial, he replied that 'the laws should be upheld'. Tiberius had likewise been incensed by the circulation of anonymous poems (on the subject of his ruthlessness, his arrogance, and his strained relations with his mother).

73. It will not be inapposite to record the first experiments in such charges, which arose in the cases of Faianius and Rubrius, two Roman equestrians of little importance. In this way light may be thrown on the origins of the deadly curse and on how Tiberius' cunning allowed it to creep in, and how it was subsequently suppressed, but then finally flared up to engulf everything. The charge that Faianius' accuser brought against him was that he had admitted amongst the votaries of Augustus*—these were maintained in all the great houses and resembled priestly colleges—a certain Cassius, who was a mime-actor and notorious catamite; and also that in the sale of his gardens Faianius had disposed of a statue of Augustus. The charge brought against Rubrius was that he had violated Augustus' divinity by perjury.*

When the accusations came to Tiberius' notice, he informed the consuls* in writing that his father had not been decreed divine status so that the honour could be turned to the destruction of his fellow-citizens. The actor Cassius, along with others in that same profession, had, he said, regularly attended the games* that his mother had consecrated to the memory of Augustus; and for representations of Augustus, like other statues of deities, to be part of the sale of gardens and houses was not sacrilege. On the matter of the oath, that should be assessed just as if the man had sworn falsely by Jupiter—offences against the gods were the gods' concern!

74. Not long afterwards Granius Marcellus, the governor of Bithynia, was arraigned on a charge of treason by his own quaestor,

Caepio Crispinus, with Romanius Hispo supporting the accusation. Hispo then embarked on a type of livelihood* which the wretched times and shamelessness of men later made notorious. Destitute, unknown, and restless, he insinuated himself into the ruthless emperor's confidence by accusing people in private reports, and soon imperilled anyone of distinction, gaining power with one man, but earning the hatred of everybody. He thus set a pattern, following which made poor men rich, and despised men fearful, and which brought ruin on others and finally on themselves.

Crispinus accused Marcellus of making derogatory remarks about Tiberius, a charge impossible to rebut since the accuser selected the foulest characteristics of the emperor, and ascribed the comments to the accused (for, the observations being true, it was believed that they had also been given expression). Hispo added the charge that Marcellus' statue had been set in a higher position than those of the Caesars, and that in the case of another statue Augustus' head had been cut off and Tiberius' features set on it instead. Tiberius was so incensed at this that he broke his usual silence and declared that in this case he, too, would vote, openly and under oath, so that the others would have to follow suit. But even at that time there lingered traces of the freedom that was dying. Gnaeus Piso said: 'Caesar, at what point are you going to vote? If you are first,* I shall have something to follow, but if you are after everyone else I am afraid I may disagree without realizing it.'

Tiberius was shaken by this and, remorsefully submissive after his ill-advised outburst, he voted for the defendant's acquittal on the treason charges. Those of embezzlement* went before the board of assessors.*

75. Not yet having had his fill of senatorial investigations, Tiberius began to sit in the law courts, taking a place at the end of the tribunal so as not to remove the praetor from his curule chair; and because of his presence many verdicts were handed down that ran contrary to the intrigues and solicitations of the powerful. But while integrity was being served, liberty was being undermined.

Such cases included that of the senator Pius Aurelius. He complained that his house had been destabilized by the construction of a public road and an aqueduct, and appealed to the senators for assistance. The praetors of the treasury* rejected his appeal, but the emperor came to his aid and paid him the value of the house—Tiberius was ever eager to spend money on honourable causes, a virtue that he retained long after he sloughed off all his others. When the ex-praetor Propertius Celer asked to be relieved of his rank because of financial problems,* Tiberius made him a gift of a million sesterces, after he had established that the shortage of funds was due to Celer's meagre inheritance. When others tried the same line, Tiberius told them to justify their cases before the Senate, his passion for austerity making him strict even in matters where he was acting correctly. As a result, the others preferred silence and straitened circumstances to confession and charity.

76. That same year the Tiber, in spate after an unbroken spell of rain, had flooded the low-lying areas of the city, and there was much loss of life and property as it receded. Asinius Gallus accordingly proposed consulting the Sibylline Books. Tiberius demurred, his tendency to conceal reaching the divine as well as the human plane; but Ateius Capito and Lucius Arruntius were authorized* to find the means to hold the river in check.

Achaea and Macedonia* sought to be excused their heavy tax burden, and it was decided that they be temporarily relieved of their proconsular control and transferred to the emperor.

Drusus presided over a gladiatorial performance that he put on in his own and his brother Germanicus' name, and revealed an exces-sive delight in the bloodshed, cheap though it was. This was disturb-ing for the common people and even his father was said to have remonstrated with him. Why Tiberius himself missed the show was explained in various ways, some saying he was sick of crowds, and others putting it down to his morose temperament and fear of com-parison with Augustus, who had been a good-humoured spectator. I am not inclined to believe that he purposely furnished his son with the means to demonstrate his savagery and thus excite the disgust of the people, though that, too, was suggested.

77. Disorderly behaviour in the theatre, which had first mani-fested itself the previous year, at this point broke out more seriously. Not only members of the public but soldiers and a centurion, too, were killed—and a tribune of praetorian cohort was also wounded—as they attempted to stem abuse that was being hurled at the magis-trates and disputes amongst the common people. The fracas was discussed in the Senate, and opinions were voiced to the effect that the praetors should have the authority to flog actors. Haterius Agrippa,*

a plebeian tribune, vetoed the motion, and received a tongue-lashing from Asinius Gallus, but Tiberius, who would permit the Senate such empty shows of independence, remained silent. The veto remained in force, however, because the deified Augustus had once expressed the opinion that actors were not subject to floggings,* and Tiberius did not feel he had the right to contravene his judgements. On limiting actors' pay, and combating the unruly behaviour of their supporters, many decrees were passed. The most striking were the following: no senator was to enter the homes of mime-actors; Roman knights were not to escort actors when they appeared in public; and the actors were to be viewed nowhere but in the theatre.* Also, the praetors were to have the right to punish with exile any outrageous behaviour on the spectators' part.

78. A request from the Spaniards for a temple* to Augustus to be built in the colony of Tarraco was granted, and that meant a precedent was set for all the provinces. When there was a public outcry against the one per cent sales tax* that had been put in place after the civil wars, Tiberius made the announcement that the military treasury* depended on this support, and that, furthermore, the state was not equal to its financial burden unless the discharge of veterans took place in their twentieth year of service. Thus the ill-conceived terms granted in the recent mutiny (by which the men had extorted the right to finish after sixteen years) were rescinded for the future.

79. The next matter raised in the Senate, by Arruntius and Ateius, was whether, in order to check the flooding of the Tiber, there should be a diversion of the rivers and lakes by which its flow was increased. Delegations from municipalities and colonies* were given a hearing. There the people of Florentia begged that the Clanis not be moved from its usual bed and redirected into the River Arnus, which would be disastrous for them. The people of Interamna put forward a similar case, saying that Italy's most fertile plains would be destroyed if the River Nar were divided into a number of streams, as planned, and if it then flooded the countryside. The people of Reate did not remain silent, either; they opposed the damming of Lake Velinus at its outlet into the Nar on the grounds that its waters would burst over the lands next to it. Nature, they said, had done her best to serve the interests of mortals, giving rivers their own mouths and channels, as well as their sources and limits. Moreover, one should take into account the religious observances of the allies, who had

dedicated cults, groves, and altars to their local streams. Why, even Tiber himself would certainly not want to flow with diminished glory, deprived of his tributaries, they said. Whether the pleas from the colonies prevailed, or whether it was the difficulty of the work or just the superstition, the result was that support went to the motion of Piso, who had advocated no change.

80. Poppaeus Sabinus* had his governorship of Moesia extended, with Achaea and Macedonia added to it. This was also one of Tiberius' foibles, to extend commands and keep numerous people in the same armies or jurisdictions to the end of their lives. Various motives are given for this. Some claim that it was dislike of fresh administrative concerns that made him regard decisions once taken as perpetually binding, others that it was jealousy, a wish not to have a larger number enjoying office. There are some who think that while he had a keen intellect, his judgement was indecisive. For he did not court outstanding virtue, and yet he hated vice; he feared danger for himself from the best people, and disgrace to the state from the worst. Eventually, such indecision took him to the point of assigning provinces to some men whom he was never going to allow to leave the city.

81. On the matter of the consular elections then held for the first time* in his principate, and on those that came later, I would not venture to make any statement with confidence—so conflicting is the evidence found not only in the historians but in Tiberius' own speeches. At one time he would remove candidates' names, but describe each man's background, civil career, and military service, so their identities could be surmised.* On other occasions he would remove even these pointers and encourage the candidates not to upset the elections by canvassing, promising his own help in that regard. His usual claim was that only those whose names he had given to the consuls had declared their candidacy to him, and that others could still declare if they had confidence in their influence or merits. This sounded plausible, but was in fact a piece of meaningless chicanery, and the more it was wrapped up in a show of liberty, the more repulsive was the servitude in which it was destined to result.

BOOK TWO

1. In the consulship of Sisenna Statilius and Lucius Libo there was unrest in the kingdoms and Roman provinces of the East. The trouble started with the Parthians.* They asked Rome for a king, and accepted one, but then began to look down on the man as a foreigner, despite his being a member of the Arsacid family.* This was Vonones, who had been given to Augustus as a hostage by Phraates. For although Phraates had defeated Roman armies and commanders, he had shown Augustus every mark of respect and, to cement their friendship, had sent him some of his children, not from fear of us but from lack of confidence in his countrymen's loyalty.

2. After the death of Phraates and the kings that followed him, there was a period of civil bloodletting and a delegation came to the city from the Parthian nobility to invite Vonones, the eldest of Phraates' children, to come home. Tiberius believed this a magnificent compliment to himself, and he boosted Vonones' wealth. The barbarians, too, gladly welcomed him, as usually happens with new regimes. Soon their joy turned to shame: the Parthians had fallen into decline; a king—one corrupted by Roman manners—had been sought from another world; and now the Arsacid throne was being treated, and given away, like one of the Roman provinces. Where, they asked, was that glory that belonged to those who slaughtered Crassus and drove out Antonius*—if Caesar's slave, a man who had spent so many years in servitude, were to rule the Parthians? Their disdain was further kindled by the man himself: his interests ran counter to his ancestral traditions, for he rarely hunted, had little enthusiasm for horses, used a litter whenever he passed through the cities and had contempt for traditional Parthian banquets. His Greek attendants were also objects of ridicule, as was his keeping under seal the most worthless articles. His approachability and easygoing courtesy, on the other hand, were virtues unknown to the Parthians, and they saw them as strange vices. In fact, both his bad and decent characteristics were foreign to their culture, and so both were hated by them.

3. As a result, Artabanus* was summoned—he was of Arsacid blood but had grown up among the Dahae—and though routed in

the first clash he rallied his forces and seized the kingdom. The defeated Vonones found refuge in Armenia, which then lacked a ruler and, poised between the empires of Parthia and Rome, was trusted by neither. This was because of the crime of Antonius, who had led on King Artavasdes* of Armenia with a pretence of friendship, and then clapped him in irons and finally put him to death. Artavasdes' son, Artaxias,* furious with us because of his father's memory, defended himself and his kingdom by the might of the Arsacids. Then Artaxias was treacherously assassinated by his relatives, and Augustus gave the Armenians Tigranes, who was escorted to his kingdom by Tiberius Nero. Tigranes' reign was not of long duration, either, nor was his children's,* although—as is the practice with foreigners—these were partners in marriage as well as royal power.

4. Then, by order of Augustus, Artavasdes was placed on the throne, but was unseated, not without serious loss to us. After that Gaius Caesar* was selected to settle Armenia, and he made Ariobarzanes ruler. The man was a Mede by birth, but the Armenians acquiesced because of his outstanding good looks and brilliant mind. When Ariobarzanes met with a fatal accident, the people would not countenance his son. After experimenting with the rule of a woman, whose name was Erato, and quickly expelling her, they were unsure and wavering, more lacking a ruler than possessing liberty, and they accepted the fugitive Vonones on the throne. But then Artabanus became threatening, and Vonones had little support amongst the Armenians, while his being defended by our forces would perforce entail war with the Parthians. The governor of Syria, Creticus Silanus,* therefore sent for him and put him under arrest, though he still retained his opulent lifestyle and royal title. Vonones' efforts to escape this ludicrous situation I shall recount at the appropriate point.*

5. For Tiberius, in reality, the upheaval in the East came as something that was not unwelcome. He now had a plausible excuse for taking Germanicus away from the legions with which he was familiar, putting him in charge of new provinces and exposing him to treachery and the vagaries of fortune.* But Germanicus enjoyed the support of his men while he faced the antipathy of his uncle, and the stronger these sentiments became the keener he was to advance the day of victory. He began to reflect on battle strategies, and on the cruel reverses and the successes that had been his in the two years of

his campaign. He noted that the Germans suffered defeat in pitched battle and on neutral ground, but were favoured by woods, bogs, the short summer, and the early winter, while his own men were hurt not so much by the wounds they received as by the long distances and by losing their weapons. Also, the Gallic provinces were tired of supplying horses, and the long baggage column offered an easy opportunity for ambush, and was difficult to defend. If they took to the sea, however, they could easily occupy the country without detection by the enemy, and at the same time the war could be started earlier, with legions and supplies transported together—and cavalrymen and their mounts, ferried into river-mouths and upstream, could reach the middle of Germany intact.

6. This, then, was the strategy on which Germanicus focused his intention, and Publius Vitellius* and Gaius Antius were sent to conduct the census of the Gallic provinces. Silius, Anteius, and Caecina were put in charge of the construction of a fleet.* It seemed that a thousand ships would suffice, and the work was hurried along. Some were short, with a narrow stern, narrow prow, and broad centre, so that they might more easily cope with rough seas. Some had flat keels so they could run aground without damage. More had rudders set at both ends so that, if the rowers suddenly reversed direction, they could land on either side of the river. Many were fitted with decks on which artillery could be transported, while also being serviceable for carrying horses or provisions. Able to move under sail, or swiftly propelled by oar, the fleet was an impressive and fearful spectacle, and was rendered more so by the fervour of the soldiers.

The point selected for the rendezvous was the island of the Batavi: it offered easy opportunity for landing, and was well suited for receiving troops and taking hostilities over into Germany. For the Rhine flows as a single body to that point, or flows around some small islands; but at the start of Batavian territory it virtually splits into two branches. Where it borders Germany* it has the same name and same violent current until it meets the sea; on the Gallic side it is a broader and gentler stream, and its name changes, being now called the Vahalis by the local people. Soon there is another name-change, and it becomes the River Mosa before it also empties into the sea at its huge estuary.

7. While the ships were being brought together, Germanicus ordered his legate Silius to conduct a raid on the Chatti with a

light-armed detachment, and he himself, having been informed that a fort on the River Lupia was under blockade, led six legions to the area. But because of a sudden onset of rain all Silius managed to do was seize a small quantity of plunder, along with the wife and daughter of Arpus, a chieftain of the Chatti; and in Germanicus' case, too, the blockaders gave him no opportunity to do battle, for they slipped away on hearing of his approach. (They had, however, demolished the mound recently erected to commemorate Varus' legions, as well as an altar consecrated to Drusus. Germanicus re-established the altar and led a parade of his troops in his father's honour, but decided against rebuilding the mound. The entire area between Fort Aliso and the Rhine was also strengthened with fresh fortifications and embankments.)

8. After the fleet arrived, Germanicus entered what is called the Drusian Fosse* (he had already sent ahead his supplies and distributed the ships amongst his legions and allied troops). He offered a prayer to his father Drusus, asking that he remember the example of his own designs and exploits and now willingly and favourably assist him as he embarked on the same venture, and then he had a fair voyage through the lakes and the sea as far as the River Amisia. The fleet was moored on the left side* of the river, but he blundered in not ferrying the troops upstream for them to enter the lands on the right bank. The result was many days wasted on constructing bridges. In fact, both cavalry and the legions fearlessly crossed the first estuaries, before the tide was on the rise; but the rear of the column of auxiliaries, along with the Batavi in that part of the force, were thrown into disorder when they jumped confidently about in the waters, displaying their swimming skills, and some were drowned. As Germanicus was laying out his camp he was brought word of a revolt of the Angrivarii* to his rear. Stertinius was immediately sent off with cavalry and a light-armed contingent, and he repaid them for their treachery with burning and carnage.

9. The River Visurgis flowed between the Romans and the Cherusci. Arminius now stood on the bank with the other German chieftains and asked if Germanicus had arrived. Receiving the reply that Germanicus was there, he then asked permission to speak with his brother* (Arminius' brother, whose name was Flavus, was in the Roman army, and was well known for his loyalty, and for the eye he had lost when wounded a few years earlier under Tiberius' command).

Permission was granted,* and when Flavus came forward he was greeted by Arminius. Arminius then dismissed his bodyguard, and requested that the archers posted along our bank also withdraw; and after these retired he asked his brother how his facial disfigurement had come about. When Flavus named the place and the battle, Arminius asked what reward he had received. Flavus told him of his increase in pay, his decorative neck-chain and crown, and his other military donatives, only to have Arminius ridicule such 'cheap rewards for servitude'.

10. With that, a clash of views began. Flavus focused on the greatness of Rome, the emperor's power, the serious penalties meted out to the conquered, and the clemency that was always there for the man who surrendered—and Arminius' wife and son were not being treated as enemies, he added. Arminius pointed to the sacred claims of the fatherland, to their ancestral liberty, to the gods of the German home, and then to their mother who, he said, shared his prayers, namely that Flavus not prefer to desert and betray his kinsmen and relations, and indeed his entire race, than to be their leader. Gradually they fell to quarrelling, and they could not have been prevented from coming to blows, even with the river between them, had not Stertinius run up to restrain Flavus who, full of anger, was calling for his weapons and a horse. Arminius could be observed on the other bank uttering threats and giving notice of battle; for he threw in numerous pieces of Latin, having served in the Roman camp as leader of his countrymen.

11. The following day the German army stood in line on the other side of the Visurgis. Germanicus felt it was unacceptable for a commanding officer to expose his legions to danger without first constructing bridges and manning them with troops, and he sent the cavalry over by a ford. In command were Stertinius and Aemilius (who was of senior centurion rank), and they attacked at some distance from each other so as to divide the enemy force. The Batavian leader, Chariovalda, charged at the point where the stream was fastest. Feigning flight, the Cherusci drew him onto some level ground surrounded by woods. Then, springing to the attack, and pouring forth from all directions, they drove back those who resisted, and pressed hard on the heels of those who withdrew; and when the Batavi formed a circle, they flung them back in disorder, some fighting hand-to-hand, others with projectiles from a distance. After long

enduring the furious enemy onslaught, Chariovalda urged his men to form a body and burst through the enemy who were bearing down on them, and he himself plunged into the thickest of the foe. There he fell, with weapons raining down on him and his horse stabbed beneath him, and many of the Batavian noblemen fell around him. Others were taken out of danger by their own efforts or by the cavalry, which came to their aid led by Stertinius and Aemilius.

12. After crossing the Visurgis, Germanicus learned from information supplied by a deserter that a site for the battle had already been chosen by Arminius, that other tribes had come together at the sacred wood of Hercules and that they would attempt a night attack on the Roman camp. The informant was deemed trustworthy, and fires were also becoming visible, while scouts who got close to the enemy reported hearing the neighing of horses and the commotion of a huge, poorly disciplined army. And so, with the final outcome close at hand, Germanicus believed he should test the morale of his men, and turned his thoughts to how disinterested results could be obtained. The tribunes and centurions, he felt, more often gave reports that were optimistic rather than based on fact; the freedmen had servile characters; and his friends were given to sycophancy. If a meeting were called, there, too, he reasoned, what a few put forward at first the rest would noisily support. He needed to get an insight into the men's minds when they were on their own and unobserved— at the soldiers' mealtime, the time when they divulged their hopes and fears.

13. At nightfall Germanicus furtively left his headquarters taking a secret path unknown to the sentries; he was accompanied by one man, and wore an animal skin on his shoulders. He came to the streets of the camp, stood close by the tents and enjoyed hearing about himself. One man praised their leader's noble character, another his good looks, and most of them his tolerance and affability, his even temper in his serious moments and times of amusement, and they acknowledged that they had to show their gratitude in the field of battle. At the same time, they said, the traitors who had broken the peace had to be sacrificial victims to their vengeance and their glory.

In the meantime, one of the enemy who knew Latin rode up to the rampart and, in Arminius' name, loudly promised rewards to any who deserted—wives, lands, and a daily pay of a hundred sesterces* for as long as the war lasted. This insult intensified the fury of the legions. Just let daylight come, they said, and let them be given the chance to fight! The Roman soldiers would *take* the Germans' lands, and *drag off* the wives. They accepted the omen, they added, and they saw their enemies' wives and money as their spoils of war. At about the third watch, there was an assault on the camp, without a weapon being thrown: the Germans realized that there were cohorts stationed at close intervals along the fortifications, and vigilance had not been relaxed.

14. That same night brought Germanicus a pleasant dream in which he saw himself offer sacrifice and then, when his toga was spattered with the victim's blood, take another more attractive one from the hands of his grandmother Augusta. Encouraged by the omen, and the auspices also being favourable, he called a meeting of the troops and discussed the precautions that his own judgement had suggested to him, and other items appropriate for the coming battle. It was not just open country that favoured the Roman soldier in battle, he said; so did woods and forest glades, if shrewdly used. For the oversized shields of the barbarians and their huge spears were not as effective amidst tree-trunks and undergrowth as the Roman javelins, swords, and body-hugging armour. They should strike repeatedly, said Germanicus, and aim at the face with the points of their weapons. The Germans had no breastplate and no helmet—not even shields reinforced with iron or animal tendons (in place of which they carried wickerwork structures or flimsy, painted boards). The first line was equipped with some kind of spears, he added, but the rest had only short weapons hardened by fire. While their physique presented a grim spectacle and was strong enough for a brief attack, they had no resistance to wounds. They were men who would leave the field and flee with no thought for the disgrace of it, and no concern for their leaders—panic-stricken in defeat and oblivious to any law, human or divine, in their moments of success. If the Romans were sick of marching and seafaring and wanted an end to it, he said, this was the battle by which that could be acquired. The Elbe was now closer than the Rhine, and there would be no fighting* beyond it as long as they made him the victor in that very region where he was treading in the footsteps of his father and his uncle.*

15. The leader's speech was received with fervour by the men, and the signal was given for battle. On their side, Arminius and the other German chieftains did not forget to call on their various peoples to witness that these Romans were the swiftest to flee in Varus' army, men who had turned to mutiny to avoid going to war. Now, they said, with the gods against them and with no hope of success, these were again facing a wrathful foe, some exposing backs covered with wounds, and others limbs that had been shattered by waves and storms. For they had resorted to their ships and the remote water-ways to avoid any opposition as they came, and any pursuit when they were driven back—but winds and oars would prove ineffectual safeguards when the two sides came to grips! They should simply remember the greed, the ruthlessness, and the arrogance of the Romans! Were they now left any option other than retaining their liberty, or dying before becoming slaves?

16. This inflamed the men, who clamoured for battle, and their officers led them down into the plain called Idistaviso. This lies between the Visurgis and the hills, being irregularly contoured because of receding river-banks and projecting spurs of the mountains. To the rear of the Germans rose a forest with towering branches and clear ground between the tree-trunks. The plain and fringes of the forest were occupied by the barbarian battle-line, apart from the Cherusci, who alone were ensconced on the mountain heights so they could charge down on the Romans during the fighting.

Our army advanced in the following order. The Gallic and German auxiliaries were in front, with the foot-archers behind them; next came four legions, and Germanicus at the head of two praetorian* cohorts and some elite cavalry; then there were the other legions (in the same number), the light-armed troops with the mounted archers, and the other allied cohorts. The soldiers were alert and ready to form up the battle-line in the order of the march.

17. The hordes of the Cherusci made an impulsive rush forward. When Germanicus spotted them he ordered his strongest horsemen to charge their flank, and instructed Stertinius to work his way around with the other cavalry squadrons and attack the rear. Germanicus himself would present himself at the appropriate moment.

Meanwhile a fine omen caught the commander's eye, eight eagles that were spotted heading for and entering the woods. They should go ahead and follow the Roman birds, the special deities of the legions, Germanicus cried; and in a simultaneous movement the infantry line made its charge, and the cavalry that had been sent forward attacked the rear and the flanks. And then, strange to say, two columns of the enemy went in headlong flight in opposite directions, those who had been deployed in the woods heading for the open country, and those positioned on the flat ground into the wood. Between the two, the Cherusci were being dislodged from the hills, and amongst them, a striking figure, was Arminius, trying to keep the battle alive by fighting, shouting and taking his wounds. He had swooped down on the archers, intending to break through at this point, only to find his way blocked by the Raetian, Vindelician, and Gallic cohorts. Even so, with great physical effort and by the momentum of his horse, he did make his way through, after smearing his face with his own blood to avoid recognition. Some have claimed that he was actually recognized and let through by the Chauci who were serving amongst the Roman auxiliaries. Similar courage—or similar treachery—enabled Inguiomerus to escape. The rest were slaughtered indiscriminately. Some tried to swim across the Visurgis, but were overpowered by a volley of weapons or the force of the current, and eventually by the rushing mass of fugitives and the collapsing banks. Some, in a shameful attempt to escape, struggled up to the treetops and hid in the branches, but these were scornfully shot down when the archers were brought up, or crushed when the trees were felled.

18. It was a great victory* and not dear in blood for us. The enemy were massacred from the day's fifth hour until nightfall, covering a ten-mile stretch with corpses and weapons, and amongst the spoils were discovered chains that they had brought for the Romans, believing the result a foregone conclusion. The men hailed Tiberius as *Imperator** on the site of the battle, and raised a mound on which they set weapons (as one does with trophies), with an inscription bearing the names of the conquered tribes at its foot.

19. As for the Germans, their wounds, their grief, and their losses did not incite as much pain and wrath as did the sight of this. Men who had been preparing to leave their homes and retreat across the Elbe now wanted a fight, and seized their weapons. Common people and chieftains, young and old, suddenly launched attacks on the Roman column, throwing it into disorder. Finally they selected a spot confined by a river and some woods, with a flat piece of boggy terrain in between; and there was also a deep swamp surrounding the woods, except that on one side the Angrivarii had raised a broad mound to mark their frontier with the Cherusci. Here the German infantry took up a position, but the cavalry they set under cover in

some nearby copses so they would be to the rear of the legions when these entered the woods.

20. None of this escaped Germanicus' attention. He was cognizant of their plans and positions, of their overt and covert movements, and he set about turning the ruses of the enemy to their own destruction. He put the cavalry and its operations on the flat land in the hands of his legate, Seius Tubero.* The infantry line he deployed in such a manner as to have some entering the wood on the level ground, with others climbing the mound that blocked their path. The hardest tasks he assumed himself, leaving the rest to his subordinates.

Those who had been assigned the level ground charged ahead with ease; those who had to attack the mound found it was like scaling a wall, and they were under severe pressure from projectiles delivered from above. The commander sensed the disadvantage in a battle fought at close quarters. He therefore brought the legions back a short distance and ordered his slingers and artillery to launch their weapons and drive off the enemy. Spears were discharged from the throwing devices, and the more in evidence the defenders were, the more numerous were the wounds by which they were brought down. The earthwork captured, Germanicus took the praetorian cohorts and was the first to direct an attack into the woods. There they fought hand-to-hand. To their rear the enemy was restricted by the marshland, the Romans by the river or the mountains. Each was under pressure from his position, where hope lay only in courage, and safety only in victory.

21. The Germans were not inferior in courage, but they were outdone by the nature of the fighting and weaponry. With their large numbers they could not, in the restricted space, adequately thrust and withdraw their huge spears, and, forced into stationary combat, they could not profit from their sudden charges and speed, either. The Roman soldier, by contrast, with shield pressed to his breast and hand on sword-hilt, was stabbing at the broad frames of the barbarians and their unprotected faces, and was opening up a path by cutting down the enemy. And Arminius was by now holding back because of the constant risks he was facing, or because a wound he had just received had slowed him down. As for Inguiomerus, who had been darting all over the battlefield, he was let down by fortune rather than his courage. Germanicus, too, so he would be more easily

recognized, had removed his headgear and was begging his men to keep up the slaughter. No need to take captives, he told them—only total extermination of that people would end the conflict. It was already late in the day when he withdrew a legion from the battle-line to make camp; the other legions glutted themselves with the enemy's blood till nightfall. The cavalry battle was indecisive.

22. Germanicus commended his victorious troops at an assembly, and piled up a heap of weapons, adding a proud inscription stating that the army of Tiberius Caesar had consecrated that memorial to Mars, Jupiter, and Augustus after reducing the tribes* between the Rhine and the Elbe. He added nothing about himself, fearing to provoke envy or else believing that awareness of his achievement was sufficient. Presently he authorized Stertinius to make war on the Angrivarii,* unless they surrendered first. In fact, they came as suppliants and, by refusing no condition, received a full pardon.

23. With summer now far advanced,* a number of the legions were sent back to winter quarters overland; most of them Germanicus put aboard his fleet and transported to the Ocean along the River Amisia. At the start there was a calm sea, disturbed only by the sound of the oars of a thousand ships and their scudding under sail. Soon black clouds gathered, and there was a downfall of hail, while at the same time the waves kept shifting in the winds that were blowing from every direction; and this removed all visibility and hampered the steering. The soldiers, panic-stricken and unfamiliar with the hazards of the sea, obstructed the sailors or brought ill-timed assistance, thus impeding the experts in the performance of their duties. Then the whole sky and the whole sea fell under the power of the south wind, which draws strength from the wet terrain of Germany, its deep rivers, and huge tracts of cloud, and is made the more grim by the freezing cold of its neighbour, the north wind. This seized and scattered the ships over the open sea, or towards islands* that had sheer cliffs or were fraught with danger because of hidden shoals. For a short while these were avoided, though with difficulty. Then the tide started to turn and flow with the wind, and it proved impossible to hold to the anchors, and to bale out the waters that came crashing over the vessels. Horses, pack-animals, baggage, and even weapons were jettisoned to lighten the hulls, which were shipping water through their sides and from the waves flooding over them.

24. As the Ocean* is more violent than any other sea, and Germany transcends other countries in the brutality of its climate, just so did that disaster surpass others in its bizarre nature and magnitude. They had hostile shores all around, and a deep so vast that it is believed to be the final sea, where land ends. Some of the ships were sunk, more cast up on far-off islands. Because of the lack of human habitation there, soldiers starved to death, apart from those sustained by the cadavers of horses cast up on the same shore. Germanicus' trireme put in alone at the land of the Chauci. He, through all those following days and nights, would cry out amidst the rocks and on the coastal headlands that he was to blame for such a great disaster; and his friends had difficulty holding him back from suicide in that same sea.

Finally, with the ebbing tide and a favourable wind, some ships returned, disabled, a few with their oars, or with clothing stretched out as sails, and some towed by others that were in better shape. These Germanicus hurriedly repaired and sent off to reconnoitre the islands. A number of men were picked up as a result of his solicitude. The Angrivarii, whose submission had been recently accepted, ransomed large numbers from inland tribes and restored them to us; some had been swept away to Britain and were returned by its tribal chieftains. Everyone returning from afar brought wondrous tales of violent whirlwinds, unknown birds, sea-monsters, and creatures part-human and part-beast—things they had seen or, in their fear, believed they had seen.

25. Now, while reports of the loss of the fleet roused the Germans to hopes of war, it also inspired Germanicus to hold them in check. He ordered Gaius Silius to march on the Chatti* with thirty thousand infantry and three thousand cavalry, and he himself launched an invasion on the Marsi with a larger force. The leader of the Marsi, Mallovendus, whose surrender had recently been accepted, told him that the eagle of one of Varus' legions lay buried in a grove close by, and was only lightly guarded. A band of men was immediately sent to draw the enemy away from the front of the position, while others were to encircle the rear and dig up the ground. Both groups achieved success. Germanicus therefore marched into the interior with all the greater determination, pillaging and wreaking destruction on an enemy who dared not engage or, wherever he resisted, was immediately driven back and intimidated (so it was gathered from prisoners) as never before. For they kept declaring that the Romans were invincible, that they could be cowed by no reverses. When their fleet was destroyed and their weapons lost, and after the shores were littered with the bodies of horses and men, they had charged upon them with the same courage, and with just as much ferocity—and even, so it seemed, with increased numbers!

26. The men were then led back to winter quarters, happy in their hearts at having compensated for their disaster at sea with a success-ful operation. In addition, Germanicus showed his generosity by covering whatever losses anyone declared. And there was no doubt now that the enemy was wavering and considering plans to sue for peace, and that a further campaign the following summer could see the war brought to a conclusion. Tiberius, however, in a succession of letters, kept advising him to return for the triumph* that had been decreed for him—there had been enough successes, enough misfor-tunes. His battles had been great victories, he was told, but he should also bear in mind the losses brought on by the winds and waves—losses which, while not the leader's fault, were heavy and serious none the less. He himself had been sent into Germany nine times by the deified Augustus, Tiberius added, and he had achieved more by diplomacy than force—that was how the Sugambri had been brought to surrender, and how the Suebi and King Maroboduus had been made to accept peace. Since the vengeance of Rome had been satisfied, he concluded, the Cherusci and the other rebellious tribes could also be left to their internal discords.

When Germanicus pleaded for a year to complete his undertaking, Tiberius worked more keenly on his modesty with an offer of a second consulship, the duties of which required his presence in Rome. He made the further point that, if the war must be continued, Germanicus should leave the wherewithal for his brother Drusus to acquire *his* glory. With no other enemy then available, it was only in the German provinces that Drusus could acquire the title of *Imperator* and bring home the laurel crown. Germanicus no longer hesitated, although he understood these were simply falsehoods, and that jealousy was the reason for his being torn away from distinction already won.

27. About this same time, Libo Drusus,* a member of the Scribonian family, was accused of fomenting revolution. I shall give a rather detailed account of how this matter began, progressed, and ended because that was the start of practices that gnawed away at the state for so many years. Firmius Catus, a senator, was on very friendly terms with Libo, and he pushed the thoughtless young man, who was prone to delusions, to turn to the assurances of Chaldeans,* to magic rites and even to interpreters of dreams. Catus did this by drawing Libo's attention to the fact that his great-grandfather had been Pompey,* and his great-aunt was Scribonia, who had once been the wife of Augustus; that he had Caesars as his cousins; and that his house was full of his ancestors' images. And so he encouraged him into a life of extravagance and debt, sharing his vices and financial difficulties so as to have more evidence to ensnare him.

28. When he had found sufficient witnesses, and some slaves to acknowledge the truth of their information, Catus requested an audience with the emperor, having already made him aware of the charge and the identity of the accused through the Roman knight Flaccus Vescularius, who was on closer terms with Tiberius.

Tiberius did not reject the information, but declined the meeting, saying that their communication could be continued with Flaccus as their intermediary. In the meantime he paid Libo the honour of conferring a praetorship* on him, invited him to his dinner-parties,* and revealed no alienation from him in his expression, and no irritation in his speech—such was the extent to which he had suppressed his anger. All Libo's words and acts he could have held in check, but he preferred to have knowledge of them—until, eventually, a certain Junius, who had been approached by Libo to call up shades of the dead with his spells, brought this information to Fulcinius Trio.* Trio was renowned amongst the informers for his talent, and was thirsting for an evil reputation. He immediately pounced on the accused man, went to the consuls and demanded a judicial inquiry by the Senate. The senators were then summoned, and were also informed that they must debate an important and heinous matter.

29. Libo, meanwhile, changed into mourning clothes and, escorted by ladies of the highest distinction, went from house to house, begging his wife's relatives for aid and asking them to voice support to ward off his peril. All refused, proffering different excuses, but from the same fear. On the day of the Senate meeting he was worn out from trepidation and sickness, or perhaps (as some have recorded) he was feigning illness. He was carried to the doors of the Curia in a litter, and then, leaning on his brother, he stretched out his arms and made suppliant pleas to Tiberius, but was met by a face devoid of expression. Presently the emperor read aloud the list of charges along with the denouncers' names, controlling his delivery to avoid the impression of either lightening or aggravating the accusations.

30. Fonteius Agrippa and Gaius Vibius* had also joined Trio and Catus as Libo's accusers, and they were now at odds over who should be granted the privilege of conducting the case against the defendant. Eventually, Vibius declared that, because they would not defer to each other, and because Libo had made his entrance without counsel, he would lay the charges one by one.* He then produced documents so absurd as to include Libo making consultations about whether he was going to have wealth enough to cover the Appian Way with money all the way to Brundisium! There were others of the same type: stupid, senseless, or, if one looked at them more charitably, pathetic. In one document, however, the accuser maintained that some sinister or mysterious characters had been added, in Libo's handwriting, beside the names of imperial family members or senators. When the defendant denied this, it was decided that some slaves who recognized the handwriting be interrogated under torture.* There was, however, an old decree* of the Senate by which such an investigation was prohibited when it was a matter of a capital charge against a master; and so Tiberius, a clever man even in devising legal precedents,* ordered the slaves sold off individually to the treasury agent.* And this was done, of course, so the investigation of Libo through his slaves could be effected with no contravention of the senatorial decree! In the light of this the defendant requested an adjournment till the following day and, going home, put his final pleas to the emperor in the hands of his relative, Publius Quirinius.*

31. The answer he was given was that he should address his appeal to the Senate. Meanwhile his house was surrounded by soldiers, and these created a disturbance even in the vestibule so that they would be both heard and seen. Then, tortured by the very dinner that he had put on to provide his last pleasure, Libo called for someone to kill him and, grasping the hands of some slaves, tried to place his sword in them. The slaves, in confusion and shrinking back, knocked over a lamp set on a table nearby and, in what was for him already the darkness of death, Libo delivered two blows to his own vital organs.

In response to the groan as he fell, his freedman ran to the spot, and the soldiers, seeing him dead, stood back. The accusation was none the less seen through with the same formality, and Tiberius swore* that he would have asked for Libo's life, guilty though he was, had he not been too hasty in committing suicide.

32. Libo's goods were divided* amongst his accusers, and those of them who belonged to the senatorial order were granted extraordinary praetorships. Then Cotta Messalinus* proposed that Libo's image* not attend the funeral of any of his descendants, and Gnaeus Lentulus that no Scribonius should take the *cognomen** Drusus. Days of public thanksgiving were ordained on a motion of Pomponius Flaccus,* and Lucius Plancus, Gallus Asinius,* Papius Mutilus, and Lucius Apronius* sponsored a decree that gifts be offered to Jupiter, Mars, and Concord, and that 13 September, the day on which Libo had killed himself, be regarded a holiday. (I have brought up these proposals and instances of obsequiousness so it may be known that this has been a long-standing plague in the state.)

There were also senatorial decrees* passed expelling astrologers and magicians from Italy. One of these, Lucius Pituanius, was hurled from the rock,* and the consuls had Publius Marcius executed in the ancient manner* outside the Esquiline Gate, after ordering a trumpet to be sounded.

33. At the next meeting of the Senate, a long disquisition on extravagance in the state was delivered by the ex-consul Quintus Haterius* and the former praetor Octavius Fronto. It was then decided that vessels for serving food* should not be made of solid gold, and that men not dishonour themselves by wearing silk clothing. Fronto went beyond this to demand limits on ownership of silver, furniture, and domestic slaves (for it was still common practice for senators, when it was their turn to vote, to bring up anything they believed beneficial to the state).

Gallus Asinius spoke against the motion. As the empire had grown, he argued, private means had also increased, and that was nothing new but was in line with ancient practice. Money was one thing in the days of the Fabricii, and another in those of the Scipios—all was measured against the condition of the state. When this was weak, the households of citizens were impoverished; but after it reached such a level of opulence as now, individuals also prospered more. With regard to domestic slaves and silver, and all acquisitions with a utilitarian purpose, nothing was excessive or modest except in relation to the fortune of its owner. Different property classifications existed for the Senate and for the knights, Asinius continued, not because these people were intrinsically different, but because, as they were pre-eminent in theatre-seating, in social ranking, and political office, so they should have priority in those things that promote mental relaxation and physical health. That is, he added, unless every man of distinction should face more anxieties and greater dangers—and also be deprived of things that make the anxieties and dangers bearable! Gallus' admission of vice in fine-sounding terms won him easy assent from his like-minded listeners. Furthermore, Tiberius had added the remark that this was not the time for moral correction, but if there were a slide in ethical standards someone to address it would not be lacking.

34. During this discussion Lucius Piso* launched into a tirade against influence-peddling in the Forum, corrupt practices in the courts, and the callousness of orators, with their threats of impeachment, and he declared that he was retiring and abandoning the city to live in some secluded and remote part of the countryside. So saying, he proceeded to leave the Curia. Tiberius was concerned, and though he tried to placate Piso with gentle words he also prevailed upon the man's relatives to use their influence, or even entreaties, to halt his leaving.

Piso soon provided a further instance of his readiness to vent his indignation, by taking to court Urgulania,* whom friendship with Augusta* had set above the law. In fact, Urgulania did not comply with the summons, but instead ignored Piso and had herself transported to the emperor's home. Piso did not back down, either, despite Augusta's protests that she was being dishonoured and humiliated. Tiberius considered that he had the right as a citizen to indulge his mother to the extent of saying he would attend the praetor's court to support Urgulania, and so he left the Palatium after ordering his soldiers to follow at a distance. As people flocked towards him, he could be seen, with an unruffled expression, drawing out the time and the journey with various topics of conversation. Finally, when his relatives failed to hold Piso back, Augusta ordered the payment of the amount of money that was claimed. And that was the end of the matter—from which Piso derived some prestige, and Tiberius also saw his reputation enhanced. In fact, Urgulania's power was so oppressive on the state that she did not deign to appear as a witness in a certain case that was being dealt with before the Senate. A praetor was dispatched to put questions to her at home, despite the long-standing convention of Vestal Virgins* being heard in the Forum law courts whenever they gave evidence.

35. I would not mention that year's suspension of public business* were it not that the difference of opinions between Gnaeus Piso and Asinius Gallus on the matter is worthy of note. Tiberius had said that he would not be attending the Senate. Piso then expressed his opinion that this of itself made the continuation of business there all the more necessary—the fact that the Senate and knights could continue to discharge their duties in the emperor's absence would be to the credit of the state. Seeing that Piso had pre-empted him with this display of independence, Gallus insisted that no public business could be sufficiently impressive, or be in keeping with the dignity of the Roman people, unless it were conducted in the presence, and under the eyes, of Tiberius. Accordingly, he said, matters relating to deputations from all of Italy and those flooding in from the provinces should be held over until he was present. Tiberius listened to this and remained silent. The issue was hotly debated on both sides, but the suspension came into effect.

36. Gallus also found himself pitted against Tiberius. He moved that the elections serve to appoint magistrates for the next five-year period,* and further that legionary commanders who were serving in the field before holding the praetorship should be made praetors-designate at that time, with the emperor nominating twelve candidates per year. There was no doubt that the proposal had a deeper purpose, with some probe being made into the secrets of the imperial power. Nevertheless, Tiberius spoke as if his authority was actually being extended—so many elected to office and so many deferred put a heavy burden on him, given his self-restraint, he said. One could barely avoid causing offence even with annual appointments—but at least there was some consolation for rejection in hope for the near future. How great would the resentment be on the part of those who would be cast aside for more than five years! Over so long a period of time how could one predict the thinking, the domestic situation and the fortunes of each individual? Men became above themselves even with the appointment on a yearly basis—what if they had that office reserved for a five-year period? In fact, the magistracies

were being quintupled, and the laws defining the periods for candidates to put in their work, and for seeking or acquiring offices, were
being subverted. With this speech, which looked conciliatory,
Tiberius kept intact the substance of his power.

37. Tiberius also helped some senators with their wealth-
qualifications. This makes his disdainful reaction to the pleas of the
young nobleman, Marcius Hortalus,* all the more surprising, as
Hortalus was clearly in financial difficulties. He was the grandson of
the orator Hortensius, and had been induced by a generous gift of a
million sesterces from the deified Augustus to take a wife and raise
children so that a famous family would not die out. The Senate was
then being held in the Palatium,* and Hortalus' four sons were
standing before the threshold of the Curia. When his turn came to
give his opinion, Hortalus looked at one moment towards the statue
of Hortensius among the orators, and at another towards that of
Augustus, and began to speak:

'Senators: it was not my idea to have these children—and you see
how many they are and how young—but I did so at the emperor's
prompting. At the same time, my ancestors deserved to have descendants. I, in these changing times, was unable to inherit or gain wealth,
popular support, or—the heirloom of our family—eloquence,* and it
was enough for me if my straitened circumstances proved to be neither a disgrace to me nor a burden to others. On the emperor's
instructions I married. See, here, the offspring and progeny of so
many consuls and so many dictators!* And I mention that not to
make invidious comparisons, but to win your pity. While you
flourish in power, Caesar, they will gain the offices you grant them.
Meanwhile, keep the great-grandsons of Quintus Hortensius, the
foster-children of Augustus, out of penury.'

38. The favourable reaction of the Senate was an incentive for
prompt opposition on the part of Tiberius, whose words were much
like this:

'If all the poor start coming here asking for money for their children, individuals will never be satisfied and the state will go bank-
rupt. Certainly, allowance was made by our ancestors for the occasional
digression from the motion in the Senate, when it was one's turn to
express his opinion, and for making proposals for the public benefit.
But the point of that was certainly not so that we could further our
private interests and family affairs, exposing thereby the Senate and

the emperors to resentment, whether they granted or refused the award. For that was no appeal, but a threatening demand, one ill-timed and unexpected—to stand up when members were discussing other matters and, by citing the number and age of his children, to embarrass and constrain the Senate. It is likewise putting pressure on me, and virtually breaking into the treasury—and if we empty that through improper influence, it will have to be refilled by crime!

'Hortalus, the deified Augustus gave you money, but not because he was called upon for it and not on the condition that it be continually given. In any case, individual effort will decline, and lethargy will be bolstered, if fear and hope are totally unrelated to personal responsibility, and all men will nonchalantly expect help from others—becoming useless to themselves, and a burden on us.'

These and other such comments met with approval from those who habitually praise every move, honourable or dishonourable, that emperors make; the majority heard them in silence or with a hushed murmur. Tiberius felt it, and after a brief pause stated that he had given his reply, but if such were the senators' decision, he would give each of Hortalus' children who were of the male sex 200,000 sesterces. Some members thanked him; Hortalus remained silent, fearful or because even in his straitened circumstances he still clung to his ancestral nobility. Nor did Tiberius show any compassion after that, though the house of Hortensius declined into shameful penury.

39. That same year, had not action been quickly taken, the reckless behaviour of a single slave might have brought down the state with dissension and civil war. On learning of the death of Augustus, a slave of Postumus Agrippa, whose name was Clemens, conjured up an idea one would not expect of a slave: he would proceed to the island of Planasia, take Agrippa by subterfuge or force, and bring him to the armies in Germany. What checked his bold venture was the slowness of his merchant vessel. The murder of his master having been perpetrated in the meantime, Clemens turned to a more ambitious and more dangerous plan. He stole Postumus' ashes, sailed to Cosa, a promontory in Etruria, and shut himself away in hiding until he could grow his hair and beard longer (for in age and appearance he was not unlike his master). Then, using suitable agents who were party to his secret, he saw to it that word spread that Agrippa was alive.* First there were whispered conversations—as is usual with forbidden topics—and presently a vague rumour that would

reach the welcoming ears of the naive or else come to dissidents who were eager for revolution. In addition, Clemens would come to the towns when day turned to dusk, never being in full view or remaining too long in the same spot. He knew that the truth gains validity through seeing and the passage of time, and deception from haste and uncertainty, and he would leave behind him a rumour of his appearance, or arrive before it started.

40. In the meantime the story was spreading throughout Italy that, by a gift of the gods, Agrippa had been saved, and it was beginning to be believed in Rome. When the man sailed into Ostia, a huge crowd welcomed him, and in the city, too, many gathered in secret for the occasion. At that point Tiberius was torn by conflicting thoughts. He wondered whether to use the military to suppress his own slave,* or allow this idle fancy to disappear with the passage of time; and, wavering between shame and fear, he would at one moment think that nothing should be taken lightly, and at the next that not everything need be feared. Finally he put the matter in Sallustius Crispus' hands. Crispus selected two of his clients—some have it that they were soldiers—and urged them to approach Clemens with a pretence of collaborating with him. They were to offer him money, loyalty, and their willingness to face the dangers. The two followed their orders. Then, watching out for a night when he was unguarded, they took a sufficiently large group of men, and dragged Clemens, bound and gagged, into the Palatium. It is said that when Tiberius asked him how he had 'become Agrippa', Clemens replied: 'The way you became Caesar.' He could not be compelled to identify his accomplices. Not daring to punish him in public, Tiberius ordered him to be killed in a secret area of the Palatium, and the body surreptitiously removed. It was claimed that many of the emperor's household and many knights and senators had supported Clemens with their financial resources, but there was no inquiry.

41. At the end of the year the following dedications were made:

An arch near the temple of Saturn, in thanks for the recapture, under Germanicus' command, and under the auspices of Tiberius, of the standards* lost with Varus.

A temple of Fors Fortuna on the banks of the Tiber, in the gardens that the dictator Caesar had left the Roman people in his will.

A shrine to the Julian family, and a statue to the deified Augustus, at Bovillae.*

In the consulship of Gaius Caelius and Lucius Pomponius, on 26 May, Germanicus Caesar celebrated a triumph* over the Cherusci, the Chatti, the Angrivarii, and the other tribes as far as the Elbe. Spoils, prisoners, and representations of mountains, rivers, and battles formed part of the procession; and because Germanicus had been prevented from finishing off the war, it was regarded as finished. For the onlookers the spectacle was enhanced by Germanicus' handsome appearance and by the chariot with its cargo of five children. But there was subliminal apprehension, too. People thought back on the fact that the favour of the crowd had not been to his father Drusus' advantage, that his uncle Marcellus* had been swept away, in his youth, while he had the ardent support of the commons, and that such love affairs of the Roman people were short-lived and ill-starred.

42. Tiberius gave each of the plebeians 300 sesterces in Germanicus' name, and designated himself his colleague for the consulship. Even so, he did not convince people of the sincerity of his affection, and he resolved to remove the young man from Rome with some specious promotion. He then invented grounds for this, or seized on those offered by chance.

King Archelaus had been in power in Cappadocia for fifty years,* and was hated by Tiberius because, during his time on Rhodes, the king had not paid his respects to him. In fact, Archelaus had omitted to do so not from any disdain for the man, but on the advice of close friends of Augustus. For Gaius Caesar was then much in favour, and had been sent to effect a settlement in the East, so that friendship with Tiberius was deemed risky. When Tiberius gained power after the extinction of the line of the Caesars, he enticed Archelaus to Rome with a letter, written by his mother, in which Livia, without concealing her son's hard feelings, held out the prospect of mercy if Archelaus came to beg for it. Unaware of the trick, or fearing violent treatment if he were thought to know of it, Archelaus rushed to the city, where he was met by an unforgiving emperor and presently impeached* in the Senate. Then, not because of the charges, which were trumped up, but from anxiety (and also because he was exhausted with age, and because kings are unused to equality, much less humiliation), he came to the end of his life, either through suicide or from natural causes. His kingdom was reduced to a province. Tiberius declared that with the income from it the one per cent tax could be reduced,* and he fixed it at half of one per cent for the future.

At about the same time, with the death of Antiochus, king of Commagene,* and Philopator,* king of Cilicia, there was unrest amongst their peoples, most wanting Roman rule, but others the monarchy. Furthermore, the provinces of Syria and Judaea, weary of their tax burdens, were pleading for a reduction of their tribute.

43. Tiberius therefore discussed with the senators these matters, and those of Armenia which I noted above, and declared that the disturbances in the East could be settled only by Germanicus' sound judgement. For he himself was in his declining years,* he said, and Drusus was not yet senior enough. Then, by senatorial decree, the overseas provinces were assigned to Germanicus, who was also to have, wherever he went, greater authority* than those who held provincial governorships through sortition or imperial mandate.

Tiberius had, however, removed from Syria Creticus Silanus, who had a marriage tie with Germanicus, Silanus' daughter being engaged to Germanicus' eldest son. He had then appointed as governor Gnaeus Piso,* who had a violent nature and could not accept authority. His restive character derived from his father Piso who, in the civil war, gave vigorous support to the renascent opposition to Caesar in Africa. (Piso subsequently followed Brutus and Cassius and, when allowed to return home, refused to stand for office until actually pressed to accept a consulship* offered him by Augustus.) But his father's restlessness aside, there were also the noble station and wealth of his wife Plancina to fire his spirit. He was barely deferential to Tiberius, and he looked down on Tiberius' children as being very much his inferiors. And Piso had no doubt that his choice as governor of Syria was intended as a check on Germanicus' ambitions. Some believed that he was also given secret instructions by Tiberius; and Augusta, prompted by female jealousy, certainly advised Plancina* to persecute Agrippina. For there were divisions and schisms in the court, with support tacitly given either to Drusus or Germanicus. Tiberius favoured Drusus as his own son and his own flesh and blood. In Germanicus' case, being alienated from his uncle had served to increase affection for him amongst everyone else, as also had the advantage he enjoyed in the distinction of his mother's family—he claimed Marcus Antonius as his grandfather, and Augustus as a great-uncle. For Drusus, on the other hand, his

great-grandfather Pomponius Atticus,* a Roman knight, only seemed
to bring discredit on the family images of the Claudii, and Germanicus'
wife Agrippina eclipsed Drusus' wife Livilla* in child-bearing and
reputation. Nevertheless the brothers had an exceptionally harmonious relationship, unshaken by the rivalries of their kinsfolk.

44. Not much later Drusus was sent into Illyricum* in order to
gain military experience and win over the support of the troops.
Tiberius also felt that the young man, running amok in the high
living of the city, was better off in a camp, and that he himself would
be safer if both his sons had legionary commands. The alleged
reason, however, was a Suebian plea for assistance against the
Cherusci. With the departure of the Romans, and their release from
an external threat, the Germans, reverting to tribal custom and competing for glory, had turned their arms against each other. The
strength of the two tribes and the courage of their leaders were on a
par; but his royal title made Maroboduus* hated amongst his compatriots, while Arminius enjoyed popularity as a fighter for freedom.

45. As a result, it was not simply a matter of Arminius' old soldiers, that is, the Cherusci and their allies, taking up the fight; even
from Maroboduus' realm, two Suebian tribes, the Semnones and
Langobardi, defected to him. With such reinforcements, Arminius' superiority was assured—but for Inguiomerus' desertion to Maroboduus
with a group of his clients (the only reason for which was an aged uncle's
proud refusal to take orders from his brother's young son).

The battle-lines were being deployed with equally high expectations on both sides, and there were no random charges or attacks by
scattered companies, in the old German fashion. Through their long
campaigning against us, they had developed the practice of following
standards, using reserves to support the main body, and obeying
their commanders. On this occasion, too, Arminius ranged over the
whole field on his horse. As he rode up to each unit he pointed out to
them the freedom they had regained, the legions they had slaughtered, and the spoils and javelins that had been seized from the Romans
and which were now in the hands of many of his men. Maroboduus,
by contrast, he styled as a man quick to flee and lacking battle
experience. He had sought protection in the hideouts of Hyrcania,
and had soon asked for a treaty, using gifts and delegations—a traitor to his country and a hanger-on of the emperor. They should
chase him out with as much loathing as they felt when they killed

Varus Quinctilius. They only had to think back on all those battles whose outcome, with the final expulsion of the Romans, showed clearly enough with which side lay the final result of the war.

46. Maroboduus did not let slip the opportunity for self-glorification or vituperation of the foe, either. Grasping Inguiomerus, he declared that in that person resided all the glory of the Cherusci, and that it was because of his plans that all their successes had been achieved. Arminius was a madman with no practical know-how, he said; and he was appropriating to himself credit due to another for having treacherously taken by surprise three straggling legions and their commander, who was unaware that trickery was afoot. (And the result of that, he added, was disaster for Germany and dishonour for Arminius personally, since his wife and son were still enduring servitude.) Now when he, Maroboduus, was attacked by twelve legions* under Tiberius' command, he had kept the glory of Germany unsullied, the two sides presently parting on equal terms*—and he felt no regret that they now had the choice between war against the Romans with their strength intact and a bloodless peace, now rested in their hands.

The two armies were roused by these speeches, and they had their own motives to stimulate them, as well: for the Cherusci and Langobardi the struggle was for their glory of old or their fresh liberty, and on the other side it was for the extension of power. Never was an engagement so fiercely fought, and the result so indecisive, with the right wings routed on both sides. It was expected that the fight would be renewed, but Maroboduus withdrew his camp to the hills. This was the sign of his defeat and, when he was gradually stripped of troops by desertions, he withdrew to the Marcomani and sent spokesmen to Tiberius to beg for assistance. The reply was that he had no right to call upon Roman arms against the Cherusci since he had provided no help to the Romans when they were fighting that same enemy. Even so, Drusus was sent out, as we have noted, to consolidate the peace.

47. During that same year twelve famous cities in Asia collapsed in an earthquake,* which occurred at night and so made the damage all the more unexpected and serious. Even rushing out into the open, the normal means of escape in such events, proved of no help because people were swallowed up by fissures in the earth. There are accounts of huge mountains subsiding, of land that was level being seen raised

up, and of fire flashing out amidst the destruction. The worst losses fell on the people of Sardis, and this also brought them the most compassion. The emperor made them a commitment of ten million sesterces, and granted them five years' relief from all payments owing to the treasury or imperial exchequer.* Second in terms of losses, and relief provided, were thought to be the people of Magnesia near Sipylus. Then there were the people of Temnus, Philadelphia, Aegeae, and Apollonis, and the so-called Mosteni or Hyrcanian Macedonians, as well as Hierocaesaria, Myrina, Cyme, and Tmolus. It was decided that these should also receive relief from tribute-payments for the same period of time, and that a representative of the Senate be sent to see how matters stood and to aid recovery. One of the ex-praetors, Marcus Ateius, was chosen for the job. For the governor of Asia was of consular rank, and there was fear of rivalry between men of equal status, which could cause problems.

48. To his impressive generosity on the official level Tiberius added private liberality that was no less appreciated. The property of Aemilia Musa,* a rich lady but intestate, had been claimed for the imperial exchequer, but the emperor passed it on to Aemilius Lepidus,* to whose family she appeared to have belonged. He also passed on the inheritance of a rich Roman knight Pantuleius (even though Tiberius himself was selected as co-inheritor) to Marcus Servilius,* whose name he had discovered had been entered in an earlier, authenticated will. The nobility of both these men, he declared, needed financial support. He also would not touch anyone's inheritance unless he had earned it from friendship, and kept his distance from strangers and people who named the emperor as an heir because of their quarrels with others. But while he alleviated the honourable poverty of the guiltless he also removed from the Senate, or permitted them to leave of their own accord, prodigals whose neediness arose from their vices. Such were Vibidius Virro, Marius Nepos, Appius Appianus, Cornelius Sulla, and Quintus Vitellius.

49. In this same period Tiberius also dedicated the following temples that were in ruins through age or from fire, and whose restoration had been started by Augustus:

The temple to Liber, Libera, and Ceres* (which the dictator Aulus Postumius had promised in a vow), close to the Circus Maximus.

The temple to Flora, in the same location, which had been established by Lucius and Marcus Publicius* during their aedileship.

The temple to Janus, which Gaius Duilius* had built in the Forum Holitorium. Duilius was the first man to achieve success for Rome at sea and earn a naval triumph over the Carthaginians.

A temple to Hope was dedicated by Germanicus (Aulus Atilius* had promised it in a vow during the same war).

50. Meanwhile, the law of treason was coming to maturity, and an informer arraigned Appuleia Varilla, granddaughter of Augustus' sister.* The basis for the charge was that she had ridiculed the deified Augustus, Tiberius, and Tiberius' mother in scurrilous conversations, and that, though a relative of the emperor, she was guilty of adultery. Sufficient provision was made for the adultery under the Julian law,* it was decided. As for the charge of treason, the emperor demanded that it be broken down, that Appuleia be condemned if she had made any impious comments about Augustus, but that he did not want gibes at himself made the subject of an inquiry. When asked by the consul what he thought about the offensive remarks that Appuleia was said to have made about his mother, Tiberius remained silent. Then, on the next day the Senate met he earnestly requested in his mother's name that no one be charged for having made any kind of comment on her. So he acquitted Appuleia of treason; and, in the matter of the adultery, he made a plea against the heavier penalty,* urging that tradition* be followed and she be removed by her relatives to a point beyond the two-hundredth milestone. Her lover, Manlius, was forbidden residence in Italy and Africa.

51. A dispute arose over the praetor to replace Vipstanus Gallus, who had been removed by death. Germanicus and Drusus—both were still in Rome at the time—favoured Haterius Agrippa,* a relative of Germanicus. For the other side several people were pressing for the number of children to be the predominant factor in the case of the candidates, as the law* stipulated. Tiberius was delighted to see the Senate as the arbiter between his sons and the laws. Of course, the law was the loser, but not immediately and only by a few votes, which was how laws were defeated even when they had force.

52. During that same year war broke out in Africa, where the enemy leader was Tacfarinas.* He was a Numidian by nationality who had done service as an auxiliary soldier in the Roman camp, but had soon turned deserter. He initially put together a collection of drifters, who were practised in banditry, for pillaging and robbery, but then he formed them up as detachments and squadrons, in military

fashion, and finally he came to be regarded as the leader, not of a disorganized rabble, but of the Musulamians. This was a powerful tribe that lived close to the deserts of Africa, and which even at that time was ignorant of city living. The Musulamians then took up arms and also drew into the war their neighbours the Mauri, who had their own leader, Mazippa. The army was divided such that Tacfarinas could keep in his camp some elite troops armed in the Roman manner, whom he would familiarize with discipline and the command structure, while Mazippa took a light-armed detachment and spread fire, carnage, and terror around the country. They had also forced the Cinithii, a tribe not to be underestimated, to join the same cause. At that point Furius Camillus, proconsul of Africa, brought together as a single force his legion* and all the auxiliaries serving under his standards, and led it against the enemy. This was a small unit if one considered the huge numbers of Numidians and Mauri, but Camillus was trying more than anything to ensure that the enemy would not avoid combat through fear.

So Camillus' legion was positioned in the centre, and the light-armed cohorts and two cavalry squadrons on the wings. Tacfarinas did not decline the fight, either. The Numidians were routed, and after a hiatus of many years military glory was acquired for the name Furius. For, after that famous regainer* of the city and his son Camillus, praise accruing to generals had gone to other families; and this man of whom we speak was regarded as no soldier. So Tiberius was all the more inclined to praise his exploits in the Senate; and the senators decreed triumphal insignia for him, something which, because of his unassuming way of life, brought no harm to Camillus.

53. The following year saw Tiberius consul* for the third time, and Germanicus for the second. Germanicus, however, entered the office in the Achaean city of Nicopolis. He had reached there by journeying along the Illyrian coastline after visiting his brother Drusus, who was then in Dalmatia, and after a stormy passage in the Adriatic and then the Ionian Sea. He therefore spent a few days on repairs to the fleet, and at the same time he visited the gulf made famous by the victory at Actium, the spoils consecrated by Augustus, and the camp of Antonius—all of them reminders of his own ancestors. For, as I noted,* Augustus was Germanicus' great-uncle and Antonius his grandfather, and in that place there were images evoking for him much sadness and pleasure.

From here, Germanicus came to Athens, where respect for the treaty with this city, allied to us and of great antiquity, led him to make use of only one lictor.* The Greeks welcomed him with elaborate honours, drawing attention to the historical deeds and sayings of their people so that their flattery would have more dignity.

54. Germanicus then headed for Euboea and crossed to Lesbos, where Agrippina gave birth to Julia, her last child. After that he moved into the outer reaches of Asia, and to the Thracian cities of Perinthus and Byzantium, entering then the narrow straits of the Propontis and the mouth of the Pontus, desirous as he was to acquaint himself with these ancient and fabulous places. At the same time he sought to aid the recovery of the provinces, exhausted now from internal wrangling and the malpractice of their magistrates. On his return journey he tried to visit the Samothracian Mysteries,* but encountered northerly winds that drove him off course. He therefore went to Ilium and the sites there venerable for their shifting fortunes and for our own origins,* and after that he skirted the coast of Asia again, putting in at Colophon to consult the oracle of Clarian Apollo. There it is not a priestess, as at Delphi, but a priest who officiates, a man selected from certain families (usually from Miletus) and he is told only the number and names of those consulting the oracle. He then goes down into a cave, drinks water from a secret spring, and, though generally unversed in letters and poetry, gives his responses in formal verse to questions that each of the enquirers has only framed in his mind. And it was said that he predicted a premature end for Germanicus, but did so in riddles, as is the way with oracles.

55. Meanwhile, to get his plans under way the more quickly, Gnaeus Piso cowed the citizens of Athens by his tumultuous arrival, and then berated them in a savage address. In this he launched a sidelong attack on Germanicus for dishonouring the Roman name by his excessive affability towards a people who were not really the Athenians—those had been wiped out by their many disasters*—but merely a trashy collection* of various tribes. These, he said, had been the allies of Mithridates against Sulla, and of Antonius against the deified Augustus. He even cast up their faults of old, their unsuccessful operations against Macedon, and their violence towards their own citizens. His resentment also sprang from a personal grievance—their refusal to surrender, despite his pleas,

a certain Theophilus who had been found guilty of forgery by the court of the Areopagus.

After that Piso made a swift voyage by a shorter route through the Cyclades, and overtook Germanicus at the island of Rhodes. Germanicus was not unaware of the verbal attacks made on him; but he conducted himself with such forbearance that, when a storm blew up and was driving Piso towards some rocks, he sent triremes to help rescue him from danger, even though his enemy's death could be attributed to an accident. Piso was not mollified, however, and after allowing barely a day to pass he left Germanicus, and went on ahead. On reaching Syria and its legions, his conduct was so corrupt that he was, in the conversations of the rank and file, referred to as 'the father of the legions'. He gave gifts, used bribery, helped out the lowest of the common soldiers, and dismissed old centurions and strict tribunes, giving their posts to his own clients and all the most unsavoury individuals. He tolerated idleness in camp and licence in the towns, and allowed the men to wander and run riot throughout the countryside. Nor did Plancina remain within the bounds of feminine propriety, either. She attended cavalry drills and cohort manoeuvres, and would make insulting comments on Agrippina and on Germanicus. Even some of the good soldiers were ready to lend her a dishonourable compliance because a muted rumour was spreading that what was going on was not against the emperor's wishes. This was all known to Germanicus, but attending to Armenia was a more pressing concern.

56. The Armenians have been an undependable people from early times, a result of their national character and geographical position, for the country borders our provinces for a great distance and stretches as far as Media. They thus lie between great empires, and more often than not are at variance with them, feeling hatred for the Romans and envy with regard to the Parthian. At that time, with the removal of Vonones, they had no king; but the national inclination was towards Zeno, son of Polemo,* king of Pontus. This was because, from his earliest years, Zeno had imitated the practices and lifestyle of the Armenians, and with his hunting, feasting, and other favourite barbarian pursuits had earned the affection of the chieftains and common people alike. So it was that Germanicus, in the city of Artaxata, to the approval of the nobles and with a huge crowd around him, placed the royal diadem on Zeno's head. The whole attendance

then paid homage to him, saluting him as 'King Artaxias', a title they
had conferred on him from the name of the city. (Cappadocia, by
contrast, was turned into a province, and was given Quintus
Veranius* as its governor; and a number of the tributes that had been
imposed by the kings were reduced to foster the hope that Roman
authority would be more benign. In the case of Commagene, then for
the first time put under the jurisdiction of a praetor,* Quintus
Servaeus* was made governor.)

57. Germanicus' uniformly successful arrangement of the affairs
of the allies did not, for all that, bring him pleasure. This was because
of the high-handedness of Piso who, ordered to take part of the
legions into Armenia in person or send them under his son's leadership, had failed to do either. The two men finally came together at the
winter quarters of the Tenth Legion in Cyrrus, both with fixed
expressions, Piso not to show fear and Germanicus not to be thought
menacing—and, as I have noted, he tended towards clemency. But
his friends, who were clever at stoking up his resentment, proceeded
to stretch the truth, to pile up lies, and to attack Piso, Plancina, and
their sons in various ways. Eventually, with just a few close associates present, Germanicus talked to him in terms prompted by anger
that he was trying to hide, and Piso replied with pleas insolent in
tone. They parted on openly hostile terms.

Following this Piso was rarely to be seen on Germanicus' tribunal;
and whenever he did take a seat there, he was grim-faced and made
clear his opposition. Furthermore, when, in a banquet at the court of
the king of Nabataea, some heavy gold crowns were offered to
Germanicus and Agrippina, and light ones to Piso and the others,
Piso's voice was heard declaring that the banquet was being given in
honour of the son of a Roman emperor, not of a Parthian king. At the
same time Piso flung aside his crown, adding a long diatribe on
luxury which, cutting though it was, Germanicus tolerated.

58. Meanwhile ambassadors arrived from Artabanus, king of
Parthia. Artabanus had sent them to call attention to his treaty of
friendship with Rome and his desire for a renewal of the pledges
between them, and also to report that he would, as a mark of respect
for Germanicus, come to the bank of the Euphrates. In the meantime, said the ambassadors, he requested that Vonones not be kept in
Syria and thus be allowed to draw tribal chieftains into quarrels by
sending them messages from close at hand. Germanicus gave an

impressively worded reply on the subject of the Romano-Parthian alliance; on the matter of the king's coming and the honour paid to himself he was dignified and modest. Vonones was taken away to Pompeiopolis, a town on the coast of Cilicia. This was not simply a case of acceding to Artabanus' pleas; it was also an insult to Piso, who was very well disposed towards Vonones because of the numerous services and gifts through which the man had put Plancina under obligation to him.

59. In the consulship of Marcus Silanus and Lucius Norbanus, Germanicus left for Egypt to acquaint himself with its antiquities. The pretext given, however, was his concern* for the province, and he did, in fact, lower the price of grain by opening up the granaries, and take up many crowd-pleasing practices. He would walk out without military escort, with feet uncovered, and dressed just like the Greeks—in emulation of Publius Scipio* who, we have been told, used to do the same thing in Sicily although the war with the Carthaginians was still raging. Tiberius used some gentle words of rebuke for his appearance and dress, but was bitingly critical of him for entering Alexandria without the emperor's authorization, which was a breach of the practice established by Augustus. For amongst the various arcane policies of his regime, Augustus had one by which he kept Egypt in isolation, forbidding entry to senators or eminent Roman knights unless they had his permission.* This was to prevent anyone from putting pressure on Italy with food shortages by establishing himself in the province, and holding the key access points to it by land and sea—for there he could hold back mighty armies with the flimsiest of forces.

60. Germanicus, however, starting out from the town of Canopus, sailed up the Nile before learning that his journey was meeting with disapproval. (The Spartans founded Canopus in honour of their helmsman Canopus, who was buried there when Menelaus, heading back to Greece, was driven off course to the land of Libya in a distant sea.) From Canopus, he came to the next mouth of the Nile, which is dedicated to Hercules, who, the natives claim, was born in their land and was the most ancient Hercules. (Others who later demonstrated a similar fortitude were simply given his name, they say.) His next visit was to the extensive ruins of ancient Thebes. There still remained on the piles of masonry Egyptian inscriptions giving a summary of the city's earlier wealth. One of the senior priests was instructed to translate his native language, and he reported that seven hundred thousand men of military age had once lived in Thebes. It was with such an army, he said, that King Rhamses* had taken control of Libya, Ethiopia, the Medes and the Persians, and Bactria and Scythia, as well as all the lands inhabited by the Syrians and the Armenians, and by their neighbours the Cappadocians. Rhamses' empire had comprised the area from Bithynia on one side to the Lycian sea on the other, said the priest. The lists of the tribute imposed on the various nations could also be read—the weight of silver and gold, the quantity of weapons and horses, the gifts of ivory and perfumes for the temples, and the amounts of grain and all other provisions that each people had to contribute. These were all no less impressive than the duties now levied by the might of Parthia or the power of Rome.

61. Germanicus, however, had his attention focused on other wonders, too. Foremost amongst these were the stone figure of Memnon* that emitted the sound of a voice when struck by the rays of the sun; the pyramids that, because of the rivalry of wealthy kings, were erected like mountains amidst the shifting and barely passable sands; a lake* sunk in the ground to receive the overflow of the Nile; and, elsewhere, narrow gorges, and river depths* that none can plumb. After that he came to Elephantine and Syene; these formerly represented the limits of the Roman empire, which now extends as far as the Red Sea.*

62. While Germanicus' summer was being spent that year* in several provinces, Drusus won not inconsiderable glory for enticing the Germans into disharmony and, with Maroboduus' power broken, for pressing on with the man's total destruction. There was among the Gotones a young nobleman called Catualda, who had once been forced into exile by Maroboduus, and who now ventured to exact his revenge while the king was in difficulties. Catualda took a strong body of men and entered the territory of the Marcomani where, by bribing their leading men to join him, he broke into the palace and a nearby fortress. In them were discovered Suebian plunder from the distant past and, from our provinces, camp-followers and traders. These had been lured into enemy territory* from their various homes first by trading privileges,* then by their desire to increase their wealth, and finally by their forgetfulness of their country.

63. Maroboduus was now totally deserted, and his only recourse was the emperor's mercy. He crossed the Danube at the point where it skirts the province of Noricum, and wrote Tiberius a letter not as a refugee or suppliant, but as one who remembered his former status. For, he said, although many peoples had issued invitations to him as a formerly glorious king, he had preferred the friendship of Rome. The reply from the emperor was that Maroboduus would have a safe and honourable residence in Italy, if he remained there, but that if some other arrangement were more advantageous he would leave with the same guarantees with which he had come. In the Senate, however, Tiberius claimed that the Athenians had had less reason to fear Philip,* or the Roman people Pyrrhus or Antiochus,* than they had to fear Maroboduus. The speech still survives in which he underlined the man's importance, the violent character of the tribes subject to him, his proximity to Italy as an enemy, and also the measures Tiberius had himself taken to bring him down. And Maroboduus was actually detained at Ravenna, with the threat of his return being held out in the event of the Suebi ever becoming recalcitrant. In fact, he did not leave Italy for eighteen years, and grew old in much diminished glory simply because he was too eager to stay alive.

Catualda faced a similar fate, and found no other escape when, not long after this, he was driven out by the powerful Hermunduri under the leadership of Vibilius. He was granted refuge by the Romans and dispatched to Forum Julii, a colony in Narbonese Gaul. It was feared, however, that the barbarians accompanying the two men might disturb the peace if they were merged into the population of the provinces. They were therefore relocated between the rivers Marus and Cusus, and given Vannius, one of the Quadi, as their king.

64. Just as the news arrived that the Armenians had been assigned Artaxias as their king by Germanicus, the senators decreed that Germanicus and Drusus should enter the city with an ovation. Arches were also erected flanking the temple of Mars the Avenger and bearing portraits of the Caesars, and Tiberius was happier for having established peace through shrewd diplomacy than if he had finished off a war by armed confrontation. He therefore also employed ingenuity to deal with Rhescuporis, king of Thrace.

The whole of that nation had been under the rule of Rhoemetalces,* and on the king's death Augustus granted half of the

kingdom of Thrace to his brother Rhescuporis, and half to his son
Cotys. In this division the arable land, towns, and the areas bordering Greece came to Cotys; and what was uncultivated, barbarous,
and adjacent to hostile peoples came to Rhescuporis. This matched
the characters of the kings themselves, one being mild and affable,
the other grim, rapacious, and incapable of collaboration. At first
their relationship was one of duplicitous co-operation, but Rhescuporis soon began to cross his boundaries, to appropriate what had
been awarded to Cotys and to attack him when he resisted. He did
this with some hesitation under Augustus, since he feared the
founder of the two kingdoms would punish any violation of his
arrangement. When he heard of the change of emperor, however, he
proceeded to send in bands of marauders and destroy fortresses, thus
providing reasons for war.

65. Nothing made Tiberius as anxious as his fear of settlements
being upset. He selected a centurion to notify the kings that they
must avoid an armed resolution; and Cotys straightway demobilized
the auxiliary forces he had prepared. With a pretence of compliance,
Rhescuporis insisted that they come together at a meeting place—
their differences could be settled by discussion. There was no long
hesitation over the time, location, and then terms for the meeting:
both conceded and accepted everything, one because of his easygoing
nature, the other with treachery in mind. Rhescuporis also hosted a
banquet—to seal the treaty, he said. The festivities were drawn
out until late at night, and Cotys was completely off guard in an
atmosphere of feasting and heavy drinking. At this point Rhescuporis
put Cotys in chains and he, on recognizing the treachery, appealed
to the sanctity of the throne, the gods of the family to which the
two belonged, and the sacred hospitality of the table. Now in
command of all of Thrace, Rhescuporis wrote a letter to Tiberius
informing him that a plot had been mounted against him, but that he
had caught the plotter first. At the same time, on the pretext of
opening hostilities against the Bastarnae and Scythians, he proceeded to strengthen himself with new troops of foot and horse. He
received a gently worded reply. If there were no treachery involved,
Rhescuporis could feel secure in his innocence, but neither Tiberius
nor the Senate would decide on the rights or wrongs of the case without hearing it first. He should therefore surrender Cotys and, coming
to Rome, there transfer to his brother the odium of guilt.

66. This letter the propraetor of Moesia, Latinius Pandusa, sent into Thrace along with the soldiers to whom Cotys was to be surrendered. Rhescuporis hesitated, caught between fear and anger, but he decided on being tried for a crime perpetrated rather than merely started. He ordered Cotys to be put to death, and fabricated a story that it was a suicide. Even so, his course adopted, Tiberius did not change it. Instead, on the death of Pandusa, who Rhescuporis claimed was hostile to him, he made Pomponius Flaccus governor of Moesia. Flaccus was a campaign-hardened veteran who was on close terms with the king, and thus better placed to dupe him, and that was the main reason for his appointment.

67. After crossing to Thrace, Flaccus used lavish promises to induce Rhescuporis to enter the Roman fortifications, uneasy though the man was and fretting over his crimes. Then, in an apparent gesture of respect, a large contingent of soldiers surrounded the king. Tribunes and centurions were giving advice, urging him on, and making more evident the reality of his arrest the further he was taken; when his dire situation finally dawned on him, they dragged him off to Rome. He was accused by Cotys' wife* in the Senate and condemned to detention far from his kingdom. Thrace was partitioned between his son Rhoemetalces—it was established that he had opposed his father's policies—and the sons of Cotys.* As these were not yet of age, Trebellenus Rufus, a former praetor, was assigned the interim administration of the realm, the precedent for that being our ancestors' sending of Marcus Lepidus* to Egypt as guardian for Ptolemy's children. Rhescuporis was shipped off to Alexandria and was there killed attempting to escape, or after being falsely charged with doing so.

68. In this same period, Vonones (whose removal to Cilicia I mentioned above*) bribed his guards and attempted to escape to Armenia, and from there to the Albani, the Heniochi, and the king of Scythia, who was a relative of his. He left the coastal region on a pretence of going hunting and headed for the remote forests, subsequently using a swift horse to reach the River Pyramus. However, the local people had broken down the bridges when they heard of the king's escape, and fording the river was impossible. Vonones was thus captured on the river-bank by Vibius Fronto, a prefect of the cavalry; and later Remmius, a senior soldier* earlier assigned to guarding the king, ran him through with his sword, ostensibly in a fit of anger. Hence a growing belief that Vonones' death occurred through Remmius' complicity in his crime and fear of denunciation.

69. On his return journey from Egypt, Germanicus discovered that all the orders that he had left relating to the legions or the cities had been cancelled or reversed. This gave rise to scathing reproaches against Piso, but Piso's attacks on Germanicus were no less cutting. After that, Piso decided to leave* Syria, but was held back by Germanicus' ill-health. He was then told that Germanicus had recovered, and when vows that had been made for his safety were being discharged, Piso had his lictors forcibly remove* the sacrificial victims that had been brought to the altars, and the paraphernalia of sacrifice, along with the common people of Antioch, who were now in festive mood. He then left for Seleucia to await the outcome of the illness that had once more struck Germanicus.

The patient's conviction that he had been poisoned by Piso served to heighten the cruel effects of the disease. And, in fact, disinterred remains of human bodies were found in the soil and walls, along with incantations, curses, and Germanicus' name inscribed on lead tablets;* there were also half-burned ashes smeared with some putrid matter, and other black-magic implements by which it is believed souls are consigned to the infernal deities. In addition, accusations were being made that men sent by Piso were closely examining the adverse symptoms of the disease.

70. Germanicus received such reports with as much indignation as fear. If his home were under siege, he thought, and if he had to let out his last breath before his enemies' eyes, what then would happen to his poor wife, what to his infant children?* Poisoning was evidently too slow for Piso—he was now making haste and pressing on with his plans for sole possession of the province and the legions. But he himself had not become as weak as all that, Germanicus mused, nor were the prizes of murder going to remain in his killer's hands. He wrote a letter formally renouncing* his friendship with him; and many further state that Piso was ordered to quit the province. Piso delayed no longer. He set sail, and slowed his progress in order to shorten the return journey if Germanicus' death left Syria open to him.

71. Germanicus was momentarily roused to hope. Then he lost strength and, his end approaching, he addressed the friends at his bedside in the following manner: 'Were I facing a natural death,

I would still feel a justified resentment towards the gods for taking me away, in my youth, from my parents, children, and country by an early death. As it is, I have been cut down by the criminal act of Piso and Plancina, and I leave these last prayers of mine in your hearts. Report to my father and brother the agonies I suffered, and the treachery by which I was beset, as I ended my wretched life with the worst of deaths. Any inspired by their hopes in me, or by kinship with me, and any even who were roused to envy towards me in my lifetime—these will shed tears that a man formerly successful, and one who survived so many wars, has been brought low by a woman's treachery.

'You will have the opportunity to lodge a complaint in the Senate, and to appeal to the laws. The prime duty of friends is not to attend a dead man with faint-hearted lamentation, but to remember his wishes and follow his instructions. Even strangers will weep for Germanicus; but it will be for you to avenge him, if it was me you loved rather than my station in life. Show the Roman people the deified Augustus' granddaughter, who was also my wife; count out for them her six children. Pity will be on the side of the accusers, and men will either not believe or not forgive those falsely claiming that they were following criminal orders.'

Grasping the dying man's right hand, his friends swore they would let go of life sooner than revenge.

72. Turning then to his wife, Germanicus begged her—by the memory she would have of him and by the children they shared—to set aside her pride,* submit to the cruelty of fortune, and, on her return to Rome, not enrage those stronger than her by competing for power. Such were his open pronouncements, and he made others in private, in which, it was thought, he alerted her to the threat posed by Tiberius. Not much later he expired,* bringing great sorrow to the province and surrounding peoples. Foreign nations and kings mourned for him: such had been his good humour with the allies, and his leniency with the enemy.* He commanded respect with his looks and his speech alike, and while he retained the eminence and dignity of his lofty position, he had avoided envy and arrogance.

73. The funeral, with no family portraits or procession, was marked by eulogies that recalled Germanicus' virtues. There were those, too, who made comparisons with the death of Alexander the Great, based on his looks, his age, the manner of his passing, and

even the proximity of the region in which he perished. For both men were physically attractive, of distinguished pedigree, and not much beyond thirty,* and they had died amongst foreign peoples through the treachery of compatriots. Germanicus, however, had been gentle with his friends, they said, and restrained in his pleasures; he had had one marriage and legitimate children. Nor had he been any less a warrior even if he lacked the other's recklessness and had, after crushing the Germanys with so many victories, been prevented from completing their submission. Had matters been entirely under his control, and had he had the authority, and the title, of a king, he would just as easily have won the military glory of Alexander as he had surpassed him in mercy, self-control, and all other virtues.

Before cremation, Germanicus' corpse was exposed naked in the forum of Antioch, the appointed place for the funeral, but there is little agreement on whether it bore indications of poisoning.* Views differed according to whether one felt pity for Germanicus and was predisposed to suspicion, or else tended to favour Piso.

74. There followed discussion amongst the legates, and other senators present, of who should take charge of Syria.* After some weak jockeying by the other candidates, it came down to a decision, which was long debated, between Vibius Marsus and Gnaeus Sentius; then Marsus gave in to Sentius, who was older and making his case more forcefully. Sentius sent to Rome a woman called Martina, who was infamous in that province for cases of poisoning, and who was very dear to Plancina's heart. He did this at the insistence of Vitellius and Veranius and the others, who were framing charges and a formal accusation against individuals as if they had already been indicted.

75. Agrippina was exhausted from grief and physically weakened, but she could not tolerate anything that would delay her revenge. She boarded ship with Germanicus' ashes and her children. All pitied her. She was a woman of the highest birth who had recently enjoyed the finest marriage, one who had been used to being regarded with respect and esteem. Now, they said, she carried in her arms funerary remains, being uncertain of revenge, apprehensive for herself, and, because of her unlucky fertility, exposed to multiple blows of fortune!

Piso meanwhile was overtaken by the news of Germanicus' death when he was on the island of Cos. He received it with effusive joy, and he then slaughtered sacrificial animals, and visited the temples.

He could not set bounds to his elation, but Plancina was even more outrageous, then for the first time laying aside her mourning for her dead sister to put on clothes of rejoicing.

76. Centurions* now came streaming in to inform Piso of the support he enjoyed in the legions. He should head back to the province that had been unjustly taken from him* and was now vacant, they said. As he debated what to do, his son Marcus Piso suggested that he make haste for Rome. So far, he said, there had been no inexcusable action taken, and feeble suspicion or idle bits of hearsay were not to be feared. His differences with Germanicus might perhaps earn him unpopularity, but not punishment, and his personal enemies had gained their satisfaction when he was deprived of his province. Going back to Syria, on the other hand, meant the start of civil war, if Sentius opposed him; and the centurions and the men would not remain firmly on his side—the still-fresh memory of their commander and their deep-seated love of the Caesars were what counted with them.

77. Domitius Celer, on the other hand, who was one of Piso's closest friends, maintained that he should take advantage of the situation. It was Piso, not Sentius, who had been made governor of Syria, he said, and it was to him that the fasces and praetorian authority had been given, and to him the legions. In the face of an attack, who would have more justification for armed resistance than the man who had received a legate's authority* and personal instructions? Furthermore, rumours should be given time to weaken with age— when resentment is fresh, innocent men often cannot rise above it. If he kept the army, however, and increased his strength, much that could not be foreseen would, through the workings of chance, turn out for the better. 'Are we hurrying to put in at Rome along with Germanicus' ashes,' he added, 'so that Agrippina's breast-beating and the uninformed masses may sweep you away when the rumours start, with no hearing and no defence? You have Augusta as your accomplice, and Tiberius supporting you, but in secret; and none are making more of a show of sorrow for Germanicus' passing than those most delighted by it.'

78. Piso was a man inclined to impetuous action, and it took no great effort for him to be brought to this opinion. He sent a letter to Tiberius accusing Germanicus of prodigality and arrogance. He himself had been driven out so that an opportunity could be provided for

revolution, he said, but he had now taken charge of the army once more, with the same loyalty with which he had earlier commanded it. At the same time he put Domitius aboard a trireme, ordering him to avoid the sea coast and head for Syria on the open sea, skirting the islands. As deserters* came flocking to him, he formed them into companies, and he armed the camp followers. He also took some ships over to the mainland, where he intercepted a detachment of recruits en route for Syria, and he wrote to the petty kings of the Cilicians,* requesting that they assist him with auxiliary troops. Meanwhile, the younger Piso was not slack in making preparations for the war, despite having been against undertaking it.

79. While they were skirting the coast of Lycia and Pamphylia, they met the ships carrying Agrippina. As there was animosity on both sides, they initially made ready their weapons; but then, having fear of each other, they went no further than verbal abuse, with Marsus Vibius announcing to Piso that he should come to Rome to plead his case. Piso, as a gibe, replied that he would be present there when the praetor who investigated poisonings set a date for the defendant and his accusers.*

Meanwhile Domitius had put in at the Syrian city of Laodicea. He headed for the winter quarters of the Sixth Legion, thinking it would be the most suitable force for his revolutionary plans, but he was anticipated by the legate Pacuvius. Sentius made this known to Piso by letter, and warned him against trying to destabilize his camp by bribery, and the province by war. He then brought together the men who were loyal to Germanicus' memory or opposed to his enemies, time after time impressing on them the greatness of the emperor and the fact that the state was facing an armed assault. After that he led out a strong force that was ready for battle.

80. Although Piso's undertakings were proving unsuccessful, he did not fail to take the safest course in the circumstances, seizing a well-fortified stronghold in Cilicia called Celenderis. For, by adding in the deserters, the recently intercepted recruits, and his own and Plancina's slaves, he had formed the Cilician auxiliaries that the petty kings had sent into what matched a legion in terms of numbers. He insisted that he was a legate of Tiberius, and was being kept out of a province that Tiberius had given to him—and not by the legions (for it was in response to their call that he came) but by Sentius, who was masking personal animosity with baseless accusations. They should

take their places in the line, he said—Sentius' soldiers would not fight, not when they saw Piso, once called 'father' by them, a man with superior claims in terms of justice, and not weak militarily, either.

Piso then deployed his companies before the fortifications of the stronghold, on a steep and sheer hill (for the rest of the area was surrounded by sea). Facing him were veteran* troops, drawn up in ranks and auxiliary squadrons. On one side were rugged soldiers; on the other there was rugged terrain, but no spirit, no hope, and even no weapons, apart from some rustic or makeshift specimens. When the two sides engaged, the issue remained indecisive only until the Roman cohorts clambered up to the level ground, at which point the Cilicians turned tail and shut themselves away in their stronghold.

81. Piso meanwhile made an unsuccessful attempt to attack the fleet,* which was waiting not far off. Then, returning, he stood before the walls, and tried to incite a mutiny. He would be beating his breast at one moment, and at another calling on individuals by name, trying to win them over with rewards; and he had in fact touched them sufficiently for the standard-bearer of the Sixth Legion to come over to him with the standard. Then Sentius called for blasts on the trumpets and bugles, and for an attack to be launched on the embankment. He ordered ladders to be raised, and for all the most valiant to climb them, while others were to launch volleys of spears, rocks, and firebrands from the catapults. His obstinacy finally overcome, Piso asked that he be allowed to hand over his weaponry and remain in the stronghold while Tiberius considered to whom he should assign Syria. His terms were not accepted, and all that Piso was granted was some ships and a safe passage to the city.

82. Meanwhile, in Rome, after word spread of Germanicus' illness and all reports began to be exaggerated for the worse, as happens with far-off events, there was pain and anger, and an outburst of protest. Of course, that was why Germanicus had been shipped off to the ends of the earth, people said. That was why the province had been granted to Piso, and this was what Augusta's clandestine conversations with Plancina had brought about! What the older people had said about Drusus* was certainly true: rulers do not like their sons having libertarian tendencies, and the sole reason that the lives of both men had been cut short was that they considered extending equal rights over the Roman people, restoring their liberty. Such conversations amongst the common people became so heated with

the news of Germanicus' death that, before any edict came from the magistrates or any decree from the Senate, business came to a halt, forums were deserted and homes shut up. Everywhere there was silence and sobbing, with nothing done for appearances' sake. And while they did not shun the insignia of mourning,* they grieved more deeply in their hearts.

As it happened, some traders who had left Syria when Germanicus was still alive brought more cheerful news about his illness. This was immediately believed, and immediately spread; and as people met, they passed on what they had heard to others, no matter how dubious the authority, and these passed it on to more people, adding to it in their joy. They ran through the city, and broke open temple doors. Night heightened their credulity, and positive assertions came the more easily in the dark. And Tiberius did not block the false reports, either, allowing them to fade with the passage of time—and so the people's grief for Germanicus was the keener, as if he had been twice taken from them.

83. Honours* were dreamed up and decreed, according to a man's affection for Germanicus or his ingenuity. His name was to be sung in the Saliarian hymn;* curule chairs* were to be set up in the places reserved for the Augustal priests, with oak crowns on them; an ivory statue* of him was to lead off the games in the Circus; and no flamen* or augur was to be inaugurated in Germanicus' place unless he belonged to the Julian family. There were arches decreed, as well, at Rome, on the Rhine bank and on Mt. Amanus in Syria, each with an inscription listing his achievements and stating that he had died for his country. There was also to be a cenotaph at Antioch, where he had been cremated, and a monumental tribunal at Epidaphna,* where his life had ended. As for statues and places where his worship was to be established, their number would not be easy to assess. When a proposal came forward that he be granted a gold shield of remarkable size amongst the leading orators,* Tiberius declared that he would dedicate to him a conventional one like the others. In eloquence, he explained, judgement was not based on one's rank, and to be given a position amongst the writers of old was distinction enough. The equestrian order applied the name 'Germanicus' block'* to the so-called 'Juniors' Section', and arranged that their squadrons* should follow his effigy on 15 July. Many of these institutions remain in place; some were immediately dropped, or have been effaced by the passage of time.

84. Now while grief for Germanicus was still fresh, his sister Livilla, who was married to Drusus, gave birth to twins of the male sex.* This is an unusual and happy occurrence even for lowly households, and it brought such great joy to the emperor that he could not help boasting to the senators that no Roman of such high rank had ever before been blessed with a twin birth—for he would turn everything, even chance events, to self-glorification. But to the common people, given the circumstances, this too brought pain, as they felt that the increase in Drusus' children put greater pressure on the house of Germanicus.

85. That same year, restraints were placed on female sexuality by coercive senatorial decrees, and a woman was barred from engaging in prostitution if she had a grandfather, father, or husband who was a Roman knight. For Vistilia, who came from a praetorian family, had made an open declaration before the aediles* of her readiness to engage in illicit sex, an accepted procedure in past times which believed there was sufficient punishment for unchaste women in the actual admission of their wrongdoing. Vistilia's husband, Titidius Labeo, was also called on to explain why he had ignored the punishment provided by the law* in the case of a wife manifestly guilty of the offence. Labeo's excuse was that sixty days were granted for consideration of the matter, and these had not expired. It therefore appeared sufficient to fix a punishment in the case of Vistilia, and she was banished to the island of Seriphos.

There was also discussion of driving out Egyptian and Jewish rites,* and a senatorial decree was passed ordering 4,000 persons of the freedman class who had been infected with such superstition, and who were also of appropriate age, to be transported to the island of Sardinia. There they were to be employed in putting down banditry, and if they perished because of the oppressive climate the loss would be slight. The others were under orders to leave Italy unless they cast aside their profane religious observances before a specific date.

86. After this Tiberius put forward a motion for the selection of a virgin to replace Occia, who had presided over the rights of Vesta for fifty-seven years* with irreproachable purity. He also offered thanks to Fonteius Agrippa and Domitius Pollio for actually competing with each other in their service of the state by offering their daughters for the post. Preference was given to Pollio's daughter for no other reason than that her mother had remained in the same marriage, for Agrippa had lowered the standing of his household by divorce. And Tiberius offered solace to the lady in second place in the form of a dowry of a million sesterces.

87. The plebeians were complaining about the atrocious cost of food, and Tiberius fixed the price that the buyer should pay for grain,* undertaking to give the merchants two sesterces extra per measure. For this, however, he did not accept the title 'Father of the Nation', which had also been offered him earlier,* and he sharply criticized those who had spoken of his 'divine occupations' and referred to him as 'the lord'. * So language was a restricted and hazardous area under an emperor who feared liberty, but hated flattery.

88. In the works of authors and senators of the period I find the statement that a letter of Adgandestrius, a prince of the Chatti, was read out in the Senate, in which the prince promised the death of Arminius if he were sent poison to carry out the assassination. The answer given, according to these sources, was that the Roman people did not use treacherous and underhand means to avenge themselves on their enemies, but did so openly and under arms. With this vainglorious comment Tiberius was putting himself on a par with the generals of old* who had forbidden the use of poison against King Pyrrhus, and then made the affair public. As for Arminius, he aimed at kingship during the Roman withdrawal and after the expulsion of Maroboduus, and this clashed with his compatriots' love of freedom. Facing armed attack, he fought with intermittent success, and fell through the treachery of his relatives. He was without doubt the liberator of Germany, one who had challenged the Roman people not at its beginnings, like other kings and leaders, but when its empire was at its zenith; and while he had varied success in battle, in the war he was undefeated. His life lasted thirty-seven years, his power twelve,* and he is still a subject of song amongst the barbarian tribes. He is, however, unknown to the history of the Greeks, whose admiration is restricted to their own achievements, and not much celebrated in that of the Romans, for we, who praise the deeds of antiquity, have little interest in those of recent times.

BOOK THREE

1. With no interruption* of her journey over the winter sea,* Agrippina reached the island of Corcyra, which lies opposite the Calabrian coast. She spent a few days there to compose herself: her grief was ferocious, and she was unused to suffering. Meanwhile, hearing of her arrival in Corcyra, all her closest friends and numerous military officers, all of whom had served under Germanicus, hurried to the town of Brundisium, the destination a voyager would most quickly reach and the safest landing-point. There were many strangers, too, who came from the neighbouring towns, some believing this a mark of respect to the emperor, more simply following the leaders.

Once the fleet was sighted out at sea, it was not merely the harbour and areas closest to the seas that filled up with crowds of mourners; so too did the city walls and the roofs of houses, and any points from which a distant view could be had. These people asked each other whether they should receive Agrippina in silence as she stepped ashore, or with words of some kind. They were still not agreed on what suited the occasion when the fleet gradually approached, not with the usual vigorous rowing, but with everything arranged to betoken sadness. When Agrippina stepped from the ship with her two children,* clutching the funeral urn and with her eyes fixed on the ground, a concerted groan arose from the whole gathering. And one could not tell relatives from strangers, men's lamentations from those of women. All one could tell was that Agrippina's attendants, exhausted from protracted grief, were surpassed in its expression by those who met them, and whose pain was fresh.

2. Tiberius had despatched two praetorian cohorts and had also sent instructions for the magistrates of Calabria, together with the Apulian and Campanian officials, to pay their last tributes to his son's memory. Germanicus' ashes* were therefore carried on the shoulders of tribunes and centurions, and before the procession the standards were unadorned and the fasces reversed. And when they passed through the colonies, the plebs were dressed in black and the knights in the *trabea,** and they burned garments, incense, and other traditional funerary offerings, according to the resources of the district.

Even those whose cities lay far off came to meet them, and as they offered sacrificial victims and altars to the spirits of the dead they made clear their pain with tears and lamentations.

Drusus went ahead to Tarracina with Claudius, brother of Germanicus, and with those of Germanicus' children who had been in the city. The consuls* Marcus Valerius and Marcus Aurelius (they had already started their terms), the Senate, and large numbers of the public filled the road, in scattered groups, all weeping as they felt inclined. For there was no sycophancy: all knew that Tiberius was happy with Germanicus' death, and that he was having difficulty concealing it.*

3. Tiberius and Augusta avoided making a public appearance; open grieving they thought beneath their imperial dignity, or else they feared hypocrisy would be recognized if the eyes of all searched their faces. I find no mention—not in the historians and not in the daily record, either—of Germanicus' mother, Antonia,* playing any significant part in the ceremonies, despite all other relatives (in addition to Agrippina, Drusus, and Claudius*) being listed by name. It may be that she was prevented by illness, or perhaps her grief-stricken spirit could not cope with the magnitude of the misfortune she had to look upon. I would find it easier to believe that constraints were put upon her by Tiberius and Augusta—who did not set foot outside their home—to give the impression of sorrow shared, with grandmother and uncle kept indoors by the example set by the mother.

4. The day on which the remains were being taken to the tomb of Augustus* was marked alternately by desolate silence and loud outbreaks of lamentation. The city streets were choked, and torches blazed throughout the Campus Martius.* Present there were the soldier under arms, the magistrate without his insignia, the people arranged in their tribes, all sending up the cry that the state had collapsed and no hope remained. And they did this too readily and overtly for one to believe that they remembered those who ruled them. But nothing struck home with Tiberius more than the ardent support shown for Agrippina. The glory of the nation, they called her, the lone survivor of Augustus' bloodline,* the one surviving model of the past; and turning to heaven and the gods, they prayed that her progeny would remain safe, and survive those who wished her ill.

5. There were some who missed the splendour of a state funeral*
and made comparisons with the magnificent honours that Augustus
had paid to Germanicus' father, Drusus. In the fiercest days of
winter, they said, Augustus had travelled as far as Ticinum,* and,
without leaving the body, had come into the city with it. The ancestral busts of the Claudii and Julii had surrounded the funeral couch.
There had been mourning in the Forum, a eulogy before the Rostra,
and all the marks of esteem that our ancestors conceived, or their
descendants devised, had been heaped upon him. Germanicus, by
contrast, had not even been accorded the usual honours due to any
nobleman. Naturally, because of the length of the voyage, the body
had been given some sort of cremation in foreign parts; but the tributes paid to him should have been all the greater since chance had
denied them to him initially. To meet him, his brother* had made
but a day's journey; his uncle* had not even come as far as the city
gate. Where were those institutions of the ancients? Where was
the effigy* set before the funeral couch, the poems performed to
commemorate the man's virtue, the encomia, and the tears—or at
least some semblance of grief?

6. Tiberius was aware of all this, and to suppress the gossip of
the crowd he reminded them with an edict that, while many famous
Romans had died for the state, none had been honoured with such
an intense feeling of loss. And, said Tiberius, if moderation were
observed, that would be a great favour to him, and all involved. For
the things that were appropriate to lowly houses and lowly communities were not appropriate to emperors and an imperial people.
While their mourning, and the consolation that grief provides, had
been appropriate when the pain was fresh, it was now time for them
to steel their hearts, just as the deified Julius had once resolutely set
aside his sorrow after losing his only daughter,* and the deified
Augustus when his grandchildren* were taken from him. There was
no need, he continued, to cite ancient examples of all those occasions
when the Roman people had steadfastly borne disasters befalling
their armies, the deaths of commanders and the complete annihila-
tion of noble families. Emperors were mortal, the state everlasting,
he told them. They should therefore go back to their usual occupations and, since the spectacle of the Megalesian Games* was at hand,
resume their pleasures, as well.

7. The suspension of business put aside, people returned to their duties, and Drusus set off to rejoin the armies in Illyricum.* There was now universal excitement and anticipation of vengeance being visited on Piso, and there were frequent protests that, with high-handed and crafty delaying tactics, the man was destroying the evidence of his crimes as he spent the interval roaming the beautiful areas of Asia and Achaea. For the news had spread about Martina, the notorious poisoner who had (as I noted above) been sent to Rome by Gnaeus Sentius: she had died suddenly at Brundisium, poison had been hidden in a knot of her hair, and no indications of a self-inflicted death were found on the body.

8. Piso had meanwhile sent his son ahead to Rome, and given him instructions on how to mollify the emperor. He then set off to see Drusus, who he hoped would be not so much embittered by a brother's death as well disposed towards him for the elimination of a rival. To exhibit his open-mindedness, Tiberius gave the young man a warm welcome, bestowing on him the generosity he usually showed to the sons of the nobility.

Drusus' reply to Piso was that, if there was truth in the allegations being put about, he would be the person most aggrieved, but he preferred to think them false and without foundation, and that Germanicus' death would prove to be nobody's undoing. This was said openly, with all private conversation avoided. No doubt was felt, however, that the wording was supplied by Tiberius; for an otherwise guileless person, with the easygoing character of youth, was on that occasion revealing the diplomatic skills of an old man.

9. Piso crossed the Dalmatian Sea and left his ships at Ancona. Then, making his way through Picenum and subsequently along the Flaminian Way, he overtook a legion that was being taken from Pannonia to the city (and which after that was to serve as the garrison for Africa*). What became a particular topic of rumour was how he had frequently put himself on show for the men on the road during the march. From Narnia he sailed down the Nar, and then the Tiber—to avoid suspicion, or because men's plans shift when they are fearful—and increased the anger of the common people by land-ing at the tomb of the Caesars. And he did this in the daylight, too, when the river-bank was crowded and he himself was attended by a long train of clients, and Plancina by a retinue of ladies, the two of

them striding ahead with cheerful expressions. Amongst the things that roused ill-will against them were the house towering above the Forum and its festal decorations, the dinner-party and banquet that he hosted, and the fact that nothing was done discreetly in such a public place.

10. The following day Fulcinius Trio began criminal proceedings* against Piso before the consuls. However, Vitellius, Veranius, and the other former members of Germanicus' retinue insisted that Trio had no role in the process, adding that they themselves were not undertaking the prosecution but that, as informers and witnesses, they would bring forward Germanicus' instructions. Trio then abandoned the prosecution of that area of the case but gained the right to direct charges against Piso's earlier career, and the emperor was invited to take over the investigation. Even the defendant had no objection to this, fearing as he did the temper of the people and the senators, and believing that Tiberius, by contrast, would be strong enough to dismiss hearsay, and that he was also compromised by his mother's complicity. He further believed that the truth could be more easily disentangled from accepted calumnies by a single judge, while animosity and envy prevailed amongst large numbers.

Tiberius was well aware of the problems involved in the investigation, and the savage rumours to which he was being subjected. He accordingly heard the threats of the accusers and the pleas of the defence before a few of his close friends, and then referred the whole case to the Senate.

11. Drusus, meanwhile, was on his way back from Illyricum. The senators had voted that his return to Rome should be marked with an ovation because of the surrender of Maroboduus, and because of the successful campaign the previous summer,* but he deferred the honour and came straight into the city.

The defendant requested Lucius Arruntius, Publius Vinicius, Asinius Gallus, Aeserninus Marcellus, and Sextus Pompeius as his advocates,* but they gave various reasons for declining, and Marcus Lepidus, Lucius Piso, and Livineius Regulus came to his aid. The entire community was now excitedly speculating on the depth of the loyalty of Germanicus' friends, the confidence the defendant had in his case, and whether Tiberius would succeed in suppressing and controlling his own feelings. On no other occasion were the people more alert, allowing themselves an unprecedented measure of whispered criticism of the emperor, or of suspicious silence.

12. On the day of the Senate meeting, the emperor delivered a speech of studied restraint. Piso, he said, had been his father's legate and friend, and he himself had assigned him to Germanicus, on the recommendation of the Senate, to help* with the administration of the affairs in the East. Whether he had there irritated the young man by his wilfulness and quarrelling, and had then expressed pleasure at his death, or whether he had criminally put an end to Germanicus' life—that was for them to decide with minds unprejudiced.

'For,' he continued, 'if as a legate he overstepped his authority, and cast aside his obedience to his commanding officer, and was then pleased with the man's death, and my grief, then I shall hate him and bar him from my house, satisfying personal grudges without the use of the imperial power. If, however, a crime is revealed that should be punished, a crime that has taken the life of any human being whatsoever, then it is for you to bring due solace both to the children of Germanicus and to us, his parents. And at the same time you must consider whether Piso was a seditious troublemaker in his handling of the armies, whether he used corrupt practices to win the support of the soldiers, and whether he employed armed force to recover the province*—or whether these are groundless charges, exaggerations put about by his accusers.

'And the over-zealousness of the plaintiffs makes me justifiably angry. For what purpose did it serve to strip the body naked and let the eyes of the crowd run over it? Or to have it spread abroad, and amongst foreigners, too, that his life was cut short by poison, if such allegations remain uncertain and in need of verification?

'I weep for my son and will always weep for him, but I do not, even so, oppose the defendant's efforts to bring to light everything that would substantiate his innocence or demonstrate any wrongdoing on Germanicus' part. Furthermore, I entreat you not to accept charges laid as being proven just because they are connected with my own sorrow. If a blood relationship or loyalty has brought any of you to Piso's defence, you must each put all the strength of your eloquence and all your commitment into helping him in his hour of danger; and I urge the prosecution to make the same effort, and show the same determination. Only one thing above the law shall we be seen to have accorded Germanicus: the inquiry into his death is taking place in the Curia,* not the Forum, before the Senate, not the judiciary. Let everything else be handled with similar restraint. No one should take account of Drusus' tears and my own sorrow, or of any stories fabricated against us, either.'

13. A two-day period was then scheduled for the deposition of charges, and after an interval of six days the defence of the accused was to last three days.

Fulcinius began with some dated and pointless accusations regarding the corruption and avarice that marked Piso's administration of Spain* (even if proved these would not hurt the defendant, if he cleared himself of the recent allegations, while a successful defence would not acquit him either, if he were found guilty of the greater crimes). After Fulcinius came Servaeus, Veranius, and Vitellius.* With much the same passion—and Vitellius with considerable eloquence—they alleged that, from hatred of Germanicus and desire for revolution, Piso had corrupted the common soldiers by sanctioning indiscipline and maltreatment of the allies, so much so that he was called 'father of the legions' by the worst of them. On the other hand, they said, he was ruthless with all the finest soldiers, especially the companions and friends of Germanicus. And, finally, he had done away with the man himself by curses and poison—hence Piso's and Plancina's ceremonies and unspeakable sacrifices, Piso's armed assault on the state, and (so he could be brought to justice) his defeat in battle.

14. On all charges but one the defence was in trouble (for there was no denying allegations of the corruption of the soldiers, of the province being left at the mercy of all the most unscrupulous types, and even of the insults against the commander). The only charge that Piso appeared to have refuted was that of poisoning. Even the prosecution could not satisfactorily establish a case that he had, at a dinner hosted by Germanicus, who occupied a place above him,* poisoned the commander's food with his own hands. Indeed, it seemed inconceivable that he would have made such an attempt amidst another man's slaves, with so many present, and in Germanicus' presence; and the defendant also insisted on torture for his own household slaves and for the waiters.

The judges, however, were immovable, for various reasons, Tiberius because war had been brought to a province, the Senate because it had never truly believed that Germanicus' death had not involved foul play <. . .> their demand for what they had written Tiberius refused as firmly as Piso. At the same time cries could be heard coming from the public before the Curia: they would not refrain from violence if the man avoided sentencing by the Senate, they said. They had also dragged statues of Piso onto the Gemonian Steps* and had started hacking them to pieces—but these were rescued and put back on the emperor's orders. Piso was therefore placed in a litter and escorted home by a tribune of a praetorian cohort: rumour varied on whether the man was with him to protect his life, or ensure his death.

15. Plancina faced the same hostility, but she had greater influence, and so it was long unclear how far the emperor would be allowed to go with her. And, in fact, while Piso's hopes hung in the balance, she herself promised to share his fate, whatever it was, and, if needs be, go to her death with him. But when she gained a pardon, through discreet appeals from Augusta,* she began, little by little, to distance herself from her husband and to separate her defence from his. The defendant realized that this spelled his end, and wondered whether to continue his efforts. His sons encouraged him, however, and he steeled himself and entered the Senate again. There he endured a renewed attack, abuse from the senators, a completely hostile and cruel reception; but nothing frightened him more than seeing Tiberius—no pity, no anger, and his mind shut tight against any emotional appeal.

Piso was taken home, where he wrote a few things, ostensibly in preparation for his defence the next day, and then sealed the document and passed it to a freedman. After that he gave the usual care to his personal grooming. Later, when much of the night had passed, his wife left the bedroom, and he ordered the door to be shut. At break of day he was found with his throat pierced, a sword lying on the ground.

16. I remember* being told by older people of a document that was quite frequently seen in Piso's hands, the nature of which he never made public. But apparently his friends used to assert that it contained a letter from Tiberius with instructions relating to Germanicus, and that, had he not been tricked by Sejanus with empty promises, Piso intended to put this before the senators and to demonstrate Tiberius' guilt. They also said that his death had not been suicide, but that an assassin had been sent to him. I would not confidently affirm either of these claims, but at the same time I felt

obliged not to conceal an account given by people who lived on into the period when I was young.

With features composed to affect sadness, Tiberius \<complained\> to the Senate that Piso's intention by such a death was to rouse animosity against him. \<He ordered Marcus Piso to be summoned\> and with intense questioning asked him how the elder Piso had spent his last day and night. The man's replies were mostly discreet, though some were ill-advised, and Tiberius then read out a letter drawn up by Piso, which went much like this:

'I have been overwhelmed by a conspiracy of my enemies and by the resentment generated by a false accusation and, since there is no place anywhere for truth and my innocence, I swear by the immortal gods, Caesar, that I have lived loyal to you, and have been just as devoted to your mother. I beg the two of you to look out for my children. Gnaeus Piso* is totally unconnected with my fortunes, whatever they have been, since he spent all the time in question in the city; and Marcus Piso urged me not to return to Syria. And I only wish that I had given in to my young son, rather than he to his aged father! I therefore entreat you all the more earnestly not to let a guiltless man pay the penalty for my wrong-headedness. By my forty-five years of loyal service, by the joint consulship* we held, and as one who once earned the approval of your father, the deified Augustus, and as your friend who will ask you for nothing after this—I ask you for my unfortunate son's life.' About Plancina he added nothing.

17. After this Tiberius acquitted the young man of the charge of civil war; the orders had come from his father, he said, and a son could not have disobeyed. At the same time he expressed pity for the noble pedigree of the family, and for the sad plight of Piso, whatever it was he deserved. For Plancina he made an embarrassed and disgraceful appeal, proffering as an excuse the entreaties of his mother, against whom the criticisms of all decent people were flaring up more intensely in secret. It was morally acceptable, then, for a grandmother to look her grandson's killer in the face, they said, and to talk to her and rescue her from the hands of the Senate. The laws were there to benefit all citizens, they said—in Germanicus' case alone they had not been applied! There had been *lamentation* for Germanicus in the speeches of Vitellius and Veranius; Plancina had actually been *defended* by the emperor and Augusta. So now she should turn her poisons and magical practices—so successfully tested!—on

Agrippina and her children, and give a fine grandmother and uncle their absolute fill of blood from a tragic household.

Two days were spent on this charade of a trial, as Tiberius pressed the sons of Piso to defend their mother. And since the prosecution and its witnesses competed with each other in the length of their speeches, eliciting no response, it was pity that grew rather than rancour.

The first to be asked his opinion was the consul Aurelius Cotta* (for when the emperor presided, the magistrates fulfilled that function, too). He proposed that Piso's name be deleted from the Fasti, that half his property* be confiscated, the other half being given to his son Gnaeus Piso, and that the son should change his *praenomen*.* Marcus Piso should be stripped of his rank,* he added, and relegated for ten years, being made a grant of five million sesterces. Plancina, in view of Augusta's pleas, should be exonerated.

18. Many facets of this proposal were softened by the emperor. Piso's name would not be removed from the Fasti, since the name of Marcus Antonius, who had made war on the fatherland, remained, as did that of Iullus Antonius,* who had dishonoured the family of Augustus. He also spared Marcus Piso his diminution in rank, and granted him his father's property. Tiberius was, as I have often said, firmly resistant to financial temptation, and at that moment he was more lenient because of embarrassment over Plancina's exoneration. Likewise, when Valerius Messalinus* suggested setting up a gold statue in the temple of Mars the Avenger, and Caecina Severus* an altar of Vengeance, he rejected the proposals, declaring that such monuments were consecrated for victories abroad, and setbacks at home should be veiled in sadness. Messalinus had made the further suggestion that thanks be offered to Tiberius, Augusta, Antonia, Agrippina, and Drusus for the vengeance they had taken for Germanicus, and he had omitted mention of Claudius.* In fact Lucius Asprenas* actually enquired of Messalinus before the Senate whether the omission was intentional, and only then was the name of Claudius added to the list. Personally, the more I consider recent or earlier history, the more I find myself face to face with the farcical nature of all human affairs. For in terms of reputation, hopes, and respect, everyone was more likely to succeed to power than the man whom fortune was keeping under cover as the future emperor.

19. A few days later Tiberius proposed to the Senate the award of priesthoods* to Vitellius, Veranius, and Servaeus, and he committed

himself to support for Fulcinius for public office, but warned him against ruining his eloquence by aggressiveness.

That spelled the end of the punitive measures for Germanicus' death, but the affair remained a subject of conflicting rumours not only amongst men of that epoch but in the years that succeeded them as well. So true is it that the greatest events are fraught with ambiguity: some regard as certain any hearsay at all, while others turn the truth inside out; and both versions balloon in succeeding generations.

Drusus* had now left the city to take up his command again, but he soon re-entered with an ovation. A few days later his mother Vipsania* died, the only one of all of Agrippa's children to meet a non-violent end. The others were killed,* some, as was manifest, by the sword, others, it was believed, by poison or starvation.

20. This same year Tacfarinas (whose defeat the previous summer* at the hands of Camillus I have noted above) renewed hostilities in Africa. First there were sporadic depredations, too swift for retaliation, and then he proceeded to destroy villages and haul off plunder on a large scale. Finally, he encircled a Roman cohort not far from the River Pagyda. There, in command of the Roman stronghold, was an energetic and campaign-seasoned man, Decrius, who felt the siege a matter of disgrace. Encouraging his men, he deployed his battle-line before the encampment to give them an opportunity for a fight on open ground. The cohort was driven back with the first onset, and Decrius darted nimbly between the weapons to face his fleeing men, berating the standard-bearers for letting Roman soldiers turn tail before undisciplined troops or deserters. At the same time he received multiple wounds and, though one eye was pierced, he turned his face towards the enemy and did not give up the fight until he collapsed, deserted by his men.

21. When the news reached Lucius Apronius* (he had succeeded Camillus), he was more distressed by the shameful performance of his own men than by the glory won by the enemy, and he employed a procedure rarely used at the time and harking back to days of old. Drawing by lot one in every ten men* from the disgraced cohort, he had these men clubbed to death. So successful was his savage measure that a detachment of veterans, no more than five hundred strong, put those very same troops of Tacfarinas to flight when they attacked a fortress called Thala. In that engagement Rufus Helvius, a common soldier, earned the distinction of saving a citizen's life and was presented with

a necklace and spear by Apronius. Tiberius added the civic crown,*
complaining (but without being genuinely upset) that Apronius had
not made this further award to Helvius in his position as proconsul.

When Tacfarinas saw the Numidians routed and reluctant to conduct siege-warfare, he spread out his operations, giving ground when
under pressure, and then rounding on his adversaries' rear. While
that remained the barbarian's strategy, he could, with impunity, toy
with his enemy, frustrating and exhausting him. Then he veered
to the coastal districts and there, encumbered with plunder, stuck
close to his base camp. At this point Apronius Caesianus, sent out by
his father with some cavalry and auxiliary cohorts (to which he had
added the swiftest of his legionary troops), fought a successful battle
against the Numidians and drove them into the desert.

22. At Rome, meanwhile, Lepida* (who, apart from her distinguished connection to the Aemilii, also had Lucius Sulla and Gnaeus
Pompey as her great-grandfathers) was accused of falsely claiming
to have borne a child fathered by the rich and childless Publius
Quirinius. Further charges were added: adultery, poisoning, and
consulting astrologers on the subject of the emperor's household.*
The brother of the accused, Manius Lepidus, conducted her defence.
By his continued hostility after giving notice of the divorce, Quirinius
had generated some sympathy for the woman, despite her bad reputation and her guilt.

One could not easily fathom the thoughts of the emperor in this
inquiry, so confused and mixed were the signals of anger and clemency
that he gave. At first he appealed to the Senate that treason charges
not be admitted; later he induced the former consul Marcus
Servilius and other witnesses to bring forward the information he
had apparently wanted to exclude from the case. Similarly, he transferred Lepida's slaves to the authority of the consuls when they were
being held in military custody, and would not allow them to be
interrogated under torture on matters relating to his own household.
He also exempted Drusus, who was consul-designate, from the duty
of giving his opinion first.* This a number of people judged a libertarian gesture, freeing the others from the obligation of agreeing with
Drusus, though some saw in it a more ruthless motive: Drusus would
have ceded his place only if he were duty-bound to convict.

23. The games* had interrupted the trial, and during that
time Lepida went into the theatre* in the company of some ladies

of distinction. There, with tearful lamentations, she called upon her ancestors and on Pompey himself, whose monument that building was, and whose statues stood in full view, and such was the compassion she evoked that the audience burst into tears and shouted savage and abominable insults against Quirinius. A woman once destined to be Lucius Caesar's wife and the deified Augustus' daughter-in-law, they said, was being sacrificed to an old and childless man from a family of no repute. Then, with the torture of her slaves, her misdeeds came to light, and the voting favoured the proposal of Rubellius Blandus,* who was for refusing her 'fire and water'. Drusus supported Blandus, though others had been more forgiving in their votes. Later, as a favour to Scaurus,* who had had a daughter by the woman, it was decided that her property not be confiscated. Then Tiberius finally disclosed that he had also discovered from Publius Quirinius' slaves that an attempt had been made by Lepida to poison Quirinius.

24. The misfortunes befalling illustrious families—for there had been little time between the Calpurnii losing Piso and the Aemilii losing Lepida—were somewhat relieved by the restoration of Decimus Silanus to the Junian family. Silanus' tribulations I shall briefly recapitulate. Whereas the deified Augustus' fortunes flourished in public life, on the family plane they were unhappy because of the immorality of his daughter and granddaughter,* both of whom he expelled from the city, punishing their lovers with death or exile. For, in applying the severe terms 'sacrilege' and 'treason' to such widespread misconduct amongst men and women, he exceeded the humane penalties sanctioned by our ancestors and his own legislation.* (The fate of other individuals, and the rest of the events of that period, I shall relate in future if, after completing my proposed schedule of work, I find I live long enough to take on further literary endeavours.)

Now Decimus Silanus was the adulterer in the case of Augustus' granddaughter. Although the severity of his punishment went no further than exclusion from Augustus' friendship, he was aware that he was being shown the door into exile, and it was only under Tiberius' rule that he presumed to make an appeal to the Senate and the emperor. He did this relying on the influence of his brother Marcus Silanus,* who enjoyed some pre-eminence because of his high rank and eloquence. Tiberius, when Silanus thanked him, replied in the presence of the Senate that he, too, was happy at his brother's return from his long journey abroad, and that it was quite justifiable as his exile had not been sanctioned by a senatorial decree or by law. He added, however, that he retained his father's resentment towards the man unaltered, and that Augustus' wishes had not been effaced by Silanus' return. After that Silanus remained in the city, but did not gain public office.

25. There followed a motion on softening the *Lex Papia Poppaea*,* which Augustus had authorized at an advanced age as a follow-up to the Julian enactments, in order to increase the penalties for remaining unmarried and to augment the exchequer. But, given the power that lay in being childless, there was no increase in marriages and the upbringing of children. The numbers now in danger from its provisions, however, were growing, since every home was being subverted by the interpretations denouncers put on them; and while the problem before had been the transgressions, now it was the actual laws.*

This fact prompts me to go more deeply into the origins of the legislation, and the ways in which we arrived at this limitless and varied array of laws.

26. The earliest humans, having no perverse desires, lived without fault and without crime, and so without punishment and coercion. Rewards were unnecessary since decency was sought after for its own sake; and as people had no outlandish appetites they were not barred from anything by the use of deterrents. After egalitarianism was sloughed off, however, and ambition and violence began to replace restraint and modesty, despotisms sprang up, remaining a permanent fixture among many peoples. Some, either from the start or after tiring of monarchy, preferred a system of laws. These were quite basic at first, the people being unsophisticated. The greatest celebrity has been accorded to those of Crete, drafted by Minos, those of Sparta, drafted by Lycurgus, and later the more elaborate and comprehensive system drafted for Athens by Solon.*

In our case, the rule of Romulus* was arbitrary, and then Numa* used religious injunctions and god-given legislation to keep the people in check (and some innovations were added by Tullus* and Ancus*). Servius Tullius,* however, was our principal legislator, producing laws with which even the kings should have complied.

27. After Tarquin's* expulsion, the people opposed the intrigues of the senatorial class by taking numerous measures to protect their freedoms and strengthen their unity. Decemvirs* were appointed and, with fine additions incorporated from all quarters, the Twelve Tables were drawn up, the epitome of fair legislation. For while the laws that followed were sometimes aimed at felons, with specific reference to their crime, more often they arose from class struggles and were carried by force with the aim of gaining office illegally or banishing distinguished men, or for other unprincipled motives. This gave rise to rabble rousers like the Gracchi and Saturninus, and Drusus* (who was no less prodigal, but on the part of the Senate). The allies were bribed with hope and bamboozled with the veto. Not even in the Italian war, which was soon a civil war, was there any halt to the flood of contradictory legislation until the dictator Lucius Sulla* rescinded or changed earlier laws (while adding further ones) and produced some slowdown in this process, though it was short-lived. The fractious bills of Lepidus* quickly appeared, and not long afterwards the tribunes saw the return of their licence to incite the people any way they wanted. And from now on legislation was focused not on the community as a whole but on particular individuals, and laws were most numerous when the state was most corrupt.

28. Then, in his third consulship, Gnaeus Pompey* was chosen to effect moral reform, but his cures proved more severe than the offences. Creator and subverter of his own laws, he lost by armed force what he had used armed force to protect. There followed twenty years* of constant discord, with no morality and no law; the worst outrages went unpunished, and decent acts often proved fatal. Finally, in his sixth consulship, Caesar Augustus, secure in his power, annulled all the measures of his triumvirate and produced legislation to ensure us peace and an emperor.

Then the shackles grew tighter. Guards were set over us and, in cases of men relinquishing the privileges of parenthood, these guards had the inducement of rewards under the *Lex Papia Poppaea* to ensure that the people, the parent of all, as it were, took over the unclaimed inheritances. But they began to take too deep a hold, fastening their grip on the city, on Italy and citizens everywhere, and many people found their fortunes severed from them. Everyone was threatened with terror, but Tiberius, to provide a cure, selected by lot five ex-consuls, five ex-praetors and a like number from the rest of the Senate; and in the hands of these men many of the legal knots were loosened, and, for the time being, some slight relief provided.

29. Nero,* one of Germanicus' children, had just reached the formal status of a young man, and at this time Tiberius commended him to the Senate. He asked that Nero be released from the obligation of taking up a vigintivirate,* and that he stand for the quaestorship five years* before the legal age, which provoked some derisive laughter in his audience! His claim was that, at the request of Augustus, he and his brother had been granted the same authorization. (In fact, I would not doubt that even then there were men who would have secretly ridiculed such a petition; and yet that was only the beginning of the hegemony of the Caesars, and it was a time when old traditions loomed larger in people's minds, and, moreover, the bond between stepfather and stepson is weaker than that between grandfather and grandson.) Nero was also granted a priesthood,* and on the day that he first entered the Forum* largesse was distributed to the plebs, who were delighted at the sight of a child of Germanicus now come to puberty. Their joy was increased after that by the marriage of Nero to Drusus' daughter, Julia. But the positive comments circulating on this stood in contrast to the hostile reaction to the news that Sejanus was marked out to be the father-in-law of Claudius' son.* It seemed that Tiberius had sullied his family's nobility, and gone too far in his elevation of Sejanus, a man already suspected of inordinate ambition.

30. The end of that year saw the demise of two distinguished men, Lucius Volusius* and Sallustius Crispus. Volusius belonged to an old family, but one that had never gone further than the praetorship. He himself brought a consulship into it; he also held the authority of a censor for the selection of equestrian *decuriae*,* and was, moreover, the first to amass the fortune by which that household achieved its enormous success.

Crispus came from an equestrian background. That outstanding author of Roman history, Gaius Sallustius, adopted him—Crispus was his sister's grandson—and gave him his name. And though the way to public office lay open to him, Crispus followed Maecenas' example and, without achieving senatorial status, exceeded in influence many who had enjoyed triumphs and consulships. But he departed from old-time tradition in his elegance and sophistication, and in financial resources and extravagance he bordered on profligacy. But underneath lay a vigorous intellect that was equal to great endeavours, and the greater his outward show of sleepiness and lethargy, the keener that intellect was. So it was that, in Maecenas' lifetime, he was the second, and afterwards the primary, person to whom imperial secrets would be entrusted. He was party to the murder of Agrippa Postumus, but as he aged he retained an artificial rather than an active friendship with the emperor. That had also happened to Maecenas. Such is the way with influence, which is rarely everlasting; or else one or other of the parties becomes satiated, one after giving everything, or the other finding there is nothing left to wish for.

31. There followed Tiberius' fourth, and Drusus' second, consulship,* noteworthy because of the partnership of father and son. Three years earlier Germanicus had shared the same office with Tiberius, but this had not been a pleasure for the uncle, and the family relationship had not been so close.

At the start of that year Tiberius retired to Campania,* ostensibly to build up his health, but he was really practising by degrees for his long, continuous absence from Rome or else giving Drusus leeway to fulfil his consular duties on his own with his father absent.

And, as it happened, a trivial event, which developed into a serious conflict, furnished the young man with the means of winning public favour. An ex-praetor, Domitius Corbulo,* lodged a complaint in the Senate about a young nobleman, Lucius Sulla.* Sulla, he said, had not ceded his seat to him at a gladiatorial show.* On Corbulo's side there was his age, ancestral custom, and the support of the older generation. Against him were Mamercus Scaurus, Lucius Arruntius, and other relatives of Sulla. These started a battle of speeches, with examples adduced of ancestors who had censured young men's disrespect with punishing decrees, until finally Drusus produced some appropriate remarks for calming ruffled feelings. Then satisfaction was given to Corbulo through the agency of Mamercus, who was both uncle and stepfather to Sulla, and also the most articulate orator of the period.

It was Corbulo, too, who raised a commotion about many of the roads* throughout Italy being in disrepair and impassable because of the fraudulent practices of contractors and the indifference of magistrates.* He happily accepted to look after the business, but this proved not so much a boon for the public as ruinous for many people, whose capital and good name he savaged with condemnations in court and public auctions of property.

32. Not much later Tiberius sent a letter to the Senate informing the members of further destabilization in Africa arising from an incursion by Tacfarinas. The senators should be discriminating in their selection of a proconsul, he said; he should be a man with military experience and a strong physique, and one capable of such a campaign. Sextus Pompeius* took this as an opportunity to start venting his hatred on Manius Lepidus,* accusing him of being a listless pauper who was a disgrace to his ancestors and who should therefore be kept from the assignment of Asia, as well as Africa. The Senate demurred. Lepidus they regarded as a placid rather than idle individual—his straitened circumstances derived from his father, and they thought the nobleman's life that he had led without reproach was a credit rather than a disgrace to him. He was therefore dispatched to Asia,* and in the matter of Africa it was decided that the emperor should choose the man to whom it should be assigned.

33. During these proceedings Severus Caecina made a proposal* that no magistrate allotted* a province should have his wife accompany him there. He devoted a long preamble to his harmonious relationship with his wife, and to the six children she had borne him, and declared that he maintained within his own family the principle he wanted to establish as public policy. For, he said, she had been kept back in Italy although he had himself served forty* campaigns in numerous provinces. The policy of old, namely not to have women dragged along amongst the allies and foreign peoples, had some point to it, he said. In a retinue of women there were those who interfered with peacetime operations by their extravagance, and wartime operations by their fear, and they had given a Roman army on the march the appearance of a barbarian parade. Nor was their sex merely weak and unsuited to hardship; given the chance, it was also ruthless, self-seeking, and greedy for power. Women would strut amongst the soldiers, and have centurions at their beck and call; and recently a woman had presided over drills of cohorts, and legionary manoeuvres.* They themselves should bear in mind, Caecina continued, that when men were on trial for extortion the charges were mostly levelled at the wives. It was to them that all the vilest provincials immediately became attached; it was by them that business was taken in hand and transacted. Respects were accorded to two people when they left their residence, and there were two headquarters; and it was the wives' orders that were the more oppressive and headstrong. They had once been constrained by the Oppian* and other laws, he said: today, having thrown off their bonds, they were running the home, the law courts, and now the army, too.

34. Few were in agreement when they heard this. More noisily objected that there had been no motion on the question, and also that Caecina was no appropriate censor* in such an important issue. Presently Valerius Messalinus replied (his father was Messala, and Messalinus retained some semblance of the paternal eloquence), and he argued that the severity of the past had been largely improved and softened. For, he said, the city was not besieged by conflicts as it once was, nor were the provinces hostile; and the few concessions made to women's requirements were not a burden even on their husbands' household, much less the allies. All else was shared with the husband, and that presented no problem as far as peace was concerned. In the case of war, clearly, men have to be ready for action; but when they return after the ordeal what more decent solace is there than that of a wife? But some women have slipped into self-seeking ways and avarice, it is said. So? Have not a number of the magistrates themselves become subject to various kinds of cupidity? But that did not mean that no one was sent out to a province. Husbands have often been corrupted by their wives' moral depravity! Are all unmarried men then without fault?

The Oppian laws found favour of old, Messalinus continued— that period of the republic's history required them. Subsequently there was some relaxation and mitigation, because that was expedient. There was simply no point in having our own inertia given other names: for it was men who were at fault if a woman went beyond the limit. In addition, it was wrong that the weak spirit of one or two should lead to husbands in general being deprived of companionship for their good times and bad; and it was also wrong for a naturally weak sex to be left to itself, exposed to its own sensuality and the carnal desires of others. Marriages were with difficulty kept inviolate when they were under constant surveillance—what would happen if they were consigned to oblivion for several years by what was virtually a divorce? When confronting wrongdoings elsewhere they should be remembering the misdeeds in Rome!

Drusus* made a few additional remarks about his own marriage— for the imperial family had to visit distant parts of the empire quite often, he said. How often, he continued, had the deified Augustus travelled to the east and the west* accompanied by Livia! Drusus himself had made the journey to Illyricum, and should it serve a purpose he would go to other nations, too, though not always cheerfully if he were to be torn from his beloved wife, the mother of their numerous children. So it was that Caecina's motion was outmanoeuvred.*

35. The next day that the Senate met, Tiberius, in a dispatch, levelled some indirect criticism at the members for referring back to the emperor all matters of concern, and he proceeded to name Marcus Lepidus and Junius Blaesus as the men from whom the proconsul of Africa should be chosen. The statements of both were then heard. Lepidus was the more insistent in his plea to be excused, adducing ill-health, the ages of his children, and a marriageable daughter;* and what he left unsaid was also picked up, namely that Blaesus was Sejanus' uncle and so the stronger candidate. Blaesus' response was ostensibly a refusal, but one lacking the same determination, and he was assisted by the united front of his sycophants.

36. Something then surfaced which had been kept hidden, though many complained in secret. More and more, all the most worthless people had been taking advantage of the practice of grasping an image of the emperor* as a means of avoiding punishment for making insulting and hateful remarks against decent people; and even freedmen and slaves had actually become objects of fear to their patron or master with their threatening words and gestures.

The senator Gaius Cestius* accordingly made the point in his speech that emperors were indeed on the level of gods, but it was only the just entreaties of suppliants that were entertained by gods. No one, he added, sought refuge in the Capitol or other temples of the city with the intention of using these places to support criminal activity. The laws had been discontinued or totally overturned, he said, when insults and threats were directed at him in the Forum, on the threshold of the Curia, by Annia Rufilla, a woman whom he had had convicted of fraud in court, and he did not himself dare seek legal redress because he was confronted with the emperor's likeness! Members raised a din all round him, complaining of not dissimilar—and some even of more distressing—abuses, and they repeatedly begged Drusus to set an example by inflicting punishment. Finally, Drusus sent for Rufilla, had her convicted, and ordered her detained in a public prison.

37. Punitive measures were also taken against the Roman knights Considius Aequus and Caelius Cursor* for having brought trumped-up charges against the praetor Magius Caecilianus. This was done on the emperor's authority and with a decree of the Senate, and both factors redounded to Drusus' credit. Because Drusus presented himself at people's gatherings and conversations in the city, it was thought that the effects of his father's reclusive behaviour were softened. And the young man's extravagance did not find much disfavour, either. Let him indulge such inclinations, it was felt, spending his days on putting up buildings* and his nights on feasting; better that, than that he be alone with no pleasures to distract him, prey to gloomy sleeplessness and fiendish thoughts.

38. For Tiberius was not flagging, and neither were the informers. Indeed, Ancharius Priscus accused the proconsul of Crete, Caesius Cordus, of extortion, adding a charge of treason, which at that time accompanied all accusations. Antistius Vetus, one of Macedonia's leading men,* had been cleared of a charge of adultery. The emperor excoriated his judges and brought Vetus back to face trial for treason, alleging that he was seditious and implicated in the plots of Rhescuporis, at the time when the latter had contemplated war with us (after his assassination of Cotys). Vetus was accordingly 'forbidden fire and water', with the further condition added that he be detained on an island inconveniently situated in relation both to Macedonia and Thrace.

In fact, through lack of familiarity with us, Thrace* had been in discord ever since the division of the realm between Rhoemetalces and the children of Cotys, who, because of their young age, had as their guardian Trebellenus Rufus. The Thracians accused Rhoemetalces as much as they did Trebellenus of allowing the wrongs done to their countrymen to go unpunished. The Coelaletae, the Odrysae, and the Dii, who were powerful tribes, then took up arms, but under different leaders who were comparable only in their lack of nobility; and this was what occasioned their failure to come together and make it a bloody campaign. One group brought chaos to the immediate neighbourhood; and others crossed Mt. Haemus to galvanize the distant tribes. The majority, and the best organized, blockaded the king in Philippopolis, a city founded by Philip of Macedon.

39. When word of this was brought to Publius Vellaeus—he commanded the closest army*—he sent out his auxiliary cavalry and

light-armed cohorts against those who were drifting about pillaging or attempting to raise reinforcements, while he personally took the main body of his infantry to raise the siege. All operations met with simultaneous success: the raiding parties were cut to pieces; quarrelling broke out amongst the blockaders; the king made a timely sortie; and the legion arrived. 'Pitched battle' or 'engagement' would be an inappropriate term for something in which poorly armed and straggling men were butchered with no blood spilled on our side.

40. That same year the Gallic communities* started a rebellion because of the heavy burden of their debts.* The leading agitator amongst the Treveri* was Julius Florus,* and amongst the Aedui, Julius Sacrovir. Both were blessed with noble birth, and with ancestors who had given good service and who had therefore been granted Roman citizenship, in the early days when this was a rarity* and exclusively the reward of merit. These men now held secret talks, in which they involved all the most aggressive types, or men absolutely forced to crime by straitened circumstances and guilty fears arising from their heinous acts. At the talks Florus undertook to stir up the Belgae, and Sacrovir the more closely located Gauls. And so, at meeting points and gatherings, they held seditious conversations about their never-ending taxes, the punishing rates of interest, and the viciousness and arrogance of those in power over them. They noted, too, that the Roman soldiers were disaffected after hearing of Germanicus' death. It was an excellent occasion for taking back their independence, they said. They themselves were flourishing, and they should reflect on how defenceless Italy was, and how weak the urban proletariat, and on the fact that there was no strength in the armies apart from what came to them from abroad.

41. Hardly any community remained untouched by the seeds of the uprising, but the first to erupt were the Andecavi and the Turoni. The Andecavi were checked by the legate Acilius Aviola,* who summoned a cohort on garrison duty in Lugdunum. The Turoni were crushed by legionary troops that Visellius Varro,* legate of Lower Germany, had sent. These were again led by Aviola, along with some Gallic chieftains who brought him help in order to conceal their defection and reveal it more effectively at an appropriate moment. Sacrovir was also on prominent display, urging on the fight on behalf of the Romans with his head uncovered—to display his courage, so he said. Captives, however, claimed that he had made

himself recognizable so that he would not be a target* for weapons. When Tiberius was consulted on the matter, he disregarded the evidence and by his scepticism fuelled the war.

42. Florus meanwhile forged ahead with his plans and attempted to induce a cavalry squadron—it had been recruited among the Treveri but kept in our service, and under our discipline—to open the war with a massacre of some Roman traders. Though a few of the cavalrymen succumbed to his bribes, most remained loyal. The general crowd of debtors and dependants took up arms, however, and began to head for the woodlands called Arduenna. They were, however, headed off by legions sent from opposite directions* by Visellius and Gaius Silius* from their two armies in order to block them. Julius Indus was then sent ahead with an elite detachment— he came from the same community as Florus, but had differences with him and so was all the more enthusiastic to render the service— and he scattered the still disordered crowd of insurgents. Florus eluded the victors by shifting his hiding-places, but eventually, at the sight of soldiers who had invested his escape routes, he died by his own hand. And that marked the end of the uprising of the Treveri.

43. Amongst the Aedui the problem was the greater for their having a richer community, and the forces to suppress them being at a distance. Sacrovir had, with some armed cohorts, seized the tribal capital of Augustodunum, along with the most noble children of Gaul, who were engaged in liberal studies* there, his aim being to use them as hostages to bring their parents and relatives over to his cause. At the same time he distributed amongst the young men weapons that had been manufactured in secret.

Sacrovir's supporters numbered forty thousand, a fifth of them equipped with legionary weapons, the rest carrying hunting-spears, knives, and other implements used for the hunt. In addition to these there were some slaves marked out for a gladiatorial career who were, in the fashion of their country, completely covered with iron body-armour (they call these men *cruppellarii*, and while they are ill-suited to delivering wounds, they are also invulnerable). These forces were on the increase, for while there was as yet no open unity amongst the neighbouring communities, support on the individual level was enthusiastic. There was also conflict between the Roman commanders, each wanting conduct of the war for himself. Presently Varro,* feeble with age, gave way to the energetic Silius.

44. At Rome, however, it was thought that not only the Treveri and the Aedui but all sixty-four Gallic communities had defected, with the Germans also supporting their cause, and that the Spanish provinces were vacillating. As is the way with rumour, everything was believed, and exaggerated. All the most loyal people were stricken with anxiety for the state. Many, from hatred of the status quo, and desire for change, were even enjoying their own danger and were criticizing Tiberius for spending his time on the briefs of informers while things were in such turmoil. Was Sacrovir to be brought up on a charge of treason in the Senate? they asked. At last, men had come forward to suppress with weapons the bloody letters, they said—for a miserable peace even war was a good exchange! But Tiberius was all the more intent on appearing unconcerned. Changing neither his location nor his expression, he carried on as usual throughout those days, either from his deep reserve or because he had ascertained that the incidents were minor and less serious than commonly reported.

45. Silius, meanwhile, had been advancing with two legions. Sending ahead an auxiliary detachment, he plundered the country districts of the Sequani that lay on the edge of their territory (these areas were also on the frontiers of the Aedui, with whom they were brothers-in-arms). Soon, he made for Augustodunum at a rapid pace, the standard-bearers racing each other, and even the rank and file noisily demanding that there be no halting for the usual rest or to pass the night. Just let them see their enemy and be seen by them— that would be enough for victory, they cried. At the twelfth milestone Sacrovir and his troops came into view on open ground. He had deployed his heavily armoured troops at the front, his cohorts on the flanks, and his poorly armed men at the rear. Sacrovir himself went forward amongst the front ranks on a magnificent horse. He reminded them of the ancient glories of the Gauls and the defeats they had inflicted on the Romans, of how splendid freedom would be for them in victory, and how much more unbearable their servitude if they were defeated again.

46. The address was short, his audience sullen. For the legions were approaching in battle order, and the ill-organized townsmen, who had no knowledge of soldiering, were incapable of putting their ears or their eyes to profitable use.

On the other side, anticipation of success had removed the need for exhortation; but Silius, even so, kept calling out that it was insulting for them, conquerors of the Germanys, to be led against Gauls as though against an enemy! 'A single cohort recently crushed the insurgent Turoni,' he said, 'a single cavalry troop crushed the Treveri, and a few squadrons of this very army crushed the Sequani. The Aedui are the more unwarlike from being wealthy, and extravagant in their pleasures; crush them, and spare the fugitives!'

A mighty roar met these words. The cavalry poured round the enemy; the infantry attacked their front; and there was no hesitation on the flanks, either. The iron-armoured men occasioned some small delay since their metal plating was resistant to javelin and sword, but the soldiers seized their axes and picks and cut through the body-armour and bodies as if breaching a wall. Some, using poles and pitchforks, knocked over the lumbering masses. These then lay there, making no effort to get up again, and were left for dead. Sacrovir and a few of his most loyal men made for Augustodunum first, and then, fearing betrayal, for a country house close by. There they died, Sacrovir by his own hand, the others exchanging mortal blows. The house was burned over them, cremating them all.

47. Only then did Tiberius inform the Senate by letter* of a war begun and terminated.* He neither detracted from nor embellished the truth, saying that his legates and he had prevailed, they by their loyalty and courage, and he by his planning. At the same time he also furnished explanations for why neither he nor Drusus had left for that campaign; he stressed the size of the empire, and the fact that it was inappropriate for emperors <. . .> to leave the city, the centre of government for the whole realm, over unrest in one or two communities. Now that his motivation could not be attributed to fear, he would go to inspect and settle matters on the spot. The senators decreed vows for his return, prayers of thanksgiving and other 'appropriate' measures. Only Cornelius Dolabella* (with the intention of outdoing the others) went to absurd lengths of sycophancy and moved that Tiberius, on returning from Campania, enter the city in ovation. The result was a letter from the emperor. After crushing the most savage tribes and accepting or declining so many triumphs* in his youth, he said, he was not now, in his advancing age, so lacking in glory as to seek the hollow prize of a journey in the suburbs.

48. It was about the same time that Tiberius requested of the Senate that the death of Sulpicius Quirinius* be marked with a state funeral. Quirinius had no connection with the old patrician family of

the Sulpicii, having been born in the municipal town of Lanuvium. However, through being an active soldier, and by his energetic service, he had gained a consulship under the deified Augustus and later, because of his storming the strongholds of the Homonadenses in Cilicia, he had won triumphal insignia.* He was also assigned as an adviser to Gaius Caesar during his governorship of Armenia. He had, in addition, cultivated Tiberius' friendship during his time on Rhodes. This fact Tiberius revealed to the Senate on that occasion, praising the man's services to him while also criticizing Marcus Lollius,* who he claimed was responsible for Gaius Caesar's vicious and quarrelsome tendencies. The others, however, had no pleasant memory of Quirinius because of the dangers to which Lepida had been exposed (as I have narrated), and because of his miserly old age, in which he had too much power.

49. A Roman knight, Clutorius Priscus, had been awarded a sum of money by the emperor following a celebrated poem of his in which he had lamented the death of Germanicus. At the end of the year Priscus found himself in the clutches of an informer, who charged him with having composed a poem during Drusus' illness, hoping for an even greater reward should Drusus die. Clutorius had, showing off, given a reading of the piece at the home of Publius Petronius,* in the presence of Petronius' mother-in-law Vitellia and many ladies of distinction. When the informer came forward, these were all frightened into giving evidence—all except Vitellia, who insisted that she had heard nothing. But more credence was given to those whose allegations were aimed at destroying Priscus, and on a motion of the consul-designate Haterius Agrippa* the death penalty was sought for him.

50. Marcus Lepidus demurred, and proceeded with the following speech:*

'Senators, if we are looking at only one thing, namely the heinous words with which Clutorius Priscus sullied his own mind and the ears of his audience, then neither prison nor the noose, and not even the torture inflicted on slaves, would suffice to punish him! But while scandalous and criminal conduct may have no limit, our emperor's judiciousness, and your ancestors' and your own examples, set bounds to punishment and corrective measures. And if there is a difference between silliness and crime, between words and evildoing, then there is room for a proposal by which this man's offence would not be left unpunished and by which you, too, would have no reason to regret either your mercy or your severity.

'I have often heard our emperor complain of people whose suicide has prevented his exercise of mercy. Clutorius' life is as yet untouched; spared he will be no danger to the state, and executed no deterrent. His works are as inconsequential and ephemeral as they are full of delusion; and one need fear no grave or serious threat from a man who betrays his own crimes, worming his way into the minds not of men but of poor little women. Let him leave the city, lose his property, and be refused water and fire. And this I propose just as if he were liable to prosecution under the law of treason.'

51. The only man to agree with Lepidus was Rubellius Blandus, one of the ex-consuls. The others went along with Agrippa's motion, and Priscus was led away to prison and immediately put to death. Tiberius complained about this before the Senate with his customary equivocation, praising the loyalty of those who actively avenged wrongs, however slight, done to their emperor, but disapproving of mere words being punished in so precipitous a manner. He commended Lepidus, but did not criticize Agrippa. The result was a decision of the Senate that decrees of its members not be deposited in the treasury for nine days, and that condemned prisoners be given a reprieve for that length of time. The Senate, however, had no latitude to reverse its decisions, and Tiberius tended not to soften in the intervening period.

52. The next consuls were Gaius Sulpicius* and Decimus Haterius. It was a year without trouble in external affairs, but at home there was anticipation of severe measures against luxurious living, which had erupted on a massive scale in every sphere on which money can be lavished. Now, other forms of expenditure, though more excessive, could be masked by concealing the prices involved; but the provisions for eating and gluttony, being a topic of widespread conversation, had given rise to concern that an emperor of old-time thrift might produce rather stringent measures. For, when Gaius Bibulus first raised the matter, the other aediles* had also observed that the sumptuary law* was being flouted and that, despite prohibitions, food prices were daily on the rise and could not be stemmed by feeble measures. When the senators were consulted, they passed the whole business on to the emperor, untouched.

Tiberius had frequently wondered to himself whether such intemperate appetites could be restrained, and whether restraining them would do more harm than good to the state. He was aware, too, of how humiliating it would be to take on a challenge that he could not meet, or which (if he did have success) would inevitably ruin the name and reputation of illustrious men. Finally, he composed a letter to the Senate, which went essentially like this:

53. 'Senators: in other matters it may perhaps be more expedient that, when it comes to what I think serves the republic's interests, I be present to be questioned by you and to give my reply. In the case of this particular proposal, it is preferable that my eyes be removed from it, for fear that, when you note the fearful faces of individuals who might be accused of shameful extravagance, I might also see them, and catch them out, as it were. If those energetic men, the aediles, had earlier discussed it with me, I may well have urged them to overlook inveterate, firmly established vices rather than achieve only the result of publicizing failings we are unable to control. Now, they have, in fact, done their duty, and in a way in which I should like to see the other magistrates fulfil their own functions; but for me, while remaining silent is not honourable, speaking out is not easy, either, because mine is not the role of aedile, praetor, or consul. Something greater and more elevated is required of an emperor; and while everybody tries to appropriate credit for things well done, the unpopularity for collective misconduct devolves upon a single individual.

'For what is the first thing I should repress and cut back to traditional standards? Country houses* of immense dimensions? The number of slaves of different nationalities? The weight of silver and gold? Marvellous bronze artefacts and wonderful pictures? The clothing worn by both men and women, and those items, exclusively used by women,* for which our money is shipped to foreign and enemy races?

54. 'I am not unaware that such things are criticized at dinner-parties and social gatherings, and that demands are made for curbs on them. But should a person enact a law and lay down penalties, those same complainants will cry out that the state is being destroyed, that society's most splendid people are facing ruin, and that no one is immune from prosecution. But the fact is that, even with the body, it is only by harsh and painful treatment that you can stem long-standing maladies which have had time to grow; and a mind that is at once corrupted and a corrupting influence, one that is both languid and feverish, has to be neutralized with remedies no less potent than the passions with which it burns. But while there are so many laws of our ancestors' devising, and many that the deified Augustus enacted, the former have become ineffectual because they are forgotten, the latter (which is worse) because they have been flouted. This has only bolstered confidence in the life of luxury. For if you hanker after what is not yet forbidden, you may fear its being forbidden in the future. But if you have transgressed in a prohibited area and not been punished, there is no fear and no shame after that.

'So why was thrift so prevalent in the past? Because everybody practised self-control, because we were citizens of a single city. Even when our dominion was confined to Italy, we did not have the same temptations as now. From victories abroad we learned to devour other peoples' goods, and from the civil wars our own as well. How trifling is the matter of which the aediles warn us! How insignificant it must be thought if you consider things in general! Good heavens, no one mentions in a motion that Italy is reliant on supplies from abroad, that the livelihood of the Roman people lurches along each day through shifting seas and tempests! And if the resources of the provinces fail to assist our landowners and slaves and our own agricultural lands, then, naturally, it will be our own groves and country houses that will provide us with subsistence!

'This, senators, is the responsibility that the emperor shoulders, and neglect of it will entail total ruin for the state. For other problems the remedy must be sought within a person: let embarrassment improve us senators, and let necessity improve the poor, and satiety the rich. Alternatively, if any of the magistrates promises to show such energy and stringency as to meet the problem head-on, then I applaud this man and I also confess that I am thus relieved of some of my burdens. If, however, people want only to censure the vices and then, after winning a fine reputation for doing that, they cause quarrels and leave them to me—in that case, senators, you can be sure, that I, too, am not hungry for animosity. I *do* accept it on behalf of the state, serious and often unjust though it may be, but I have every right to refuse it when it is pointless and fruitless, and unlikely to serve my interests or yours, either.'

55. When the emperor's letter had been heard, the aediles were relieved of responsibility* in the matter, and extravagant cuisine (which was practised with prodigal expenditure for a hundred years, from the end of the battle of Actium to the armed conflict in which

Servius Galba gained power*) faded out by degrees. I would like to examine the reasons for this change.

Earlier, rich noble families, or families with an illustrious reputation, had been collapsing because of their fondness for splendour. For it was even at that time permissible to cultivate the friendship of the plebs, the allies, and the tributary kingdoms, and to be cultivated by them—and a man was the more distinguished in terms of reputation and clients according to the magnificence of his wealth, his home, and his personal effects. After the savage butchery,* and when a great renown came to mean death, those who remained turned to a more sensible course. Along with this there were the 'new men' who were frequently enlisted in the Senate from the municipal towns and colonies,* and even the provinces. They brought with them the frugality of their own background, and although a number of them reached an affluent old age through good fortune or hard work, their earlier attitudes remained with them. But the outstanding proponent of thrifty behaviour was Vespasian,* who was himself old-fashioned in his style of life. After that, deference to the emperor and the fervent wish to emulate him were more effective than any legal penalty or deterrent. Or perhaps there is a sort of cycle in all things, with changes of morality coming around again like seasonal changes. (And not everything was better in our ancestors' days, either—our own age, too, has produced many instances of excellence and artistic merit deserving to be imitated by posterity. At all events, let us continue to promote such honourable competitiveness with our ancestors!)

56. Having thus gained a reputation for judiciousness by checking the assault of the accusers,* Tiberius now sent a letter to the Senate seeking 'tribunician authority' for Drusus. This term* Augustus had thought up for the top position of power, in order not to assume the title of 'king' or 'dictator'* but still have precedence over the other offices. Subsequently he chose Marcus Agrippa as his colleague in that authority and then, on Agrippa's death, he chose Tiberius Nero—so as to leave no doubt about his successor. His thinking was that in this way the misguided hopes of others would be checked, and at the same time he had confidence in Tiberius' moderation and his own stature.

In following this precedent Tiberius now brought Drusus close to supreme power, although when Germanicus was still alive he had been non-committal in judging between the two. At the start of his letter was a prayer to the gods that they further his plans to the benefit of the state, and then he had some low-key remarks (without any false exaggeration) on the young man's character. Drusus had a wife and three children, he said, and was at the age* when Tiberius himself had been called on by the deified Augustus to take on this responsibility. Nor was this a hasty decision, he added; after an eight-year trial period of suppressing mutinies* and finishing wars,* Drusus, who had held a triumph* and twice been consul,* was now being enlisted to share work that he knew well.

57. The senators had anticipated Tiberius' address, and the sycophancy was therefore the more studied. Even so there was no innovation, nothing beyond proposals for statues of the emperors, altars of the gods, temples and arches and the other standard honours—except in the case of Marcus Silanus. Silanus sought a way to honour the emperors by debasing the consulship, proposing* that, for recording dates on public and private monuments, it should not be the consuls' names that topped the inscription, but those of the holders of the tribunician authority. Quintus Haterius'* motion that the resolutions of the Senate for that day be set up in gold letters in the Curia only made him a laughing stock—an old man who would gain from the affair only disgrace for his disgusting sycophancy!

58. Meanwhile, Junius Blaesus' tenure of the governorship of Africa was extended, and Servius Maluginensis, the flamen of Jupiter,* requested that he have Asia allocated to him. The common belief that flamens of Jupiter were not allowed to leave Italy was erroneous, Maluginensis insisted, and his legal status was no different from that of the flamens of Mars and Quirinus—so if *they* had been allotted* provinces, why was this forbidden for flamens of Jupiter? There were no plebiscites* on the ruling, he said, nothing to be found in the books on ritual procedure. The pontiffs had regularly performed the rites of Jupiter if the flamen was prevented from doing so by ill-health or a public responsibility. For seventy-five years after Cornelius Merula's suicide* nobody had been appointed in his place, and yet there had been no interruption in the performance of the rites. If no appointment had been made throughout all those years, with no detrimental effect on the religious ceremonies, how much easier would be his absence for a single year of proconsular *imperium*? In the past, he said, a ban by the various supreme pontiffs* on the flamen's travel to the provinces had been a result of private feuds.

Now, through the gift of heaven, the supreme pontiff was also the supreme man, and he was not susceptible to jealousy or animosity, or to personal prejudices.

59. Since the augur Lentulus and others had various objections to this, their solution was to await the opinion of the chief pontiff. Tiberius postponed an inquiry into the flamen's legal status, but cut back on the ceremonies decreed in honour of Drusus' tribunician authority, expressly criticizing the outrageous proposal of Silanus and also the gold letters ('contrary to ancestral tradition', he said). A letter from Drusus was also read aloud, and though it aimed at modesty it was perceived as being very arrogant. So, people said, things had now reached the point that even a young man receiving such a great honour did not deign to come before the city's gods, to enter the Senate, or even to take the auspices on his native soil. It must be a war, they said, or he is being detained in some far-off land—this man who at that very moment was on his journey around the beaches and lakes of Campania! Such was the training of a ruler of the human race, and this was his first lesson from his father! Of course, the old emperor might be reluctant to look upon his fellow-citizens, and could plead in his defence the exhaustion of age, and the works he had accomplished. In Drusus' case, what stopped him but his arrogance?

60. Tiberius was thus consolidating for himself the true essence of imperial power, but he also offered the Senate a glimpse of earlier times by sending the demands of the provinces* for its members to examine. For unchecked licence in establishing places of sanctuary had been on the increase throughout the Greek cities. Temples were filling up with the worst kinds of slaves; debtors were also receiving the same protection against and refuge from their creditors, as also were men suspected of capital crimes.* And there had been no authority strong enough to suppress the seditious behaviour of a people that harboured the misdemeanours of men as part of religious practice. The decision reached, therefore, was for the states in question to send proof of their rights, and spokesmen to present it. Some who had made spurious claims to such rights voluntarily relinquished them; many others relied on old superstitions and their services to the Roman people. It was a great spectacle on that day, when the Senate examined the benefits conferred by our ancestors, treaties made with our allies, and decrees of kings who had held power before

Roman hegemony, along with the cults of the gods themselves. And they had the liberty, as in earlier days, to ratify or emend.

61. The very first to come forward were the people of Ephesus. They claimed that, contrary to the common belief, Diana and Apollo were not born on Delos. There was a River Cenchreus in their lands, they said, and a grove of Ortygia, where Latona, in the advanced stages of pregnancy, had leaned against an olive tree (which was still there) and given birth to the two deities. It was at the behest of the gods that the grove had been consecrated, and there Apollo himself had avoided the anger of Jupiter after the killing of the Cyclopes. Later, Father Liber, after his victory in the war, had there pardoned the suppliant Amazons* when they sat at the altar. The temple's sacrosanctity had been enhanced by permission of Hercules when he was in control of Lydia, they added, and its privileges had not been diminished under the Persian empire, after which the Macedonians,* and then we, kept them in force.

62. The people of Magnesia were next, and they sought support from the ordinances of Lucius Scipio* and Lucius Sulla.* After Scipio had defeated Antiochus, and Sulla Mithridates, the two had paid tribute to the loyalty and courage of the Magnesians by granting the temple of Diana Leucophryne inviolability as a sanctuary. Then came the peoples of Aphrodisias and Stratonicea. These presented a decree of the dictator Caesar, awarded for their historic services to his cause, and a recent one of the deified Augustus, in which they were praised for facing the Parthian assault* without the slightest weakening in their loyalty to the Roman people. (In fact, the state of Aphrodisias patronized the worship of Venus, and Stratonicea that of Jupiter and Trivia.)

The people of Hierocaesaria brought to light a claim of earlier date, noting that they had in their land a Persian Diana and a shrine dedicated to her in the time of King Cyrus. Perpenna's* name was mentioned, and those of Isauricus* and numerous other commanders who had granted the same sacrosanctity, not just to the temple but to an area of two miles' radius around it. The people of Cyprus then made a claim for three shrines. The oldest of these, to Paphian Venus, had been inaugurated by its founder, Aerias; the second, to Venus Amathusia, by Aerias' son Amathus; and the third, to Salaminian Jupiter, by Teucer, when he was fleeing the anger of his father.

63. Deputations from other states were also heard. Wearied by their number and also by the intensity of the debates, the senators left the matter to the consuls. These were to examine the legitimacy of each case and, if there were some irregularity, to refer the entire matter back to the Senate. Apart from the city-states that I have mentioned, the consuls reported that they had found there to be a genuine sanctuary of Aesculapius* at Pergamum, but that the other cases relied on traditions obscure because of their antiquity. For example, the people of Smyrna, they said, cited an oracle of Apollo, on whose instructions they had dedicated a temple to Venus Stratonicis, and the people of Tenos cited an oracular pronouncement of the same god by which they were ordered to consecrate a statue and temple to Neptune. The people of Sardis had appealed to more recent events, saying their grant of sanctuary was a gift from the victorious Alexander; and the people of Miletus' claim likewise relied on King Darius. (But in these cases the objects of worship of the cults were, respectively, Diana and Apollo.) The Cretans also claimed a sanctuary, on the basis of a statue of the deified Augustus.

Senatorial decisions were then passed, and by these, very respectful though they were, a limit was set. The various peoples were instructed to set up bronze fixtures in the actual temples, to commemorate solemnly the occasion, and to prevent them from masking with religion a lapse into self-interested rivalry.

64. At about this same time a critical illness* of Julia Augusta obliged the emperor to make a speedy return to the city, there being still some genuine harmony between mother and son, or veiled hatred. For, a little earlier, Julia had been dedicating a statue* to the deified Augustus not far from the theatre of Marcellus, and she had inscribed Tiberius' name after her own. It was believed that Tiberius took this as a slight to his majesty as emperor, but had concealed his heavy resentment and stored the episode away in his mind.

At all events, propitiatory ceremonies were decreed by the Senate on that occasion, and Great Games to be staged by the pontiffs, augurs, and quindecimvirs, in company with the septemvirs* and members of the Augustal fraternity.* Lucius Apronius proposed that the Fetials* should also preside at these games. Tiberius, however, opposed the motion, noting the distinction between the various priesthoods and citing examples from the past. The Fetials, he observed, had never enjoyed that level of prestige, and the addition of the

Augustals was a result of their priesthood's special connection with the family for which the vows were being discharged.

65. I have not set myself the goal of recording senatorial proposals, except in cases where they are remarkable for their integrity, or notoriously discreditable. For I think it is a special duty of history to see that virtues are not left unrecorded, and also that fear of disgrace in posterity attends iniquitous words and actions. But those times were so corrupt and contaminated with sycophancy that men competed with each other in standing up and making foul and outrageous proposals. And it was not just the leading citizens of the community who did so, either, men who had to protect their distinction with servility; so, too, did all the ex-consuls, most ex-praetors, and even many of the lower-ranking senators.* The story goes that, whenever he left the Curia, Tiberius was in the habit of declaring, in Greek: 'Ah, men ready to be slaves!' Clearly, while he objected to the freedom of the people, he was also sickened by such abject submission from his 'slaves'.

66. Then, by degrees, they passed from degradation to savagery. Gaius Silanus,* proconsul of Asia, was prosecuted for extortion by the provincials. Mamercus Scaurus,* an ex-consul, Junius Otho,* a praetor, and Bruttedius Niger,* an aedile, pounced on him together, charging him with dishonouring the divinity of Augustus and being disrespectful of Tiberius' majesty. Mamercus also tossed in some ancient precedents—Lucius Cotta's* indictment by Scipio Africanus, Servius Galba's* by Cato the Censor and Publius Rutilius'* by Marcus Scaurus. (Naturally, these were the kinds of activities for which Scipio, Cato, and the well-known Scaurus sought punishment—Scaurus, who was Mamercus' grandfather and whom he, a disgrace to his ancestors, was dishonouring with his shameful endeavours! Junius Otho's old occupation was running an elementary school. Subsequently he became a senator through Sejanus' influence, and by his shameless and outrageous behaviour brought further disgrace upon his mean beginnings. Bruttedius was a man of many honourable accomplishments, headed for all manner of distinction had he simply kept to the straight path; but impatience drove him to try to surpass his equals, then his superiors, and eventually his very own ambitions. This has been the downfall of many men—good men, too—who, rejecting success that is attainable slowly but surely, chase after that which can be reached early, even if it brings ruin.)

67. The number of accusers was raised by the addition of Gellius Publicola and Marcus Paconius,* respectively quaestor and legate of Silanus. There was thought to be no doubt of the defendant's guilt on the charges of brutality and peculation, but there were many factors piling up against him that would have imperilled even the guiltless. Apart from having so many senators against him, he, on his own and knowing nothing of oratory, had to respond to the most eloquent men in all of Asia, men chosen to prosecute him for that very reason. And Silanus had his own particular grounds for fear (which has a debilitating effect even on trained eloquence), for Tiberius did not stop browbeating him with his tone of voice and his looks, and frequently putting questions to him himself. He was given no opportunity to rebut or evade, either, and often had to admit to things simply so Tiberius' questions would not have been asked in vain. In addition, a public agent had taken possession of Silanus' slaves so they could be interrogated under torture.* And, to prevent any of his friends from helping him in his predicament, treason charges were added, making silence a binding obligation on them. Silanus therefore requested a few days' discontinuance and abandoned his defence, after venturing to send the emperor a petition that was a mixture of resentment and entreaties.

68. To make what he was preparing for Silanus seem more excusable by means of a precedent, Tiberius ordered the documentation of the deified Augustus' case against Volesus Messala* (who was similarly a proconsul of Asia) to be read out, along with the decree of the Senate against the man. He then asked Lucius Piso* for his opinion. After a long preamble on the emperor's clemency, Piso recommended that Silanus be forbidden fire and water, and relegated to the island of Gyarus. So too the others, except Gnaeus Lentulus, who stated that the property of Silanus deriving from his mother should be kept separate—for his mother was Appia—and restored to Silanus' son. Tiberius agreed.

69. Cornelius Dolabella, however, took his sycophancy further. After condemning Gaius Silanus' character, he subjoined that nobody who had an unsavoury record and was steeped in infamy should be eligible for the provincial sortition, and that the emperor should decide on this proposal. Misdemeanours, he noted, were punished under the law, but how much gentler it would be on the individuals themselves, and how much better for the provincials, to have antimalpractice provisions in place beforehand!

The emperor spoke against the proposal, saying that while he was not unaware of the rumours circulating about Silanus, decisions should not be based on hearsay. The actions of many in their provinces had belied the hopes or fears that people had entertained, with some being inspired to better things by their great responsibilities, and others enfeebled by them. And, he added, an emperor could not have all-embracing knowledge, nor was it expedient for him to be influenced by the ambition of others. It was precisely because future actions were unknowable that the laws were established to deal with those of the past. This was why it had been established by their ancestors that punishment should follow crimes that were committed earlier; and they should not subvert what had been wisely conceived and accepted ever since. Emperors bore enough burdens, he said, and enough power, too. People's rights were diminished as central power grew, and one should not have recourse to authority when matters can be conducted under the law.

The rarity of Tiberius' popularity-seeking pronouncements meant that they were received with all the more pleasure. And the emperor, prudent in steering his way forward when not urged on by personal resentment, then added that the island of Gyarus was a grim place devoid of human habitation.* As a concession to the Junian family, and because Silanus was a man once holding the same rank as they, he said, they should allow him to go to Cythnus instead. That, said Tiberius, was also the request of Silanus' sister, Torquata,* a Vestal Virgin of traditional virtue. The matter went immediately to the vote.

70. After that the people of Cyrene were given an audience, and, with Ancharius Priscus conducting the prosecution, Caesius Cordus was found guilty of extortion. The Roman knight Lucius Ennius was arraigned on a charge of treason for having transformed an effigy of the emperor into silver plate for everyday usage, but Tiberius forbade his case to go to trial. This prompted open protest, in what looked like a gesture of independence, from Ateius Capito. The Senate should not be stripped of its power to decide cases, he said, and a crime of such magnitude should not go unpunished—by all means let the emperor be slow to anger when personally hurt, but he should not condone injury done to the state! Tiberius took this for what it was, not for what was actually being said, and maintained his veto. Capito's debasement was all the more marked because, an expert in secular and religious law as he was, he was thought to have dishonoured a fine public career and his own personal qualities.

71. There next arose a matter of religion, namely in which temple the offering should be placed that the Roman knights had vowed to Equestrian Fortune* for Augusta's recovery. For while there were numerous shrines of the goddess Fortune in the city, none bore such a cult title. It came to light that there was a temple at Antium bearing that name, and that in the towns of Italy all religious rites, temples, and statues of the deities fell under the jurisdiction and governance of Rome. The offering was accordingly set up at Antium.

And since religious procedure was under discussion, Tiberius brought forth his response—which he had recently postponed—to the flamen of Jupiter, Servius Maluginensis. He read out a decree of the pontiffs stating that, whenever illness struck a flamen of Jupiter, he could take more than two nights' leave with the permission of the Pontifex Maximus, provided that the absence did not fall during days of public sacrifice or occur more than twice per year. These ordinances, established in the principate of Augustus, made it sufficiently clear that flamens of Jupiter were not allowed leave of a year and provincial governorship. Mention was also made of the precedent set by the Pontifex Maximus Lucius Metellus, who had kept the flamen Aulus Postumius* in Rome. The allotment of Asia was therefore bestowed upon the ex-consul next in rank to Maluginensis.

72. At about the same time <Marcus> Lepidus* requested permission from the Senate to repair and refurbish at his own expense the basilica of Paulus, a monument of the Aemilian family. Even then munificence on behalf of the state was still in vogue; and earlier Augustus had not stopped Taurus, Philippus, or Balbus* from contributing spoils from the enemy, or from their excessive resources, in order to beautify the city and earn renown for their descendants. This was the example that Lepidus, despite his modest means, was following in reviving the glory of his ancestors.

Pompey's theatre,* however, destroyed by an accidental fire, Tiberius undertook to rebuild on the grounds that no member of that family could afford the restoration. Pompey's name would be left unchanged. At the same time he had high praise for Sejanus, whose efforts and vigilance, he said, had ensured that the great violence of the fire had been confined to the destruction of one building. (The senators also voted for a statue to Sejanus, which was to be placed in the theatre of Pompey.) And not long afterwards, when Tiberius was bestowing the honour of triumphal insignia on Junius Blaesus, proconsul of Africa, he said he was granting this as a mark of respect for Sejanus, whose uncle Blaesus was. In fact, though, Blaesus' record did merit such a decoration.

73. Tacfarinas had suffered many defeats, but he had rebuilt his forces in the interior of Africa. He had now reached such a pitch of arrogance that he sent representatives to Tiberius and actually demanded a dwelling place for himself and his army, with threats of interminable war as the alternative. They say that Tiberius never felt as pained over an insult to himself and the Roman people as he did over this deserter and bandit comporting himself like a genuine enemy. Not even Spartacus* had been allowed the privilege of surrendering on agreed terms, he thought, not even when he was burning Italy with impunity, after defeating so many consular armies, and when the republic was collapsing under the huge wars with Sertorius* and Mithridates!* And now that the Roman people were at the height of their glory, the bandit Tacfarinas was certainly not going to be bought off with a peace-treaty and a grant of land!

Tiberius entrusted the matter to Blaesus, who was to coax the others into hopes of laying down their arms without punishment but use all available means to apprehend the actual leader. That pardon resulted in the surrender of many. Presently the war was directed against the wiles of Tacfarinas in a manner not dissimilar to his own.

74. Tacfarinas could not match his enemy in the solid mass of his infantry, but was better in guerrilla warfare. He therefore used several bands for conducting raids and then eluding the enemy, and also for setting ambushes. To combat him, three lines of attack were prepared, and the same number of divisions. One of these, commanded by the legate Cornelius Scipio, covered the area where there were raids being made on the Lepcitani, and where the raiders received shelter amongst the Garamantes. On the other flank, Blaesus' son led a company of his own, his mandate being to prevent the unrequited pillaging of the country districts of Cirta. In the centre was the commander himself with an elite unit, establishing fortresses and strongholds at appropriate points. Blaesus had thus put the enemy in a tight and dangerous situation because, wherever they turned, some part of the Roman force was before them, on their flank, and, often, to their rear as well; and many were cut down or surrounded by this strategy.

Blaesus then split his tripartite army into several units, putting centurions of proven courage in charge of them. Nor did he follow the usual practice of withdrawing his forces at summer's end, or billeting them in winter quarters in the old province. Instead, as though he were on the threshold of war, he established forts here and there and, employing light-armed men who knew the deserts, kept hounding Tacfarinas from one native hut to another. Eventually, after capturing the man's brother, he returned, but too soon for the good of the allies, as he left behind men who could revive the war.

Tiberius, however, regarded the war as terminated, and he also granted Blaesus the privilege of being saluted as *Imperator* by his legions. This was an honour conferred on generals in antiquity who, after rendering good service to the state, were acclaimed with joyful enthusiasm by the conquering army; and there would be several such *Imperatores* at the same time, but they were not above the others in rank. Augustus,* too, granted the title to a number of men, and then—its last conferral—Tiberius granted it to Blaesus.

75. Two illustrious men died that year. One, Asinius Saloninus,* was famed for having Marcus Agrippa and Asinius Pollio as his grandfathers, and Drusus as his brother, as well as for being the intended husband of Tiberius' granddaughter. The other, Ateius Capito, whom I mentioned above, gained a leading position in the state through his legal studies, but he had one of Sulla's centurions for a grandfather and an ex-praetor for a father. Augustus had accelerated his promotion to consul so that he would, by the status conferred by that office, overshadow Antistius Labeo,* a leading man in the same branch of knowledge. For that generation produced two distinguished representatives of peacetime activity at the same time; but while Labeo was possessed of an unequivocal outspokenness* and therefore had the greater reputation, Capito's servility* earned him the approval of his rulers. Labeo's failure to advance beyond the praetorship won him esteem because of the injustice, and Capito's attainment of the consulship hatred because of people's resentment.

76. Junia,* too, now saw her last day, in the sixty-fourth year after the battle of Philippi.* She was born to have Cato as her uncle, and was the wife of Gaius Cassius and sister of Marcus Brutus. Her will was the subject of much gossip amongst the common people because, in disposing of her great resources, she had named nearly all the leading people in complimentary terms, but omitted Tiberius. This was accepted with good grace, and the emperor did not prevent the

funeral from being honoured with a eulogy before the Rostra and all the other formalities. Twenty ancestral busts* of the most distinguished families were carried ahead of the procession—the Manlii,* the Quinctii, and others with equally aristocratic names. But conspicuous above all were Cassius and Brutus, precisely because their portraits were not on view.

BOOK FOUR

1. The consulship of Gaius Asinius and Gaius Antistius saw Tiberius experiencing his ninth year of stability in the state and prosperity in his family—for Germanicus' death he counted amongst the providential events. Then, suddenly, fortune began to run riot, and Tiberius himself to turn brutal, or to foster brutality in others. The origin and cause lay with Aelius Sejanus, prefect of the praetorian cohorts,* whose influence I mentioned above. Now I shall give an account of his origins, his character and his criminal attempt to seize absolute power.

Sejanus was born in Vulsinii, and his father was Seius Strabo, a Roman knight. In his early youth he cultivated the friendship of Gaius Caesar, grandson of the deified Augustus, and was also rumoured to have sold sexual favours to the rich and profligate Apicius.* Subsequently, by various means, he cast such a spell on Tiberius, who was inscrutable in his dealings with others, that he made him feel relaxed and off his guard only with him. This was not the result of his cleverness—it was, after all, by such qualities that Sejanus was eventually undone—but of the anger of heaven towards the Roman state, for which Sejanus' heyday and fall were equally disastrous.

He had a physique that could endure hard work, and an enterprising spirit. Secretive about himself, he slandered others; he was a blend of sycophancy and arrogance; on the surface there was calm reserve, inside lust for supreme power (in the pursuit of which there was occasionally lavish gift-giving and extravagant living, but more often hard work and vigilance—qualities just as deadly when developed for acquiring a kingdom).

2. To the prefecture, formerly of slight importance, he gave added power by concentrating in a single camp the cohorts dispersed throughout the city.* They would thus receive their orders at the same time, and from their numbers and strength, and from the very sight of each other, they would gain self-confidence, while fear would be inspired in everyone else. Sejanus' claim was that soldiers become unruly when they are separated, that in the event of an emergency a united response was more effective, and that they would be more disciplined if their base were established far from the city's attractions.

When the camp was completed, Sejanus little by little wormed his way into the soldiers' favour by fraternizing with them and addressing them by name, and at the same time he took personal charge of the selection of centurions and tribunes. He did not stop short of courting the Senate, either, furnishing his supporters with offices or provinces. Tiberius accepted this, and in fact was so compliant as to hail Sejanus as his 'partner in toil' (and not just in informal conversation, but in addressing the Senate and the people) and to permit honours paid to the man's statues in the theatres* and forums, and in the legionary headquarters.*

3. The imperial house, however, was full of Caesars—a son who was a young man and grown-up grandchildren*—and that was arresting Sejanus' ambitions; and since violently sweeping away so many at once would be unsafe, a canny approach called for intervals between the crimes. Sejanus, however, decided to take an even more stealthy approach and start with Drusus, against whom he was driven by a recent angry spat. Drusus had no time for his rival, and was prone to anger. A quarrel had chanced to arise, he had raised his hand to Sejanus and then struck* him in the face when he offered resistance.

Examining all aspects of the matter, Sejanus felt the most practicable course was to turn to Drusus' wife, Livilla,* the sister of Germanicus, who, though plain-looking in her early years, had later developed into an outstanding beauty. With a pretence of passionate love for her, he tempted her into an adulterous relationship. Having succeeded with his first criminal step—and a woman, after losing her virtue, would be unlikely to refuse other inducements—he pushed her further, to hopes of marriage and to thoughts of sharing the realm and killing her husband. She also had Augustus as her great-uncle, Tiberius as her father-in-law, and children by Drusus; and she was now bringing shame upon herself, her ancestors, and descendants by taking a small-town* lover, sacrificing an honourable and stable situation for degrading and uncertain prospects. Eudemus, friend and doctor to Livilla, was taken into their confidence, his profession being a pretext for frequent clandestine meetings. To allay his mistress's suspicions, Sejanus removed his wife Apicata, by whom he had had three children,* from his home. But the enormity of the crime occasioned fear, postponements, and, sometimes, opposing plans of action.

4. Meanwhile, at the start of the year, one of Germanicus' children, Drusus, took up the *toga virilis*, and the honours that the Senate had decreed in the case of his brother Nero were repeated for him. The emperor also made a speech that was full of praise for his own son Drusus for showing a father's benevolence towards his brother's children. For, difficult though it is for power and concord to live under the same roof, Drusus was sympathetic* towards the boys, or at least not hostile to them.

Next an old plan was revived, one that Tiberius had often pretended to have had, namely visiting the provinces. The reason the emperor adduced was the large number of veterans being discharged and the need to fill vacancies in the armies with troop-levies.* There was a dearth of volunteers, he claimed, and even if they were available they lacked the usual courage and discipline because, generally, it was the indigent and homeless who took up military service by choice. He then cursorily enumerated the legions and the provinces they defended. I feel that I should do that, as well, giving an account of Rome's strength in armed forces,* of its client kings and of the comparatively restricted scope of its empire.

5. Two fleets,* based at Misenum and Ravenna, stood guard over Italy on the two seas, and the adjacent Gallic coast had the protection of warships that Augustus had captured in the victory at Actium and dispatched with strong crews to Forum Julii. But our principal military strength lay on the Rhine, where there were eight legions serving as a defensive force against the Germans and Gauls alike. The Spanish provinces, only recently subdued, were garrisoned by three. King Juba* had been given Mauretania as a gift by the Roman people; the rest of Africa was garrisoned by two legions, and Egypt by the same number. After that the huge expanse of territory lying between the start of Syria and the River Euphrates was held by four, and on its borders the Iberian, Albanian, and other kings were protected against foreign domination by our great power.* Thrace was held by Rhoemetalces* and the sons of Cotys, and the Danube bank by two legions in Pannonia and two in Moesia, and the same number stationed in Dalmatia. The latter, because of the area's geographical position, were to the rear of the others, and could be easily brought in from close at hand in the event of Italy calling for swift assistance (although the city had its own defensive force, three urban and nine praetorian cohorts, raised mostly in Etruria and Umbria or in old Latium* and the ancient Roman colonies). At appropriate points in the provinces there were also allied triremes, cavalry squadrons, and auxiliary cohorts, with a combined strength not much different from that of the legions. But a detailed account would be unreliable as they moved about in various directions according to the needs of the moment, their numbers swelling and, sometimes, diminishing.

6. I am inclined to think it would be appropriate to review other areas of government as well, and how they were administered to that date, since that was the year that initiated the change for the worse in Tiberius' principate. At the start of his rule, public business—and the most important items of private business—was handled in the Senate,* with leading men given the opportunity for discussion, and the emperor himself arresting any lapses into sycophancy. Tiberius would also assign offices with an eye on noble ancestry, military distinction, and outstanding attainments on the domestic front, so that there was general agreement that there were no better candidates. Consuls and praetors enjoyed the prestige that was appropriate to them; the lesser magistrates also exercised their authority; and the laws—if exception be made for the treason trials—were properly enforced.

Administration of grain-dues, indirect taxes, and all other state revenues, however, was in the hands of companies* of Roman knights. His own affairs* Tiberius entrusted to men whose qualities he knew well, and to some strangers on the basis of their reputation. Once employed, they were retained indefinitely, a number growing old in the same functions.

The common people were hard pressed by a seriously difficult grain supply, but no blame attached to the emperor who, in fact, spared no expense or effort in battling the infertility of the soil and the rigours of the sea. He also ensured that there was no distress amongst the provincials* from new burdens and, by suppressing the rapacity and cruelty of officials, that they could tolerate the old ones—there were no physical beatings or confiscations of property. The emperor's lands in Italy were sparse, his slaves few, and his household maintained by a handful of freedmen; and if ever he had differences with private citizens, they went to court in the Forum.

7. All of this Tiberius kept up, not with good grace, but in a severe and often frightening manner—but keep it up he did, until change

came with Drusus' death. As long as Drusus lived, the status quo
obtained because Sejanus, his influence still in the early stages,
wanted to gain a reputation for giving good advice. There was also
his fear of an avenger in the form of a man who did not hide his
hatred, but often complained that, although a son still lived,
another was being styled 'assistant to the empire'. And how short
a time would it be, Drusus asked himself, before that man was
called 'colleague'? Imperial ambitions encounter difficulties at first,
he reasoned, but take the first step and support and helpers are
on hand! Why, a camp had already been built on the prefect's suggestion, and soldiers had been put in his hands! His statue was to be
seen amongst the monuments of Gnaeus Pompey! The man would
share grandsons* with the family of the Drusi! After this one simply
had to pray for self-control on the man's part so that he could rest
content!

And it was not just on rare occasions and before a few people that
Drusus would throw out such reflections, either; and his secrets were
also being passed on, as a result of his wife's seduction.

8. Sejanus therefore felt he should speed matters up, and he
chose a poison whose gradual working would resemble some ordinary sickness. This was given to Drusus by the eunuch Lygdus (as was
discovered eight years after the event). Throughout the days of
Drusus' illness, Tiberius still went into the Curia, either free from
apprehension or else wishing to show strength of character, and he
did so even after Drusus died but was not yet buried. The consuls,
as a mark of their mourning, took ordinary seats,* but Tiberius
reminded them that their seating was a sign of their office; and when
the senators burst into tears he suppressed his own sobbing and at
the same time raised their spirits with a smoothly flowing oration. He
was not unaware that he could be criticized for subjecting himself to
the eyes of the Senate when his grief was still so fresh, he said—most
people in mourning can barely tolerate words of support from their
own relatives, can barely stand the light of day. Nor were these individuals to be criticized for weakness, he continued—but in his case
he had sought stronger consolation in the arms of the state. After an
expression of lamentation for Augusta's extreme old age, his grandsons' immaturity, and his own declining years,* he requested that the
children of Germanicus—his one solace in his current misfortune,
he said—be ushered in.

The consuls left and, after reassuring the boys, brought them in and had them stand before the emperor. Tiberius took them by the hand, and said:

'Senators: when these children lost their father, I put them in their uncle's care. I begged him to look after them, although he had children of his own, to cherish them as though they were his own blood, to set them on their feet, and to mould their character in his own and posterity's interests. Now that Drusus is taken, I redirect my entreaties to you, and appeal to you before the gods and our fatherland. Adopt and guide these great-grandchildren of Augustus, product of the most distinguished forefathers, and thus discharge your duty and mine together. Nero and Drusus, these men will serve as your parents. Such is your birth that any good or evil in your character must affect the state.'

9. This was received with floods of tears, and then prayers for a propitious outcome; and had Tiberius but curtailed his speech, he would certainly have left his audience full of pity for him and full of pride. Instead, he lapsed back into the fatuous topics so often ridiculed—restoring the republic, and the duty of the consuls or someone else to take over the administration—and in doing so deprived even a sincere and noble sentiment of credibility.

Drusus' memory was honoured with the same decrees as had been passed for Germanicus, with a number of additions (as is usual with flattery repeated at a later date). The funeral was particularly remarkable for its parade of images. On view, in a long line, were Aeneas,* initiator of the Julian family, all the Alban kings, and Romulus, founder of the city of Rome; and after these came the Sabine nobles, Attus Clausus, and the rest of the effigies of the Claudii.

10. In my account of Drusus' death I have recorded what is given by most sources, and by the most reliable ones, but I should not omit a rumour in circulation at the time, one so prevalent that it is still not fading away. After seducing Livilla into crime, Sejanus, it is alleged, also secured the eunuch Lygdus' allegiance by means of a sexual liaison, Lygdus being dear to his master, because of his age and good looks, and one of his foremost servants. Then, when the place and time for the poisoning had been agreed upon by the conspirators, Sejanus became so bold that he altered the scenario. He secretly warned Tiberius that Drusus intended to poison his father, and advised him to avoid the first drink he would be offered when

dining at his son's house. The old man fell for this trick and, after arriving at the banquet, passed on to Drusus the cup he had been given. Drusus, in his ignorance, drained it with a young man's gusto, thereby increasing the suspicion that, from fear and shame, he was actually inflicting on himself the death he had planned for his father.

11. This rumour gained wide circulation but, even overlooking the lack of support in any reliable source, one may reject it out of hand. For what moderately intelligent man (much less Tiberius, with his expertise in such important matters) would inflict death on his son without hearing him out, and do so with his own hand at that, leaving no possibility of a change of heart? Would he not, rather, torture the man who served the poison, and seek out the plot's instigator? In short, in the case of his only son, till then found guilty of no wrongdoing, would he not demonstrate that characteristic hesitation and wariness that he even employed towards outsiders? But Sejanus was held to be the author of all manner of wickedness and, since Tiberius felt inordinate affection for him, while everybody else hated both men, the most implausible and monstrous stories were actually believed (and rumour is always more outrageous where the deaths of rulers are concerned).

In any case, the way the crime really progressed* was divulged by Sejanus' wife, Apicata, and then brought out into the open by the torture of Eudemus and Lygdus. And there has appeared no writer so hostile to Tiberius as to impute the act to him, despite their penchant for raking up and throwing all other charges at him. I had my own motive for recording and criticizing the rumour. With this glaring example I wanted to dispel the fictions of hearsay, and to ask people into whose hands my book may come not to prefer widely circulated and eagerly accepted fantasies over truth uncorrupted by sensationalism.

12. When Tiberius delivered his son's eulogy from the Rostra, the Senate and people assumed the demeanour and tones of mourning, but out of pretence rather than inclination; secretly, they were pleased at the revival of the house of Germanicus. This incipient popularity, however, and Agrippina's failure to conceal her ambition,* only accelerated the family's destruction.* When Sejanus saw that Drusus' death brought no punishment to his killers, and no grief to the public, he became brazen in his criminal designs, and his early success led him to ponder ways of destroying Germanicus' children,

whose succession was now assured. Poison could not be dispensed to all three: the loyalty of their bodyguards was exceptional, and Agrippina's virtue* unassailable. He therefore proceeded to target the woman's wilfulness, and to work on Augusta's long-entrenched hatred* of her, and on Livilla's recent complicity. He prompted the two of them to criticize Agrippina in Tiberius' presence; her pride in her fertility and her support amongst the people were giving her imperial ambitions, they were to say. And he relied on cunning informers to further his plans. These included Julius Postumus* who, because of an adulterous relationship with Mutilia Prisca,* was among the close confidants of the grandmother—Prisca had a great influence on Augusta—and so very suitable for Sejanus' designs. Prisca kept trying to forge a rift between the old woman (who was by her very nature anxious about her own influence) and her granddaughter-in-law. Agrippina's closest friends were also inveigled into constantly provoking her proud spirit with mischievous remarks.

13. Tiberius allowed no interruption of his official business. He took solace from his work, handling judicial cases of citizens and appeals from the provincials. Senatorial decrees were also passed on his initiative granting aid, in the form of a three-year remission of tribute, to the city-states of Cibyra in Asia, and Aegium in Achaea, both of which had suffered earthquakes. In addition, Vibius Serenus,* proconsul of Further Spain, was found guilty of public violence,* and was deported to the island of Amorgos for his barbarous conduct. Carsidius Sacerdos* was accused of aiding an enemy of the state, Tacfarinas, with grain supplies, but was acquitted, as was Gaius Gracchus* on the same charge. Gracchus' father Sempronius had taken him, when he was a very young child, to share his banishment on the island of Cercina. There he grew up amongst exiles who had no culture, and subsequently supported himself by trafficking in cheap wares in Africa and Sicily; but he still did not avoid the pitfalls of a great background. In fact, had it not been for Aelius Lamia* and Lucius Apronius, both of whom became governors of Africa, and gave the innocent man their protection, he would have been swept to destruction by the distinction of his ill-starred family* and his father's misfortune.

14. That year also saw embassies arrive from two Greek city-states: the people of Samos were seeking confirmation of the ancient right of asylum for their shrine of Juno, and those of Cos for their shrine

of Aesculapius. The Samians based their claim on a decree of the Amphictyonies, whose judgement in all such matters was supreme in the epoch when the Greeks, who had established cities throughout Asia, controlled the sea-coast. The Coans had as much antiquity on their side, and they also had a good deed connected with the place as a further claim. For they had taken Roman citizens into the temple of Aesculapius when these were being butchered on King Mithridates' orders throughout the islands and cities of Asia.*

Next, after various, and more often than not futile, complaints from the praetors, Tiberius finally raised the matter of the disreputable behaviour of actors;* they were, he claimed, responsible for much public disorder and their behaviour in private homes was disgraceful. The old Oscan show,* the lightest form of mass entertainment, had become so shocking, and had taken such a hold, that it had to be checked by the authority of the Senate, he said. The actors were then expelled from Italy.

15. The same year also brought fresh grief to the emperor: it took the life of one of Drusus' twins, and—just as painful—brought the death of a friend. This was Lucilius Longus,* Tiberius' constant companion in sadness and joy, and the only senator to have accompanied him during his retreat on Rhodes. Thus, 'new man' though he was, the Senate voted Longus a state funeral* and a statue in the Forum of Augustus,* at public expense. At that time all business was still handled in the Senate, so much so that Lucilius Capito,* the procurator of Asia, had to plead his case before the body when the province arraigned him. The emperor insisted that the jurisdiction he had granted Capito was limited to the imperial slaves and finances. If the man had encroached on the praetor's authority and used military force, he said, he had in doing so disregarded his orders—and the senators should heed the provincials. The matter was accordingly investigated, and the accused found guilty. In thanks for this redress, and also because of the punishment of Gaius Silanus the previous year, the cities of Asia decreed a temple in honour of Tiberius, his mother and the Senate. Permission was granted for the building, and Nero* gave the requisite vote of thanks to the Senate and his grandfather. This aroused feelings of delight in his audience, for, with the memory of Germanicus still fresh, people felt that he was the man they were looking at, he the man they were hearing. In addition, the youth had the modesty and good looks

appropriate to an emperor, and since Sejanus' hatred of him was common knowledge, his jeopardy made these features all the more attractive.

16. At about this same time, Tiberius discussed the choice of a flamen of Jupiter to replace the late Servius Maluginensis, and about passing new legislation relating to it. The ancient custom, he explained, required the simultaneous nomination of three patricians born of parents who had been married by *confarreatio*,* with one of the candidates to be elected. Now, however, there was not the quantity of candidates that existed earlier, because the practice of *confarreatio* marriage had been discontinued, or was retained only by a few. (Tiberius put forward a number of explanations for this, the main one being lack of interest on the part of men and women alike, though another factor was the difficulties inherent in the ceremony, which led to deliberate avoidance of it. Furthermore, the man who obtained the office of flamen, and the woman who married him, left parental* jurisdiction.) This, then, should be remedied through a senatorial decree or a law,* Tiberius concluded, just as Augustus had modified certain severe elements of ancient morality to suit contemporary practice.

After a discussion of the religious implications, it was decided that the structure of the office of flamen should remain unchanged, but a law was passed by which the wife of the flamen of Jupiter would remain under her husband's authority for religious purposes, but in all else have the same rights as other women.

Maluginensis' son was then appointed as his father's replacement. Further, to increase the prestige of religious officers and make them readier to perform their rites, it was decided that a grant of two million sesterces be made to the Vestal Virgin Cornelia, who was then being appointed as Scantia's successor, and that Augusta should take her seat amongst the Vestals* whenever she entered the theatre.

17. In the consulship of Cornelius Cethegus and Visellius Varro, the pontiffs and (following their example) the other priests offered prayers* for the well-being of the emperor, but they also commended Nero and Drusus to the same gods as him. They did so, not out of affection for the young men, but from sycophancy which, in a corrupt society, is as dangerous when taken to extremes as when it is absent. For Tiberius, never well disposed towards Germanicus' family, could not bear the boys receiving as much honour as he did in his

advancing years. He summoned the pontiffs and asked them if they had done this as a concession to Agrippina's pleas, or her threats. Despite the pontiffs' denials, they received a reprimand, though it was mild (most were relatives of his, or leading men of the community). In the Senate, however, Tiberius made a speech with a warning for the future—no one was to encourage arrogance in the boys' capricious spirits with premature honours. In fact, there was pressure coming from Sejanus, who was warning him that the state was divided, virtually by civil war. There were men styling themselves 'members of Agrippina's party',* he said, and left unopposed their numbers would grow. And the only remedy for the growing discord, he added, was for one or two of the ringleaders to be brought down.

18. For this reason Sejanus launched an attack on Gaius Silius and Titius Sabinus. Friendship with Germanicus proved deadly to both, but in Silius' case there was also the fact that, his fall being greater, fear would be more widely spread amongst others (for he had been the leader of a huge army for seven years, had won triumphal insignia in Germany, and had emerged victor in the war with Sacrovir). Many believed that Silius' offence had been compounded by his own lack of judgement in making extravagant boasts about his own men remaining steadfastly loyal* while others were slipping into mutiny. Tiberius would not have remained in power, he said, if those legions had also felt the urge to revolt. Tiberius thought that his own position was being undermined by such comments, and that he was incapable of repaying a service of such magnitude. For favours are welcome only to the point where reciprocity seems possible. When they go far beyond that, hatred replaces gratitude.

19. Silius' wife* was Sosia Galla, detested by the emperor for her affection for Agrippina. This couple, it was decided, would be the victims—Sabinus would be left aside for the moment—and the consul Varro was set upon them. Varro, with the excuse of following up his father's quarrels,* indulged Sejanus' hatred, to his own shame. The defendant, Silius, requested a brief moratorium until his prosecutor should leave the consulship, but Tiberius demurred. It was normal for magistrates to arraign private citizens in court, he said, and one should not infringe the rights of a consul, for it was on this officer's vigilance that he relied to see that 'the state suffered no harm'.* (It was Tiberius' way to cloak recently invented crimes in old-fashioned terminology.)

It was therefore with great earnestness that the senators were convened—as though the case of Silius were based on law, and as if Varro were really a consul and this were the republic! The defendant remained silent or, if he started to defend himself, made no secret of whose resentment he was the victim. The charges presented were: Sacrovir's guilt long concealed because of Silius' complicity in his rebellion; Silius' victory sullied by rapacity; and his wife being his accomplice. There was no doubt that they were caught on the extortion charges, but everything was conducted as a treason trial, and Silius pre-empted his looming conviction by suicide.

20. Nevertheless, the attack on Silius' estate* was savage, and not in order to provide refunds for the provincial taxpayers, none of whom sought them. Gifts from Augustus were ripped out of it, and sums sought for the imperial exchequer were itemized individually. That was the first time that Tiberius paid attention to another's finances.

Sosia was driven into exile on a motion from Asinius Gallus, who had proposed the confiscation of half of her estate, with the rest being left to her children.* A counter-proposal from Marcus Lepidus, however, saw a quarter go to the accusers, as the law required, and the rest to the children.

I am beginning to see that this Lepidus was a wise and perspicacious man in his day; for he assured a better result for many issues by steering them away from the brutal sycophancy of others. But he was not without a sense of proportion, either, since he was consistently influential with Tiberius and favoured by him. This makes me wonder whether it is, as in other matters, through fate and one's lot at birth that emperors incline towards some people, and resent others. Or can it rather be that there is something in our own plans enabling us to trim a path between downright obstinacy and degrading sycophancy, a path free from favour-seeking and danger alike? Whatever the case, Messalinus Cotta,* whose ancestors were just as distinguished as Lepidus', was a very different character. He proposed ensuring by senatorial decree* that magistrates, no matter how innocent and unaware of another's wrongdoing they be, should be punished for crimes committed in the provinces by their wives just as if the crimes were their own.

21. There followed the case of Calpurnius Piso,* a nobleman and a fractious character. It was Piso who had, as I noted earlier, cried out

in the Senate that he would leave the city because of the intrigues of informers, and who, in defiance of Augusta's power, had dared to bring Urgulania to trial, summoning her from the imperial home. Tiberius treated this with an ordinary citizen's patience for a while; but even if an offence had lost its initial impetus, in a mind that would brood on angry thoughts the memory remained strong. Piso's accuser was Quintus Veranius, who charged him with holding a private conversation of a treasonable nature, and added that he kept poison at home and would enter the Curia wearing a sword.* The last charge was dropped as being too appalling to be true; the others were mounting in number, however, and he was listed for trial but, through a timely death, not prosecuted.

There was also discussion of the exiled Cassius Severus. He was of low birth, and led the life of a reprobate, but he was a powerful orator who, through the severe vendettas he had fomented, succeeded in having himself banished to Crete by a judgement of the Senate that was taken under oath. There, by continuing with the same activities, he brought on himself fresh antagonisms in addition to the old. He then lived to old age on the rock of Seriphos, deprived of his property and forbidden fire and water.

22. At about this same time, for reasons unknown, Plautius Silvanus,* a praetor, hurled his wife Apronia down from the upper part of his house. Haled before Tiberius by his father-in-law Lucius Apronius, Silvanus responded, with a confused air, that he had been in a deep sleep, and thus oblivious to everything. His wife's death had been self-inflicted, he claimed. Without a moment's hesitation, Tiberius proceeded to the house and went to see the bedroom, in which there were evident indications that the woman had resisted and been pushed. He referred the case to the Senate and, when a jury had been formed, Urgulania, Silvanus' grandmother, sent her grandson a dagger. Because of Augusta's friendship with Urgulania, it was believed that this was done on the emperor's advice. The accused man failed in his attempt with the weapon, and had his veins opened. Subsequently, an earlier wife of Silvanus, Numantina, was accused of having induced insanity in her former husband by spells and sorcery, but was found not guilty.

23. That year finally released the Roman people from the long-drawn-out war against the Numidian Tacfarinas. As soon as they believed their records qualified them for triumphal honours, earlier

commanders* had been leaving the enemy in peace, and by now there were three statues adorned with laurel in the city, and Tacfarinas was *still* pillaging Africa. He had support from Moorish auxiliaries who, finding that Juba's son, Ptolemy, ruled with a young man's negligence, had chosen to fight rather than accept the rule of freedmen and the orders of slaves. Serving as the receiver of Tacfarinas' plunder, and an associate in his raids, was the king of the Garamantes. He, however, did not advance to Tacfarinas at the head of an army, but sent out light-armed units, whose numbers were exaggerated in hearsay by the distance involved. From the province itself, too, all the indigent and disorderly elements rushed to join the rebel, and the more keenly because, following Blaesus' success, the emperor had ordered that the Ninth Legion* be brought home, as if there were no longer enemies left in Africa. Nor had the proconsul for that year, Publius Dolabella,* dared keep the legion in place, since he was more fearful of the emperor's orders than he was of the vicissitudes of war.

24. Tacfarinas therefore spread the word that the power of Rome was being torn to shreds by other tribes as well, and that it was, for that reason, gradually withdrawing from Africa. The Romans remaining behind could be cut off, he said, if all who preferred liberty to slavery simply applied themselves to the task. In this way Tacfarinas increased his forces, and, encamping at the town of Thubursicum, he proceeded to lay siege to it. Dolabella, however, brought together all the troops under his command and, through the terror inspired by the Roman name (and also because Numidians are incapable of facing infantry in battle), he raised the siege with his first attack and fortified a number of strategic points. At the same time he beheaded some chiefs of the Musulamians* who were in the initial stages of rebellion. It was now understood, after numerous campaigns against Tacfarinas, that a roving enemy was not to be hunted down with a heavily armed force in a single assault. Dolabella accordingly called on the help of King Ptolemy and his people, and put together four columns, giving command of them to legates or tribunes. There were also raiding parties under hand-picked Moors. Dolabella himself was on hand as overall adviser.

25. Not much later, news arrived that the Numidians had pitched their huts close to a half-destroyed stronghold called Auzea, which had earlier been put to the torch by the Numidians themselves; they

had confidence in the position because it was surrounded by deep forests. Then some light-armed cohorts and cavalry squadrons were hurried along by forced marches, and were kept ignorant of their destination. At daybreak, with a blast of trumpets and a fierce shout, they fell upon the barbarians, who were half-asleep, with their horses still tethered or roaming through distant pastureland. On the Roman side the infantry were in close formation and the cavalry squadrons deployed—preparations for battle were complete. The enemy, by contrast, unaware of anything, had no weapons, no order, no plan; like sheep, they were dragged off, butchered, or captured. The Roman soldiers were furious when they remembered their hardships and their frequent wish to engage an elusive enemy, and they all took their fill of bloody revenge. The word was spread amongst the companies that it was on Tacfarinas, familiar to them from their many battles, that they should concentrate their efforts—there would be no respite from war unless the leader were killed. Tacfarinas' bodyguard was cut down around him, his son was put in irons, and Romans were pouring in from every side. Tacfarinas rushed into their weapons and escaped capture by death, which did not come without a price for the Romans. That spelled the end of the conflict.

26. Dolabella applied for triumphal honours, but Tiberius refused, out of regard for Sejanus (he did not want to see the reputation of Sejanus' uncle Blaesus* eclipsed). However, Blaesus did not gain kudos from this, while the refusal of the honour brought renown to Dolabella who, with a smaller army, had brought home famous prisoners, the distinction of killing the leader, and the glory of terminating the war. He was also attended by ambassadors of the Garamantes, a rare sight in the city. This tribe had been shaken by the death of Tacfarinas and, aware of its own guilt, had sent the ambassadors to make amends to the Roman people. Then, when Ptolemy's support throughout this war was recognized, an honour of some antiquity was revived for him. One of the senators was sent off to make him an award of an ivory sceptre and an embroidered toga*— gifts conferred by the Senate in days of old—and to address him with the titles king, ally, and friend.

27. That same summer the seeds of a slave war that had begun to stir in Italy were crushed by pure chance. The prime mover of the disorder was Titus Curtisius, formerly a soldier in a praetorian cohort. Starting with secret meetings in Brundisium and the neighbouring

towns, and then openly posting pamphlets, Curtisius called on the fierce agricultural slaves* living in the remote countryside to strike a blow for their freedom. Then, like a gift from heaven, three biremes put in there, their commission being to serve commercial vessels in those waters. Also in that same region was Curtius Lupus, a quaestor who had been allotted the ancient post of supervisor of the pasture-lands* as his sphere of responsibility. Lupus deployed a force of marines and quashed the conspiracy just as it was starting. Furthermore, Staius, a tribune, was swiftly dispatched there by Tiberius at the head of a strong detachment, and he dragged back to Rome the ringleader himself and the boldest of his partisans. The city was already in a state of alarm over its large numbers of household slaves, which were growing at an enormous rate, while the freeborn population was diminishing every day.

28. The same consulship witnessed a terrible example of suffering and cruelty. A father and son (both named Vibius Serenus*) were ushered into the Senate, the father as defendant, the son as prosecutor. The father had been dragged back from exile and, in a filthy and squalid condition, and now in irons, too, he stood facing his son's formal charges. The young man cut a very elegant figure and had an air of enthusiasm as he gave an account, acting as informer and witness together, of a plot mounted against the emperor, and of men sent to Gaul* to foment war. He added that an ex-praetor, Caecilius Cornutus, had provided the finance. Sick with worry, and also because a prosecution was seen as tantamount to a death penalty, Cornutus accelerated his own end. The defendant, by contrast, not at all daunted, turned to his son and shook his chains. He called out to the gods of vengeance and prayed that they return him to exile to live far from behaviour like this, and that punishment eventually catch up with his son. He repeatedly declared that Cornutus was innocent, that he had panicked before a false accusation. This would be easy to understand if other names were produced, he said—for he had certainly not considered assassinating the emperor and starting a revolution with only one accomplice!

29. The accuser then put forward the names of Gnaeus Lentulus and Seius Tubero.* This caused Tiberius great embarrassment* since the men being charged with inciting an enemy uprising and foment-ing revolution were leaders of the community and close friends of his. In addition, Lentulus was very old, and Tubero physically infirm.

In fact, however, the two were immediately excused from appearing. In the case of Serenus the father, his slaves* were interrogated, and the interrogation went against the prosecutor. The man was now crazed with guilt, and also terrified by the rumours passing amongst the people, who were threatening him with imprisonment and the rock,* or the punishments reserved for parricides,* and so he left the city. He was brought back from Ravenna and forced to continue with the indictment, since Tiberius made no secret of his inveterate hatred for Serenus the exile. For, after the condemnation of Libo, Serenus had sent a letter of reproach to the emperor, saying that his efforts alone had been left unrewarded,* and he had added some remarks too forward to be safely confided to ears that were proud and easily offended. Tiberius brought these matters up eight years after the event, adding various complaints for the intervening period, even though torture had yielded negative results because of the slaves' tenacity.

30. The opinions then expressed favoured Serenus being given the traditional punishment* but, in order to soften public antipathy, Tiberius used his veto. When Gallus Asinius proposed imprisonment on Gyarus or Donusa, he rejected this as well, replying that both islands were short of water, and that a man granted his life should also be provided with the necessities of life. Serenus was therefore taken back to Amorgos. Because Cornutus had died by his own hand, there was also discussion of quashing rewards for accusers if anyone prosecuted for treason committed suicide before the conclusion of the case. The voting was going in support of this view, but Tiberius protested, quite forcefully and with uncharacteristic openness, in favour of the informers. The laws would be rendered ineffectual, he said, and the state set on a precipitous course—better to destroy legislation than remove its guardians! So it was that the informers, a class of men devised for the destruction of society, and never sufficiently checked even by legal penalties, were now being given the inducement of rewards.

31. This unremitting train of depressing events saw one slightly pleasurable interval. Gaius Cominius, a Roman knight, had been found guilty of writing poetry that was insulting to the emperor, and in response to the pleas of his brother, who was a senator, Tiberius spared him. It was therefore found all the more surprising that someone who knew the better course of action, and the reputation that

attended clemency, should prefer the harsher course. This failing of his was not due to stupidity; and it is not difficult to see when the pleasure with which the actions of emperors are praised is genuine and when it is insincere. In fact, Tiberius himself usually had an unnatural air, his words virtually struggling to get out, but whenever he was coming to someone's aid his speech was freer and more articulate.

But then there was Publius Suillius,* a former quaestor of Germanicus, who was facing banishment from Italy after being convicted of accepting bribes in a court case. Tiberius expressed the opinion that the man should be removed to an island, and did so with such passion that he swore on oath that it was in the interests of the state. This was poorly viewed at the time, but it presently redounded to Tiberius' credit after Suillius' return. The following generation saw him as a very powerful and venal man who long used his friendship with the emperor Claudius for selfish, and never honourable, ends. The same penalty was fixed for the senator Catus Firmius* for having trumped up charges of treason against his sister. It was Catus, as I have noted, who had lured Libo into a trap, and then brought about his destruction by informing on him. Tiberius remembered the service and interceded to spare him exile, but adduced other factors for doing so. He did not object to Catus' expulsion from the Senate.

32. I am well aware that many of the things that I have recounted, and will recount, may seem trivial and too unimportant for the historical record; but nobody should compare my *Annals* with the writings of those who have composed early histories of the Roman people. They, with freedom to digress, would recount the history of mighty wars, the storming of cities, or the defeat and capture of kings; and if ever they turned to internal affairs, it would be to the quarrels of consuls with the tribunes, the agricultural and grain legislation, and the struggles of the plebs and aristocracy. My area of work is restricted and without glory: peace unbroken or only weakly challenged, grim episodes in the city, and an emperor with no interest in extending the empire. Even so, it may not be without profit to examine these incidents, which initially seem trivial, but by which important events are often set in motion.

33. All nations and cities are governed by the people, by the aristocracy, or by monarchs. (A political system that is a selected blend

of these is easier for one to praise than it is for it to evolve, or if it does evolve it is perforce short-lived.) Formerly, the plebs were strong or else the senators were dominant. Then one needed to have a knowledge of the nature of the proletariat and how it could be kept under control, and, in the other case, those thoroughly conversant with the temper of the Senate and the aristocrats were thought to possess political sense and wisdom. Circumstances have now changed, and the safety of the state depends entirely upon one man exercising power. Thus it will prove edifying for these apparent trivialities to be gathered together and recorded, because few have the foresight to distinguish the decent from the dishonourable, or the useful from the harmful—most people learn from the experiences of others. However, useful though such information will be, it has little entertainment value. For the topography of peoples, fluctuating battles, the famous deaths of leaders—these are what hold and refresh the minds of readers. In my case, I am presenting a series of cruel orders, endless accusations, faithless friendships, and calamities befalling innocent people, with the causes of their ruin being always the same—for I am faced with a tedious abundance of recurrent material. There is the further consideration that those who censure the authors of old are few, and nobody cares whether one accords more fulsome praise to the Carthaginian* or the Roman army. But many who suffered punishment or disgrace under Tiberius have descendants still alive; and even in cases where the families themselves have died out, one will still find those who, because of the similarity of their behaviour, believe that, when others' misdeeds are recounted, it is they who are being pilloried. Even glory and virtue excite hostility by seemingly indicting the opposite qualities with too close a contrast. But I return to my subject.

34. In the consulship of Cornelius Cossus and Asinius Agrippa, Cremutius Cordus* was arraigned on a new charge, then heard of for the first time: publishing a history in which he praised Marcus Brutus and referred to Gaius Cassius as 'the last of the Romans'. His accusers were Satrius Secundus and Pinarius Natta, both clients of Sejanus. This fact spelled doom for the defendant, as did the severe frown with which Tiberius heard his defence. Cremutius, who was resolved upon leaving this life, began to speak in this manner:

'Senators: it is my words that are being put on trial—so innocent are my actions! But even these words do not apply to the emperor or the emperor's mother, with whom the treason law* is concerned. It is said that I praised Brutus and Cassius,* whose history many have written, and of whom none has spoken unfavourably. Titus Livius,* who enjoys an outstanding reputation for his style and reliability, gave such high praise to Gnaeus Pompey that Augustus called him 'the Pompeian', and that had no effect on their friendship. Scipio,* Afranius,* this very Cassius and this Brutus of whom we speak he never called 'bandits' and 'parricides', terms applied to them now, and he frequently referred to them as 'distinguished men'. The writings of Asinius Pollio* pass on to us a highly favourable account of those same men, and Messalla Corvinus* praised Cassius as his 'commander'. And both authors kept on living lives of wealth and honour. How did Caesar, when he was dictator, respond to the book of Marcus Cicero* in which he praised Cato to the skies? He wrote a speech refuting him, as though he were answering a case in court.

'Antonius' letters and Brutus' speeches contain material insulting to Augustus, which, though untrue, is very caustic, and the poems of Bibaculus* and Catullus,* still read today, are full of abuse of the Caesars. The deified Julius and the deified Augustus themselves put up with this, and left the authors alone. Whether that was from self-restraint or wisdom on their part I should find it difficult to say. What is ignored just fades away; resentment looks like acknowledgement of the truth.

35. 'I make no mention of the Greeks, amongst whom licence, not just freedom of expression, went unpunished; or if anyone did seek redress, he took revenge for words with words.

'But an area that was particularly open, and free from criticism, was speaking of those whom death had removed from hatred or favour. For by telling of Cassius and Brutus under arms, and occupying the fields of Philippi, I am not inflaming the people to civil war with public speeches, am I? They were taken from us seventy years ago.* They are recognized today in their statues,* which even their conqueror did not banish, and do they not likewise also keep their memory alive, in part, in the historians? Posterity grants everybody the glory he is due. And if condemnation faces me, there will be no shortage of people to remember not just Brutus and Cassius, but me as well.'

Cremutius then left the Senate and ended his life by starvation. The senators voted that his books should be burned by the aediles, but they survived,* being hidden and then republished. This makes one all the more inclined to laugh at the stupidity of those who believe that the memories of succeeding generations can be stifled by power in the present day. Quite the reverse is true. The authority wielded by talent that is punished continues to grow, and foreign kings, or those employing the same sort of brutality, have succeeded only in bringing shame on themselves and glory on their victims.

36. That year saw a series of arraignments so constant that when Drusus,* as prefect of the city, ascended the tribunal during the days of the Latin Festival in order to take the auspices, Calpurnius Salvianus accosted him with a denunciation of Sextus Marius.* This drew a public rebuke from Tiberius and brought about Salvianus' exile.

The people of Cyzicus* were officially impeached for neglecting the worship of the deified Augustus, and they were also charged with violence against Roman citizens. And so they lost the independence they had earned in the war with Mithridates, when they endured a siege and drove off the king, a feat due as much to their own determination as to military assistance from Lucullus. However, Fonteius Capito,* a former proconsular governor of Asia, was acquitted when it became clear that the charges brought against him were trumped up by Vibius Serenus. Even so, the affair did not damage Serenus, whom the hatred of the people served to protect. Readiness to strike made an informer almost inviolate; it was the insignificant nonentities who were punished.

37. About this same time Further Spain sent a delegation to the Senate requesting permission to follow the example of Asia and build a shrine to Tiberius and his mother. Tiberius was generally firm in refusing honours, and now felt a reply was needed for those whose rumour-mongering was accusing him with a tendency to vanity. And so, on this occasion, he proceeded with a speech along these lines:

'I know, senators, that many have regretted a lack of consistency on my part in not denying a similar request made recently by the communities of Asia. Accordingly, I shall lay before you my defence of my earlier silence and, at the same time, the procedure I have decided to follow in future. The deified Augustus had not forbidden the establishment at Pergamum* of a temple to himself and to the city of Rome, and I regard all his actions and utterances as law. I followed that precedent, which had his approval, and did so all the more readily because in this case veneration of the Senate was actually being combined with a personal cult of myself. But while a single acceptance may be forgivable, to be worshipped throughout the provinces with a statue, like the gods, would be pretentious and arrogant; and the honour paid to Augustus will fade if it is cheapened by such indiscriminate flattery.

38. 'I am mortal, senators, my functions are those of humans and I am satisfied if I have the highest position amongst them. I call on you to witness that, and I want posterity to remember it. The latter will show enough, and more than enough, respect to my memory if they believe me worthy of my ancestors, judicious in my stewardship of your interests, steadfast in the face of danger, and not afraid of giving offence for the good of the state. These thoughts of me in your minds will serve as *my* temples; these will be *my* finest, *my* enduring statues. For if posterity's judgement turns to hatred, those made of stone are disregarded like sepulchres. So I make a prayer to the provincials and Roman citizens, and to the gods themselves. I pray that the gods grant me, till my life's end, an easy mind that knows human and divine law, and that provincials and citizens will, when I leave this world, have only praise and happy memories of my actions and my name.'

And after this, even in his private conversations, Tiberius continued to reject such worship of his person. Some saw this as modesty, many as a lack of self-confidence, and a number of people as a sign of a degenerate spirit. The best of men, they said, had the highest aspirations. This was why amongst the Greeks Hercules and Liber, and amongst us Quirinus, had been added to the list of the gods. Augustus had done better in that he entertained hopes of immortality. Emperors immediately had everything they wanted but one thing, they said, and that had to be worked for incessantly—a happy memory of themselves amongst posterity. Despising fame meant despising virtues.

39. Now, too much good fortune had made Sejanus incautious, and he was also spurred on by a woman's passion, for Livilla was demanding the marriage she had been promised. He therefore composed a petition to the emperor (it was at that time the custom to address him by letter even if he was present in Rome). The purport of the letter was as follows. Thanks to the kindness of Tiberius' father Augustus, and subsequently to the many marks of Tiberius'

esteem, Sejanus had become accustomed to bringing his hopes and prayers to the ears of the emperors as readily as to the gods. He had never asked for glittering honours—he preferred vigilance and labour for the emperor's security, like a regular soldier. He had, nevertheless, gained what was the finest thing of all, being deemed worthy of a family connection with the emperor. This was what had started him hoping, he continued, and he had also heard that Augustus, in betrothing his daughter, had given some consideration even to Roman knights.* Accordingly, if a husband was being sought for Livilla, he asked that Tiberius keep in mind his friend, whose only gain from the relationship would be the glory of it. He was not trying to slough off the duties assigned to him; he thought it enough that the family be strengthened against the unjustified resentment of Agrippina—and this for the children's sake. For him, living out his life under such an emperor would be more than enough!

40. Tiberius' response was to praise Sejanus' loyalty, cursorily run through his own kindnesses to him, and ask for time to consider the question objectively. He added that other mortals' plans depended on self-interest, but emperors were in a different position, having to direct their most important business with an eye on public opinion. Thus, he continued, he was not resorting to that response which was ready at hand, namely that Livilla could decide for herself whether she should remarry after Drusus, or carry on in the same household, and that she had a mother and grandmother to give her closer counsel. He would be more straightforward than that. First, there was the matter of Agrippina's hostility, which would burst into much fiercer flames should Livilla's marriage tear the house of the Caesars into two factions. Even as it was, there were outbreaks of rivalry between the women, and his grandsons were being torn apart by the conflict. What if the strife were intensified by such a match?

'For', he went on, 'you are wrong, Sejanus, if you think you are going to remain at your present rank, and that Livilla, formerly married to Gaius Caesar and then Drusus, will be content to grow old with a Roman knight. Granted that I myself should allow it, do you think men who have seen her brother, her father, and our ancestors in the top positions of power are going to accept it? Yes, you want to remain within your present station. But those magistrates and dignitaries who burst in on your privacy against your will and consult you on every matter—these are spreading the word, and not discreetly, that it is quite some time since you rose above the ceiling of the equestrian rank and that you have gone far beyond my father's friends.* And, through jealousy of you, they also criticize me.

'Now, you say that Augustus considered giving his daughter to a Roman knight. He was distracted by many cares and foresaw the enormous advancement given to whomsoever he raised above other men by such a match. Surprising then that he mentioned Gaius Proculeius* in his conversations and certain others who were leading remarkably tranquil lives and were not involved in the affairs of state! But if we are concerned by Augustus' hesitation, how much more important is the fact that he actually betrothed her to Marcus Agrippa,* and then to me?

'In view of our friendship I have not concealed these reflections from you; but I shall not oppose your plans or Livilla's. I shall for the moment refrain from mentioning what I have been mulling over in my mind, the new ties by which I intend to strengthen our relationship. This only will I state openly: there is nothing, however exalted, that your virtues and loyalty to me do not deserve, and when the moment is granted me* I shall not remain silent on that score, either in the Senate or in a public meeting.'

41. Sejanus was no longer concerned about the marriage; his dread was deeper, and he begged Tiberius to ignore the hushed suspicions, the rumour-mongering of the street and the jealousy that was threatening him. He feared he would weaken his power if he kept away the bands of regular visitors to his house, but feared also that he would be furnishing material to his accusers if he received them. He turned, therefore, to the idea of nudging Tiberius into passing his life in some attractive location far from Rome. Indeed, he saw many advantages in this. Access to Tiberius would be in his hands, and he would, by and large, have control of his correspondence, since this came and went in soldiers' hands.* Tiberius was already in his declining years, and soon, relaxed by a secluded environment, he would be more ready to delegate some of the functions of government. In addition, the antipathy towards Sejanus himself would decrease if he got rid of the crowd of morning callers, and with the empty trappings removed his real power would be increased. He therefore proceeded, little by little, to criticize the aggravations of the city with its bustling population and crowds of visitors, while he extolled the blessings of peace and solitude, where there was nothing to upset or annoy a person,

and the most important affairs of state could be given one's close attention.

42. As it happened, the trial of Votienus Montanus,* a man of renowned intellect, was being held at that time, and it was this that convinced the wavering Tiberius that he should avoid Senate meetings and the comments there made to his face, which were usually true and usually offensive. Votienus had been arraigned for making insulting comments on the emperor and, in his eagerness to prove the case, a witness, Aemilius,* who was a soldier, went into all the details. Despite the remonstrations of the senators, Aemilius pressed ahead with great persistence, and Tiberius heard the cutting gibes with which he was being secretly assailed. He was so shaken that he cried out that he would clear his name, either then and there or in the course of the trial, and it was only after pleas from his friends, and flattery from all present, that he was able—and only with difficulty—to regain his composure. Votienus did, indeed, suffer the penalty for treason; and Tiberius clung all the more tenaciously to his policy of severity towards defendants with which he had been reproached. Aquilia, denounced for adultery with Varius Ligus,* he punished with exile even though the consul-designate Lentulus Gaetulicus* had secured her condemnation under the Julian law,* and Apidius Merula* he struck off the senatorial register for not having sworn obedience to the measures passed by the deified Augustus.*

43. Delegations from Sparta and Messene were then heard on the question of jurisdiction over the temple of Diana Limnatis. The Spartans appealed to historical records and the poetic tradition in support of their claim that the temple had been dedicated by their ancestors, and in their territory. It had been wrested from them by force of arms, they said, by Philip of Macedon,* with whom they had been at war, and was subsequently restored to them by a judgement made by Julius Caesar and Marcus Antonius. The Messenians countered by bringing up the old division of the Peloponnese between the descendants of Hercules, in which, they claimed, the Denthaliate territory, in which the shrine stood, had passed into the hands of their king. Monuments testifying to this still survived, engraved in stone and ancient bronze, they said. But if they were called on to adduce poets and historical records in evidence, they had more of them and more reliable ones. Philip's decision had not been an arbitrary use of power, either, but based on fact. King Antigonus* had

reached the same conclusion, and so had the commander Mummius.*
The Milesians who were made official arbiters* of the case had
decided likewise and, finally, so had Atidius Geminus,* governor of
Achaea. The case thus went in the Messenians' favour.

The people of Segesta then applied for renovations to their temple
of Venus on Mt. Erycus, which had fallen into ruin with age. They
gave the celebrated account of its origins, which pleased Tiberius,
who gladly took on the responsibility for the restoration, as a family
member.*

Discussion of a petition from Massilia followed, and the precedent
set by Publius Rutilius* was accepted. When he was banished by law
from Rome, the people of Smyrna had awarded Rutilius citizenship;
and on this basis Vulcacius Moschus,* granted Massilian citizenship
when he was exiled, had left his property to the state, which he
regarded as his fatherland.

44. That year saw the deaths of the noblemen Gnaeus Lentulus
and Lucius Domitius.* Apart from a consulship and triumphal
insignia for victories over the Getae, Lentulus had the distinction of
having borne straitened circumstances with dignity, and then having
innocently gained, and modestly employed, a great fortune.*
Domitius' renown came from his father,* a powerful commander at
sea during the civil war, until he sided with Antonius, and then
Caesar. His grandfather* had fallen in the battle of Pharsalus,
fighting for the aristocrats. Domitius himself had been selected to be
married to the younger Antonia,* daughter of Octavia, and he later
crossed the River Elbe* with an army, driving further into Germany
than any of his predecessors and gaining triumphal insignia for his
achievements.

Another death was that of Lucius Antonius,* member of a very
illustrious but ill-starred family. His father, Iullus Antonius,
received the death penalty for adultery with Julia, and Augustus then
banished Lucius, who was his own sister's grandson and still just a
boy, to the city of Massilia* (where the term 'exile' could be masked
by a façade of intellectual pursuits). Honour was accorded to his
funeral, however, and his bones were, by senatorial decree, interred
in the tomb of the Octavii.*

45. In the same consulship a heinous crime was committed in
Nearer Spain by a peasant of the Termestine tribe. The governor of
the province, Lucius Piso,* was incautious because of the peaceful

conditions, and the man surprised him while he was travelling, striking him dead with a single blow. Making good his escape on a swift
horse, the assassin turned the animal loose when he reached a wooded
region, and then eluded his pursuers in the rugged, trackless country.
But he was not long undetected. The horse was caught and led
through the neighbouring villages, and its owner was thus identified.
The man was found, but when he was being tortured to reveal his
accomplices he cried out in a loud voice, and in his native language,
that the interrogation was pointless—his associates could come and
observe, he said, as there was no pain fierce enough to elicit the truth
from him! The next day, when he was being brought back for further
interrogation, he broke away from his guards and smashed his head
on a rock, with such force that death was instantaneous. It is believed,
however, that Piso's death was plotted by the Termestines: money
had been embezzled from the public purse, and Piso was trying to
recover it with a rigour greater than the barbarians could bear.

46. In the consulship of Lentulus Gaetulicus and Gaius Calvisius,
Poppaeus Sabinus was decreed triumphal insignia for crushing some
Thracian tribes who lived uncivilized lives in the high mountains,
and were all the more ferocious for it. The cause of the uprising
(apart from the natural disposition of the tribesmen) was their refusal
to tolerate troop conscription* and to surrender all their strongest
fighters for service with us. They were not used to obeying even their
own kings unless it suited them; if they did send them auxiliary
troops, they would have their own leaders command them, and they
would go to war only against their neighbours. At that time, too, a
rumour had spread that they were to be split up and incorporated
with other tribes, and then hauled off to distant lands.

Before commencing hostilities, the Thracians sent delegates to
remind the Romans of their friendship and loyalty, adding that these
would remain unchanged if they were not provoked by any new
burden. If, however, they had slavery imposed on them as a conquered people, they had their weapons, manpower, and a spirit ready
to claim freedom or face death. At the same time they pointed to
their strongholds perched upon the cliff-tops, and to their parents
and wives gathered there, and threatened the Romans with a war that
would be difficult, rigorous, and bloody.

47. Until he could unite his army, Sabinus made conciliatory
replies. However, after Pomponius Labeo* arrived from Moesia with

a legion, and King Rhoemetalces came with an auxiliary force of his countrymen (those who had not changed their loyalties), he added to them the troops then at his disposal, and marched on the enemy, now deployed in some wooded gorges. Some of these, with greater bravado, showed themselves on the open hills, but the Roman general moved in on them in battle formation and chased them off without difficulty, though little barbarian blood was shed because of the proximity of places of refuge. Sabinus then established camp on the spot and, with a strong unit, occupied a narrow mountain ridge that ran, unbroken and level, as far as the nearest stronghold, which was manned by a large force of soldiers and irregulars. At the same time he sent forward an elite band of archers to tackle the boldest of these, who after the manner of their race were leaping around, singing and dancing, before their rampart. While the archers were shooting from a distance, they inflicted wounds frequently without suffering loss, but as they came closer they were thrown into chaos by a sudden charge and were rescued only by the assistance of a Sugambrian cohort. The Roman commander had deployed this cohort not far away, since the Sugambrians were ready to face danger and, because of the noise the men generated with their songs and weapons, were just as intimidating as the Thracians.

48. The camp was then moved close to the foe, but the Thracians who had come to support us (as I noted above) were left at the earlier fortification. They were given leave to plunder, burn, and haul away booty, provided that their raiding was confined to the daylight hours and that they spent the night in camp, in safety and keeping watch. The condition was initially observed; but they soon turned to self-indulgence and, enriched by their plunder, abandoned their posts for unruly feasting, or lay prostrate in a drunken stupor. The enemy, learning of their negligence, prepared two columns. The Thracian raiders were to be attacked by the one, while the other was to assault the Roman camp, not with the expectation of taking it, but so that everyone there, focusing on his own personal danger, would be insensible to the noise of the other engagement. In addition, to increase the panic, the time chosen was after dark. In fact, those attacking the legionary rampart were easily driven off, but the Thracian auxiliaries were terrified by the sudden assault. Some were lying next to the fortifications, but most were wandering about outside, and they were cut down all the more ferociously for being seen as

turncoats and traitors bearing arms to enslave themselves and their fatherland.

49. The next day Sabinus paraded his army on level ground, hoping that the barbarians, elated with their success during the night, would risk an engagement. When they failed to descend from their stronghold or the adjacent heights, he proceeded with a blockade, employing the forts which he was already building at appropriate points. Next he constructed a combined trench-and-breastwork configuration with a four-mile circumference; then he gradually tightened his grip, hemming the foe into a restricted area, in order to deprive him of water and fodder. Work also began on a mound from which rocks, spears, and firebrands could be hurled at an enemy who was now in close range. But nothing caused more distress than thirst: a huge crowd of soldiers and non-combatants were limited to the use of one remaining spring. At the same time, the horses and cattle that were enclosed with them (as is the way with barbarians) were dying because of the shortage of fodder, and alongside them lay human corpses finished off by wounds or thirst. It was one foul mess of pus, stench, and disease.

50. A final misfortune was then added to the chaotic situation: dissension. Some advocated surrender; others were for death by wounds delivered to each other; and there were those who urged a sortie instead of death unavenged. It was not just the cowards who reacted against these last two suggestions. One of the leaders, Dinis, who was of advanced age and had long experience of Roman might and clemency, argued that they should lay down their arms, that this was the sole remedy for their predicament; and he was the first to surrender himself, together with his wife and children, to the victor. Those handicapped by age or sex followed, as did those who had a greater love for life than glory.

The younger warriors, however, were split between Tarsa and Turesis. Both were determined to die with their freedom, but Tarsa, crying out for a swift end, and for their hopes and fears to be quenched together, set an example by plunging a sword into his chest. And there was no shortage of men who sought death by the same means. Turesis, with his band of followers, waited for nightfall, but our commander was not ignorant of his plan, and he strengthened his outposts with more troops. Darkness fell with a terrible rainstorm, and the enemy, their wild shouting alternating with periods of desolate silence, shook the besiegers' resolve. Then Sabinus did the rounds of his men, urging them not to let strange noises or the phoney silence fool them into giving the enemy an opportunity for his tricks. Each man should stick to his post, he told them, without moving or hurling weapons at an illusory target.

51. Meanwhile, the barbarians came charging down the hill in bands. At one moment they hurled stones, fire-hardened stakes, and severed branches at the rampart; at the next they filled the ditches with brushwood, hurdles, and corpses. Some had earlier constructed gangways and ladders, and now they brought them up to the defence-works, which they grasped and tore down, afterwards struggling hand-to-hand with the defenders. The Roman soldiers for their part pushed back the enemy with their missiles, beat them off with their shield-bosses, parried them with wall-javelins* and rolled piles of rocks onto them. Adding courage to the Roman side was the hope that victory was already theirs, and the feeling that infamy would be the more conspicuous if they gave way; in the case of the Thracians it was that this was their last chance of salvation, and for some, too, the presence of mothers and wives, and their lamentations. The night fostered daring in some, fear in others. There were blind lunges, wounds out of nowhere. And the inability to distinguish friend from foe, and the cries echoing back from the mountain gorges—seemingly coming from behind—had caused such general confusion that the Romans abandoned some of their positions, assuming them breached. In fact, of the enemy only a handful made it through. The rest, with their bravest fighters dead or wounded, the Romans pushed back into their mountain stronghold at the approach of daylight, and there they were finally compelled to surrender. Neighbouring areas were taken with the agreement of the inhabitants; the premature onset of a cruel winter in the Haemus range saved the others from being reduced by assault or siege.

52. In Rome, meanwhile, the imperial family had been shaken. The steps that would lead to Agrippina's destruction began with the arraignment of her cousin Claudia Pulchra,* her accuser being Domitius Afer.* Afer had recently held the praetorship, had little reputation, and was in a hurry to gain celebrity by any deed. His charges against Pulchra were immorality, with Furnius her adulterer, and acts against the emperor involving poison and magical curses. Agrippina was always a formidable woman, but she was then

also incensed by a relative's danger. She went straight to Tiberius, whom she chanced to find sacrificing to his father.* This aroused her indignation; the same person should not be offering sacrifices to the deified Augustus and also persecuting his descendants, she declared. Augustus' divine spirit had not been transferred into a stone representation of him—*she* was his true image, a descendant of his heavenly blood! She knew the danger she was in, she added, and was therefore adopting mourning attire. There was no point in using Pulchra as a pretext; the sole cause of her ruin was that she had foolishly chosen Agrippina as a friend, forgetting that Sosia had been brought low for the same reason.

These words drew a response from that secretive breast, a rare occurrence. Tiberius seized Agrippina and, in a line of Greek verse,* advised her that 'because she did not rule did not mean she was being mistreated'. Pulchra and Furnius were condemned. Afer became ranked among the leading orators now that his talent had been given exposure, and a comment of the emperor followed that he had 'a genuine fluency'. Subsequently, in taking on prosecutions or conducting defence, his eloquence earned more fulsome praise than his ethics. His later years took much away from that eloquence, for he still retained, even with a weakened mental capacity, an inability to remain silent.

53. Agrippina meanwhile persisted in her anger and was also overtaken by physical illness. When Tiberius came to visit her, she long shed tears in silence, and then addressed him with angry entreaties: he should help her in her loneliness and supply a husband for her. She was still young enough,* she said, and the only solace for decent women lay in marriage*—and there were in the city <men who> would deign to accept Germanicus' wife and children. The emperor, however, understood what the request entailed for the state, but so as not to show any resentment or fear he left her without making a reply, despite her insistence. This episode, which is not recorded by historians, I found in the journals* of her daughter Agrippina who, as mother of the emperor Nero, gave posterity an account of her life and the fortunes of her family.

54. Agrippina was now sorrowful and unwary, and Sejanus deepened her anxiety by sending men to warn her, ostensibly out of friendship, that a scheme to poison her was afoot, and that she should avoid dining with her father-in-law.* But she could not dissemble,

and when she reclined next to Tiberius she did not soften her expression or tone of voice, and would not touch her food, until Tiberius noticed, by chance or because he had been told. To test matters further, he recommended some fruit when it had been served, and passed it to his daughter-in-law with his own hand. Agrippina's suspicion was heightened by this and, without tasting it, she passed the fruit on to the slaves. However, Tiberius made no comment to her face. Instead, he turned to his mother and said that it should be no surprise if he took rather stern measures with a woman by whom he was being accused of poisoning. From this arose a rumour that her downfall was in preparation, but that the emperor did not dare to act openly, and a way of effecting it secretly was being sought.

55. To deflect such gossip, Tiberius regularly attended the Senate, and spent several days hearing deputations from Asia dispute the choice of city-state where his temple would be erected. There were eleven cities in contention, all equally ambitious, but disparate in strength. There was little difference between their arguments, which were based on the antiquity of their race, and support of the Roman people in the wars with Perses, Aristonicus, and other monarchs.* Hypaepa and Tralles, however, along with Laodicea and Magnesia, were rejected as having too weak a case; and even the people of Ilium, despite their reference to Troy as parent of the city of Rome, had no strong claim beyond a glorious antiquity. There was some momentary hesitation over Halicarnassus because its people had claimed that its site had been undisturbed by earthquakes for twelve hundred years, and that the temple's foundations would be on natural rock. Pergamum, it was believed, had received sufficient honour because there was already a temple of Augustus situated there (the very point on which it based its claim!). Ephesus and Miletus were seen as fully occupied with the worship of Diana and Apollo respectively. Consideration was thus limited to Sardis* and Smyrna.

The people of Sardis read out a decree of the Etrurians, with whom they claimed consanguinity. For, they said, because of its great numbers, Tyrrhenus and Lydus, sons of King Atys, divided their race. Lydus had then stayed behind to settle in the land of his fathers, while Tyrrhenus was charged with founding a new settlement; and these peoples, one in Asia, and the other in Italy, were named after their leaders. The power of the Lydians was further increased when groups of colonists were sent to that area of

Greece which later took its name from Pelops. The Sardians also called attention to letters from Roman commanders and treaties struck with us during the war with Macedon, as well as to the ample flow of their rivers, their temperate climate, and the rich lands around them.

56. The people of Smyrna on their side recalled their antiquity—whether they owed their foundation to Tantalus, son of Jupiter, to Theseus, also of divine stock, or to one of the Amazons—and then moved on to the points in which they had most confidence. First came their services to the Roman people, including their sending of naval forces, not only for wars abroad* but also for those endured in Italy.* Then there was their having been the first to build a temple dedicated to the city of Rome, in the consulship of Marcus Porcius,* a time when Roman power was great but had not yet reached its peak, a time when the Punic capital was still standing and there were still powerful kings in Asia. The Smyrnaeans also cited Lucius Sulla* as witness on their behalf. His army had been in very serious danger because of the severity of the winter and lack of clothing, they said, and when that announcement was made at a public meeting in Smyrna, all present had taken the outer garments from their bodies and sent them to our legions.

Thus, when asked their opinion, the senators gave Smyrna as their first choice. Vibius Marsus* moved that Marcus Lepidus, to whom that province had been allotted, should be assigned a supernumerary legate* to take responsibility for the temple. And because, from modesty, Lepidus declined to make the choice himself, one of the ex-praetors, Valerius Naso, was sent out after being selected by lot.

57. Meanwhile the emperor, who had long considered the idea and often deferred it, finally left for Campania. The pretext was his dedication of a temple to Jupiter in Capua, and one to Augustus in Nola,* but really he was determined to live away from Rome. As to the reason for his retirement, I have followed the majority of historians* in putting it down to the wiles of Sejanus. However, Tiberius lived in the same seclusion for six years in succession after his execution of Sejanus, and so I am sometimes prompted to wonder whether it would not be more correctly put down to the man himself, and a wish to conceal by his location the cruelty and lust that he was exhibiting in his behaviour. There were some who believed that, in his old age, he was also ashamed of his physical appearance, since he

was of tall stature, very thin and stooped, his head devoid of hair, and his face covered with sores and streaked with ointments (at Rhodes, too, he had made a habit of avoiding company and keeping his pleasures secret). It is also reported that Tiberius was driven away by his mother's domineering manner. He refused to have her sharing his rule,* but could not remove her because he had received that rule as a gift from her. For Augustus had considered putting Germanicus, his sister's grandson and a man praised by everybody, at the head of the Roman state. He was, however, overcome by his wife's entreaties, and arranged for Germanicus to be adopted by Tiberius, and Tiberius by himself. Augusta was continually casting this up, and demanding her repayment.

58. His departure took place with a limited entourage.* There was one senator, Cocceius Nerva, an ex-consul and a legal expert; another Roman knight in addition to Sejanus, Curtius Atticus, who was a leading member of the order; and the rest were men with a liberal education, mostly Greeks,* whose conversation was meant to provide him with entertainment. Astrologers claimed that Tiberius' departure from Rome coincided with a movement of the planets that indicated there would be no return. That caused the downfall of many people, who surmised that his death was at hand and spread the word, failing to foresee the incredible circumstance that he would, for eleven years, voluntarily exile himself from his native city. The narrow line between science and error, and in what obscurity the truth is veiled, presently became clear. For the prediction that he would not return to the city* proved not untrue; but on everything else the astrologers revealed their ignorance, for, while he took up quarters in the nearby countryside or coastal districts, and often right by the city walls, he managed to reach a very ripe old age.

59. It so happened that a dangerous accident befell Tiberius at that time, increasing the idle rumours and giving him grounds for putting greater confidence in Sejanus' friendship and loyalty. They were taking a meal in a villa called 'The Cavern', which was in a natural cave between the sea at Amyclae and the hills of Fundi. There was a sudden rock-slide at the mouth of the cave that buried a number of servants, precipitating universal panic and the flight of those attending the meal. Sejanus positioned himself over the emperor on his hands and both knees, setting himself against the falling stones, and such was the position in which he was found by the soldiers who

came to the rescue. Sejanus' authority grew after this, and, disastrous though his advice might be, he was listened to with confidence as being a man with no concern for himself. And he assumed the role of judge with regard to Germanicus' children, bribing men to play the part of accusers, and to pick on Nero in particular. Nero was the next in line of succession and, though he had the modesty of youth, he often forgot what was appropriate in the present circumstances. And he was also being goaded by his freedmen and clients, all of them rushing to acquire power, to show himself bold and confident. This was what the Roman people wanted and what the armies truly desired, they told him, and Sejanus, at the moment mocking an old man's passivity along with a young man's indolence, would not venture to oppose him.

60. Listening to these and similar comments, Nero harboured no criminal thoughts, but occasionally trenchant and ill-considered remarks would emerge from him. Those assigned to watch him took note of these and exaggerated them in their reports, while Nero was given no chance to defend himself. So various forms of anxiety began to manifest themselves. One person would avoid meeting him; another would exchange a greeting and immediately turn away; some would break off speaking in mid-conversation—while Sejanus' supporters who were present just stood by and laughed. As for Tiberius, he met him with a grim expression, or a false smile; and if the young Nero spoke, or if he said nothing, silence showed his guilt, and so did talking.

Even night was not safe, since his wife* disclosed his waking moments, his sleep times, and his sighs to her mother Livilla, and Livilla disclosed them to Sejanus. Sejanus had also brought Nero's brother Drusus* over to his side, offering him hope of the supreme position if he removed his elder brother, who was already in difficulties. Apart from his lust for power, and the hatred that usually exists between brothers, Drusus had a frightful character that was further inflamed by envy over his mother Agrippina's preference for Nero. Even so, Sejanus' backing of Drusus was not such as to prevent him from sowing the seeds of *his* future destruction, too, for he knew him to be particularly headstrong, and so more easily trapped.

61. The end of the year saw the deaths of two distinguished men, Asinius Agrippa* and Quintus Haterius.* Agrippa's ancestors were distinguished rather than ancient, and he was not their inferior in his

own life. Haterius came from a senatorial family, and was celebrated for his oratory throughout his life, though the surviving literary monuments to his genius are not so highly regarded. Indeed, his success derived more from his lively delivery than the care he took; and whereas the preparation and industry of others gains them appreciation with later generations, Haterius' resonant and flowing style died with him.

62. In the consulship of Marcus Licinius and Lucius Calpurnius an unforeseen catastrophe brought loss of life on the scale of some major wars, and no sooner had it begun than it was over. A certain Atilius, a man of freedman status, had begun work on an amphitheatre near Fidenae for the staging of a gladiatorial show, but he did not set its foundations on solid ground and did not bind the wooden superstructure securely with firm joints, either. In fact, he had sought the contract not because he possessed great wealth or had political ambitions in the town, but as a sordid commercial venture.

People flocked in, eager for such entertainment, for under Tiberius they had been deprived of their diversions. There were men and women of all ages, and the numbers were swollen by the location's proximity to town, which made the mishap all the more catastrophic. The structure became crowded, then broke apart, collapsing inward or spreading over the area outside, and it dragged down with it, and buried, a huge mass of humanity, people engrossed in the spectacle or just standing around. Those killed in the initial destruction escaped the real agony, as far as that can be said of such a tragedy; more to be pitied were those whom life had not left after suffering some partial mutilation of their bodies. These recognized their wives and children by sight in the daylight, but at night only from the sound of their lamentations and groaning. Soon all others in the area were brought there by the news—and one found himself lamenting the loss of a brother, another a relative, and a third his parents. Even those whose friends or kinsfolk were away from home for other reasons were still terrified; and while the victims of the disaster remained unidentified the fear was more widespread because of that uncertainty.

63. When the removal of debris began, there was a rush to the dead bodies, which people embraced and kissed; and often there was a spat when features were quite indistinct but similarity of shape or age caused errors in identification. Fifty thousand people* were

disabled or crushed to death in that accident; and by decree of the
Senate provision was made for the future that no one with capital of
less than 400,000 sesterces was to stage a gladiatorial show, and that
an amphitheatre was to be built only on land of proven stability.
Atilius was driven into exile. As a consequence of this disaster, however, the homes of leading citizens were thrown open, and dressings
and doctors were made universally available. During those days the
city, despite her mournful appearance, lived up to the tradition of the
ancients who, after great battles, supported the wounded with their
generosity and care.

64. The memory of that disaster had not yet faded when a raging
fire* brought an exceptional amount of damage upon the city, completely consuming the Caelian Hill. It was a fateful year, people said,
and the emperor had decided to remain absent despite unfavourable
omens. They—as the crowd usually does—were taking chance events
as being a causal factor; but then Tiberius faced the problem head-
on by doling out money in proportion to losses incurred. Thanks
were offered him in the Senate by distinguished members, and his
reputation improved amongst the people because, without being
influenced by canvassing or the entreaties of relatives, he had with
his liberality assisted even people unknown to him and encouraged
them to come forward. There were also proposals made that the
Caelian Hill be henceforth called the Augustan Hill,* since the only
thing that remained untouched, while everything went up in flames
around about, was a statue of Tiberius that stood in the home of the
senator Junius. That, people declared, had happened earlier to
Claudia Quinta.* Her statue had on two occasions escaped a violent
fire, and so their ancestors had consecrated it in the temple of the
Mother of the Gods. The Claudian family was holy and dear to the
gods, they said, and the spot on which heaven had shown their
emperor such honour should receive additional veneration.

65. It would not be inappropriate to note that, in early times, that
hill bore the name 'Querquetulanus'* because it produced wood of
that species in great abundance, and that it was only later renamed
'Caelian', after Caeles Vibenna. Vibenna was a leader of the Etruscan
race, who had brought assistance to Rome and for that had been
granted the hill as a place to settle by Tarquinius Priscus,* or another
of the kings—historians are in disagreement on his identity.* The
other elements of the story are not in doubt: Vibenna's large forces

also settled on the level ground there and in the district close to the Forum, the 'Tuscan Street' thus taking its name from the newcomers.

66. Now, while the nobility's public spirit and the emperor's generosity had brought relief in the case of disasters, there was no let-up in the violence of informers, which was growing and becoming more virulent each day. Domitius Afer found a victim in Quinctilius Varus,* a wealthy man related to the emperor. Afer had earlier secured a guilty verdict against Varus' mother, Claudia Pulchra, and now no surprise was felt that, long penniless and having squandered his recently won reward, he should be preparing himself for further outrages. What *was* surprising was the appearance on the scene of Publius Dolabella* as a partner in the denunciation: coming from distinguished ancestors, and being related* to Varus, he was setting out to ruin his own noble class, and his own family, too. Resistance came from the Senate, however, which voted to await the emperor,* the one thing that provided some temporary shelter from the pressing troubles.

67. Tiberius had in the meantime finished dedicating the temples in Campania. He had also issued an edict advising people that his peace was not to be disturbed, and crowds of townspeople were kept at bay by soldiers stationed for that purpose. Even so, his distaste for the municipal towns, colonies, and everything lying on the mainland led him to shut himself away on the island of Capreae, which is separated from the tip of the promontory of Surrentum by a strait three miles wide. I am inclined to believe that it was the solitude that pleased him most: surrounded by the sea, the island has no harbours and barely any havens even for smaller craft, and no one could put in there without a sentry knowing about it. The climate is mild during winter because of a mountain barrier by which it is protected from savage gales, and in summer the island is delightful because it is exposed to the west wind and surrounded by open sea. In addition, it enjoyed the view of a beautiful bay, until Mt. Vesuvius' eruptions* changed the landscape. Tradition has it that Greeks colonized the area, and that Capreae was inhabited by the Teleboans.

At this time, however, it was Tiberius who settled there, occupying twelve villas,* individual structures with their own names and, as totally as he had been engrossed with public affairs, he now similarly relaxed into private extravagances and pernicious leisure. For there still remained his excessive tendency to suspicion and credulity.

This Sejanus had persistently cultivated in Rome, as well, and now he was stoking it more fiercely, his traps for Agrippina and Nero no longer kept a secret. Soldiers, assigned to the two, would take note of messages and visits they received, and all their open and private activities, as accurately as for a work of history. Men were actually given the task of advising them* to seek refuge with the armies in Germany, or to embrace the statue of the deified Augustus when the Forum was particularly crowded, and call on the people and Senate for help. Such courses of action were rejected, but they were charged with intending to accept them.

68. The year of the consulship of Junius Silanus and Silius Nerva began in an atrocious manner with a distinguished Roman knight, Titius Sabinus,* dragged off to prison for his friendship with Germanicus. For Sabinus had not given up paying his respects to the man's wife and children, visiting their home, and accompanying them in public. Of all their clients, he was the only one who remained, and he was therefore praised by decent men and disliked by the wicked. He was pounced on by Latinius Latiaris, Porcius Cato, Petillius Rufus, and Marcus Opsius. These were ex-praetors who wanted the consulship; the only way to it was through Sejanus, and Sejanus' favour was to be gained only by crime.

The arrangement between them was that Latiaris, who had some slight familiarity with Sabinus, should set the trap; the others would be present as witnesses; then they would begin the accusation. Latiaris, therefore, engaged Sabinus in some casual conversation, and then praised his loyalty in not, like the others, having deserted in its adversity a family with which he had been friendly when it prospered. At the same time, he referred respectfully to Germanicus and expressed pity for Agrippina.

The human heart is soft in times of misfortune, and Sabinus burst into tears. He then added some complaints and, his confidence growing, proceeded to berate Sejanus for his ruthlessness, his arrogance, and his ambitions. He did not even stop short of verbal abuse of Tiberius, and these conversations, as an exchange of illicit confidences, gave the impression of close friendship between the men. And with that Sabinus actually began to seek out Latiaris, to visit his home, and to bring to him his tales of woe as though to a most trusted friend.

69. The above-mentioned individuals now discussed how these conversations could be heard more widely. Their meeting place, they thought, had to retain the appearance of being private; and if they were standing behind doors, there was fear of their being seen, or of their making a noise, or of Sabinus simply becoming suspicious. The three senators hid themselves in a spot between the roof and the ceiling—a hiding-place whose squalor matched the vileness of the treachery— and put their ears to various chinks and cracks. Latiaris, meanwhile, found Sabinus in the street and, pretending he was going to give him some fresh news, took him into the bedroom of his home. There he piled up accounts of past and current events—and there were plenty—and added the most recent terrors. Sabinus concurred, and at greater length, for once grief breaks forth silence is more difficult.

The accusation was then speeded up. In a letter, the men briefed Tiberius on the steps in the plot and their own shameful actions. Never had the city known greater tension and panic,* with people tight-lipped even with their closest relatives. They avoided meetings and conversations, and the ears of friend and stranger alike. Even mute and lifeless objects— roofs and walls—were eyed with suspicion.

70. In a letter to the Senate on 1 January, Tiberius offered the customary prayers for the start of the year, and then turned on Sabinus, charging him with corrupting some of his freedmen and making an attempt on his life; and he was not unclear about the punishment he wanted. There was no delay* with the judgement. The condemned man was dragged off, crying out (as well as he could with clothes pulled over his head and his neck choked) that such were the new year's celebrations, and these the sacrificial victims offered to Sejanus! And wherever he fixed his gaze, wherever his words fell, there was wholesale flight, leaving roads and forums deserted. Some indeed came back and showed themselves again, frightened of the very fact that they had shown their fear. For, they thought, what day could be free from punishment when, amid the sacrifices and prayers—a time when it was customary to avoid even profane language—chains and the noose were being brought into use? Tiberius had not exposed himself to such intense resentment unthinkingly, they reasoned. No, it was a deliberate and premeditated step, to make people realize that there was nothing to prevent the new magistrates from opening up the prison as they did the shrines and altars.

A letter followed offering thanks to the senators for having punished a man who was an enemy to the state. Tiberius added that he
lived in constant anxiety, and that he suspected treachery on the part
of his enemies, but he named no names. There was no doubt, however, that the reference was to Nero and Agrippina.

71. Were it not for my plan of assigning all events to their appropriate year, I would have liked to jump ahead and immediately
record the ends that Latinius, Opsius, and the other architects of that
piece of villainy experienced, not only after Gaius Caesar came to
power, but even during Tiberius' lifetime. (While Tiberius was loath
to see the agents of his crimes brought down by others, he often
became fed up with them and, when offered fresh men for the same
work, he got rid of the older ones who had become repugnant to
him.) But these and other punishments of the guilty parties I shall
record at the appropriate point.

Asinius Gallus, to whose children Agrippina was aunt,* then
expressed his opinion that the emperor be asked to divulge his fears
to the Senate, and allow them to be dispelled. Tiberius prized none
of what he considered to be his virtues as highly as he did his ability
to dissemble, and so he was all the more annoyed at what he wanted
to hide being brought into the open. Sejanus, however, calmed
him down, not from any affection for Gallus, but to see how the
emperor's hesitation would turn out. He knew that he was slow in
his deliberations but that, once his temper burst forth, he swiftly
followed grim words with terrible action.

About this same time Julia,* Augustus' granddaughter, died.
Augustus had convicted her of adultery, passed sentence on her, and
cast her away on the island of Trimetus, not far from the Apulian
shoreline. There she endured twenty years of exile, helped along by
support from Augusta,* who secretly contrived her stepchildren's
destruction in their heyday, and made a show of pity for them when
they were brought low.

72. That same year a people beyond the Rhine, the Frisians, abandoned their peace, more through our rapacity than because they were
chafing at their subjection. Drusus had levied from them a modest
tribute, taking account of their straitened circumstances: their payment was to be oxhides for military use. However, nobody had paid
attention to the firmness or measurements of the hides until
Olennius, a man of senior centurion rank who had been appointed to

govern the Frisians, chose the skin of the auroch as the yardstick of acceptability. That would even have posed a problem for any other tribes, but in the case of the Germans it was particularly difficult to tolerate in that, while they have woods teeming with huge beasts, their domestic animals are quite small. At first, they were surrendering just the oxen; then it was their lands; and finally it was their wives or children delivered into slavery. From this came rage and protests; and when no relief arrived, war was the solution. The soldiers who were there to take the tribute were kidnapped and nailed to gibbets. Olennius escaped the fury of the Frisians by flight, and was taken in at a fortress called Flevum. There a unit of no mean size, comprising citizens and allies, stood watch over the Ocean coastline.

73. When word of this reached Lucius Apronius, propraetorian governor of Lower Germany, he called in detachments of legions from the upper province, along with an elite group of auxiliary infantry and cavalry. He then shipped both armies together down the Rhine and marched with them against the Frisians. (Their siege of the fortress had by now been raised, and the rebels had left in order to defend their own territory.)

Apronius used a network of embankments and bridges in the neighbouring estuaries to provide a solid thoroughfare for transporting a more heavily armed column. Moreover, having meanwhile discovered a ford, he ordered the Canninefate cavalry, along with all the German infantry serving in our ranks, to move around to the rear of the enemy (who were already deployed for battle, and were driving back the allied squadrons and legionary cavalry sent as reinforcements). Then three cohorts of light infantry were sent into the fray, followed by two others and, after an interval, by the mounted auxiliaries. This was a strong enough force—had they attacked together. By arriving in stages, however, they had not strengthened the resolve of the disordered units and were themselves being swept back by the panic of those in retreat.

Apronius set the remainder of the auxiliaries under the command of Cethecius Labeo, legate of the Fifth Legion, and Labeo, put gravely at risk by his men's precarious situation, dispatched a message with a plea that the entire strength of the legions be sent in. The men of the Fifth Legion charged forward ahead of the others, drove back the enemy in a fierce engagement, and rescued the cohorts and cavalry, who were exhausted from their wounds. The Roman commander did not seek retribution, nor did he bury the dead, despite the fact that numerous tribunes and prefects, and some out-standing centurions, had fallen. It was subsequently learned from deserters that nine hundred Romans had been killed in a grove they call Baduhenna, having drawn out the battle to the following day, and that another contingent of four hundred, who had occupied a villa belonging to Cruptorix, a former mercenary, had fallen by each other's hands when it was feared that treachery was afoot.

74. After that the Frisian name enjoyed some cachet amongst the Germans, but Tiberius, to avoid entrusting the conduct of the war to anyone, hid the losses. The Senate, too, was unconcerned about an ignominious reverse on the fringes of the empire; fear within had seized their attention, and the cure for it was being sought in syco-phancy. And so, although they were being consulted on other mat-ters, the senators voted an altar* to Clemency and an altar to Friendship, with statues of the emperor and Sejanus on either side. They also, with frequent entreaties, petitioned the two men to let themselves be seen in person. The two did not, however, come into the city or its environs; they felt it enough to leave the island and be on view in the closest part of Campania. To this area came senators, knights, and large numbers of the plebs, all of them worried with regard to Sejanus, to whom access had become more difficult and had to be gained by intrigue and becoming associated with his designs. There was general agreement that his arrogance was increased when he looked upon this foul servility openly displayed. For at Rome comings and goings are the norm, and because of the city's size it is unclear to what business each person is proceeding. There, however, lolling around on the plain or the shore, day and night alike, they experienced the favour or the disdain of the doorkeepers—until that, too, was forbidden. Then they came back to Rome. Those whom Sejanus had not graced with a conversation or a look were terrified, and some were in high spirits—unwisely, since the deadly outcome of that unlucky friendship was looming over them.

75. Tiberius, meanwhile, had personally engaged his grand-daughter Agrippina* Germanicus' daughter to Gnaeus Domitius,* and he issued orders for the marriage to be celebrated in the city. In Domitius, in addition to the antiquity of his family, Tiberius had also selected a relative of the Caesars, for the man could boast Octavia as grandmother and, through her, Augustus as a great-uncle.

BOOK FIVE (FRAGMENT)

1. The consulship of Rubellius and Fufius, both of whom bore the surname Geminus, saw the passing of Julia Augusta,* at a very advanced age. She was a woman of the most brilliant aristocratic lineage because of her membership in the Claudian family* and her adoption into those of the Livii and Julii. She was first married to Tiberius Nero,* with whom she had her children. Nero was exiled during the Perusine War* and after peace was concluded between Sextus Pompeius and the triumvirs, he returned to the city. It was after this that Augustus, from physical attraction, took her from her husband—whether she was an unwilling bride is not clear—and in such haste that he did not even allow time for the birth but took her into his home while she was pregnant.* She produced no other child after this but, becoming connected to Augustus' bloodline through the union of Agrippina and Germanicus, she had grandchildren in common with him. In the purity of her household she preserved the old morality, though her sociability exceeded the approved norms of women of antiquity. She was an overbearing mother but a compliant wife, who was a good match for her husband's craftiness and her son's hypocrisy.

The funeral was modest, her will* long not put into effect. Her eulogy from the Rostra was given by Gaius Caesar, her grandson, who soon afterwards came to power.

2. With no change in his hedonistic lifestyle, Tiberius by letter pleaded the great pressure of business as his excuse for failing to attend the final ceremonies for his mother. A wide range of honours to her memory were decreed by the Senate, but he (ostensibly from modesty) reduced them, accepting a very small number and adding that Livia should not be decreed divine honours,* and that such had been her own preference. Furthermore, in part of the same letter he criticized 'women's friendships', which was an oblique dig at the consul Fufius.* Fufius had risen to prominence through Augusta's favour, being an adept at gaining the attentions of women. He was also witty, and he made a practice of mocking Tiberius with caustic jokes, which live long in the memory of men in supreme command.

3. But from that point it was an out-and-out oppressive tyranny. When Augusta was alive there was still some refuge because of Tiberius' long-standing deference to his mother, and Sejanus would not presume to supersede a parent's authority. But at this time they both charged forth, as though freed from the reins, and a letter attacking Agrippina and Nero was sent off. (It was commonly believed that this had been brought earlier and kept back by Augusta, for its public reading came about not long after her death.) It contained expressions of calculated harshness, but the charges Tiberius levelled against his grandson were not of armed rebellion or revolutionary designs, but of love affairs with young men and lewd behaviour. He had not the audacity to trump up even a charge like that against his daughter-in-law, and instead accused her of arrogant language and recalcitrant temper. This brought a deep, fearful silence on the Senate. Then a few members, who had no hopes of gaining anything from decent behaviour (and public misfortunes are used by individuals as a way of ingratiating themselves), demanded a motion on the question, the most enthusiastic being Cotta Messalinus who came up with a savage proposal. But there was fear on the part of the other leading senators, especially the magistrates, for though Tiberius' tirade had been savage, he had left everything else unclear.

4. One member of the Senate, Junius Rusticus, was Tiberius' choice as secretary of the senatorial proceedings,* and he was therefore believed to have some understanding of the emperor's way of thinking. Rusticus fell prey to some deadly impulse—for he had not earlier given any evidence of moral fibre—or to a misguided shrewdness that made him fearful of uncertainties while remaining oblivious to dangers right before him. He joined the ranks of the waverers and warned the consuls not to entertain a motion. The most important matters, he added, were swayed by the slightest influences, and it could be that the old man would some day regret the destruction of Germanicus' line.

At the same time the people* encircled the Curia carrying portraits of Agrippina and Nero and, with prayers wishing the emperor well, protested that the letter was a forgery and that the emperor would not consent to his house being threatened with destruction.

So it was that no dreadful deed was perpetrated that day. There were even false motions directed at Sejanus being circulated under the names of some ex-consuls, since numerous individuals were

allowing their imaginations to run free, and all the more extrava-
gantly because of their anonymity. That made Sejanus' anger more
violent and gave him material for accusations. The Senate cared
nothing for the emperor's suffering, he said, and the people had
abandoned their loyalty. Already seditious tirades were being heard
and read, and seditious decrees of the Senate. What was left for them
to do now but take up the sword and choose as their leaders and
commanders those whose portraits they had followed like military
standards?

5. Tiberius therefore repeated his reproaches against his grandson
and daughter-in-law, and he rebuked the people in an edict. To the
Senate he protested that, through the duplicity of a single member,
his imperial majesty had been publicly insulted, but he demanded
that all decisions in the matter be left in his hands.* There was no
further discussion. Not that they decreed the ultimate penalty—that
had been forbidden—but they declared that, ready to exact
vengeance though they were, they were held back by the emperor's
authority. . . .

BOOK SIX

At this point there is a gap in the manuscript. It appears that only a few letters from the manuscript are missing, but it is evident that at some earlier stage in the copying process a large section of the narrative, covering almost two years, has been lost. The events described before the gap all belong to the early part of AD 29, after it to late AD 31, and these later events clearly belong to Book 6. Hence the assignment of the next six chapters to Book 5, made in the sixteenth century, is universally accepted as erroneous, but the resulting flawed chapter numbering has become hallowed by tradition.

The missing narrative would have contained the conviction of Drusus, son of Germanicus, and the death of his brother Nero, through the machinations of Sejanus. The downfall of Sejanus himself followed soon after, and the text resumes shortly after that momentous event.

[5] **6.** . . . forty-four speeches* were delivered on that subject, a few from fear, more through the habit . . . 'I thought* . . . would bring disgrace to me or resentment against Sejanus. There has been a change of fortunes, and the man who had accepted Sejanus as colleague and son-in-law* finds forgiveness for his own mistake; all the others, who earlier debased themselves supporting Sejanus, now wickedly attack him. Which is the more pitiful I cannot decide—being accused because of a friendship, or accusing a friend. I shall not put to the test anyone's heartlessness or clemency; I shall head off the danger as a free man with my self-esteem intact. But I beg you to remember me with happiness, not sorrow, adding me to the list of those who, by a noble end, escaped the country's misfortunes.'

[5] **7.** After that he spent part of the day detaining or bidding farewell to individual visitors, as people were inclined to stay and talk with him. There was still a large company present, all of them gazing on his fearless expression, and believing that time still remained before the end, when he fell on a sword he had hidden in his clothing. And Tiberius levelled no accusations or abuse against the deceased, although he had made many shameful charges against Blaesus.*

[5] **8.** Next came discussion of Publius Vitellius* and Pomponius Secundus.* In the case of Vitellius, informers claimed that he had

offered the keys of the treasury* (which was in his charge), and
the military fund, for revolutionary action. The charge against
Pomponius—made by the ex-praetor Considius—was one of
friendship with Aelius Gallus* who, after Sejanus' punishment, had
fled to Pomponius' gardens, assuming that to be his safest haven.
And the defendants' only help in their predicament lay in the steadfast loyalty of their brothers, who put up bail for them. There were
numerous deferments, and, under the stress of being suspended
between hope and fear, Vitellius asked for a sharpener,* ostensibly
for his literary studies, and, making a slight cut in his veins, ended
his life in a state of depression. Pomponius, by contrast, a man of
refined character and outstanding intellect, bore his misfortune with
equanimity, and outlived Tiberius.

[5] **9**. It was next decided that Sejanus' remaining children* should
face punishment (despite the fact that the anger of the plebs was
subsiding, and that most people had been appeased by the earlier
executions). They were therefore carried into prison, the son aware
of what lay ahead, but the girl so naive as to repeatedly ask what she
had done wrong, and where they were dragging her. She would not
repeat her offence, she said, and could be corrected with the beating usually accorded a child. Contemporary authors record that, capital punishment for a virgin being unheard of, she was raped by the
executioner, with the noose lying beside her. The two were then
strangled and their bodies—at that tender age—thrown on the
Gemonian Steps.

[5] **10**. At about the same time there was consternation in Asia and
Achaea over a rumour (which was rampant but not long-lived) that
Germanicus' son Drusus had been spotted in the Cyclades, and later
on the mainland.* In fact, there was a young man, not much different
from Drusus in age, who had been 'recognized' by a number of
imperial freedmen; and when these joined him, knowing it was a
hoax, some ignorant people began to be won over, thanks to the fame
of Drusus' name and the Greek propensity for the bizarre and the
incredible. They fabricated a tale—and immediately believed it
themselves—that Drusus had given his guards the slip, and was
heading for his father's army with the intention of invading Egypt
and Syria. Already attracting crowds of young men, and winning
support amongst the people, the boy was enjoying his immediate
success and entertaining idle hopes, when news of the phenomenon

reached Poppaeus Sabinus.* Sabinus was then preoccupied with Macedonia, but he also had charge of Achaea. He decided to head off danger, whether real or fictitious. He swiftly passed the gulfs of Torone and Thermae, then went on to Euboea, an island in the Aegean, and to Piraeus on the Attic coastline, fetching up at the shore of Corinth and the narrow isthmus; after that, sailing the other sea,* he entered the Roman colony of Nicopolis. There, finally, Sabinus learned that the man had been subjected to some careful cross-questioning on his identity, and had said that he was the son of Marcus Silanus, adding that, when many of his supporters slipped away, he had boarded a ship (intending, apparently, to head for Italy). Sabinus told Tiberius this by dispatch, and I have discovered nothing more on how the matter began or ended.*

[5] 11. At the end of the year a feud that had long been growing between the consuls finally erupted. Trio, with a knack for making enemies and with experience in court, had indirectly criticized Regulus* for being slow in crushing the agents of Sejanus. Regulus, who was cool-headed except when provoked, not only rebuffed his colleague's attack but initiated a judicial inquiry against him for complicity in the plot. Though many of the senators begged them to lay aside animosities that were likely to end in their destruction, the two went on hating and threatening each other until they left office.

6.1. When Gnaeus Domitius and Camillus Scribonianus commenced their consulship, Tiberius crossed the channel between Capreae and Surrentum and proceeded to skirt the Campanian coast.* He was either undecided about entering the city, or, having decided against it, was making a pretence of coming there. After frequent landings in the vicinity, and paying a visit to the gardens on the Tiber, he headed back once more to his rocks and lonely seascape, ashamed of his crimes and debaucheries. So uncontrollably inflamed with these had he become that, in the manner of a king, he was defiling free-born children with his lechery. Nor was it just good looks and shapely bodies that titillated his libido—in some cases it was a boy's shyness, in others his ancestors' portraits.* Then, too, previously unknown terms were invented: *sellarii* and *spintriae*, named respectively from the foul locations where they operated, and their wide range of pathic sexual activities.* Slaves were assigned the task of searching out and dragging in the victims, with gifts for the willing and threats for the reluctant; and if a relative or parent held them back they resorted to seizure by force and satisfied their own lusts on them, as though on prisoners of war.

2. In Rome, meanwhile, at the start of the year, savage motions were being put forward relating to Livilla's statues and memory—as if her crimes had just come to light, and had not been punished long before. Sejanus' property was also withdrawn from the public treasury for transfer to the imperial exchequer, as if it made any difference!* People like Scipio, Silanus, and Cassius were very earnestly supporting these proposals, in the same or slightly altered wording, when, suddenly, Togonius Gallus edged his undistinguished self into the company of the great names, and was listened to with derision. He begged the emperor to choose a number of senators, twenty of whom would assure his security whenever he entered the Curia, the men being drawn by lot and armed with swords. Togonius had evidently given credit to the letter in which Tiberius demanded one of the consuls as his bodyguard, so that he could safely make for the city from Capreae!

Nevertheless Tiberius, whose way it was to mix jest and earnest, expressed his thanks for the senators' kindness; but who, he asked, could be passed over, and who chosen? Always the same individuals, or different ones in rotation? Those who had held office, or young men, and private citizens, or some of the magistrates? And what sort of figure would they cut, he then added, taking out their swords on the threshold of the Curia? His life was not worth so much to him if it needed to be protected by weapons!

Such was the response he made to Togonius, restraining his language, and asking nothing other than the withdrawal of the motion.

3. For Junius Gallio,* however, Tiberius had severe criticism. Gallio had proposed that members of the praetorian guard should, on the completion of their service,* gain the right to sit in the fourteen rows.* The emperor, as though addressing him face-to-face, asked what he had to do with the military, who had no right to take orders or rewards from anyone but the emperor. Gallio had clearly come across something that had escaped the deified Augustus' foresight! Or was it a case of discord and sedition being fomented by a supporter of Sejanus, who wanted to use an apparent honour to drive simple minds into breaches of military discipline?

This was the prize Gallio won for his studied flattery: immediate expulsion from the Curia, and later from Italy. And then, because it was alleged that his exile would be easy, since he had chosen the famous and delightful island of Lesbos, he was brought back to the city and put under house arrest in various senators' homes. In that same letter Tiberius also struck down Sextius Paconianus, much to the delight of the Senate; for Paconianus was a headstrong and evil man who ferreted out everybody's secrets and had been chosen by Sejanus to help with the destruction of Gaius Caesar.* When this came to light, long-simmering hatreds erupted, and only his willing-ness to denounce others saved the man from the death penalty that was being passed on him.

4. When Tiberius proceeded to attack Latinius Latiaris, however, accuser and accused alike—being both hated—provided the most delightful spectacle. It was Latiaris (as I noted above*) who had been primarily responsible for the fraudulent conviction of Titius Sabinus, and he was then the first to pay the penalty. In the mean-time Haterius Agrippa attacked the previous year's consuls, asking them why they now remained silent after their rounds of mutual recrimination. Obviously, fear and complicity in guilt served as a bond between them, he said—but the senators must not remain silent about what they had heard. Regulus replied that he was wait-ing for the right moment for vengeance, and that he would follow the matter up before the emperor;* Trio said that any rivalry between colleagues, and any negative comments made in the heat of argu-ment, were better forgotten. When Agrippa pressed the matter, the ex-consul Sanquinius Maximus* begged the Senate not to increase the anxieties of the emperor by stirring up further troubles—Tiberius was capable of finding the remedies himself. That meant salvation for Regulus, and a postponement of destruction for Trio.* Haterius was all the more hated because, languid from oversleeping or from nightly debaucheries though he was—and thus not needing to fear the emperor (no matter how cruel he was) because of his own indolence—he would plot the destruction of illustrious men* amidst his gluttony and lechery.

5. Next it was the turn of Cotta Messalinus, mover of all the most savage proposals, and so an object of long-standing hatred. As soon as an opportunity presented itself, he was accused of making numer-ous remarks about Gaius Caesar's 'dubious manhood', and of refer-ring to a banquet he attended with the priests on Augusta's birthday as 'a funeral dinner'.* There was also a charge that, when he was

complaining about the power of Marcus Lepidus and Lucius Arruntius,* with whom he was in dispute over a financial matter, he had added that '*They* will be defended by the Senate, but *I* shall be defended by my little Tiberius.'

On all charges Cotta's guilt was being exposed by leading men of the state, and as they kept up the pressure he appealed to the emperor. Not long afterwards a letter was brought, drafted like a defence oration, in which Tiberius recalled the early days of his friendship with Cotta and noted the man's numerous services to him. He then demanded that words that had been malevolently twisted, or candid dinner conversations, not be made grounds for a criminal charge.

6. The opening of that letter from the emperor seemed particularly significant, beginning as he did with these words:* 'May the gods damn me to worse punishment than I feel myself suffer every day if, at this time, I know what I should write to you, senators, how I should write it, and what I certainly should not write.' So true was it that his own crimes and wickedness had turned into punishment for him. And what the leading man of philosophy used to claim* is not untrue: if the minds of tyrants were opened up, gashes and wounds would become visible, since the soul is torn apart by cruelty, lust, and evil designs, no less than the body is torn by beatings. For neither Tiberius' fortune nor his isolation could keep him from confessing the torments in his breast, and the punishments he himself was suffering.

7. The members were granted authority* to decide the case of the senator Caesilianus, who had provided most of the evidence against Cotta, and their will was that he suffer the same penalty as Aruseius and Sangunnius, the accusers of Lucius Arruntius. No honour greater than that was ever paid to Cotta. He was a noble, it is true, but one impoverished through extravagance, and infamous for his vices; and now, in the vengeance with which he was honoured, he was being put on a level with Arruntius and his unblemished virtues.

Next was the trial of Quintus Servaeus and Minucius Thermus.* Servaeus was a former praetor who had once been a member of Germanicus' retinue, and Minucius was of equestrian rank; they had been restrained in their friendship with Sejanus, and so they enjoyed greater sympathy. Tiberius, by contrast, censured them as being leaders in the criminal conspiracy and told the elder Gaius Cestius* to inform the Senate of the contents of the letter he had written to the emperor. Cestius then undertook the prosecution.

This was the most pernicious feature of that period: leading members of the Senate practising, some openly, and many covertly, the lowest forms of delation. And whether this involved outsiders or family-members, friends or strangers, whether recent acts or those from the dimly remembered past—there was no discernible difference. Whatever people had talked about, whether in the Forum or at dinner, furnished the basis for an accusation, with each man rushing to beat the others in finding someone to accuse, a number doing so from self-defence, more as if they had caught some contagious disease.

Minucius and Servaeus were condemned, and then they joined the ranks of the informers. Drawn into the same misfortune were Julius Africanus from the Gallic community of the Santoni, and Seius Quadratus (whose origin I have not discovered). I am not unaware that the dangers and punishments experienced by many people have been omitted by a number of historians, wearied by the numbers involved, or else fearing to inflict on potential readers the same ennui with what they themselves found to be an overabundance of depressing material. Numerous instances have come to my notice which I feel, though they are not recorded by others, do deserve to be known.

8. For example, at that time, when others had hypocritically disavowed their friendship with Sejanus, a Roman knight by the name of Marcus Terentius* had the courage to cling to it when tried on that account. He addressed the Senate thus:

'In my circumstances, acknowledging the charge may perhaps be less expedient than denying it; but, no matter how things turn out, I am going to admit that I was a friend of Sejanus, that I actively sought to be so, and that I was happy to have attained that end. I had seen him commanding the praetorian cohorts as his father's colleague, and then simultaneously discharging civil and military duties. His kinsmen and in-laws were honoured with magistracies; and closeness to Sejanus strengthened one's friendship with the emperor, while those out of favour had to contend with fear and suppliant rags.* I cite no specific example. All of us who had no part in the man's final plan I shall defend with risk only to myself.

'For we were cultivating the friendship not of Sejanus of Vulsinii, but of a member of the Julian and Claudian families, into which he had entered by a marriage connection. He was your son-in-law, Tiberius, your colleague in the consulship, one performing your duties in the state. It is not for us to judge any man whom you raise above the others, and your reasons for doing so. To you the gods have granted supreme governance in all matters, and the glory of obeying you is what is left to us. Moreover, we see only what is put in our view—we see the man granted wealth and office by you, and those who are given the greatest power to help or harm. And no one could deny Sejanus had all of this. But an emperor's inner thoughts, and what he is planning in secret—to seek that out is forbidden and dangerous. And one would not succeed, anyway.

'Do not, senators, think about Sejanus' last day; think of his sixteen years.* We even used to pay our respects to Satrius and Pomponius;* and becoming personally known to the man's freedmen and door-keepers was thought a splendid thing. So, is this line of defence to be offered to all indiscriminately and without reserve? No, of course not; there must be a clear dividing line. Plotting against the state and planning to assassinate the emperor should be punishable offences; but when it comes to friendship and its obligations, ending these at the same time as you must acquit you and us together, Tiberius.'

9. The courage of Terentius' speech, and the fact that someone had been found to express what everybody was thinking, proved so effective that his accusers, when their earlier misdeeds were also taken into consideration, were punished with exile or execution.

Then came a letter from Tiberius targeting the ex-praetor Sextus Vistilius,* whom the emperor had transferred into his own cohort because he was a close friend of his brother Drusus. What caused his displeasure with Vistilius was either the fact that he had been the author of some writings impugning Gaius Caesar for his immorality, or Tiberius' mistaken belief that he had done so. Excluded from the emperor's circle, Vistilius tried the knife with his ageing hand, but retied the veins. Then, after sending a letter begging for pardon and receiving a heartless reply, he opened them once more.

Following that, an entire group* was accused of treason: Annius Pollio, Appius Silanus, Scaurus Mamercus, Sabinus Calvisius, and also Vinicianus, and his father Pollio along with him. These men were from renowned families and had held the highest offices as well. A shudder ran through the senators—how few were not related, by marriage or by friendship, to so many distinguished men? Then Celsus, tribune of one of the urban cohorts, and at that time one of the informers, came to the rescue of Appius and Calvisius. The emperor deferred the cases of Pollio, Vinicianus, and Scaurus for the moment so that he could personally look into them with the Senate, though he made some ominous hints against Scaurus.

10. Not even women* were out of danger. They could not be charged with trying to seize power, and so they were arraigned for their tears; and the old lady Vitia,* mother of Fufius Geminus, was put to death for weeping over the execution of her son.

Such were proceedings in the Senate. Cases were no different before the emperor. Vescularius Flaccus and Julius Marinus* were driven to their deaths, although the two were amongst Tiberius' oldest friends, had gone with him to Rhodes, and been inseparable from him on Capreae. Vescularius had been his intermediary in the plot against Libo, and Marinus had participated in Sejanus' crushing of Curtius Atticus. All the greater the satisfaction, then, that the examples had recoiled on their authors.

About this same time the pontiff Lucius Piso* succumbed to a natural death, a rare occurrence when a man was as famous as he. Piso never voluntarily produced a servile proposal, and whenever under pressure to agree he showed a prudent restraint. I noted above that his father had been a censor. He lived to his eightieth year, and had won triumphal honours in Thrace. But his greatest glory lay in the tact he showed as city prefect, an office only recently made permanent and thus much resented because people were unaccustomed to its authority.

11. In earlier days, in fact, to ensure that the city would not be without government when the kings (and later on the consuls) left home, a temporary official would be appointed to administer justice and cope with emergencies. Denter Romulius, they say, was assigned that position by Romulus, and later on so was Numa Marcius by Tullus Hostilius, and Spurius Lucretius by Tarquinius Superbus.* Then it was the consuls who made the choice, and a trace of the system remains in the consular duties an appointee is charged with taking on for the Latin Festival. In the civil wars Augustus gave Cilnius Maecenas,* who was of equestrian rank, authority over everything in Rome and Italy. Later, when he came to power, the size of the population and the slowness of legal redress led him to select one of the ex-consuls to restrain the slaves, as well as that

section of the citizens who would be reckless and unruly without the threat of violent reprisals. Messala Corvinus* was the first to take on that responsibility, only to renounce it within a matter of days claiming ignorance of how to use it. Next, Taurus Statilius* did an excellent job, despite his advanced age, and after that Piso won equal approval, holding the office for twenty years, and was honoured with a state funeral by senatorial decree.

12. A motion relating to a book of the Sibyl* was then brought before the senators by the tribune Quintilianus.* The quindecimvir Caninius Gallus* had demanded the inclusion of this book amongst the others of the same prophetess, and ratification of it by senatorial decree. This passed on a division alone, and Tiberius sent a letter,* mildly rebuking the tribune's ignorance of ancient custom, which he attributed to his youth. Gallus, however, he severely reprimanded: after long experience in the science of religious ceremonial he had, on dubious authority, brought the matter up in a poorly attended Senate, before the college had expressed an opinion, and when the verses had not been read and evaluated by the 'masters' (as was the usual procedure). He also reminded him that, because many spurious works were in circulation under that famous name, Augustus had set a date within which they should be brought before the urban praetor, and after which private ownership of them would be forbidden. Such a decree had also been passed by our ancestors, Tiberius added, after the burning of the Capitol in the Social War.* At that time verses of the Sibyl (whether there was one prophetess or more) were sought out in Samos, Ilium, and Erythrae, and even throughout Africa, Sicily, and the Italian colonies, and the priests were authorized with identifying, as far as was humanly possible, those that were genuine.

So, on this occasion, too, that book was submitted to the quindecimvirs for examination.

13. In the same consulship rioting almost broke out over the oppressively high price of grain,* and many demands, voiced in the theatre over a period of several days, were addressed to the emperor in unusually bold language. Upset at this, Tiberius criticized the magistrates and senators for not having used their official authority to restrain the people, and he also pointed out to them the provinces from which he was importing grain, noting how much greater the supply was than under Augustus. And so, to chasten the plebs, a senatorial decree of old-time severity was framed, and the consuls'

edict was no less stringent. Tiberius' own silence in the matter was not seen as the appropriate response of an ordinary citizen, but as arrogance.

14. At the end of the year the Roman knights Geminius, Celsus, and Pompeius* succumbed to a charge of conspiracy. Of these, Geminius, because of his extravagance and effeminate ways, was a friend of Sejanus, but not party to any serious wrongdoing. When Julius Celsus, a tribune, was put in irons, he loosened his chain, wound it around him and, pulling it in different directions, broke his own neck. Rubrius Fabatus* was put under surveillance, suspected of despairing of the fortunes of Rome and intending to throw himself on the mercy of the Parthians. He was actually found close to the Straits of Sicily, and when he was brought back by a centurion he could provide no plausible reasons for his distant voyage. Even so he remained unharmed, forgotten rather than forgiven.

15. Tiberius had long been considering the choice of husbands for his granddaughters, and now, in the consulship of Servius Galba and Lucius Sulla, with the girls' marriageable age approaching, he selected Lucius Cassius and Marcus Vinicius.* Vinicius came from a provincial town. Born at Cales, with a father and grandfather who had both been consuls (though otherwise his family was entirely equestrian), he was a man of gentle disposition and refined eloquence. Cassius was from a plebeian family in Rome, but one that was ancient and venerable. He was brought up under his father's strict discipline, but was more often acclaimed for his congeniality than his industry. To these Tiberius engaged Germanicus' daughters, Drusilla to Cassius and Julia to Vinicius, and he wrote a letter to the Senate on the matter, with some lukewarm tributes to the young men. Then, after giving some extremely vague reasons for his absence, he turned to more weighty matters, the animosities he had incurred on behalf of the state, and requested that the prefect Macro* and a few tribunes and centurions go with him whenever he entered the Curia. A broadly worded senatorial decree was passed with no restriction placed on the composition or numbers of the escort, but he never approached even the roofs of Rome, much less its deliberative council, though he would often go round his native city by circuitous routes, and avoid it.

16. Meanwhile a large body of informers rushed down on those who kept augmenting their fortunes by usury, breaching the legislation of

the dictator Caesar, with its provisions concerning moneylending and property-possession within Italy. (In fact, this legislation had long been disregarded, because the public good comes second to private interests.) Moneylending was, to be sure, a long-standing blight on the city, and very often the cause of sedition and discord, so that there were efforts to check it even in days of old when morals were less corrupt. First there was the provision in the Twelve Tables* against lending at interest above one-twelfth,* whereas previously the rate was set at the whim of the rich; then, by a bill of the tribunes, the rate was lowered to one twenty-fourth; and finally interest was prohibited altogether.* And there were numerous plebiscites to counter the frauds that, though often suppressed, would keep rising again as a result of some amazing ingenuity.

On that occasion, the inquiry had fallen to the praetor Gracchus, and he was obliged by the large number of people in danger of prosecution to refer the matter to the Senate. The senators were alarmed*— none was free from guilt of this sort—and asked the emperor for a pardon. Tiberius granted it, and the following year and six months were granted as the period within which they were all to settle their personal finances to comply with the legal prescriptions.

17. This led to a shortage of ready money*—debts were simultaneously called in, and the cash that was raised after so many were condemned, and their property sold, was kept locked away in the imperial chest or public treasury. To meet this situation, the Senate had regulated that every creditor should invest two-thirds of his capital in land in Italy. The creditors, however, called in the full amount, and the debtors were honour-bound not to break faith. And so, at first, there was a great scramble and entreaties, and then uproar at the praetor's tribunal; and the measures that had been devised as a remedy—the sales and purchases—had the opposite effect, because the moneylenders had invested all their money in buying land. The large number of sales was followed by depressed prices, and the more indebted a man was the greater the difficulty he had in selling, so that many people were stripped of their wealth. The destruction of the family fortune began to hurl down rank and reputation, but then Tiberius brought aid by distributing a hundred million sesterces among the banks,* and also by providing opportunities for interest-free loans over a three-year period if the borrower gave the people security in land for double the amount borrowed. Credit was restored

by these measures, and gradually private lenders were also found. The purchase of land, however, was not conducted in conformity with the senatorial decree, the energy of the early stages being followed, as usual, by final indifference.

18. After this, the earlier fears returned, with Considius Proculus* being prosecuted for treason. He was celebrating his birthday, fearing nothing, when he was rushed into the Curia and no sooner convicted than executed! (His sister Sancia, too, who was prosecuted by Quintus Pomponius,* was deprived of water and fire. Pomponius was a restless character who claimed that his motive for this and other such acts was to ingratiate himself with the emperor and thereby help his brother Pomponius Secundus in the perils he was facing.) A sentence of exile was even passed on Pompeia Macrina, whose husband Argolicus and father-in-law Laco—leading Achaeans—the emperor had destroyed. Macrina's father, too, who was an illustrious knight, and her brother, an ex-praetor, committed suicide when faced with conviction. The charge against these was that Gnaeus Magnus* had counted amongst his friends their great-grandfather, Theophanes of Mytilene,* and that on Theophanes' death the sycophantic Greeks had accorded him divine honours.

19. Following these, the richest man in the Spanish provinces, Sextus Marius, was denounced for having had incestuous relations with his daughter, and he was thrown down from the Tarpeian Rock. And to leave no doubt that it was really the extent of the man's wealth that had brought about his downfall, Tiberius set aside his gold and silver mines for himself, although they were state confiscations. Excited now by the executions, he ordered all imprisoned on charges of complicity with Sejanus to be put to death. The carnage was enormous,* with bodies lying around—both sexes, all ages, the famous and the unknown, all scattered about or heaped together. Neither relatives nor friends were permitted to stand close to them, to shed tears, or even to look on them for any length of time. Guards were posted around the area, noting each person's grief; and they accompanied the putrefying corpses until they were dragged to the Tiber. There they floated around or were pushed to the banks by the current, and nobody cremated them or touched them. Ordinary human interaction had been destroyed by the power of fear, and with the growth of the savagery came the exclusion of pity.

20. About this same time Gaius Caesar, who had attended his grandfather when he left for Capreae, married Marcus Silanus' daughter Claudia.* Gaius concealed a monstrous personality beneath a deceitful veneer of moderation, and had uttered not a word at his mother's condemnation or his brothers' ruin.* Whatever Tiberius' mood for the day seemed to be, he would adopt the same, using language little different from his. Hence the ingenious comment of the orator Passienus,* which gained currency later on, that 'never had there been a better slave, or a worse master'.

I should not omit the prophecy of Tiberius concerning Servius Galba, consul at the time. After summoning him and sounding him out on various topics, Tiberius finally made a comment in Greek, along these lines: 'You, too, Galba, will at some point taste command,' a reference to Galba's power, which arrived late and was short-lived. This came from Tiberius' knowledge of the art of the Chaldeans,* acquired during his retirement at Rhodes. There he had as his teacher Thrasyllus,* whose expertise he had put to the test in the following way.

21. Whenever Tiberius was making this sort of consultation, he employed the top of the house, and had one sole freedman as his confidant. The freedman, who was illiterate but physically strong, would proceed along a wild and precipitous path (for the house was perched on a cliff) ahead of the man whose astrological skill Tiberius had decided to put to the test. On the return journey, the freedman, if any suspicion had arisen that the man had no ability or was a fraud, would hurl him down into the sea below, so he should not survive as witness to Tiberius' secret.

Now, Thrasyllus had been led along the same rocky path, and he had impressed Tiberius, when he questioned him, by cleverly revealing his forthcoming reign and events in the future. He was then asked if he had discovered the hour of his own birth, and what sort of year, and what kind of day, he was then having. Thrasyllus calculated the positions and distances of the planets, and first of all hesitated, but then grew fearful. The more he looked into the matter, the more agitated he became in his surprise and fear, until he finally cried out that he was threatened with a situation that was dangerous and virtually fatal. At that Tiberius threw his arms around him and congratulated him on his foreknowledge of his dangers, which he would now avoid. The emperor took predictions he had made as having oracular authority, and he kept Thrasyllus as one of his closest friends.

22. When I listen to this and other such stories, I am undecided whether the affairs of human beings evolve by fate, and an immutable inevitability, or by chance. Indeed, you will find disagreement on this amongst the greatest sages of antiquity and the adherents of their schools.* Many have the belief ingrained in them that our beginnings and our end, and, in fact, humankind in general, are of no concern to the gods, and that this explains why misfortune frequently comes upon the good, while the worse sort enjoy prosperity. Others, by contrast, think that fate accords with events, but that it is not influenced by wandering stars, that rather it follows the principles and sequences of natural causation. These people do, however, leave us free to choose our lives—but the choice once made, there is a fixed order for future events. They also disagree with the common interpretation of bad and good. Many who seem to be struggling with misfortune are happy, they contend, whereas some people are absolutely miserable in the midst of great wealth—the result of courage in bearing hardship in the former case, and foolishness in the use of prosperity in the latter.

However, the notion that a person's future is marked out at the moment of birth cannot be dispelled from the minds of most human beings. They believe that things turning out differently from what was predicted is due to the chicanery of false prophets, and that this is the reason for the loss of confidence in an art for whose validity both antiquity and our own day provide clear proof. For the prediction of Nero's reign* that was made by this same Thrasyllus' son* will be related in due course, so that I do not at this time digress too far from my subject.

23. In this same consulship news spread of the death of Asinius Gallus.* That he died from starvation was not in doubt; what was thought uncertain was whether it was voluntary or forced on him. When asked if he would allow burial for him, the emperor did not blush to grant his permission—nor indeed to deplore the circumstances that had taken the defendant off before he could be convicted in his presence! Naturally, there had not been enough time in the past three years for this aged ex-consul, father of numerous ex-consuls, to be brought to trial!

Drusus' death* came next; he had kept himself alive for eight days on a wretched diet, eating the stuffing from his bed. Some have recorded that Macro had been given orders, in the event of an armed uprising being attempted by Sejanus, to take the young man out of detention—he was being held in the Palatium—and set him up as the people's leader. Presently, as a rumour spread of the emperor's forthcoming reconciliation with his daughter-in-law and grandson, he chose brutality over a change of heart.

24. Tiberius went further and cast slurs on the dead man, charging him with sexual perversions and planning murder within his family and treason towards the state. He also ordered the daily record that had been kept of Drusus' actions and words to be read out, and that seemed the cruellest stroke of all. That men had been at Drusus' side for so many years to take note of his expression, his sighs, and even a suppressed murmur, and that his grandfather could have heard all this, and read it and made it public—it simply beggared belief. But it was borne out by the letters of the centurion Attius and the freed-man Didymus, which gave the names of all the slaves who had beaten and terrorized Drusus whenever he tried to leave his bedroom. The centurion had even subjoined, as something creditable, his own remarks at the time, which were full of savagery, along with Drusus' dying words. At first Drusus had begun to aim some maledictions against Tiberius, apparently in a fit of madness, but then, as he lost hope of remaining alive, his curses became studied and carefully worded. Just as Tiberius had murdered his daughter-in-law, his brother's son, and his grandchildren, and had filled his entire house with carnage, so, Drusus prayed, may he too pay the penalty to their ancestors' name and family-line, and to posterity.

There were repeated remonstrations from the senators, seemingly to ward off the curse, but in reality fear and amazement were sinking into their hearts. This man had earlier been cunning and secretive in the concealment of his crimes, they thought; but now he had reached such a pitch of confidence as to take away the walls, so to speak, revealing his grandson beneath a centurion's whip, and facing punches from slaves, as he begged in vain for the final necessities of life!

25. That painful episode had not yet faded when news came of Agrippina.* After Sejanus' death I think she had lived on buoyed by hope, and then, as there was no let-up in Tiberius' savagery, she took her own life—unless perhaps she was refused food to produce a death that could be taken for suicide. Tiberius, it is true, flared up

with the foulest reproaches against her, charging her with moral turpitude,* with Asinius Gallus as her lover, and claiming that it was Gallus' death that had made her tired of life. (In fact, Agrippina, intolerant of equality and yearning for power, had thrown off female weaknesses and developed masculine ambitions.) Tiberius added that she had died on the same day that Sejanus had paid his penalty two years earlier, and that this was something that should be recorded. He also congratulated himself on the fact that she had not been strangled and thrown on the Gemonian Steps. Official thanks were given to him for that, and a decree was passed authorizing the consecration of an offering to Jupiter every year on 18 October, the anniversary of the two deaths.

26. Not much later Cocceius Nerva, a constant companion of the emperor, and an expert in all divine and secular law, took the decision to die, though his position was secure and he was in good health. When Tiberius learned of it, he sat at Nerva's bedside, asked his reasons, added entreaties, and finally admitted that it would be hard on his conscience, and hard on his reputation, if his closest friend should run away from life when he had no reasons for dying. Nerva refused to converse and persisted in abstaining from food. Those familiar with his thought processes claimed that anger and fear, arising from the closer view he had of the ills of the state, had made him wish for an honourable end, while he was still safe and not yet under attack.

Barely credible though it is, the destruction of Agrippina dragged Plancina* in its wake. She had once been married to Gnaeus Piso, and had openly shown pleasure over Germanicus' death; and during Piso's downfall her protection had come from Augusta's pleas for her, and no less from the antipathy of Agrippina. When hatred and influence ceased to act, justice prevailed. Arraigned for crimes that were well known,* she paid with her own hand a penalty that was late in coming rather than undeserved.

27. While the city mourned so many grievous events, a part of its sorrow was for the marriage of Drusus' daughter Julia,* formerly wife of Nero, into the house of Rubellius Blandus, whose grandfather many remembered as a Roman knight from Tibur.

At the year's end, the death of Aelius Lamia* who, finally released from his chimerical governorship of Syria, had become city prefect, was honoured with a censor's funeral. He had a famous family, and an active old age, and not being allowed to administer the province had added to his stature. Then, on the death of Flaccus Pomponius,* propraetor of Syria, a letter from the emperor was read out in which Tiberius complained that all the finest men who were fit to command armies declined the office. He was thus, out of necessity, driven to entreaties, he said, in the hope that some of the former consuls might be pushed into taking on provinces. He was evidently forgetting that it was now the tenth year that Arruntius was being held back* from proceeding to Spain.

That year also saw the death of Marcus Lepidus,* to whose judicious and discerning character I have assigned sufficient space in earlier books. Nor does his noble background require further elucidation: the family of the Aemilii has produced good citizens in abundance, and even the corrupt characters from that family still enjoyed outstanding fortunes.

28. In the consulship of Paulus Fabius and Lucius Vitellius,* the phoenix* came to Egypt, after a long cycle that lasted centuries, and this offered the greatest scholars of the native Egyptians and the Greeks scope for lengthy treatises on that miraculous phenomenon. My aim here is to present particulars on which they agree, as well as a greater number that are controversial but not too far-fetched for notice.

That the phoenix is a creature sacred to the sun, and one differing from all other birds in the shape of its beak and the peculiarities of its plumage, is something agreed upon by all who have described its features. On the number of years between its appearances, accounts vary. The most common is a period of five hundred years, but some insist on an interval of 1,461 years. These claim that the earlier birds first flew to the city called Heliopolis during the reign of Sesosis,* then in that of Amasis, and afterwards in that of Ptolemy (the third Ptolemy of the Macedonian dynasty). The phoenix, they claim, was then attended by a large flock of birds of all the other species, which were astonished by its strange appearance. What happened in antiquity is unclear; but between Ptolemy and Tiberius was a period of less than two hundred and fifty years. Some people have for this reason believed that the bird in this case was a false phoenix, one not originating in the lands of the Arabs, and that it did none of the things that ancient tradition claims for it, which are as follows. After it has completed the sum of its years and death is approaching, it builds a nest in its own lands and pours over it a procreative force, from which arises its offspring. The young bird's first concern, when grown, is to bury its father, which is not done without great care. It picks up a load of myrrh, and tries out its strength carrying it on a long journey; when it is equal to its burden and equal to its journey, it picks up the father's body and takes it to the altar of the sun and cremates it. These particulars are uncertain and exaggerated by mythical elements; but there is no doubt about the bird's occasional appearance in Egypt.

29. In Rome the slaughter went on. Pomponius Labeo, whom I mentioned above* as governor of Moesia, cut open his veins and let out his lifeblood, and his wife Paxaea followed his example. (Fear of the executioner occasioned the ready acceptance of such deaths, as also did the fact that condemned men had their property confiscated and were forbidden burial—those taking the initiative themselves received burial of their bodies, and the continued validity of their wills, as a reward for expediting matters.) Tiberius, however, in a letter to the Senate, observed that it had been their ancestors' custom to forbid a person entry to their home whenever they broke off friendships, and that this gesture ended the amicable relations. That is what he had tried to do in Labeo's case, he said. Labeo, however, charged with malfeasance in his province and other crimes, had tried to cover up his own guilt by fomenting resentment against him, and had needlessly frightened his wife, who faced no danger, guilty though she was.

Then Mamercus Scaurus was arraigned for a second time, a man who was distinguished for his noble background and forensic oratory, but dissolute in his personal life. His downfall had nothing to do with Sejanus' friendship, but rather with the hatred of Macro, which was just as deadly (for he practised the same arts, but with greater secrecy). Macro had laid information regarding the plot of a tragedy that Scaurus had written, but he had also specified in the accusation some verses* that could be applied to Tiberius. However, the charges brought against Scaurus by the informers Servilius and Cornelius were adultery with Livilla* and magical rites. Scaurus, in a manner befitting the Aemilii of old, forestalled his condemnation, egged on by his wife Sextia, who encouraged, and shared, his death.

30. And yet accusers were also punished, if an opportunity arose. Servilius and Cornelius, infamous for ruining Scaurus, were removed to islands and 'forbidden fire and water' for having accepted payment

from Varius Ligus to drop a denunciation. Then there was the former aedile Abudius Ruso. He was actually threatening to bring a charge against Lentulus Gaetulicus* (under whom he had commanded a legion) for having intended to make Sejanus' son his son-in-law, when he was himself condemned and banished from the city.

At that time Gaetulicus was commander of the legions in Upper Germany, and he had gained his men's affection to a remarkable degree for his excessive clemency and his tempered discipline. Through his father-in-law Lucius Apronius* he was also popular with the neighbouring army. Hence the persistent rumour that he dared to send a letter to the emperor noting that his relationship with Sejanus had not been *his* idea but one suggested by Tiberius. It was as easy for him to be duped as Tiberius, he reportedly argued, and for the same mistake not to harm the emperor but to prove deadly for others was wrong. His loyalty was intact and would remain so, if he were not the target of plotting—but a successor he would accept as indicating a death sentence. They should strike a treaty, as it were, whereby the emperor would remain in control of everything else while Gaetulicus retained his province.

This is an amazing story, but it gained credibility from the fact that Gaetulicus was the only person connected with Sejanus to remain unharmed and in high regard; for Tiberius reflected on the hatred the people felt for him, his very advanced age, and the fact that his position now rested more on reputation than actual strength.

31. In the consulship of Gaius Cestius and Marcus Servilius, some Parthian noblemen came to Rome without King Artabanus' knowledge.* Fear of Germanicus had kept Artabanus loyal to the Romans, and fair in his dealings with his own people, but presently he began to exhibit arrogance towards us and brutality towards his countrymen. His confidence came from success in his wars with the surrounding peoples, but he was also contemptuous of the aged Tiberius,* whom he considered incapable of fighting. Furthermore, he coveted Armenia, over which he had installed the eldest of his children, Arsaces, on the death of its king Artaxias (adding the insult of sending men to reclaim the treasure left by Vonones in Syria and Cilicia). At the same time he would boast about the ancient boundaries of Persia and Macedonia, and make blustering threats about invading the territories held first by Cyrus and later by Alexander.

Amongst the Parthians the strongest proponent of this secret mission was Sinnaces, famed for his family and wealth alike, and next after him was Abdus, a man who had been castrated (a condition not looked down upon amongst barbarians, and which actually confers authority). Other leading Parthians were also enlisted, and because they were unable to put any member of the Arsacid family on the throne, most having been put to death by Artabanus, or not yet grown to manhood, they urgently requested that Phraates, son of King Phraates, be sent from Rome. There was need only of a name and the authorization, they said, for an Arsacid descendant to be seen on the bank of the Euphrates, if such was Tiberius' will.

32. That was what Tiberius wanted. He gave Phraates the insignia and assistance needed to assume his father's high position, thus maintaining his policy of transacting foreign affairs by strategic planning and intrigue,* and avoiding armed confrontation. Artabanus, meanwhile, had discovered the plot. He was at one moment held back by fear, and at the next he was aflame with desire for revenge; and in the eyes of barbarians hesitation is a servile reaction, and immediate response a kingly quality. However, pragmatism prevailed. Inviting Abdus to dinner under the pretence of friendship, Artabanus caught him in his trap with a slow-working poison, while he delayed Sinnaces with deception and gifts, and also by keeping him occupied. Moreover, in Syria, Phraates abandoned the Roman lifestyle, to which he had been habituated for many years, and adopted Parthian customs, but he was insufficiently robust for his ancestral regime, and he died from a disease.

Tiberius, however, did not abandon his plans. He selected Tiridates (a member of the same family) to be Artabanus' rival; and for the recovery of Armenia he chose the Iberian Mithridates, effecting a reconciliation for him with his brother Pharasmanes, who was the sovereign in their country. He made Lucius Vitellius overall supervisor of the operations in the East.

As regards Vitellius, I am not unaware of his sinister reputation in Rome, and the many unsavoury stories told about him, but his provincial administration was characterized by old-time integrity. After his return, out of fear of Gaius Caesar and then because of friendship with Claudius, he lapsed into a disgusting servility, to become for following generations an example of shameful sycophancy.

His early career is overshadowed by its end, the noble actions of his youth wiped out by the scandals of his old age.

33. Of the petty kings, Mithridates moved first, inducing Pharasmanes to support his efforts with trickery and force, and men were found to bribe Arsaces' attendants (with a large amount of gold) to commit the crime.* At the same time the Iberi invaded Armenia with a powerful force and took possession of the town of Artaxata. When news of this was brought to Artabanus, he equipped his son Orodes* to exact his revenge, giving him Parthian troops and sending men to hire auxiliary forces. Pharasmanes' response was to make an alliance with the Albani and send for help from the Sarmatians—whose satraps then followed their national policy of accepting gifts from the two parties and supporting both sides of the conflict. The Iberi, however, had the territorial advantage, and they swiftly sent their Sarmatians pouring into Armenia by the Caspian route. Those coming to the aid of the Parthians were easily repulsed, however. The enemy had blocked all approaches apart from the one between the sea and the outermost Albanian mountains, and that was impassable in summer because the shallows are flooded by the Etesian gales. (In winter, the south wind rolls back the waves and with the consequent receding of the sea a narrow strip of shoreline is left exposed.)

34. Orodes was thus short of allies. Pharasmanes, strengthened now with his reinforcements, proceeded to challenge him to engage and, when he refused battle, to harass him, riding up to his camp and plundering his sources of forage. Often he would surround him with outposts, as though blockading him, until the Parthians, unused to such insults, crowded around their king and demanded battle.

The Parthians had strength only in their cavalry; Pharasmanes also had powerful infantry. For, living as they did in forested areas, the Iberi and Albani had become more attuned to a life of hardship and endurance. They claim also to be descended from the Thessalians, this dating back to when Jason, some time after he had taken Medea away and had children by her, returned to the empty palace of Aeetes and Colchis, which now lacked a king. They celebrate the name of Jason in many ways and maintain an oracle of Phrixus,* where nobody would sacrifice a ram since it is believed that it was a ram—whether a real animal or the figurehead of his ship—that brought Phrixus there.

When the battle-lines had been deployed on both sides, the Parthian king addressed his men on their empire in the East, and the fame of the Arsacids, which he contrasted with the unknown Iberi and their mercenary forces. Pharasmanes for his part declared that his people were free from Parthian domination. The greater their aims, the more glorious would be their victory, he said; but should they turn to flight, the greater would be their disgrace and peril. At the same time he pointed out to them their own menacing battle-line, and the gold-embroidered columns of the Medes—men on this side, he said, booty on that.

35. In fact, the leader's voice was not the only one to be heard amongst the Sarmatians; they were all encouraging one another, saying they should not let it become a battle of arrows—better to anticipate that by charging and fighting at close quarters! As a result, the battle took on a variety of forms. The Parthians, practised in pursuing and retreating with equal skill, spaced out their squadrons, seeking space for discharging arrows; the Sarmatians put aside the bow (theirs had a shorter range) and charged with lances and swords. At one moment it resembled a cavalry battle, with attacks from front and rear in turn. At other times, when the two lines came together, men drove forward, or were driven back, using their bodily force and thrusting their weapons.

By now the Albani and Iberi were also grappling with their enemy, unseating the riders and so making it a twofold battle for them, since they had the cavalry attacking from above and the infantry inflicting wounds at closer range.

Meanwhile Pharasmanes and Orodes stood out prominently as they brought support to the valiant and assistance to the irresolute, and the two recognized each other. With a shout, with weapons poised and with horses galloping, they clashed, but Pharasmanes with greater force, for he inflicted a wound on his adversary through his helmet. He could not repeat the action as he was swept ahead by his horse, and the bravest of his enemy's bodyguards offered protection to the wounded man. Nevertheless, a false report that Orodes had been killed was believed, and this terrified the Parthians, who conceded victory.

36. Shortly afterwards, Artabanus threw all his kingdom's resources into seeking revenge. The fighting favoured the Iberi, because of their knowledge of the region, but Artabanus was not,

even so, ready to withdraw. Vitellius, however, brought his legions together and circulated a rumour that he was about to invade Mesopotamia, thus raising fears of a war with Rome. Armenia was then abandoned, and Artabanus' fortunes reversed, since Vitellius enticed the Parthians to abandon a king who was merciless in peace, and a disastrous failure in war. And so Sinnaces (whose earlier hostility I have already mentioned) drew into revolt his father Abdagaeses, along with others who had been secretly contemplating it, and who were then readier after the incessant Parthian defeats. Others gradually joined the movement, too, people who had been held in subjection through fear rather than goodwill, and who had plucked up courage when leaders were found.

Artabanes was now left with nothing other than some foreigners who formed his bodyguard—all of them exiles from their own homes, who had no understanding of decency, and no scruples about evil-doing, men who are kept and paid as abetters in crime. Taking these along, he made a hurried flight into the distant areas next to Scythia, hoping to find help there because he had marriage ties with the Hyrcanians and Carmanians. He thought, too, that the Parthians, ever sympathetic towards the absent and fickle towards those present, could change and regret their actions.

37. With Artabanus in flight, and the attention of his countrymen turned towards a new king, Vitellius urged Tiridates to seize the opportunity offered him, and led the core of the legionary and allied troops to the bank of the Euphrates. There they sacrificed, Vitellius making the traditional Roman offering of the *suovetaurilia*,* while Tiridates adorned a horse for placating the river. During the ceremony the local people reported to them that, although there had been no heavy rainfall, the Euphrates was spontaneously rising to an extraordinary height, and that it was forming circles of white foam in the shape of a diadem, which was an omen of a successful crossing. Others were more ingenious in their interpretation, arguing that the initial stages of the operation would be successful but success would be short-lived. Portents coming from the earth or sky were more reliable, they said, whereas the changeable character of rivers meant that they revealed, and then swept away, the omens.

A pontoon bridge was constructed and the army taken over. The first to come to their camp, at the head of several thousand cavalry, was Ornospades, a former exile who had assisted Tiberius, not without glory, during his mopping up of the Dalmatian war,* for which he had been awarded Roman citizenship. Subsequently, he had regained his king's friendship and was held in great honour by him, being made governor of the plains that were given the name 'Mesopotamia' because they are enclosed by the famous Euphrates and Tigris rivers.

Shortly afterwards Sinnaces augmented their troops, and Abdagaeses, the pillar of their side, contributed his royal treasure and appurtenances. Vitellius considered it sufficient just to have made a display of Roman arms, and he left Tiridates and the leading noblemen of his force with a word of advice. Tiridates should keep in mind his grandfather Phraates and his foster-father Tiberius, and the fine qualities of the two men, he said; and the others should maintain their obedience to their king, their respect for us, and their individual honour and loyalty. With that, Vitellius returned to Syria with his legions.

38. I have here put together the events of two summers so that the reader's mind can have some respite from domestic tragedies. For in Tiberius' case, despite three years having passed since Sejanus' killing, the things that normally soften other people—time, entreaties, saturation—did not appease him, and stop him inflicting punishment in cases that were dubious, or far in the past, as though they were extremely serious and of recent date. From fear of this, Fulcinius Trio* refused to await the threats of his accusers, and in his will he put together numerous vicious attacks on Macro and the leading imperial freedmen. Tiberius himself he charged with being mentally decrepit from senility, and virtually living in exile with his continuous absence. These allegations were covered up by Trio's heirs, but Tiberius ordered them read out—parading his tolerance of others' freedom of expression, and showing indifference to his own bad reputation. Or perhaps, after his long ignorance of Sejanus' crimes, he preferred to have remarks about him made public, no matter what was said, and so become informed, even through insults, of the truth that flattery impedes.

During those same days a senator, Granius Marcianus, who had been arraigned for treason by Gaius Gracchus, violently ended his own life, and an ex-praetor, Tarius Gratianus, was condemned to capital punishment under the same law.

39. The deaths of Trebellenus Rufus and Sextius Paconianus were not dissimilar from these. Trebellenus fell by his own hand, and

Paconianus was strangled in prison for verses that he composed there against the emperor. Tiberius received news of these cases, not when he was cut off by the sea, as he had been earlier, nor through messengers travelling from afar. He had taken up a position near the city,* so that, on that same day, or after the interval of a night, he could answer the letters of the consuls, while he was virtually looking upon the private homes awash with blood, and the work of his executioners.

At the year's end Poppaeus Sabinus left this life. He was a man of humble background who, through his friendship with emperors, had gained the consulship and triumphal honours and had, over a period of twenty-four years, been put in command of the most important provinces. This was not through outstanding ability on his part, but simply through being up to the task and no more.

40. The consulship of Quintus Plautius and Sextus Papinius followed. That year neither the fact that Lucius Aruscius* <. . .> were put to death was regarded as frightful, since people were habituated to misery, but what did cause terror was the fate of Vibullius Agrippa, a Roman knight. Right in the Curia, when his accusers had finished their summing up, he drew poison from a fold in his clothing and drained it. Collapsing, he was, in his death throes, rushed off to prison by the swift hands of the lictors, and there was strangled with the noose, although he was already dead. Even Tigranes,* former ruler of Armenia and then facing trial, was not saved by his royal title from the punishments faced by citizens. The ex-consul Gaius Galba,* however, and the two Blaesi* died by suicide, Galba because he had been kept from the sortition for his province by a grim letter from the emperor. In the case of the Blaesi, priesthoods had been earmarked for them when their family was intact, but Tiberius had suspended them after its collapse, and then conferred them on others as though they were vacant. This they took as a death sentence, which they executed. Then there was Aemilia Lepida,* whom I have mentioned as the wife of the young Drusus. She had tormented her husband with repeated accusations and, detestable though she was, she went on living unpunished while her father Lepidus survived. Later she was attacked by informers for adultery with a slave, and there was no doubt about her guilt. She therefore abandoned her defence and ended her life.

41. At about the same time as this, the Cietae, a tribe subject to Archelaus of Cappadocia,* withdrew to the heights of the Taurus

range because they were being forced to follow our system of returning census figures and submitting to tribute payment. There, because
of the nature of the terrain, they successfully defended themselves
against the feeble troops of the king, until the legate Marcus
Trebellius was sent by Vitellius, governor of Syria, with four thousand legionaries and some elite auxiliary troops. Trebellius threw
earthworks around the two hills that the barbarians had occupied (the
smaller called Cadra, the other Davara), and forced them to capitu-
late—those daring to make a sortie, with the sword, the others, by
thirst.

Tiridates* meanwhile, with the agreement of the Parthians, took
possession of Nicephorium, Anthemusias, and the other cities
which, though founded by the Macedonians, have Greek names. He
also took over the Parthian towns of Halus and Artemita. And the
inhabitants of these places were overjoyed: Artabanus, brought up
amongst the Scythians, they had hated for his ruthlessness, and now
they hoped to find in Tiridates a good nature that derived from
Roman culture.

42. The greatest show of sycophancy came from the people of
Seleucia, a powerful, walled city which had not declined into bar-
barism but retained the character of its founder Seleucus. Three
hundred men, selected for their wealth or wisdom, form their Senate,
and the people have their own political prerogative. Whenever the
two are agreed, no attention is paid to the Parthian; when they are at
odds, each side calls for assistance against the opposition, and the
Parthian, being invited to help one of the two parties, dominates the
entire population. This had happened recently when Artabanus was
king. He, serving his own interests, had delivered the common
people up to the nobles; for the dominance of the people is close to
freedom, while the ascendancy of the few is closer to the arbitrary
rule of a king.

On this occasion, when Tiridates arrived the people of Seleucia
heaped on him the honours paid to their kings of old, and others more
lavish that were recent inventions. At the same time they poured
insults on Artabanus—an Arsacid on his mother's side, but in all else
degenerate! Tiridates transferred the government of Seleucia to the
people. He next considered the date for his coronation ceremony,
but meanwhile he received a letter from Phraates and Hiero, who
held the strongest provinces,* requesting a short postponement.

He decided to wait for these very powerful men, and in the meantime headed for the imperial capital, Ctesiphon. But as they continued to procrastinate, the Surena* bound Tiridates' head with the royal diadem, in traditional manner, before a large and appreciative crowd.

43. Had Tiridates now marched on the other tribes in the interior, the misgivings of the reluctant would have been crushed, and the whole population would have passed exclusively into his hands. But by besieging a fortress where Artabanus had stored his money and his concubines, he allowed time for the breaking of pacts. For Phraates and Hiero, and all the others who had not attended the coronation day celebrations, went over to Artabanus, some from fear, and some from jealousy of Abdagaeses, who now had the court and the new king under his control. Artabanus was discovered amongst the Hyrcanians, covered with filth, his bow providing his food.

At first he feared it was a trap; but when assured that the aim of the visit was the restoration of his rule, he was relieved and asked the reason for the sudden change. Hiero then railed against the immaturity of Tiridates. The kingship did not now belong to an Arsacid, he said. An empty title lay with a weakling softened by foreigners, and the power was really in the house of Abdagaeses.

44. With his long experience of ruling, Artabanus realized that, false in affection though they were, they were not faking their hatred. He delayed no longer than it took to muster Scythian auxiliaries, and then set off at a rapid pace, not giving his enemies time for tricks, or his friends time to change their minds. Nor had he altered his filthy appearance, hoping to win over the common people with pity. Nothing was left untried, not trickery and not entreaties, to entice the wavering and encourage the willing.

As Artabanus approached the environs of Seleucia with a large force, Tiridates, shaken by the report of his coming, and simultaneously by the man's presence, was torn by doubts. Should he march against him or protract the war by delay? Those who favoured battle and a speedy decision claimed that Artabanus' men were dispersed and exhausted from their lengthy march, and had not even united in spirit to obey him—they were, just recently, traitors and enemies to the very man they were once again supporting. Abdagaeses, however, advocated returning to Mesopotamia. There, using the river as a barrier, they could meanwhile call to their aid the Armenians, the

Elymaeans* and the other tribes to their rear. They could then put fortune to the test when they were reinforced by these allied troops, and any that the Roman commander might send. That was the suggestion that prevailed, since Abdagaeses wielded the greatest authority amongst them, and Tiridates was a coward in the face of danger. But their departure resembled a flight. It started with the tribe of Arabs,* but then the others also left for their homes or the camp of Artabanus, until Tiridates* returned to Syria with a few men and so relieved them all of any shame over deserting him.

45. That same year brought a serious fire upon the city, with a section of the Circus bordering the Aventine being burned down, along with the Aventine itself; but the emperor turned the loss into self-promotion by covering the costs of the houses and apartment buildings affected. A hundred million sesterces* were spent on that magnanimous act, and this was all the more gratifying to the people in that he was sparing with buildings of his own.* Even on behalf of the state he erected only two works, a temple to Augustus and the stage of the theatre of Pompey (and when these were completed he did not dedicate them, either disdaining popularity or from old age). Four of Tiberius' grandsons-in-law were appointed to assess each person's loss—Gnaeus Domitius, Cassius Longinus, Marcus Vinicius, and Rubellius Blandus—with Publius Petronius* added to the list as a nominee of the consuls. And, the result of individual creativity, various honours were devised and decreed for the emperor. Which ones he refused or accepted was unclear because the end of his life was near.

For not long afterwards the last consuls of Tiberius' reign, Gnaeus Acerronius and Gaius Pontius, took office, at a time when Macro was excessively powerful. Macro had never neglected Gaius Caesar's favour, but now he was courting it with greater enthusiasm every day. In fact, after the death of Claudia (whose marriage to Gaius I have mentioned*), Macro had pushed his own wife Ennia* into leading the young man on by feigning love for him, and then binding him to a promise of marriage. And Gaius would refuse nothing provided that he could gain power; for despite his mercurial temper he had nevertheless learned the arts of dissimulation in his grandfather's lap.

46. This was known to the emperor, and it made him hesitate over the transfer of the state. He wavered first between his grandchildren.

Drusus' son* was closer to him in blood and in terms of affection, but he had not yet entered puberty. Germanicus' son had a young man's strength, and the enthusiastic support of the people, which for his grandfather was a reason for hatred. Tiberius even considered Claudius, because he was at a settled age and had a keen interest in the liberal arts, but his diminished mental capacity stood in the way. If, however, a successor were sought outside the family, he feared that the memory of Augustus and the name of the Caesars would be open to ridicule and insult—for Tiberius was less concerned with popularity of the moment than with winning the approval of posterity. Subsequently his indecision and failing health left to fate the choice he could not make. He did, however, throw out some remarks to let it be understood that he had some insight into the future. His reproach to Macro that he was leaving a setting sun to look at one that was rising* was no abstruse riddle. And when Gaius was mocking Lucius Sulla in some casual conversation, Tiberius made the prediction that he would have all Sulla's vices and none of his virtues. On the same occasion, he embraced the younger of his grandsons with floods of tears and, seeing the other's grim expression, said: 'You will kill him, and another will kill you.'*

However, though his health was declining, Tiberius did not relax his debaucheries in any way, faking good health in his suffering. And he constantly ridiculed the physicians' skills and those people who, after the thirtieth year of their life, needed a stranger's advice in distinguishing what was good from what was harmful for their own bodies.

47. In Rome, meanwhile, the seeds were being sown even for post-Tiberian killings. Laelius Balbus had arraigned Acutia, former wife of Publius Vitellius, on a charge of treason. When she was found guilty, and the reward was being decreed to her accuser, the plebeian tribune, Junius Otho, used his veto, which precipitated hatred between the two men, and soon afterwards destruction for Otho. Then there was Albucilla,* notorious for her affairs with many men and once married to Satrius Secundus, who had disclosed the conspiracy. She was denounced for impiety towards the emperor, and linked with her in the charge as accomplices and as her lovers were Gnaeus Domitius, Vibius Marsus, and Lucius Arruntius. Of the distinction of Domitius I have spoken above; Marsus, too, was a man with ancestral honours and renowned for his learning. But records*

sent to the Senate indicated that Macro had overseen the examination of witnesses and the torture of slaves. And the fact that there was
no letter from the emperor against the men raised the suspicion—
given Macro's well-known antagonism towards Arruntius—that
much of the evidence had been made up when Tiberius was sick and,
possibly, unaware of the facts.

48. The result was that Domitius and Marsus prolonged their
lives, Domitius preparing his defence, and Marsus apparently determined to starve himself. Arruntius, when friends urged procrastina-
tion and delay, replied that the same course was not honourable for
everybody. His life had been long enough, he said, and he had no
regrets, apart from having tolerated an old age plagued by anxiety,
and facing ridicule and danger. Long hated by Sejanus, he was now
hated by Macro—it was always by one of the powerful—and not
from any fault of his own, but from his intolerance of iniquity.
Certainly, avoiding death was possible for the few days up to the
emperor's last moments—but how would he escape the youth of the
man waiting in the wings? After all his experience, Tiberius was still
shaken and transformed by the force of absolute power, he said.
Would Gaius Caesar, his boyhood barely at an end, and totally ignorant, or else brought up on evil, take a better course, with Macro as
his guide? Macro, who was chosen to crush Sejanus because he was
worse than him, and who had inflicted more crimes on the state than
Sejanus! Now he could foresee a harsher servitude, he said, and so he
wanted to escape the ills of the past and those to come. Uttering these
words in prophetic manner, he opened his veins.

That Arruntius did well in choosing death will be demonstrated
by what followed. Albucilla, after dealing herself a wound that
proved unsuccessful, was carried off to prison by order of the Senate.
The sentencing in the case of those who abetted her promiscuity was
that the ex-praetor Carsidius Sacerdos* was to be deported to an
island; Pontius Fregellanus was to lose his senatorial rank; and the
same punishment was decreed for Laelius Balbus. (The last of these
sentences, at least, was delivered with rejoicing, because Balbus was
seen as possessing a ferocious eloquence, and was ready to attack the
innocent.)

49. During those same days Sextus Papinius,* who came from a
consular family, chose a sudden and frightful end by throwing
himself down from a height. The motivation for this was attributed

to his mother. She had been divorced some time before and, by indulging him in his extravagant ways, had driven the young man into an impasse from which death was the only escape. She therefore stood accused in the Senate, where she grovelled before the members' knees and made a lengthy plea, appealing to the grief that all humans shared and the weaker spirit of women in such circumstances, and adding other sad and doleful remarks in the same pitiful strain. She was, nevertheless, banished from the city for ten years, to allow time for her younger son to exit from the slippery years of youth.

50. By now Tiberius' body and strength were failing him, though not yet his dissimulation. His inflexible will was unaltered; and, firmly controlling his conversation and looks, he would sometimes try to conceal his evident decline with contrived affability. After numerous changes of residence,* he finally settled in a villa which Lucius Lucullus had once owned, on the promontory of Misenum. There the fact that he was nearing the end was discovered in the following manner.

There was a doctor called Charicles who was well known for his skill and who, while not regularly employed in treating the emperor's illnesses, made himself available to him for consultation. When Charicles was leaving, ostensibly to conduct some private business, he grasped Tiberius' hand as a mark of respect and felt his pulse, though he did not fool him in doing so. For Tiberius, possibly offended and so concealing his anger all the more, ordered the banquet to be renewed and reclined at the table longer than he usually did, as if to honour his departing friend. Charicles even so assured Macro that Tiberius' breathing was failing and that he would last no more than two days. All arrangements were then accelerated, with discussions held amongst those present, and messages sent to legates and armies. On 16 March his breathing failed, and he was thought to have ended his mortal existence; and, surrounded by a large crowd of well-wishers, Gaius Caesar was going out to initiate his reign when, suddenly, word came that Tiberius' voice and vision were returning and that people were being called on to bring food to revive him after his fainting spell. At this there was total panic, and all fled in various directions, everyone feigning grief or ignorance—all but Gaius. Frozen in silence, he was now, after the highest hopes, anticipating the worst. Undaunted, Macro gave orders for the old man to be smothered by piling bedclothes on him,* and for people to leave the doorway. Thus, in the seventy-eighth* year of his life, Tiberius met his end.

51. His father was Nero, and on both sides he was descended from the Claudian house, although his mother, by various adoptions, passed into the Livian and then the Julian family. From earliest infancy he experienced the vicissitudes of fortune. His father was proscribed, and he went with him into exile. When he entered Augustus' house as a stepson, he faced competition from numerous rivals during the entire time that Marcellus and Agrippa, and then Gaius and Lucius Caesar, were figures of importance. Even his brother Drusus enjoyed greater popularity with the citizens. But he was on a particularly slippery path when he married Julia, and put up with, or avoided, his wife's promiscuity. Then, on his return from Rhodes, he occupied for twelve years the emperor's house that was now without heirs, and subsequently took control of the Roman empire for almost twenty-three years.

His character also saw different phases. The period he spent as a private citizen, or holding various commands under Augustus, was, both for his life and his reputation, a noble one. The interval while Germanicus and Drusus remained alive was one of secrecy and hypocrisy as he affected virtue. While his mother still lived he was a mixture of good and bad. He was atrocious in his brutality, but his lechery was kept hidden while he loved, or feared, Sejanus. In the end, he erupted into an orgy of crime and ignominy alike, when, with all shame and fear removed, he simply followed his own inclinations.

Books 7–10 are entirely lost.

BOOK ELEVEN

1. . . . for Messalina* thought that Valerius Asiaticus, who had twice been consul, was a former lover of Poppaea's, and at the same time she hankered after his gardens (these had been laid out by Lucullus, and Asiaticus was improving them in a singularly lavish manner). She therefore had Suillius* bring an accusation against the pair of them. Suillius was given an associate—Sosibius, the tutor of Britannicus.* Sosibius' role was to warn Claudius, apparently as a favour, to be wary of a power and wealth that was hostile to the imperial family. He would say that Asiaticus had been primarily responsible for Gaius Caesar's* assassination, that he had not been afraid to admit it in an assembly of the people—and was, in fact, seeking credit for the deed. He had gained notoriety in the city from it, his fame had spread through the provinces, and he was preparing a journey to the German armies—for, born in Vienne, he enjoyed the support of many powerful connections and had the means to incite the tribes of his country to insurrection.

Claudius enquired no further into the matter. He sent off the prefect of the praetorian guard, Crispinus,* and a body of troops, at maximum speed, as though to put down a rebellion. Asiaticus was found at Baiae by Crispinus; he was then put in irons and rushed to Rome.

2. Refused an audience with the Senate, Asiaticus was heard in private chambers, in Messalina's presence. Suillius accused him of corrupting the troops—Asiaticus had, through bribery and sexual misconduct with them, put them under obligation to commit all manner of crimes—then of adultery with Poppaea,* and finally of passive homosexuality. At that the defendant broke his silence and blurted out: 'Ask your own sons,* Suillius. They will tell you I'm a man!'

Proceeding then with his defence, his effect on Claudius was more marked, but he also drew tears from Messalina. As she slipped from the room to wipe them dry, she warned Vitellius not to let the accused man slip through his fingers. Messalina herself now rushed on with Poppaea's destruction, bribing people to drive her to suicide with the terrifying prospect of the dungeon. Claudius was unaware of this, so much so that when Poppaea's husband Scipio* dined with him a few days later, the emperor enquired why he had come to the table without his wife, and Scipio replied that she had passed away.

3. Now when Claudius sought his opinion on acquitting Asiaticus, Vitellius wept as he recalled their long-standing friendship, and the respect they had both had for the emperor's mother, Antonia. Then after reviewing Asiaticus' services to the state, including his recent military campaign against Britain,* and other things that seemed designed to arouse sympathy, Vitellius recommended that Claudius grant the man free choice over his means of death. And Claudius' announcement following this showed the same compassion.

When some urged him to accept starvation as a gentle exit from life, Asiaticus replied that he declined their kind advice, and he went ahead with his customary physical exercises, took a bath, and enjoyed a cheerful dinner. Then, remarking that his death would have been more honourable had it come from Tiberius' cunning or Gaius Caesar's fury rather than a woman's treachery and Vitellius' filthy mouth, he opened his veins. First, however, he visited his pyre, and ordered that it be moved to another location so that the shade from the trees not be diminished by the heat of the fire. Such was his nonchalance to the end!

4. The senators were convened after this, and Suillius proceeded to add to his list of victims some Roman knights surnamed Petra. The cause of their death was really that they had provided their house as a meeting place for Mnester and Poppaea. But the charge against one of them centred on a dream he had had at night. In this, it was alleged, the defendant had seen Claudius wearing a garland of wheat with the ears of wheat upside down, and then, on the basis of that image, he had predicted difficulties with the grain supply. (Some have recorded that the dream involved a vine-garland with whitening leaves, which was then interpreted as indicating the emperor's death at the end of autumn. What is not disputed is that it was as a consequence of some sort of dream that destruction was brought on the man and his brother.)

A decree was passed authorizing one and a half million sesterces and praetorian insignia for Crispinus. Vitellius proposed a further award of a million for Sosibius for help he was giving to Britannicus by his instruction and to Claudius by his advice. When Scipio was also asked his opinion he replied: 'Since I feel the same as everybody else about Poppaea's offences, just assume I say the same thing as everybody else'—an elegant compromise between conjugal love and his senatorial obligation.

5. After that Suillius' prosecutions were incessant and relentless, and many rivalled him in audacity; for the emperor's appropriating to himself all the functions of the laws* and magistrates had opened up fine opportunities for plunder. And there was nothing in the public marketplace so saleable as the perfidy of advocates. In fact, a distinguished Roman knight, Samius, gave Suillius four hundred thousand sesterces and, on discovering his collusion with the other party, fell on his sword in Suillius' house. Thus, on the initiative of the consul-designate Gaius Silius,* whose power and fall I shall relate at the appropriate point, the senators rose up together to demand the application of the Cincian law* which, enacted long before, forbade the acceptance of money or a gift for pleading a case.

6. There was a noisy protest from the people for whom this insult was intended. Then Silius launched a virulent attack on Suillius, with whom he had differences, citing examples of the orators of old who had considered the rewards of eloquence to be limited to their reputation and their standing with posterity. What would otherwise be the finest and greatest of the liberal arts was being degraded by vulgar transactions, he said, and even integrity could not remain intact when eyes were fixed only on the size of the profits. If lawsuits were conducted for no pay, they would be fewer. As it was, quarrels and accusations, hatred and injustices were being encouraged so that the corruption of the Forum could bring money to advocates, just as violent diseases brought fees to doctors. They should remember Gaius Asinius, Marcus Messala, and, more recently, Arruntius and Aeserninus. These had risen to the top of their profession without tarnishing their lives or their eloquence. When the consul-designate made such comments, others agreed, and a motion was prepared that would make offenders liable under the extortion law. Then Suillius, Cossutianus* and the rest of them could see that what was being arranged for them was not a trial—for they were clearly guilty—but punishment, and they stood around Claudius begging pardon for their past actions.

7. After Claudius nodded his assent, they proceeded to make their case. Who had such arrogance, they asked, as to suppose he could hope for eternal fame? Their service was providing practical

assistance for people and their affairs, they said, so that none would be at the mercy of the powerful through a shortage of advocates. And yet eloquence did not come without a cost: in order for a man to focus on the affairs of another, his own family concerns were neglected. Many made a living by military service, a number by agriculture; nobody sought an occupation unless there were some prospect of income. It was easy for Asinius and Messala, or the likes of Aeserninus and Arruntius, to assume their magnanimous attitude— the former loaded with the prizes of the wars between Antonius and Augustus, the latter heirs of wealthy families! But, they continued, they had their own examples to hand: the large fees that Publius Clodius or Gaius Curio* habitually received for their speeches. They themselves were senators of modest means seeking only peacetime remuneration at a time of tranquillity in the state. Claudius should consider the plebeians who had brilliant careers in oratory. Remove the fees earned from liberal studies and the studies, too, would perish.

The emperor thought these arguments, while less dignified, were not completely unfounded, and he limited fees that could be taken at ten thousand sesterces, with any exceeding that liable to prosecution for extortion.

8. I noted above* how Mithridates became king of Armenia, and was later imprisoned on the orders of Gaius Caesar. Now at about this time, on Claudius' advice, and relying on the support of Pharasmanes, the king returned to his kingdom. (Pharasmanes, king of the Iberi, was also Mithridates' brother, and he kept reporting to him that there was discord amongst the Parthians, and that with the supreme power in dispute less important matters were receiving no attention.)

In fact, Gotarzes had taken a number of ruthless measures, including the hasty murder of his brother Artabanus, together with Artabanus' wife and son. Fear then spread to everybody else, and they called in Vardanes. Vardanes, ever ready for a great enterprise, marched into the country, covering three thousand stades* in two days. Taking Gotarzes by surprise, he drove him out in terror, and showed no hesitation in seizing the closest prefectures, the Seleucians alone repudiating his authority. As these had also defected from his father, he was motivated by anger rather than by the needs of the moment, and became mired in the siege of a powerful city that was further strengthened by a river that served as a protective barrier, and by a wall and lines of supply. In the meantime Gotarzes, bolstered by assistance from the Dahae and the Hyrcanians, renewed the war, and Vardanes, forced to abandon Seleucia, moved his camp to the Bactrian plains.

9. Then, with the forces of the East divided and unsure where to direct their support, Mithridates was given a chance to occupy Armenia: he had the powerful Roman infantry to destroy the highland strongholds and at the same time the Iberian troops scoured the plains. There was no resistance from the Armenians after the rout of their prefect, Demonax, who had risked an engagement. A slight delay was caused by Cotys, king of Armenia Minor, to whom a number of the chieftains had rallied, but he was then brought into line by a dispatch from Claudius. Everything now went in favour of Mithridates who, however, was harsher than was appropriate for a new regime.

As they were preparing for battle, however, the Parthian commanders suddenly concluded a treaty: they had learned of a conspiracy amongst their compatriots, which Gotarzes revealed to his brother. They came together, initially with some hesitation; then they clasped hands and swore before the altars of the gods to take revenge for the treachery of their enemies, and to make reciprocal concessions. Vardanes seemed the better choice for maintaining the kingdom; Gotarzes, so no trace of rivalry would remain, withdrew deep into Hyrcania. And when Vardanes returned, Seleucia surrendered to him six years* after its defection, bringing disgrace on the Parthians, whom a single city had flouted for so long.

10. Vardanes then visited the strongest prefectures. He longed to recover Armenia, but was stopped by Vibius Marsus, legate of Syria, who threatened him with war. Meanwhile, Gotarzes regretted having conceded the throne, and when the nobles (who find servitude harder to bear in peacetime) called him home, he mobilized an army. He was met by Vardanes' forces at the River Erindes, and there was a hard-fought battle during the crossing, from which Vardanes emerged the clear victor. Then, in a number of successful engagements up to the River Sindes, which forms the frontier between the Dahae and the Hyrcanians, Vardanes brought to heel the tribes between the two rivers. At that point a limit was placed on his success, for the Parthians, victors though they were, refused to

serve far from home. He therefore erected monuments as a testament to his power, and to the fact that tribute from those races had been won by none of the Arsacids* before him, and he went home with great glory—and was all the more arrogant and insufferable to his subjects because of it. These, indeed, after plotting together, caught him unawares while engrossed in a hunt and assassinated him. He was still in early manhood, but had a renown enjoyed by few long-lived monarchs—or would have, had he but sought affection amongst his own people as keenly as he sought to inspire fear in his enemies.

The Parthian situation was destabilized by the assassination of Vardanes, and there was uncertainty over an acceptable candidate for the throne. Many favoured Gotarzes, but some were for Meherdates, a descendant of Phraates, who had been given to us as a hostage. Gotarzes then emerged the winner. But after he gained the throne his ruthlessness and profligacy obliged the Parthians to send a secret entreaty to the Roman emperor begging for Meherdates to be allowed to assume his forefathers' throne.

11. It was during this same consulship* that the Secular Games* were put on, in the eight-hundredth year after Rome's founding, and the sixty-fourth after their staging by Augustus. The chronological calculations of the two emperors I pass over, since they were sufficiently covered in the books I devoted to the history of the emperor Domitian.* For Domitian also staged Secular Games, and I attended those with special interest since I had been accorded a quindecimviral priesthood and was then a praetor. I mention this not to boast, but because, from antiquity, that was the responsibility of the quindecimviral college, and the magistrates were the people especially charged with overseeing the ceremonial duties.

When Claudius was seated at the games in the Circus, boys from noble families put on the Game of Troy* on horseback. Amongst them was Britannicus, son of the emperor, and Lucius Domitius,* who would soon be taken by adoption into the ruling family, with the *cognomen* Nero. The support of the crowd, which was more enthusiastic for Domitius, was taken as an omen. It was also put about that snakes had looked after the boy like guardians during his infancy, a tall tale made up to match the wondrous stories of foreign nations. In fact, Nero, no man to downplay himself, used to recount that no more than one serpent was seen in his bedroom.

12. In reality, the support of the people arose from the memory of Germanicus,* whose sole male descendant Nero was. And sympathy for his mother Agrippina was heightened by the savagery of Messalina. She had always hated Agrippina, but was at that time particularly exasperated, being deterred from fabricating charges against her, and finding people to lay them, only by her new infatuation, which bordered on insanity. For she had developed a passion for Gaius Silius, the best-looking of Rome's young men, and so much so that she chased Junia Silana,* a woman of noble descent, from her marriage and then assumed possession of her now-unattached lover. Silius was not oblivious to the disgrace and risks involved; but refusal meant certain death, there was some chance of escaping notice, and at the same time the rewards were great. He therefore consoled himself with simply letting the future take its course and enjoying the present. As for Messalina, she made regular visits to the man's house, and not secretly, either, but with a large retinue; she hung on his arm when he came out of doors; and she lavished riches and honours on him. Eventually, it seemed as if there had been an exchange of fortunes, with the slaves, freedmen, and trappings of the emperor on view at the lover's house.

13. Claudius, oblivious to his matrimonial situation, was busy with his duties as censor. He passed strict edicts that chastised public misbehaviour in the theatre, because people had hurled abuse at the ex-consul Publius Pomponius (who presented verses on stage) and at some distinguished ladies. He produced legislation to curb the severity of creditors, forbidding them to lend young men* money at interest repayable on their fathers' deaths. He had spring water* diverted from the Simbruine hills and brought into the city. Furthermore, he added, and put into everyday use, new alphabetic letters,* after discovering that the Greek alphabet was also not begun and completed all at one time.

14. It was the Egyptians who first gave written form to ideas, using representations of animals. These are the most ancient documents in the history of mankind, and are still to be seen engraved on stones. And the Egyptians lay claim to being the inventors of letters, saying that it was from Egypt that the Phoenicians—because of their dominance at sea—brought them to Greece, winning the renown of having discovered what in fact they had taken from them. For the story goes that Cadmus* initiated the still-barbarous Greek peoples in this art, after arriving with a Phoenician fleet. Some have it that the Athenian Cecrops, or the Theban Linus (or even the Argive Palamedes, at the time of the Trojans) invented sixteen letter forms, and that others—Simonides, in particular—later invented the others. In Italy, however, the Etruscans learned them from Demaratus the Corinthian, and the Aborigines from the Arcadian Evander; and the shape of the Latin letters is that of the most ancient Greek letters. But in our case, too, the letters were originally few in number, with additions made later. With this as his precedent, Claudius added three letters.* They were employed during his reign, but later fell out of use, though they are to be seen even today on bronze plaques set up for public display in the forums and temples.

15. Claudius next brought before the Senate the matter of establishing a college of soothsayers,* to prevent Italy's oldest art from falling into disuse through lack of practice. It had often happened, he said, that soothsayers had been called in when the state was in trouble, and through their advice ceremonies had been revived and more strictly observed for the future. Furthermore, the leading men of Etruria had, of their own accord or at the prompting of the Roman Senate, kept this branch of knowledge alive, and passed it down in certain families. Now less attention was being paid to it through the apathy of the people towards the noble arts, and because of the growth of superstitions from abroad. And while all was going well for the moment, they should show gratitude for the kindness of the gods, and see to it that sacred rites practised in times of crisis did not disappear when times are good. A decree of the Senate was therefore passed authorizing the pontiffs to examine which of the soothsayers' institutions should be retained and strengthened.

16. This same year the tribe of the Cherusci asked for a king appointed by Rome. Their nobility had been wiped out in civil wars, and there remained only one person of royal descent, a man called Italicus,* who was detained in the city. On his father's side, Italicus was the son of Arminius' brother Flavus,* and his mother was the daughter of Actumerus, chieftain of the Chatti. He was a good-looking man who had been trained in weaponry and horsemanship after both his and our ancestral manner. Claudius accordingly provided him with funds, gave him bodyguards in addition, and urged him to assume with confidence that position of honour amongst his own people. He was, said Claudius, the first man born in

Rome—and one not a hostage but a citizen—who was leaving to take up a foreign throne.

The initial German reaction to Italicus' arrival was one of joy, and he was fêted with praise and honour because, untainted by their quarrels, he was equally affable in his dealings with everybody. Sometimes his behaviour was marked by courtesy and restraint— qualities disliked by no one—more often with drunkenness and lechery, qualities that appeal to barbarians. As his fame now began to grow amongst those close by, and then further afield, the men who had flourished during the periods of factional strife became suspicious of his power. They went off to the neighbouring peoples proclaiming that the old independence of Germany was being taken from them and Roman power was on the increase. Was there really no one born in those same lands of theirs capable of filling that supreme office, they asked, without the offspring of Flavus the scout having to be elevated above everyone? There was no point in appealing to Arminius' name. Even if it had been *his* son coming to the throne after growing up on enemy soil, there could still have been grounds for fear since the boy would have been tainted with foreignness in everything—in his upbringing, his servility, and his dress. But suppose Italicus had the mentality of his parent—no one else had made war more aggressively on his own country and the gods of his home than his father had.

17. With these and other such arguments they amassed mighty forces, and Italicus could count no fewer on his side. For, he would remind them, he had not forced himself on them against their will, but had been invited because he surpassed all others in noble birth— and they should put his courage to the test to see if he was worthy of his uncle Arminius and his grandfather Actumerus. And he felt no embarrassment for his father, either, for his unflagging loyalty to the Romans, which he had initially maintained with the approval of the Germans. And the word 'liberty' was being put forward as a specious pretext by men who, coming personally from low families, and being ruinous to the public cause, had no prospects except through civil discord.

Italicus received enthusiastic applause from the crowd, and in a great battle between the barbarian tribes he emerged the victor, but then because of his success he slipped into arrogance. He was driven out, and subsequently restored through the support of the Langobardi;

and whether things went well or badly for him, he continued to oppress the Cheruscan nation.

18. In this same period, having no dissension at home and in high spirits after the death of Sanquinius,* the Chauci made raids into Lower Germany while Corbulo* was still on his way. They were led by Gannascus, a Canninefate by race who had long served as an auxiliary, and had subsequently deserted. Now a privateer with some light vessels, he concentrated his depredations on the coastline of the Gauls, whom he knew to be rich, and poor fighters.

Corbulo entered the province with considerable caution, and soon began to acquire his renown (which actually began with that campaign). He brought his triremes* up the channel of the Rhine, and the rest of his ships by way of estuaries and canals, according to their capabilities. He sank the enemy boats and drove out Gannascus. After settling the present situation to his satisfaction, he restored to the legions—which had become slack vis-à-vis their duties and hard work, but loved to plunder—the old form of discipline that forbade anyone to leave the marching column or enter battle without orders. Outpost and sentry duty, and fatigues performed by day or night, were all conducted under arms, and they say that one soldier was punished with death for digging an earthwork unarmed, and another for doing so armed only with a dagger. These instances are extreme and may be false rumours, but they do derive from the commander's severity; and one can be sure that he was strict and inflexible in dealing with the serious misdemeanours when he was believed to be so hard on the trivial.

19. In fact, the terror Corbulo inspired impacted differently on our soldiers and the enemy: it meant increased courage for us, but a crushing of the barbarians' spirit. The Frisian tribe* had been openly hostile or undependable since the rebellion that began with the defeat of Lucius Apronius, but they now gave hostages and settled in the territory assigned to them by Corbulo, who also imposed on them a senate, magistrates, and a legal system. So they would not flout his instructions, he established among them a fortress with a garrison, and sent men to talk the Greater Chauci into surrender and also to set a trap to waylay Gannascus. And the ambush was neither unsuccessful nor dishonourable, targeting as it did a deserter who had broken his word. But there was a strong reaction from the Chauci to his killing, and it was now Corbulo who was sowing the seeds of

rebellion, news that was viewed favourably by some, but negatively by certain others. Why, they asked, provoke the enemy? A loss would damage the state; and if he were successful, a man thus distinguished would be a threat to the peace and an embarrassment to a cowardly emperor. Claudius accordingly forbade any new show of force against the German provinces, to the point of ordering the garrisons to be brought back west of the Rhine.*

20. The message was brought to Corbulo by letter as he was establishing his camp on enemy soil. The sudden blow prompted a flood of simultaneous considerations—fear of the emperor, the contempt that would come from the barbarians, the derision of the allies. But he said nothing more than 'Happy the Roman commanders of yesteryear!' and gave the signal to withdraw. However, to ensure the men had no time on their hands, he dug a canal, twenty-three miles in length, between the Mosa and the Rhine so the hazards of the ocean could be avoided. Claudius nevertheless bestowed triumphal insignia on Corbulo, although he had denied him the military operation.

Not long after this Curtius Rufus* was accorded the same honour. He had opened up a mine in the area of Mattium to search for veins of silver, but the proceeds were slim and not of long duration. For the legions it meant hard work, and financial loss,* too, as they dug out water channels and toiled underground on projects that would have been difficult in the open air. The soldiers were ground down by this, and because similar hardships were being experienced in a number of provinces, they wrote a secret letter in the name of all the armed forces, imploring the emperor to award triumphal honours in advance to officers to whom he intended to assign armies.

21. On the pedigree of Curtius Rufus, whom some have recorded to be a gladiator's son, I would not produce lies, and yet I am reluctant to go into the truth in detail. When he grew up, he became an attendant to a quaestor who had been allotted Africa as his province. In the town of Hadrumetum he was once spending some solitary moments in a portico, which was deserted in the middle of the day, when a vision* of a woman of superhuman stature appeared before him. 'Rufus,' she was heard to say, 'you are one who will come as proconsul into this province.' Encouraged in his expectations by such an omen, Curtius returned to Rome. There, through bribes put about by his friends and through his own sharp intelligence, he gained a quaestorship, and subsequently, on the imperial recommendation and despite being in competition with noble candidates, a praetorship. Tiberius, in fact, glossed over Rufus' shameful family background with the words 'Curtius Rufus seems to me a man born of his achievements'. He enjoyed a long old age after this, morosely sycophantic towards his superiors, arrogant towards his inferiors, and difficult with his peers. He gained consular power, triumphal insignia, and eventually Africa, where he died and fulfilled the prophecy of his destiny.

22. At Rome, meanwhile, for no apparent reason, and none that was later discovered, the Roman knight Gnaeus Nonius* was detected armed with a sword amidst those paying their respects* to the emperor. After his body-destroying torture began, he did not deny his own guilt, but did not name accomplices, though whether he was hiding any is unclear.

In the same consulship Publius Dolabella proposed the annual staging of a gladiatorial show* at the expense of men successful in their bid for the quaestorship. In the days of our ancestors magistracies had been awarded on merit, with all citizens allowed to seek office if they had confidence in their good qualities. There had not even been an age qualification* preventing men from taking up the consulship and dictatorships in the early years of manhood. Quaestors were first appointed when the kings were still in power, as the renewal of the *lex curiata** by Lucius Brutus* demonstrates. Their selection then remained the prerogative of the consuls until the people assumed the authority for assigning that office as well. The first elected quaestors* were Valerius Potitus and Aemilius Mamercus, in the sixty-third year after the expulsion of the Tarquins, and their function was to supervise military finances in the field. Then, as their official duties increased, two more were added with responsibilities confined to Rome. Their number was presently doubled as Italy became taxpaying and revenues also came in from the provinces. Later, under the legislation of Sulla,* twenty were elected as an addition to the Senate, to whose authority Sulla had transferred the law courts. And although the knights later recovered responsibility for the law courts, the granting of the quaestorship remained cost-free, and depended on the quality of the candidates or the indulgence of the electors—until it was more or less put on sale by Dolabella's motion.

23. In the consulship of Aulus Vitellius* and Lucius Vipstanus, there was debate over bringing up the numbers of the Senate, and the foremost men of the so-called 'Long-haired' Gaul*—who had acquired treaty privileges and citizenship* long before—requested the right to hold office in Rome. There was a lot of wide-ranging discussion of the matter. Before the emperor,* too, the issue was debated with much passion on both sides, some insisting that Italy was not so feeble that she could not provide her own capital with a senate. In the past, they said, rule by native Romans had been satisfactory for peoples who were related to them by blood, and nobody had any complaint about the republic of former times. In fact, people were still citing examples relating to virtue and achieving glory that the Roman character had produced through its old-time morality. Was it not enough that the Veneti and the Insubres had broken into the Curia, without the Romans now having a kind of captivity imposed on them with this tribe of foreigners? What honour would they be leaving for such as remained of the nobility, or for any senator of modest means coming from Latium? Those rich foreigners would swamp everything—those men whose grandfathers and great-grandfathers had commanded enemy tribes and cut down our armies in furious conflict, and besieged the deified Julius at Alesia!* But these were recent examples, they said; what about remembering those felled by the hands of the same people in the Capitol* and citadel of Rome? By all means let them enjoy being called citizens, but let them not cheapen the insignia of the Senate and the dignity of the offices of state.

24. The emperor was unmoved by these and similar comments. He immediately stated the opposite view, and he also convened the Senate* and proceeded to address them in the following manner:

'Of my own ancestors, the most ancient, Clausus,* was of Sabine origin, but he was accepted at the same time both for Roman citizenship and for membership in the patrician families of the city. Those ancestors therefore urge me to follow the same procedure in the administration of state policy, bringing here all that is excellent anywhere else. For I am not unaware that the Julii were admitted into the Senate from Alba, the Coruncanii from Camerium, and the Porcii from Tusculum, and that—not to be delving into ancient instances— men were admitted from Etruria, Lucania, and the whole of Italy. I am aware, too, that Italy itself was pushed forward to the Alps* so that whole lands and nations, and not just individual persons, might be brought together under our name. Then we had real peace* at home; and we faced foreign lands with strength when the Transpadanes were admitted to citizenship and when, under the guise of settling our legions in colonies* throughout the world, we resuscitated our weary empire by adding to it the strongest of the provincials. Surely we have no regrets about the Balbuses* having joined us from Spain, and men no less distinguished from Narbonese Gaul? Their descendants are still here, and they do not take second place to us in love for this country. What else was it that spelled destruction for the Spartans and the Athenians,* militarily powerful though they were, if not their segregation of conquered peoples as foreigners? By contrast, our founder Romulus showed such wisdom that he regarded numerous peoples as his enemies and then as his fellow-citizens on the very same day! Foreigners have ruled over us; and the granting of magistracies to the sons of freedmen is not something totally new, as many wrongly suppose, but was a practice of our people in the old days. "But we fought with the Senones," it is argued. Of course the Vulsci and the Aequi never deployed a battle-line against us! "We were captured by the Gauls!" But we also gave hostages to the Etruscans,* and passed under the yoke of the Samnites.* And yet, if one reviews all our wars, none was brought to an end in a shorter time than that against the Gauls,* since when there has been peace, uninterrupted and faithfully observed. Now they are integrated with us in culture, the arts, and family connections; let them bring us their gold and their wealth rather than keep it to themselves! Senators, everything that is now believed to be really ancient was once new. There were plebeian magistrates after patrician, Latin magistrates after plebeian, and magistrates of the other races of Italy after the Latin. This step will also become established, and what we are defending today with precedents will itself be amongst future precedents.'

25. A decree of the Senate followed the emperor's speech, and the Aedui* became the first to gain the right to become senators in Rome. This was granted them in view of their long-standing treaty,* and also because they are the only Gauls who retain the title of 'brothers' of the Roman people.

At about the same time Claudius admitted to the ranks of the patricians* all senators with long service or who had eminent parents. (By now few of the families that Romulus had designated 'Greater',* and those that Lucius Brutus had termed 'Lesser', were still in existence, and even those that the dictator Caesar had appointed as replacements under the *Lex Cassia*, and the emperor Augustus under the *Lex Saenia*,* were finished.) These duties, which were deemed to be in the interests of the state, were begun with great pleasure on the part of the censor.

Claudius was now concerned over how he could expel from the Senate those with a reputation for immorality, and he applied a clement and recently devised technique instead of the old-fashioned hard line. He advised these people to consider their own records, and then request permission to leave the senatorial rank. Permission would readily be given, he told them, and he would publish the names of those removed from the Senate alongside those who were excused. In this way, he said, the mixing of the negative judgement of the censors with the modesty of those retiring of their own volition would alleviate the shame.

In recognition of this, the consul Vipstanus proposed that Claudius be formally called 'Father of the Senate', for, he said, the title 'Father of the Nation' was held by others, too, and these new services to the state deserved to be honoured in terms not in regular use. Claudius, however, checked the consul, thinking his flattery too effusive. He also performed the census-purification,* at which time the count of the citizens* was 5,984,072.

This point also spelled the end of Claudius' ignorance about his family situation. Not long afterwards he was forced to take note of, and to punish, his wife's scandalous behaviour, and the outcome of this was a passion that would lead him to an incestuous marriage.*

26. The adulterous affair going too easily, Messalina became bored and began to drift into bizarre sexual practices. At this point Silius himself started to push for a swift end to their secrecy; either he was suffering from a fatal delusion, or he thought that the remedy for the dangers hanging over them lay in acts that were themselves dangerous. They had not come so far just to wait for the emperor's old age, he told her. To the innocent, planning ahead brought no harm; but when offences were in the open, assistance had to be sought from bold action. They had associates at hand who had the same fears as they. He himself was unmarried, childless, and ready to marry her and adopt Britannicus. Messalina's power would remain the same, he said, but safety would be added if they pre-empted Claudius, who was not on his guard against treachery but was swift to anger.

These remarks were received with little enthusiasm. This was not because of Messalina's love for her husband, but from fear that Silius, having reached the heights, would shun his lover, and would come to assess at its true value a crime to which he had given his approval only in time of peril. But she passionately desired the title 'wife' because the notion was utterly scandalous—and that, for the profligate, is the ultimate pleasure. Waiting only for Claudius to leave for Ostia* to hold a sacrifice, she went through a marriage ceremony with all its formalities.

27. I am well aware that it will seem incredible* that, in a city that knows all and conceals nothing, any members of the human race could have been so reckless. Even more incredible that a consul-designate, on a prearranged date and with signatories present, should have come together with an emperor's wife 'for the purpose of having legitimate children'! Incredible that she heard the words of the auspices, took vows, and sacrificed to the gods! That they took their places for dinner with guests, that there were kisses and embraces, and that they finally spent the night together freely as a married couple! But nothing in my account has been invented for sensationalism; it is what our elders heard and passed down in writing.

28. So a shudder had run throughout the emperor's court. In particular there were indignant protests—and no longer in hushed conversations, but openly expressed—from those with whom the power lay, and who would live in fear were there a change of regime. When an actor* had been defiling the emperor's bedroom, they said, an insult had certainly been delivered but there had been little prospect of destruction. Now a young nobleman cutting an elegant figure, possessed of a strong intellect, and with a consulship forthcoming was preparing for a greater prospect. For what lay beyond such a marriage was quite clear. There is no doubt that alarm swept over them as they thought about Claudius' naivety and his subservience to his wife, and about the many killings brought off on Messalina's orders. On the other hand the emperor's easygoing nature itself gave some reason for confidence that Messalina could be crushed, condemned before she was even tried—if they won him over first with the enormity of the charge. It was in whether her defence would be given a hearing that the danger lay, and in whether his ears could be closed to her even if she confessed.

29. Initially, Callistus*—whom I have already discussed in connection with the assassination of Gaius Caesar—came together with Narcissus,* who had engineered the murder of Appius,* and with Pallas,* who was then at the height of his influence. They discussed whether to use secret threats to divert Messalina from her passion for Silius while at the same time concealing everything else. Then two backed out, fearing that it might actually entail their own downfall, Pallas through faint-heartedness, and Callistus because he had also had experience of the previous regime, from which he was aware that power was more safely maintained by wary than by impetuous policies. Narcissus went ahead, making only one change: in no conversation would he let Messalina have any foreknowledge that she was being charged and who was accusing her.

Narcissus kept watching for an opportunity, and then while Claudius was on a prolonged stay in Ostia he induced two prostitutes, with whose sexual services Claudius had been very familiar, to take on the role of informers. He did that by financial rewards and promises, and by pointing out to them the increased power they would enjoy once the wife was removed.

30. Next Calpurnia (as one of the prostitutes was called) was given a private audience with Claudius. She flung herself before his knees and declared that Messalina had married Silius, and at the same time she asked Cleopatra, who was standing beside her waiting for the question, whether she had also learned of it. Cleopatra nodded and Calpurnia then requested that Narcissus be called.

Narcissus asked for Claudius' pardon for his past conduct in having concealed from him his knowledge of the likes of Titius, Vettius, and Plautius.* He then added that he would not make adultery an issue even on this occasion, in case Claudius set about demanding back his own home, his slaves, and all the other trappings of his station. No, Silius could have the benefit of those things, he said—but he should restore the wife and break the wedding tablets. 'Are you aware that you are divorced?' Narcissus asked him. 'For the people, the Senate, and the soldiers saw the wedding, and if you do not move quickly the husband controls the city.'

31. Claudius then called in his closest friends, and first of all interrogated Turranius,* prefect of the grain supply, and after him Lusius Geta,* who was in command of the praetorians. When these confessed the truth, the others all proceeded to shout each other down, urging Claudius to go to the camp, secure the praetorian cohorts, and see first to his security before his revenge. It is well established that Claudius was so overwhelmed with panic that, time after time, he asked if he was master of the empire, and if Silius was still a private citizen.

Messalina's extravagant behaviour was wilder than ever. Autumn was well advanced, and she was staging a tableau of the grape-harvest throughout the house. Presses were in operation, vats were overflowing, and there were women dressed in animal skins leaping about like maenads sacrificing or driven into a frenzy. Messalina herself, her hair streaming, brandished a thyrsus, and beside her was an ivy-garlanded Silius, wearing high boots and tossing his head, while all around them rose the din of a dissolute chorus. They say that, in fun, Vettius Valens* struggled up a very tall tree, and when people asked him what he saw he replied that there was a terrible storm in the area of Ostia. Perhaps such a thing had started to appear, or perhaps it was just a casual remark that became regarded as prophetic.

32. Meanwhile actual messengers—not simply a rumour—were coming in from all quarters to report that Claudius was aware of everything and that he was on his way, eager to exact vengeance. Messalina accordingly left for the Gardens of Lucullus and, to hide his fear, Silius left to take up his duties in the Forum. The others slipped away in all directions, centurions appeared, and any found in the streets or in hiding were put in irons. The setback prevented any planning, but Messalina boldly determined to meet and be seen by her husband—an approach that had often proved effective in the past—and she sent instructions for Britannicus and Octavia to go and embrace their father. She also begged Vibidia,* the senior of the Vestal Virgins, to seek an audience with the supreme pontiff and try to gain his mercy. Meanwhile, with only three companions—so alone did she suddenly find herself—she walked the whole length of the city and then set out on the road for Ostia on a cart employed for garden refuse. There was no pity from anyone; her atrocious crimes outweighed everything.

33. There was no less alarm on Claudius' part, for his men did not have much confidence in the praetorian prefect Geta, who was equally unreliable whether the cause were honourable or wicked. Narcissus therefore enlisted the support of others who harboured the same fears and declared that the only hope of saving Claudius' life

lay in the emperor transferring command of the troops, for that one day, to one of the freedmen; and he offered to take it on himself. Also, so that Claudius would not be influenced by Lucius Vitellius and Largus Caecina* to regret his decision on the return journey to Rome, Narcissus demanded a seat in the same carriage and was taken on board.

34. It was frequently reported later that the emperor's remarks were inconsistent, as at one moment he would berate his wife's scandalous conduct, but then he would occasionally lapse into recollections of his marriage and the early years of their children. Meanwhile, it was said, Vitellius murmured only, 'Ah, such a crime! Such villainy!' Narcissus pressed him to clarify his ambiguous remarks and let the truth be known, but succeeded only to the extent of having him reply with vague comments capable of being interpreted as required; and Caecina Largus followed his example.

Messalina was now in view and shrieking out that he should listen to the mother of Octavia and Britannicus. Her accuser shouted her down with the story of Silius and the wedding. At the same time, to take Claudius' eyes from her, he passed him some writing tablets that detailed her depravities. Shortly afterwards, as the emperor was entering the city, the children they shared were brought to him— but Narcissus had them removed. He could not, however, push to one side a highly indignant demand from Vibidia that a wife not be consigned to her death without a defence. He therefore replied that the emperor would hear her and she would have the opportunity of rebutting the charge. Meanwhile, the Vestal Virgin should go away and attend to her sacral duties.

35. During all of this Claudius maintained a strange silence, while Vitellius seemed stunned; and everything was passing under the freedman's control. Narcissus issued orders for the adulterer's home to be opened up and the emperor to be taken there. First he showed Claudius the statue of Silius' father* on display in the vestibule (though this had been banned by senatorial decree), and then pointed to all the heirlooms of the Nerones and Drusi* that had accrued to this household in payment for its depravity. Claudius was fuming, and broke into threats. Narcissus then took him to the camp, where an assembly of the troops had been arranged. At the prompting of the freedman, Claudius spoke briefly, for shame would not let him express his indignation, justified though it was. Then from the

cohorts came one long cry as they demanded the names of the mis-
creants and their punishment; and when Silius was brought before
the tribunal he did not try to defend himself or seek a delay, asking
only that his execution come quickly. The same resolution was also
found in some distinguished Roman knights. Claudius ordered the
following accomplices given over for execution: Titius Proculus,
appointed as guardian for Messalina by Silius and now offering to
denounce her; Vettius Valens, who confessed his guilt; Pompeius
Urbicus; and Saufeius Trogus. Decrius Calpurnianus, the prefect of
the watch, Sulpicius Rufus, procurator of a gladiator school, and the
senator Juncus Vergilianus also received the same penalty.

36. Only Mnester's case caused some hesitation. Tearing his
clothes, he cried out that Claudius should inspect his stripes from the
lash and remember the words he had used to make him subject to
Messalina's bidding. Others were guilty through bribery or excessive
ambition, he said, but he was so from necessity, nor would anyone
have been facing death earlier than he if Silius were in power. Claudius
was impressed by such arguments and was inclining towards mercy
when the freedmen prevailed upon him not to concern himself about
an actor when so many distinguished men had now been put to
death. Whether Mnester had acted of his own accord or under
coercion was irrelevant when the crime he had committed was so terrible, they said. Not even the defence of the Roman knight Traulus
Montanus was accepted. He was a decent but good-looking young
man who had actually been sent for by Messalina, and then pitched
out by her, in the space of a single night, for she was as fitful in taking
dislike as she was in developing a passion. Suillius Caesoninus* and
Plautius Lateranus* were spared the death penalty, Lateranus
because of his uncle's outstanding service. Caesoninus' protection
lay in his perversions: in that disgusting gathering he had played only
the woman's role.

37. Meanwhile, in the Gardens of Lucullus, Messalina was trying
to extend her life. She was drafting a plea, not without hope and with
bursts of anger—such was her pride even in this desperate situation!
And had not Narcissus accelerated her death, destruction would
have recoiled on the accuser. For on returning home Claudius had
been calmed by a protracted dinner, and when he felt the mellowing
effects of wine he ordered a man to go with a message for the 'poor
woman' (his exact expression, they say) that she should appear to

plead her case the following day. The words were noted. Anger was subsiding and love returning, and there was fear for the oncoming night and Claudius' reminiscing about his wife's bedchamber. Narcissus therefore rushed out and instructed the centurions and the tribune on duty to carry out the execution—it was on the emperor's order, he said. One of the freedmen, Euodus, was to oversee the deed and ensure its completion. He swiftly went ahead to the gardens, where he found Messalina prostrate on the ground. Sitting beside her was her mother Lepida* who, estranged from her daughter in her heyday, had been brought round to compassion in her bleakest hour, and was now urging her not to wait for the executioner. Her life was over, she told her, and all that remained was to seek death with honour. But the woman's mind, corrupted by debauchery, had no spark of decency left in it. There were tears and lamentations, uselessly prolonged, and then the doors were broken in with a charge from the new arrivals. Before her, in silence, stood the tribune, but there too was the freedman, berating her with a torrent of abuse appropriate for slaves.

38. That was when Messalina first understood her situation. She took a blade and, as she fumbled with it, vainly trying to put it to her throat or breast, she was run through by a sword-thrust from the tribune. The body was given up to her mother. Claudius was dining when he was brought the news that Messalina had died, whether by her own hand or another's being left unclear. And he did not ask; he simply called for a cup and carried on with the routine of the banquet. Even in the days that followed he gave no sign of resentment or joy, anger or sadness, or any other emotion of a human being—not even when he saw the delight of her accusers, and not when he saw the grief of his children. The Senate helped him to erase her memory, decreeing that her name and statues be removed from private and public locations. The insignia of a quaestor were awarded by decree to Narcissus, a mere trifle for a haughty man who comported himself as the superior of Pallas and Callistus. . . . †It was certainly honourable, but from it would come terrible consequences.*

BOOK TWELVE

1. The emperor's household was in convulsions as a result of the killing of Messalina. Conflict had arisen amongst the freedmen over which of them would choose a wife for Claudius, who could not bear the single life and always bowed to his wives' commands. And no less a rivalry had flared up amongst the women, all of them flaunting their noble birth, beauty, and wealth as being superior to the others' and highlighting their claims to such a great marriage. But the contest was mainly between Lollia Paulina,* daughter of the ex-consul Marcus Lollius, and Julia Agrippina, who was a child of Germanicus. As supporters, Agrippina had Pallas and Paulina Callistus, while Aelia Paetina,* from the Tubero family, had the backing of Narcissus. As for Claudius, he at one moment inclined towards one, at the next towards another (depending on which of the advocates he had been listening to). Finally he called a meeting of the feuding parties and ordered each to give his opinion and his reasons for it.

2. Narcissus' arguments centred on Claudius' marriage of old, the daughter the couple had had together (Antonia was his child by Paetina), and the fact that there would be no change in his domestic situation if a wife with whom he was familiar returned. She would certainly not look with a stepmother's hatred upon Britannicus and Octavia, children next to her own in her affection. Callistus claimed she was disqualified by the long period of the divorce, and being taken back would itself make her insufferably arrogant. Far preferable, he said, for Lollia to be brought in: having no children, she would be free of jealousy and would serve as a mother for the stepchildren. As for Pallas, his recommendation for Agrippina centred on her bringing with her the grandson of Germanicus. His noble pedigree was worthy of the imperial rank, he argued, and he could join together the descendants of the Julian and Claudian families—and they should ensure that a woman of proven fertility, and in the bloom of her youth, did not take the glory of the Caesars into another house.

3. These arguments prevailed, aided as they were by Agrippina's charms. Using their family connection as a pretext, she made frequent

visits, and so captivated her uncle that she was preferred to her rivals and, though not yet a wife, now wielded a wife's power. For, once certain of her own marriage, she began to make greater plans, and to engineer a marriage between Domitius, the son she had had by Gnaeus Ahenobarbus,* and Claudius' daughter Octavia. This could not be brought off without some criminal act. Claudius had promised Octavia to Lucius Silanus,* and had brought the young man, already distinguished, popularity with the masses by granting him triumphal insignia and staging a magnificent gladiatorial show in his honour. But there seemed no difficulty in manipulating the mind of an emperor whose favour and animosity were always implanted and programmed by others.

4. Now Vitellius, who screened his servile intrigues behind his title of censor, and had the ability to foresee the rise of despotic regimes, began to associate himself with Agrippina's schemes in order to win her favour. He brought charges against Silanus, whose sister, Junia Calvina,* was indeed attractive and precocious (and she had also been Vitellius' daughter-in-law shortly before). It was on this that the allegations were based, with Vitellius putting a sordid interpretation on an affection between the siblings which, while indiscreet, was not incestuous. And Claudius lent an ear, more pre-pared to listen to innuendo against a son-in-law because of his love for his daughter. Silanus, who was ignorant of the plot and happened to be praetor that year, was suddenly removed from the senatorial order by an edict of Vitellius, despite the fact that the list of senators had long been drafted and the census-purification performed. At the same time Claudius broke off the engagement, and Silanus was forced to resign his magistracy,* the one remaining day of his praetorship being conferred on Eprius Marcellus.*

5. In the consulship of Gaius Pompeius and Quintus Veranius the matrimonial compact made between Claudius and Agrippina was being strengthened in part by popular opinion and in part by their illicit lovemaking. They did not yet dare to hold a wedding cere-mony, however, as there was no precedent for a brother's daughter being escorted* to the house of her uncle. In fact, it was incest, and disregard of that, it was feared, might lead to dire consequences for the state. Their hesitation did not end until Vitellius undertook to use his own special skills to solve the problem. He asked Claudius if

he would accept the orders of the people and the authority of the Senate, and when the emperor replied that he was one of the citizens and unable to resist their united voice Vitellius told him to wait within the Palatium.*

Vitellius entered the Curia and, declaring that it was a matter touching on the highest interests of the state, begged permission to speak ahead of the others. He then began by saying that crushing labours were placed on the emperor in his governance of the world, and support was needed for him to attend to the public good free from domestic worries. And where could the mind of a censor* find more honourable solace than in the taking of a wife, a companion in good times and bad, to whom he could entrust his most intimate thoughts and his little children? For he was a man who was not used to the life of luxury and pleasure, but one who from his earliest youth had lived in obedience to the laws.

6. Many expressions of agreement followed these preliminary remarks, which were couched in terms designed to win approval. Vitellius then made a fresh start, declaring that, since all were in favour of the emperor marrying, a woman known for noble birth, childbearing, and the purity of her life ought to be selected. And no long investigation was needed, he continued, to determine Agrippina's superiority in family distinction; her fertility had been proven; and she had the corresponding moral attributes. But there was one outstanding benefit: by divine providence a widow would be united with an emperor whose experience of women was confined to his own marriages. They had heard from their parents, and seen for themselves, he said, how wives could be torn away from husbands at the whim of the Caesars*—that was far removed from the respectable situation now proposed. Indeed, a precedent should be set for the emperor receiving his wife from the Senate.

Now, it might be argued that marriage with daughters of brothers is unfamiliar to us, Vitellius continued; but it was regular practice in other societies, and was prohibited by no law. Marriages with cousins had long been unfamiliar to us, too, but had become frequent with the passage of time. Custom became adapted to expediency, he concluded, and this, too, would soon become part of common Roman practice.

7. There was no shortage of senators rushing from the Curia declaring that they would resort to force if Claudius hesitated; and a

motley crowd gathered, crying out that the Roman people joined the Senate in its entreaty. Claudius waited no longer. Meeting them in the Forum he accepted their good wishes, and then, entering the Senate, asked for a decree* whereby marriage between uncles and their brothers' daughters would, in future, too, be recognized in law. (Only one man, however, was found seeking such a marriage, the Roman knight Alledius Severus, and many claimed that his sole motivation was to ingratiate himself with Agrippina.)

With that the state was transformed, and everything passed under a woman's control, one who, unlike Messalina, did not capriciously tamper with the Roman government. It was a strict despotism with a masculine character. In public there was austerity and, more often, arrogance, and at home no sexual impropriety, unless it helped gain power. She had an excessive greed for gold, her pretext for accumulating it being to assist the imperial power.

8. On the wedding day Silanus took his own life. Either he had reached that point buoyed with hopes of staying alive, or he chose the day to increase public resentment. His sister Calvina was banished* from Italy. Claudius went further, calling for ceremonies in conformity with the laws of King Tullus,* with expiatory rites celebrated by the pontiffs in the grove of Diana; and it brought general amusement that this was the time chosen for punishment and expiation for incest! But not to have a reputation only for evil deeds, Agrippina successfully petitioned for remission in the case of Annaeus Seneca's* exile, and a praetorship for him along with it. She thought this would have public approval in view of Seneca's literary fame, and she also planned to have Domitius' early years mature under such a teacher. Moreover, they could profit from the man's advice in their imperial aspirations, for (it was believed) Seneca would be loyal to Agrippina through remembrance of her benefaction, and hostile to Claudius because he was piqued by the wrong he had suffered.

9. It was decided that there be no further delay, and the consul-designate Mammius Pollio* was induced with lavish promises to put forward a motion in which Claudius would be entreated to sanction the engagement of Octavia to Domitius. At the age of the two this was not inappropriate, and it would open the way to greater things. Pollio made the proposal in terms not dissimilar to those recently employed by Vitellius. Octavia was then engaged and, in addition to

his previous family connection, Domitius now became the emperor's promised son-in-law and Britannicus' equal—all because of his mother's intrigues and the machinations of those who, having accused Messalina, feared retribution from her son.

10. At about this time the Parthian representatives* who (as I noted above) had been sent to ask for the return of Meherdates, made their appearance in the Senate and delivered their message in the following terms. They were not unaware of their treaty, they said, and in coming they were not revolting against the Arsacid family. They were, rather, calling upon the son of Vonones, grandson of Phraates, to counter the despotism of Gotarzes, which their nobility and common people alike found unbearable. Brothers, kinsmen, and more distant relatives had been wiped out in Gotarzes' massacres; and pregnant women and little children were being added to the list while he, inactive at home and unsuccessful in war, covered up his cowardice with ruthlessness. They had a long-standing friendship with us that had been inaugurated officially, they said, and we should aid allies who, our equals in strength, nevertheless deferred to us out of respect. There was a reason that the children of their kings were given as hostages, they concluded: if the Parthians grew dissatisfied with the regime at home, they had recourse to the emperor and the senators, so that a king could be installed who would be all the better for exposure to their culture.

11. After the Parthians made these and similar arguments, Claudius proceeded with a speech on the grandeur of Rome and Parthian deference to it, and compared himself with the deified Augustus who, he noted, had also been asked for a king* (he omitted mention of Tiberius, though he too had sent them kings). He added some words of advice, since Meherdates was present. Meherdates should not think in terms of mastery over slaves, he said, but of being a director amongst citizens, and he should follow a policy of clemency and justice, qualities which, being unknown to barbarians, would be all the more appreciated. Then, turning to the representatives, he heaped praise on this 'foster-child of Rome', a man of exemplary self-discipline to that point. However, he added, the character of monarchs had to be tolerated, and frequent regime-changes were not beneficial. The Roman state, having acquired all too much glory, had arrived at the point of wanting settled conditions in foreign nations, too. Gaius Cassius,* the governor of Syria,

was then given the responsibility of escorting the young man to the bank of the Euphrates.

12. At that time Cassius was pre-eminent for his jurisprudence; for military skills remain an unknown quantity in tranquil times, and peace keeps the energetic and the indolent on the same level. Even so Cassius (as far as he was allowed when there was no war) set about reviving the discipline of old, drilling the legions, and employing as much care and caution as if there were an enemy threat. For he thought this was in keeping with the dignity of his ancestors and the Cassian family,* which was also famous throughout the peoples in that area. He therefore mobilized the people on whose recommendation the request for the king had been made, and encamped at Zeugma, from which there is a very easy river crossing. After the arrival of the Parthian notables and Acbarus* the Arab king, Cassius warned Meherdates that the great zest of barbarians flagged with delay, or turned into treachery, and so he should press ahead with his enterprise. The advice was disregarded through Acbarus' treachery. The young man lacked experience and thought the height of good fortune lay in dissipation; and Acbarus thus detained him for several days in the town of Edessa. And although Carenes* summoned him, and pointed out that success was at hand if they arrived swiftly, Meherdates did not head directly for Mesopotamia but took a detour into Armenia, which the onset of winter made impracticable at that time.

13. Then, worn out by the snow and mountainous terrain, they approached the plains and joined up with Carenes' forces. Crossing the River Tigris, they made their way through the Adiabeni,* whose king, Izates,* had publicly taken up an alliance with Meherdates, but secretly favoured Gotarzes and had greater loyalty to him.

En route, the city of Ninos, the ancient Assyrian capital, was captured, as was a stronghold that had become famous as the site of the final battle* between Darius and Alexander, which signalled the collapse of the power of Persia. Meanwhile Gotarzes offered vows to the local deities on a mountain called Sanbulos, the prime cult in the area being that of Hercules who, on a fixed date, tells his priests during their sleep to station horses beside the temple geared up for hunting. When they have had quivers filled with arrows placed on them, the horses wander through the woodlands and eventually return at night panting heavily and with the quivers empty. The god then makes a second appearance during the night and indicates where he has wandered in the forests, and wild animals are found killed at various points.

14. His army not yet sufficiently strengthened, Gotarzes relied on the River Corma as a line of defence. Though challenged to fight by taunting messages, he manufactured delays, changed positions and, sending men with bribes to undermine the enemy's loyalty, bought off a number of them. These included Izates and Acbarus, who left with the Adiabene and Arab armies respectively. This was an illustration of their national fickleness, but in addition—a well-established fact—barbarians are more content to ask for kings from Rome than to keep them!

Stripped of his powerful auxiliary troops, and suspecting treachery on the part of the others, Meherdates decided on the one remaining course of action, namely to trust to luck and risk a battle. Gotarzes did not decline the fight, either, his confidence boosted by the diminished enemy numbers. The clash yielded great carnage and an unclear result, until Carenes advanced too far after driving back those before him and was cut off to his rear by a fresh detachment. Then, losing all hope, Meherdates listened to promises made to him by Parraces, a client of his father, only to be tricked by him and delivered to the victor. Gotarzes reprimanded him as being no relative of his and no member of the Arsacid family, but a foreigner and a Roman. Then, to demonstrate his clemency and humiliate us, he ordered Meherdates to be left alive with his ears cut off. Gotarzes died of an illness after this, and Vonones, then ruler of the Medes, was invited to assume the throne. Vonones had neither successes nor reverses to make him noteworthy. His rule was short and undistinguished, and the Parthian empire then passed on to his son Vologaeses.*

15. Mithridates of Bosporus* had been roaming around after losing his power. He then learned that the Roman general Didius* and the cream of his forces had withdrawn, leaving the callow youth Cotys in his new kingdom, along with a few cohorts under the Roman knight Julius Aquila. With contempt for both men, Mithridates roused the local tribes to action and enticed deserters to his cause, and finally, mobilizing an army, drove out the king of the Dandaridae and took possession of his territory. When this became

known to Aquila and Cotys, and it was expected that Mithridates would attack Bosporus at any moment, they felt no confidence in the strength of their own forces (for King Zorsines of the Siraci had now resumed hostilities against them). They accordingly sought outside help themselves, sending envoys to Eunones, who ruled over the tribe of the Aorsi. And for people who could point to the power of Rome facing the rebel Mithridates, negotiating an alliance was no difficult matter. They agreed therefore that Eunones would take charge of fighting the cavalry battles while the Romans would be responsible for besieging cities.

16. They then headed out in a combined column, the Aorsi giving protection to the front and rear, and the cohorts and Bosporani (who were armed in the Roman manner) to the centre. Defeating the enemy with this formation, they reached Soza, a town in Dandarica that had been deserted by Mithridates and which, given the ambivalent sympathies of its people, they thought should be secured by leaving a garrison in place. They next advanced on the Siraci and, after crossing the River Panda, blockaded Uspe, which stood on high ground and was protected by fortifications and ditches. However, the ramparts were not constructed of stone, but of wickerwork panels and frames with earth between them, making them weak in the face of attack; and our siege-towers rose up above them, creating havoc amongst the besieged population when torches and spears were discharged from them. In fact, had nightfall not cut short the fighting the siege would have started and been brought to an end the same day.

17. The next day the townspeople sent spokesmen to beg for a pardon for all free persons, and they offered to surrender ten thousand slaves. The victors rejected their entreaty because it would be barbaric to butcher men who surrendered, and difficult to surround such huge numbers with guards. Better, they reasoned, for them to die by the rules of war, and the soldiers who had scaled the walls on ladders were given the signal for a massacre.

The destruction of Uspe struck fear into the other tribes. They now thought they had no security, not when armies, defences, terrain difficult or high, rivers, and cities were all alike surmounted by the enemy. Zorsines therefore long considered whether he should consider Mithridates' dire predicament or the kingdom of his forefathers.

The interests of his people prevailed, and he gave hostages and flung himself before the effigy of Claudius—to the great glory of the Roman army, for it was now well known that it was only three days' march from the River Tanais, unbloodied and triumphant. On the return journey, however, fortunes were different. A number of ships—they were returning by sea—were driven on to the shores of the Tauri, where the barbarians surrounded them, killing a prefect of a cohort and several auxiliaries.

18. Meanwhile Mithridates, with no help to be sought in battle, wondered on whose mercy he should throw himself. His brother Cotys, once a traitor to him and then his enemy, inspired fear; of the Romans there was nobody at hand of sufficient authority for his assurances to carry much weight. He turned to Eunones, who had no private grudges against him, and who had recently been strengthened by an alliance with us. So, with dress and expression as much as possible adapted to his present fortunes, Mithridates entered Eunones' palace and threw himself before his knees.

'I, Mithridates,' he said, 'am here of my own accord, having been hunted by the Romans over land and sea for so many years. Deal as you wish with a descendant of the great Achaemenes*—the one thing my enemies have not taken from me.'

19. Eunones was touched by the man's distinction, his reversal of fortune, and his entreaty, which did not lack dignity. He raised the suppliant and commended him for choosing the Aorsi people and Eunones' right hand for making his appeal for forgiveness. At the same time he sent delegates to Claudius with a letter that ran like this. Friendship between the emperors of the Roman people and the rulers of great nations rested primarily on the equivalence of the positions, he said, but between himself and Claudius there was also the common bond of victory. The best ending to hostilities was one that came with forgiveness, he continued, and thus it was that Zorsines had faced no expropriation after defeat. Mithridates did deserve harsher treatment, he said, and his plea was not that the man should retain his power and his throne, only that he not be paraded in a triumph or face the death penalty.

20. Claudius was indulgent with foreign nobles, but he now wondered whether it would be better to accept Mithridates as a prisoner of war with his life guaranteed, or to recover him by armed force. Resentment over his injuries and a lust for revenge urged the second

course; but the argument made against it was that the war would be undertaken in trackless countryside and on a harbourless sea. In addition there were aggressive rulers, nomadic peoples, and a barren terrain. Delay would arouse ennui, and haste would create dangers, while there would be little praise for victory and great disgrace if they were defeated. Why not take what was being offered and save the exile for whom, being destitute, a longer life meant only greater punishment?

Moved by these arguments, Claudius wrote to Eunones telling him that Mithridates deserved punishment of the choicest kind, and that he did not lack the power to inflict it, but his ancestors' procedure was to show kindness to suppliants and determination against enemies in equal measure. For, he said, triumphs were won only when the powers of the defeated peoples and kings were unimpaired.

21. Mithridates was then handed over and taken to Rome* by Junius Cilo,* procurator of Pontus, and it was said that he spoke more aggressively before Claudius than his situation warranted. One of his statements that came to the notice of the public went like this: 'I have not been sent back to you but have come back; and if you don't believe that, release me and try to catch me!' He also maintained his fearless expression when he was put on show for the people, surrounded by guards, beside the Rostra. Consular insignia were bestowed by decree on Cilo, and on Aquila praetorian insignia.

22. Agrippina was savage in her hatred, and she resented Lollia for having competed with her to marry the emperor. Now, in this same consulship, she engineered charges against her, finding an informer to accuse her of resorting to Chaldeans and magicians, and of having consulted the statue of Apollo of Clarus regarding the emperor's marriage.

Without hearing the accused, Claudius prefaced an address to the Senate with many remarks on Lollia's illustrious background. She was the daughter of Lucius Volusius' sister,* he said; her great uncle was Cotta Messalinus; and she had once been married to Memmius Regulus (he was careful to say nothing about her marriage to Gaius Caesar). He then added that her machinations were injurious to the state, and that she should be deprived of the wherewithal to commit crime. Accordingly, he said, her property should be confiscated and she should leave Italy. As a result she was, in exile, left only five million sesterces from her enormous possessions.

Calpurnia,* a lady of great distinction, was also ruined, because the emperor had praised her looks. There was no sexual interest; it was merely a remark made in passing, and Agrippina's wrath therefore stopped short of extreme measures. In Lollia's case* a tribune was sent to see that she was driven to suicide. Cadius Rufus* was also condemned, under the law of extortion, the charge brought by the people of Bithynia.

23. Because of its deep respect for the Senate, Narbonese Gaul was granted the privilege (already enjoyed by Sicily) of senators from the province being allowed to visit their estates without first consulting the emperor. On the death of their kings, Sohaemus* and Agrippa,* Ituraea and Judaea were annexed to the province of Syria.

It was decided that the Augury of Safety, abandoned for twenty-five years, should be revived and continued in future. Claudius also expanded the *pomerium** of the city in accordance with the ancient custom by which those who extended the empire* are also granted the right to enlarge the boundaries of the city. In fact, despite the subjection of great peoples, Roman commanders had not exercised the right, with the exception of Lucius Sulla and the deified Augustus.

24. As for the kings, there are various popular accounts of their pretensions or praiseworthy actions in this matter, but I think it pertinent to investigate the initial foundation of the *pomerium* and its dimensions as Romulus fixed them. Now, a furrow was used to mark out the town limits. It began at the Forum Boarium (where we see the bronze statue of a bull, since this is the species of animal that is yoked to the plough) and was made to include the great altar of Hercules. After that there were stones set at regular intervals along the foot of the Palatine Hill* up to the temple of Consus,* then to the ancient *curiae*,* and after that to the shrine of the Lares. As for the Roman Forum and the Capitol, the general belief has been that these were added to the city not by Romulus but by Titus Tatius.* Later the *pomerium* was extended as Rome's fortunes increased, and the bounds that Claudius at that time established are easily recognizable and are registered in the official records.

25. In the consulship of Gaius Antistius and Marcus Suillius, the adoption of Domitius was swiftly pushed ahead through

Pallas' influence. Pallas felt bound to Agrippina as the arranger of her marriage, and later because of a sexual relationship, and he now kept urging Claudius to take thought for the good of the state and provide protection for Britannicus in his early years. He cited the parallel of the deified Augustus in whose family, though he had grandsons to rely on, stepsons had a prominent role, and the case of Tiberius, who had children of his own but also adopted Germanicus. Claudius, too, he said, should equip himself with a young man who would assume some of his responsibilities.

Convinced by this, Claudius set Domitius, who was three years older, ahead of his own son, making a speech in the Senate along the lines of what he had heard from the freedman. Experts observed that there had been before this no case of adoption amongst the patricians of the Claudian family,* and that they had survived without interruption from Attus Clausus* on.

26. The emperor was thanked, and the flattery of Domitius was particularly well constructed; and a law was passed* that provided for his adoption into the Claudian family with the name 'Nero'. Agrippina, too, received elevation with the *cognomen* Augusta.* When this was done, there was nobody so heartless as not to be touched by sadness for Britannicus' lot. The boy was gradually deprived even of the service of his slaves, and he treated with derision the poorly timed solicitude of his stepmother, aware of its hypocrisy. For they do say that he was not slow-witted by nature. That may be true, or perhaps sympathy for his danger allowed him to keep that reputation without it being put to the test.

27. To demonstrate her power to the allied peoples, as well, Agrippina successfully petitioned for a colony* of veterans—its title was derived from her own name—to be established in the chief town of the Ubii, in which she had been born. And it so happened that this was the tribe that her grandfather Agrippa had taken under Roman protection when it crossed the Rhine.

In the same period there was alarm in Upper Germany with the arrival of the Chatti on a plundering expedition. The legate Publius Pomponius responded by dispatching auxiliaries of the Vangiones and Nemetes, with allied cavalry support, under orders to head off the raiders, or to surprise and surround them if they split up. Spirited action from his men followed up the commander's plan. They split into two columns, and those who had headed out to the left encircled some of the enemy who had recently returned and who, after squandering their plunder on dissipation, were heavy with sleep. The joy of the Romans was increased by the fact that they had, after forty years, delivered from slavery some survivors of the disaster of Varus.

28. Those who had taken the right-hand, shorter routes inflicted greater loss on the enemy, who confronted them and risked pitched battle. Charged with spoils and glory, they returned to Mt. Taunus where Pomponius was waiting with the legions in case the Chatti, eager for revenge, offered him the chance of battle. But the Chatti feared being outflanked on the one side by the Romans and on the other by the Cherusci (with whom they were constantly feuding), and they sent spokesmen into the city with hostages. Pomponius was voted triumphal honours, a modest contribution to his standing with posterity, with whom the glory of his poetry takes precedence.

29. At this same time Vannius* was driven from his throne. Imposed on the Suebi by Drusus Caesar, he had, in the early years of his reign, enjoyed the respect and affection of his people. Presently, as time passed, he changed and became tyrannical, and found himself beleaguered by the hatred of his neighbours, along with civil disturbance at home. The ringleaders were Vibilius,* king of the Hermunduri, and Vangio and Sido,* the sons of Vannius' own sister. And Claudius, despite numerous appeals, refused military intervention in this struggle between barbarians, promising only a safe refuge for Vannius were he driven out. He also sent written instructions to Palpellius Hister,* governor of Pannonia, to station a legion, and auxiliaries raised from the province itself, along the riverbank. These were to provide assistance to the conquered, and also intimidate the victors so they would not, elated with their good fortune, disturb our peace, as well. For there was an enormous force approaching—Lugii and other tribes—drawn by reports of the wealth of the kingdom that Vannius had built up through thirty years' of plunder and taxation. Vannius had his own infantry force, and cavalry that came from the Sarmatian Iazyges. This was no match for the enemy numbers, and so he had decided to rely on his strongholds for defence, and to draw out the war.

30. The Iazyges, however, could not tolerate a siege, and as they drifted through the nearby plains they made battle inevitable, since the Lugii and Hermunduri had advanced into that area.

Vannius therefore came down from his strongholds and was defeated in the field, winning praise—despite his failure—for taking part in the battle himself and for receiving frontal wounds. He nevertheless sought refuge with the fleet that was waiting at the Danube. His clients soon followed and were settled in Pannonia with grants of land. Vangio and Sido divided the kingdom between them and maintained exceptional loyalty towards us; but because of their own character, or because such is the character of servitude, they won great affection from their subjects while gaining their fiefdoms, and greater hatred after doing so.

31. In Britain,* meanwhile, the propraetor Publius Ostorius* was faced with a state of turmoil. The enemy had poured into the territory of our allies with all the more fury because they believed that a new commander would not confront them with an army unfamiliar to him, and with winter already begun. Ostorius knew that fear or confidence is inspired by initial results, and he hurried along his light-armed cohorts, annihilated resistance, and hunted down the scattered fugitives. His aim now was to prevent the enemy from regrouping, and to avoid a peace negotiated with hostility and lack of faith that would permit neither the general nor the common soldier to be at ease. He therefore prepared to disarm those he suspected, and to hold in check with encampments the entire area as far as the rivers Trisantona* and Sabrina.

The first to oppose these measures were the Iceni,* a powerful tribe that had not been crushed in battle, having voluntarily entered into alliance with us. At their prompting, the surrounding tribes selected for the battlefield an area that was enclosed by a country dyke, with a narrow entrance that would make it impassable to cavalry. Such were the defences that the Roman commander prepared to breach, despite the fact that he was at the head only of allied troops* without the strength of the legions. He deployed his cohorts, and applied even his cavalry squadrons to the duties of infantrymen. He then gave the signal, and the men broke through the dyke and caused mayhem amidst the enemy, caught within a barrier of their own making. The Britons, from a guilty conscience over their rebellion and with escape routes blocked, brought off many brilliant exploits; and in that battle the legate's son Marcus Ostorius won the prize of honour* for saving a citizen's life.

32. After the defeat of the Iceni, calm prevailed amongst those who were wavering between war and peace, and the army was led

against the Decangi.* Lands were plundered, and booty carried off in all areas, since the enemy would not risk battle, and their trickery was punished if they tried to harass the column from concealed positions. By now the Romans had reached a point not far from the sea facing the island of Hibernia when trouble arising among the Brigantes made the commander turn back, for he was resolutely determined not to undertake new conquests before consolidating earlier gains.

The Brigantes were, in fact, pacified when the few who initiated hostilities were put to death and the others pardoned. However, no cruel punishment, and no clemency, could change the hearts of the tribe of the Silures and deter them from continuing the war, and they had to be suppressed by the installation of a legionary camp.* So that this could be effected more easily, a colony comprising a large unit of veterans was established on conquered lands at Camulodunum.* This would serve as a defensive force against rebellion and inculcate respect for the laws in the allies.

33. Next came an expedition against the Silures who, apart from being naturally recalcitrant, also had confidence in the might of Caratacus,* whom many indecisive and many successful engagements had raised to a level above the other commanders of the Britons. But on that occasion, being inferior in numbers, Caratacus relied on cunning and a treacherous terrain to gain advantage, shifting the theatre of war to the land of the Ordovices. There, reinforced by all those who feared a peace with us, he took the ultimate risk, after selecting a site for the battle where everything—advancing and pulling back alike—was unfavourable to us, but to his own men's advantage. There were high mountains on one side, and any area that was reachable by a gentle incline Caratacus blocked with rocks that formed a kind of rampart. Before the site flowed a river with a ford of varying depth, and bands of armed men had taken a position before the defences.

34. Moreover, the tribal chieftains were doing the rounds of their men, giving encouragement and building confidence by easing fears, kindling hopes, and providing other incentives to battle. As for Caratacus, he was darting this way and that, proclaiming that this was the day and this the battle that would begin their recovery of liberty or else their eternal slavery. He also called out the names of their ancestors, who had driven back the dictator Caesar, and thanks to whose courage they had been spared the axes and tribute-payments,

and had kept the persons of their wives and children free from violation. As he made these and similar comments, the crowd noisily
applauded, and all swore by their tribal gods that no weapons and no
wounds would make them give ground.

35. This fervour astounded the Roman commander. The river
that stood in his way, and the fortifications that had been added, also
caused him alarm; so did the towering mountains, and the whole
grim scene bristling with defending forces. But the men were clamouring for battle, crying out that everything could be overcome by
courage; and prefects and tribunes intensified the ardour of the
troops with similar comments.

Ostorius looked around him to see what was impenetrable and
what accessible, and then, at the head of his frenzied troops, he
crossed the river without difficulty. When the men reached the rampart, wounds were more numerous on our side, and there were considerable losses, as long as the fighting was confined to projectiles.
Then, with the use of a tortoise formation, the crude and shapeless
stone structure was dismantled, and close-quarter fighting began on
equal terms. At that point the barbarians retreated to the hilltops.
There, too, the skirmishers and heavy infantry broke in upon them,
the skirmishers attacking with their spears, the infantry advancing in
close order. And on the side of the Britons, who had no breastplates
or helmets for protection, the ranks were thrown into disorder.
If they attempted to resist the auxiliaries, they were cut down by the
swords and javelins of the legionaries; and if they turned to face
the legionaries they were felled by the broadswords and lances of the
auxiliaries. It was a brilliant victory. Caratacus' wife and daughter*
were taken prisoner, and his brothers surrendered.

36. Caratacus himself sought the protection of Cartimandua,*
queen of the Brigantes, but (as insecurity generally attends adversity)
he was put in chains and handed over to the victors, eight years* after
the commencement of hostilities in Britain. His fame had thus
passed beyond the island and spread through the nearby provinces,
becoming known throughout Italy, as well. People were therefore
eager to see who this man was who had for so many years disdained
our might. Even in Rome the name of Caratacus was not unknown;
and while Claudius sought to enhance his own repute, he also added
lustre to the defeated man. For the people were invited to what was
apparently a remarkable spectacle; and the praetorian cohorts stood

under arms on the level ground before their camp. Then, as the king's clients filed past, Caratacus' ornaments, necklaces, and the prizes that he had garnered in foreign wars were carried along; and after that his brothers, his wife and daughter, and finally the man himself, were put on display. The other prisoners, out of fear, resorted to unbecoming entreaties. Not so Caratacus, who sought pity neither with a downcast expression nor with his words. Halting at the tribunal, he said:

37. 'Had I, in my successes, observed a moderation that was as great as my nobility and rank, I would have come into this city as a friend rather than as a prisoner of war. Nor would you have objected to accepting into a peace-treaty a man descended from famous forefathers, and one ruling over many nations. My present lot, degrading to me, is glorious for you. I had horses and men, arms and wealth. Is it surprising if I was loath to lose them? For if *you* want to be masters of the world, does it follow that the world should welcome slavery? If I were being brought here after an immediate surrender, there would have been no fame attaching either to my misfortune or your great success. And forgetfulness will follow my execution, whereas if you keep me alive I shall be an everlasting illustration of your clemency.'

Claudius' response was to grant pardon to Caratacus himself, and to his wife and brothers. Freed from their chains, these also paid their respects to Agrippina, who was highly visible on another dais close by, praising her and thanking her in the same terms as they had the emperor. Of course, it was something new, and out of step with the traditions of old, for a woman to be seated before the Roman standards; she was making it clear that she had a share in the empire that her forefathers* had won.

38. After this, the senators were convened, and they made long, grandiose speeches on the capture of Caratacus. The event was as glorious as when Publius Scipio put Syphax* on display for the Roman people, they said, or when Lucius Paulus displayed Perses,* and other generals other conquered kings. Ostorius was voted triumphal insignia. Until then his record was one of success, but it subsequently became patchy, either because our own military precautions declined—as though the war was concluded with Caratacus' removal—or because the enemy's desire for retribution flared up more fiercely through compassion for such a great king. They surrounded a camp prefect and

the legionary cohorts which had been left behind to construct garrison-posts amongst the Silures; and these would have been wiped out had not help swiftly arrived in response to messages sent from the neighbouring fortresses. Even so the prefect, eight centurions, and the most intrepid of the rank and file lost their lives. And not much later the enemy overwhelmed a foraging party of ours, along with the cavalry squadrons sent to support it.

39. Ostorius next used his light cohorts to check the Britons, but even then he would have failed to stem the rout if the legions had not taken up the fight. Through their strength, evenness was restored to the battle, which then turned in our favour. Because the day was fading, the enemy fled with only meagre losses.

There were frequent battles after that, more often than not looking like guerrilla engagements. They were fought in woods and marshes, the outcome dependent on individual luck or courage, and they could be fortuitous or planned. They arose from anger or to gain plunder, sometimes on the orders of the commanders, and sometimes without their knowledge. The resolution made by the Silures was remarkable. What enraged them was a remark of the Roman commander that had gained currency. Just as the Sugambri* had earlier been destroyed, or moved to the Gallic provinces, he had said, so now the Silurian name should be completely wiped out. The Silures therefore cut off two auxiliary cohorts which, because of the greed of their officers, were pillaging with too little caution; and by making gifts of spoils and prisoners of war they also began to bring over other tribes to join the revolt. It was now that Ostorius departed this life, weary and exhausted by his responsibilities. The enemy were delighted that a leader who was not to be underestimated had been removed by the war, even if it was not in battle.

40. When he learned of the death of his legate, Claudius replaced him with Aulus Didius so the province would not be without a governor. Didius sailed quickly, but still did not find a healthy situation in the province, for in the meantime the legion that Manlius Valens* commanded had been defeated in battle. The report of this had actually been exaggerated by the enemy to demoralize the incoming commander, and the commander further exaggerated the reports he was given—he would have greater praise if the rebels were pacified, or, if they held out, a more acceptable excuse for failure.

It was once again the Silures who had inflicted the damage, and they continued their sweep of the land until driven back by Didius' arrival. After Caratacus' capture, however, the leading British military strategist was Venutius, whose origins in the Brigantian community I have already mentioned,* and he long remained loyal and enjoyed Roman military protection, while he remained married to Queen Cartimandua. Presently there was a divorce, which was immediately followed by war, and Venutius took up hostilities against us, as well. At first, however, the struggle was just between the two, and Cartimandua with some clever tactics captured Venutius' brother and close relatives. The enemy were incensed over this, and the shame of being subjected to a woman's power further exacerbated them; and so a powerful and exceptionally well-armed body of young warriors swept into her kingdom. This we had foreseen, and cohorts that were sent to assist Cartimandua fought a fierce battle, in which a happy conclusion followed a shaky beginning. In these operations similar success attended the legion,* which Caesius Nasica commanded (for Didius, with the weight of his years upon him, and covered with honours, was satisfied to act through his subordinates and keep the enemy at bay).

Although these campaigns were conducted over a number of years by two propraetors, I have put them together in case, related separately, they would not appear in my account as being as important as they were. I now return to the chronological narrative.

41. In the consulship of Tiberius Claudius (his fifth) and Servius Cornelius, Nero was granted the *toga virilis* before his time* so that he would appear ready for a political career. And Claudius happily acceded to the sycophantic request of the Senate that Nero enter the consulship in his twentieth year,* and that in the meantime he hold consular power outside the city as consul-designate, and be given the title 'Prince of the Youth'.* There was, in addition, largesse for the soldiers along with gifts for the people, all made in Nero's name. Moreover, at the games in the Circus—put on to win over the favour of the masses—Britannicus rode past in the procession wearing the boy's toga and Nero triumphal dress.* The people were supposed to see one in the insignia of a commander, and the other in the clothes of a boy, and to anticipate on that basis the future prospects of each. At the same time, any centurions and tribunes commiserating with Britannicus' lot were removed on spurious grounds, and some with

the pretence of promotion. In the case of freedmen, too, anyone whose loyalty remained untainted was ejected when opportunities like the following arose. When the two met, Nero greeted Britannicus by name, but Britannicus called Nero 'Domitius'.* Agrippina brought this to her husband's notice with bitter complaints, saying it was the start of internal dissension: the adoption was being disregarded, the vote of the senators and the command of the people repudiated within their home. Unless the evil influence of those inculcating such hostility were checked, she added, it would erupt with disastrous consequences for the state. Disturbed by these veiled charges, Claudius punished all the finest tutors of his son with exile or execution, putting his stepmother's appointees in charge of the boy.

42. However, Agrippina did not yet dare attempt her supreme coup without Lusius Geta and Rufrius Crispinus being first relieved of their command of the praetorian cohorts. She believed that they remained faithful to Messalina's memory, and were devoted to her children. So when the emperor's wife insisted that there was dissension in the cohorts because the two were jockeying for position, and that discipline would be stricter if the troops were commanded by one man, authority over the cohorts was transferred to Burrus Afranius.* (Burrus had an outstanding reputation as a soldier, but he also knew on whose wishes his appointment depended.) Agrippina was also raising even further her own already high profile. She would enter the Capitol in a carriage, a privilege confined in the old days to priests and to sacred paraphernalia, and that increased the reverence felt for a woman whose position was, and remains to this day, unparalleled. For she had been daughter of a commander, and sister, wife, and mother of men* who gained the supreme power.

Meanwhile, Agrippina's special champion Vitellius, who was at the height of his influence and well on in age, suddenly found himself hit with an arraignment—so capricious are the fortunes of the great—with the senator Junius Lupus as his accuser. Lupus brought against him charges of treason and reproached him with designs on the throne. Claudius would have lent an ear to this, had his mind not been changed by what were threats rather than entreaties emanating from Agrippina, which made him instead forbid water and fire to the accuser. That was all Vitellius* had wanted.

43. That year there were many prodigies. Ill-omened birds roosted on the Capitol. There were frequent earthquakes causing the

collapse of houses, and in the spreading fear all the weak were trodden underfoot by the panicking crowds. There was a shortage
of crops that led to a famine, and that too was taken as a prodigy.
Nor were there only muted protests. People surrounded Claudius
with boisterous shouting as he was dispensing judgements,
drove him to the far end of the Forum, and kept jostling him until
he burst through the ugly mob with a body of troops. It was established that the city had fifteen days' worth of food left—and no more
than that—and that it was only because of the great bounty of the
gods and the mildness of the winter that relief was brought to a
desperate situation. (For heaven's sake, Italy once used to transport
supplies for our legions to the distant provinces! Even now there is
no problem with sterility, but we prefer to cultivate Africa and
Egypt, with the livelihood of the Roman people left to shipping and
its hazards!)

44. That same year war broke out between the Armenians
and Iberi, and it had serious repercussions for Parthian-Roman
relations. The Parthian race was under the rule of Vologaeses.
On his mother's side, Vologaeses was the son of a Greek concubine,
and he had gained the throne because it was ceded to him by his
brothers.* The Iberi had long been under the sway of Pharasmanes,
and the Armenians were, with our support, under his brother
Mithridates. Pharasmanes had a son called Radamistus who, tall and
handsome, had remarkable physical strength, was well trained in the
skills of his country, and enjoyed an illustrious reputation amongst
his neighbours. Radamistus would proclaim—too insistently and
frequently for him to mask his ambition—that the insignificant
realm of Iberia was being kept from him by his father's lingering
old age.

Now Pharasmanes feared the young man, who was eager for
power and buttressed by the support of his people, while he himself
was already in his declining years. He therefore tried to attract his
son to other prospects, and drew his attention to Armenia which, he
reminded him, he had given to Mithridates after driving out the
Parthians. But, added the king, the use of force must be postponed,
and a trick with which to take Mithridates by surprise was preferable. And so Radamistus, feigning a rift with his father, and appearing unable to take his stepmother's hatred, went to his uncle, by
whom he was subsequently treated with great kindness, just like

one of Mithridates' own children. He then proceeded to entice the leading Armenians to revolt. Mithridates knew nothing of this, and was showing him great honour to boot.

45. Radamistus then made a pretence of reconciliation and returned to his father, reporting that all that could be achieved by trickery was ready, and that the rest had to be accomplished by armed force. Meanwhile, Pharasmanes concocted pretexts for war. When he was fighting the king of the Albani,* he said, and calling on the Romans for assistance, his brother had opposed him, and now he would avenge that wrong by killing him. At the same time, he put large forces in his son's hands. Radamistus then terrified Mithridates with a surprise attack, drove him from the plains, and forced him into the stronghold of Gorneae, which was safeguarded by its position and by a garrison of Roman soldiers under a prefect, Caelius Pollio, and a centurion, Casperius.*

Barbarian ignorance is nowhere greater than in engines and stratagems for assaulting towns. Radamistus' attacks on the defences proved futile, or resulted in loss, and he proceeded with a blockade. Then, abandoning force, he tried to buy off the avaricious prefect, although Casperius objected to the wrongful overthrow by bribery of an allied king and of Armenia, which had been a gift of the Roman people. In the end, however, because Pollio kept dwelling on the enemy numbers, and Radamistus on his father's instructions, the centurion negotiated a truce and left. If he could not deter Pharasmanes from the war, he would tell Ummidius Quadratus,* governor of Syria, how matters stood in Armenia.

46. Feeling released from surveillance by the centurion's departure, the prefect urged Mithridates to conclude a treaty. He emphasized the ties between brothers, Pharasmanes' seniority in age, and the other ways in which the two were connected—Mithridates being married to Pharasmanes' daughter, and being also father-in-law to Radamistus. The Iberi were not averse to peace, he said, despite having the upper hand at the moment; the treachery of the Armenians was well known; and the only defence he had was a stronghold without provisions. He should therefore not choose an unpredictable outcome in battle over terms without bloodshed. Mithridates was hesitant in the face of such arguments, and he suspected the prefect's advice—the man had seduced a royal concubine and could be bribed, it was thought, to commit any wanton act.

Casperius meanwhile came to Pharasmanes and called on him to raise the siege. Pharasmanes' responses in public were non-committal, and quite often conciliatory, but by secret messages he warned Radamistus to accelerate the siege at all costs. The price of dishonour went up, and by covert bribes Pollio induced the soldiers to demand a peace-treaty and to threaten to abandon the garrison. This obliged Mithridates to accept a date and location for negotiating the treaty, and he left the stronghold.

47. Radamistus first of all threw himself into Mithridates' embrace, pretending to defer to him and using the terms 'father-in-law' and 'father'. He then added an oath, that he would do no violence to him, either by the sword or by poison. At the same time he took him into a nearby copse, saying that preparations for a sacrifice had been made there so the ratification of their treaty could be witnessed by the gods.

When kings meet to form an alliance, it is their custom to grasp each other's right hand and bind the thumbs together, fastening them tightly with a knot. Then, when the blood has flowed to the thumb-tips, they let it out with a slight nick and each of them licks it in turn. Such a treaty is regarded as having mystical qualities, being sanctified by each other's blood. On that occasion, however, the man who was doing the fastening pretended that he had tripped, and he seized Mithridates' knees and bowled him over. At the same moment several men ran up, and Mithridates was put in chains and dragged off in leg-irons, which is shameful to barbarians. Soon the common people, because they were harshly dealt with under him, began to direct abuse and blows at him. But there were also those who felt sympathy for such a change of fortunes, and his wife, who followed with their young children, filled the whole area with her laments. The prisoners were hidden in separate covered wagons until Pharasmanes' orders could be ascertained. For him, desire for the kingdom counted for more than his brother and daughter, and in his heart he was ready to commit crimes—but he spared his eyes the sight of having them killed before him. Radamistus, likewise, seems to have remembered his oath—he did not bring out a sword and did not bring out poison to use on his sister and uncle. Instead he had them thrown to the ground and killed by burying them under a large amount of heavy clothing. Mithridates' sons were also led to the slaughter for having wept at the murder of their parents.

48. When Quadratus learned of Mithridates' betrayal and the occupation of the kingdom by his murderers, he called a meeting of his staff,* informed them of what had happened and sought advice on whether to take punitive measures. A few were concerned about the honour of the state; more talked about security. All crime abroad should be welcomed with joy, they said, and one should even sow the seeds of disaffection, just as Roman emperors had often offered this same Armenia, seemingly as a gift, in order to create confusion in the barbarians' minds. Let Radamistus enjoy what he had dishonourably gained, as long as he was hated and disgraced, since that was more useful for us than if he had won it gloriously. This was the opinion that was accepted. But they wished to avoid the impression of having approved a crime when Claudius' orders might turn out to be different, and so messengers were sent to Pharasmanes with orders for him to leave Armenian territory and remove his son.

49. The procurator of Cappadocia was Julius Paelignus, a man contemptible both for his idle intellect and his physical deformity. He was, however, very close to Claudius—for when the emperor was still a private citizen he added amusement to his leisure time by fraternizing with buffoons. This Paelignus had raised some auxiliary troops amongst the provincials with the avowed aim of recovering Armenia. Instead, he pillaged the allies more than the enemy, and when his men deserted him, and he had no help in the face of barbarian attacks, he came to Radamistus. Won over by his gifts, Paelignus actually encouraged Radamistus to assume the royal diadem, and when he did so was present as his promoter and assistant. The disgraceful story spread abroad and, so the other governors would not be judged by Paelignus' standard, the legate Helvidius Priscus* was sent with a legion to deal with the troubles as circumstances required. Priscus, therefore, swiftly crossed Mt. Taurus, and restored tranquillity in more cases by exercising restraint than by using force. He then received orders to return to Syria, in order to avoid anything that might start a war with Parthia.

50. For Vologaeses thought an opportunity had arrived to invade Armenia, once possessed by his ancestors and now, through an outrageous crime, in the hands of a foreign king. He accordingly mobilized his troops and prepared to put his brother Tiridates on the throne, so that no member of his family would be without a kingdom. The Iberi were driven back without a battle by the advancing

Parthians, and the Armenian cities of Artaxata and Tigranocerta submitted to the yoke. Then a savage winter, an inadequate stockpiling of supplies, and a wasting disease arising from the combination of the two forced Vologaeses to drop his immediate plans. Armenia being once more leaderless, Radamistus invaded, more ruthlessly than before, feeling he was facing rebels who would, when the time was ripe, rise against him again. And the Armenians, used to servitude though they were, threw off their submissiveness and surrounded the palace in arms.

51. All that Radamistus had to help him was the speed of his horses, and on these he and his wife rode off. But his wife was pregnant. The first part of the flight she managed to endure somehow because of her fear of the enemy and her love for her husband. Later, her uterus shaken, and her insides jostled in their unremitting haste, she begged to be spared the indignities of captivity by an honourable death. Radamistus at first held her in his arms, and consoled and encouraged her, wavering between admiration for her courage and a sickening fear of someone possessing her if she were left behind. Finally, urged on by the violence of his love, and being no novice in atrocities, he drew his sabre, stabbed her, and dragged her to the bank of the Araxes; then he consigned her to the river so that even her corpse would be taken from the enemy. Radamistus himself rode speedily to his native kingdom of Iberia.

Meanwhile, Zenobia (as his wife was called) was spotted in a calm backwater by some shepherds, breathing and showing vital signs. Judging from her distinguished appearance that she was not of low birth, the shepherds bound her wound, applied their rustic cures and, on learning her name and circumstances, conveyed her to the city of Artaxata. From there she was officially escorted to Tiridates,* by whom she was cordially received and accorded regal treatment.

52. In the consulship of Faustus Sulla and Salvius Otho, Furius Scribonianus* was driven into exile on a charge of employing Chaldean astrologers to make enquiries about the emperor's death. His mother, Vibia, was linked with the accusation for not willingly accepting her earlier misfortune (she had been relegated). Camillus, the father of Scribonianus, had fomented armed insurrection in Dalmatia, and Claudius used this to illustrate his clemency, in that he was for a second time sparing a hostile family. However, the exile did not have long to live after that, and people spread the word of a natural death or murder by poison according to their personal beliefs. On the matter of driving astrologers out of Italy, there was a senatorial decree that was harsh, and ineffectual.

After this, in a speech by the emperor, praise was heaped on those who voluntarily withdrew from the senatorial order* because of financial difficulties in the family, and those who added brazenness to the poverty by choosing to remain were expelled.

53. During this session, Claudius brought before the senators the question of punishment for women involved in sexual relationships with slaves. It was decided* that women descending to that level without the knowledge of the slave's master should be considered to have servile status; if the master gave his consent, they would be regarded as freedwomen. Claudius declared Pallas to be the author of the proposal, and a motion that the freedman be awarded praetorian insignia and fifteen million sesterces was made by the consul-designate, Barea Soranus.* A rider to the motion, that Pallas be given official thanks, was proposed by Cornelius Scipio on the grounds that, though descended from Arcadian* royalty, Pallas saw his ancient nobility as secondary to the common good, and permitted himself to be regarded as one of the emperor's servants. Claudius stated that Pallas was satisfied with the honour* paid him, and would remain within the bounds of his earlier modest condition. So it was that a decree of the Senate was set up in public, engraved on a bronze plaque, in which a freedman in possession of three hundred million sesterces had praise heaped on him for his old-fashioned thrift.

54. However, Pallas' brother, who was surnamed Felix,* did not behave with the same moderation. He had been made governor of Judaea some time before and, enjoying as he did such powerful support, he thought that all his misdeeds would go unpunished. The Jews had, in fact, given indications of an uprising when disaffection broke out after* <. . .> but, when they learned of his assassination, they had not carried out the order. Still, the fear remained that some emperor would issue the same instructions. Meanwhile, Felix was only aggravating the mischief with ill-timed remedies, and Ventidius Cumanus,* under whose authority a part of the province lay, rivalled him in the worst of his actions.

The division of power was such that Ventidius had the tribe of the Galileans under him, and Felix the Samaritans,* the two peoples having long been at odds, with their animosities now less suppressed because of their contempt for their governors. They were, as a result, pillaging each other, sending out bands of marauders, laying traps, and occasionally fighting pitched battles; and they would bring back the spoils of their looting to the procurators. The procurators were pleased at first but, as the destruction increased, they intervened with armed force, and some soldiers were cut down. The province would then have gone up in the flames of war had not Quadratus, governor of Syria, brought assistance. With respect to the Jews who had rushed into killing the soldiers, there was little hesitation over the death penalty. Cumanus and Felix gave some pause because, on hearing the reasons for the revolt, Claudius had given Quadratus authority to decide the case of the procurators, as well. But Quadratus put Felix on view amongst the judges, welcoming him to his tribunal in order to temper by fear the enthusiasm of the accusers. Cumanus was condemned for the wrongdoings of the two, and calm returned to the province.

55. Not long after this the wild Cilician tribes called the Cietae, which had also caused trouble on numerous other occasions, chose some rugged mountains for a camp, under their leader Troxoborus. From there they would sweep down to the coastline or to the cities, where they had the temerity to inflict violence on the country people and urban dwellers, and very frequently on traders and shipowners. The community of Anemurium was blockaded, and a cavalry force sent to its aid from Syria, under the prefect Curtius Severus, was routed; for the harsh terrain in the area, though suited to fighting on foot, was not conducive to cavalry engagements. Then Antiochus,* who was the ruler of that shoreline, broke the unity of the barbarian troops by using inducements on the rank and file and trickery on their leader. After executing Troxoborus and a few of the chiefs, he established peace amongst the others by showing clemency.

56. At about this same time excavation of a passage through the mountain between the Fucine lake* and the River Liris was completed and, to enable this magnificent achievement to be viewed by more spectators, a naval battle was staged on the lake itself. It was like the one that Augustus had once put on (though his vessels were lighter, and the personnel fewer) when he constructed his lagoon close to the Tiber. Claudius fitted out triremes and quadriremes, and armed nineteen thousand men. He surrounded the battle area with rafts in order to prevent stragglers from escaping; but he enclosed

enough space for the rowers to demonstrate their power and the helmsmen their skill, and also for charges to be made by the ships and for other standard features of battle. On the rafts companies and squadrons of the praetorian cohorts were deployed, with a barricade before them from which their catapults and ballistas were to be operated. Marines on decked ships covered the rest of the lake. The immense crowd, coming from the neighbouring towns, and some from the city itself, filled the banks, the higher ground and the hill-tops like a theatre, wishing to see the spectacle or out of respect for the emperor. Dressed in a magnificent military cloak, Claudius presided over the event in person, along with Agrippina, who was not far from him in a mantle of gold cloth. Although it was a battle between criminals, they fought with the spirit of courageous men, and after they had received many wounds their lives were spared.

57. But when, on the conclusion of the spectacle, the passageway was opened for the waters, defects in the construction became clear, for it had not been excavated deeply enough to reach the bottom of the lake. And so, later on, the tunnel was dug deeper and, in order to bring together a crowd once again, a gladiatorial display was put on, with pontoons set down for an infantry battle. In fact, there was even a banquet laid out at the outlet of the lake, and there was intense alarm amongst all present because the force of the gushing waters swept away everything close by, and areas further off were shaken or filled with terror from the crashing and roaring. At the same time Agrippina took advantage of the emperor's fright to accuse Narcissus,* the man responsible for the scheme, of avarice and fraud. And Narcissus did not remain silent, either, criticizing her typically female lack of restraint, and her inordinate ambition.

58. In the consulship of Decimus Junius and Quintus Haterius, Nero, now aged sixteen,* married Claudius' daughter Octavia.* And to gain a brilliant reputation for honourable pursuits and public speaking, he took up the cause of the people of Ilium. After an eloquent disquisition on the Roman people's Trojan descent, on Aeneas as the founder of the Julian family, and other old tales not far removed from legend, he succeeded in having the people of Ilium granted immunity from all public taxation. Thanks to the same public speaker, the colony of Bononia, which had been razed by fire, was assisted with a grant of ten million sesterces. The Rhodians* had their freedom restored—it had often been taken from them, or

confirmed, depending on their service in foreign wars, or their misdeeds in time of civil discord—and Apamea, shaken by an earthquake, was excused payment of tribute for a five-year period.

59. Claudius, however, was being pushed into committing the most heinous crimes, also by the wiles of Agrippina. She destroyed Statilius Taurus,* who was renowned for his wealth, because she coveted his gardens, and Tarquitius Priscus* provided the accusation. Priscus had been Taurus' legate in Africa when Taurus governed there with proconsular powers. After their return from the province, Priscus brought a few charges of extortion against him, but in particular he accused him of practising magic. Taurus did not tolerate a lying accuser and his own unmerited defendant's rags for long; he violently ended his life before the Senate passed sentence. Tarquitius, however, was driven from the Curia, something the senators, who hated the informer, managed to achieve despite Agrippina's canvassing on his behalf.

60. That same year the emperor was quite often heard to comment that judgements made by his procurators should have as much authority as if he had made them himself.* And so it should not be seen as a slip on his part, a senatorial decree was passed to that effect which was fuller and more comprehensive than before. In fact, the deified Augustus had authorized judicial proceedings to be held before knights who governed Egypt,* with their decisions regarded as being as binding as if Roman magistrates had made them. After that, in other provinces and in Rome, several more judicial matters, which were formerly decided by praetors, were put in the hands of equestrians.

Claudius now surrendered to them the entire legal system, over which there had been so much class struggle* or armed conflict. By the Sempronian proposals the equestrian order had been put in charge of the judicial process; the Servilian laws* then restored it to the Senate; and it was over this especially that Marius and Sulla went to war. On those occasions, however, it was a matter of the classes having different interests, and the victories won by them had validity for the whole state. Gaius Oppius and Cornelius Balbus* were, with Caesar's support, the first to be able to negotiate peace terms and take decisions about war. There would be no point in bringing up the people who followed, people like the Matii, the Vedii,* and other Roman knights with influential names—not when Claudius raised up to his own level, and that of the laws, freedmen whom he had set in charge of his personal wealth.

61. Claudius' next proposal was tax-exemption for the people of Cos, and he presented a long discourse on their antiquity. The oldest inhabitants of the island, he said, were the Argives or Coeus, father of Latona; and presently, with the arrival of Aesculapius, the art of healing was introduced, and this gained great fame in the time of his descendants. (At that point Claudius mentioned the names of the various individuals and the *floruit* of each.) Indeed, he continued, Xenophon*—on whose medical knowledge he himself relied—came from that same family, and they should answer Xenophon's prayers by granting that the Coans should live, from then on, free of tribute on a sacred island that ministered exclusively to that god. There is no doubt that many of those same islanders' services* to the Roman people could have been cited, along with victories in which they had participated. Claudius, however, had no need of extraneous arguments to cloak a favour that he had, with his customary indulgence, granted to one individual.

62. Not so the people of Byzantium who, in an appeal to the Senate for relief of their heavy tax burden, listed all *their* services when granted permission to speak. They began with the treaty they had struck with us in the days of our war with the Macedonian king* who was of low birth and so given the title 'Pseudo-Philip'. After that they brought up the forces they had sent against Antiochus, Perses, and Aristonicus,* and the help given to Antonius* in the war against the pirates. Next came the offers they had made to Sulla, Lucullus, and Pompey, and then their recent services to the Caesars. This was all possible, they said, because they occupied an area convenient for the passage of generals and their armies, travelling by land or sea, and also for the transport of provisions.

63. In fact, the Greeks founded Byzantium* at the far edge of Europe, on the narrowest part of the strait between Europe and Asia. When they consulted Pythian Apollo on where to establish the city, the answer from the oracle was that 'they should seek a site opposite the lands of the blind'. It was the people of Chalcedon who were being referred to in this riddling phrase because they had arrived there earlier and seen the advantages of the region first, but had then chosen an inferior* one. For Byzantium possesses fertile soil, and teeming sea-waters, the result of the immense fish shoals that come pouring

out from the Pontus; frightened by the slanting rocks beneath the surface, these avoid the winding shoreline opposite and are brought into the harbours on this side. As a result, the people were initially rich and prosperous. Later, under the weight of their tax burdens, they made urgent requests for them to be ended or curtailed. The emperor supported them, noting that they had recently been exhausted by wars in Thrace and the Bosporus* and needed help. So it was that their tribute was remitted for five years.

64. In the consulship of Marcus Asinius and Manius Acilius, it was understood from a succession of prodigies that a warning of change for the worse was being given. Soldiers' standards and tents burned with fire that came from the sky; a swarm of bees settled on the top of the Capitol; hermaphroditic babies had been delivered, and a pig with hawk's talons. One phenomenon included amongst the portents was the diminished number of all the magistrates, since a quaestor, an aedile, a tribune, a praetor, and a consul all died within the space of a few months.

But Agrippina was especially frightened. She was alarmed at a remark of Claudius'—which he had let drop when he was drunk— that it was his fate to suffer, and then to punish, the sexual misconduct of his wives. She decided to take action and take it quickly, though first she destroyed Domitia Lepida, and for typically female motives. Lepida was a daughter of the younger Antonia;* she had had Augustus as her uncle; she was first cousin once removed to Agrippina; and she was the sister of Agrippina's former husband Gnaeus—and so she thought herself on Agrippina's level of distinction. Nor was there a great difference in beauty, age, and wealth; and both were immoral, disreputable, and violent, rivals no less in vices than in the blessings granted them by fortune. But the most bitter rivalry between them was over whether aunt or mother would have the greater influence on Nero.* For Lepida was trying to win over the young man's mind by cajoling and liberality; Agrippina, by contrast, was grim and threatening—able to give her son an empire, unable to stand him as emperor.

65. The charges brought against Lepida, however, were those of having made the emperor's wife the object of magical spells, and causing disturbance of the peace in Italy by not keeping her troops of slaves in Calabria sufficiently under control. On these grounds she was condemned to death, despite Narcissus' vigorous

opposition. For Narcissus was becoming ever more suspicious of Agrippina, and he was said to have remarked amongst his cronies that, whether it was Britannicus or Nero who acceded to power, his death was certain, but that Claudius had done so well by him that he would lay down his life in his service. Messalina and Silius had been condemned, he said, and there were similar grounds for another accusation should Nero become emperor. If Britannicus were the successor, as emperor he would have nothing to fear.* But now the whole royal house was being rent asunder by his stepmother's intrigues, which would be a greater crime than if he had said nothing about the sexual impropriety of the earlier wife. Not that there was even a lack of sexual impropriety now, he added, since she had Pallas as her lover—just so no one could doubt that honour, morals, and her body all meant less to her than supreme power! Uttering these and similar comments, he would embrace Britannicus* and pray for him to acquire the strength of age as quickly as possible. Let him grow up, he would say, stretching out his hands at one moment to the gods, at another to the boy himself; let him drive off his father's enemies, and even take revenge on his mother's killers.

66. Burdened with all these anxieties, Narcissus fell ill and went to Sinuessa to restore his strength in its mild climate and wholesome waters. Agrippina had long been set on committing the crime, was quick to grasp the opportunity she was offered, and was not short of agents for it; and so she considered the type of poison to be used. The act should not be betrayed by an effect that was swift and deadly, she thought. If she chose one that was slow and lingering, however, Claudius might, as he reached the end, become aware of the trick played on him and regain affection for his son. Something recherché was what was wanted, something to disrupt his reasoning while delaying his end. A specialist in such matters, whose name was Locusta,* was selected for the job; she had recently been found guilty of murder by poison, and had long been retained as one of the instruments of the palace. A poison was concocted with this woman's expertise, and the agent to administer it was one of the court eunuchs, Halotus,* whose usual occupation was to bring in, and act as taster for, the imperial dinners.

67. The whole story soon gained such notoriety that writers of the period have recorded that the poison was smeared on a particularly

succulent mushroom, and that its immediate effects went unnoticed, either from inadvertence or Claudius' drunkenness. At the same time, a bowel movement appeared to have come to his aid. Agrippina was terrified. Fearing the worst, she ignored the odium immediate action might arouse and relied on the complicity of the doctor Xenophon, which she had secured in advance. As if he were helping Claudius in his efforts to vomit, Xenophon, it is thought, put down his throat a feather smeared with fast-working poison. He was not unaware that the greatest crimes involve risk at the beginning, but bring reward* on completion.

68. Meanwhile, the Senate was being called together, and the consuls and priests were beginning to recite their vows for the preservation of the emperor's life. And this was when the already dead Claudius was being covered with blankets and dressings—a time during which the appropriate arrangements were being made to secure Nero's accession to power. First of all, Agrippina, seemingly overwhelmed with grief and seeking consolation, held Britannicus in her arms, calling him the very image of his father, and using various devices to stop him leaving his room. She likewise kept back his sisters Antonia and Octavia, and she had blocked with guards* all access to the scene, making frequent announcements that the emperor's health was improving. This was so that the soldiers would have their hopes raised, and the auspicious moment could arrive as the Chaldeans had advised.

69. Then, in the middle of the day, on 13 October, the doors of the palace suddenly opened. With Burrus accompanying him, Nero came out to the cohort that, following regular military routine, was on guard duty. There, at the prompting of the commanding officer, he was cheered and placed in a litter. They say that some had hesitated, looking round and asking where Britannicus was, but presently, as no one suggested an alternative, they went along with the choice that was on offer. Nero was carried into the camp, and after a few preliminary words appropriate to the occasion he promised largesse on the scale of his father's generous distributions,* and was hailed as emperor.

The decision of the troops was followed by decrees from the Senate, and there was no indecision in the provinces either.

Claudius was voted divine honours, and the funeral ceremony for him matched that of the deified Augustus, since Agrippina was trying to rival the pomp of her great-grandmother Livia. The will was not read out, however, for fear that the shameful injustice of the stepson being preferred to the son might upset the common people.

BOOK THIRTEEN

1. The first death* under the new principate was that of Junius Silanus,* proconsul of Asia, and it was brought off by the machinations of Agrippina, without Nero's knowledge. Silanus had not provoked his own downfall because he had a violent nature; he was an indolent man, and despised under the earlier regimes, to the point that Gaius Caesar used to call him 'the golden sheep'. It was rather that Agrippina, having engineered the killing of his brother Lucius Silanus, feared vengeance from him. For it was now common talk that Silanus was to be preferred to Nero who was scarcely beyond boyhood and had gained power by a crime. Silanus, it was said, was a man of mature age,* innocent character, and noble birth, who was also one of the descendants of the Caesars, a point then regarded as important (Silanus was also a great-great-grandson* of the deified Augustus).

This was the motive for his murder. The perpetrators were Publius Celer,* a Roman knight, and the freedman Helius,* who were responsible for the emperor's affairs in Asia. By them the proconsul was given poison at dinner, too obviously for them to escape notice.

No less speedy was the death of Claudius' freedman Narcissus (whose quarrels with Agrippina I have related above*), which was forced on him by a pitiless imprisonment and the most dire of circumstances. This was against the wishes of the emperor, to whose as-yet hidden vices Narcissus' avarice and extravagance were admirably suited.

2. The general slide towards carnage was opposed only by Afranius Burrus and Annaeus Seneca. These were the men guiding the emperor's youth and (a rare phenomenon when power is shared) they acted in harmony, exercising equal influence, but in different spheres, Burrus with his military interests and strict morality, Seneca with his oratorical teaching and principled cordiality. The two worked together so they could the more easily confine the unsteady age of the emperor (if he rejected virtue) to acceptable diversions.

The one struggle both faced was with Agrippina's headstrong character. Ablaze with all the passions of a criminally acquired rule, she had on her side Pallas, the man responsible for Claudius' ruining himself with his incestuous marriage and disastrous adoption. But it was not in Nero's nature to defer to slaves, and by his surly arrogance Pallas had exceeded the parameters of a freedman's conduct, making himself offensive to the emperor. In public, however, all sorts of honours were heaped on Agrippina, and when the tribune, following military routine, asked for the password, Nero gave him 'excellent mother'. By decree of the Senate, she was also granted two lictors,* a priesthood* of the cult of Claudius, and, along with these, a public funeral for Claudius, with deification* to follow.

3. On the day of the funeral, Nero proceeded with the eulogy of Claudius. While he held forth on the antiquity of his family, and his ancestors' consulships and triumphs, he and everyone else remained serious. His comments on Claudius' cultural pursuits,* and the fact that during his rule there had been no mishap in external affairs, also received a favourable hearing. But when he turned to Claudius' foresight and wisdom, no one could hold back his laughter. And yet the speech, being a composition of Seneca's, had a large measure of sophistication, the man being possessed of a talent that charmed, and was well adapted to the contemporary ear.

Older people, whose spare time is spent comparing past and present, observed that Nero was the first of all the holders of the supreme power to have needed another man's rhetoric. For the dictator Caesar* was a match for the best orators, and Augustus had a ready and articulate delivery, and one befitting an emperor. Tiberius, too, had a skilful manner of weighing his words, and was able to express his sentiments with force or with deliberate ambiguity. Even Gaius Caesar's disturbed mind did not spoil the power of his speaking. In Claudius, too, when he was delivering a prepared speech, one would not find elegance lacking. In Nero's case, his lively intellect turned elsewhere right from his early years—to engraving, painting, singing, and chariot-driving. Sometimes, too, in his verse-composition he demonstrated that he had the basic elements of literary skill.

4. The charade of sorrow completed, Nero entered the Curia and, after some preliminary remarks on the authority of the senators and the consensus of the military, he observed that he had advice and examples available to make his administration exceptional. Furthermore, his youth had not been steeped in civil wars or domestic strife, he said, and he brought with him no animosities, no wrongs to be righted, and no thirst for revenge. He then sketched the outlines of his coming

principate,* avoiding especially matters that had recently caused burning resentment. He would not be a judge in all cases, he said, with informers and defendants confined in one house where the influence of a few would be at work. There would be no bribery in his home, no room for influence-peddling. His house and the state were separate. The Senate should retain its ancient functions; Italy and the 'public' provinces should address themselves to the tribunals of the consuls. They would grant them access to the Senate, while he himself would see to the armies that were his charge.

5. Nero did not break his word, either, and many measures were implemented on senatorial authority. Pleading a case for payment or gifts* was to be disallowed, and quaestors-designate* would not be obliged to give gladiatorial shows. The second of these Agrippina opposed as being a reversal of Claudius' legislation, but the senators carried it none the less. (They used to be summoned to the Palatium just so that Agrippina could be present, standing at a doorway added at the back and separated from the proceedings by a curtain, which kept her out of sight but did not prevent her hearing.* In fact, when representatives of the Armenians were pleading the cause of their people before Nero, she was preparing to mount the emperor's tribunal and preside with him, and would have but for Seneca who, while the others were paralysed with fear, advised the emperor to go to meet his mother as she approached. Thus disgrace was obviated by a show of filial devotion.)

6. At the year's end disturbing rumours arrived of another incursion of the Parthians and of their raids on Armenia after the expulsion of Radamistus (who, after often taking control of the realm and then becoming a fugitive, had now also abandoned the war). As a result, in a city avid for gossip, questions were being asked. How could an emperor scarcely past seventeen shoulder this burden or stave off the crisis? What support was to be expected from a man ruled by a woman? Could battles, the blockading of cities, and all the other military operations also be conducted by teachers? Others felt differently. What had transpired, they said, was better than having Claudius, enfeebled with age and indolence, being called on to undertake the hardships of a campaign, a man who would be taking orders from slaves! In fact, Burrus and Seneca were known for their broad experience; and, people asked, how far could their emperor be lacking in strength when Gnaeus Pompey* took on the burden of

civil war in his eighteenth year and Caesar Octavianus in his nineteenth?* At the highest level of government, more was achieved by
authority and policy than by weapons and physical strength. Nero
would give proof positive that he was relying on friends who were
honourable (or otherwise) if, setting jealousy aside, he were to select
an outstanding commander, rather than a rich man relying on favour
gained through influence-peddling.

7. As people passed these and other such observations around,
Nero ordered the young men recruited in the neighbouring
provinces to be brought up to supplement the legions of the East, and
for the legions themselves to be deployed closer to Armenia. He further ordered the two veteran kings Agrippa and Antiochus* to make
ready forces for an offensive into Parthian territory, and bridges were
also to be built over the Euphrates. Armenia Minor Nero assigned
to Aristobulus,* and the area of Sophene to Sohaemus,* both of
them also receiving royal diadems. And then, opportunely, a rival to
Vologaeses emerged in the person of his son Vardanes, and the Parthians
left Armenia, apparently postponing hostilities.

8. In the Senate, however, all was celebrated with hyperbolic
proposals. Members voted public thanksgiving to the gods and triumphal dress* for the emperor on the thanksgiving days; they voted
that he enter the city in ovation, and that he be granted a statue on
the same scale as that of Mars the Avenger, and in the same temple.
But, the routine sycophancy apart, they were happy that Nero had
given Domitius Corbulo responsibility for securing Armenia, and
that an avenue was apparently being opened up for merit.

The troops in the East were divided in the following manner.
Some of the auxiliaries, along with two legions, were to remain in the
province of Syria under its governor Quadratus Ummidius. Corbulo
would have an equal number of citizen and allied forces, plus the
infantry and mounted troops wintering in Cappadocia. The allied
kings had instructions to take orders from either commander,
depending on the requirements of the war, but their support leaned
more towards Corbulo. To capitalize on his reputation (which is of
utmost importance in new ventures), Corbulo marched swiftly, but
was met at the city of Aegeae in Cilicia by Quadratus. Quadratus had
come there fearing that, if Corbulo entered Syria to take over his
troops, he would have all eyes turned on him; for Corbulo was a man
of large physique and flamboyant speech and, beyond his experience

and intelligence, he made an impression even with his unimportant attributes.

9. In fact, both men sent messengers to King Vologaeses, advising him to choose peace over war and supply hostages, thereby maintaining the deference to the Roman people customarily shown by earlier kings. To allow himself to prepare for war on his own terms, or else to remove suspected rivals by calling them hostages, Vologaeses put the leading members of the Arsacid house in the Romans' hands. They were accepted by the centurion Insteius, who had been sent by Ummidius and happened to be there first, visiting the king on that business. When this came to Corbulo's notice, he ordered Arrius Varus,* prefect of a cohort, to go and take possession of the hostages. This led to a quarrel between the prefect and the centurion and, not to prolong this spectacle before foreigners, the hostages and Roman officers who were escorting them were left to decide the matter. They preferred Corbulo, whose renown was fresh and who enjoyed some sort of popularity even with the enemy. The result was friction between the generals. Ummidius protested that the gains made by his plans were taken from him; Corbulo for his part claimed that the king had been brought to offer hostages only when he himself was chosen as commander for the war and thereby transformed Vologaeses' hopes into fear. To settle their quarrel, Nero had a proclamation made that laurel was being added to the imperial fasces* because of the successes of Quadratus and Corbulo. These events I have put together, though they actually extended into the next consulship.

10. That same year Nero petitioned the Senate for a statue in honour of his father Gnaeus Domitius,* and for consular insignia for Asconius Labeo, whom he had had as a guardian; and he also refused the offer of solid silver or gold statues for himself. Furthermore, despite a vote of the fathers that the calendar year should commence with the month of December (the month in which Nero was born), he kept 1 January as the start of the year because of its venerable religious associations. Nor were charges entertained in the cases of the senator Carrinas Celer (who was accused by a slave) or the Roman knight* Julius Densus, the charge against whom was based on his support for Britannicus.

11. In the consulship* of Claudius Nero and Lucius Antistius, when the magistrates swore the oath to uphold the legislative measures of the emperors, Nero forbade his colleague Antistius to swear

to uphold the measures he himself had passed. This drew fulsome praise from the senators, who hoped that his young mind, elated by the glory arising from even trivial gestures, might immediately proceed to more substantial ones. Then came his clemency towards Plautius Lateranus, who had been demoted from his rank for adultery with Messalina. Nero restored him to the Senate, committing himself to leniency in a string of speeches which Seneca, by putting them in Nero's mouth, brought to public notice, either to attest to the nobility of his instruction, or to showcase his talent.

12. Meanwhile the power of the mother was gradually weakened. Nero had fallen in love with a freedwoman called Acte,* and had at the same time enlisted as his confidants Marcus Otho* and Claudius Senecio, good-looking young men (Otho came from a consular family,* and Senecio had an imperial freedman for a father). Acte had wormed her way deeply into the emperor's affections—without the mother's knowledge, and later despite her attempts to oppose it—by assisting his extravagances and by secret meetings of a dubious nature. Not even the emperor's older friends objected to seeing a young girl satisfy his urges, with no one harmed. For—whether by some stroke of fate, or because the illicit is always more appealing—Nero detested his wife Octavia, a noblewoman of proven virtue; and there were fears that, if disallowed that indulgence, he would go on a rampage of unlawful sex with illustrious ladies.

13. But Agrippina, just like a woman, grumbled about the 'freedwoman rival', the 'serving-girl daughter-in-law', and the like, and she would not wait until her son regretted or tired of the liaison. In fact, the fouler her reproaches, the more she fired his passion, until eventually he was driven by the power of his love to throw off all deference to his mother, and put himself in the hands of Seneca. (One of Seneca's friends, Annaeus Serenus,* had, in fact, screened the young ruler's early desires by affecting passion for the same freedwoman, and had put his name at Nero's disposal, publicly lavishing on her gifts that the emperor was really giving her in secret.)

Agrippina then changed her tactics. She approached the young man with endearments, and offered him the privacy of her own bedroom for concealing those activities that his early years and exalted position might demand. Indeed, she even admitted her ill-timed severity, and put at his disposal her own great riches, which fell not far short of the emperor's—as excessive in her obsequiousness to her son as she had earlier been in restraining him. The change did not fool Nero, and his closest friends were also afraid. They begged him to be on guard against the wiles of a woman who had always been ruthless, and was now also being duplicitous.

As it happened, Nero had during those days been examining the attire that had graced wives and parents of emperors. He selected a garment and gems, which he sent as a present to his mother, and there was no penny-pinching—he was, unasked, making her a gift of choice items coveted by others. Agrippina, however, proclaimed that her wardrobe was not being increased by these things; rather, she was being kept from the rest, and her son was merely dividing up all the things that he possessed thanks to her.

14. There was no shortage of people to put a more sinister interpretation on this, and Nero, furious with those who supported such female arrogance, relieved Pallas of the responsibility vested in him by Claudius, through which he exercised virtual control over the realm. It was said that, as the man left with a large crowd of attendants, Nero made the not inappropriate remark that Pallas was 'going to take his resignation oath'.* In fact, Pallas had negotiated an agreement that he not be subject to enquiry regarding any past action, and that his accounts with the state be taken as balanced.

After this Agrippina charged headlong into fearful threats, not stopping short of declaring in the emperor's hearing that Britannicus was now grown, the rightful and worthy heir to his father's power, which was currently wielded by an adopted interloper as a result of wrongs done by his mother. She had no objection, she said, to the exposure of all the ills of that unhappy house, her own marriage first of all, and her use of poison. The one precaution taken by heaven and by herself was leaving her stepson alive! She would go to the camp with him, she said. The daughter of Germanicus should be heard on one side, the cripple Burrus and the exile Seneca on the other, men laying claim to the governance of the human race—with a mutilated hand, of course, and a professorial tongue! At the same time she threw up her hands, showered abuse on him, and called upon the hallowed Claudius, the shades of the Silani below and all the crimes she had committed for nothing.

15. Nero was worried by this, and the day was also approaching on which Britannicus was to complete his fourteenth year.* He pondered at one moment on his mother's impetuosity, at the next on the character of the boy himself, which had lately been put to the test and demonstrated in a trifling incident, but one that had gained Britannicus widespread approval. During the festal days of Saturn,* one of the games that Nero's companions played was drawing lots for the 'kingship', and the lot had fallen to Nero. He therefore gave the others various commands that would not cause embarrassment, but he ordered Britannicus to get up, go to the middle of the group, and begin a song. He was expecting to provoke laughter at the expense of a boy who had no experience even of sober gatherings, much less drunken ones. Britannicus, however, confidently launched into some verse in which there were allusions to his own removal from his father's home and from supreme power. The result was an awakening of a sympathy for him that was the more obvious since the gaiety of the night had banished all insincerity. Awareness of the ill-will he had himself incurred increased Nero's hatred, and he was now also under pressure from Agrippina's threats. But there was no viable charge, and he dare not give an order openly for his brother's death. He therefore set to work in secret and ordered a poison to be prepared. He used the services of Julius Pollio, tribune of a praetorian cohort, in whose care the condemned poisoner called Locusta— a woman with a great reputation for her criminal acts—was being detained. For arrangements had been made long before for all closely associated with Britannicus to have no scruples or loyalty.

Britannicus was given his first dose of poison by his very own tutors, but because of a bowel movement he excreted it—it was too weak, or perhaps had been diluted so its effect would not be immediately lethal. But the time the crime was taking taxed Nero's patience. He threatened the tribune and ordered the poisoner's execution; while they were keeping an eye on public opinion, he claimed, and preparing to defend themselves, they were putting his security on hold. At this they promised a death as swift as from a sword-thrust, and a poison was brewed close to the emperor's bedroom, its virulence guaranteed by the previously tested* toxins it contained.

16. It was the custom for emperors' children to take their meals sitting with the other young nobles* at their own, less copiously provided table, in sight of their relatives. There Britannicus was dining and, since a chosen member of his staff would taste what he ate and drank, the following ruse was found so that the protocol would not be broken, or the crime betrayed by the death of both individuals.

Britannicus was handed a drink that was innocuous, and also very hot, and which had gone through the tasting process. Then, when it was refused because of its heat, poison was added in some cold water, and that spread so effectively throughout the boy's body that the power to speak and breathe were both taken from him. There was alarm amongst those sitting around him, and the less discerning scattered; but those with a keener understanding remained fast in their seats, staring at Nero. He, reclining and seemingly unaware of the situation, remarked that this was a regular occurrence connected with the epilepsy with which Britannicus had been afflicted since early infancy, and that his sight and senses would gradually return. But from Agrippina, for all her efforts to control her expression, came a fleeting glance of such panic and confusion that it was clear that she knew just as little as Britannicus' sister Octavia. She was beginning to realize, in fact, that her last support had been removed, and a precedent had been set for murdering a family member. Octavia, too, despite her tender years, had learned to hide grief, affection, and all her emotions. And so, after a brief silence, the revelry of the banquet recommenced.

17. The one night saw Britannicus' killing and his funeral pyre in tandem, for preparations (which were modest enough) for his funeral had already been put in place. He was, however, interred in the Campus Martius,* during a downpour so violent that the masses took it as a sign of the gods' anger over a crime that even many men could forgive, when they considered the ancient animosities between brothers, and the indivisibility of regal power. Many authors of the period record that, on numerous days prior to the death, Nero took advantage sexually of the young Britannicus—and his end might therefore be seen as neither too early nor cruel. And that despite its being hurriedly brought upon the last of the Claudian bloodline* (amid the sacred observances of the table, without his being given even the time to embrace his sisters, and before the eyes of his enemy), who was defiled by sexual misconduct before he was by poison.

Nero defended the hurried obsequies in an edict, declaring that it was the established practice of their ancestors* to remove from the gaze of the people bitterly untimely funerals, and not hold them back with encomia and ceremony. But with his brother's aid now lost to him, he added, all his remaining hopes rested in the state; and the senators and people should give all the more support to their emperor as the lone survivor of a family born to the supreme power.

18. Nero then bestowed largesse upon his greatest friends. And there was no lack of people criticizing men with pretensions to austerity for having, at that time, divided houses and country estates amongst themselves like plunder. Others believed that pressure was applied by the emperor, who was conscious of his guilt and hoping for forgiveness if he put all the most powerful under obligation with lavish gifts.

His mother's wrath, however, could be appeased by no munificence. She became close to Octavia, and often held clandestine meetings with her friends, appropriating cash from all sources which— her congenital rapacity apart—she considered an emergency fund. She gave a warm welcome to tribunes and centurions, and showed respect for the names and virtues of such nobles as still survived, as if she were searching for a leader and a party.

Nero learned of this, and ordered the withdrawal of the military watch*—earlier maintained for her as the emperor's wife, and now as the imperial mother—and likewise of the Germans* recently added as sentries as the same mark of respect. Moreover, to cut down on the large numbers of her morning-callers,* he separated their home, and transferred her to Antonia's former abode. Whenever he visited there in person, he came surrounded by a large group of centurions and left after a hurried kiss.

19. Nothing in the world is as flimsy and fleeting as a reputation gained for power that has no strength of its own. Agrippina's threshold was immediately deserted. Nobody offered consolation; nobody visited her, apart from a few ladies; and whether they did so from affection or hate is unclear. One was Junia Silana, who, as I noted above,* had been driven out of her marriage to Gaius Silius by Messalina. She was reputed for her nobility, her looks, and her easy virtue, and was for a long time a favourite of Agrippina. Subsequently private animosities arose between the two, for Agrippina had put the young nobleman Sextius Africanus* off marrying Silana by repeatedly telling him she was a slattern who was getting on in years. (This was not to set Africanus aside for herself, but to keep the potential husband from coming into possession of the childless Silana's riches.)

Now offered the prospect of revenge, Silana arranged for two of her clients, Iturius and Calvisius, to provide the accusation. The charges were not the old, hackneyed ones—Agrippina lamenting the death of Britannicus, or making public the wrongs done to Octavia—but rather that she had decided to encourage Rubellius Plautus* (who on his mother's side was as closely related as Nero to the deified Augustus) to foment revolution, and then, by marrying Plautus and getting him into power, to reassert her control over the state. These charges Iturius and Calvisius made known to Atimetus, a freedman of Nero's aunt Domitia.* Delighted with this gift—for bitter rivalry existed between Agrippina and Domitia—Atimetus pushed the actor Paris,* who was also a freedman of Domitia, to go quickly and ferociously denounce Agrippina.

20. The night was far advanced, and Nero was spinning it out in a drinking bout when Paris entered. Normally his arrival at this hour would stimulate the ruler's excesses, but on that occasion Paris affected a gloomy air. He laid out the charge in detail, and struck such terror into the emperor as he listened that Nero decided not only to kill his mother and Plautus, but even to remove Burrus from his prefecture—Burrus had been promoted through Agrippina's favour, he thought, and was now repaying her. Fabius Rusticus* records that a letter was actually written to Caecina Tuscus,* assigning to him responsibility for the praetorian cohorts, and that it was only through Seneca's influence that Burrus retained the post. Plinius* and Cluvius,* however, make no mention of there being suspicions about the prefect's loyalty. (Of course, Fabius tends to eulogize Seneca, to whose friendship he owed his success. For my part, I shall follow the consensus of the sources, but in the case of their giving divergent accounts I shall transmit these accounts under the writers' own names.)

Nero was in a panic and eager to kill his mother. He could be brought to delay matters only when Burrus promised him her death if she were proven guilty. But, said Burrus, anyone should be allowed a defence, and a mother above all. And there were no accusers in this instance, only the words spoken by one man, and emanating from a hostile family. Nero should note that it was now the hour of darkness, that he had been awake all night carousing, and that all the circumstances favoured a precipitate and misguided response.

21. The emperor's fear was allayed by this, and at daybreak a delegation went to Agrippina so that she could be apprised of the charges— she was to refute them,* or else pay the penalty. Burrus discharged

this commission, in Seneca's presence, and there were also some freedmen present to witness the conversation. Then, after revealing the charges and their authors, Burrus struck a threatening pose. Agrippina, remembering her pride, retorted: 'I am not surprised that Silana, not having borne a child, has no idea of a mother's feelings—for mothers do not change their children the way a slut does lovers! Iturius and Calvisius, after exhausting their entire fortunes, are repaying the old lady with one last service, namely undertaking this accusation. But that is no reason for me to incur the disgraceful suspicion of murder within the family, or the emperor of being an accomplice. As far as Domitia is concerned, I would thank her for her animosity if she were trying to rival me in goodwill towards my Nero; as it is, she is merely composing what seem to be dramas for the stage, using her bedfellow Atimetus and the actor Paris. When, through my planning, preparations were being made for his adoption, for his proconsular power, for his post as consul-designate, and for all the other measures preparatory to his taking power—at that time she was embellishing her fishponds on her Baiae estate!* Or else let someone stcp forward with proof that the city cohorts have been corrupted, that the loyalty of the provinces has been undermined, or finally that there has been bribery of slaves or freedmen for criminal purposes!

'Could I have remained alive with Britannicus in power? And suppose Plautus, or some other who would judge me, took over the government. Naturally, people to accuse me are in short supply, people to charge me not only with the odd imprudent comment arising from impulsive affection, but with crimes for which I could be pardoned only by a son!'

Those present were moved, and were actually attempting to calm her, but she insisted on talking to her son. There she said nothing about her innocence, which might have indicated some lack of confidence, and nothing about her services, which might have implied a reproach, but she gained from him revenge on her accusers and rewards for her friends.

22. Faenius Rufus was entrusted with authority over the grain-supply,* Arruntius Stella* with supervision of the games that were now being prepared by the emperor, and Claudius Balbillus* with Egypt. Syria was earmarked for Publius Anteius,* but his hopes were subsequently frustrated by various stratagems and he was finally kept back* in the city. Silana, however, was driven into exile, and Calvisius

and Iturius, too, found themselves relegated. Atimetus was executed, but Paris was too important a figure amidst the emperor's debaucheries to face punishment. Plautus was, for the moment, passed over in silence.

23. After that Pallas and Burrus were accused of conspiring to have Cornelius Sulla* summoned to imperial power because of his distinguished lineage and family connection with Claudius, whose son-in-law he was through his marriage to Antonia. The man responsible for the charge was a certain Paetus, who was notorious for his dealings with the treasury in confiscated goods, and at that time he was clearly caught out in a lie. However, Pallas' proven innocence brought people less pleasure than his arrogance brought indignation. For when the names of the freedmen who were his alleged accomplices were given, Pallas replied that, at home, he never communicated anything except by a nod or a wave of the hand, and if further explanation were necessary, he used writing so as to avoid conversing with them. Although he was also in the dock, Burrus joined the judges in expressing his opinion.* A sentence of exile was imposed on the accuser, and the records he used to retrieve the forgotten claims of the treasury were incinerated.

24. At the end of the year the cohort usually stationed to keep watch over the games* was removed. The point of this was to provide a greater impression of freedom, to lessen corruption amongst the military by isolating them from the permissive atmosphere of the theatre, and to test whether the plebs would maintain order if their guardians were removed. The emperor conducted a purification of the city, in accordance with a response from the soothsayers relating to lightning that struck the temples of Jupiter and Minerva.

25. The consulship of Quintus Volusius and Publius Scipio saw peace abroad, but shameful dissolution at home, where Nero made a practice of wandering through the city streets, the brothels, and the taverns dressed as a slave to conceal his identity. He would be attended by men whose task it was to snatch objects displayed for sale, and to inflict beatings on those they met; and so unaware were the latter that even Nero himself received blows and sported bruises on his face. It then became common knowledge that the emperor was the perpetrator, and assaults on men and women of rank began to multiply, with some (now that indulgence had been granted) doing the same things with their own gangs—and with impunity, as they

did so using Nero's name! And the night in Rome resembled that in a captured city.

Julius Montanus, who was a member of the senatorial order* but had not yet held office, happened to meet the emperor in the dark. When Nero made a violent attack* on him, Montanus vigorously resisted, but then he recognized him and begged his pardon. For that he was forced to commit suicide—as if he had reproached him! Nero, however, was more wary after that, and he surrounded himself with soldiers and numerous gladiators. These were to allow brawls to go on if they began on a small scale and were apparently between individuals; but any stiff resistance from the victims they would meet with weapons. He also created virtual battles from unruly behaviour in the theatre and the factions supporting the actors, by granting amnesty and awarding prizes, and even by viewing the troubles himself, sometimes hidden, but very often quite openly. Finally, with the people at each other's throats and the frightening prospect of more serious disturbances, the only remedy that was found was the banishment of actors from Italy, and the return of a military presence in the theatre.

26. At about this same time the misconduct of freedmen was discussed in the Senate, and a demand was made for patrons to have the right to revoke emancipation in cases of the undeserving. There was no shortage of supporters, but the consuls did not dare put the motion while the emperor remained unaware of the matter, though they did give him a written report of the consensus of the Senate. Nero <deliberated> whether to sponsor the resolution < . . . > his advisers being few and divided in their opinions. Some grumbled that freedmen's disrespect, reinforced by their new liberty, had become so out of control that they could consider dealing violently, or at least on terms of equality, with their patrons; and they even raised their fists to beat them, impudently urging on them the punishment appropriate to themselves! In fact, they asked, what recourse* did an injured patron have other than to relegate the freedman to the Campanian coast* beyond the hundredth milestone? Apart from that, the legal processes were undiscriminating and the same for both parties. A patron should be provided with a weapon that could not be held in contempt. Moreover, it would not be hard for the manumitted to preserve their liberty by the same deference through which they had gained it, while those clearly guilty of crimes deserved to be brought back into servitude to ensure that those whom kindness had not reformed could be restrained by fear.

27. The argument of the opposition went like this. The wrong-doing of the few should bring ruin upon them, but the rights of all should not be curtailed—they were a widely diffused class of people. It was from them largely that the tribes* and the decuries were drawn, along with magistrates' and priests' attendants, as well as the cohorts conscripted in the city.* It was from here, and nowhere else, that most equestrians* and many senators* traced their origins, and if freedmen were set on one side, the fewness of the freeborn would become apparent. It was no accident, they said, that when their ancestors differentiated honours for the various orders they had made freedom the common attribute of all. In fact, they had even put in place two forms of manumission, so that room could be left for a change of heart or a further benefit. Those whom the patron did not free by the formal act* were still virtually held by the chain of servitude.* Everyone should carefully review the merits of a case, they concluded, and be slow in granting what cannot be removed once given.

This was the view that prevailed, and the emperor gave the Senate written instructions to deal with cases individually, whenever freed-men were accused by their patrons, and not curtail rights in a global manner. And not long after this Nero's aunt saw her freedman Paris taken from her, ostensibly by civil law—and not without some disgrace falling on the emperor, by whose order the judgement that the man was freeborn* had been obtained.

28. Nevertheless, there still remained some semblance of the republic. An altercation broke out between the praetor Vibullius and the plebeian tribune Antistius* over an order given by the tribune for the release of some supporters of actors imprisoned by the praetor for disorderly conduct. The senators endorsed Vibullius' decision, censuring Antistius for his permissiveness. At the same time the trib-unes were ordered not to encroach on the authority of praetors and consuls,* or bring in from Italy* people who could be subject to legal proceedings there. The consul-designate Lucius Piso* made the further motion that tribunes should not inflict in their own homes* any penalty that lay within their powers, and that quaestors of the treasury not enter in the public records* any fine levied by them until four months had passed. In the meantime, there should be right of

appeal, and the consuls would decide the issue. Restrictions were also placed on the power of the aediles,* with limits set on the capacity of both curule and plebeian aediles to levy fines and seize goods for non-payment of them. And the plebeian tribune Helvidius Priscus* engaged in a personal feud with a quaestor of the treasury, Obultronius Sabinus,* charging him with treating the poor unmercifully in the exercise of his authority to confiscate and sell. After that the emperor transferred charge of the public records from the quaestors to prefects.*

29. The structure of the treasury department had taken various forms* and undergone frequent changes. Augustus granted the Senate the right to choose its administrators. Subsequently, as suspicions arose of irregularities in the voting, those who were to take charge of it were drawn by lot from the body of praetors. That did not last long, either, because the lot would stray to the incompetent. Claudius then put quaestors in control again, and, so they should not be remiss through fear of causing offence, promised them extraordinary honours; but as this was their first public office, they lacked the firmness of maturity. Accordingly, Nero selected* instead those who had held the praetorship and had proven experience.

30. In this same consulship, Vipsanius Laenas was convicted of rapacity in administering his province of Sardinia; and Cestius Proculus was acquitted on a charge of extortion that the people of Crete brought against him. Clodius Quirinalis was accused of having oppressed Italy, as though it were the lowest of nations, by his extravagance and brutality when he was commander of the rowers stationed at Ravenna, and he took poison to forestall condemnation. Caninius Rebilus, one of the country's leading men in jurisprudence and wealth, escaped the torments of a sick old age by letting the blood flow from his arteries. (In fact, he had been thought incapable of the resolution to commit suicide because of the effeminate predilections for which he was notorious.) Lucius Volusius, however, went out enjoying great esteem. He had had a life that covered ninety-three years, an outstanding fortune honourably gained, and harmonious friendships with many emperors.

31. In the consulship of Nero (his second) and Lucius Piso, there were few events worth recording, unless one wishes to fill volumes with a panegyric on the foundations and timbers* that the emperor used to raise his massive amphitheatre in the Campus Martius.

(In fact, it has been found in keeping with the dignity of the Roman people to set only remarkable incidents in the history books, consigning material of this nature to the city's daily record.) However, it is true that the colonies of Capua and Nuceria were strengthened by the addition of veterans; the plebs were granted largesse to the sum of four hundred sesterces per person; and forty million were deposited in the treasury to sustain the people's credit. In addition, the four per cent sale-tax* on the sale of slaves was remitted, though this was more in appearance than reality because the vendor was now ordered to pay it, and purchasers found it passed on as an addition to the price.

The emperor also issued an edict forbidding any magistrate or procurator to stage a show of gladiators or wild animals, or put on any other entertainment, in the province of which he was the governor. For before that governors had been oppressing their subjects* no less by such 'largesse' than they had by their peculation, attempting as they did to shield, by courting popularity, wrongs they had committed through greed.

32. A decree of the Senate,* calculated to provide both punishment and security, was also passed: if a man had been murdered by his slaves, the death penalty was to be inflicted even on those who had been manumitted by his will but remained under the same roof, as well as on the slaves. Lurius Varus, an ex-consul who had earlier been brought down on charges of rapacity, was restored to his rank. A lady of distinction, Pomponia Graecina, married to Aulus Plautius (whose ovation* over the Britons I mentioned earlier), was accused of foreign superstition,* and left to be judged by her husband. Plautius followed the ancient procedure of holding an inquiry before their relatives, since it related to her legal status and reputation, and pronounced her innocent. (Pomponia had a long life of unremitting sorrow. For, after Drusus' daughter Julia* was put to death through Messalina's scheming, she lived for forty years wearing only clothes of mourning, and remaining ever sick at heart. This went unpunished during Claudius' reign, and later redounded to her glory.)

33. That same year saw more people on trial, including Publius Celer, who faced a charge brought by Asia. The emperor could not acquit him, and instead dragged the process out until Celer died of old age. For with his murder of the proconsul Silanus (which I related earlier), Celer by the magnitude of the crime put all his

other misdemeanours in the shade. The people of Cilicia had
brought charges against Cossutianus Capito. He was a man of tainted
and despicable character who believed he had the right to behave as
unscrupulously in the province as he had in the city. He was, however, hounded by a relentless prosecution, so that he finally abandoned his defence and was found guilty* under the law of extortion.
In the case of Eprius Marcellus, from whom the Lycians were seeking damages, influence-peddling was so effective that some of his
prosecutors were punished with exile for having endangered an innocent man!

34. When Nero was consul for the third time, Valerius Messala
entered the consulship as his colleague; and by now only a few old
men* remembered Messala's grandfather, Corvinus the orator, as
being the colleague of the deified Augustus, Nero's great-great-
grandfather, in the same office. However, that noble family's honour
was augmented by an annual grant of 500,000 sesterces so Messala
could endure his poverty innocently. The emperor also established
an annual fund for Aurelius Cotta* and Haterius Antoninus,* despite
their having wasted their inherited wealth on dissipation.

The war between Parthia and Rome over the possession of
Armenia had been dragging on after a feeble start, but at the beginning of that year it was prosecuted with vigour. Vologaeses would
not permit his brother Tiridates to be deprived of a kingdom that he
had given him, or to possess it as a gift of a foreign power; and
Corbulo thought it in keeping with the greatness of the Roman
people to recover territory earlier won by Lucullus and Pompey.*
Furthermore, the Armenians, whose loyalty was dubious, were inviting in the armies of both sides, although they were geographically
and culturally closer to the Parthians, with whom they were also connected by intermarriage, and to whom, in addition, they inclined
through their ignorance of liberty.

35. Corbulo, however, had more trouble coping with the lethargy
of his troops than with enemy treachery. The legions transferred
from Syria,* listless after a long peace, had little tolerance for camp
fatigues. It was clear that there were veterans in that army who had
not done sentry duty or the night watch, and who looked upon the
rampart and ditch as something unfamiliar and strange. Without
helmets and without breastplates, they were sleek and prosperous,
having spent their service only in towns.

Corbulo therefore discharged those disadvantaged by age or ill-health, and requested reinforcements. Troop-levies were then held throughout Galatia and Cappadocia, and a legion was added from Germany,* together with auxiliary cavalry and cohorts of infantry. The entire army was kept under canvas,* despite a winter so severe that the ground, covered with ice, would not afford a place for tents without digging. Many had limbs frostbitten from the intense cold, and some died on watch. The case was noted of a soldier who, carrying a load of firewood, had his hands frozen to the point where they stuck to his load and fell off, leaving his arms as stumps. Corbulo himself, lightly dressed and bare-headed, was regularly in the marching-line and among the working parties, giving praise to the stout-hearted and consolation to the sick, and setting an example for all. Then, because many could not bear the harshness of the climate and campaign, and were beginning to desert, Corbulo looked to severity as a remedy. He did not treat the first or second offences with leniency, as happened in other armies: anyone leaving the standards was summarily executed. That this was beneficial, and more effective than clemency, became clear from the results: there were fewer desertions from that camp than from those where leniency was shown.

36. Meanwhile, Corbulo kept his legions in camp until spring set in, and deployed the auxiliary cohorts in appropriate locations, ordering them not to be the first to risk engagement. Command of these garrisons he confided to Paccius Orfitus, who had held the post of first centurion. Now Orfitus told Corbulo by letter that the barbarians were off their guard and that the Romans were offered a chance of a successful operation, but he was instructed to stick to his fortifications and await a stronger force. However, when a few cavalry squadrons arrived from nearby strongholds and were, through inexperience, demanding action, he broke his orders, engaged the enemy, and was routed. Moreover, the troops that were to have brought support were unnerved by Orfitus' losses, and fled back in panic to their respective camps. Corbulo was angry. He reprimanded Paccius, and ordered him, along with his officers and men, to encamp outside the rampart.* They were kept in that ignominious position until they were released in response to entreaties from the entire army.

37. In addition to his own vassals, Tiridates had the support of his brother Vologaeses, and he now proceeded to put pressure on Armenia,

not furtively but with open warfare. He conducted raids on all he thought to be loyal to us, and if troops were led out against him he took evasive action, flitting here and there and spreading more terror through rumour than by fighting. Frustrated in his prolonged efforts to engage, Corbulo was obliged to follow the example of the enemy and take the war around the country, splitting his forces so that his legates and prefects could make simultaneous attacks on different locations. At the same time he told King Antiochus to launch an assault on the prefectures closest to him. For after executing his son Radamistus as a traitor, Pharasmanes* was venting his old hatred on the Armenians the more actively in order to prove his loyalty to us. That was also the first time the Moschi were won over—a tribe ahead of all others in its alliance with Rome—and they raided the wild areas of Armenia.

Tiridates' plans were thus being completely reversed. He therefore proceeded to send spokesmen to ask, on his own account and on behalf of the Parthians, why, after recently giving hostages and renewing a treaty that was supposed to open the door to further benefits, he was being driven from Armenia, which had long been his possession. If Vologaeses had not made any move himself, he said, it was only because they preferred to settle issues by negotiation rather than by force, but if the Romans persisted with the war, the Arsacids would not lack the courage and good fortune that had been frequently demonstrated by a Roman debacle.* Corbulo, however, was reliably informed that Vologaeses was being delayed by a revolt of Hyrcania, and he urged Tiridates to approach the emperor with a petition. It was possible for him to gain a secure throne and to reign without bloodshed, Corbulo told him, if he abandoned a long-term hope for a better one close at hand.

38. The interchange of messages was doing nothing to advance the cause of peace, and so it was decided that a date and location should be arranged for the two leaders to parley. Tiridates said that a thousand cavalry would escort him, but he did not specify the size and composition of the force that might attend Corbulo, provided that it seemed peaceful, with breastplates and helmets set aside. To anyone in the world, much less a veteran commander with foresight, the barbarian trick would have been obvious. The number being restricted for one side, and a larger one offered to the other, was clearly to bait the trap: if bodies were exposed unprotected to a

cavalry force with expertise in archery, large numbers would be of no advantage. Corbulo, however, hiding his awareness of this, replied that it would be more fitting for them to discuss matters that were of national concern before their entire armies. He then chose a location of which half was made up of gently rising hills—suitable for ranks of infantry—while the other half spread out into flat country where cavalry squadrons could be deployed.

On the agreed day Corbulo made the first move, positioning the allied cohorts and the auxiliary forces of the kings on the wings, with the Sixth Legion in the centre. He had, however, integrated into the legion three thousand men from the Third, whom he had brought in from another camp at night, but there was only one eagle, giving the appearance that it was the same legion unchanged. It was late in the day when Tiridates took up his position, at a distance, where he could be seen rather than heard. And so, without the parley, the Roman commander ordered his men to retire to their various camps.

39. The king now left in a hurry. Either he suspected a ploy, since the Romans were moving in several directions at once, or he was intending to intercept our supplies that were coming by way of the Pontic sea and the town of Trapezus. He was, however, unable to make an attack on the supplies because they were being brought over mountains garrisoned by us, and Corbulo meanwhile, to prevent the war dragging on to no purpose, and to force the Armenians to defend their own possessions, prepared to destroy their fortresses. The strongest in that prefecture, which was called Volandum, he kept for himself; the minor ones he assigned to his legate Cornelius Flaccus, and to the camp prefect Insteius Capito.* Then, after examining the fortifications and making appropriate arrangements for the assault, he encouraged his troops to chase from his home this vagrant enemy, prepared neither for peace nor for war, and who, by his flight, admitted his perfidy as well as his cowardice. They should think about the spoils as well as the glory, he said.

Corbulo next divided his army into four parts. One he grouped in tortoise formation and brought forward to undermine the rampart; a second he ordered to move ladders up to the walls; and a large contingent he ordered to launch firebrands and spears from the engines. The slingers and throwers were allocated a position from which to shoot their projectiles over a considerable distance, so that fear would be equally spread amongst the enemy, and no unit would be able to bring assistance to those in difficulties.

Such was the fervour and drive of the army that, by the third part of the day, the walls had been stripped of defenders, the barriers of the gates demolished, the fortifications taken by scaling, and all adults slaughtered—with not a soldier lost and a mere handful wounded. The horde of non-combatants was auctioned off, and the rest of the plunder went to the victors. The legate and the prefect were just as fortunate. Three fortresses were stormed in one day, and of the others some capitulated in terror, and others surrendered through the decision of their inhabitants.

This inspired them with confidence for an attack on the tribal capital, Artaxata. The legions were not led there by the shortest route, however: crossing the River Araxes (which laps the city walls) by the bridge would put them in range of projectiles. They went over it at a distance, using a ford of some width.

40. Tiridates felt both shame and fear. Accepting a prospective blockade would make it appear that he had no strength; interfering with it, he might tie himself and his cavalry down on difficult ground. He finally decided to display his battle-line and, if given an opportunity to engage, either to proceed with the battle or, pretending to flee, to put an ambush in place. He therefore suddenly encircled the Roman column, a move not unforeseen by our commander, who had marshalled his army both for marching and for battle. On the march the Third Legion was on the right flank, and the Sixth on the left, with handpicked men of the Tenth in the centre. The baggage had been taken into the lines, and a thousand cavalrymen gave protection to the rear, under orders to parry any attack at close quarters, but not to pursue a retreating enemy. On the wings were the infantry bowmen and the remainder of the cavalry, with the left wing extended further, along the base of some hills, so that if the enemy broke through he would find troops in front of him, and outflanking him.

Tiridates launched assaults from various points without actually coming into javelin-range. He would by turns threaten and feign fear, hoping to loosen our ranks and attack them when they were separated. But no act of bravado broke our solidarity; and all that resulted was that a cavalry officer, who advanced too recklessly, strengthened the obedience of the rest by his example when he was run through by arrows. Tiridates then fell back with the approach of darkness.

41. Corbulo established his camp on the spot, and considered whether to march on Artaxata by night, with his legions unencumbered by baggage, and lay siege to the city, for he assumed Tiridates had withdrawn there. Scouts then brought word that the king was on a lengthy journey, and that it was unclear whether he was heading for the Medes or the Albani. Corbulo therefore waited for dawn, sending ahead his light infantry in the meantime to invest the walls and commence the blockade at a distance. In fact, the townspeople of their own accord threw open the gates and put themselves and their possessions at the mercy of the Romans. That move saved their lives. Artaxata was put to the torch, destroyed, and levelled to the ground; for, because of the size of its walls, it could not be held without a strong garrison, and we did not have forces enough to split between strengthening the garrison and prosecuting the war. On the other hand, if the town remained untouched and unguarded, there was no advantage or glory forthcoming from its capture. There was, in addition, a seemingly god-sent prodigy.* Up to this point everything had been brightly illuminated by the sun. Suddenly, however, the area enclosed by the walls was covered with black cloud and cut off by flashes of lightning, so that it was believed that the gods were attacking and the town was being consigned to destruction by them.

Nero was hailed as *Imperator* because of this success and, following a senatorial decree, prayers of thanksgiving were held. There were statues voted to the emperor, and arches and repeated consulships; and the day on which the victory was won, on which it was announced, and on which it had been discussed in the Senate, were all to be set among the festal days. Other measures of this sort were also put to the vote, so outrageous that Gaius Cassius, who had supported the other honours, declared that, if thanks given to the gods were to be commensurate with the blessings of fortune, a whole year would be insufficient for their prayers. Accordingly, he said, there should be a distinction made between holy days and business days, that is, days on which they could hold religious observances without suspending human activity.

42. Then a defendant who had been storm-tossed by various fortunes, and had earned the hatred of many, was condemned, though not without bringing unpopularity to Seneca. This was Publius Suillius, a fearful and corrupt figure during Claudius' reign, who had not been brought as low as his enemies would have liked by the change in the times, and who was the sort who preferred to be seen as a criminal rather than as a suppliant. It was with the purpose of crushing him, it was thought, that the decree of the Senate was revived, along with the penalty prescribed by the Cincian law, against those who had pleaded in court for pay. And Suillius did not hold back his protests and reproaches. Naturally fierce-tempered, he had also become outspoken in his extreme old age; and he reproached Seneca for being hostile to the friends of Claudius, under whom Seneca had endured a very well earned exile. At the same time, he continued, Seneca, accustomed to impractical studies and inexperienced youth, envied those who employed a lively and genuine eloquence in the defence of their fellow-citizens. He, Suillius, had been Germanicus' quaestor, while Seneca had been an adulterer in that man's house. Was gaining a reward, volunteered by a litigant for an honourable service, to be considered more reprehensible than desecrating the bedrooms of imperial ladies? What was the wisdom, what the philosophical tenets by which Seneca had acquired three hundred million sesterces within a four-year period of friendship with the emperor? In Rome, the wills of childless men were being caught in his net, while Italy and the provinces were being drained by his unscrupulous usury. He, on the other hand, had only limited funds, which were earned by his labours. But he would face accusation, trial, everything rather than have his time-honoured, and independently earned, reputation at the mercy of this nouveau riche!

43. There was no shortage of people to carry these remarks back to Seneca, verbatim or with a more pejorative slant. Accusers were found who charged Suillius with plundering the allies during his governorship of the province of Asia, and with embezzlement of public funds. Presently, they were granted a request for a year to gather evidence, and it seemed that starting with crimes relating to the city would shorten the process, there being witnesses readily available. These charged Suillius with driving Quintus Pomponius* to civil war by a vicious accusation; with forcing Drusus' daughter Julia and Sabina Poppaea into suicide; with the entrapment of Valerius Asiaticus,* Lusius Saturninus* and Cornelius Lupus;* and with the condemnation of hordes of Roman knights—in fact, with all Claudius' cruel measures.

Suillius defended himself by saying that none of these acts had been voluntary, that he had been following the emperor's orders—until

Nero checked him in mid-speech. He knew from his father's documents, said Nero, that no accusation had been brought against anyone through compulsion from him. Then Suillius' excuse became that they were Messalina's orders, and his defence began to collapse. For why, he was asked, was no one else chosen to put his voice at the service of that merciless whore? The perpetrators of those atrocious acts must be punished, he was told: after taking payment for their crimes they were ascribing those very crimes to others.

Suillius was deprived of half his possessions (his son and granddaughter* were granted the other half, and what these had received in the will of the mother, or grandmother, was also exempted from confiscation). He was banished to the Balearic Islands, not cowed in spirit during the actual proceedings, nor after his condemnation; and it was said that he bore his secluded existence by living a life of ease and luxury. When informers attacked his son Nerullinus, capitalizing on the father's unpopularity and using charges of extortion, the emperor intervened on the grounds that enough vengeance had been taken.

44. A plebeian tribune, Octavius Sagitta, was madly in love with a married woman, Pontia, and at about this time he used extravagant gifts to bribe her into an adulterous affair, and then into leaving her husband. He promised to marry her and gained her agreement to the wedding. When the woman was unattached, however, she began fabricating reasons for delay, and claimed that her father was opposed to the idea; and then, when faced with the prospect of a richer husband, she reneged on her promises.

Octavius for his part alternated protests and threats, pointing to his lost reputation and drained resources, and finally putting his life—the only thing he had left, he said—in her hands. Continually rejected, he asked of her a single night to console him; soothed by that he would be able to exercise self-control in future. A night was agreed upon, and Pontia assigned a maid who was her confidante to watch over the room. Octavius then came, in the company of a single freedman, with a dagger hidden in his clothing. As usually happens when love and anger combine, there were outbursts and pleas, reproaches and making up, and part of the night was reserved for sex. Then, as though in a fit of passion, and when Pontia had no fear, Octavius ran her through with the dagger. When the maid ran forward, he frightened her away with a slash of the knife and charged from the room.

Next day the murder came to light, the perpetrator's identity not being in doubt—it was a proven fact that he had spent the night with her. However, the freedman laid claim to the crime, saying that he had avenged the wrongs done to his patron. In the event, he did move a number of people by his magnanimous gesture—until the maid recovered from her wound and revealed the truth. Octavius was arraigned before the consuls by the murdered woman's father and, after he retired from his tribunate, he was condemned by the judgement of the senators under the murder law.*

45. A no less scandalous case of immorality that year proved to be the start of deep troubles for the state. One Sabina Poppaea lived in the city. She was the daughter of Titus Ollius, but she had adopted the name of her maternal grandfather, Poppaeus Sabinus, who had an illustrious history and was pre-eminent as an ex-consul who had also celebrated a triumph. For Ollius had been brought low by his friendship with Sejanus* before even holding the high offices. This lady had to her credit everything but decency. Her mother had surpassed all women of her generation in beauty, and had bestowed on her both distinction and good looks, and Poppaea's finances were in line with the renown of her family. She had refined conversation, and was not dim-witted. She had a modest air, and a salacious lifestyle. She rarely made an appearance in public, and did so with face partially veiled so as not to satisfy men's glances, or because that suited her appearance. She had no concern for her reputation, making no distinction between husbands and lovers. She was not controlled by feelings, either her own or another's, ever redirecting her sexuality to where material benefit was in evidence. So it was that, while she was living married to a Roman knight, Rufrius Crispinus, by whom she had had a son,* Otho seduced her by his youth and his luxurious lifestyle, and by the fact that he was a notoriously close friend of Nero's. The affair was quickly followed by marriage.*

46. Otho now proceeded to sound the praises of his wife's looks and refinement in the emperor's presence, either because love made him incautious or to rouse Nero's passions and have the bond of their possessing the same woman increase his influence. He was often heard rising from the emperor's dinner table saying that he was going to her, that he had been granted a nobility and beauty that all wanted, and that the fortunate enjoyed.

With these and other such incitements, it did not take long. Accepting an audience, Poppaea first established herself by her sweet talk and wiles, pretending she could not control her passion and was captivated by Nero's looks. Presently, as Nero's infatuation intensified, she began to give herself airs. If kept there beyond one or two nights, she would say repeatedly that she was a married woman and could not abandon her marriage—she was bound to Otho by a quality of life that none could match. Otho was a man of magnificent spirit and refinement, she would say; in him she could see qualities deserving the highest fortune. But as for Nero—he was bound to a chambermaid-whore in his relationship with Acte, and he had drawn from his cohabitation with a slave nothing that was not degrading and sordid!

Otho was cut off from his normal intimacy with Nero, and then from his position as courtier and member of the imperial retinue. Finally, so he would not be in the city as Nero's rival, he was made governor of the province of Lusitania.* There he lived right up to the civil war,* not in the disreputable fashion of earlier days, but in an upright and virtuous manner, mischievous in his leisure-time, but quite self-controlled in his exercise of power.

47. Such was the extent to which Nero sought to cloak his shameful and criminal acts. He was especially suspicious of Cornelius Sulla,* whose slow-wittedness he took as being its opposite, regarding him as a clever man putting on an act. Graptus, one of the imperial freedmen who—because of his experience and old age—was an expert in the house of the emperors from Tiberius' time, intensified Nero's fears with the following lie.

The Mulvian Bridge was, in that period, famous for its night life, and Nero used to frequent the place so he would have greater leeway for his lechery outside the city. Now Graptus fabricated the story that a trap had been set for him on his return journey along the Flaminian Way; that Nero had had a fortuitous escape because he came back by another route to the Gardens of Sallust; and that the man responsible for the plot was Sulla. (Graptus hit upon this story because it so happened that the uproarious behaviour of some young people—a widespread phenomenon at the time—had earlier struck groundless panic into a number of the emperor's servants on their way home.) No slave or client of Sulla's had actually been identified, and the man's nature, which was universally despised, and incapable of any enterprising act, was at odds with the accusation. Even so, Sulla received orders to quit the country, just as if he had been found guilty, and to remain within the confines of the walls of Massilia.

48. In this same consulship, two different delegations from Puteoli were granted a hearing. These had been sent to the Senate* by the town council* and the people respectively, the former protesting against the violence of the mob, the latter against the avarice of their officials and leading citizens. There was fear that the discord, which had reached the stage of stone-throwing and threats of arson, might lead to bloodshed and armed conflict, and Gaius Cassius was chosen to remedy the situation. As both sides would not put up with the man's severe measures, responsibility for the problem was passed on to the brothers Scribonius,* at Cassius' own request, and they were assigned a praetorian cohort. The terror inspired by this, along with a few executions, restored harmony to the townspeople.

49. I would not record a very ordinary decree of the Senate, by which the city of Syracuse was allowed to exceed its prescribed number of gladiatorial shows,* had not Thrasea Paetus* spoken against it and thereby provided his critics with an opportunity to criticize his vote. If Paetus believed the workings of the commonwealth required the independence of the Senate, why, they asked, was he following up such inconsequential matters? Why did he not speak for or against questions of war or peace, of taxation and legislation, and other matters vital to the functioning of the Roman state? Whenever they were authorized to express an opinion, the senators were allowed to say what they wished, and to demand a motion on it. Was this the only worthwhile reform—to see that Syracuse was not too bountifully provided with shows? Was everything else, in every corner of the empire, in such fine shape—as fine as if Thrasea, and not Nero, were in control? But if the most important matters were passed over and ignored, how much greater was one's obligation to leave trivialities alone!

When his friends asked him for an explanation, Thrasea replied that it was not from ignorance of the current situation that he offered amendments to such decrees, but that he was, rather, showing respect for the senators. He was demonstrating that men who gave their attention to the slightest matters would not conceal their concern for the important ones.

50. That same year, following persistent demands from the people, who had been accusing the *publicani* of excesses, Nero considered whether he should order the suspension of all indirect taxes and make that his finest gift to the human race. However, after high praise for his magnanimity, his senior advisers curbed his enthusiasm, explaining to him that curtailing the revenues, which were the underpinnings of the state, would lead to the break-up of the empire. Once port-duties* were lifted, the next step would be a demand for the abolition of direct taxes. Many of the tax companies had been established by the consuls and plebeian tribunes when the liberty of the Roman people still had its vitality, they told him, and the provisions subsequently introduced were designed to see that there was a balance between total revenue and necessary expenditures. It was clear, however, that the rapacity of the *publicani* needed to be curtailed so that they did not, by fresh irritations, bring into disfavour what had been tolerated without complaint for so many years.

51. The emperor accordingly issued an edict ordering the public posting of the regulations concerning each tax, which had been kept secret until that time. The *publicani* were not, after the lapse of a year, to take up again claims that had been dropped. At Rome the praetor, and in the provinces propraetorian or proconsular governors, should give priority to lawsuits against *publicani*. Soldiers' tax-free status was to be preserved, except in the case of goods they were trading. There were also some other very fair measures that were respected for a short while, and then disregarded. However, the abolition of the 'fortieth' and 'fiftieth',* and the other names the *publicani* had invented for their illegal tax-levies, remains in force. The cost of transporting grain was lowered in the overseas provinces, and it was decided that the ships of traders would not be counted in their assessments, and that they would not be taxed on them.

52. The emperor acquitted Sulpicius Camerinus* and Pompeius Silvanus* of charges relating to the province of Africa, where they had held proconsular authority. Camerinus' adversaries were a few private citizens, who levelled against him accusations of brutality rather than embezzlement. Silvanus had found himself in the midst of a horde of accusers who were demanding time to summon witnesses, but the accused insisted on defending himself there and then. And he had his way, thanks to his being wealthily childless and to his old age—which he extended beyond the lifetimes of those whose graft had secured his acquittal.

53. To that point things had been quiet in Germany.* This was because of the shrewdness of the commanders who, now that triumphal insignia were commonplace, were hoping for greater glory from maintaining the peace. Paulinus Pompeius and Lucius Vetus* were at the head of the army at that time. To avoid having their men idle, Pompeius completed the embankment for containing the Rhine that had been started by Drusus sixty-three years earlier,* and Vetus prepared to connect the Mosella and the Arar by constructing a canal between the two. (The aim here was to enable merchandise that was transported by sea, and then taken up the Rhône and the Arar, to travel by way of the canal, and then the Mosella, to the Rhine, and from there to the ocean. With the difficulties of the journey removed, there could be a shipping connection between the shores of the west and those of the north.) Aelius Gracilis, legate of Belgica, looked on the project with envy, and he deterred Vetus from bringing his legions into another man's province and courting popularity in Gaul. The emperor, he kept telling him, would find this alarming—the argument by which honourable endeavours are often blocked.

54. Now, because of the prolonged inactivity of the armies, a rumour arose that the legates had been stripped of their authority to lead them against an enemy. As a result, the Frisians brought their soldiers to the bank of the Rhine by way of the woods and marshes, transporting over the lakes those who were not of fighting age. There, led by Verritus and Malorix, who were the rulers of the tribe (to the extent that Germans can be ruled), they settled on unoccupied lands that had been set aside for the use of the troops. They established homes, seeded the fields and were tilling the land as though it had belonged to their fathers. At that point Dubius Avitus,* who had taken over the province from Paulinus, threatened the Frisians with a violent Roman response if they did not go back to their old location, or if they did not have a request for a new site granted by the emperor. He thus forced Verritus and Malorix into undertaking the petition.

The two left for Rome where, while waiting for Nero, who was busy with other concerns, they saw the sights usually shown to barbarians, including the theatre of Pompey, which they entered in order to observe the size of the population. While they were idling around there (for, being ignorant, they found no pleasure in the performances), they made enquiries about the audience in the seating area and the class distinctions there (which seats were for the knights, and where the Senate sat). They also noticed some people in foreign dress in the senators' seats* and, when they asked who they were, were told that this was an honour accorded to ambassadors of peoples who were particularly noted for their courage and their friendship with Rome. The two then announced that there were no people alive superior to the Germans in combat and loyalty, and they went down and sat amongst the senators. This was taken in good part by the onlookers, who saw in it a primitive impulse and an honourable spirit of competition.

Nero conferred Roman citizenship on both men, but ordered the Frisians to leave the territory. And when they disobeyed, auxiliary horsemen were suddenly sent into their midst, and these, capturing or killing all who put up a spirited resistance, left them no alternative.

55. The Ampsivarii took over those same lands, a stronger tribe, not only through their own resources but also from having the sympathy of the neighbouring peoples—they had been driven out by the Chauci and, now homeless, were begging only for a safe exile. They were also helped by a man called Boiocalus, who was famous amongst those peoples and who was also loyal to us. Boiocalus declared that he had been put in irons on Arminius' orders during the Cheruscan uprising;* that he had later served under the leadership of Tiberius and Germanicus; and that he was now further adding to his fifty years of faithful service by bringing his people under our sway. And it was such a small portion of the plain,* he said, serving only to have the flocks and herds of the soldiers occasionally driven into it! Of course they should hold in reserve refuges for their animals while men go hungry—but not so much as to prefer empty desert to friendly peoples! These fields once belonged to the Chamavi, he continued, then to the Tubantes and after them to the Usipi.* As heaven had been allocated to the gods, so the earth had been granted to the race of mortals; and whatever was unoccupied belonged to everybody. Then, looking up at the sun and invoking the other heavenly bodies, he kept asking, as though face-to-face with them, whether what they wanted to look upon was empty soil. Better, he said, for them to pour the sea over it to combat these robbers of land!

56. Avitus was annoyed by this, and replied that commands from one's superiors must be obeyed. Those gods that they were invoking had decided, he said, that judgement of what was to be given and what taken away should remain with the Romans, and the Ampsivarii should accept no arbiters other than them.

Such was Avitus' official response to the Ampsivarii; to Boiocalus personally he said he would grant him land in memory of their friendship. Boiocalus dismissed the offer as a bribe for his betrayal, adding: 'We may be short of land to live on, but not land to die on.' And with that they parted, with bad feeling on both sides.

The Ampsivarii now called on the Bructeri, the Tencteri, and tribes even further afield to become their allies in the war. Avitus wrote to Curtilius Mancia,* legate of the upper army, requesting that he cross the Rhine and appear in force to their rear; and Avitus himself led his legions into the land of the Tencteri, threatening them with destruction unless they dissociated themselves from their allies' cause. And so the Tencteri withdrew, and the Bructeri now faced the same intimidation. When the rest also proceeded to abandon a dangerous campaign that was not their concern, the tribe of the Ampsivarii was left isolated and withdrew to the Usipi and Tubantes. Driven from their lands, too, they made for the Chatti, and then the Cherusci. In their long migrations they were regarded successively as guests, as indigents, and as enemies on foreign soil; and on that soil all their fighting men fell, while those not of military age were distributed as plunder.

57. That same summer a great battle was fought between the Hermunduri and the Chatti. Both were trying to appropriate by force a river that was a rich producer of salt and which formed the boundary between them. In addition to their love of deciding everything by warfare, the tribes also had a deep-seated superstition that the region was particularly close to heaven, and that mortals' prayers were nowhere heard by the gods in closer proximity. (Hence, they believed, it was through divine indulgence that, in that river and those woods, the salt was produced not, as amongst other peoples, from the evaporation of tidal overflows, but from water poured over a pile of burning trees.* Its crystallization was thus the result of two elements that are opposites, fire and water.) The war went in favour of the Hermunduri, and was all the more ruinous for the Chatti in that both peoples vowed to sacrifice the enemy battle-line to Mars and Mercury in the event of victory, a vow which meant the extermination of horses, men, and all living things.

In this case, at least, the threats made by the enemy recoiled upon themselves. Not so with the community of the Ubii, allied to us, which was afflicted with an unforeseeable disaster. Fires emanating from the earth engulfed farms, cultivated land, and villages far and wide, and were carried right to the walls of the recently established colony. They could not be extinguished, not by rainfall and not by water drawn from the river or any other source, until a number of peasants, at a loss for a remedy and angry over the calamity, began to hurl stones at them from a distance. Then, as the flames came to a halt, the peasants came closer and proceeded to drive them off like wild animals by beating them with clubs and other instruments. Finally they stripped the clothes from their bodies and threw these on, and the dirtier and more soiled they were, the more effective they were in dousing the fires.

58. In this same year the Ruminal tree* in the *comitium*, which had given shelter to Remus and Romulus in their infancy eight hundred and thirty years earlier, became shrivelled, with its branches dead and its trunk suffering desiccation. The phenomenon was regarded as an evil portent, until the tree revived and put out fresh shoots.

BOOK FOURTEEN

1. During the consulship of Gaius Vipstanius and Gaius Fonteius, Nero put off no longer the fiendish act* he had been mulling over for quite some time. His rule was well enough established to bolster his confidence, and his love for Poppaea was burning hotter every day. Poppaea could not herself hope to be married, or for Octavia to be divorced, while Agrippina lived, and with frequent taunts and occasional teasing she would jeer at the emperor, calling him 'the ward' and saying that he was subject to the orders of others and, so far from wielding power, did not even have his own freedom. Why else was her wedding being put off? she asked. Nero must be displeased with her looks and her triumph-celebrating forebears!* Or was it with her fertility and the sincerity of her feelings? No, it was fear that, as his wife, she would reveal the insults heaped on the senators and the resentment felt by the people over his mother's arrogance and greed.* But if Agrippina could countenance only a daughter-in-law who hated her son, she concluded, then Poppaea should return to her marriage to Otho*—she would go anywhere in the world where she would only *hear* the vilification of the emperor and not be personally witnessing it while also sharing his perils. Tearfully directed with the artfulness of an adulteress, these and other such comments were beginning to strike home, and no one tried to stop them. Everybody wanted to see the mother's power destroyed, and none thought the son's hatred would harden to the point of his murdering her.

2. According to Cluvius' account, Agrippina was so far driven by her desire to hold on to power that at the mid-point of the day, when Nero—even at that hour—was flushed with wine and feasting, she quite often appeared before her inebriated son all dressed up and ready for incestuous relations. People close to them began noticing the salacious kisses and the sweet talk that is usually the precursor to sexual relations; and to counter female charms Seneca sought to enlist a woman's aid. He brought in the freedwoman Acte, who was worried both about her own parlous situation and the disgrace facing Nero. Acte was to report to the emperor that the incest was common knowledge since his mother boasted of it, and that his soldiers would not accept the sovereignty of a depraved emperor. Fabius Rusticus claims that the desire for such relations was not Agrippina's, but Nero's, and it was then frustrated by the freedwoman's ploy. But the other sources give the same version as Cluvius, and popular opinion leans that way, too. Possibly Agrippina really did envision such a ghastly act, or perhaps contemplating this sexual deviation seemed more plausible in her case. She had, after all, had illicit intercourse with Marcus Lepidus* as a girl because of her lust for power; with that same craving she had abandoned herself to the appetites of Pallas; and she had been trained in all manner of immorality through marriage to her uncle.

3. Nero accordingly avoided private meetings with her, and applauded her for taking a break whenever she left for her gardens or her estate at Tusculum or Antium. Concluding finally that she was a real problem wherever she was kept, he decided to kill her off, considering only the question of whether to use poison, or the sword, or some other violent means. At first he favoured poison. If, however, it were administered at the imperial dinner, the incident could not be ascribed to chance, since Britannicus had already met a similar end; and it was evidently difficult to suborn servants of a woman whose own criminal experiences made her wary of treachery. Besides, she had already built up her body's immunity by the prior taking of counter-agents. As for death by the sword, no one could find a method of concealment; and he was afraid that someone chosen for such a heinous crime might disregard his orders.

It was the freedman Anicetus who came up with the brilliant idea. He was prefect of the fleet at Misenum,* had been the young Nero's tutor,* and was hated by Agrippina with a loathing that was mutual. Anicetus explained that a vessel could be constructed with a section designed to fall apart on the open sea, pitching the unsuspecting woman overboard. Nothing offered such latitude for accident as did the sea, he said, and, if Agrippina were overtaken by shipwreck, who would be so unreasonable as to attribute to crime the mischief done by wind and waves? The emperor would then also grant the deceased a temple, altars, and everything else for demonstrating filial devotion.

4. The plan's ingenuity won approval, and the timing helped, too, as Nero used to celebrate the festival of the Quinquatrus* at Baiae.* To this spot he enticed his mother, frequently remarking that one should tolerate the outbursts of parents and try to soothe their anger— all this to generate a rumour of their reconciliation, which Agrippina

would swallow with the gullibility of a woman receiving good news. When she arrived Nero went to the shore to meet her (she was coming from Antium). He welcomed her with outstretched hands and an embrace, and took her to Bauli. (This was the name of a villa lapped by the waters of an inlet between the promontory of Misenum and the lake of Baiae.) At anchor amongst the others was one particularly fine vessel—apparently a further mark of respect for his mother, for she had been used to sailing in a trireme with a crew of marines. She was also now invited to dinner, so that there should be darkness, too, to hide the crime.

It is well established that there was an informer, and that when Agrippina heard of the plot she could not decide whether to believe it, and used a litter as her transport to Baiae. There, some sweet talk alleviated her concerns; and she was warmly welcomed and seated above Nero himself. As conversation flowed freely, Nero alternating a juvenile chattiness with an earnest expression as he apparently communicated some serious points, the dinner-party became a protracted affair. Nero then escorted Agrippina as she departed, hanging on her gaze and clinging closely to her. Either he was putting the finishing touch to his charade or the last sight of his mother going to her end made even his heart falter, inhuman though it was.

5. As if to provide proof of the crime, heaven provided a night bright with stars and peaceful with a tranquil sea. The ship had not gone far. Two of Agrippina's personal friends were with her: Crepereius Gallus* stood near the helm, and Acerronia* was leaning over the feet of her mistress (who was lying down), cheerfully talking about the son's change of heart and the mother's reinstatement in his good graces. Then a signal was given, the ceiling covering the spot collapsed, weighted as it was with a large quantity of lead, and Crepereius was immediately crushed to death. Agrippina and Acerronia were protected by the sides of the bed that jutted up above them and which happened to be too strong to crumple under the weight. The disintegration of the vessel did not follow, either; there was general confusion, and most of the sailors, unaware of the plot, kept obstructing the conspirators. The oarsmen then thought it best to throw their weight on one side and capsize the ship like that, but they could not reach a quick consensus about dealing with the emergency, and others countered their efforts, making it possible for the victims to slip gently into the sea. Acerronia, misreading the

situation, cried out that she was Agrippina and that the emperor's mother should be helped, whereupon she was battered to death with poles, oars, and any marine implements that came to hand. Remaining silent, Agrippina decreased the chance of recognition (though she did receive one wound to the shoulder). Then, swimming off, she met some skiffs that took her to the Lucrine lake, and from there was transported to her own villa.

6. There Agrippina reflected on the motive for the duplicitous letter of invitation, and for her particularly respectful treatment. Also, she noted, the ship had been close to shore, was not driven by the winds, and had not struck any rocks; and yet it had collapsed from the top like some apparatus on land. She also thought about Acerronia's murder, and at the same time looked at her own wound; and she realized that the only way of dealing with the plot was by seeming not to recognize its existence. She sent her freedman Agermus to report to her son that, because of the benevolence of the gods and Nero's own good fortune, she had escaped a serious accident. Despite his alarm over the danger his mother had faced, she added, she begged him to postpone the visit he was anxious to make—she had need of rest for the moment. Meanwhile, feigning nonchalance, she applied medication to her wound and lotions to her body. She ordered a search for Acerronia's will and had her belongings sealed up*—her one act that was not a pretence.

7. Nero was waiting for news that the deed was done when word came that Agrippina had escaped with a slight wound and had been close enough to danger for no doubt to be left about who was responsible. He was petrified with fear, declaring that she would be there at any moment, intent on swift revenge. She would arm her slaves, or incite the soldiery; she would get to the Senate and the people, laying at his door the shipwreck, her wound, the killing of her friends. And what help was there for *him*? Unless Burrus and Seneca could come up with something . . . He had had them summoned immediately, though whether they had no prior knowledge of the plot is unclear.

Both were silent for a long while. Either they feared that trying to hold him back would fail, or else they believed that things had gone so far that Nero was done for unless Agrippina were stopped. Then Seneca took the lead to the extent of looking at Burrus and asking whether soldiers should be ordered to kill her. Burrus replied that the praetorian guards had sworn loyalty* to the entire house of the

Caesars, and that, remembering Germanicus, they would take no violent action against his progeny. Anicetus should live up to his promise, he added.

With no hesitation, Anicetus asked to be put in charge of the crime. Responding to his request, Nero declared that this was the day on which he was given an empire, and the giver of such a great gift was his freedman. Anicetus should go swiftly, he said, and take with him the men most ready to follow orders. On being told that Agermus had arrived with a message from Agrippina, Nero took the initiative and provided the scenario for an accusation of his own. He threw a sword at Agermus' feet as the freedman delivered the message entrusted to him, then ordered him clapped in irons as though caught in a treasonous act. He would fabricate a story of his mother plotting the emperor's assassination, and then committing suicide from shame when the crime was detected.

8. Meanwhile news had spread of Agrippina's perilous episode, which was represented as an accident, and as people learned of it they all rushed to the shore. Some clambered up the embankments, some boarded the closest skiffs; others waded into the sea as far as was physically possible; some stood with arms outstretched. The whole shoreline was filled with the noise of moaning, prayers, and cries as people asked various questions or gave vague replies. A huge crowd surged to the spot with torches, and when it was known that Agrippina was safe they prepared to offer their felicitations, until they were scattered by the sight of a column of men, armed and menacing.

Anicetus cordoned off the villa and broke down the door. He threw aside any slaves in his way until he reached the bedroom door. Before it stood only a few attendants; the rest had been frightened off, terrified by the break-in. In the bedroom there was a dim light and one of the maids, and Agrippina, growing more and more worried that nobody had come from her son, not even Agermus. Things would look different had her plan gone well, she thought; as it was, there was only solitude broken by sudden uproar, and indications that it had gone very badly.

Her maid then began to leave. 'Are you deserting me, too?' asked Agrippina and, looking round, she saw Anicetus, who was accompanied by the trierarch Herculeius and by Obaritus, a centurion of the marines.* If Anicetus had come to visit the patient, she said, he could report that she was recovered. If he had come to commit a crime, she did not believe her son was involved—he had not given the order for parricide. The assassins stood around the bed, and the trierarch took the lead, striking her on the head with a club. The centurion then drew his sword to deliver the death blow. 'Strike me in the belly,' she cried, thrusting out to them her womb, and was finished off by a welter of stab-wounds.

9. On these events there is agreement. As for whether Nero looked upon his dead mother and praised the beauty of her corpse, there are some who have recorded it and some who deny it. She was cremated that same night on a dining couch* in a paltry funeral, and during the whole of Nero's reign the burial ground was not heaped in a mound or granted an enclosure. (Later on, through the devotion of her servants, she was given a modest tomb alongside the road to Misenum and close to the villa of Caesar the dictator which, from its lofty elevation, looks out over the bays below.) When Agrippina's pyre was set alight, her freedman, a man named Mnester, ran himself through with a sword, though whether it was from affection for his patroness or from fear of execution is moot.

That such would be her end Agrippina had believed many years earlier, and had made light of it. When she consulted the Chaldeans* about Nero, they replied that he would be emperor and kill his mother. 'Let him kill me,' she replied, 'as long as he comes to power.'

10. As for Nero, it was only after the crime had been committed that its enormity came home to him. He spent the rest of the night petrified and silent at one moment, but more often rising to his feet in panic and dementedly awaiting the dawn that he thought would bring his undoing. It was the obsequiousness of the centurions and tribunes, orchestrated by Burrus, that first encouraged him to hope; they grasped his hand and congratulated him on evading the unforeseeable danger of his mother's criminal act. His friends then visited the temples and, the example set, the adjacent towns of Campania bore witness to their joy with sacrifices and ambassadorial missions; and Nero, with a contrary pretence, was dejected, apparently displeased with his own deliverance and in tears over his mother's death. However, unlike men's expressions, the appearance of landscapes does not change, and the grim sight of that sea and shoreline was continually before his eyes (and there were those who believed that the sound of a trumpet could be heard in the surrounding hills, and lamentations coming from his mother's tomb). Nero therefore

withdrew to Neapolis and sent a letter to the Senate. The gist of it was that Agermus, one of Agrippina's closest freedmen and his would-be assassin, had been caught with a sword and that Agrippina, conscience-stricken over the crime she had engineered, had paid the penalty.

11. Nero added 'crimes' from earlier times. She had entertained hopes of joint rule,* he declared, and of having the praetorian guard swear allegiance to a woman, with the Senate and people subjected to the same humiliation. When she was disappointed in this, her resentment against the military, the senators, and the plebs had led her to oppose the cash distributions for the soldiers and the people, and to hatch plots against illustrious men. What an effort it had been, he said, for him to stop her bursting into the Curia* and giving replies to deputations* from foreign peoples!

He followed this with a sidelong attack on the Claudian period, attributing to his mother all the atrocities of that regime, and claiming that her extermination was for the public good. He even discussed the shipwreck, though there was no one to be found who was stupid enough to think it accidental—or to believe that a lone man had been sent with a weapon by a shipwrecked woman to smash his way through the emperor's bodyguard and navy! As a result, it was no longer Nero (whose villainy surpassed all criticism) but Seneca* who was the subject of nasty rumours—with a speech like that he had signed his confession!

12. But it was with an amazing spirit of rivalry amongst the notables that public prayers* were officially authorized at all the couches, and the Quinquatrus—the period when the 'plot' was brought to light—was to be celebrated with annual games. A gold figure of Minerva was also to be set up in the Curia with a statue of the emperor next to her, and Agrippina's birthday was to be placed among the days unfit for public business.* It had been Thrasea Paetus' practice to let earlier instances of sycophancy pass by remaining silent, or with a brief indication of assent, but on this occasion he walked out of the Senate, thus exposing himself to danger, but without providing the others with an impulse to assert their independence.

There were also, at the time, frequent but meaningless prodigies. A woman gave birth to a serpent, and another was killed by a lightning bolt while making love with her husband. The sun was suddenly darkened, and the fourteen districts of the city were struck by lightning. But all of this was far from being the result of divine intervention—Nero extended his reign and crimes for many years thereafter!

To deepen resentment against his mother, and to make it clear that his own clemency was increased by her removal, he reinstated in their ancestral homes two illustrious ladies, Junia and Calpurnia, as well as the ex-praetors Valerius Capito and Licinius Gabolus. These had earlier been banished by Agrippina. He even allowed the ashes of Lollia Paulina to be brought back and a tomb erected for her, and Iturius and Calvisius, men whom he had himself recently relegated, he relieved of their punishment. In the case of Silana, she had passed away on her return to Tarentum from her distant exile, at a time when Agrippina, whose hostility was the cause of her downfall, was already losing influence, or had relented.

13. Nero nevertheless hung back in the towns of Campania, nervously wondering how he should enter the city, and whether he would find the Senate fawning and the plebs supportive. He did, however, have all the worst characters—and no palace ever had a richer crop—telling him that the name of Agrippina was detested, and that his popularity with the people had been boosted by her death. Proceed with confidence, they told him, and feel their veneration in person. At the same time they begged permission to go ahead of him. And, in fact, they found a warmer welcome than they had promised, with the people coming to meet him in tribes,* the Senate in festive garb, wives and children marshalled by sex and age, and spectators' seats erected along the route he would be taking, just as triumphs are viewed. So now he approached the Capitol* with pride, as victor over a servile people, and gave his thanks—and then let himself loose on all the forms of depravity which, though repressed with difficulty, respect for his mother (such as it was) had managed to check.

14. Nero had long had a hankering to drive a four-horse chariot, and a no less disgraceful desire to sing accompanied by the lyre like a stage-performer. Horse-racing,* he would say, was the sport of kings, one in which leaders of old would frequently indulge, and it was celebrated in the panegyrics of the bards and put on in honour of the gods. Furthermore, he said, singing was sacred to Apollo, and it was dressed for this activity that this outstanding, prescient deity stood not only in the cities of Greece, but also in the temples of Rome. There was now no holding him, and Seneca and Burrus thought that, to prevent him from gaining both ends, they should

grant him one. And so an area was fenced off in the Vatican valley* for him to drive his horses without making a public spectacle of it. Soon the Roman people were actually invited to watch, and they praised Nero to the skies, the crowd being ever eager for amusements and delighted if their emperor is similarly inclined. However, the exposure of his humiliating activities did not induce weariness of them, as his advisers had expected, but further stimulation. He now thought that his disgrace would be lessened if he degraded a greater number, and he paraded on the stage* the descendants of noble families whom poverty had made corruptible. They have passed away now, and I think their ancestors should be accorded the respect of my not transmitting their names. Nero also used extravagant gifts to induce well-known Roman knights to promise their services in the arena—though payment from a man who can command carries the force of an order.

15. Not yet ready to be disgraced in the public theatre, however, Nero established the so-called 'Juvenalian Games',* for which there was widespread enrolment. Neither noble birth nor past magistracies stopped anyone from plying the actor's art, whether Greek or Roman,* right down to its unmanly body movements and music. Women of rank, too, put on lewd performances; and low dens and taverns were built in the grove that Augustus planted around the 'Naval Pond',* with items promoting dissipation put on sale there. Spending-money was also distributed, which decent people used under pressure, and the salacious with proud abandon. The result was an increase in degenerate and scandalous behaviour, and nothing contributed more depravity to a long-corrupt moral climate than did that cesspool. Decency is with difficulty maintained even amongst honourable pursuits; much less could morality, propriety, or any trace of probity be kept alive amid these competing vices.

Finally, the man himself came on stage, carefully tuning his lyre and warming up before his music teachers. A cohort of soldiers had also come for the performance, along with centurions and tribunes, and Burrus, who both grieved and applauded. That was the first occasion on which Roman knights were recruited under the title of 'Augustiani',* young men of remarkable strength, some brazen by temperament, others ambitious for power. Day and night these shouted applause, using epithets reserved for the gods to describe the emperor's appearance and voice. They enjoyed fame and honour, apparently earned by their merits.

16. But so as not to have the imperial fame restricted to theatrical skills, Nero also adopted the pursuit of poetry, gathering around him men who had some as-yet unrecognized proficiency in composition.* These would sit with him and string together lines of verse they had brought along, or which they improvised on the spot, and they supplemented Nero's own words in whatever metre he had used. (This process is betrayed by the very features of the poetry, which in its flow has no drive or inspiration or uniformity of style.) Nero would also devote some time to professors of philosophy, after-dinner affairs at which he could also enjoy the conflict of opposing opinions. And there was no shortage of people wanting to be seen at the royal entertainments with their gloomy faces and expressions.

17. At about this same time, following a trivial incident, terrible carnage broke out between the peoples of the two colonies of Nuceria and Pompeii.* It occurred at a gladiatorial show that Livineius Regulus (who, I noted above,* had been removed from the Senate*) was holding. Jeering at each other with the usual high spirits of small towns, they progressed from insults to stone-throwing and finally the sword, with the Pompeian crowd—amongst whom the spectacle was being held—having the upper hand. As a result, many of the Nucerians were taken off to Rome maimed by their wounds, and a large number were shedding tears over dead children or parents. The emperor left adjudication of the matter to the Senate, and the Senate left it to the consuls. When it was again referred back to the senators, the people of Pompeii received a public injunction against gatherings of that type for ten years, and the associations* they had established in contravention of the laws were disbanded. Livineius and the others responsible for the disturbance were punished with exile.

18. Pedius Blaesus* was also expelled from the Senate when the people of Cyrene* charged him with plundering the treasury of Aesculapius and with corrupt practice, involving bribery and influence-peddling, in a miltary levy. The Cyreneans also indicted Acilius Strabo.* Strabo had held the praetorship, and had been sent out by Claudius to arbitrate in the matter of the lands that had once been the ancestral estate of King Apion* and which, along with his kingdom, had been left by him to the Roman people. All the neighbouring landowners had appropriated these, basing their claim on the long-standing indifference to their unlawful possession, as though that were just and equitable. Thus, when the lands were taken from them by his verdict, animosity arose against the judge. The Senate's response was that it did not know Claudius' instructions, and that the emperor should be consulted. Nero upheld Strabo's finding, but wrote that even so he was coming to the assistance of the allies, and granting them the lands they had wrongfully seized.

19. There followed the deaths of the illustrious Domitius Afer and Marcus Servilius.* Both had enjoyed successful careers, filling the highest offices and displaying great eloquence. Afer was famous for forensic pleading, and Servilius for his long practice in the Forum, though he was later renowned for works of Roman history and a refined lifestyle (which made him the more famous, as he was the other's intellectual equal but different in character).

20. During the consulship of Nero (his fourth) and Cornelius Cossus, Quinquennial Games* were established at Rome on the model of the Greek competition and, as with nearly all innovations, opinions were mixed. There were some who declared that Gnaeus Pompey had similarly been criticized by an older generation for having established a permanent theatre building. Before that, performances were put on with makeshift seating and a temporary stage, they said, or if one went further back the people actually watched them on their feet*—for fear that being seated in a theatre might lead to their spending entire days doing nothing! The old type of performances should be maintained, they said, any time that a praetor presided over them,* with no obligation placed on citizens to compete. However, they added, their traditional morality, which had been gradually eroding, was now being totally subverted by an imported degeneracy. The result was that anything capable of being corrupted or of causing corruption was on view in the city, and young people were becoming decadent through fads from overseas—visiting the gymnasia, loafing around, and indulging in degrading love affairs. And the emperor and Senate were responsible: not only did they countenance such vices, but they put pressure on Roman noblemen to demean themselves on stage on the pretext of delivering speeches and poetry. What now remained but to strip off, take up boxing-gloves, and train in that sort of fighting rather than military drills and weaponry? Would justice be furthered and would the decuries* of knights better fulfil their noble function as jurors for having listened with a virtuoso's ear to falsetto notes and

melodious voices? Night, too, had been devoted to shameful conduct, they said, so that no time would be left to decency and, instead, in a motley crowd, every profligate could dare to pursue in the dark the lusts he had conceived in daylight.

21. Most were actually pleased with the permissive climate, but they still cloaked it with respectable terms. Their ancestors, too, had not shunned agreeable spectacles, as far as the resources of the day allowed, they would say, and so actors had been brought in from Etruria* and horse-racing from Thurii. With the annexation of Achaea and Asia,* games were staged more elaborately, but in the two centuries since the triumph of Lucius Mummius, the first to have put on this kind of show in the city, no Roman of decent background had disgraced himself by taking up professional acting. Economy had also been taken into account with the establishment of a permanent location for the theatre, rather than having one raised and dismantled every year at enormous cost. Nor, they said, would magistrates exhaust their personal wealth,* or the people have reason to demand of them Greek-style competitions, when it was the state defraying the costs. Victory in the oratorical or poetic spheres would be an incentive for talent, and no judge would find it offensive to lend his ear to honourable intellectual activities and legitimate diversions. It was, they said, a case of a few nights during a five-year period being given over to hilarity—not promiscuity—and during these, because of the bright illumination, no impropriety could be concealed.

And, in fact, the spectacle passed with no obvious scandal. Moreover, there was not the slightest flare-up of partisan enthusiasm among the people because, although the *pantomimi** had been brought back on to the stage, they were barred from the sacred competitions.* Nobody took the prize for oratory, but Nero was pronounced the victor. Many people had appeared at the event in Greek clothing, but this subsequently fell out of fashion.

22. It was during this period that a blazing comet* appeared which, in the view of the common people, presages a change of ruler. Thus, as though Nero had already been deposed, people began to ask who might be selected. And the man frequently on the lips of all was Rubellius Plautus,* whose noble blood came, on his mother's side, from the Julian family. Plautus held to the ideas of his ancestors, being austere in appearance, and moral and reclusive in his private

life; but the more cloistered he became through fear, the greater the reputation he acquired. The prevailing rumour was intensified by an interpretation (just as unwarranted) put on a lightning-bolt. Nero was dining in his villa, called the Sublaqueum, near the Simbruine lakes, when the meal was struck and the table shattered, and because this had happened in the territory of Tibur, homeland of Plautus' family on his father's side, people believed that Plautus was being designated as the successor by divine will. He also had widespread support from the sort of men who have a voracious (and often misguided) ambition to be ahead of others in espousing new and risky causes. Worried by this, Nero drafted a letter to Plautus, telling him to consider the peace of the city and distance himself from those who were spreading malicious gossip. Plautus had ancestral lands throughout Asia, Nero said, and in these he could enjoy his youth in safety and without trouble. And so Plautus retired there with his wife Antistia and a few close friends.

At that time, too, Nero's extreme self-indulgence brought him into disrepute and danger when he went for a swim in the source of the Marcian water* that was channelled to the city. By bathing his body there he was thought to have befouled the holy waters and the sanctity of the location. A serious illness that followed only confirmed the anger of the gods.

23. After the destruction of Artaxata,* Corbulo felt that he should capitalize on the fresh panic to seize Tigranocerta: by destroying it he could heighten the enemy's fears, or by sparing it he could gain a reputation for clemency. He therefore set off for the town. The army was not on an offensive footing—he did not want to quash hopes of pardon—but he did not relax his guard, either, knowing as he did the volatility of the race, which, reluctant in the face of danger, was treacherous when offered opportunities.

The barbarians' reaction differed with their temperament: some came to him with entreaties, and others deserted their villages and dispersed into the wilderness, while there were also those who hid themselves and their dearest possessions in caves. The Roman commander accordingly varied his approach, showing compassion towards suppliants, swiftly pursuing fugitives, and dealing ruthlessly with those who had occupied hiding-places—he filled the mouths and exits of the chambers with brushwood and twigs, and burned them out. And then Corbulo himself came under attack from the

Mardi (practised marauders who had mountains to defend them against an invader) as he was skirting their territory. He sent in his Iberians, and plundered their country, spilling foreign blood* to punish the enemy's effrontery.

24. Though Corbulo and his army sustained no losses in the battle, they were beginning to experience exhaustion from food-shortages and their labours, being reduced to stave off hunger with animal flesh. In addition, there was a lack of water, an intense summer heat, and long marches, lightened only by the endurance of the commander, who bore as much as—and more than—the rank and file. They then reached a cultivated region, where they harvested the crops and took by assault one of two strongholds in which the Armenians had sought refuge (the other, which had repulsed the first attack, was reduced by siege). Passing from there into the lands of the Tauronites, Corbulo managed to avoid an unexpected danger. Not far from his tent a barbarian of some distinction was discovered with a weapon, and under torture the man gave a detailed account of a plot against the commander, identifying himself as its instigator and naming his accomplices. There followed the conviction and execution of those who, under a pretence of friendship, had been plotting treachery.

Not much later representatives sent from Tigranocerta brought news that the city's defences were open to Corbulo and that their fellow-citizens were ready to follow his orders, and at the same time they handed over to him a golden crown as a gift of welcome. The Roman accepted it respectfully, and the city suffered no loss: unharmed, they would adopt a compliant attitude all the more readily, he thought.

25. The fort of Legerda, however, which a group of defiant young warriors had closed against him, was not taken without a fight. The enemy ventured to do battle before the walls; furthermore, when they were driven back within their fortifications, they could be forced to yield only when faced with a siege-mound and an armed assault.

These ends were achieved the more easily because the Parthians were distracted by the Hyrcanian war. The Hyrcanians had sent representatives to the Roman emperor with a petition for an alliance, calling attention to the fact that, as a pledge of their friendship, they were obstructing Vologaeses. As the representatives were returning,

Corbulo, fearing they might be surrounded by enemy patrols after crossing the Euphrates, gave them an armed guard and escorted them to the shores of the Red Sea.* From there they returned home, steering clear of Parthian territory.

26. Furthermore, Tiridates* was now advancing into the fringes of Armenia by way of Media. In response, Corbulo sent his legate Verulanus ahead with the auxiliaries, and then himself followed with the legions by forced marches, thus obliging the Parthian to withdraw a long way and abandon his hopes for war. Those he found opposed to us he subjected to wholesale slaughter and burning, and he was proceeding to take control* of Armenia when Tigranes,* chosen by Nero to assume the throne, arrived on the scene. Tigranes was a member of the Cappadocian nobility, and a grandson of King Archelaus, but a long period as a hostage in Rome had brought him into a state of abject submissiveness. And his welcome there was not unequivocal, either, since there still remained some support for the Arsacids, though most people, from a loathing for the high-handedness of the Parthians, preferred a king given them by Rome. Tigranes was also provided with military assistance—a thousand legionaries, three cohorts of allies, and two squadrons of cavalry. In addition, to facilitate his defence of his new kingdom, various portions of Armenia were instructed to accept submission to whichever king they were contiguous to—Pharasmanes,* Polemo,* Aristobulus or Antiochus.* Corbulo withdrew into Syria which, left vacant by the death of the legate Ummidius, had now been assigned to him.

27. That same year one of Asia's famous cities, Laodicea, collapsed in an earthquake, but recovered through its own resources with no help from us. In Italy, the ancient town of Puteoli* received from Nero the rights and official designation of a colony. Veterans were enrolled as settlers in Tarentum and Antium, but did nothing to stem the depopulation of these places since most slipped away into the provinces in which they had completed their service. And as they did not usually marry or rear children, they left behind empty homes without descendants. For it was not, as in the past, a matter of entire legions being settled in colonies along with their tribunes, centurions, and serving men from the same unit, so that they would form a community based on concord and affection. Instead, the colonists were unknown to each other, drawn from different maniples,* without a leader and without mutual feelings. It was as if they had been

suddenly brought together from another race of mortals entirely, an assemblage rather than a colony.

28. Because the praetorian election, usually held under senatorial authority, had roused rather keen and heated competition, the emperor settled the matter by appointing the three extra candidates* to legionary commands. He also enhanced the dignity of the senators by ruling that those appealing to the Senate from the civil courts* should be liable to the same forfeit as those petitioning the emperor (for before this the procedure had been unrestricted and free from penalty). At the end of the year a Roman knight, Vibius Secundus,* was found guilty of extortion in a case brought by the people of Mauretania.* He was banished from Italy, his efforts to avoid a worse sentence succeeding through the resources of his brother, Vibius Crispus.

29. During the consulship of Caesennius Paetus and Petronius Turpilianus there was a serious reverse in Britain. There the legate Aulus Didius had, as I noted above,* merely held on to what he had gained, while his successor Veranius,* after some minor pillaging expeditions against the Silures, was prevented by death from pushing ahead with his offensive. Throughout his life Veranius was famed for his austere character, but an egotism was clearly demonstrated by the final words of his will where, with gross flattery of Nero, he added that he would have brought the province to heel for him had he lived a further two years.

Paulinus Suetonius* then took over the governorship of Britain. He was Corbulo's rival in military science and in the esteem of the people (which permits nobody to be without a competitor), and he passionately wanted to match the glory of the recovery of Armenia by crushing the foe. Accordingly he prepared for an assault on the island of Mona, home to a strong population and a haven for refugees, and he built flat-bottomed boats to counter the precarious shallows. Thus the infantry crossed; the cavalry followed through the shoals, or by swimming alongside their mounts where the waters were deeper.

30. Facing them on the shore was the enemy line, a dense array of arms and men, and amongst them rushed women who, like furies, wore funereal clothing, had dishevelled hair, and brandished torches. Around stood Druids,* their hands raised to heaven, pouring out terrible curses; and the extraordinary spectacle struck such fear into the

men that they presented their bodies motionless to enemy weapons, as if their limbs were paralysed. Then, with encouragement from their commander, and urging each other not to be alarmed at a horde of fanatical women, they charged forward, mowing down those in their way and engulfing them in their own flames.

A garrison was imposed on the defeated enemy after that, and the groves sacred to their barbarous superstitions were cut down (for they held it morally acceptable to make their altars reek with prisoners' gore and to consult the gods with the entrails of humans). While Suetonius was thus engaged he was brought news of a sudden uprising of the province.

31. Prasutagus, king of the Iceni, famed for a wealth that he had long enjoyed, had entered in his will as his heirs the emperor and his own two daughters, thinking that such an act of obsequiousness would keep his realm and household out of harm's way. The reverse turned out to be the case, so much so that the realm was pillaged by centurions, and his household by slaves,* as if they were spoils of war. Right at the start Prasutagus' wife Boudicca was flogged and his daughters raped. All the leading Iceni were divested of their ancestral property, as though the Romans had been made a gift of the entire region, and the king's relatives were dealt with as slaves.

Prompted by this humiliation and the fear of worse (since they had been formally made into a province), the Iceni took up arms. They also incited the Trinovantes to join the revolt, along with other peoples who, still not broken by oppression, had committed themselves by covert intrigues to reasserting their independence—their most bitter animosity being directed towards the veterans. These had recently been settled in the colony of Camulodunum, and had been driving its inhabitants from their homes and throwing them off their lands, calling them 'prisoners of war' and 'slaves'. The common soldiers were also abetting the lawlessness of the veterans—their way of life was similar, and they hoped for the same lack of constraint upon themselves. Furthermore, a temple erected to the deified Claudius* lay before the natives' eyes like a bastion of everlasting domination, and the men chosen as its priests were pouring away whole fortunes* in the name of religion. And wiping out a colony surrounded by no fortifications did not seem a difficult undertaking—our commanders, paying more attention to aesthetics than utility, had taken too little precaution in this regard.

32. Meanwhile, for no apparent reason, the statue of Victory in Camulodunum toppled over and turned around as though giving ground to an enemy. In addition, women who had been driven into a frenzy uttered prophecies that destruction was at hand. Foreign cries had been heard in their curia, they said, and the theatre had rung with wailing, while an apparition of the colony overthrown had been seen in the Thames estuary.* In addition, the ocean had taken on a bloody hue, and the imprint of human corpses had been left behind by the ebbing tide, all of which fed the Britons' hopes, and the veterans' fears.

Because Suetonius was far off, however, the veterans sought help from the procurator Catus Decianus.* He sent no more than two hundred improperly armed men, and there was also a small group of regulars in the town. The defenders had to rely on the temple building for protection. They were also impeded by clandestine accomplices of the rebellion who were trying to sabotage their plans, with the result that they dispensed with a ditch or a rampart, and failed to remove the old and the women and leave only the young men in the fighting line. Showing as little caution as if they were in the midst of peace, they were surrounded by a horde of barbarians. Everything else was pillaged or burned by their onset, but the temple in which the soldiers had gathered was subjected to a two-day blockade and then taken by storm. Moreover, the triumphant Britons met Petillius Cerialis,* legate of the Ninth Legion,* who was coming to relieve the Romans, and they put his legion to flight and killed all his infantry. Cerialis escaped to his camp with the cavalry and found protection within his fortifications. Alarmed by this disaster, and by the hostility of the province that his rapacity had driven into war, the procurator Catus crossed to Gaul.

33. Suetonius, however, showing amazing determination, headed for Londinium* through the midst of his enemies. While it did not have the distinction of being designated a 'colony', the town was nevertheless much famed for its large concentration of businessmen and saleable goods. There Suetonius vacillated over whether he should choose it as his base of operations; but when he considered his small numbers, and the clear evidence of the severe penalty Petillius had paid for headstrong action, he decided on saving the overall situation by the sacrifice of a single town.* The tearful lamentations of people begging his aid could not avert him from giving the signal to move

out and taking into the body of his column only those able to accompany him. All who were held back because their sex disqualified them from fighting, or because they were feeble with age or had attachments to the locality, were overwhelmed by the enemy.

The same disaster befell the town of Verulamium, because the barbarians, who revelled in plunder and were averse to hard work, bypassed strongholds and garrisoned positions to make for the military granary—rich pickings for a looter and difficult for its defenders to secure. It is well established that some seventy thousand Roman citizens and allies lost their lives in the locations I have mentioned. For the Britons did not take captives, or sell them, or indulge in any other wartime trafficking; rather, they hastily resorted to slaughter, the gallows, burning, and crucifixion, accepting that they would face punishment, but meanwhile taking revenge for it ahead of time.

34. Suetonius had under his command the Fourteenth Legion,* the *vexillarii* of the Twentieth, and some auxiliaries from the nearby settlements—a total of about ten thousand men under arms—and he now prepared to take the field, delaying no further. He selected a location* where there was a narrow defile and he had the cover of a wood to his rear, and he had ascertained for sure that the only enemy presence was before him where an open plain guaranteed no fear of ambush. The legionaries therefore stood in close-ordered lines, with the light infantry deployed around them and the cavalry bunched on the wings. The troops of the Britons, by contrast, darted about in squadrons and companies all over the field in unprecedented numbers, and such was their confidence that they also brought their wives along with them to witness their victory, placing them in carts which they had set at the far edge of the plain.

35. Boudicca rode in a chariot with her daughters before her, and as she approached each tribe she declared that, while it was quite normal for the Britons to fight under a woman's command, she was not on that occasion seeking vengeance for a kingdom and possessions as a woman descended from great ancestors. No, she said, she sought it as one of the people, sought it for liberty lost, a flogging received and the sexual abuse of her daughters. The cupidity of the Romans, she said, had reached the point of not leaving people's bodies undefiled, or even old age, or girls' virginity. But, she added, the gods were with them to exact their just revenge. The legion that

had dared to engage had been destroyed; the others were hiding in their camp, or looking around for an escape. The Romans would not stand up even to the roar and shouts of so many thousands of men, much less to their charge and their sword-arms! If they themselves assessed their own troop numbers and their motives for war, she said, then in that engagement they had to win—or fall. That was the decision a woman had taken—let the men live on and be slaves!

36. Suetonius did not remain silent at such a critical juncture, either. Though he had confidence in the valour of his men, he none the less delivered a mixture of exhortation and pleas, urging them to pay no heed to the barbarians' noise and empty threats—there were more women than young men visible among them, he said. Lacking fighting ability and weapons, they would immediately give ground when they recognized the arms and courage of their conquerors—so many were their past defeats! Even when legions were many, he said, only a handful of men decided the outcome of battles, and it would further redound to their glory that, small force as they were, they would win the fame of an entire army. They should just keep close order and, after discharging their javelins, continue the bloody slaughter with shield-bosses and swords, and with no thought for plunder—everything would come to them when victory was won! Such was the enthusiasm that followed the commander's words, and such the eagerness with which his veterans, with their long battle-experience, had made ready to hurl their javelins, that Suetonius, certain of the outcome, gave the signal for battle.

37. At first, the legion, not taking a step, held on to the restricted terrain for its defence, but when the enemy closed in, and the legionaries had used up their well-aimed javelins on them, they burst out in wedge-formation. The auxiliaries' charge was equally spirited, and with lances levelled the cavalry smashed through any stiff resistance they encountered. The rest of the Britons turned tail, escape being difficult because the wagons deployed around them blocked all the exits. And the troops did not refrain even from the slaughter of women, while pack animals that had been run through with spears also increased the pile of corpses.

The glory won that day was spectacular, equal to that of victories of old, for some reports* put the British dead at not much below eighty thousand, with roughly four hundred Roman soldiers killed and not many more wounded. Boudicca ended her life with poison.

Poenius Postumus,* camp prefect of the Second Legion, also stabbed himself with his sword when he learned of the success of the legionaries of the Fourteenth and Twentieth: he had cheated his own legion of similar glory and violated military procedure by disobeying his commander's orders.

38. The entire army was then brought together and kept under canvas with a view to finishing off what remained of the war. The emperor increased its strength by dispatching two thousand legionaries from Germany, along with eight cohorts of auxiliaries and a thousand cavalry, on the arrival of which the shortages in the Ninth were made good with regular legionaries. The cohorts and cavalry squadrons were placed in new winter quarters, and any tribes that had been vacillating or resisting were devastated by fire and the sword. But nothing caused the enemy as much suffering as famine: they had been negligent about sowing crops, with men of all ages being diverted to the war effort, while they assumed our provisions were going to be theirs. In addition, these savage tribes were all the slower in inclining towards peace because of Julius Classicianus,* who had been sent out to succeed Catus. Classicianus, at loggerheads with Suetonius, was undermining the national interest by his personal feuds, and he had put about the idea that they should await the arrival of a new legate who would deal humanely with those who surrendered, without an enemy's resentment or the pride of a victor. At the same time he was sending reports to Rome that they should expect no end to the hostilities unless a successor were found for Suetonius, whose setbacks he ascribed to bad judgement, and his successes to luck.

39. One of the freedmen, Polyclitus,* was therefore sent out to review the situation in Britain, for Nero greatly hoped that, through the man's authority, not only would harmony be established between legate and procurator, but the barbarians' rebellious spirit might also be pacified. Polyclitus proved burdensome to Italy and Gaul with his enormous retinue, and after crossing the ocean he did not fail to cut a frightening figure for our soldiers, either. But to the enemy he was a joke. The spirit of freedom still burned strongly amongst them, and they were as yet unacquainted with the power of the freedmen; and they were amazed that a commander and an army that had brought such a great war to an end should defer to slaves. Everything was toned down in the report to the emperor, however, and Suetonius

was kept in charge of operations. But after losing a few vessels on the shore and the oarsmen along with them, he was commanded to pass on his army to Petronius Turpilianus (who had now left the consulship) on the grounds that a state of war still existed. Not provoking the enemy, and unprovoked by them, Turpilianus gave his listless inaction the honourable title of 'peace'.*

40. That same year saw two remarkable crimes committed in Rome, one through the gall of a senator, the other that of a slave. Domitius Balbus* was a man of praetorian rank who, thanks to the combination of his advanced age, lack of children, and wealth, was a likely target for fraudulence. His relative Valerius Fabianus, who was marked out for a political career, forged a will in Balbus' name, having engaged as his co-conspirators two Roman knights, Vinicius Rufinus and Terentius Lentinus, who, in turn, took on Antonius Primus* and Asinius Marcellus* as accomplices. Antonius was a recklessly enterprising man; Marcellus enjoyed distinction because of his great-grandfather Asinius Pollio,* and was not lacking respect for his moral principles, either—apart from his believing that poverty was the worst of misfortunes! And so, having enlisted the men I mentioned above, and others of lesser distinction, Fabianus sealed the tablets. This was proved in the Senate, and Fabianus and Antonius, together with Rufinus and Terentius, were convicted under the Cornelian law.* In the case of Marcellus, the memory of his ancestors and the pleas of the emperor saved him from punishment, though not from disgrace.

41. That day also brought down Pompeius Aelianus, a young ex-quaestor, on a charge of being privy to the crimes of Fabianus, and he was debarred from Italy and from Spain, the land of his birth. Valerius Ponticus was subjected to similar humiliation for having attempted to prevent some defendants being tried before the city prefect:* he had brought evidence against them to the praetor in order to evade justice temporarily by legal pretexts, and later on by collusion. A rider was added to the senatorial decree that anyone buying or selling such services should face the same penalty as if he were convicted in a public court of false accusation.

42. Not much later the city prefect Pedanius Secundus* was murdered by his own slave. Either Secundus had refused him his freedom, after negotiating the price for it, or the man, fired with passion for a catamite, could not bear having his master as a rival. In any

case, in accordance with long-standing custom, all the household slaves that had been lodged under the same roof were required to face execution; but the plebs gathered together in their desire to safeguard so many innocents, and matters reached the point of a riot. The Senate then came under siege, and in the house support came from some who opposed such extreme severity, though most were for not breaking with tradition. One such was Gaius Cassius* who, when granted his turn to give his opinion, spoke as follows:

43. 'Senators: I have on many occasions been present in this assembly when demands were made for new decrees of the Senate that contravened the institutions and laws of our forefathers; and I did not oppose them. That was not because I had any doubts about the superiority and greater justice of the earlier provisions, and that such modifications as were introduced were changes for the worse. No, it was so that I would not appear to be advertising my own profession, by an overstated affection for the past. At the same time, I did not feel that whatever influence I possess should be squandered by my constantly opposing measures—I wanted it to remain intact for a time when the state was in need of advice. That time has come today, after a former consul's murder in his own home at the treacherous hands of a slave, without anyone intervening or denouncing the plot, even though the senatorial decree* that threatened all the household slaves with execution had not yet been challenged. By God, grant them impunity by your decree! But who will find protection in his rank, when that did not help a city prefect? Who will be protected by the number of his slaves when four hundred failed to safeguard Pedanius Secundus? Who will be brought help by his domestics, when even fear does not make them aware of the danger we are in? Or (since some do not blush to fabricate stories) was the murderer avenging wrongs he had himself suffered? Had he been dealing with money left him by his father, or was a family slave being filched from him? Let us go all the way and declare that the master's murder appears justified!

44. 'Do we want to cast about for arguments on a matter already carefully considered by wiser men? But even if this were the first time that we had to decide on it, do you think a slave would have raised the courage to kill his master without some sinister words falling from his lips, without some ill-considered remark? Granted, he concealed his plan and prepared his weapon amongst others

326 BOOK FOURTEEN AD 61

ignorant of the plot. But could he really have slipped by the guards, opened the bedroom doors, carried in a light, and brought off the murder without anyone knowing? There are many indications that a crime is afoot. If slaves divulge them, then we can live one amongst many, in safety amongst their fears, and, if we must die, not unavenged amongst the guilty.

'Our ancestors suspected the temperament of slaves, even when they were born on the same estates, or in the same houses, as they, and thus conceived an affection for their masters right from the start. But now we have in our households tribes of foreigners who have different rites, and alien religions, or no religion at all. You will not hold scum like that in check except by intimidation. But some innocents will die, you will say. Yes, and when every tenth man from a defeated army is struck with the club,* brave men also draw the lot. Every great example involves a measure of injustice, but wrongs done to individuals are counterbalanced by the common good.'

45. No one senator dared rebut Cassius' argument, but a confused shouting answered him, as members showed pity for the numbers involved, their ages, their sex, and the undeniable innocence of the majority. Even so, the party supporting the death penalty won the day. The sentence could not be carried out, however, since a mob had gathered and was threatening violence with stones and torches. Then Nero issued an edict reproaching the people, and set a barrier of troops all along the route by which the condemned were to be led to execution. Cingonius Varro* had proposed that, in addition, freedmen who had been under the same roof be deported from Italy, but that was rejected by the emperor in case a time-honoured custom, which pity had not softened, be made harsher through cruelty.

46. During the same consulship Tarquitius Priscus was convicted on a charge of extortion laid by the people of Bithynia. This brought great pleasure to the senators, who remembered that Statilius Taurus, Priscus' own proconsul, had been accused by him. There were censuses held in the Gallic provinces by Quintus Volusius,* Sextius Africanus and Trebellius Maximus,* during which there was rivalry between Volusius and Africanus because of their noble birth. Both felt disdain for Trebellius, and in so doing raised his profile above theirs.

47. That was the year of Memmius Regulus'* death. His prestige, determination, and reputation gave him a distinction as great as can

be gained in the shadow of an emperor's lofty eminence, to the point that when Nero fell ill, and the flatterers around his bed were saying that it would be the end of the empire if he died, the emperor answered that the state had a safeguard. When they went on to ask to whom, in particular, he was referring, he had replied 'Memmius Regulus'. Regulus lived on after this, protected by his tranquil lifestyle and the fact that he was of a family that only recently gained distinction, while his wealth was not such as to excite envy.

A gymnasium was dedicated by Nero that year, and oil* was provided for the equestrian and senatorial classes—a Greek indulgence.

48. In the consulship of Publius Marius and Lucius Afinius, the praetor Antistius (whose unruly conduct as tribune of the people I have already mentioned*) composed poetry abusive of the emperor which he recited in public at a banquet packed with guests, while he was dining at the home of Ostorius Scapula. He was thereupon charged with treason by Cossutianus Capito, who—following a petition from his father-in-law Tigellinus*—had only recently regained his senatorial rank. This was the first revival of the law, and it was believed that the aim was not so much to bring down Antistius as to exalt the emperor—when Antistius would be found guilty by the Senate, Nero could rescue him from death by using his veto as a tribune.*

Although Ostorius said in evidence that he had heard nothing, credence was given to hostile witnesses; and the consul-designate Junius Marullus proposed that the accused be divested of his praetorship and put to death in the traditional manner* of their ancestors. All the others then voiced their agreement, apart from Thrasea Paetus. With great deference to the emperor, and after sharply criticizing Antistius, Paetus argued that, acting under an exceptional ruler and not being coerced in any way, the Senate was not obliged to decree whatever a guilty defendant deserved to suffer. The executioner and his noose were things of the past, he said, and there were penalties established by the laws so that punishment could be decided without viciousness on the part of the judges, and without bringing dishonour on their times. In fact, the longer Antistius extended his iniquitous life, the more miserable he would be personally, spending it on an island with his property confiscated; and he would also be a great example of official clemency.

49. Thrasea's outspokenness broke the others' servility, and when the consul had permitted the division* all supported him in the voting, with few exceptions. (Amongst these was Aulus Vitellius,* the readiest with flattery, a man who would berate all the most decent individuals and—such is the way of cowards—fall silent when someone answered him.) The consuls, however, did not dare ratify the Senate's decree, and instead wrote a letter to the emperor to inform him of its consensus. Nero wavered between discretion and anger, eventually responding with a letter asserting that Antistius had made the most abusive insults against the emperor though he had suffered no wrong at his hands. A demand that he pay for them had been made by the senators, he said, and a punishment fitting the magnitude of the crime would have been in order. However, he would have opposed severity in their decree, and now he did not veto their moderation. They could decide as they wished, and were even free to acquit the man.

Despite these and similar remarks, and the evident dissatisfaction of the emperor, the consuls did not alter the motion. Thrasea did not retract his opinion, either, nor did the others abandon what they had approved, some of them in order not to appear to have exposed the emperor to odium, more feeling safe in their numbers. In Thrasea's case it was a matter of his habitual resolve of purpose, and a refusal to compromise his outstanding reputation.

50. Fabricius Veiento* was pursued with a charge that was not very different, namely that he was the author of numerous abusive comments on the senators and priests in books that he had entitled 'Codicils'.* His accuser Tullius Geminus claimed that he had also made a practice of trafficking in imperial privileges* and the rights to gaining public offices. This was a reason for Nero to take up the case. Finding Veiento guilty, he banished him from Italy and ordered the burning of his books, which were sought out and much read when acquiring them was risky (though presently freedom to own them swept them into obscurity).

51. The tribulations of the state were every day growing more serious, and safeguards against them were on the decline, and it was now that Burrus* died—whether from illness or poison is unclear. That it was illness was deduced from the fact that he stopped breathing at a time when there was a gradual swelling within his throat and his windpipe was choked. More people claimed that, on Nero's instructions, his palate had been smeared with a poisonous ointment that was supposedly applied as a cure. Burrus, they said, saw through the

.crime, and when the emperor came to visit him he averted his gaze and, in answer to Nero's queries, said only '*I* am all right.'

He was, and remained, sorely missed by the state, because his integrity was remembered, and also because of the ineffectual guilt-lessness of one of his successors and the monstrous crimes of the other. For the emperor had appointed two men to command the praetorian cohorts—Faenius Rufus, because of the popular support he enjoyed from not profiteering in his handling of the grain supply, and Ofonius Tigellinus, whose attraction lay in his long-standing depravity and disreputability. And the men's performance accorded with their known characteristics. Tigellinus had the stronger hold on the emperor's mind, and was enlisted by him to join his private debaucheries; and Rufus stood in high esteem amongst the people and the soldiers, which he found to be a disadvantage in his relations with Nero.

52. The death of Burrus broke the power of Seneca. Good qual-ities carried less weight with one of their champions removed, and in addition Nero was turning more towards worse characters. These attacked Seneca on various charges. He was, they said, still adding to his huge riches, which were already excessive for any private citizen; he was turning to himself the support of the citizens; and in the charm of his gardens and the magnificence of his country homes he was apparently trying to outdo the emperor. They also accused him of monopolizing all recognition given for oratory, and of composing verses more frequently after Nero developed a passion for them. He was openly hostile to the emperor's diversions, they said; he was dis-missive of his ability in driving horses and ridiculed his singing voice. How long would nothing in the state have distinction unless it were thought to be Seneca's creation? Nero's boyhood was certainly over, they added, and a young man's vigour was upon him. He should slough off his teacher—he had brilliant enough educators in his ancestors!

53. Seneca, in fact, was not unaware of the allegations; people with some regard for decency disclosed them to him, and the emperor was avoiding his company more than usual. He therefore requested time for a word with him, and when granted it he began like this:

'Caesar: it is the fourteenth year* since I was brought in to assist your prospects for the future, and the eighth that you have been in power. During that time you have heaped upon me so many honours and riches that nothing is lacking to complete my good fortune, except the ability to make proper use of them. I shall cite great examples, not from my station in life, but yours. Your great-great-grandfather,* Augustus, granted Marcus Agrippa retirement* at Mytilene, and to Gaius Maecenas* he granted, within the city itself, what was tantamount to a retreat abroad. One had been his partner in the wars, and the other beleaguered by many heavy responsibilities at Rome. They had then received their rewards, large indeed, but in line with the greatness of their services. In my case, what have I been able to contribute to justify your munificence, other than my studies, which have been fostered in the shade, so to speak, and become renowned only because I am thought to have aided your education in your youth (a great reward for such service)? Even so you have surrounded me with enormous influence, and wealth beyond measure, so much so that I often inwardly wonder, "Am I, born of an equestrian father in the provinces, actually numbered among the leaders of the state? Has my newcomer presence achieved distinction amongst noblemen who can put on display a long series of glittering decorations?* Where is that spirit that was happy with little? Is it out building gardens such as mine? Is it strutting through these suburban retreats? Is it awash with such extensive lands and such far-flung investments?"* Only one line of defence comes to mind—I had no right to resist your generous gifts.

54. 'But we have both reached the limit, you of what an emperor could bestow on a friend, and I of what a friend could accept from an emperor. Everything beyond that increases envy. Like all mortal things, this lies beneath your greatness,* but it weighs heavily on me, and I need help. Just as I would ask for a stick if I were exhausted on military service or a journey, so on this journey through life, as an old man and one unequal to the most insignificant cares, I am seeking assistance since I can no longer bear the burden of my riches. Give the order for my property to be managed by your procurators and to be incorporated into your fortune. I shall not be forcing myself into poverty, but after surrendering the things whose lustre dazzles me I shall direct back to the intellect the time now reserved for the care of my gardens and country homes. You have an abundance of stamina, and over many years you have wielded supreme power. We older friends of yours can claim their repose. This, too, will be counted to

your credit—that you elevated to the highest positions men who could also put up with modest ones.'

55. Nero's response was much like this:

'The fact that I can reply immediately to your prepared speech is what I consider your first gift to me—you have taught me impromptu as well as prepared delivery. My great-great-grandfather Augustus did permit Agrippa and Maecenas to enjoy a period of rest after their labours, but at a time in his life when his prestige could guarantee anything he conceded them, whatever its nature. And yet he did not strip either of them of the rewards earlier granted by him. They had earned them in warfare and danger—for that was where Augustus' youth was spent. Not that your weapons and sword-hand would have failed me had I been in combat; but, instead, as the immediate circumstances required, you nourished my boyhood and then my youth with your reason, advice, and principles. And, in fact, *your* gifts will always be with me as long as my life goes on, while those that you have from me—gardens, investments, villas—are all exposed to the vagaries of fortune. And while they may seem a lot, many men have had more, men in no way equal to you in accomplishments. I am ashamed to mention the freedmen who have greater riches than you on display. And so it makes me blush that you, who come first in my affections, do not yet surpass them all in prosperity.

56. 'But you are vigorous in your years, capable of conducting state business and enjoying its rewards, and I am taking my first steps in power. Or perhaps you think less of yourself than you do of Vitellius,* who was three times consul, or less of me than you do of Claudius— and perhaps my generosity to you cannot accumulate as much as Volusius' long-lasting thrift* did for him! If my youthful unsteadiness goes awry at some point, why not bring me back to the path and guide my strength more intensely, providing it with your support? It is not your moderation that will be on the lips of all if you return the money, nor your retirement if you leave your emperor. Rather it will be my greed and the fear of my cruelty. Even if your restraint is praised to the skies, it will still prove dishonourable for a philosopher to acquire glory from something that brings infamy to his friend.'

These words he followed with an embrace and kisses, for he had a natural propensity, further trained by habit, for cloaking his hatred with treacherous flattery. Seneca offered the thanks that mark the conclusion of all conversations with a master. However, he changed the routine associated with his former authority. He kept away the crowds of well-wishers, avoided entourages, and was rarely in evidence in the city, ostensibly kept at home by poor health or philosophical studies.

57. After Seneca's downfall, undermining Faenius Rufus'* position with a charge of friendship with Agrippina was easy. Tigellinus' power, moreover, was growing daily, and he now felt that his evil qualities, on which his power entirely depended, would be more appealing to Nero if he could put the emperor under obligation by association in crime. He therefore proceeded to pry into his fears. Discovering that his anxieties were focused mostly on Plautus* and Sulla*—both recently removed from Italy, Plautus to Asia and Sulla to Narbonese Gaul—he began commenting on their noble birth and the fact that both had armies close to them (Plautus that in the East, and Sulla the one in Germany). He had not the conflict of interest* that Burrus had, said Tigellinus—Nero's safety was his only concern! And for that all possible precautions were being taken against treachery in Rome by his action on the spot. But how could distant insurrections be quelled? The Gallic provinces were all agog at the name of the dictator,* he said, and the peoples of Asia were no less excited by the fame conferred by having Drusus as a grandfather.* Sulla was poor, and hence his excessive recklessness; and he was faking apathy until he found an opportunity for some bold stroke. As for Plautus, with his great wealth he did not even feign a desire for tranquillity. Instead he ostentatiously aped the Romans of old, even adopting the arrogant teachings of the Stoics* which made men mutinous and ambitious.

There was no further delay. Five days later, before any rumour arrived to cause alarm, Sulla was killed as he was reclining for dinner, after assassins had sailed to Massilia. His head was brought back to Nero, who poked fun at the premature greyness that disfigured it.

58. That Plautus' assassination was being planned was less of a secret: more people were concerned for his safety, and the length of the land and sea journey and the time interval involved had given rise to rumour. The lie being put about was that Plautus had headed for Corbulo, who was then at the head of mighty armies, and who would himself be in a particularly parlous situation if the famous and blameless were targeted for murder. Furthermore, it was said that Asia had taken up arms in support of the young man, and that

soldiers sent to do the deed, being neither strong in numbers nor inwardly committed, had been incapable of carrying out their orders and joined the revolt.

These idle speculations were enhanced, as happens with rumour, by credulous people with time on their hands; but a freedman of Plautus arrived, thanks to some swift winds, ahead of the centurion* and delivered to Plautus instructions from his father-in-law Lucius Antistius.* Antistius told him to avoid a cowardly death while there was still a way out. He would, through the sympathy generated by his great name, find good men to help, and would enlist brave allies. Meanwhile, no assistance should be rejected. He needed to drive off sixty soldiers, the number then en route, and while the news was being carried back to Nero and while a second force was on its way, much might transpire that could develop into war. In short, said Antistius, either Plautus' salvation would be gained by such a plan or he would have to suffer nothing worse for showing spirit than playing the coward.

59. This, however, made no impression on Plautus. Either he could see no future for himself as an unarmed exile, or he was tired of his fluctuating hopes. Or possibly it was because of his love for his wife and children, thinking the emperor would be more lenient to them if he had no worries to bother him. There are some who record that a second message arrived from his father-in-law reporting that he was facing no terrible danger, and also that his philosophy teachers, Coeranus and Musonius*—the former of Greek, the latter Tuscan, stock—urged him to await death with resolution rather than live in incertitude and fear.

At all events, he was found in the middle of the day stripped for physical exercise. Such was his condition when he was cut down by the centurion, before the eyes of the eunuch Pelago, whom Nero had set over the centurion and his unit like a royal minister over retainers. The head of the murdered man was brought back and at the sight of it Nero said (I shall quote the emperor's actual words): 'Why, Nero <. . .>.'*

His fear now removed, he proceeded to hurry on his marriage to Poppaea, which had been delayed by such anxieties, and to remove his wife Octavia (who, for all her modest demeanour, was offensive to him because of her father's name* and her popularity with the people). He did, however, send a letter to the Senate in which, without admitting to the assassination of Sulla and Plautus, he said that both had a turbulent character and that he took great care over maintaining the safety of the state. On this account decrees were passed for prayers of thanksgiving and the removal of Sulla and Plautus from the Senate—a farce that was now more disgusting than the crimes.

60. Receiving the decree of the Senate, Nero saw that all his crimes were accepted as good deeds, and so he drove out Octavia, claiming she was barren. He then married Poppaea. She had long been Nero's bedfellow, controlling him first as her adulterer and subsequently as her husband, and now she pushed one of Octavia's servants into accusing her mistress of a love affair with a slave. A man called Eucaerus, an Alexandrian native who was an expert flute-player, was marked out as the defendant. Octavia's maidservants were interrogated under torture and, though some were so overcome by the severity of their ordeals as to make false statements, more resolutely defended the virtue of their mistress (and, when Tigellinus pressed her, one replied that Octavia's private parts were more pure than his mouth). She was removed, none the less, first under the pretext of a civil divorce, when she was given Burrus' house and Plautus' estates (two inauspicious gifts), and later she was banished to Campania where she was also put under a military guard. There followed repeated and unconcealed protests amongst the common people, who have less prudence than others and who, because of their meagre fortunes, face fewer dangers. From this <arose the rumour> that Nero had regretted his outrageous conduct and recalled* Octavia to the marriage.

61. Then the people joyfully climbed the Capitol and at last paid homage to the gods. They threw down Poppaea's statues, lifted effigies of Octavia on their shoulders, scattered flowers over them, and set them up in the Forum and temples. There was even praise for the emperor and they once more competed with each other in their homage to him. They were already filling the Palatium with their numbers and their shouting when companies of soldiers were sent forth who broke up the gathering and dispersed them with beatings and drawn swords. The changes they had brought about with the riot were reversed, and Poppaea's honours were re-established.

Ever vicious in her hatred, she was now wild with fear of increased violence from the mob, or a change of heart in Nero because of the mood-swing of the people, and she flung herself at his knees. Her situation was not such that she was fighting for her marriage, she said, although that meant more to her than her life. No, she said, that very life had been put in extreme jeopardy by Octavia's clients and slaves, who called themselves 'the plebs', and who had the audacity to commit in peace acts that scarcely took place in war. That armed insurrection had been directed against the emperor; all it had lacked was a leader, and one would easily be found once things got under way! That woman, at whose nod, even in her absence, rioting was set in motion, now had only to quit Campania and come to the city in person! And what had been Poppaea's wrongdoing, anyway? What offence had she caused anyone? Could it be because she was going to give the house of the Caesars legitimate offspring? Did the Roman people prefer the scion of an Egyptian flute-player to be brought to the empire's highest post? In short, if it was in his interests, he should bring home the woman who controlled him, but of his own will rather than under duress—or else he should take thought for his own safety. The initial disturbances had been settled through fair retribution and gentle correctives, she said, but if the people lost hope of Octavia being Nero's wife they would give her another husband!

62. Her address, with its varying tone, and adapted to stir up both fear and anger, both terrified and incensed her listener. But suspicion was too weak in the case of the slave, and had been undermined by the interrogation of the maidservants. It was accordingly decided that a confession should be obtained from someone on whom a charge of subversion could also be pinned. And for that Anicetus seemed a good choice, the perpetrator of his mother's murder. He was, as I noted, prefect of the fleet at Misenum and, while he had enjoyed some slight favour after committing the crime, he had then become the object of a deepening hatred, for the agents of one's nefarious acts are viewed as a standing reproach.

Summoning Anicetus, Nero reminded him of his earlier service. He alone had taken measures for his safety against a scheming mother, the emperor told him, and now he had the opportunity to do no less a favour by clearing away a hateful wife. No violence, no weapon was required—he need only admit adultery with Octavia. Though these would remain secret for the moment, Nero promised him great rewards and a delightful retirement property, threatening him with death if he refused. With his deranged viciousness and a facility he demonstrated in his earlier crimes, Anicetus fabricated even more than he had been ordered to, and made a confession before friends whom the emperor had brought together as though for an advisory council. He was then banished to Sardinia where he endured an exile that was far from impoverished, and died a natural death.

63. Nero issued an edict in which he declared that the prefect had been seduced by Octavia, who had hoped thereby to enlist the support of the fleet. Then, forgetting the barrenness of which she had been accused shortly before, he added that she had undergone an abortion through guilt over her sexual excesses, and this had become known to him. He then shut her away on the island of Pandateria. No woman in exile ever inspired more pity in those who saw her. Some could still recall Agrippina's banishment by Tiberius,* and there was also the more recent memory of Julia,* banished by Claudius. But those women had with them the strength of age;* they had seen some happy days and could find comfort for the brutality of the present in the recollection of better fortunes in the past. For Octavia her wedding day* was, first of all, tantamount to a funeral, when she was escorted to a home in which she would encounter only grief, her father being snatched from her by poison, and her brother, too, immediately thereafter. Then came the maidservant* who was more powerful than her mistress; then Poppaea, whose marriage served only to destroy the wife; and finally the accusation more agonizing than any death.

64. So, in her twentieth year,* the girl, surrounded by centurions and soldiers, had been removed from the living by the presentiment of her doom, but not yet could she enjoy the tranquillity of death. After a few days' interval, the order for her death was given. She declared that she was now a widow and merely a sister,* and she appealed to Nero by calling upon their common kinsmen the Germanici* and, finally, upon the name of Agrippina, in whose lifetime she had endured a marriage that, while unhappy, had not carried a death sentence.

She was chained up, and the veins were cut in all her limbs; and because the blood, arrested by her fear, flowed too slowly, her life was terminated by the steam of an overheated bath. An act of even more atrocious savagery followed: her head was cut off and taken to Rome, where Poppaea viewed it.

In thanks for this, offerings were decreed at the temples—but how long shall I go on relating such events? Any who learn about the tribulations of those times from me, or from other authors, can take it for granted that, whenever the emperor authorized exile or assassination, prayers were always offered to the gods, and that the former indicators of success had now become those of public disaster. And yet I shall not keep silent about any senatorial decree that marked new stages of obsequiousness or extremes of servility.

65. That same year Nero was believed to have murdered by poison two of his most powerful freedmen—Doryphorus* for his opposition to the marriage to Poppaea, and Pallas for living too long in possession of immense riches. Romanus had laid secret charges against Seneca of collaboration with Gaius Piso,* but was himself more effectively brought down on the same grounds by Seneca. From that arose fear on Piso's part, and against Nero arose a conspiracy that was momentous, and ill-starred.

BOOK FIFTEEN

1. Meanwhile* Vologaeses, king of Parthia, had learned of Corbulo's exploits and discovered that Tigranes, a foreigner,* had been placed on the throne of Armenia; and at the same time he wanted to avenge the expulsion of his brother Tiridates, which was an insult to the dignity of the Arsacids. However, when he considered Roman greatness and his past respect for the treaty, which had remained unbroken,* he was drawn in two different directions at once. He was hesitant by nature, and also encumbered by the defection of a mighty people, the Hyrcanians, and the numerous campaigns arising from it.

In fact, he was still wavering when news of a further insult galvanized him into action. On emerging from Armenia, Tigranes had inflicted damage on the bordering tribe of the Adiabeni too extensively, and for too long, for his action to be simply predatory raiding, and the chiefs of the Parthian races were infuriated. They had now become so despised, they said, that it was not even from a Roman general that they were under attack, but from an overambitious hostage treated for years by the Romans as one of their slaves. Monobazus,* who was the ruler of the Adiabeni, further inflamed their anger by asking what assistance he could look for, and from whom. They had already given up on Armenia, he said, and the lands bordering it were being seized. If the Parthians did not defend them . . . well, serfdom to the Romans was easier for those who surrendered than for those who were captured, he declared.

Tiridates, a fugitive from his kingdom, had an even deeper effect through his silence or with his mild protests. Great empires were not held together by idleness, he said. There had to be competition in men and weapons. At the topmost levels of power might was right. And while maintaining one's possessions befitted a private household, a king won praise by contending for those of others.

2. Impressed by these comments, Vologaeses called a council meeting,* set Tiridates next to him, and began to speak:

'This man, born of the same father* as myself, ceded to me the supreme title in view of our ages, and I put him in possession of Armenia, which is regarded as the third-ranking kingdom in power— for Pacorus* had already taken the Medes. And breaking with the traditional hatreds and squabbles between brothers, I thought I had found an appropriate settlement of our family's issues. The Romans are standing in our way, and are breaking a peace accord, the violation of which has never done them any good—and it will mean destruction for them. I shall not deny it: I should have preferred to preserve the gains made by our forefathers by an appeal to justice rather than by bloodshed, by negotiation rather than arms. If I have erred by vacillating, I shall make amends by courage. Your strength and prestige are, at least, undiminished, and to them is now added a reputation for moderation, which the greatest of mortals should not disdain, and which is esteemed by the gods.'

With that he bound a diadem around Tiridates' head, and he placed a cavalry detachment, which was at the ready and which usually attended the king, under the command of the nobleman Monaeses, adding some auxiliaries of the Adiabeni, and charged him with the responsibility of driving Tigranes from Armenia. Vologaeses himself set aside his differences with the Hyrcanians, mustered his internal forces, and initiated a massive war, threatening the Roman provinces.

3. When Corbulo heard this from reliable reports, he sent two legions under Verulanus Severus* and Vettius Bolanus* to assist Tigranes, but secretly instructed them to act at all times with deliberation rather than speed. For, he explained, he wanted to be in a state of war rather than fighting one. He had also informed Nero by dispatch that Armenia needed its own commander for its defence, and Syria would be in more serious danger if Vologaeses attacked. In the meantime he deployed his remaining legions along the bank of the Euphrates, put a makeshift company of provincials under arms, and closed with armed detachments the points of entry open to the enemy. And because the region lacked water, he established forts at the springs, and some of the streams he hid from view under piles of sand.

4. While Corbulo was taking such measures for the protection of Syria, Monaeses marched swiftly in order to outstrip word of his coming, but still failed to take Tigranes by surprise or catch him off his guard. Tigranes had seized Tigranocerta, a town of some strength thanks to the number of its defenders and the extent of its fortifications. Furthermore, the River Nicephorius, which has a considerable width, flows past a section of its walls, and a huge ditch had been dug where the river could not be relied on for protection. Inside were

regular troops and supplies that had been laid up in advance. (In bringing these up to the town a few of the men had been over-enthusiastic in their advance and had been cut off by the sudden appearance of the enemy, which had inspired anger rather than fear in the others.)

In fact, the Parthian completely lacks the daring in hand-to-hand fighting needed for successful siege operations; firing off the odd arrow he fails to unnerve those under siege and simply becomes frustrated. When the Adiabeni proceeded to move up ladders and siege-engines, they were easily thrown back and, presently, cut down in a sortie of our men.

5. Despite his success, Corbulo felt he should not press his luck, and he sent off a deputation to Vologaeses to deplore the violence brought against the province,* and the fact that a king who was his ally and friend was under siege, along with Roman cohorts. He would do better to raise the siege, said Corbulo, or he, too, would pitch his camp in enemy territory!

The centurion Casperius, who had been chosen for this deputation, came to the king at the town of Nisibis, thirty-seven miles from Tigranocerta, and there delivered his instructions in strongly worded terms. Vologaeses had a long-standing and firmly held principle of avoiding armed confrontation with the Romans and, in addition, things were not running well for him at the time. The siege was a failure; Tigranes was secure, thanks to his manpower and supplies; those who had undertaken the assault on the town had been routed; legions had been sent into Armenia; and others were on the Syrian border ready to launch an offensive. As for his own situation, his cavalry was weakened from lack of forage, for the sudden appearance of a swarm of locusts had left nothing in the way of grass or foliage. Vologaeses therefore concealed his unease and, assuming a more conciliatory approach, replied that he would send spokesmen to the Roman emperor about his petition for Armenia and strengthening the peace. He ordered Monaeses to quit Tigranocerta, and proceeded to pull back himself.

6. Most praised this as a magnificent achievement brought off by the king's fear and the threats of Corbulo. Others explained it as a secret agreement whereby Tigranes would also leave Armenia after both sides abandoned hostilities and Vologaeses departed. Why else, they asked, had the Roman army been withdrawn from Tigranocerta?

Why had they abandoned in peacetime what they had defended in war? Was it better to have wintered on the fringes of Cappadocia in hurriedly erected huts rather than in the capital of a kingdom they had just succeeded in holding? Armed conflict had been deliberately postponed, they said, so Vologaeses could clash with someone other than Corbulo, and so Corbulo would not further jeopardize the glory he had earned over the years. For, as I have observed, Corbulo had requested that Armenia have its own commander for its protection, and the news was that Caesennius Paetus* was close at hand.

Soon Paetus was there. The troops were then divided, with the Fourth and Twelfth legions, plus the Fifth (recently summoned from Moesia), put under Paetus' command, along with the auxiliaries from Pontus, Galatia, and Cappadocia. The Third, Sixth, and Tenth legions, and the troops earlier serving in Syria, would remain with Corbulo. All else they would share, or divide up, according to the exigencies of the moment. But Corbulo could not stand a rival, and Paetus, for whom being second to him should have been glory enough, kept disparaging Corbulo's achievements. There had been no 'bloodshed or spoils', he would say, and the 'storming of cities' that Corbulo often referred to applied in name only. It would be he, Paetus, who would impose on the conquered peoples tribute and laws, and, instead of a phantom king, Roman jurisdiction.

7. Vologaeses' representatives, whom I mentioned above as having been sent to the emperor, returned at about this same time, empty-handed; and so the Parthians turned to open warfare. Paetus did not demur. He took two legions—the Fourth, which Funisulanus Vettonianus commanded at that time, and the Twelfth, which was under Calavius Sabinus*—and entered Armenia accompanied by a grim omen. For on their way over the Euphrates, which they crossed by a bridge, the horse carrying the consular insignia took fright for no apparent reason and escaped to the rear of the troops. Furthermore, a sacrificial animal that was standing beside the winter quarters, which were under construction, burst through the half-finished works in flight, and ran out from the rampart. Soldiers' javelins also burst into flames, a prodigy of significance because, in combat, the enemy fights with projectiles.

8. Paetus, however, disregarded the omens and, although he had not yet adequately fortified his winter quarters or made any provision for his grain supply, he hurriedly marched his army over the

Taurus range. His aim, he kept saying, was to retake Tigranocerta and lay waste the areas that Corbulo had left untouched. He did take a number of strongholds and acquire a measure of glory and plunder—but failed to exercise moderation in the pursuit of glory, or circumspection in the pursuit of the plunder. With forced marches he overran areas that could not be held, only to lead back his army when the provisions that had been captured had rotted and winter was coming on. Then, as though the war were over, he wrote a letter to Nero framed in grandiose terms, but devoid of substance.

9. Meanwhile Corbulo secured the bank of the Euphrates—which he had never neglected—with more closely spaced guard-posts. In addition, to ensure that enemy cavalry squadrons would not obstruct his establishing a bridge on the river—for they were already racing about on the nearby plains, an impressive sight—he drew a line of sizeable ships, connected with planking and built up with turrets, across the river. From these, using catapults and ballistas, he drove back the barbarians, whom rocks and missiles could reach at a range that arrows shot back in response could not match. Then the bridge was completed, and the hills on the far side were taken over by the allied cohorts, and subsequently by the legionary camp. Such was the speed of the Romans, and such their show of strength, that the Parthians abandoned their preparations for invading Syria and directed all their hopes towards Armenia. This was where Paetus was, ignorant of the looming threat and with the Fifth Legion stationed far off in Pontus; and the remaining legions he had weakened by indiscriminately granting leave to his men. Then word came that Vologaeses was approaching with a large army ready to attack.

10. The call went out for the Twelfth Legion, but this move, which Paetus had hoped would spread the word of an increase in his forces, only betrayed his weakness. Even so, the camp could have been held, and the Parthian could have been foiled by an extension of the war, had Paetus held consistently to his own plans or those developed by others. Instead, as soon as his confidence to face immediate crises had been bolstered by his military advisers, he would switch to other—and less effective—strategies so as not to seem dependent on other men's ideas. And so, at that time, he left winter quarters and, proclaiming that it was not a ditch and a rampart, but men and weapons, that he had been given to face the enemy with, he led his legions forward as though for pitched battle. Then, after losing

a centurion and a few soldiers whom he had sent ahead to observe the enemy troops, he fell back in panic. Vologaeses, however, put less pressure on him than he might have, and Paetus experienced another surge of misplaced confidence. He stationed three thousand elite infantry on the closest heights of the Taurus range to bar the king's passage; and he also deployed his mounted Pannonian auxiliaries, the cream of his cavalry, on part of the plain. Paetus' wife and son were placed in hiding in a fort called Arsamosata,* with a cohort assigned to protect them. Thus a force, which, if kept together, might more readily have stood up to the wide-ranging enemy troops, was dispersed.

They say that Paetus was only with difficulty made to acknowledge the enemy pressure to Corbulo. And there was no haste on Corbulo's part—as the dangers mounted, credit for relieving Paetus would also grow. He did, however, give orders for a thousand men from each of the three legions, along with eight hundred auxiliary cavalry and a similar number from the cohorts, to prepare for the march.

11. Vologaeses had received word that the roads had been blockaded by Paetus at various points with infantry or cavalry, but he did not change his strategy at all. With a forceful and threatening advance he struck panic into the allied cavalry and crushed the legionaries. One centurion alone, Tarquitius Crescens, had the fortitude to defend the tower in which he was on garrison duty: he made repeated counter-attacks and cut down any barbarians who came too close, until he was overwhelmed by the firebrands the enemy hurled at him.

All the uninjured foot-soldiers made for points distant and remote, while the wounded headed back to camp, exaggerating from fear every detail of the battle—the courage of the king, and the savagery and number of the tribes involved—and finding ready belief among those sharing the same fears. Even the commander failed to cope with the disaster. He had relinquished all his military duties after once more sending an entreaty to Corbulo to come quickly and protect the standards, eagles, and whatever remained of the honour of the hapless army. In the meantime, while life remained, they would maintain their loyalty, he said.

12. Corbulo was undaunted. He left some of his troops in Syria to hold the defences erected on the Euphrates, and, taking the shortest route which would not be devoid of provisions, he headed for the region of Commagene, then Cappadocia, and from there Armenia. Accompanying the army—apart from the usual war apparatus— was a large number of camels laden with grain, so Corbulo could ward off both hunger and the enemy. The first of the defeated Romans that he came upon was the senior centurion Paccius, then a number of the rank and file. They proffered sundry excuses for their flight, but Corbulo advised them to return to their standards and throw themselves on the mercy of Paetus—he himself was pitiless to all but victors, he said.

At the same time Corbulo approached his own legions with words of encouragement. He reminded them of their past record, and pointed to fresh glory to come. Their goal was worth the effort, he said: not Armenian villages or towns, but a Roman camp with two legions in it. If the crown reserved for saving a citizen's life were conferred on individual soldiers by the emperor's hand, he said, then what glory—what great glory!—would be theirs when the numbers bringing deliverance and those receiving it were seen to be the same.

Inspired as a body by these and similar words—and there were some fired by the personal stimuli of having brothers or relatives in danger—they made a speedy march, day and night, without a halt.

13. Vologaeses intensified his pressure on the besieged Romans. He alternated his assaults between the rampart of the legions and the fort that sheltered those too young to fight, and approached more closely than was the Parthian norm, in the hope of enticing the enemy into combat by such temerity. The Romans, however, could hardly be drawn out of their tents, and then they did no more than defend their fortifications, some under orders from the commander, and others because of their own cowardice or because they were waiting for Corbulo. In addition, if a violent attack was impending, they had the peace-treaties of Caudium and Numantia* as precedents— and the Samnites, an Italian people, or the Spaniards were not on the same level of power as the Parthians, Rome's rivals for dominion! Whenever fortune went against them, the strong and praiseworthy Romans of old had made provision for their own safety, they said.

The commander was crushed by his army's despair, but he nevertheless composed an initial dispatch to Vologaeses which was not suppliant in tone but was more of a protest at the Parthian taking the offensive on behalf of the Armenians. These, he said, had always been under Roman jurisdiction, or subject to a king whom the emperor had chosen. Peace was advantageous to both sides, Paetus continued, and Vologaeses should not consider only the present—he had come with all the forces of his realm to face two legions, but the Romans could draw on the rest of the world to sustain their war effort.

14. Vologaeses' reply did not address these points; he wrote merely that he had to wait for his brothers Pacorus and Tiridates. That was the place and time at which they had decided to make a decision about Armenia, and it was the gods who had then added— something worthy of the Arsacids—that they should simultaneously settle the question of the Roman legions. After that messengers were sent by Paetus requesting a meeting with the king, but Vologaeses ordered his cavalry commander Vasaces to go in his stead. Paetus then mentioned men like Lucullus and Pompey, and whatever the Caesars had done relating to the occupation of Armenia or allocating its throne. Vasaces, however, noted that, while we had some illusion of retaining or granting it, the real power lay with the Parthians. After much arguing back and forth, Monobazus the Adiabene was called on to appear the following day as a witness to whatever they agreed. It was decided that the legions be relieved of the blockade, that all troops quit the territory of the Armenians, and that forts and supplies be surrendered to the Parthians. Vologaeses was to be given leave to send spokesmen to Nero when this was all done.

15. Meanwhile Paetus set a bridge on the River Arsanias, which flowed past the camp. He pretended to be making a path for himself, but in fact the Parthians had ordered it built as evidence of their victory—it was to them that it was useful, as our men set off in the opposite direction. Rumour added that the legions had been sent under the yoke, and suffered other indignities appropriate to a defeat which had been copied by the Armenians. For they entered the fortifications before the Roman column left, and they stood at the roadside identifying and removing slaves or beasts of burden that had been captured earlier. Even clothing was seized and weapons withheld, the frightened soldiers yielding them so there would be no grounds for a fight.

Vologaeses piled up the arms and corpses of the slain as a testimonial to our defeat, but stopped short of watching the legions in flight; after indulging his pride to the full, he was seeking a reputation for moderation. He forded the River Arsanias on an elephant, and all members of his entourage charged over on their powerful horses, for the rumour had arisen that—because of the treachery of its builders—the bridge would give way under their weight. In the event, those who had the temerity to set foot on it found it strong and reliable.

16. It is well established, however, that those under siege had such quantities of grain at their disposal that they set fire to their granaries. On the other hand, according to Corbulo's account, the Parthians, short of provisions and their forage exhausted, were on the point of raising the siege (and Corbulo himself was no more than three days' march away, he says). He adds that a sworn undertaking was given by Paetus before the standards, and in the presence of men whom the king had sent to witness it, that no Roman would enter Armenia* until the arrival of Nero's letter stating whether he agreed with the peace-treaty. While this account was intended to increase Paetus' disrepute, the other details are not unclear: Paetus covered a distance of forty miles* in one day, leaving wounded men all along the route, and the panic-stricken retreat was no less unsightly than if the men had turned tail in battle.

Corbulo met them with his own forces on the bank of the Euphrates, but he avoided such a display of insignia and weapons as would make a humiliating contrast between them. The units were downcast and deploring the lot of their comrades, and they could not even hold back their tears; greetings could barely be exchanged because of the weeping. Gone was the will to compete in valour, gone the striving for glory, which are the inclinations of successful men; pity reigned alone, and it was stronger in the lower ranks.

17. Next came a brief conversation between the commanders. Corbulo complained that his efforts had been wasted, that the war could have been ended if the Parthians had been routed. Paetus responded that everything remained unchanged for the two of them—they should turn the eagles around and together invade Armenia, now weakened by the departure of Vologaeses. Such were not the orders he had from the emperor, said Corbulo. He had left his province from concern over the danger facing the legions, and as the Parthians' intentions were unclear, he would head back to Syria.* Even so, he would still have to pray for the best of luck in order for his infantrymen, exhausted from the long distances covered, to overtake spirited cavalrymen who would outpace them over the easy terrain of the plains.

Paetus then wintered in Cappadocia. Messengers from Vologaeses were meanwhile dispatched to Corbulo to tell him to dismantle his forts across the Euphrates and make the river the boundary between them as before. Corbulo had a demand, too, that Armenia be cleared of its various garrisons. In the end the king acquiesced; the fortifications that Corbulo had established beyond the Euphrates were demolished, and the Armenians were left without a ruler.

18. At Rome, meanwhile, trophies* and arches were being erected in the middle of the Capitoline Hill for victory over the Parthians. Decreed by the Senate when the war was still undecided, they were not even now discontinued, attention being paid to appearances, despite knowledge of the facts. Indeed, to hide his concern over events abroad, Nero had the common people's grain, which had rotted with age, dumped into the Tiber in order to maintain public confidence in the grain supply. There was no addition made to the price of grain, despite the fact that a violent storm had sunk some two hundred ships right in the harbour, and a chance fire had destroyed a hundred others that had sailed up the Tiber.

Nero then put three ex consuls, Lucius Piso, Ducenius Geminus, and Pompeius Paulinus,* in charge of the public revenues,* criticizing earlier emperors for having exceeded the regular income of the state with heavy expenditures. He himself made an annual gift* of sixty million sesterces to the exchequer, he said.

19. At that time an unconscionable practice had become very common. As elections or a provincial sortition drew near, large numbers of childless men acquired sons in bogus adoptions, immediately releasing those they had adopted after they, along with genuine fathers, were allotted praetorships* or provinces. As a result, those who actually had begotten children approached the Senate in high dudgeon. They listed the rights of nature, and the hardships involved rearing children, contrasting with them the chicanery and tricks being practised in the short-term adoptions. Childless men had sufficient recompense, they argued, in that they had influence, honours, and everything else ready at their disposal without much to worry them and without any responsibilities. But what *they* had been promised by law, and had long awaited, was now being turned into a joke, for any man who became a parent without worry, and was made childless without grief, could instantly achieve what real fathers had been aspiring to over a long period. As a result a senatorial decree was passed to the effect that a sham adoption should not be of benefit in any sector of public service and could not even be of use in the acquisition of inheritances.

20. Next the Cretan Claudius Timarchus was prosecuted, the charges being those usually brought against powerful provincials whose excessive wealth gives them the confidence to oppress their inferiors; but also, in his case, there was one comment in which he had gone so far as to insult the Senate. It was reported that he had often stated that the giving of the vote of thanks to proconsuls who governed Crete lay in his power. Thrasea Paetus turned this opportunity to the common good. After stating as his opinion on the defendant that he should be banished from the province of Crete, he added the following:

'Experience has shown, senators, that fine laws and honourable precedents emerge amongst decent men from the misdeeds of others. Thus it was that the liberties taken by orators gave birth to the Cincian bill, the corrupt practices of candidates to the Julian laws,* and the avarice of magistrates to the Calpurnian resolutions.* For the crime precedes its punishment, and correction follows wrongdoing. Accordingly, to combat this recent arrogance of the provincials, let us adopt a measure in keeping with the honour and steadfast commitment of Rome, one that is in no way detrimental to the protection that our allies enjoy but which also eradicates the notion that a man's reputation can be fixed somewhere other than in the judgement of his fellow-citizens.

21. 'At one time, in fact, private citizens, and not just a praetor or consul, would be sent to inspect the provinces and report their impressions of the loyalty of each, and nations would tremble anticipating the verdict of individual Romans. Now, by contrast, we cultivate foreigners and flatter them; and just as a vote of thanks is decreed when one of them gives the nod, so (and the more readily) is an act of impeachment.

'Let those decrees be made, and let the provincials retain their ability to demonstrate their power in such a manner! But let insincere eulogies, squeezed out by entreaties, be curbed as much as malfeasance, or as much as cruelty. More wrongs are often done while we try to please than while we give offence. In fact, some virtues— uncompromising strictness and a mind impervious to favouritism, for example—provoke hatred. Thus our magistrates' terms of office tend to be better at the start; it is the end that sees a decline, when we seek votes just as candidates do. If all that could be stopped, the administration of the provinces will be fairer and more consistent. For just as greed has been suppressed through fear of an extortion charge, so influence-seeking will be checked by a ban on the vote of thanks.'

22. The proposal was warmly received, but the senatorial decree could not be passed as the consuls claimed there had been no formal motion* on the matter. Shortly afterwards, at the emperor's suggestion, they enacted a law banning any proposal at a council of the allies that votes of thanks be given in the Senate to propraetors or proconsuls, and forbidding anyone to participate in such a delegation to the Senate.

While these consuls were still in office, the gymnasium* burned down after being struck by lightning, and a statue of Nero within it melted into a shapeless mass of bronze. In addition, the populous town of Pompeii in Campania was largely destroyed by an earthquake.* The Vestal Virgin* Laelia passed away, and was replaced by Cornelia, a member of the Cossi family.

23. In the consulship of Memmius Regulus and Verginius Rufus, a daughter* was born to Nero by Poppaea, and he welcomed her with a joy transcending that of a mortal, naming her Augusta and conferring the same title on Poppaea. Her birthplace was the colony of Antium, where Nero himself had been born. The Senate had earlier commended Poppaea's pregnancy to the protection of the gods, and had undertaken vows in the name of the state, which were now multiplied and discharged. There was also a period of thanksgiving, with decrees issued authorizing a temple to Fertility and a contest modelled on the rite of Actium.* Statues in gold of the goddesses of Fortune were also to be set on the throne of Capitoline Jupiter, and circus entertainments were to be held at Antium in honour of the Claudian and Domitian families, like those for the Julian at Bovillae.

But these were all transitory: the baby was dead within four months. And then came more sycophancy, as they voted the child divine honours, complete with couch, temple, and priest. And Nero himself was as immoderate in grief as he had been in joy.

It was observed that, when the entire Senate surged out to Antium soon after the birth, Thrasea had been forbidden to attend, and that he had accepted the affront—a harbinger of the oncoming carnage—with composure. This was followed, they say, by proud remarks from Nero, in Seneca's presence, about his reconciliation with Thrasea, and Seneca's offer of congratulations to Nero. From this came increasing renown, and increasing peril, for these two exceptional men.

24. Meanwhile, at the start of spring, representatives of the Parthians arrived with King Vologaeses' instructions and a letter that ran along the same lines. The claims to sovereignty over Armenia that he had so often insisted on earlier he was now dropping, Vologaeses said. The gods, arbiters of all peoples, no matter how powerful, had delivered possession of it to the Parthians, not without some humiliation for the Romans. Recently he had blockaded Tigranes, and then released Paetus and his legions unharmed when he could have crushed them. He had given sufficient proof of his power, and also demonstrated his clemency. Tiridates would not have refused to come to Rome to accept his diadem, either, he said, had he not been held back by the religious taboos of his priesthood.* He would, however, come before the standards and statues of the emperor, there to inaugurate his reign in the presence of the legions.

25. Such was the letter of Vologaeses, and Paetus' account, suggesting that matters were still undecided, contradicted it. A centurion who had arrived with the representatives was therefore questioned on the Armenian situation, and he replied that all the Romans had quit the country. Aware now of the mockery implicit in the barbarians asking for what they had already seized, Nero consulted the leading men* of Rome on whether they preferred a dangerous war or a dishonourable peace. It was war, without question. With his many years' experience of the Roman troops and the enemy, Corbulo was put in charge of the campaign, so there would be no further bungling through another's inexperience—they had had enough of Paetus.

The representatives were therefore sent back with their mission unaccomplished, but bearing gifts to raise hopes that Tiridates would not fail with the same request if he petitioned in person.

Gaius Cestius* was entrusted with the civil administration of Syria, and Corbulo with the military forces, which were reinforced by the addition of the Fifteenth Legion, under Marius Celsus,* brought in from Pannonia. Tetrarchs,* kings, prefects, procurators, and praetors in charge of neighbouring provinces were sent written instructions to take their orders from Corbulo, whose powers were increased roughly to the level of those the Roman people had granted

Gnaeus Pompey* for the war on the pirates. Although Paetus feared worse on his return, Nero was satisfied merely with a facetious rebuke, the gist of which was that he was pardoning Paetus immediately in order that a man so prone to panic might not fall ill from chronic worry.

26. In Corbulo's view the Fourth and Twelfth legions, with their best fighters lost and the rest demoralized, were not battle-ready. He transferred them to Syria, and from there took into Armenia the Sixth and Third. This was a force with a full complement of soldiers that had been hardened by regularly and successfully facing difficult tasks. He added to it the Fifth Legion (which had been spared the disaster because it was on service in Pontus), the soldiers of the Fifteenth, recently brought into the theatre, and companies of elite troops from Illyricum and Egypt. He also added all the auxiliary cavalry and infantry that he had, and the auxiliary troops of the kings that had been concentrated at Melitene (which was where he was preparing to cross the Euphrates).

Corbulo then undertook the ritual purification of the troops, and summoned them to a meeting. There he proceeded to talk in grandiose terms about his campaigns under the emperor's auspices and his own achievements, attributing the reverses to Paetus' incompetence. And this he did with great authority, which counted as eloquence in the military man.

27. Presently Corbulo took the road once opened up by Lucius Lucullus,* clearing such obstacles as the years had thrown up. And when spokesmen came from Tiridates and Vologaeses to discuss peace he did not rebuff them, sending back with them some centurions bearing a communiqué that was not intransigent in tone. Matters had not yet reached the point where out-and-out war was necessary, it said. Much had gone well for the Romans, and some things for the Parthians—and this served as a warning against pride. Accordingly, not only was it to Tiridates' advantage to receive as a gift a kingdom spared the ravages of war, but Vologaeses would also serve the interests of the Parthian race more by an alliance with Rome than by resorting to mutual damage. Corbulo was aware of the amount of internal conflict in Vologaeses' realm, the message concluded, and of the unruliness and ferocity of the tribes he ruled over, whereas Corbulo's own ruler had undisturbed peace everywhere else, and this was his only war.

At the same time Corbulo pressed home his advice with some intimidation. He drove from their homes the Armenian grandees who had been the first to defect from us, demolished their strongholds and filled the plains and highlands, and the strong and the weak, with the same terror.

28. Even amongst the barbarians Corbulo's name did not excite animosity or the hatred felt for an enemy, and so they thought his advice to be reliable. Consequently, Vologaeses was not inflexible on the main issue, and even requested a truce in certain prefectures.* Tiridates demanded a place and day to parley. The date chosen was close, and the place was where the legions and Paetus had recently been under siege—selected by the barbarians in remembrance of a rather successful operation there. Corbulo did not shy away from it, hoping that the contrast between the two situations would only increase his prestige. Nor did Paetus' disgrace distress him, a fact made abundantly clear by the order he gave to Paetus' son, a tribune, to take some units and cover over the vestiges of that unfortunate encounter.

On the appointed day, Tiberius Alexander* and Vinicianus Annius* came into Tiridates' camp as a mark of respect for the king, and also, by this reassuring gesture, to allay any fears of a trap. (Alexander was a distinguished Roman knight who had been brought in as a military administrator, and Annius was Corbulo's son-in-law, not yet of senatorial age, but set in command of the Fifth Legion as a legate.) Then each leader took an escort of twenty cavalrymen. Catching sight of Corbulo, the king was the first to dismount. There was no hesitation on Corbulo's part, either, and, on foot, the two clasped each other's right hand.

29. The Roman then praised the young man for rejecting impetuous policies in favour of a safe and secure course. After a lengthy prelude on the nobility of his family, Tiridates proceeded modestly. He would go to Rome, he said, and bring Nero a novel honour—an Arsacid as suppliant although Parthia had suffered no reverse. It was agreed that Tiridates would set his royal diadem before the emperor's statue, and take it back only from Nero's hand. And the meeting ended with a kiss.

Then, after a few days' interval, there was a magnificent display on both sides. On the one, cavalry was deployed by squadrons and with tribal insignia; on the other, legions were standing in columns, with gleaming eagles, standards, and representations of the gods, as in a temple. In their midst was a tribunal which held a curule chair, and the chair held an effigy of Nero. Tiridates went forward to it. After the customary slaughter of sacrificial animals, he took the diadem from his head and set it at the feet of the image, which stirred deep emotions in all present, emotions magnified by the vision of the slaughter and blockade of Roman armies that still lingered before their eyes. Now, they reflected, the situation was reversed: Tiridates would go ahead to be on view for the world—and how little short of a captive was he!

30. Corbulo enhanced his glorious reputation by affability and by hosting a banquet. Moreover, the king would ask for explanations whenever he noticed something unfamiliar—the centurion's announcement of the start of each watch,* for instance, the dinner-party's end signalled by a bugle-call, and the fire on the altar before the general's tent being lit from beneath with a torch. Corbulo embellished everything and filled him with admiration for the old Roman traditions. The next day Tiridates requested time to visit his brothers and his mother, since he had such a long journey before him. Meanwhile, he handed over his daughter as a hostage, together with a letter of entreaty to Nero.

31. Setting off, Tiridates found Pacorus in Media and Vologaeses in Ecbatana. Vologaeses was not unconcerned about his brother, for he had requested of Corbulo, through his personal messengers, that Tiridates not be subjected to any outward appearance of servitude. He asked that he not surrender his sword,* that he not be barred from embracing provincial governors, nor to be made to stand at their doors, and that, in Rome, he be shown as much respect as the consuls. Vologaeses, of course, was used to the pomp of the foreigner and had no knowledge of us, people for whom the reality of power is important but its trappings irrelevant.

32. That same year Nero conferred Latin rights* on the tribes of the Maritime Alps. He positioned the seating of the Roman knights* in the Circus in front of the places assigned to the plebs, for until that date there had been no segregated entry, since the Roscian law* applied only to the 'fourteen rows'. The same year witnessed gladiatorial shows just as magnificent as those preceding them; but there were more women of distinction and senators degrading themselves in the arena.

33. In the consulship of Gaius Laecanius and Marcus Licinius, Nero was driven by a daily increasing desire to appear on the public stage.

To that point he had confined his singing to his home or gardens during the Juvenalian Games,* but he was now becoming disdainful of these as providing too small an audience and being too limited for so great a voice. He would not risk a debut in Rome, however, and he selected Neapolis* instead, it being a Greek city. That would be his starting point, he thought. He would then cross to Achaea, acquire the famous crowns, hallowed from olden times, and, his fame thus enhanced, win the acclaim of his fellow-citizens.

He therefore assembled a crowd of townspeople, and they were joined by those whom talk of the event had brought from nearby colonies and municipalities, and those who followed the emperor out of respect or to perform various services; and, in addition, there were some military units. All these filled the theatre of Neapolis.

34. In the theatre, an incident occurred that was, most thought, a sinister omen, but one which Nero found providential and a sign of divine favour. After the audience left, the now-empty theatre collapsed, without causing injuries. Nero therefore composed songs thanking the gods and celebrating the good fortune attending the recent collapse. About to set off for his crossing point on the Adriatic, he made a stop at Beneventum, where a well-attended gladiatorial show was being staged by Vatinius. Vatinius was one of the foulest monstrosities of that court. Brought up in a shoemaker's shop, he was physically deformed and had the wit of a buffoon. Taken on initially as the butt of ridicule, he acquired so much power by his vilification of all the most decent people that in influence, wealth, and ability to inflict harm he was in a class of his own even amongst scoundrels.

35. For Nero, while he was attending this man's show, there was no let-up from crime, even amid his entertainments. During those very same days Torquatus Silanus* was forced into suicide because, apart from the distinction of belonging to the Junian family, he claimed the deified Augustus as a great-great-grandfather. Accusers were instructed to charge him with profligacy in distributing largesse, and with having hope now only in revolution. They were to say that Silanus even had men he styled his secretaries 'for correspondence', 'for appeals', and 'for accounts', titles attaching to the highest office of state and suggesting preparations for it! All his closest freedmen were then put in irons and taken away; and when condemnation was looming, Torquatus severed the veins in his arms.

Nero's usual speech followed: guilty Torquatus may have been, and justifiably lacking confidence in his defence, but he would have gone on living had he awaited the mercy of his judge.

36. Not much later Nero revisited Rome, temporarily abandoning his plans for Achaea (his reasons were unclear), his private daydreams now focusing on the provinces of the East, and Egypt in particular. Then, proclaiming in an edict that his absence would not be long, and that everything would remain just as stable and prosperous in the state, he visited the Capitol for divine approval for his journey. There he paid homage to the gods, but when he also entered the temple of Vesta he began to tremble throughout his body, either because the goddess filled him with terror or because he was never free from fear through awareness of his crimes. He then abandoned his project, claiming that all his interests were less important than his love for his country. He had seen the crestfallen looks of his fellow-citizens, he said, and could hear their unspoken protests that he was going to undertake such a long voyage when they could not support even his brief absences—accustomed as they were to gaining from the sight of their emperor renewed confidence to face life's vicissitudes. In personal relationships one's nearest and dearest were the most important, he said, and just so, in the case of the state, the Roman people counted most with him, and he had to heed their appeal to stay.

These and other such comments were welcome to the plebs, who wanted entertainments, and—their overriding concern—feared a shortage in the grain-supply if he were away. The Senate and most eminent citizens could not decide whether he was more to be dreaded at a distance or close at hand. Then—as happens when fear is great—they came to believe that the worse alternative was the one that had occurred.

37. To bolster the claim that nowhere else gave him as much pleasure, Nero proceeded to provide banquets in public places, and to treat the entire city as his own house. And the banquet most celebrated for its extravagance and notoriety was that hosted by Tigellinus. I shall cite this as an illustrative case to avoid frequent descriptions of the same kind of prodigality.

Tigellinus constructed a raft on Agrippa's lake* and on it set a feast that could then be moved about, towed along by other vessels. The vessels were trimmed with gold and ivory, and the oarsmen were male prostitutes who were grouped according to age and sexual expertise. Tigellinus had sought out birds and wild animals from distant lands, and sea creatures all the way from the ocean. On the lake's banks stood brothels filled with women of distinction, and on the other side common prostitutes were to be seen in the nude. At first there were obscene gestures and body movements; and when darkness began to fall the whole of the nearby copse and the surrounding buildings rang with singing and became bright with lights. Nero himself, defiled by lawful and unlawful acts, had left untried no enormity that could deepen his depravity—except one. A few days later he married, in a formal wedding, a member of that gang of perverts, whose name was Pythagoras. The bridal veil was set upon the emperor, the augurs were sent in, and dowry, marriage bed, and wedding torches were all there. In short, everything was put on show that darkness usually shrouds, even when the bride is female.

38. A disaster followed, whether accidental or plotted by the emperor is unclear (for the sources have both versions); but it was worse and more calamitous than all the disasters that have befallen this city from raging fires.* It started in the part of the Circus adjacent to the Palatine and Caelian hills. There, amidst shops containing merchandise of a combustible nature, the fire immediately gained strength as soon as it broke out and, whipped up by the wind, engulfed the entire length of the Circus. For there were no dwellings with solid enclosures, no temples ringed with walls, and no other obstacle of any kind in its way. The blaze spread wildly, overrunning the flat areas first, and then climbing to the heights before once again ravaging the lower sections. It outstripped all defensive measures because of the speed of its deadly advance and the vulnerability of the city, with its narrow streets twisting this way and that, and with its irregular blocks of buildings, which was the nature of old Rome.

In addition, there was the wailing of panic-stricken women; there were people, very old and very young; there were those trying to save themselves and those trying to save others, dragging invalids along or waiting for them; and these people, some hanging back, some rushing along, hindered all relief efforts. And often, as they looked back, they found themselves under attack from the flames at their sides or in front; or if they got away to a neighbouring district, that also caught fire, and even those areas they had believed far distant they found to be in the same plight. Eventually, unsure what to avoid and what to head for, they crowded the roads or scattered over the fields. Even though escape lay open to them, some chose death because they had lost all their property, even their daily livelihood; others did so from love of family members whom they had been unable to rescue. And nobody dared fight the fire: there were repeated threats from numerous people opposing efforts to extinguish it, and others openly hurled in firebrands and yelled that they 'had their instructions'. This was to give them more freedom to loot, or else they were in fact under orders.

39. Nero was at Antium* at the time, and he did not return to the city until the fire was approaching that building of his by which he had connected the Palatium with the gardens of Maecenas.* But stopping the fire from consuming the Palatium, Nero's house, and everything in the vicinity proved impossible. However, to relieve the homeless and fugitive population Nero opened up the Campus Martius, the monuments of Agrippa, and even his own gardens, and he erected makeshift buildings to house the destitute crowds. Vital supplies were shipped up from Ostia and neighbouring municipalities, and the price of grain was dropped to three sesterces. These were measures with popular appeal, but they proved a dismal failure. For the rumour* had spread that, at the very time that the city was ablaze, Nero had appeared on his private stage and sung about the destruction of Troy, drawing a comparison between the sorrows of the present and the disasters of old.

40. Finally, after five days,* the blaze was brought to a halt at the foot of the Esquiline. Buildings had been demolished over a vast area so that the fire's unremitting violence would be faced only with open ground and bare sky. But before the panic had abated, or the plebs' hopes had revived, the fire resumed its furious onslaught, though in more open areas of the city. As a result, there were fewer human casualties, but the destruction of temples and porticoes designed as public amenities was more widespread. And that particular conflagration caused a greater scandal because it had broken out on Tigellinus' Aemilian estates; and it looked as if Nero was seeking the glory of founding a new city, one that was to be named after him.* In fact, of the fourteen districts* into which Rome is divided, four were still intact, three had been levelled to the ground, and in the other seven a few ruined and charred vestiges of buildings were all that remained.*

41. To put a figure on the houses, tenement buildings, and temples that were lost would be no easy matter. But religious buildings of the most time-honoured sanctity were burned down: the temple that Servius Tullius had consecrated to Luna; the Ara Maxima and sanctuary that the Arcadian Evander had consecrated to Hercules Praesens; the temple of Jupiter Stator promised in a vow by Romulus; the palace of Numa; and the shrine of Vesta holding the Penates of the Roman people. Other casualties were rich spoils taken through our many victories; fine specimens of Greek art; and antique and authentic works of literary genius. As a result, though surrounded by the great beauty of the city as it grew again, older people still remember many things that could not be replaced. There were those who observed that this fire started on 19 July, which was the date on which the Senones captured and burned the city.* Others have taken their interest so far as to compute equal numbers of years, months, and days* between the two fires.

42. In fact, Nero took advantage of the homeland's destruction to build a palace.* It was intended to inspire awe, not so much with precious stones and gold (long familiar and commonplace in the life of luxury) as with its fields, lakes, and woods that replicated the open countryside on one side, and open spaces and views on the other. The architects and engineers were Severus and Celer, who had the ingenuity and audacity to attempt to create by artifice what nature had denied, and to amuse themselves with the emperor's resources. For they had undertaken to dig a navigable channel from Lake Avernus* all the way to the mouths of the Tiber, taking it along the desolate shoreline or through the barrier of the hills. In fact, one comes across no aquifer here to provide a water supply. There are only the Pomptine marshes, all else being cliffs or arid ground—and even if forcing a way through this were possible, it would have involved an extreme and unjustifiable effort. But Nero was ever one to seek after the incredible. He attempted to dig out the heights next to Avernus, and traces of his futile hopes remain to this day.

43. As for space that remained in the city after Nero's housebuilding, it was not built up in a random and haphazard manner, as after the burning by the Gauls. Instead, there were rows of streets properly surveyed, spacious thoroughfares, buildings with height limits* and open areas. Porticoes were added, too, to protect the façade of the tenement buildings. These porticoes Nero undertook to erect from his own pocket, and he also undertook to return to their owners the building lots, cleared of debris. He added grants, prorated according to a person's rank and domestic property, and established time limits within which houses or tenement buildings were to be completed for claimants to acquire the money.

He earmarked the Ostian marshes as the dumping ground for the debris, and ordered ships that had ferried grain up the Tiber to return downstream loaded with debris. The actual edifices were, for a specific portion of their structure, to be free of wooden beams and reinforced with rock from Gabii or Alba,* since such stone is fireproof. In addition, because individuals had had the effrontery to siphon off water, watchmen would be employed to ensure a fuller public supply, and at more points. Everyone was also to have appliances accessible for fighting fires, and houses were not to have party walls but each be enclosed by its own. These measures were welcomed for their practicality, and they also enhanced the aesthetics of the new city. There were, however, those who believed that the old configuration was more conducive to health, inasmuch as the narrowness of the streets and the height of the buildings meant they were less easily penetrated by the torrid sunlight. Now, they claimed, the broad open spaces, with no shade to protect them, were baking in a more oppressive heat.

44. Such were the precautions taken as a result of human reasoning. The next step was to find ways of appeasing the gods, and the Sibylline Books* were consulted. Under their guidance, supplicatory prayers were offered to Vulcan, Ceres, and Proserpina, and there were propitiatory ceremonies performed for Juno by married women, first on the Capitol, and then on the closest part of the shoreline. (From there, water was drawn, and the temple and statue of the goddess were sprinkled with it.) Women who had husbands also held ritual feasts* and all-night festivals.

But neither human resourcefulness nor the emperor's largesse nor appeasement of the gods could stop belief in the nasty rumour that an order had been given for the fire. To dispel the gossip Nero therefore found culprits on whom he inflicted the most exotic punishments. These were people hated for their shameful offences* whom the common people called Christians.* The man who gave them their name, Christus, had been executed during the rule of Tiberius by the procurator Pontius Pilatus.* The pernicious superstition had been temporarily suppressed, but it was starting to break out again, not just in Judaea, the starting point of that curse, but in Rome, as well, where all that is abominable and shameful in the world flows together and gains popularity.

And so, at first, those who confessed were apprehended, and subsequently, on the disclosures they made, a huge number were found guilty—more because of their hatred of mankind than because they were arsonists.* As they died they were further subjected to insult. Covered with hides of wild beasts, they perished by being torn to pieces by dogs; or they would be fastened to crosses and, when daylight had gone, burned to provide lighting at night. Nero had offered his gardens as a venue for the show, and he would also put on circus entertainments, mixing with the plebs in his charioteer's outfit or standing up in his chariot. As a result, guilty though these people were and deserving exemplary punishment, pity for them began to well up because it was felt that they were being exterminated not for the public good, but to gratify one man's cruelty.

45. Meanwhile Italy had been completely devastated to raise Nero's funds; the provinces had been ruined, and so had the allied peoples and the so-called free communities. Even the gods became part of those spoils, with temples gutted in the city and their gold removed, gold that the Roman people in every generation had consecrated through triumphs or as votive offerings, after success or in time of fear. Moreover, throughout Asia and Achaea it was not simply the temple offerings, but the statues of the gods, too, that were being plundered, Acratus and Secundus Carrinas* having been sent into those provinces. Acratus was a freedman ready for any kind of villainy; Secundus had been trained in Greek philosophy (its words only!), but had not brought any morality into his soul from it. It was rumoured that, to avert opprobrium for the sacrilege from himself, Seneca had earnestly requested a place of retirement deep in the country, and that, when this was not granted, he feigned illness from a muscular disease, and refused to leave his bedchamber. Some have recorded that, on Nero's instructions, a poison was concocted for him by his own freedman, who was called Cleonicus, but that Seneca avoided it, either because of the freedman's disclosure, or his own suspicions. He then kept himself alive on a very plain diet of wild fruits and, if he felt the promptings of thirst, water from a running stream.

46. About this time gladiators* in the town of Praeneste attempted a breakout. They were arrested by the military guard stationed to keep watch over them, but already the people, with the usual wish for, and fear of, revolution, were circulating gossip about Spartacus* and the troubles of old. Not long afterwards came news of a naval disaster, but not in military action, for never had there been such a stable peace.* Nero had ordered the fleet to return to Campania before a specific date, but had made no allowance for the hazards of the sea. The helmsmen accordingly set out from Formiae in the face of churning waters, and as they tried to negotiate the promontory of Misenum they were driven on to the shores of Cumae by the violent south-westerly, losing several triremes and a number of smaller vessels all along the coast.

47. At the end of the year there was much talk of prodigies that were harbingers of imminent misfortunes. Never had there been such frequent bolts of lightning, and there was a comet*—always atoned for by Nero with illustrious people's blood. Two-headed foetuses, human and from other creatures, had been thrown out in public places or were found at those sacrifices at which it is customary to immolate pregnant animals. In the territory of Placentia, too, near a road, a calf was born with its head attached to its leg. An interpretation given by the augurs followed: another head of the world was being made ready, but it would neither gain strength nor remain concealed, because its development had been retarded in the womb and also because it had been delivered at the roadside.

48. Silius Nerva and Atticus Vestinus then entered their consulship, at a time when a conspiracy had begun and immediately escalated. Senators, knights, soldiers, and even women raced to enrol in it, from hatred of Nero and also because of the popularity of Gaius Piso.* Piso was of the Calpurnian line and was well connected with many distinguished families because of his father's noble breeding; and he enjoyed a brilliant reputation amongst the lower orders thanks to his virtue, or qualities that looked like virtues. For he used his oratorical ability to defend his fellow-citizens, showed generosity towards his friends, and was affable in his conversation and interaction even with strangers. He also enjoyed the fortuitous advantages of a tall physique and handsome looks. But he was far from possessing depth of character or moderation in his pleasures; he immersed himself in frivolity, luxury, and, sometimes, dissipation. And this had the blessing of most people who, surrounded by such sweet vices, do not want to see austerity or great strictness in the supreme power.

49. The conspiracy did not start from ambition on Piso's part; but I would not find it easy to say who the prime mover was, or who provided the inspiration for a coup that so many espoused. Its most fervent supporters proved to be Subrius Flavus, tribune of a praetorian cohort, and the centurion Sulpicius Asprus, as their resolve in facing death demonstrated. Annaeus Lucanus* and Plautius Lateranus brought to it impassioned hatred. Lucanus had personal motives for anger: Nero, fatuously thinking himself a rival, was trying to suppress the fame of his poems, and had forbidden him to give them public exposure. In the case of Lateranus, a consul-designate, it was no personal slight but rather patriotism that brought him into the plot. Flavius Scaevinus and Afranius Quintianus, both of senatorial rank, belied their reputations in embracing such a bold enterprise from the start. For Scaevinus' mental powers had been weakened by his excesses, and he therefore led a life of languid indolence. Quintianus was notorious for his effeminacy, and having been insulted by Nero in a scurrilous poem he was now set on revenge for the humiliation.

50. These men were therefore dropping hints amongst themselves or their friends about the emperor's crimes, saying that his reign was coming to an end and a man must be chosen to succour the ailing state; and they brought into their circle the Roman knights Claudius Senecio,* Cervarius Proculus, Vulcacius Araricus, Julius Augurinus, Munatius Gratus, Antonius Natalis, and Marcius Festus. Of these, Senecio had been particularly close to Nero and, since he even at that time kept up a façade of friendship, he was confronted with a multitude of dangers. Natalis was acquainted with all of Piso's secrets. For the others, fulfilment of their aspirations was being sought from revolution.

Military assistance was also enlisted—in addition to Subrius and Sulpicius, whom I mentioned above—from Gavius Silvanus and Statius Proxumus, tribunes of the praetorian cohorts, and from the centurions Maximus Scaurus and Venetus Paulus. However, their chief strength appeared to reside in the prefect Faenius Rufus.* His lifestyle and reputation won him general approval, but Tigellinus surpassed him in the emperor's estimation because of his barbarity and immorality. Tigellinus kept hounding the man with accusations, and had often frightened him by portraying him as a lover of Agrippina, bent on revenge for losing her.

Eventually the conspirators were convinced, by the frequent comments he himself made, that the prefect of the praetorian guard had joined their side, and they began to discuss more readily the timing and location of the assassination. It was said that Subrius Flavus felt an urge to make the attack on Nero as he sang on stage, or as he scurried here and there at night without an escort. In the one scenario it was Nero's isolation that had stimulated his enthusiasm, in the other the very presence of a crowd—a fine witness to a great exploit. But a wish to avoid punishment, always an impediment to great endeavours, held him back.

51. Meanwhile, a certain Epicharis had gained information about the plot—how is unclear, and she had had no prior interest in honourable causes—and as the conspirators vacillated and were deferring their hopes, and their fears, she began to incite and criticize them. She finally grew tired of their inertia and, as she was spending some time in Campania, she attempted to weaken the loyalty of the officers of the fleet at Misenum, and to enlist them as co-conspirators by taking the following steps.

Volusius Proculus* was one of the captains in the fleet there. He had been one of Nero's henchmen in his mother's murder, but had not, to his way of thinking, received the advancement that such an important crime merited. Proculus may have been known to Epicharis for some time, or possibly it was a recently made acquaintance, but he revealed to her his services to Nero, and how these had turned out to be of no benefit to him. He added further complaints and said that he would take his revenge if the opportunity arose, thus giving Epicharis hope that he could be pushed into action and win more supporters. In the fleet, too, she thought, they would have no small help, and many opportunities, because Nero enjoyed outings on the sea in the area around Puteoli and Misenum.

So Epicharis went further, listing all the emperor's crimes and saying that nothing remained sacred any more. But, she added, measures had been put in place whereby Nero could be punished for bringing down the state. Proculus need only prepare himself to do his part and bring to their cause his bravest men, for which he could expect appropriate rewards. The names of the conspirators, however,

Epicharis withheld. Thus, although Proculus reported to Nero what he had been told, his denunciation was worthless. For when Epicharis was called in and confronted with her informer, she easily confuted him since he had no witnesses to support him. But she was herself detained in custody; for Nero suspected that what was not demonstrably true was not necessarily false.

52. Prompted by fear of betrayal, however, the conspirators decided to advance the assassination, which would now take place in Piso's villa at Baiae—Nero was taken with its charming ambience, and often went there, enjoying baths and dinners, and dispensing with guards and the weighty trappings of his position. Piso, however, objected, putting forward as an excuse the antipathy they would face if the sanctity of the table, and the gods of hospitality, were stained with an emperor's blood, whatever the man's qualities. It would be better for them to carry out in the city—in that detested abode* built through the pillaging of Roman citizens, or else in a public area—the deed they had undertaken for the good of the state.

This was for general consumption, but Piso secretly harboured fears about Lucius Silanus.* Silanus had an outstanding pedigree, and had been elevated to every distinction as a result of his training under Gaius Cassius,* in whose home he had been brought up; and Piso therefore feared he might seize power. And those who had no connection with the conspiracy, and would feel sorry for Nero as the victim of a criminal assassination, would be ready to hand it to him. Several people also thought that this was Piso's way of avoiding the problem of the highly intelligent consul Vestinus, who might rise up in the cause of liberty or who, choosing another as emperor, might make the state his own personal gift to that individual. For Vestinus had no part in the conspiracy, though it was on such a charge that Nero later sated his old hatred of an innocent man.

53. They finally decided to carry out their plan on that day of the Circus games that is consecrated to Ceres.* Nero rarely went out, and kept himself shut up in his home and gardens, but he did regularly attend the entertainments in the Circus, where access to him was easier in the merry atmosphere of the show. They had established a programme for the plot. Lateranus would fall as a suppliant before the emperor's knees, pretending to be begging him for financial assistance. Surprising him, he would knock him over and, being a man with a strong will and large physique, keep him pinned down. At that

point, with Nero helpless on the ground, the tribunes and centurions, and any others who had the courage, would run up and butcher
him. (Scaevinus insisted on the leading role for himself; he had taken
down a dagger in the temple of Salus—or, according to others, of
Fortuna—in the town of Ferentinum,* and was carrying it about as
though it were consecrated to some great exploit.) Meanwhile, Piso
was to wait at the temple of Ceres. The prefect Faenius and the others
would summon him from there and carry him into the camp, and
Claudius Caesar's daughter Antonia would be with them (according
to the account of Gaius Plinius) in order to win over the support of
the mob. I did not consider suppressing this version, whatever its
value, although it does seem odd that Antonia should have lent her
name to, and taken the risk for, such a forlorn hope. Odd, too, that
Piso, whose love for his wife was well known, should have committed himself to another marriage*—unless ambition for power burns
hotter than all other feelings.

54. What is amazing is that it was all kept veiled in secrecy amidst
people of different families, class, age, and sex, and among rich and
poor alike—until, that is, betrayal* proceeded from the house of
Scaevinus. The day before the coup, Scaevinus had a long conversation with Antonius Natalis. After that he returned home, sealed his
will, and took the dagger I mentioned above from its sheath.
Complaining that it had become blunt over time, he gave orders for
it to be whetted with a stone until its point was gleaming, and this
task he confided to his freedman Milichus. At the same time he took
a more than usually sumptuous dinner, and bestowed gifts on his
slaves—freedom for his favourites, and money for others. And
Scaevinus himself was downcast and clearly deep in thought, though
he did make some rambling conversation to feign cheerfulness.
Finally he ordered dressings for wounds and articles for arresting
bleeding to be prepared, and again put this in Milichus' charge.
Either Milichus was privy to the conspiracy and remained loyal to
this point, or he knew nothing and now became suspicious for the
first time, which is what most sources have reported.

On what happened next there is agreement. When the man's
servile mind thought over the rewards of treachery, and at the same
time the unlimited money and power danced before his eyes, then
moral obligation, the safety of his patron, and the memory of the
freedom he had been given all faded away. And, in fact, he had also

accepted his wife's advice—a woman's, and quite despicable. For she worked on him with a further motive, fear, noting that numerous freedmen and slaves had been present and seen the same things as he. The silence of one man would do no good, she told him, but the rewards would come to just one man—the one who turned informer first.

55. So, at daybreak, Milichus set off for the Gardens of Servilius.* As he was being turned away from the door, he kept repeating that he brought important and dreadful news, and he was then escorted by the door-keepers to Nero's freedman Epaphroditus,* and by Epaphroditus to Nero. He then told Nero of the imminent danger, the formidable conspirators he faced, and everything else that he had heard or surmised. He also displayed the weapon that had been made ready for Nero's murder, and insisted that the culprit be brought in.

Arrested by some soldiers, Scaevinus opened his defence with the retort that the weapon that he took to be the basis of the charge was a venerated family heirloom. He kept it in his bedchamber, he said, and it had been removed by his treacherous freedman. He had on numerous occasions signed the tablets of his will, he added, without taking note of the dates. He had also previously made gifts of money or emancipation to his slaves, but had done so more generously at this time because, with his financial situation now weak and his creditors pressing, he had little confidence in his will. Moreover, he had always put on ample dinners while he could enjoy his agreeable lifestyle, one not meeting the approval of moralizing critics. No dressings for wounds had been prepared on his orders, he said. It was because the others were patently groundless that the freedman had added this accusation, one for which he could be both informer and witness!

Scaevinus backed up his statements with complete self-possession. He actually went on the offensive, calling the man a detestable scoundrel, and with such confidence in his voice and expression that the informer's case began to fall apart. It would have done so, in fact, but for Milichus' wife reminding him of Antonius Natalis' long private conversations with Scaevinus, and the fact that both were close associates of Gnaeus Piso.

56. Natalis was therefore called in, and the two men were interrogated separately on the nature and subject of their conversation. Then, because their answers did not match, suspicion arose and they were

put in irons. And at the sight and threat of torture they could hold out no longer. The first to break was Natalis, who had a fuller knowledge of the conspiracy as a whole, and more skill as a denouncer. He first confessed with regard to Piso, and then added Annaeus Seneca,* either because Seneca was actually the go-between for him and Piso, or because Natalis wanted to ingratiate himself with Nero (who, hating Seneca, was seeking any means to bring him down). Then, after learning of Natalis' disclosure, Scaevinus also showed the same weakness—or perhaps he thought that all had now been revealed and silence would do no good—and gave away the others. Of these Lucanus, Quintianus, and Senecio long denied their guilt. Later, tempted by the promise of impunity, and as a way of gaining leniency for their slowness, they named names—Lucanus naming his own mother Acilia, and Quintianus and Senecio their best friends, Glitius Gallus* and Annius Pollio* respectively.

57. Now in the meantime Nero remembered that Epicharis was being detained on information laid by Volusius Proculus and, believing that a woman's constitution could not cope with pain, he had her subjected to body rending torture. But no lashing, no burning, no furious treatment from her torturers—who piled on the pressure so as not to be bested by a woman—could break her denial of the charges. Thus the first day of the inquisition was a failure. On the next she was being brought back by means of a chair (her limbs were now dislocated and she could not stand) to face the same torments when she took the band from her breast, attached it to the chair's canopy in the form of a noose, put her neck into it and, throwing the weight of her body into the effort, choked out what little life she had left. Thus a freedwoman set all the more brilliant an example in such dire circumstances, protecting people unrelated, indeed almost strangers, to her—and that when male free persons, who were Roman knights and senators, were all betraying their nearest and dearest, without being subjected to torture. 58. For Lucanus, too, and Senecio and Quintianus did not fail to tell on their accomplices, one after the other, while Nero grew more and more frightened, despite having redoubled the guards with which he surrounded himself.

In fact, Nero virtually put the city under arrest, keeping the walls manned with military units and the sea and river under close surveillance. There were also foot- and horse-soldiers—with Germans* in

368 BOOK FIFTEEN AD 65

their ranks, trusted by the emperor as being foreigners—tearing about the forums and private houses, and even through the countryside and closest municipalities. And so never-ending columns of manacled prisoners were being dragged out and left waiting near the gates of the gardens. Then, when they went in to plead their case, it was not simply a matter of support for the conspirators being regarded as a crime; so, too, were a casual conversation, chance meetings, and attending a dinner or a show in their company. And all the while, in addition to the ruthless interrogation by Nero and Tigellinus, Faenius Rufus was piling on violent pressure. He had not yet been named by the informers, and to make people believe that he knew nothing, he was pitiless towards his accomplices. When Subrius Flavus was standing at his side, and enquired with a gesture whether he should draw his sword and assassinate Nero during the actual investigation, the same Rufus shook his head and checked the man's ardour as he was already bringing his hand to his sword-hilt.

59. After the conspiracy had been betrayed, at the time when Milichus was being given his audience and Scaevinus was hesitating, there were some who urged Piso to march into the camp, or mount the Rostra, and work on the feelings of the soldiery and the people. If his fellow-conspirators rallied in support of his effort, they told him, non-partisans would also follow; the coup, once started, would have great publicity, which was extremely important for revolutionary movements. Against this Nero had taken no precautions, and brave men, too, were unnerved by the unexpected—much less chance, then, of a counter-attack from this stage-performer, with Tigellinus and his concubines at his side! Many things that the timid think difficult are brought off just by the attempt! With the numbers involved, hoping for silence and loyalty was useless when all those minds and bodies could be worked on—torture or bribery can penetrate anything! Men would come to shackle him, too, and finally put him to an ignominious death, they said. How much more creditable to die embracing his state and calling for help for its liberty! Better that the soldiers not join him and that the plebs abandon him—provided that he himself, if his life must be prematurely taken, make his death a credit to his ancestors, and to his descendants.

Piso was not persuaded. He spent a short time in the streets, after which he shut himself up at home and stiffened his resolve to meet the end—until the arrival of military units (men of Nero's choosing, newly recruited or recently enlisted—veterans were feared as being infected with sympathy for Piso). He died by severing the veins in his arms. His will, marked by disgusting obsequiousness towards Nero, he made as a concession to his wife, whom he loved. She was of low birth with only good looks to commend her, and Piso had taken her out of an earlier marriage to a friend of his. The woman's name was Satria Galla, the former husband's Domitius Silus. Both contributed to Piso's bad name, the man by his acquiescence, the woman by her lack of shame.

60. The next murder that Nero registered was that of the consul-designate Plautius Lateranus, and with such speed as not to allow him to embrace his children or have that short moment to choose how to die. He was rushed to a location reserved for punishments for slaves and there butchered at the hands of the tribune Statius. Lateranus maintained all the while a resolute silence, and did not reproach the tribune with involvement in the plot.

Next came the killing of Annaeus Seneca, for the emperor the sweetest. Not that he had discovered any proof of Seneca's involvement in the conspiracy, but after the failure of the poison he could now go to work with the sword. In fact, Natalis alone had implicated Seneca, and only to the extent of saying that he had been sent to visit him when he was ill, and to express dissatisfaction over his refusing Piso access to him. It would be better, Natalis had said to him, if the two men developed their friendship by meeting on cordial terms; and Seneca's reply had been that conversations between the two, and frequent meetings, were of advantage to neither, but his own life depended on Piso's safety.

Gavius Silvanus, tribune of a praetorian cohort, was instructed to report these details to Seneca and ask if he acknowledged such to be Natalis' words and his own reply. Seneca, perhaps intentionally, had been returning from Campania that day and had made a stop at his country estate four miles from Rome. The tribune came to this spot as evening was coming on, and surrounded the villa with some military units. Then, as Seneca was dining with his wife Pompeia Paulina* and two friends, he brought him the emperor's message.

61. Seneca replied that Natalis had been sent to him and had expressed dissatisfaction on Piso's behalf that Piso had been kept from visiting him, and that he had then excused himself for this on the grounds of ill-health and his love of the quiet life. He had no reason to put the life of a private individual ahead of his own safety, he said, nor was he temperamentally prone to obsequiousness—and nobody knew that better than Nero, who had more often had experience of his outspokenness than his servility!

These remarks of Seneca's were reported by the tribune to Nero while he was with Poppaea and Tigellinus—the emperor's closest advisers in his savage periods. Nero asked Silvanus whether Seneca intended to commit suicide. The tribune then asserted that he had recognized no signs of apprehension, and no distress in his language or expression. He was therefore told to go back and deliver the death sentence. Fabius Rusticus records that the tribune did not return the way he had come but made a detour to the prefect Faenius. Having told Faenius about Nero's orders, he asked whether he should obey them, and was advised by him—with that fatal cowardice now common to all—to carry them out. For Silvanus, too, was one of the conspirators, and was now increasing the number of the crimes he had plotted to avenge. He did, however, spare himself from saying or seeing anything, instead sending one of the centurions to Seneca with the announcement of his final obligation.

62. Undaunted, Seneca called for the tablets of his will. The centurion refused, and Seneca, turning to his friends, declared that, since he was barred from repaying them for their services, he was leaving them the one thing he still had, but the one that was also the best, the model of his life. If they kept that in mind, he said, they would gain a reputation for good character as their reward for loyal friendship. At the same time he alternated normal conversation with sterner, coercive tones to halt their tears and revive their courage. Where were their philosophical tenets, he asked, and where that rationality they had pondered on for so many years to counter impending misfortune? For who had been unaware of Nero's ruthlessness? After killing his mother and his brother, nothing else remained but to add the murder of his guardian and tutor.

63. After these words, which had the air of a public address, Seneca embraced his wife. Then softening a little, despite his present resolve, he asked and entreated her to limit her grief, and not keep it up for ever—she should find honourable solace for the loss of her husband in reflecting on the life of virtue that he had lived. Her firm response was that she too had decided to die, and she demanded for herself the executioner's blow.

Seneca was not opposed to her noble decision, and also his love prompted him not to leave the woman he cherished above all to be maltreated. 'I showed you how to make life more palatable,' he said, 'but you prefer the glory of death, and I shall not begrudge you the fine example. For such a courageous end let us both have the same resolve, but may your leaving have the greater fame.' After that they cut their arms with the same stroke of the blade.

Seneca's ageing body, emaciated by his spare diet, allowed only slow escape for the blood, and so he also severed the veins in his legs and at the back of his knees. Worn down by the cruel torment, and not wishing to break his wife's spirit with his suffering, or have himself lapse into indecision through seeing her agonies, he persuaded her to retire to another bedroom. And since his eloquence still remained even in his very last moments, he summoned his scribes and dictated a long work* to them. As this has been published in his own words, I refrain from paraphrasing it.

64. Nero, in fact, had no personal grudge against Paulina, and fearing a surge of animosity over his cruelty he ordered her suicide to be arrested. Prompted by the soldiers, her slaves and freedmen bandaged her arms and staunched the bleeding, though whether she was unconscious is unclear. (For, the public being ever ready to believe the worst, there was no shortage of people who thought that she had sought the renown of dying with her husband as long as she feared that Nero was implacable, but fell victim to life's charms when offered a more favourable prospect.) To her life she then added only a few years, maintaining a laudable fidelity to her husband's memory, and with face and body so pale and white as to show that much of her life force had been sapped away.

Meanwhile, Seneca's death was long-drawn-out and slow. He begged Statius Annaeus,* who had proved himself a steadfast friend and skilful doctor over a long period, to bring out the poison that was used for executing those condemned in the public court of Athens* and which had been prepared some time before. When this was brought, Seneca drained it, but in vain—his limbs were already cold, rendering his body immune to the poison's effects. Finally, he went into a pool of hot water, spattering the slaves closest to him, and adding the comment that with that liquid he was making a libation to Jupiter the Liberator. He was then taken into the bath, where he suffocated in the steam. He was cremated with no funeral ceremony.

Such was the instruction he had left in his will when he was—even at the height of his wealth and power—thinking about his end.

65. There was a rumour that Subrius Flavus had formulated a secret plan with the centurions, of which Seneca was not unaware. The plan was that, after Nero had been assassinated through Piso's initiative, Piso would also be killed, and the imperial command would be transferred to Seneca, an innocent man and chosen for supreme power on the basis of his renowned virtues. In fact, there was also a saying of Flavus' in circulation that the disgrace remained the same if a lyre-player was removed and a tragic actor succeeded him (for while Nero sang with the lyre, Piso did so in tragic costume).

66. The soldiers' part in the conspiracy no longer remained secret, either, as the informers were burning to denounce Faenius Rufus, whom they could not bear, as both conspirator and inquisitor. So, as he was pressured and threatened, Scaevinus said with a smile that no one knew more than Faenius himself, and he urged him to do such a fine emperor a favour of his own accord.* Faenius had no reply to this, nor was he silent; instead, he stumbled over his words and was clearly panic-stricken. Then, after a concerted effort by the other conspirators, particularly the Roman knight Cervarius Proculus, to have him convicted, he was, on the emperor's orders, seized and put in irons by Cassius, a soldier who was in attendance because of his remarkable strength.

67. Presently the tribune Subrius Flavus was brought down by the same men's denunciation. At first he tried to make difference in character his defence, arguing that a soldier such as he would not have associated with unarmed and effeminate individuals for so great a deed. Then, under pressure, he seized on the glory of confessing. Interrogated by Nero on the reasons that brought him to forget his military oath, Subrius declared: 'I hated you, but none of your soldiers was more loyal to you while you deserved our affection. I started to hate you when you became the murderer of your mother and wife, and a charioteer, actor and arsonist.' I have given the man's very words because, while they were not published like Seneca's, the powerful, rough-and-ready sentiments of a military man were no less worth recording.

It was well known that nothing in that conspiracy was more painful to Nero's ears, for while he was ready to commit crimes he was unused to being told what he was doing. Flavus' execution was entrusted to the tribune Veianius Niger. Niger ordered a pit to be dug in a neighbouring field, and Flavus criticized it for being shallow and narrow. 'Not even this accords with military standard,' he remarked to the soldiers standing around him. When he was told to be firm in stretching out his neck, he replied, 'I just wish your blow could be as firm!' The tribune was trembling a lot and had difficulty decapitating him with two blows. He then bragged about his callousness to Nero, saying Flavus had been killed by him with a 'stroke and a half'.

68. The next instance of fortitude was provided by the centurion Sulpicius Asper who, when Nero asked why he had conspired to murder him, briefly replied that nothing else could be done for all his atrocities. He then suffered the prescribed penalty. The other centurions did not disgrace themselves in facing execution, either, though Faenius Rufus did not have the same resolve, and even entered lamentations in his will.

Nero was waiting for the consul Vestinus, whom he thought a violent man who detested him, to be included in the charge. However, none of the conspirators had communicated their plans to Vestinus, some because of old quarrels with him, more because they thought him a reckless and difficult person. Nero's loathing of Vestinus had arisen from a close companionship with him. In the course of this Vestinus came to know well, and to despise, the emperor's cowardice, while Nero came to fear his friend's outspokenness; he had many times been the butt of his biting witticisms, which, when they have drawn largely on the truth, leave behind a bitter recollection. There was, in addition, a recent motive for his animosity: Vestinus had married Statilia Messalina,* though he was not unaware that Nero was one of her lovers.

69. Thus, with no charge and no accuser forthcoming, and as Nero was therefore unable to adopt the guise of judge, he resorted to the force of the despot, sending the tribune Gerellanus to him at the head of a cohort of soldiers. Gerellanus was under orders to take pre-emptive measures against the consul's designs, seizing Vestinus' 'stronghold' and overwhelming his 'handpicked young men' (Vestinus owned a house overlooking the Forum, and a number of handsome slaves, all of the same age).

On that day Vestinus had completed all his consular duties, and was hosting a dinner-party—fearing nothing, or else concealing his fear—when the soldiers entered and told him he was summoned by the tribune. With not a moment's delay he got up, and everything was hurriedly carried out at once. He shut himself in his bedroom; the doctor was in attendance; the veins were cut; still strong, he was carried into the bath, and immersed in hot water, letting out no exclamation of self-pity. Meanwhile those who had been reclining at table with him were surrounded by guards, and were not released until late at night. By then Nero had pictured with amusement their fright as they awaited death following the dinner, and he remarked that they had been punished sufficiently for their consular feast.

70. Nero next ordered the murder of Annaeus Lucanus. As the blood flowed, Lucanus felt his feet and hands grow cold, and his life gradually slip away from his extremities, though his breast was still warm and his mental powers intact. At that point he remembered a poem* he had composed in which he had represented a wounded soldier dying a similar kind of death. He recited those very verses, and they were his last words. Following that, Senecio, Quintianus, and Scaevinus met their ends, in a manner at variance with their soft living of earlier days, and the remainder of the conspirators soon followed, though without any memorable deed or saying.

71. Meanwhile the city was filling up with funerals, and the Capitol with sacrificial animals. After the killing of a son, or of a brother or relative or friend, people gave thanks to the gods, decorated their homes with laurel, fell at the knees of Nero himself, and plied his right hand with kisses. And Nero, believing this to be a manifestation of joy, rewarded Antonius Natalis and Cervarius Proculus for their speedy denunciations with a grant of impunity. Milichus, who was enriched with gifts, adopted the name 'Saviour', but using the Greek word for it.

Of the tribunes, Gavius Silvanus died by his own hand, although acquitted; and Statius Proxumus wasted the pardon he had received from the emperor by making a vainglorious exit. Then Pompeius <. . .>, Cornelius Martialis, Flavius Nepos, and Statius Domitius* were relieved of the tribuneship; the grounds were not that they hated the emperor but that they were, nevertheless, thought to do so. Novius Priscus* was given exile (for his friendship with Seneca), as were Glitius Gallus and Annius Pollio (for being discredited rather than found guilty). Priscus was accompanied by his wife Artoria Flaccilla, and Gallus by Egnatia Maximilla* (who had great wealth, which was initially left untouched, but later confiscated, and both circumstances redounded to her glory).

Rufrius Crispinus* was also exiled, and though the conspiracy supplied the grounds he was actually hated by Nero for having once been married to Poppaea. In the case of Verginius Flavus* and Musonius Rufus it was the fame of their names that ensured their exile, for Verginius promoted the studies of our young people by his eloquence, Musonius by his philosophical teaching. Cluvidienus Quietus, Julius Agrippa, Blitius Catulinus, Petronius Priscus, and Julius Altinus—as though to round out the numbers and the list—were granted islands in the Aegean Sea. Scaevinus' wife Caedicia, however, and Caesennius Maximus* were forbidden residence in Italy, and it was only from the sentence that they discovered they had been prosecuted. Annaeus Lucanus' mother Acilia was simply ignored, with no acquittal and no punishment.

72. On finishing this business, Nero held an assembly of the troops. There he distributed two thousand sesterces to every member of the rank and file, and made them the further gift of complimentary grain-rations,* which previously had cost them market rate. Then he convened the Senate, as though he were going to discuss achievements in war, and conferred triumphal honours on the ex-consul Petronius Turpilianus,* the praetor-designate Cocceius Nerva,* and the praetorian prefect Tigellinus. Tigellinus and Nerva he honoured to the extent of placing their busts in the Palatium, in addition to their triumphal statues in the Forum. Consular insignia were decreed for Nymphidius Sabinus,* and since this is the first time he has come up I shall give a brief résumé, for he, too, will be part of the calamities that befell Rome. He had as his mother a freedwoman who had spread her fine body around the slaves and freedmen of the emperors, and he claimed to have been fathered by Gaius Caesar. For, by some chance, he was tall of stature and had a grim-looking face—or else Gaius Caesar, who lusted even after whores, did in fact have his way with Nymphidius' mother, too <. . .>

73. After his speech among the senators, Nero also delivered an edict to the people, to which he added evidence that had been gathered together on writing scrolls, and confessions of those convicted. For in fact he was being lambasted regularly in talk amongst the masses for having put to death famous and innocent men out of jealousy or fear. However, that a conspiracy had begun, had come to

fruition, and had been suppressed was not doubted at the time by any with a care to discover the truth, and it was also later admitted by those who returned to the city after Nero's death. But in the Senate all were debasing themselves with flattery (and the greater their sorrow, the more they flattered). During this, Junius Gallio,* fearful after the death of his brother Seneca, and pleading for his life, was denounced by Salienus Clemens, who called him an enemy and a murderer. Finally Clemens was restrained by a unanimous appeal from the Senate that he not give the impression of profiting from public misfortunes to satisfy a private animosity, and not give rise to fresh savagery by dragging up things that, through the emperor's clemency, had been laid to rest or forgotten.

74. Decrees were then passed for gifts and thank-offerings to the gods, with special honours for the Sun for having uncovered the secrets of the conspiracy with his power (he has an old temple in the Circus, the prospective location for the coup). The Games of Ceres in the Circus were also to be held with an increased number of horse-races, and the month of April was to receive the name 'Nero'. A temple was to be erected to Salus in place of the one from which Scaevinus had taken his weapon. Nero himself consecrated the dagger in the Capitol, bearing the inscription 'To Jupiter the Avenger'. (Although it was not noticed at the time, this was, after the armed insurrection of Julius Vindex,* taken to be an omen foretelling future vengeance.) I find in the records of the Senate* that the consul-designate Anicius Cerialis* proposed that a temple be erected as soon as possible to the deified Nero, at public expense. Cerialis surely made this motion on the grounds that Nero had gone beyond the limits of mortality and deserved the worship of human beings, but Nero himself vetoed it in case it be interpreted by some as an omen of his death. For divine honours are not paid to an emperor before he has ended his days amongst humans.

BOOK SIXTEEN

1. Fortune then made a fool of Nero, because of his own credulity and the promises of Caesellius Bassus, a man of Punic origin who was mentally unbalanced. Bassus interpreted a dream he had had while asleep at night as presenting him with a sure prospect, whereupon he sailed to Rome and bought himself an audience with the emperor. He then disclosed to Nero that there had been discovered on his land a cavern of enormous depth containing a large quantity of gold, not struck as coin, but in a crude mass as used in antiquity. Indeed, there were massive ingots lying about and, elsewhere in the cavern, standing columns of gold, he said, all hidden over a long period of time to increase the prosperity of the present. He added that, on his hypothesis, it was the Phoenician Dido who had concealed these riches after fleeing from Tyre and founding Carthage. Her aim was to avoid overindulgence in her new population from excessive wealth, or to see to it that the Numidian kings, who were hostile for other reasons, would not be incited to war through lust for gold.

2. Nero paid insufficient attention to the reliability of the informant or the plausibility of the business itself, and he did not send men through whom he could verify the truth of the report, either. He actually exaggerated the information, and sent people to bring back the plunder he assumed was waiting for him. They were given triremes and a hand-picked crew of oarsmen to improve their speed. And during those days there was no other topic of conversation, the ordinary people gullibly accepting it, and thinking people having very different comments. As it happened, the Quinquennial Games* were being celebrated for the second time, and this incident became the prime topic taken up the orators for eulogizing the emperor. Not only were the ordinary crops being now produced by the earth, they said, and gold mixed with other metals; now she was fruitful with a new kind of fertility, and the gods were sending unsolicited riches. And they produced other servile compositions of supreme eloquence, and no less sycophancy, confident of Nero's ready belief.

3. Meanwhile Nero's extravagance increased as a result of this futile hope, and his older resources were being consumed in the belief that others were being offered for many years of squandering.

Indeed, he was already distributing largesse from this source, as well, and his anticipation of riches was one of the reasons for shortages in the exchequer. Bassus had actually dug up his own land and the broad fields around it, proclaiming that here or there was the location of the promised cavern, and he was attended not only by soldiers but by a whole population of peasants enlisted to carry out the work. Finally he came out of his delusion, declaring in bewilderment that his dreams had never proved false before, and this was the first time he had been fooled by them; and he avoided humiliation and fear by suicide. Some have recorded that he was imprisoned and subsequently released, his property being seized as compensation for the royal treasure.

4. Meanwhile, as the five-year games approached, the Senate, wishing to avoid a scandal, offered the emperor victory in singing, and added the crown for eloquence, in order to keep hidden a scandalous stage performance. Nero, however, kept saying that he had no need of the influence or authority of the Senate: he was as good as his competitors, and would win the praise he deserved through the impartial decision of the judges. He began by reciting a poem* on stage. Then the crowd insisted that he 'put on show his entire repertoire' (these were their very words), and he entered the theatre again.* This time he followed all the rules of lyre-playing—not sitting when he tired, wiping away the sweat only with the garment he was wearing, and keeping from view any emissions from his mouth or nose. Finally, bending his knee and with a respectful wave of his hand to the crowd, he awaited the verdict of the judges with feigned anxiety. And the city plebs, used to encouraging the body movements even of actors, thundered its applause, in time and with orchestrated clapping. One might have thought them delighted, and perhaps they were delighted, with no concern for the public disgrace.

5. Not so those from the distant municipalities and from an Italy still strict and clinging to the old morality, and those on official delegations or private business from far-off provinces, where they had no experience of degeneracy. These could not endure the spectacle, and neither were they up to their degrading task. Their hands unpractised, they became tired, thus disorienting those experienced in the role, and they received frequent blows from the soldiers standing amongst the blocks of seats to make sure that not an instant be lost to discordant cheering or heavy silence. It was well known that

several knights were trodden under foot as they struggled through the narrow passageways and the crowds bearing down on them, and that others fell victim to a fatal disease as they kept to their seats day and night. For there was fear of a more serious fate if they missed the show, since there were people present to take note of names and faces—many openly, more in secret—and of the enthusiasm and displeasure shown by those in attendance. The result was, for the lowly, punishment inflicted immediately; and, in the case of the illustrious, hatred hidden momentarily but satisfied later. People said that Vespasian* was berated by the freedman Phoebus for dozing with his eyes closed, and was only with difficulty protected by the pleas of decent people. Later, they say, he avoided his oncoming doom thanks to his greater destiny.

6. After the end of the games Poppaea died, victim of a chance outburst of anger in her husband, from whom she received a kick during pregnancy. Though some authorities record it—more from animosity than belief—I would not give credit to poison. Nero wanted children, and was captivated by love for his wife. Her body was not cremated, the normal Roman practice.* It was embalmed, after the fashion of foreign royalty, by being filled with aromatic spices, and then taken into the Mausoleum of the Julii.* There was, however, a state funeral,* and Nero himself, on the Rostra, eulogized Poppaea for her beauty, for having been the mother of a now-deified child, and for other gifts of fortune which he represented as virtues.

7. Poppaea's death brought sadness in public, but joy to those with a memory of the past, because of her promiscuity and ruthlessness. Nero added the finishing touches by a fresh display of spite when he forbade Gaius Cassius to attend the funeral—the first sign of trouble to come. That trouble was not long delayed, with Silanus also included in his case. There had been no crime, apart from the preeminence of the two, Cassius for his ancestral riches and austere character, and Silanus for his distinguished pedigree and youthful modesty. And so, in a speech that he sent to the Senate, Nero said that both should be removed from public life, and he reproached Cassius with having also honoured the bust of Gaius Cassius* amongst the images of his ancestors, inscribing on it 'To the leader of the cause'. Cassius' aim, he said, had been to sow the seeds of civil war and encourage treason against the house of the Caesars. And, he added, so as not to rely only on the memory of a hated name to

spread disaffection, Cassius had recruited Lucius Silanus, a young nobleman of headstrong disposition, whom he could flaunt as a supporter of revolution.

8. Nero then brought against Silanus himself the same charges as he had against his uncle Torquatus: he was already distributing imperial responsibilities and assigning to freedmen the oversight of accounts, petitions, and correspondence. The charges were both trifling and false—fear had made Silanus more circumspect, and the destruction of his uncle had terrified him into taking precautions. After that so-called 'informers' were brought in to level false accusations against Lepida (wife of Cassius and aunt of Silanus), charging her with incest with her brother's son and holding ghastly religious rites. The senators Volcacius Tertullinus and Marcellus Cornelius and the Roman knight Calpurnius Fabatus* were dragged in as accomplices. These eluded immediate condemnation by appealing to the emperor and later, when Nero was preoccupied with crimes of the utmost gravity, they slipped by him as being too unimportant.

9. Sentences of exile were then passed on Cassius and Silanus by decree of the Senate; and Nero was to fix the sentence for Lepida. Cassius was deported to the island of Sardinia, where his old age was expected to finish the job. Silanus was taken off to Ostia on the assumption that he would be shipped to Naxos, but later he was kept confined to the Apulian municipality called Barium. There, as he prudently tolerated his thoroughly undeserved lot, he was apprehended by a centurion sent to kill him. The centurion urged him to open his veins, but Silanus replied that, while he had, indeed, decided on death, he would not let the killer off his glorious assignment. Though Silanus was unarmed, the centurion could see that he was very strong and more angry than fearful, and so he ordered his soldiers to overpower him. Silanus did not fail to struggle and strike out at him as strongly as he could with his bare hands, until he was brought down by the centurion, his wounds all on the front, as though in battle.

10. No less ready to face death were Lucius Vetus,* his mother-in-law Sextia, and his daughter Pollitta. They were hated by the emperor; he felt that, simply by living, they were a reproach to him for the killing of Rubellius Plautus, Lucius Vetus' son-in-law. But the first opportunity for Nero to reveal his ruthlessness was provided by Vetus' freedman Fortunatus who, after defrauding his patron,

turned to accusing him. Fortunatus also enlisted the aid of Claudius Demianus, who had been imprisoned for criminal activity by Vetus when he was proconsul of Asia, but then released by Nero as a reward for turning informer. When the accused learned of this, and realized that he and his freedman were in a struggle on equal terms,* he withdrew to his country estate at Formiae.

At Formiae, some soldiers secretly kept watch on Vetus. Present with him was his daughter who, quite apart from the impending danger, had long been tormented with grief—ever since she had set eyes on the men who came to assassinate her husband Plautus. She had put her arms around his bloody neck, and still retained his blood-stained clothing—a widow unkempt and in constant sorrow, taking no nourishment but what would stave off death. Then, at her father's urging, she went to Neapolis. Refused access to Nero, she kept watch on his exits, and then cried out to him, begging him to hear an inno-cent man and not surrender to a freedman his former colleague in the consulship. She would use at one time the plaintive cries of a woman, but sometimes aggressive shouts that belied her sex, until the emperor made it clear that he was insensible to pleas and reproaches alike.

11. Pollitta therefore reported to her father that he should aban-don hope and accept the inevitable, and at the same time news came that a trial in the Senate and a grim sentence were in the offing. And there was no lack of people advising Vetus to name Nero as a princi-pal heir,* and in this way look after his grandchildren's interests with respect to the remainder. This option he rejected so as not to sully a life lived more or less in freedom by an act of servility at its end, and he distributed all his available money amongst his slaves. He also told them all to take away for themselves any portable chattels; only three couches were to be kept back for the final moments.

Then they cut their arteries, in the same bedroom and with the same weapon. They were hurriedly carried to the baths, each covered with a single article of clothing, for decency's sake. Father looked at daughter, grandmother at granddaughter, and Pollitta looked at them both; and the three made rival prayers—praying that their halting breath be brought to a speedy end, each wanting to leave the others alive, and yet on the point of death. Fortune preserved the rightful order. The elder two expired first, and the young Pollitta after that. They were charged after their burial, and the verdict was that they receive the traditional punishment. Nero interposed his veto, allowing them death without supervision. Such were the insults heaped upon them when the killing was already done.

12. Because he had been on intimate terms with Faenius Rufus and had some passing acquaintance with Vetus, the Roman knight Publius Gallus found himself refused fire and water. His freedman was also his accuser, and as payment for his service the man was granted a seat in the theatre amongst the couriers of the tribunes.* The months following April (also called Neroneus) were renamed, Maius now being Claudius and Junius being Germanicus.* The man who had made this proposal, Cornelius Orfitus, declared that the change of nomenclature for the month Junius arose because the two Torquatuses, who had been executed for their crimes, had now made 'Junius' an inauspicious name.

13. This year, defiled by so many crimes, was further marked by the gods with storms and diseases. Campania was devastated by a hurricane that tore apart farms, orchards, and crops everywhere, and brought its destructive force to areas close to the city; and in the city mortals of every sort were ravaged by a virulent pestilence, though there was no noxious atmosphere in evidence. Homes were filling up with dead bodies, streets with funerals. Neither sex, and no age, was out of danger. Slaves and freeborn plebeians alike were snuffed out suddenly, amidst the lamentation of wives and children, whose bedside care and mourning often led to their cremation on the same pyre. The deaths of knights and senators, just as common though they were, drew fewer tears—they were apparently forestalling the emperor's brutality by sharing the common lot of humanity.

That same year there were troop-levies throughout Narbonese Gaul, Africa, and Asia for the purpose of complementing the legions in Illyricum, from which men were receiving discharge on the basis of age or illness. To the disaster in Lugdunum* the emperor brought relief with a grant of four million sesterces to replace what the city had lost. That was the amount that the people of Lugdunum had earlier offered to assist with our city's misfortunes.

14. By the consulship of Gaius Suetonius and Luccius Telesinus, Antistius Sosianus had learned of the honour paid to informers, and how ready the emperor was to kill. Sosianus was the man I have already mentioned* as having been punished with exile for his scurrilous poetry against Nero. He was a restless character who was not slow to seize opportunities. There was in exile in the same place one

Pammenes, who was famous in the Chaldean art, through which he had a large network of acquaintances, and Sosianus played on the fact that their fortunes were similar in order to gain his friendship. He felt it was not for nothing that messengers were constantly coming to consult Pammenes, and at the same time he discovered that the man was being furnished annually with money by Publius Anteius. Sosianus was also not unaware that Nero hated Anteius because of his affection for Agrippina, and that his wealth would be a particularly effective goad to the emperor's cupidity, which had been the cause of death for many.

Sosianus accordingly intercepted a letter sent by Anteius, and also stole some documents hidden in Pammenes' private papers relating to the day of Anteius' birth and his future. At the same time he came upon what Pammenes had written down about Ostorius Scapula's birth and life. He then wrote to the emperor saying that, if he could be granted relief from his exile for a short time, he would bring him some important information that would promote his security. Anteius and Ostorius, he added, were a threat to the empire, and were examining their own destinies as well as the emperor's.

With that, Liburnian galleys were dispatched and Sosianus was quickly brought back. When his information was made known, Anteius and Ostorius were regarded as convicted rather than accused men, to the point that nobody would witness Anteius' will.* Then Tigellinus gave his authorization, having first warned Anteius not to dally in making his final testament. Anteius took poison but, enraged at its slowness, he accelerated his death by cutting his veins.

15. Ostorius at that time was on a distant estate on the Ligurian border. A centurion was sent there to kill him quickly. The reason for the haste was that Ostorius had a great reputation as a soldier, and had earned the civic crown in Britain; and also that he had a massive physique and was adept with weapons. All this had made Nero afraid of an attack from him, for the emperor lived in fear, and was even more terrified after the recently discovered conspiracy. And so, after closing off escape-routes from the villa, the centurion revealed the emperor's orders to Ostorius, who turned on himself the courage he had often displayed against the enemy. He cut his veins, but the blood flowed too slowly. He therefore employed the hand of a slave, but only to the extent of having him firmly hold out a dagger. He then drew the man's right hand towards him, and met the dagger with his throat.

16. Even if I were writing about foreign wars, and deaths incurred in the service of the state that were so closely similar in their circumstances, I myself would have been overcome with tedium, and I would be anticipating ennui on the part of others. For they would have been repelled by the sad continuum of deaths, honourable though they might be, of our citizens. In this case,* the servile acceptance of death, and the spilling of so much blood within the country, fatigue the mind and paralyse it with despondency. And the one indulgence I ask of those who will come to know of these events is for my not showing abhorrence for those who perished so tamely. It was the wrath of heaven visited on the Roman state, and one cannot simply mention it and pass on, as one may in the defeat of armies or the capture of cities. And let this concession be made to the posthumous fame of illustrious men: as in their funerals they are kept apart from the common burial, so too in the historical record of their end let them be granted, and let them retain, their own memorial.

17. In fact, within a matter of days Annaeus Mela, Cerialis Anicius, Rufrius Crispinus, and Titus Petronius all fell one after the other. Mela and Crispinus were Roman knights of senatorial status. Crispinus had once been prefect of the praetorian guard* and had been presented with consular insignia,* though recently he had been banished to Sardinia on a charge of conspiracy. He committed suicide on receiving word of his death sentence. Mela, who had the same parents as Gallio and Seneca, had eschewed the quest for political office from an eccentric ambition to gain power equal to that of ex-consuls while remaining a Roman knight. At the same time he believed a shorter way to the acquisition of wealth to be through procuratorships linked with the administration of the emperor's business interests. He was also Annaeus Lucanus' father, which greatly aided his distinction. After Lucanus' killing, Mela was zealous in calling in the debts* owing to his estate, and thus earned a denunciation from Fabius Romanus, one of Lucanus' close friends. A charge that father and son were both accomplices in the plot was fabricated, and a letter from Lucanus was forged.* Nero examined it and had it brought to Mela, whose wealth he coveted. Mela took what was at the time the easiest route to death and opened his veins, having already written his will, in which he left a large sum of money to Tigellinus and his son-in-law Cossutianus Capito, so that he could have the rest remain intact. There was an addition made to the will—a statement that Mela was dying when there were no good reasons for his punishment, whereas Rufrius Crispinus and Anicius Cerialis were enjoying their lives despite their hostility to the emperor. This was believed to be a forgery because, in the case of Crispinus, he had already been put to death, and, in that of Cerialis, because it provided a rationale for his death. Not long afterwards Cerialis committed suicide, exciting less pity than the others because people remembered that it was by him that the conspiracy had been divulged to Gaius Caesar.*

18. In Petronius' case, a brief background sketch is necessary. His days were spent sleeping, his nights on the duties and delights of life. While others had been brought fame by industry, in his instance it was by idleness; and yet he was not considered a glutton and a spendthrift, like most who squander their fortunes, but a man of educated extravagance. The more outrageous his words and actions, which had a distinctive sort of nonchalance about them, the more acceptable they became as a demonstration of his sincerity. As proconsul of Bithynia, however, and subsequently as consul, he showed himself to be a man of energy who was competent in business. Then, sliding back into his vices, or through imitating vices, he was taken into Nero's small band of cronies as his 'arbiter of good taste';* in his jaded state, Nero considered nothing delightful or agreeable unless it had Petronius' approval. Hence Tigellinus' envy, directed against a rival who outclassed him in the science of pleasure. Tigellinus therefore went to work on the emperor's ruthlessness, to which all his other passions took second place, accusing Petronius of friendship with Scaevinus. He also bribed one of Petronius' slaves to inform on him, removed any means of defence and imprisoned most of his household staff.

19. As it happened, Nero had set off for Campania during the days in question, and Petronius, who had gone as far as Cumae, was detained there; and he did not let fear or hope further delay him. He was, however, in no rush to end his life. Having cut his veins, he bandaged them and opened them again, as he felt inclined, in the meantime chatting with his friends, but not on serious matters or topics that would win him glory for his resolve. He listened in turn to their words—nothing on the immortality of the soul or the tenets of philosophers, but light poetry and playful verses. To some of his slaves he presented gifts, to others a whipping. He started dinner and let himself drop off to sleep so that his death, though imposed, might

look natural. Even in his will he did not, like most who perished, flatter Nero, Tigellinus, or any other of the powerful. Instead, he itemized in writing the emperor's depravities, naming the male prostitutes and women involved, and describing all their novel sexual acts, and sent it to Nero under seal. He then broke his signet ring to prevent its later use for manufacturing danger.

20. Nero now wondered how his exotic nocturnal pastimes were becoming known, and then Silia came into his mind. A woman of some note through her marriage to a senator, she had been involved with all Nero's sexual activities, and had also been very friendly with Petronius. She was driven into exile on the grounds that she had not kept secret what she had seen and had done to her—a personal grudge on Nero's part. The ex-praetor Minucius Thermus, however, Nero surrendered to the hatred of Tigellinus. A freedman of Thermus had come with some incriminating information about Tigellinus, for which the man himself paid with the agonies of torture, and his patron with an undeserved death.

21. After butchering so many distinguished men, Nero finally conceived a deep desire to exterminate virtue itself by killing Thrasea Paetus and Barea Soranus. He had long nursed a grudge against both, and there were additional motives for his resentment of Thrasea: he had left the Senate when the matter of Agrippina was under discussion, as I have noted,* and at the Juvenalian Games his services had not been conspicuous. That particular offence went deeper because at Patavium, his birthplace, Thrasea had actually sung in tragic costume at the Cetastian Games established by the Trojan Antenor. Furthermore, on the day that the praetor Antistius was being sentenced to death for the lampoons he composed against Nero, he successfully proposed a lighter penalty; and, after deliberately missing the meeting when divine honours were decreed to Poppaea,* he had missed her funeral. Capito Cossutianus* would not allow these things to be forgotten. He was of a criminal disposition, anyway, but he also resented Thrasea because it was to his influence that he owed an earlier conviction. That was when Thrasea gave assistance to the Cilician delegation that was indicting Capito for extortion.

22. In fact, Capito made the following accusations against him, as well. At the beginning of the year Thrasea would avoid the customary oath.* Though vested with a quindecimviral priesthood he did not attend the formal prayer-offerings.* He had never offered sacrifice on behalf of the emperor's safety or his heavenly voice. He had not entered the Curia in three years, though at one time he had attended diligently* and tirelessly, conspicuously championing or opposing even quite ordinary senatorial resolutions. And most recently, when people were racing to put a stop to Silanus and Vetus, he had preferred to spend that time on the private affairs of his clients. This was already dissidence and partisanship, said Capito, and it was outright war if many dared do the same thing.

'Once our state, with its love of discord, used to talk about Gaius Caesar and Marcus Cato*—and now it talks of you and Thrasea, Nero! And he has followers—or, more correctly, his retinue—who, while not yet adopting his perverse opinions, do ape his bearing and looks. They are stiff and gloomy,* their way of reproaching your love of fun. This man alone has no concern for your safety, no respect for your art. He is contemptuous of his emperor's successes. Are your grief and pain not enough for him? Not accepting Poppaea's divinity shows the same disposition as failing to swear allegiance to the enactments of the deified Augustus and Julius.* He disdains religion, ignores the law. The daily record of the Roman people is the more attentively read throughout the provinces and throughout the army—so people can learn what Thrasea has refused to do!

'Either let us switch to his doctrine, if it is better, or else let those wanting revolution be deprived of their leader and prime motivator. That was the sect that produced the likes of Tubero and Favonius,* names unbeloved even by the republic of old. They parade the flag of freedom to overturn the empire; but if they overthrow it they will attack freedom itself. You have wasted your time removing Cassius if you allow the rivals of the Brutuses to grow and flourish.* Finally, write no memo yourself about Thrasea; let the Senate be our umpire.'

Nero stimulated Cossutianus' already fierce temper, and also brought on side Marcellus Eprius and his trenchant eloquence.

23. As for the indictment of Barea Soranus,* the Roman knight Ostorius Sabinus had already laid a personal claim to it on the basis of Soranus' proconsulship of Asia. During his mandate, Soranus had increased the emperor's resentment by his fairness and industry, and also because he had carefully cleared the harbour of Ephesus,* and omitted to punish the state of Pergamum for forcefully preventing Nero's freedman Acratus from making off with statues and art works.

However, the charges laid were friendship with Plautus and courting popularity to induce his province to revolt. The date chosen for Soranus' condemnation was that on which Tiridates* was coming to accept the throne of Armenia. This was in order to shade a crime at home by turning talk to foreign affairs—or so that Nero could flaunt his imperial greatness by a king-like* act of putting illustrious men to death.

24. The whole city poured out to welcome the emperor and see the king, but Thrasea was barred from the gathering. He was not despondent and, in fact, he wrote a petition to Nero asking to be informed of the accusations against him, and declaring that he would clear himself if he were given notification of the charges and an opportunity to refute them. Nero quickly accepted the petition, hoping that a fearful Thrasea had written something that might promote the emperor's renown, and discredit his own reputation. When this turned out not to be the case, it was Nero's turn to become frightened—at the prospect of the innocent man's facial expression, spirit, and independence—and he had the Senate convened.

25. Then, surrounded by his closest friends, Thrasea deliberated whether he should attempt or decline to defend himself. Varying suggestions were put forward. Those feeling he should enter the Curia said they were confident about his firmness of purpose—he would say nothing that would not increase his brilliant reputation. It was the feckless and cowardly who shrouded their last moments in secrecy, they told him. He should let the people see a man ready to face death, and let the Senate hear words greater than a man's, and almost divine. It could be that even Nero would be moved by the wonder of it; and if he persisted with his brutality, at least the record of an honourable end would be set apart among posterity from the cowardice of those who died in silence.

26. There were, on the other hand, those who thought he should wait at home. They said the same thing about Thrasea himself, but believed that he would face mockery and humiliation, and that he should turn his ears away from abuse and insults. It was not only Cossutianus and Eprius who were ready for heinous acts, they explained; there were others, too, whose inhumanity might lead them to raise their hands in violence, and even good men might follow from fear. Better, they said, to keep such infamous misconduct out of the Senate, to which he had always lent distinction, and

leave unknown what the senators would have decided had they seen Thrasea on trial. To imagine that Nero would be overtaken by shame for his actions was to entertain futile hopes; much more real was the fear that he would vent his wrath on Thrasea's wife, daughter, and other relatives. So he should go to his end still pure and unsullied, attaining the glory of those men in whose steps and learning he had directed his life.

Present at the meeting was a hot-headed young man named Rusticus Arulenus* who, hungry for praise, offered to veto the senatorial resolution (he was a tribune of the plebs). Thrasea curbed his enthusiasm, telling him not to embark on a futile* plan that would be of no help to the accused and deadly to its author. His own days were numbered, he said, and he should not desert a pattern of life he had assiduously maintained over so many years—Arulenus, by contrast, was starting his official career, and his future was not compromised. He should weigh up far ahead what course, in times like these, he should follow in his political life. But Thrasea kept to himself his thoughts on whether he should enter the Senate.

27. The next day, two praetorian cohorts, under arms, occupied the temple of Venus Genetrix. A body of civilians, their swords not concealed,* had taken up a position blocking the approach to the Senate, and at various points throughout the forums and basilicas were detachments of soldiers. Under the threatening gaze of these men the senators entered the Curia,* and a speech of the emperor was heard from the lips of his quaestor.* With no one mentioned by name, he criticized the senators for dereliction of their official duties and for drawing Roman knights into indifference by their example. Was it surprising that no one came from distant provinces, he asked, when many former holders of the consulship and priesthoods gave their attention instead to embellishing their gardens? This weapon the accusers seized.

28. Cossutianus took the lead, and then with greater vehemence Marcellus declared that the highest interests of state were at stake, that the mercy of their leader was being taxed by the stubbornness of his inferiors. The senators had been too tolerant up to that time, he said, allowing people to get away with making fools of them. There was the dissident Thrasea, and his son-in-law Helvidius Priscus,* victim of the same madness; and along with them Paconius Agrippinus,* who had inherited his father's hatred of emperors, and

Curtius Montanus,* ever scribbling his detestable poems. In the Senate he missed the presence of an ex-consul, he said, in the taking of vows he missed a priest, and in taking the oath of allegiance he missed a citizen. But perhaps Thrasea was rejecting the institutions and ceremonial rites of their ancestors, and openly taking on the part of traitor and public enemy! In short, let him come and state his opinion on what corrections or modifications he would like to see made—this man who was ever playing the senator and protecting those who disparaged the emperor! They would more easily bear his voice when he criticized specific items than they could his silence now as he condemned everything! Was he dissatisfied with worldwide peace,* or with victories won without loss to our armies? He was a man saddened by the prosperity of the state, one who regarded forums, theatres, and temples as deserts, and who kept threatening to exile himself—and they should not fulfil his perverted ambition for him! He had no regard for these senatorial decrees, the magistrates, and the city of Rome. Let him detach his life from this city which he had long ago ceased to cherish and now does not even look at!

29. As Marcellus made these and other such remarks, with his customary grim and menacing look, there was fire in his voice, in his face, and in his eyes. But there was not in the Senate the familiar despondency that had now become normal from the frequent perils; instead there was a new and deeper dread at the sight of the soldiers' hands on their weapons. At the same time the venerable image of Thrasea himself loomed up in their minds, and there were some who felt compassion for Helvidius, too, who would pay the penalty for a guiltless relationship. What charge had been brought against Agrippinus but the sad fate of his father?* For he, too, equally innocent, had fallen before Tiberius' brutality. And in Montanus' case, he was a young man of integrity, not really an author of slanderous verse, and he was being driven into exile for having shown talent.

30. Meanwhile Ostorius Sabinus, the accuser of Soranus, came into the Senate. He opened his address by adverting to Soranus' friendship with Rubellius Plautus and to his proconsulship of Asia, which, he claimed, Soranus had accommodated to his own glory-seeking—by promoting sedition in the various communities!—rather than the common good. These were old allegations. But there was a new one, too, which tied Soranus' daughter to her father's predicament, namely that she had given generous amounts of money

to magicians. This had actually taken place, thanks to the filial piety of Servilia (which was the girl's name). Through love for her father, and the indiscretion of her years, she had made a consultation, but only on the question of the safety of her family, on whether Nero could be appeased, and whether the senatorial inquiry would have no terrible outcome.

Servilia was therefore called into the Senate, and the two stood facing each other before the consuls' tribunal*—the aged father and, opposite him, a daughter not yet twenty years old, widowed and forlorn, since her husband Annius Pollio had recently been driven into exile. And she did not even look at her father, whose dangers she seemed to have aggravated.

31. Her accuser then asked whether she had sold her wedding gifts, and taken the necklace from her neck to put on sale, to raise money for the performance of magical ceremonies. At first she threw herself on the ground, and for a long time wept in silence. Then, grasping the altar steps and the altar,* she said: 'I have appealed to no impious gods and laid no curses. In my unhappy prayers I have asked for nothing other than that you, Caesar, and you, senators, save the life of this excellent father. Yes, I gave my jewels, my clothes, and the insignia of my rank, as I would have given my blood and my life had they asked for them. It is up to those men—unknown to me before this—to tell you what name they go by, and what arts they practise. I made no mention of the emperor except as one of the gods. But my poor father is unaware of all this, and if it is a crime I alone committed it.'

32. She was still speaking when Soranus interrupted, proclaiming that she had not gone to his province with him, could not have been an acquaintance of Plautus because of her age, and was not connected with the charges against her husband. She was guilty only of too much filial affection, and they should separate her case from his. As for himself, he would suffer any fate, no matter what. With that he sped to the arms of his daughter, who was running to him, but the lictors came between the two and stopped them.

Next it was the turn of the witnesses, and the pity that the savage accusation had excited was equalled by the anger aroused by Publius Egnatius'* testimony. He was a client of Soranus, now bribed to crush his friend. He affected the magisterial gravity of the Stoic sect,* and he was practised in putting on the outer appearance of integrity in bearing and expression, but at heart he was treacherous and cunning, keeping hidden his greed and lechery. These traits were laid bare by the money, and Egnatius provided an object lesson that one should be just as wary of those who, while putting on a show of good character, are false and perfidious in their friendship, as of those wrapped in crime and stained with infamy.

33. The same day, however, also produced the honourable example of Cassius Asclepiodotus,* who was a very prominent man in Bithynia because of his great riches. He had honoured Soranus with a loyal devotion in his prosperous days, and did not desert him in his decline. And so Asclepiodotus was entirely stripped of his fortune and driven into exile, such being the indifference of the gods to examples of good and evil.

Thrasea, Soranus, and Servilia were allowed to choose their manner of death. Helvidius and Paconius were banished from Italy. Montanus was pardoned as a concession to his father, on condition that he not continue in public life. The accusers Eprius and Cossutianus were each granted five million sesterces,* and Ostorius twelve hundred thousand, plus the insignia of a quaestor.*

34. Thrasea was in his gardens when, as evening approached, the consul's quaestor was sent to him. He had gathered together a large crowd of illustrious men and women, and was focusing his attention mostly on Demetrius,* a professor of the Cynic philosophical school. With him, as could be judged from the earnestness of his expression, and from the more audible parts of their conversation, he was examining the nature of the soul and the separation of the spirit and the body. Then one of his close friends, Domitius Caecilianus, arrived and told him of the Senate's decision. Thrasea therefore urged all present, who were weeping and protesting, to leave quickly, and not incur danger themselves by association with a man doomed to die. Arria's* aim was to accompany her husband to his end, after the example of her mother Arria, but Thrasea advised her to hold on to her life and not remove the only support enjoyed by the daughter they shared.

35. He then went to the colonnade, where the quaestor found him almost joyful because he had learned that his son-in-law Helvidius had merely been barred from Italy. He accepted the decree of the Senate, and took Helvidius and Demetrius into his bedroom. He offered the veins of both arms and, letting the blood flow freely,

sprinkled it on the ground. He then called the quaestor over and said 'We are making a libation to Jupiter the Liberator. Look, young man!* I pray the gods avert the omen, but you have been born into a time when it is helpful to toughen the mind with examples of firmness.' Then, as his slow death brought agonizing pains, turning to Demetrius . . .

The rest of the text is lost.

APPENDIX 1

LIST OF VARIATIONS FROM THE TEUBNER TEXT

	Teubner:	*This edition*:
3.43.1	ut nobilissimam . . . et eo pignore	<et> nobilissimam . . . ut eo pignore
3.49.1	iecerat	legerat
3.53.4	lapidum causa	*words omitted*
4.26.2	<s>ed culpae nescia	et culpae conscia
4.49.1	immuniebat	iam muniebat
4.59.2	vultuque	utroque
4.73.3	Cethego	Cethecio
12.36.1	Cartimandus	Cartimanduae
12.40.2	Cartimandum	Cartimandam
12.40.3	Cartimandus	Cartimandua
15.44.2	Chrestianos	Christianos
15.47.2	aut iter	et iter

I have noticed only a couple of misprints in Heubner's text: 2.8.3 aderescente (for adcrescente), 14.38.3 cuisus (for cuius).

APPENDIX 2
THE JULIO-CLAUDIAN FAMILY TREE
(SIMPLIFIED)

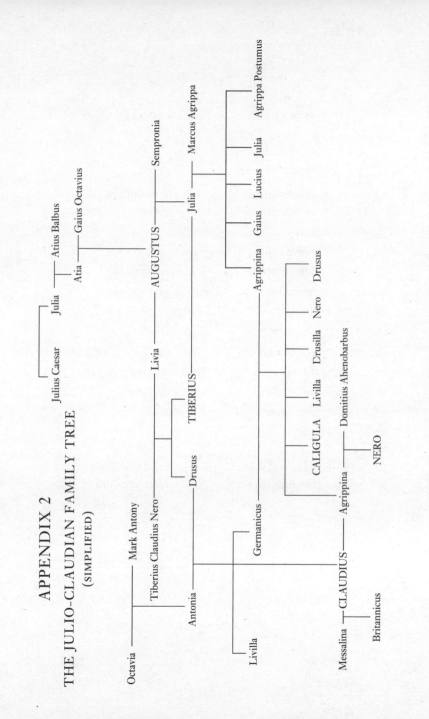

EXPLANATORY NOTES

BOOK ONE

3 *Kings . . . Lucius Brutus*: Tacitus sets the principate within the history of Rome, showing that one-man rule had long been in evidence in one form or another. The notion of the traditional first six kings of Rome owes more to legend than to fact, as does the tradition surrounding Lucius Brutus, who established 'liberty', a term that to Tacitus meant essentially the old republic. The traditional date of the first consulship is 509 BC.

decemvirs: successive boards of ten patricians were set up in 451 BC to create a legal code. They produced the law of the Twelve Tables.

military tribunes: before 367, at which point plebeians were allowed to hold the consulship, a temporary expedient was devised of substituting consuls by tribunes with consular authority, open to both plebeians and patricians.

Cinna: the last century BC saw the emergence of powerful generals as the dominating political force in Rome. Cinna, who held four consulships in a row, was killed in 84 BC while marching against his enemy Sulla, who was appointed dictator in 82 BC but gave up the office in the following year.

Crassus: the alliance of Pompey, Julius Caesar, and Crassus in 60 BC is loosely referred to as the first triumvirate. Crassus died at Carrhae in 53, Pompey after the battle of Pharsalus in 43. The second triumvirate, more properly so named, resulted from the partnership, legally established in 43 BC, of Augustus (then Octavian), Antonius, and Marcus Aemilius Lepidus. Lepidus was a spent force from 36 BC, and the defeat of Antonius, at Actium in 31 left Augustus in effective control.

without rancour or bias: *sine ira et studio*, possibly the most famous phrase of Tacitus. His evident antipathy towards the Julio-Claudian ruling family makes his claim unconvincing.

Brutus and Cassius: Marcus Junius Brutus and Gaius Cassius Longinus, leading figures in the conspiracy against Julius Caesar, committed suicide after the battle of Philippi in 43 BC.

Pompeius: Sextus Pompeius, the son of Pompey, and an able sea-commander. He opposed Octavian, over whom he gained two naval victories in 38 BC, but was crushed at the battle of Naulochus off Sicily in 36.

Caesar Octavian: after his adoption by Julius Caesar, Octavius followed Roman custom when he assumed his adopting father's name with an adjectival form of his own, *Octavianus*.

provinces: Tacitus plays down the benefits that the principate, with its heightened central control, brought to the provinces, which under the republic had frequently suffered from the greed of corrupt officials.

4 *Augustus*: this name was bestowed on Octavian when he reached a settlement with the Senate in 27 BC. It was assumed by each emperor thereafter.

Claudius Marcellus: the betrothal of Marcellus, son of Augustus' sister Octavia, to his daughter Julia, and his promotion to public office, were the first signs that the emperor hoped to be succeeded from within his own family, one of the features of the monarchical system that Augustus supposedly abjured. Marcellus died in 23 BC.

Marcus Agrippa: a capable and loyal soldier, and one of the main supporters of Augustus, he had been offended by the advancement of Marcellus. After the latter's death, he was married to Julia and his children Gaius and Lucius were adopted by Augustus. He died in 12 BC.

Tiberius Nero and Claudius Drusus: sons of Augustus' wife Livia by her former husband. Both were able and distinguished soldiers. Drusus died when crushed by his horse on campaign in 9 BC. Tiberius would succeed Augustus as emperor in AD 14.

Livia: Tacitus consistently depicts Livia as an evil schemer, hell-bent on the succession of her son Tiberius. The deliberate, if imprecise, use of the negative term *noverca*, 'stepmother', reinforces the unsympathetic impression. Other historical sources are far less hostile towards Livia than is Tacitus.

Gaius and Lucius . . . by a wound: the circumstances of their deaths, particularly in the case of Gaius, who died in AD 4 (Lucius died in AD 2), all but preclude sinister agency.

Agrippa Postumus: the posthumous son of Agrippa was exiled in AD 7, ultimately to Planasia, a small island between Elba and Corsica, for reasons that are unclear. He may have been mentally unstable.

Germanicus: the grandson of Livia was married to Augustus' granddaughter Agrippina (the Elder), and Tiberius was obliged to adopt him as his son at the time of his own adoption by Augustus in AD 4, another clear indication of Augustus' desire to be succeeded ultimately from within his own line.

adolescent son: Tiberius was married to Julia in her third 'political' marriage. To enable this he was obliged to divorce his first wife Vipsania (daughter of Agrippa) of whom he reputedly remained very fond. They had a surviving son, Drusus, born about 13 BC.

Quinctilius Varus: consul in 13 BC with Tiberius, and married to a daughter of Agrippa. His loss of four legions in the Teutoburg Forest in AD 9 was the greatest military setback of Augustus' reign and marked the end of his ambitions in Germany. Tiberius took command in the area and was largely responsible for preventing the aftermath becoming even more disastrous.

5 *arrogance*: the Claudian pride was notorious, and could be traced back to at least Appius Claudius in the mid-fifth century BC, a distinguished lawgiver but also a ruthless defiler of women.

Rhodes: resentment over the advancement of Gaius and Lucius provoked Tiberius to withdraw from Rome in 6 BC and lead a retiring, scholarly life in Rhodes. He remained there for eight years, returning only in AD 2 after the deaths of his supposed rivals.

Fabius Maximus: a literary figure of some standing, Paullus Fabius Maximus was a friend of Ovid and Horace. He was also an intimate of Augustus, held the consulship in 11 BC and was governor of Asia and legate in Spain. He was a plausible individual to be involved in the expedition.

Planasia: the story of Augustus' supposed reconciliation with Agrippa Postumus and the visit to Planasia is considered by most modern historians to be highly unlikely, perhaps an imaginative reconstruction after the event to provide Livia with a motive for wanting to eliminate her husband.

Whatever the truth: Tiberius had accompanied Augustus and Livia to Campania. He then left them to proceed to his command in Dalmatia; he was soon summoned back to Augustus' villa at Nola. The story of the guards securing the spot and issuing regular bulletins is suspiciously reminiscent of the measures taken by Agrippina as Claudius lay dying (12.68).

6 *Nola*: on a visit to Campania in AD 14, Augustus fell ill and retired to his family estate at Nola, where he died, on 19 August.

The first criminal act: the phraseology is echoed at the beginning of Book 13, when the new reign of Nero is introduced.

The more likely explanation: the supposed roles of Tiberius and Livia in the death of Agrippa are no more than speculation, and the rhetorical use of 'stepmother' is once again to be noted.

Sallustius Crispus: the great-nephew and adopted son of Sallust the historian, he was an entrepreneur and close adviser to both Augustus and Tiberius (see 2.40, 3.30).

In Rome: the nature of the oath sworn to Tiberius is far from certain, nor is its constitutional significance clear. It does not seem to be the oath of allegiance later taken to uphold the enactments of the emperor.

7 *Seius Strabo*: father of Sejanus.

Gaius Turranius: he disappears from the narrative until AD 48 (11.31).

prefect . . . grain supply: the prefectures of the praetorian guard and of the grain supply were the two most important offices open to equestrians.

Germanicus: he enjoyed a special grant of *imperium*, which gave him authority in Gaul and over the two commanders of Lower and Upper Germany, with their four legions. He had in fact given no sign that he was interested in seeking the principate. All of his actions suggest loyalty to Tiberius.

Vestal Virgins: the temple of Vesta, tended by the special order of Vestal Virgins (normally six), was regularly used for the depositing of important documents.

7 *Livia*: the posthumous adoption of Livia was remarkable. Technically, it ensured that Tiberius, already adopted by Augustus, would be a Julian on both sides. Testamentary adoptions were rare (although there was a precedent in Augustus' own case, since he was adopted by Julius Caesar in his will) and there is no known parallel for such adoptions of females, let alone of wives. Livia's assumption of the Julian title may have led her to believe that she inherited with it some of the Augustan prerogatives, a belief that caused constant friction between her and Tiberius.

8 *Asinius Gallus*: consul in 8 BC, the governor of Asia, son of the famous literary patron Asinius Pollio, consul in 40 BC. The son was considered ambitious by Augustus. Tiberius' personal dislike and mistrust of him contributed to his arrest in AD 30 and his death later by starvation.

triumphal gate: the gate, of uncertain location, through which generals entered Rome to celebrate their triumphs.

Lucius Arruntius: consul in 3 BC, a distinguished lawyer who incurred the wrath of two guard commanders, Sejanus and Macro. Towards the end of Tiberius' reign, he was falsely accused of being involved in a plot against the emperor and committed suicide.

Messala Valerius: Marcus Valerius Messalla Messalinus was consul in 3 BC. He was the son of Marcus Valerius Messalla Corvinus (see note to p. 155).

deified Julius: there were riots at Caesar's funeral, when the bier was set on fire in the Forum (Suetonius, *Jul*. 84; Plutarch, *Caes*. 68; Dio 44.50).

consulships: Augustus held the office thirteen times, Marcus Valerius Corvinus held it six times in the fourth century BC, Marius seven times between 107 and 86 BC.

9 *marvellously embellished*: Suetonius (*Aug*. 28) famously records Augustus as saying that he had found a city of brick and left one of marble.

consul's legions: two legions deserted Antonius for Octavian in November 44 BC.

Pompeian party: the old party of Pompey, opposed to Antonius and courted by Octavian out of political expediency.

Hirtius and Pansa: consuls of 43 BC; Pansa was killed as a result of an attack by Antonius; Hirtius was killed at the battle of Mutina. Suspicion was attached to the deaths of both (Suetonius, *Aug*. 11).

Pompeius: i.e. Sextus Pompeius.

Tarentum and Brundisium: treaties in 40 and 37 respectively. The marriage of Octavia to Antonius bought a temporary truce between the two men.

10 *Lollius*: Marcus Lollius, consul 21 BC, was defeated by the Germans in 17 or 16 BC.

Varro, Egnatius, and Iullus: men executed for involvement in conspiracies, or suspicion of involvement. Iullus Antonius (son of Marcus Antonius) was one of Julia's lovers and was forced to commit suicide.

Nero's wife: Tiberius Nero seems to have been willing to give up his wife to Augustus, but much criticism attached to the fact that she was pregnant (with Drusus) at the time of her second marriage.

Vedius Pollio: notorious for his wealth and cruelty. His friendship seems later to have been a source of embarrassment to Augustus.

temples: Pergamum was granted the right to construct a temple to Rome and Augustus in 27 BC.

11 *document*: Suetonius (*Aug.* 101) observes that Augustus had deposited three documents, apart from his will: (i) instructions for his funeral; (ii) a list of his achievements (*Res Gestae*); (iii) an outline of the military and financial resources of the state. It is clearly the last that Tiberius read out loud.

Vipsania: Tiberius had been betrothed to Agrippa's daughter. Gallus married her after her forced divorce from Tiberius in 11 BC.

12 *Marcus Lepidus*: consul in AD 6 and legate of Tiberius in the campaign against the Dalmatians, governor of Nearer Spain in 14, and of Asia in 26. His daughter Aemilia Lepida married Drusus, the son of Germanicus. Older readings of the MS gave M' instead of M, hence *Manius* Lepidus, an insignificant grandson of the triumvir.

Gnaeus Piso: consul in 7 BC, he plays a central role in Tacitus' later narrative (from 2.43 on), where he is implicated in the supposed murder of Germanicus.

Quintus Haterius . . . Scaurus: Haterius, an elderly lawyer, consul in 5 BC, and noted for his excitable oratorical style, was nearly 80 by this stage. Scaurus, consul in AD 21, by contrast, was considered dangerous and unethical, and committed suicide when accused of treason in 32.

adulation: the measures enacted for Livia were extraordinary, including a female version of the important title *Pater Patriae* ('Father of the Nation') and the inclusion of her filiation in Tiberius' titles. Tiberius, who had a personal aversion to honorifics, no doubt felt that in her case they would elevate her to an official state role.

Augusta: as well as being adopted into the Julian family, Livia received a female form of her husband's title (Augusta) in his will. The honour was granted sparingly during the Julio-Claudian period, more frequently after that.

lictor: as priestess of the deified Augustus, Livia was entitled to a special attendant or lictor (the emperor had twelve), but Tiberius seems to have restricted its use to the performance of her priestly duties, a restriction exaggerated by Tacitus.

13 *nominated*: the process by which the emperor approved candidates for higher office is much disputed.

elections: Tiberius gave control of the elections to the Senate in that they apparently were able to send the names of people to be elected to the popular assemblies for their formal ratification. This measure was revoked by Caligula.

13 *Augustal Games*: the *Ludi Augustales* (see also 1.54) were based on the earlier *Augustalia*, games established in October 19 BC on Augustus' return from the East.

Pannonia: at the time it was the home of the Eighth, Ninth, and Fifteenth legions.

Junius Blaesus: consul in AD 10, uncle of Sejanus, a distinguished military commander, and the last private citizen to receive the acclamation of *Imperator*, for victories in Africa.

14 *so many years*: in AD 6 the term of a legionary's service was fixed at twenty years, followed by several years' service in a special unit of veterans.

praetorian cohorts: under Augustus, the praetorian guard consisted of nine cohorts. Members enjoyed considerable privileges, including higher pay and shorter terms of service.

15 *eagles*: the general Marius (157–86 BC) was the first to give each legion its own standard, a metal eagle at the end of a pole. The smaller units (maniples) within the cohorts also had their own distinctive standards.

camp prefect: he was responsible for the practical day-to-day operations of the legionary camp. He would have field command only in the absence of the legate.

16 *Germany*: mutinies had broken out among the Rhine legions also (see below), but it is highly unlikely that news of them could have reached Pannonia by this time.

gladiators: almost certainly kept for providing local entertainment.

17 *Drusus*: Drusus' competence and leadership in Pannonia stands in contrast to Germanicus' handling of the German mutinies (see below).

German: Germans, mainly from Batavia, constituted the main element of the emperor's private bodyguard. They had been disbanded after the Varian disaster but revived shortly afterwards. They proved to be fiercely loyal.

Aelius Sejanus: this is the first mention of the sinister prefect of the praetorian guard. At this time command was split between two men, but shortly afterwards Sejanus strengthened his position by becoming sole commander.

18 *many campaigns*: Tiberius served in Pannonia, 12–9 BC and AD 6–9.

Gnaeus Lentulus: see 2.32, 3.59 and 68, and 4.29; Gnaeus Cornelius Lentulus (Augur) was consul in 14 BC and won victories on the Danube against the Getae, probably in 10–6 BC, and was awarded triumphal insignia, perhaps in 9 BC. He was a loyal supporter of the imperial house. He died in AD 25 (see 4.44). According to Seneca (*De Beneficiis* 2.27.1), he was renowned for his wealth, his stinginess, and his stupidity.

19 *moon*: the eclipse occurred at 5 a.m. Universal Time, 27 September, about 6 a.m. in Pannonia. Tacitus' description perhaps suits the preliminary phase of an eclipse, seen shortly before morning twilight.

Neros and Drususes: Nero and Drusus were the *cognomina* of the two main branches of the Claudian clan (*gens*).

21 *two armies*: at this time there were, strictly speaking, no German provinces, only two military districts housing four legions each, and each under an overall military commander.

Gaius Silius: consul in AD 13 and a distinguished soldier. He committed suicide in AD 24 when accused of treason (4.18–20). His son was the last lover of Messalina, the wife of Claudius.

Aulus Caecina: consul in 1 BC; his impressive military career has been overshadowed by a celebrated if unfortunate speech in the Senate on the dangers of allowing provincial governors to be accompanied by their wives (see 3.33–4).

levy in Rome: recruits were hastily levied in Rome to fill the gaps left after the Varian disaster.

their name: the *cognomen* 'Germanicus' had been conferred on Germanicus' father Drusus and his posterity.

22 *sixty . . . number of centurions*: after the military reforms of Marius each of the ten cohorts of the legion had six centurions.

Gaius Caesar: Caligula.

Cassius Chaerea: he assassinated Caligula on the Palatine in AD 41. He was afterwards executed by Claudius.

stepmother's: Livia was the stepmother of Agrippina's mother, Julia.

23 *victories and triumphs*: Tiberius had enjoyed a brilliant military career before his accession; he was awarded an ovation in 9 BC for his campaigns against the Dalmatians and Pannonians, and triumphs in 7 BC for victories over the Germans, and in AD 12 for victories over the Illyrians. Velleius (2.122) claims, however, that he could rightly have claimed four more triumphs.

25 *altar of the Ubii*: *ara Ubiorum*. An altar, probably to Rome and Augustus, had been established in the capital, no doubt with the intention that it might become a cult centre for a whole province, on the analogy of Lugdunum. Here the phrase simply stands for 'City of the Ubii'.

Munatius Plancus: consul in AD 13 with Gaius Silius. He is probably the brother of Plancina (2.43).

26 *descendant*: Agrippina was the daughter of Julia the Elder, and hence Augustus' granddaughter.

son: their son was the 2-year-old future emperor Caligula, who had been sent by Augustus to join his parents. In the camp he had become a mascot of the soldiers, dressed by his mother in a miniature uniform (1.41).

27 *fertility*: Agrippina bore nine children, of whom six survived infancy.

born in the camp: Tacitus is almost certainly mistaken here. Suetonius (*Cal.* 8.1) provides a useful discussion of the question and is categorical that Caligula was born in Antium (Anzio), and notes that he saw the birth entered there in the public record.

footwear: his miniature uniform included the *caligae*, or military shoes. His name is a diminutive of this word.

Quirites: originally inhabitants of the Sabine city of Cures. The Romans used the term to refer to themselves in a civil capacity. Suetonius (*Jul.* 70) places the incident in 70 BC, just before Caesar's African campaign.

Augustus: Suetonius (*Aug.* 17.4) records that Augustus dealt with the mutinous troops in Brundisium after Actium by making concessions to them, although he also records without context (*Aug.* 24.2) that he disbanded the Tenth Legion because of insubordination.

28 *entreaty*: Dio (57.6.1) provides a different account, less favourable to Germanicus, that Agrippina and Caligula were seized by the troops and reluctantly released when it was felt that their detention would achieve nothing. Suetonius (*Cal.* 48.1) reports in a later context that Caligula planned to punish the troops because they had seized him during the revolt.

29 *Augustus*: he had gone to Gaul for three years in 16 BC, at the age of 47. At the time of the mutinies Tiberius was 54. Tacitus seems to be overcome by his own rhetoric.

33 *Julia*: born in 39 BC, the daughter of Augustus and Scribonia, she had been married to Augustus' nephew, Marcellus, then to his friend and commander, Marcus Agrippa, then to Tiberius. She was involved in a major sexual scandal in 2 BC, perhaps with political overtones. Although allowed to move to a less arduous place of residence on the mainland, she remained in exile to her death.

Sempronius Gracchus: a kinsman of the Gracchus brothers and the first of the family since his famous ancestors to be mentioned in the historical record.

Lucius Asprenas: consul in AD 6, he was the cousin of Quinctilius Varus and served under him in Germany before becoming governor of Africa.

Augustal brothers: the formal consecration of Augustus as a god took place on 17 September AD 14, and a priestly college was established to tend to his cult. It was modelled on a very ancient order, the *Titii Sodales*, associated here by Tacitus with the supposed early Sabine king of Rome, although their origins are much disputed.

34 *Maecenas*: the trusted friend and adviser of Augustus, and a notable patron of literature. He died in 8 BC.

Bathyllus: a freedman of Maecenas and famous pantomime actor, who by mime gestures would act out familiar mythological stories. Pantomimes were enormously popular, with their own factions of supporters.

triumph: the triumph was the preserve of the emperor and his family. The permission for Germanicus to celebrate one despite achieving little of military significance suggests, despite Tacitus, that Tiberius did not begrudge Germanicus token recognition.

Arminius: the legendary German leader of the Cherusci, he held Roman citizenship and had served in the Roman army, but became Rome's bitterest enemy. He was responsible for the defeat of Varus. He was killed in AD 17, and later became a symbol of German nationalism, especially during the Napoleonic wars. The massive Hermannsdenkmal was erected in the Teutoburg Forest in the early nineteenth century.

Segestes: father-in-law of Arminius and a bitter opponent of him.

Lucius Apronius: consul in AD 8, a distinguished military commander, who would be awarded triumphal insignia for this campaign. He went on later to be the commander in Lower Germany and to serve in Africa against Tacfarinas.

35 *priest*: his duties would have included the cult of the deified Augustus.

36 *appropriate point*: the account of the insult must have been covered in the lost books (see 2.10 and 46).

37 *youth*: in fact, Germanicus and Arminius were more or less the same age.

Pedo: Albinovanus Pedo was a friend of Ovid and wrote a verse account (now lost) of Germanicus' campaign of the following year.

38 *first camp*: the historical accounts of the battle in Dio, Florus, Velleius, and Tacitus are confused and contradictory. Most likely the first camp is not Varus' semi-permanent headquarters but a marching camp which had been abandoned and to which the remnant of the army retreated after the major attack.

39 *augurate*: there was a general taboo on Roman priests handling dead bodies, although the severity of the prohibition may have varied from college to college. Suetonius (*Cal.* 3) has him actually handling dead bodies, which seems to have been sanitized in Tacitus' account.

Lucius Domitius: Lucius Domitius Ahenobarbus, consul in AD 16, was married to Antonia the Elder, daughter of Antonius and Augustus' sister Octavia, and grandfather of the emperor Nero. He led Roman troops across the Elbe in 2 BC (4.44; Dio 55.10a.2–3).

40 *fortieth season*: Tacitus may be using round numbers, since at 3.33, by which time (AD 21) Caecina had served at the very least in one further campaign (in AD 16), he similarly refers to his service in forty campaigns.

successes and reverses: Tacitus no doubt has in mind Caecina's less than impressive handling of the mutinies in the previous year, but Velleius (2.112.3–6) also expresses concerns about his leadership abilities in Pannonia in AD 7.

43 *Gaius Plinius*: this is one of the few occasions where Tacitus explicitly names his source, Pliny the Elder's twenty books on the wars in Germany

(*Bella Germaniae*). Pliny had served there and was supposedly asked by Drusus in a dream to record his achievements.

43 *Agrippina*: if the traditional year for the birth of Agrippina the Younger (AD 15) is correct, and we know that the month was November, Agrippina the Elder must have been in an advanced stage of pregnancy during the bridge incident, which occurred just before the autumn equinox (1.70).

woman: Tiberius had very firm views on the appropriate role for women, and especially on their involving themselves in military matters. The concerns about Agrippina will be echoed later in the account of the behaviour in Syria of Plancina, wife of Calpurnius Piso (2.55).

Publius Vitellius: uncle of the later emperor, he commanded troops in Germany under Germanicus and was later one of those who accused Piso of murdering Germanicus (2.74, 3.13). He would commit suicide in AD 31 when accused of embezzlement (6[5].8).

equinox: the autumn equinox, in late September, marked the usual end of the campaigning season.

44 *triumphal insignia*: Germanicus, as the emperor's (adopted) son, celebrated a triumph in his own right.

45 *Cassius Severus'*: a vitriolic orator, banished in AD 8 or 13. His final place of exile was the barren island of Seriphos, where he died in AD 32 (see 4.21). The ban on his works was lifted by Caligula.

votaries of Augustus: the reference is not to the official college of Augustus, the *sodales Augustales*, but to the worship of Augustus in private homes.

perjury: the swearing of oaths by the *genius* of Augustus occurred during that emperor's lifetime, from about 12 BC. Rubrius apparently had sworn a false oath by Augustus' name.

consuls: the involvement of the consuls shows that this case was brought before the Senate, not the praetor's court. The senatorial court seems to have emerged towards the end of Augustus' reign.

games: Livia established a three-day festival on the Palatine in honour of Augustus, which was celebrated by subsequent emperors.

46 *type of livelihood*: in the absence of a public prosecutor in Rome, accusations were instigated by private individuals (*delatores*), who were rewarded if the prosecution was successful. The vagueness of the *maiestas* laws encouraged the emergence of a professional class of *delatores* who saw accusations as a source of wealth.

first: Roman senators voted according to a strict order of precedence. The emperor could use the tribunician intercession to intervene at any stage.

embezzlement: oddly, when the charge against Marcellus is noted at the beginning of the chapter there is no mention of embezzlement.

board of assessors: a board of three or more judges (*reciperatores*), with a long history, established originally to handle cases involving legal issues between Roman and foreign states. It is difficult to determine a specific competence for the board in the imperial period.

praetors of the treasury: from 23 BC the treasury had been under the charge of two praetors, selected by lot.

47 *financial problems*: membership of the Senate required a census-rating that by the end of Augustus' life was set at one million sesterces.

authorized: the increasing uses of *curatores*, officials with responsibility for specific administrative taxes, was one of the hallmarks of the principate. Dio ascribes to this period the establishment of a permanent board to deal with the problems of the flooding of the Tiber. Ateius Capito had in AD 13 been appointed *curator aquarum*, responsible for Rome's water-supply. He died in 22 (3.75).

Achaea and Macedonia: the division of responsibility of the provinces made by Augustus underwent a number of adjustments. Tiberius placed these two provinces under the authority of the legate of Moesia, which would have relieved them of the considerable expenditures of the proconsul and his staff. They were restored to the Senate by Claudius in 44.

Haterius Agrippa: consul in AD 22, he was the son of Quintus Haterius. As tribune, he was able to invoke the privilege of vetoing legislation.

48 *not subject to floggings*: this is misleading. Augustus had imposed a restriction on magistrates wanting the authority to inflict summary scourging at any time. Actors could still be scourged if convicted of specific infractions.

theatre: actors were restricted to public performances, so that the state could maintain control over them.

temple: this was the first temple to be dedicated to the deified Augustus alone.

one per cent sales tax: the 1 per cent inheritance tax instituted by Augustus was very unpopular. Tiberius was under constant pressure to remove it and he does seem to have reduced it, but only temporarily, to 0.5 per cent. It was abolished by Caligula.

military treasury: the establishment of a treasury, funded by the 1 per cent tax, to provide soldiers' pensions was one of Augustus' deftest moves, since it removed the danger that discharged soldiers would look to their individual commanders to provide for them.

colonies: these were originally settlements of Roman veterans, but by this period the status could be conferred on other communities. They were distinguished from municipalities by greater privileges, in particular a greater degree of self-government.

49 *Poppaeus Sabinus*: consul in AD 9 and grandfather of Nero's second wife Poppaea, he served as Augustus' legate in Moesia for two years and was subsequently reappointed continuously by Tiberius for twenty-two years until his death in 35. Protracted periods of service were not a Tiberian

innovation. In about AD 6, Augustus had started to extend the terms of his legates to meet the crisis posed by the serious military situation in that year. Moesia comprised what is now Serbia and Bulgaria.

49 *for the first time*: candidates for AD 15 had been designated before Augustus died.

surmised: the precise procedure followed by Tiberius here is very obscure. Tacitus may possibly mean that Tiberius handed over all the names submitted to him and left it to the Senate to make the actual election, but the situation is far from clear.

BOOK TWO

50 *Parthians*: the events in Parthia during the period covered by the *Annals* are confused and obscure. In stating that difficulties started at this period, Tacitus simplifies. Eastern affairs had long been in chaos.

Arsacid family: the ruling dynasty of Parthia, named after Arsaces I (*c.*247–217). Phraates IV, who ruled from about 38 to 3/2 BC, handed over his children to the care of Augustus (Strabo 16.1.28). They included his son Vonones I, who ruled briefly in AD 8/9.

Crassus . . . Antonius: Crassus was defeated by the Parthians at the battle of Carrhae in 53 BC, and Antonius by Phraates IV in 36.

Artabanus: Artabanus II, ruler of Parthia AD 10/11–38.

51 *Artavasdes*: Artavasdes II came to power in 54 BC. He was captured by Antonius in 34 BC and handed over to Cleopatra, who put him to death.

Artaxias: Artaxias II ruled Armenia from 34 to 20 BC. On his assassination in 20 BC Tigranes III, also the son of Artavasdes, ruled until about 6 BC.

his children's: the children of Tigranes III, Tigranes IV and his sister Erato, ruled jointly from 6 BC as husband and wife. Their rule was a chequered one, as they at one point lost then regained their kingdom, and after Tigranes' death Erato briefly recovered the throne in her own right. Tacitus has chosen not to recount these complex events in detail.

Gaius Caesar: he was sent to the eastern province in 1 BC, and was wounded in Armenia in AD 3, dying of his wounds the following year. As ruler of Armenia he appointed Ariobarzanes, who died soon thereafter, to be succeeded by Artavasdes III, who remained until AD 12.

Creticus Silanus: Quintus Caecilius Metellus Creticus Silanus was consul in AD 7.

appropriate point: at 2.68.

For Tiberius . . . the vagaries of fortune: Tacitus' account of Germanicus' campaigns in AD 16 is not totally convincing, and he fails to explain why Germanicus withdrew his forces if his victories had been as decisive as presented. Another problem is Tacitus' failure to explain why so little use was made of the fleet, so carefully prepared. Finally, Tacitus' characterization of Tiberius' motives must be viewed with caution. The emperor no doubt feared that Germanicus was placing Roman troops in a seriously exposed position.

52 *Publius Vitellius*: see note to p. 43.

fleet: the ships used in AD 15 had proved unsuitable for coastal waters (1.70) and a new fleet had to be built.

Where it borders Germany: this is the Old Rhine, very minor, flowing through Leiden and Utrecht.

53 *Drusian Fosse*: this refers both to the canal, about two miles long, that Drusus built between the northern section of the Rhine and the Yssel, and also to the widened section of the Yssel itself.

left side: the passage is very confused and the precise picture that Tacitus is trying to convey has been much disputed.

Angrivarii: the reference is confusing. In 2.19 they are placed east of the Weser. For them to be to the rear of Germanicus at least part of the tribe must have been settled to the west of the river, as implied also by *Germ.* 34, which has them bordering the Frisians.

speak with his brother: the account is dubious, given the width of the Weser.

54 *Permission was granted*: some words have evidently dropped out of the text at this point. It must be assumed that in the missing section Flavus was accompanied down to the river.

55 *hundred sesterces*: that is, the equivalent of 25 denarii. Given that the annual pay for a legionary rate was 225 denarii, a promise of a daily rate of 25 would not have been taken very seriously. The mutineers in AD 14 demanded one denarius a day (1.17).

56 *no fighting*: with the friendship or neutrality of Maroboduus to the south and the Suebi beyond the Elbe there would be no serious opposition.

his father and his uncle: Drusus had reached the Elbe in 9 BC and Tiberius in AD 5.

57 *praetorian*: two praetorian cohorts had similarly been sent with Drusus to Illyricum (1.24).

58 *victory*: the speed with which the Germans regrouped demonstrates that this claim is highly exaggerated.

Imperator: Tiberius' coins do not in fact record an extra salutation until AD 20 (*Imperator VIII*) and the honour may have been declined on this occasion.

59 *Seius Tubero*: friend of Tiberius, relative of Sejanus (Velleius 2.127.3) and consul in AD 18. In Germany he had presumably replaced Lucius Apronius, who is recorded at this time in Rome (2.32).

60 *reducing the tribes*: this is a considerable exaggeration, since Germanicus had not even reached the Elbe and withdrew after each campaign.

How closely Tacitus follows the original wording of the inscription is not clear. The precedence of Mars over Jupiter might suggest some creativity.

60 *Angrivarii*: the MS reading here may be incorrect. The action is described as taking place 'presently', hence after the return to the Ems, and a reference here to a western section of the tribe must be assumed.

summer now far advanced: July. Germanicus returned early, presumably fearing the equinoctial gales he had experienced in the previous year (1.70).

islands: presumably near the mouth of the Ems or Weser. There is in fact no rocky island closer than Heligoland and the reference here is probably a piece of literary embellishment.

61 *Ocean*: the Romans thought of Oceanus as a great expanse of water that encircled the world. The term was used especially of the North Sea.

Chatti: Rome's most powerful German enemy at this time.

62 *return for the triumph*: Germanicus had been awarded a triumph in AD 15 (see 1.55). Tiberius was in an awkward position. He by now perhaps had reason to question Germanicus' competence as a commander in the field, but had to avoid any public confirmation of this lack of confidence.

Libo Drusus: the precise nature of Drusus' activities is difficult to determine. The Fasti of Amiternum (13 September) speak of his *nefaria consilia* ('wicked plans') against Tiberius and his family and other leading citizens. By focusing on the charges about astrologers and passing over those of conspiracy, Tacitus plays down the seriousness of the case against Libo. Seneca comments that he lacked imagination (*stolidus*) and had ambitions far beyond his talents (*Ep.* 70.10).

63 *Chaldeans*: the name of this ancient people of Babylonia is frequently used as a synonym for astrologers.

Pompey: Libo's mother Pompeia was the daughter of Sextus Pompeius and of Scribonia, niece of Augustus' first wife; hence Libo would have been a distant cousin of Julia (Scribonia's daughter by Augustus). It has been argued that he was the champion of a disaffected Julian faction. There was a further link to the imperial family, in that his father had been adopted by Marcus Livius Drusus Claudianus, father of Livia.

a praetorship: it is not clear to what year this refers; it is likely that he had been designated praetor for the following year, but a praetorship in 16 cannot be ruled out.

dinner-parties: a prized honour. Vespasian is said to have thanked Caligula publicly for just such an invitation (Suetonius, *Vesp.* 2).

Fulcinius Trio: a notorious *delator* and consul in 31 at the time of Sejanus' fall, he will reappear on a number of occasions, and will commit suicide in 35 (3.10, 19; 5.11; 6.38).

64 *Gaius Vibius*: he later became governor of Spain (4.13).

one by one: this would ensure that the charges would be argued separately without a lengthy speech from either side.

torture: slaves were obliged to give their testimony under torture even if they were willing to volunteer it. Otherwise it would not be valid.

old decree: even in Cicero's time there were exceptions to the rule that slaves could not testify against their master. The restriction was waived in cases involving incest and in special situations such as conspiracy.

legal precedents: Dio (55.5.4) in fact claims that this device was employed by Augustus as early as 8 BC.

treasury agent: Tacitus' term is *actor publicus*, an official whose responsibilities are unknown.

Publius Quirinius: Publius Sulpicius Quirinius was consul in 12 BC, married to Aemilia Lepida, a descendant, like Libo, of Pompey (see 3.22, 48).

65 *swore*: it is by no means clear why Tiberius needed to make this declaration on oath.

divided: traditionally, the estate of those who committed suicide before condemnation was not confiscated, but the accusers were still entitled to a share, usually one-fourth. Unusually, in this case the whole estate seems to have been divided among them.

Cotta Messalinus: consul in AD 20, son of the famous Corvinus (see note to p. 8), he was much despised by Tacitus, though admired by Ovid. He will reappear several times in the *Annals* (4.20, 5.3, 6.5).

image: a similar restriction was placed on the effigies of Brutus and Cassius (3.76), which could be owned privately but not displayed in public.

cognomen: this prohibition had republican antecedents. According to Dio, in 30 BC it was decreed that no member of the *gens* Antonia could carry the *praenomen* of Marcus.

Pomponius Flaccus: consul in 17.

Gallus Asinius: see note to p. 8.

Lucius Apronius: see note to p. 34.

decrees: Dio (57.15.8) describes the stringent measures taken against astrologers.

rock: the Tarpeian Rock, from which condemned criminals were hurled.

ancient manner: the head was fastened by the neck in a fork and the body beaten to death with rods. This form of death was decreed for Nero (Suetonius, *Nero* 49).

Quintus Haterius: see note to p. 12.

vessels for serving food: a distinction was made between the plate used at banquets and that intended for sacred rituals.

66 *Lucius Piso*: (augur), consul in 1 BC and brother of Gnaeus Piso (see note to p. 12), whom he will defend in his trial for the murder of Germanicus. Himself charged in 24, Lucius died before his own case was heard (4.21).

Urgulania: the grandmother of Claudius' wife Plautia Urgulanilla and of the consul Plautius Urgulanius.

Augusta: during Augustus' lifetime Livia had projected an image of self-effacing modesty. As Tiberius' reign progressed, she became increasingly conscious of her elevated status.

67 *Vestal Virgins*: Tacitus does not introduce Urgulania as a Vestal, but his comment, that the action taken did not conform to the usual practice applied to Vestals, implies very strongly that she belonged to the order.

suspension of public business: a reference to the vacation of the law courts and the Senate. An embarrassing point had arisen that if the vacation was timed to suit the convenience of the emperor it would coincide with the presence in Rome of a large number of Italians and provincials with legal business to be concluded.

five-year period: the precise nature of Asinius' proposal is not clear. Tacitus seems to suggest that it would somehow have limited Tiberius' authority. It was perhaps intended that all the magistracies for the next five years would be assigned, and that in succeeding years magistrates would be elected annually five years ahead. This would presumably ensure a greater independence among the men elected, since they would not depend on the *immediate* favour of the emperor.

68 *Marcius Hortalus*: his family had suffered many vicissitudes. The orator Hortensius was famously wealthy and extravagant. His son Quintus was killed at the battle of Philippi and the family property was presumably confiscated through proscription. A grandson, Hortensius Corbio, was a notorious pervert.

Palatium: the meeting would have taken place in the library in the portico of the Temple of Apollo on the Palatine Hill, where the images of great orators were displayed. Meetings of the Senate in this location were especially common in the later years of Augustus.

eloquence: it was said that only Hortensius' daughter inherited his eloquence (Val. Max. 8.3.3).

dictators: much exaggerated. In fact, from the Hortensii only one dictator (287 BC), one consul (69 BC), and one consul-designate (108 BC) can be found in the record. The Marcii could claim one dictator (356 BC).

69 *Agrippa was alive*: such fraudulent survivals were a feature of the period. Germanicus' son, Drusus, was similarly said to have survived (5.10) and a pseudo-Nero emerged after the death of that emperor (Suetonius, *Nero* 57; Tacitus, *Hist.* 2.8; Dio 66.19.3).

70 *his own slave*: Agrippa's slaves would have belonged to the *familia* of his adoptive father, Augustus; on the death of Agrippa, they would have passed to Tiberius as Augustus' heir.

standards: see 1.60, 2.25. The third eagle was in fact recovered under Claudius (Dio 60.8).

70 *Bovillae*: the association with the Julii is explained by the claim of the town to be a daughter city of Alba Longa, founded by Iulus, the son of Aeneas.

71 *triumph*: this was something of a sham, and the fact that Arminius, still pursuing the war, was not one of the captives, should have been a clear sign of how fraudulent it was.

Drusus's advantage . . . Marcellus: Drusus had died in 9 BC at the age of 30 and Marcellus in 21 BC at 20 (see notes to p. 4).

fifty years: presumably Tacitus is counting up to the accession of Tiberius in AD 14, since Archelaus was established in Cappadocia by Antonius in 36 BC. Augustus had enlarged Archelaus' kingdom with the addition of Armenia Minor and part of Cilicia.

impeached: the charges are unknown, as is the outcome. Archelaus may have died during the course of the trial.

72 *reduced*: Dio (58.16.2) claims that the tax was raised to its former amount after the fall of Sejanus.

Commagene: this was the final remnant of the great empire of the Seleucids, with whom Antiochus claimed kinship.

Philopator: he in fact held only a minor principality to the west of Cilicia.

declining years: the tone is exaggerated. Tiberius was only 59, Germanicus 31, Drusus about 29.

greater authority: the Piso Decree records that Germanicus would have greater *imperium* in any province he passed through than the proconsul of that province (*Senatus Consultum de Cn. Pisone Patre* 34–5).

Gnaeus Piso: see note to p. 14; he held the consulship with Tiberius in 7 BC and served at some point as governor of Africa. In some accounts he was one of those considered by Augustus as a potential successor and bold enough to accept it if it was offered. If there were secret instructions given to Piso they may have been more benign than as described by Tacitus, and may merely have commissioned him to act as a senior adviser to Germanicus in order to try to avert a repetition of the German adventures.

consulship: the father was consul in 23 BC.

Plancina: a close friend of Livia and daughter of the Munatius Plancus who had headed the commission sent in AD 14 to investigate the mutinies in Germany (see 1.39).

73 *Pomponius Atticus*: Marcus Agrippa's first wife was Pomponia; their daughter Vipsania was the first wife of Tiberius and mother of Drusus.

Livilla: confusingly, Tacitus calls her Livia, but the form Livilla is found in Suetonius and Dio and their practice is followed here for the sake of clarity. She was the daughter of the elder Drusus, brother of Tiberius.

Illyricum: the nature of Drusus' command is not made clear. It presumably included Pannonia, perhaps also Noricum, Raetia, and Moesia.

73 *Maroboduus*: Tacitus implies that his request for help was only a pretext for Drusus' mission, but in fact his kingdom was close to collapse, and opened up an opportunity for the Romans.

74 *twelve legions*: this seems to be an exaggeration, although it cannot be ruled out entirely. In AD 6 there were five legions in Germany, two in Raetia, and five in Illyricum, but it is unlikely that all would have been used.

equal terms: in AD 6 the initial plan had been to crush the newly emerged power of Maroboduus; the projected invasion had to be cancelled because of the major rebellion of Pannonia and Dalmatia, which was seen to pose a direct threat to Italy.

earthquake: the catastrophe of this year and Tiberius' generosity in dealing with it are covered in other sources: Strabo 13.3.5, 4.8; Seneca, *QN* 6.1.13; Pliny, *NH* 2. 200; Bianor, *Anthologia Palatina* 9.423; Phlegon 36 J; Suetonius, *Tib.* 48.2; Dio 57.17.7; Jerome, *Chronicle* P. 172H.

75 *treasury or imperial exchequer*: the distinction between the public treasury and the emperor's private funds grew difficult to maintain, since the emperor's income derived in large part from sources that might seem to belong more properly to the state, but was at the same time used to finance many public enterprises.

Aemilia Musa: the name Musa suggests that she was a freedwoman. It may be that the family of her former owner could not be definitively established and thus her property would fall to the state. Her name may simply have provided a pretext for Tiberius to help a noble family in need.

Aemilius Lepidus: he is presumably the Lepidus, probably Marcus Aemilius Lepidus, referred to later as being of limited means (3.72; see note to p. 12).

Marcus Servilius: consul in AD 3, possibly father of the consul of 35.

Liber, Libera, and Ceres: this temple was reputedly vowed by Aulus Postumius before the battle of Regillus in 496 BC and built three years later.

Publicius: the brothers Lucius and Marcus are said to have imposed fines for the illegal occupation of public lands and to have used the proceeds to establish the festival of Flora in 241 or 238 BC.

76 *Gaius Duilius*: he defeated the Carthaginians at the battle of Mylae in 260 BC.

Aulus Atilius: he was consul in 258 or 257 and 254 BC, and dictator in 249.

Appuleia Varilla . . . sister: in fact, she was the granddaughter of the elder Octavia, his half-sister (his full sister was the younger Octavia).

Julian law: the law (*de Adulteriis et Stupris*) was passed by Augustus in 17 BC as part of his policy to regulate Roman morality. The implication is that Tiberius did not wish her adultery to be considered under the heading of *maiestas*.

heavier penalty: one-third of her property and half her dowry, and relegation to an island.

tradition: this refers, not to the penalty, which would have been more severe in earlier times, but to the role given to the relatives.

Haterius Agrippa: Haterius' father was married to a daughter of Agrippa. Agrippina, Germanicus' wife, was also Agrippa's daughter.

law: the *Lex Papia Poppaea*, which among other things gave fathers an advantage in appointments, and accelerated their prospects according to the number of children they had (see 3.25, 28).

Tacfarinas: we have little information about him beyond what Tacitus provides. His previous service with the Romans parallels the career of Arminius. He was a formidable adversary.

77 *legion*: unusually Africa, although a senatorial province, housed a legion, the Ninth, at this time under the command of the proconsul.

regainer: Furius Camillus defeated the Gauls after the battle of the Allia in 390 BC. In fact, the grandson of this Furius had celebrated a triumph in 338 BC, but Tacitus seems to confuse him with his son. Marcus Furius Camillus, the descendant, was consul in AD 8.

consul: Tiberius was consul for only a few days, and was succeeded by Lucius Seius Tubero.

as I noted: see 2.43.

78 *lictor*: Germanicus would normally have been attended by twelve lictors. The usual tradition for a magistrate when entering a 'free' city, such as Athens, would be to have no lictors. The single lictor, the appurtenance of a priest, did not enforce official authority, and was in a sense equivalent to none at all.

Samothracian Mysteries: the rituals are those of the mystery religion of the Cabiri.

our own origins: Aeneas, the founder of the Roman nation, escaped from Ilium/Troy as it fell.

disasters: Attica suffered severely from Philip of Macedon (359–336) and Athens itself was stormed by Sulla in 86 BC.

trashy collection: the notoriously easy purchase of Athenian citizenship had been prohibited by Augustus (Dio 54.7.2).

79 *Polemo*: Polemo I had received his kingdom of Pontus and Armenia Minor from Antonius, and Augustus had added the Bosporus. He died about 8/7 BC and the kingdom was then ruled by his widow Pythodoris, assisted by her son, Polemo II, who succeeded her. Zeno, their other son, proved a highly successful monarch.

80 *Quintus Veranius*: Veranius was an ally of Germanicus (2.74, 3.10–19). Soon after these events he was back in Rome (2.74).

80 *a praetor*: Commagene was under the jurisdiction of the legate of Syria, who held the rank of propraetor.

Quintus Servaeus: he was not appointed as permanent governor. He would later be involved in the prosecution of Piso (see 3.13, 19), and eventually be accused of being an ally of Sejanus (6.7).

81 *concern*: Suetonius (*Tib.* 52) in fact speaks of a very serious famine, which Tacitus seems to downplay.

Publius Scipio: Livy ascribes this behaviour to Scipio under 204 BC (29.19.11–13).

permission: senators were not allowed to enter Egypt without the permission of the emperor.

82 *Rhamses*: Rhamses II, the great Egyptian king of the Nineteenth Dynasty, in the thirteenth century BC. Tacitus refers to his territories as stretching from the Black Sea (Pontus) to the northern Mediterranean.

Memnon: the reference is to one of two enormous seated statues of Amenophis III (1417–1379), identified as Memnon by the Greeks. The upper part had broken off in an earthquake, possibly in 27 BC, and consequently the lower part at sunrise emitted a sound like that of a broken harp string, until the statue was repaired by Septimius Severus, which brought the musical performances to an end.

lake: Lake Moeris; see Herodotus 2.149–50.

depths: Herodotus (2.28.4–5) tells the story of Psammeticus, who attempted to determine the depth of the Nile with a rope.

Red Sea: Tacitus might be referring to the modern Red Sea, or to the Persian Gulf. If the latter he would be writing after AD 116, to reflect Trajan's conquests in that area.

that year: there is a serious chronological problem in the following chapters. Germanicus' Egyptian tour clearly took place in AD 19, but the opening of chapter 62 refers to activities in AD 18. Also, the reports of Maroboduus' fall and the elevation of Artaxias reach Rome at the same time (chapter 64), but a year divides the two events. Moreover, Drusus left for Illyricum in AD 17, but nothing is apparently heard of him until 19. Some transpose chapters 62–7 to follow 58, so as to place events in Germany and Thrace in AD 18.

enemy territory: an interesting aspect of Tacitus' (or Drusus') preconceptions; the area had not been hostile since AD 6.

trading privileges: these were probably granted in the agreement between Maroboduus and Rome in AD 6.

83 *Philip*: see note to p. 78.

Pyrrhus or Antiochus: Pyrrhus, king of Epirus, fought a series of campaigns against the Romans between 280 and 275 BC. Antiochus III (the Great), who succeeded to the Seleucid throne in 223, fought against the Romans in Greece and Asia Minor between 191 and 188 BC.

Rhoemetalces: he died in AD 12.

85 *Cotys' wife*: Antonia Tryphaena, daughter of Polemo and Pythodoris.

sons of Cotys: Rhoemetalces, Cotys, and Polemo. They did not return to Thrace but were held by Tiberius in Rome and raised with Caligula, who would later be their generous supporter (*Inscriptiones Graecae ad Res Romanas Pertinentes* 4.145).

Marcus Lepidus: consul in 187 and 175 BC, reputedly sent to be guardian of the sons of Ptolemy Epiphanes on the latter's death in 181 (Val. Max. 6.6.1, Justin 30.3.4). The story is doubted by modern authorities.

mentioned above: at 2.58.

senior soldier: a veteran cited for special service, with the status and insignia of a centurion.

86 *decided to leave*: the Piso Decree states that Piso deserted Syria while Germanicus was still alive (*Senatus Consultum de Cn. Pisone Patre* 47–9); Tacitus, however, claims (2.70) that most authorities say that Germanicus ordered Piso from the province, and his friends after his death made the assumption that Piso had been dismissed.

Piso . . . remove: Piso's actions are baffling. It may be that we have a distorted account of public demonstrations that got out of hand.

lead tablets: these were used for 'defixions' by which the image of the targeted person was transfixed by a nail. Alternatively the name was written on the tablet with curses.

children: in addition to the infant Julia Livilla, Germanicus was accompanied by Caligula. His other children had stayed in Rome.

renouncing: this was a formal act between individuals, and even between states.

87 *pride*: an interesting admission that Agrippina was tactless and undiplomatic.

expired: 10 October AD 19.

his leniency with the enemy: Tacitus' generous assessment is not borne out by Germanicus' savagery in Germany (1.51, 2.21).

88 *thirty*: Germanicus died in his thirty-fourth year, Alexander in his thirty-third.

poisoning: Suetonius (*Cal.* 1) reports that there were dark spots on the body and foam at the mouth, and that the heart would not burn. The last point was used by the prosecution at Piso's trial to prove poisoning (Pliny, *NH* 11.187).

discussion . . . Syria: it appears that in the case of a sudden vacancy in provincial command, authority fell on the senators present, who could appoint an interim legate. Sentius' appointment was confirmed by Tiberius, and inscriptional evidence places him still in office in AD 21 (*CIL* 3.6703). Gaius Vibius Marsus was consul in AD 17 and later governor of Africa (27–30); see 6.47–8, 11.10. It is curious that Germanicus did not appoint Piso's successor.

89 *Centurions*: these would be from the Syrian legions, presumably men who owed their promotion to Piso.

taken from him: this seems to confirm the suggestions recorded in chapter 70 that Germanicus had formally deprived him of the province.

legate's authority: the advice of Celer does suggest very strongly that there was a genuine confusion over the precise authority of Germanicus in Syria. Celer's argument is that Germanicus could not countermand an official commission from the emperor.

90 *deserters*: the surprising allusion to large numbers of deserters suggests that Tacitus has given us a heavily edited account of the events in Syria.

the petty kings of the Cilicians: since the death of Philopator there remained only two kingdoms in Cilicia: Olba and Trachaea, in the western part of the province, ruled by Archelaus of Cappadocia.

when the praetor . . . and his accusers: Piso responds to Vibius with a double taunt, in which he is technically correct, that any case would follow the normal formalities of the law and Vibius' citations would have force only when a day had been determined for the appearance of both parties, usually the tenth day after the charges were received. Piso would doubtless have realized that, if there was deemed to be a case, it would almost certainly be taken directly to the emperor or, at the very least, to the Senate.

91 *veteran*: Tacitus seems to be using the word in a non-technical sense of experienced soldiers, in contrast to raw recruits.

fleet: the reference is to the *Classis Syriaca*, mentioned in inscriptions.

Drusus: he allegedly had republican sympathies (see 1.33); Suetonius (*Claud.* 1.4) links these sympathies to the rumour of his poisoning, a rumour he rejects, and Livy (*Per.* 142) asserts that his death was an accident.

92 *mourning*: the Fasti of Ostia record that a period of mourning was declared on 10 December, in AD 19, following the death on 10 October, which is surprising, since it would hardly have taken two months for the news to reach Rome from Alexandria. Suetonius (*Cal.* 6) reports that the period of mourning lasted through the Saturnalia, in December, to the following March, although that may have represented informal mourning.

Honours: on the honours decreed for Germanicus, see Introduction, p. xxiii.

Saliarian hymn: a primitive hymn, unintelligible by this period, performed by the Salii, an ancient priestly group. Augustus' name had been inserted into it during his lifetime, perhaps as early as 29 BC (Dio 51.20.1); whether other emperors were routinely added is uncertain, although we do know that Verus, son of Marcus Aurelius, was included (*Historia Augusta: Marcus Aurelius*. 21.5).

curule chairs: the curule chairs were crowned and placed in the theatre at feasts. A place would be set aside for Germanicus among the priests of Augustus since he had been a member of the college.

statue: an ivory figure of Julius Caesar was paraded during his lifetime (*RG* 10.1; Suetonius, *Jul.* 76; Dio 43.45.2) and the same honour was decreed for several members of the imperial family.

flamen: Germanicus was succeeded as *Flamen Augustalis* by Drusus.

Epidaphna: a strange error. The famous grove of Apollo some miles from Antioch led that city to be identified (in Greek) as *Antiochia epi Daphnes*.

leading orators: in the portico of the Palatine library (see note to p. 68). The *Tabula Hebana* records that the images of Germanicus and Drusus would be placed among those of famous men in the Palatine portico. These images would have been painted on shields.

block: *cuneus* (literally 'wedge') seems to refer to the section of the theatre occupied in fourteen rows by the knights, as established by the *Lex Roscia* of 67 BC, arranged in a junior and a senior section (see 6.3). The honour would be appropriate to Germanicus since he had been a *princeps iuventutis* ('leader of the youth' (Ovid, *Ex P.* 2.5.41)).

squadrons: this would be the parade of equestrians held on 15 July, as revived by Augustus.

93 *twins of the male sex*: one of them, Germanicus, died in infancy (4.15); the other, Tiberius Gemellus, would be put to death under Caligula. Tacitus' date for the birth (AD 19) is disputed, since Gemellus is said not to have reached puberty in 37, when he would have been 17 by this reckoning. Tacitus may have put the births here for dramatic effect. It is possible, however, that Gemellus was not very advanced for his age and that his puberty was late.

aediles: as magistrates responsible for the administration of the city, they had charge of establishments like brothels or taverns. The passage seems to suggest that they kept a register of prostitutes. By proclaiming herself a prostitute, a woman might seek to escape the charges associated with adultery.

law: under the *Lex Julia* a husband was obliged to divorce an adulterous wife within sixty days or be assumed to have condoned her action. Such condoning was generally tolerated; this case must have been felt to be a particularly outrageous one.

Egyptian and Jewish rites: this topic is of relatively minor interest to Tacitus and he thus deals with it rather cursorily. By contrast, Josephus (*AJ* 18.3.4.5) gives a detailed account of the two scandals that precipitated the action, the rape of a Roman lady in the Temple of Isis (subsequently demolished by Tiberius) and the embezzlement of funds sent by a Roman noblewoman to Jerusalem. Philo (*Leg.* 23, 24) speaks of a Jewish persecution, which he ascribes to Sejanus. Fears of proselytism probably underlay both incidents.

93 *fifty-seven years*: Vestals were chosen between 6 and 10 years old and were legally enjoined for thirty years, after which they could leave and marry, but usually continued in the office.

94 *grain*: the payment of compensation to merchants to keep the price of grain low was a device employed by other emperors (*RG* 5.2; Suetonius, *Aug.* 41.2; *Claud.* 18.2–19).

earlier: see 1.72.

'the lord': Dio (57.8) records that Tiberius said he was 'lord' only to his slaves.

generals of old: Livy (*Per.* 13) attributes the prohibition on poison to Gaius Fabricius, consul 282 and 278 BC.

his power twelve: his power would date from the defeat of Varus, and so his death must have occurred in AD 21, but is included here since this is the last reference to him in the *Annals*.

BOOK THREE

95 *With no interruption*: uniquely for the Tiberian books, Book 3 opens without the usual mention of the consuls to designate the year (AD 20). The preliminary events of this book may in fact belong to AD 19. Tacitus' intention clearly is to focus attention on Agrippina's dramatic arrival and to place the emphasis securely on the aftermath of the death of Germanicus.

the winter sea: the seas were technically closed to shipping until 10 March (the prohibition was at times ignored) and were considered dangerous until 27 May.

two children: Caligula accompanied his parents on the eastern missions and Agrippina had given birth to Livilla on the island of Lesbos.

Germanicus' ashes: Tacitus describes the carrying of the ashes from Brundisium to Rome as if it were part of a formal funeral procession. The event would have evoked memory of the funeral procession of his father Drusus, who had similarly died far from Rome (in Germany) and was brought back to the city in a similar pageant. Tacitus is no doubt stressing the continuity between Germanicus and Drusus, both of whom were charismatic individuals with supposedly republican leanings.

trabea: a short garment, mainly purple, worn as a formal garment by the equestrians.

96 *consuls*: mentioned parenthetically here instead of in their usual position at the beginning of the book.

concealing it: Tiberius' dissembling nature is a common motif of the Tacitean account, and a useful weapon of denigration since even generous acts can be criticized as being insincere.

Antonia: Tacitus' hostility to Tiberius and his mother borders on the irrational in this passage. He claims that out of spite they did not appear in public, although he does not specify the event from which they were conspicuously absent. He notes that there is no record of Antonia having appeared in public either, but dismisses the plausible explanation that she was ill and assumes that she was restrained in the palace by Tiberius to create a kind of parity of behaviour. In fact the *Tabula Siarensis*, a document that records the posthumous honours voted for Germanicus, shows that Tiberius played an active role in selecting the tributes from the list proposed by the Senate, and records also that he consulted Livia and Antonia, among others, in the process. Clearly all three were involved in the conferring of the honours (see Introduction, p. xxiii).

Drusus, and Claudius: curiously enough Claudius is *not* mentioned in the *Tabula Siarensis* although, as Tacitus says, Tiberius' son Drusus is recorded as being involved.

the tomb of Augustus: Augustus' mausoleum, the ruins of which are still visible, was the resting place for a number of members of the Julio-Claudian family, including Germanicus' father Drusus.

Campus Martius: bodies could not be buried within the city of Rome. Burials could take place on the Campus Martius since it lay outside the *pomerium* or city boundary.

lone survivor of Augustus' bloodline: in fact Julia, the other granddaughter of Augustus, was still alive, but in disgrace. Agrippina herself never missed an opportunity to boast of her Augustan descent.

97 *state funeral*: the funeral of Germanicus had already been held in the previous year, and the supposed complaint seems to be that Tiberius did not allow a second national funeral, which would have conflicted with Roman practice.

Ticinum: Pavia. It is striking that Tacitus omits entirely Tiberius' own journey across the Alps to visit his brother's sickbed, and his return all the way to Rome in the company of the corpse. He transfers the harshness of the journey to the far more modest expedition of Augustus to Ticinum to meet the cortège.

brother: Germanicus' natural brother Claudius is ignored. The reference here is to Tiberius' son, Germanicus' brother by adoption.

uncle: Tacitus' reference here to Tiberius' natural, rather than legal, relationship to Germanicus (father) is deliberate.

effigy: it was the custom to set a wax image of the deceased above the bier. This is recorded for the funerals of both Caesar and Augustus.

only daughter: Caesar's daughter Julia was married to Pompey, and died in childbirth in 54 BC.

grandchildren: Gaius and Lucius Caesar.

Megalesian Games: the celebration of the Megalesian Games, in honour of the eastern goddess Cybele, began on 4 April and ended on 10 April. There seems to have been an informal period of mourning that began with the first news of Germanicus' death the previous year. Tacitus' reference must surely be to this. A suspension of public business (*iustitium*) was instituted on 10 December (see note to p. 91) but it is unlikely to have remained in place until now.

98 *Illyricum*: Drusus had been given a command in Illyricum in AD 17. His sojourn on this occasion was brief. He departed from Rome after the Megalesian Games in early April and was in the city by 28 May to celebrate his ovation, or minor triumph.

  Africa: the Ninth Legion was temporarily moved from Pannonia to Africa to deal with the resumption of hostilities by Tacfarinas.

99 *criminal proceedings*: the case against Piso could have been handled before a jury presided over by a praetor, or by the Senate, presided over by the consuls, or by the emperor, meeting in camera. The last course was chosen, supposedly to the satisfaction of Piso, reasoning that Tiberius had been privy to the murder. Tiberius typically transferred the task to the Senate.

  the previous summer: AD 19; the decree for the ovation of Drusus is mentioned at 2.64, and the implication seems to be that Drusus' exploits belong to 18, in which case Tacitus' reference here to the previous summer must be in error. Much ingenuity has been exercised over this problem, which remains unresolved.

  advocates: Piso clearly had powerful friends, if not permanent ones. Of the eight names mentioned, Lucius Arruntius, Asinius Gallus (see note to p. 8), and Marcus Lepidus (see note to p. 12) had all been cited by Augustus as potential successors; three others had held the consulship: Lucius Calpurnius Piso, brother of the defendant (1 BC), Publius Vinicius (AD 2), and Sextus Pompeius (AD 14). Marcus Claudius Marcellus Aeserninus was praetor in AD 19.

100 *help*: Tiberius refers to Piso being appointed as helper (*adiutor*) to Germanicus. The imprecise nature of his role and the dividing lines between their two sets of responsibilities may have been the root cause of many of the problems between the two men.

  to recover the province: the appointment of Gnaeus Sentius Saturninus as legate of Syria following Piso's initial departure would have made Piso's attempt to recover the province an act of treason.

101 *Curia*: confusingly, the official Senate building, the Curia, was in fact located in the Forum. Here Tacitus is using *Curia* symbolically. The meeting probably took place in the temple of Apollo on the Palatine, a customary location at the time.

  Spain: Piso was legate of Hispania Tarraconensis in AD 9/10. The two charges laid against him for his conduct during that period, avarice and political ambitions, were stock complaints against governors.

  Vitellius: we know from Pliny (*NH* 11.187) that one of the arguments used by Vitellius was that Piso must have poisoned Germanicus because his heart would not burn, a detail not recorded by Tacitus, and easily countered by Piso with the assertion that hearts similarly did not burn easily following natural death (see note to p. 88).

above him: the main guest would be seated immediately to the left of the host.

102 *Gemonian Steps*: the bodies of executed criminals were dragged down the Gemonian stairs (the 'Steps of Groaning') before being thrown into the Tiber. Notoriously, Sejanus suffered this fate.

Augusta: the Pisonian Decree vindicates Tacitus here, since the Senate recorded that their actions towards Plancina were in response to a request from Livia.

I remember: it is generally assumed that Tacitus was born just after the mid-fifties AD (see Introduction). In that case his recollection cannot be dated to earlier than about 70, by which time the trial would have been over for five decades. It is worth noting also that Tacitus does not cite elderly men who had actually seen the document, but rather individuals who reported hearsay to the effect that it had been seen.

103 *Gnaeus Piso*: he not only escaped his father's fate, but went on to enjoy a successful political career, including a consulship in AD 27. Marcus was similarly spared, but in his case his association with Piso's behaviour perhaps cost him a career, since he did not apparently hold later office.

joint consulship: Piso held the consulship as colleague of Tiberius in 7 BC.

104 *the consul Aurelius Cotta*: Tacitus is a little obscure here. Normally the presiding consul would put the question and the consul-designate would have the right to first response. The implication is that on this occasion Tiberius was presiding and that the regular consul therefore had the right of speaking first.

half his property: the Piso decree indicates that in fact the whole estate was confiscated, and that half was then returned to the younger Gnaeus.

praenomen: he took the name of Lucius (see 4.62).

rank: Marcus had not yet held the consulship, but as the son of a consul he would have been entitled to wear the *laticlavus*, the broad-striped toga.

Iullus Antonius: the son of Marcus Antonius had committed adultery with Julia (see note to p. 10).

Valerius Messalinus: this may be the consul of this year, or, as many scholars believe, his father.

Caecina Severus: the commander in Germany, who will propose that wives not accompany the governors of provinces during their term (see below, chapter 33).

Claudius: the Piso Decree reveals that Claudius is mentioned last in the list of members of the family who are to be praised.

Lucius Asprenas: see note to p. 33.

104 *priesthoods*: this passage shows that the emperor exercised the right of commendation in nominations for priesthoods.

105 *Drusus*: he celebrated his ovation on 28 May, as is recorded in the Fasti. Tacitus' narrative places the ovation after the trial. This presents us with a problem, since the Piso Decree is equally securely dated to 10 December, and seems to suggest that the trial began in late November. Some have argued that the Piso Decree records a meeting of the Senate held much later than the trial itself.

Vipsania: see note to p. 4.

killed: the reference is to Agrippa's children with Julia—Gaius and Lucius Caesar, Agrippa Postumus, Julia the Younger and Agrippina the Elder, all of whom had, according to rumour, died through political murder.

previous summer: Tacitus seems to be in error here, as the campaign of Camillus belongs one year earlier, in AD 17. See 2.52.

Lucius Apronius: see note to p. 34.

ten men: the practice of decimation was said to have been introduced by Appius Claudius in the wars against the Volsci (see Livy 2.59).

106 *the civic crown*: the civic crown of oak-leaves was granted to a soldier who had saved the life of a comrade in battle under very specific conditions. Since Africa was a senatorial province, its governor was not a legate of Tiberius and was therefore entitled to bestow the honour in his own name. The award was made only rarely, and Helvius afterwards adopted the *cognomen* Civica.

Lepida: Publius Sulpicius Quirinius, a man of consular rank (see note to p. 64) had been divorced from Aemilia Lepida some time before this case. He had been considerably older than his wife, perhaps forty years, and had died in his seventies in the following year. The case described here is confusing. It is not clear whether the child in question was Lepida's, how old it was, or what she might have been hoping to achieve if there had indeed been deception. There may have been an issue of inheritance. For Manius Lepidus, mentioned below, see note to p. 12.

astrologers . . . household: this was a capital offence (see also 2.27).

opinion first: as consul-designate, Drusus would have the task of giving his opinion first. Cynics at the time claimed that, in recusing himself from giving an opinion first in any given case, Drusus was indirectly sending a signal that he was doing so because he would have voted to condemn.

games: these are probably the *Ludi Romani*, which ran 4–19 September.

theatre: the theatre of Pompey, originally built by her great-grandfather Pompey.

107 *Rubellius Blandus*: consul in AD 18, he went on to marry Julia, daughter of Tiberius' son Drusus, in 33 (see 3.51, 6.27).

Scaurus: Mamercus Aemilius Scaurus must have married Lepida after her divorce from Quirinius.

daughter and granddaughter: Julia the Elder had died in AD 6. Julia the Younger, banished in AD 8, lived until 28 (see note to p. 176). Numerous lovers are recorded for the elder Julia. Only Decimus Silanus is recorded for the younger.

own legislation: the *Lex Iulia* (see 2.50).

Marcus Silanus: consul AD 15, Marcus Junius Silanus was later father-in-law of Caligula through his daughter Junia Claudilla.

108 *Lex Papia Poppaea*: this law, passed in AD 9, modified a previous *Lex de Maritandis Ordinibus* and was part of Augustus' social legislation, intended to discourage childlessness (although it was in fact proposed by two childless consuls). Various privileges were granted to married people and parents of children, and economic and social penalties were applied to those who remained unmarried or childless. The later law excluded the unmarried from succession under a will. Its provisions were unduly stringent. Augustus' measures were no doubt intended to increase the stock of Roman citizens. Tacitus sees them as a cynical ploy to increase the revenue of the treasury.

laws: Tacitus adopts the traditional position that law is a function of modern society, which begins with a primitive period before morality declined.

Minos . . . Solon: Minos and Lycurgus are both examples of men who enacted laws; how their roles fit into the scheme described by Tacitus is far from clear. Solon was archon of Athens 594/3 BC; his state does seem to fit the category of those people who wearied of kings and chose laws.

Romulus: traditional founder of Rome, associated in legend with his twin brother Remus. After his death he was deified as the god Quirinus.

Numa: the second king of Rome is probably a historical figure but it is likely that many of the reforms that are ascribed specifically to him, in fact, reflect a long period of evolution.

Tullus: Tullus Hostilius, the third king of Rome. The legal reforms ascribed to him may be pure invention.

Ancus: traditionally the fourth king of Rome, possibly legendary, and perhaps confused with Numa. His legal contributions seem to have been minimal, beyond the building of the first permanent prison in Rome.

Servius Tulius: strictly, Servius, the sixth king of Rome, could be said to have been seen by tradition as someone who established a *constitution* rather than individual laws, although in his case also the tradition may not be reliable.

Tarquin's: Tarquinius Superbus, according to tradition expelled in 510 BC.

109 *Decemvirs*: see note to p. 3.

Gracchi . . . Drusus: the Gracchi brothers, Tiberius (tribune of the plebs in 133) and Gaius (tribune in 123), have earned an important place in history as advocates of much needed land reform in late-second-century BC Rome.

Tacitus characterizes them as demagogues, along with Lucius Apuleius Saturninus, an aggressive reformer a generation later, tribune of the plebs in 103 and 100 BC. Marcus Livius Drusus, tribune in 91, was a famous reformer (Tacitus may have added elements that more strictly belong to his father), most notably in his championing of the rights of the Italians. The failure of his measures paved the way for the Social War.

109 *Lucius Sulla*: the dictator Lucius Cornelius Sulla initiated considerable legislation, much of it with a brief life, such as his attempt to limit the veto of the tribunes and their right to initiate legislation.

Lepidus: consul in 78 BC, Marcus Aemilius Lepidus attempted to restore the tribunician powers that Sulla had repealed.

Pompey: he was elected sole consul in 52 *in absentia*, a unique procedure. He initiated legislation to end corruption at elections but the extension of his own *imperium* for five years and dispensation from the rule that candidates for office canvass in person created an impression of hypocrisy.

twenty years: from the battle of Pharsalus (48 BC) to the sixth consulship of Augustus (28 BC), who terminated the acts of the triumvirs in a single stroke. The period of Julius Caesar, who was an energetic legislator, is consigned to the general period of anarchy.

110 *Nero*: the eldest son of Germanicus was born in AD 6 and was thus 14 years old in AD 20, at which age the toga of manhood could normally be assumed.

vigintivirate: a collective term for a number of minor official functionaries, twenty under Augustus (twenty-six previously). Usually the tenure of one of these minor posts was a necessary preliminary to the quaestorship.

five years: the minimum age for offices was laid out in the *Lex Villia Annalis* of 180 BC. This was modified under Augustus, and the minimum age for the quaestorship was established at 25.

priesthood: Tacitus has confused Nero with his brother Drusus, since inscriptions show that it was the latter who was granted a priesthood.

Forum: the introduction into the Forum followed the assumption of the toga of manhood. The event is marked as occurring on 7 June in inscriptions, which also record the *congiarium*, the distribution of money to the populace.

Claudius' son: Drusus, the son of Claudius by his first wife Plautia Urgulanilla, is said by Suetonius (*Claud.* 27.1) to have died within a few days of his betrothal by choking on a pear. A daughter of Sejanus is mentioned at 5.9 (AD 31), where she is a young girl. The name Iunilla is provided in an inscription. Sejanus may have had more than one daughter. If not, the reference in this section must be to his intention rather than to an actual betrothal.

Lucius Volusius: consul in 12 BC and governor of Africa and of Syria afterwards. He was appointed by Augustus almost certainly as a member of a board of three to draw up the list of knights competent to serve as jurors. He was a cousin of Tiberius by marriage.

decuriae: the term *decuria*, literally a group of ten individuals, was usually applied to the jury panels, but here seems to refer to the general equestrian units.

111 *consulship*: Dio (57.20.1) states that people in AD 21 observed that Tiberius' previous consular colleagues, Germanicus, Quinctilius Varus, and Gnaeus Calpurnius Piso, had all died violent deaths, and that the pattern would be maintained by Drusus and Sejanus.

Campania: on this occasion Tiberius went to Campania for a brief stay, returning in the spring of the following year, when Livia fell ill. Four years later he would retire permanently from Rome.

Domitius Corbulo: the father of the famous general of Nero's reign.

Lucius Sulla: possibly Lucius Sulla Felix, consul in AD 33 (6.15).

had not ceded his seat . . . show: the location of seats at games and at theatrical performances was very important for the Romans in designating social rank.

roads: Dio (59.14) reports that a Corbulo complained about the roads under Caligula in AD 39 and was made consul in that year. Dio's Corbulo is taken by some to be the famous general, but the coincidence that both father and son complained about the roads seems too great.

magistrates: the maintenance of the roads in Italy was under the jurisdiction of the road commissioners, *curatores viarum*, a body that had been reorganized by Augustus.

112 *Sextus Pompeius*: consul in AD 14 (see 1.7).

Manius Lepidus: see note to p. 12.

Asia: the Senate controlled the governorships of the two important provinces of Africa and Asia, which normally went to the senior ex-consuls, the actual assignment being determined by lot. Since Africa had been removed from the lot process, it seems that Asia went by default to Lepidus as the senior available consul.

proposal: senators had the right to introduce a motion that was off the question under debate, provided it was in the public interest.

allotted: it is not clear here whether Caecina meant his restriction to apply only to senatorial provinces, with specific reference to Africa, or if he meant it to be inspired by the debate on Africa but to apply generally to *all* provinces, both senatorial and imperial, which is suggested by the appeal to his own career (although he did serve in Africa, he had considerable service in imperial provinces).

forty: Tacitus mentions forty campaigns at 1.64, which were followed by at least one more. Forty was no doubt intended as a round figure.

legionary manoeuvres: Caecina is alluding of course to the behaviour of Plancina (2.55), but he may also have been making an indirect allusion to

Agrippina, perhaps embarrassed by the knowledge that her conduct at the Rhine bridge saved troops under his own command.

113 *Oppian*: the *Lex Oppia*, passed in 215 BC as an economy drive during the war with Hannibal, was intended mainly to curb lavish expenditure on dress (Livy 34.1–8). It was repealed twenty years later.

censor: a contrast is understood here between Caecina and Cato the censor, who had led the debate against the repeal of the *Lex Oppia* in 195 (see previous note).

Drusus: he was probably still consul (his father stepped down from office after three months, and Drusus may have done the same), and thus presided over the debate in the Senate.

114 *the east and the west*: although such journeys by Livia in the company of Augustus are generally supposed, there is no evidence for them, apart from a highly dubious allusion to a sojourn in Gaul.

outmanoeuvred: it is likely that Caecina's motion was never presented for a vote.

daughter: she may well be the Lepida who was betrothed to the future emperor Galba.

an image of the emperor: the general reverence accorded to the image of the emperor seems to have extended to the use of his image to claim sanctuary. Agrippina, for instance, in her clash with her son Nero, will be advised (4.67) to grasp the effigy of Augustus in the crowded Forum, and there are later stories that it was an offence to beat a slave who held a coin of Tiberius.

Gaius Cestius: consul in AD 35.

115 *Considius Aequus and Caelius Cursor*: otherwise unknown.

buildings: it must be supposed here that Drusus, unlike his father, had a passion for building, a trait unattested elsewhere.

one of Macedonia's leading men: Antistius may have been a Macedonian who had received the citizenship and thus had the right to be heard before the praetor.

Thrace: for the earlier events leading up to this section, see 2.67.

closest army: the reference must be to Moesia, where two legions were based. The commander there, Publius Vellaeus, must have succeeded Pomponius Flaccus.

116 *Gallic communities*: of the four Gallic provinces, two were unaffected by the rebellion, the senatorial province Narbonese Gaul and the imperial Aquitania. The two affected ones were Belgica and Lugdunensis.

the heavy burden of their debts: there would be no exaggeration here. Indebtedness among the provinces was a constant difficulty. Extortion and mismanagement would have been aggravated by the exactions of Germanicus (see 2.5).

Treveri: since Agrippina was going to be sent there (see 1.41) they must at that time have been particularly loyal.

Julius Florus: a man of this name accompanied Tiberius to the East. He may have belonged to a family of Gallic origin that established itself at Rome. The name suggests that they were enfranchised by Caesar or Augustus, as does that of Julius Sacrovir.

rarity: Augustus reversed Caesar's practice of making lavish bestowals of citizenship, and Tiberius probably followed Augustus' example.

Acilius Aviola: he is perhaps Gaius Calpurnius Aviola, consul of AD 24 and later governor of Asia, who may have changed his name through adoption.

Visellius Varro: consul in 12 and father of the consul of 24 (see 4.17).

117 *target*: that is, of the Gauls fighting for the Romans.

opposite directions: this is confusing. The armies would have come from Upper and Lower Germany by different routes but would not have come from opposite directions.

Gaius Silius: see note to p. 21; he was still legate of Upper Germany.

liberal studies: schools were an important element in the spread of Romanization. The school at Autun is known to have been still in existence at the end of the third century.

Varro: three years after these events Visellius Varro's son would settle the score by charging that Silius concealed the rebellion of Sacrovir through complicity and extortion.

119 *by letter*: Tiberius was, of course, in Campania at the time.

begun and terminated: Velleius confirms that no official report of the war was given until it was over.

Cornelius Dolabella: consul in AD 10, Publius Cornelius Dolabella was later governor of Africa (see 4.23–6).

triumphs: see note to p. 23.

Sulpicius Quirinius: he was the fourth individual for whom Tiberius requested a public funeral (a funeral at public expense). He had held his consulate in 12 BC.

120 *triumphal insignia*: Quirinius possibly fought the successful campaign when governor of Galatia.

Marcus Lollius: see note to p. 10. The ill-feeling between him and Tiberius was noted by Suetonius (*Tib.* 12). He committed suicide after Gaius Caesar renounced his friendship because of his disloyalty and corruption.

Publius Petronius: consul in 19 and governor of Asia later; his daughter was married to the future emperor Vitellius.

Haterius Agrippa: as consul-designate, Agrippa would be the first to give his opinion in a trial held in the Senate.

speech: Lepidus' argument seems to be that the case against Priscus was not within the definition of *maiestas*, but that he proposed a punishment as if it were, namely the penalty laid down under Caesar, exile and loss of property.

121 *Gaius Sulpicius*: elder brother of the future emperor Servius Sulpicius Galba; he committed suicide in 36.

aediles: it was their duty to regulate the market.

sumptuary law: Gellius (1.54.2) alludes to a *Lex Iulia*, probably of 22 BC, that set a limit to what might be spent on dinner.

122 *Country houses*: laments about the size of private villas are a common theme of Roman literature.

those items, exclusively used by women: perhaps the most notorious example is that of Lepida, who later married Caligula. Pliny (*NH* 9.117) records that she wore forty million sesterces' worth of jewels, and carried the bills of sale to convince sceptics. The manuscript reads *lapidum causa* at this point, which Woodman persuasively argues is a gloss on 'those items . . . which'. The items themselves are the gems, so common a feature of 'female extravagance' in moralizing literature that such a reference would be easily understood by a contemporary reader (but then glossed in the margin by a later scribe).

123 *the aediles were relieved of responsibility*: nothing was done. The laws were unchanged and the aediles were excused from enforcing them rigidly. Suetonius (*Tib*. 34) says that Tiberius placed the markets under senatorial control and instructed the aediles to exercise strict control of the taverns. This measure presumably predated AD 22.

124 *a hundred years . . . gained power*: the battle of Actium occurred in 31 BC. Galba took power in AD 68.

butchery: the later years of Tiberius and of Caligula, Claudius, and Nero are presumably meant.

municipal towns and colonies: specifically, the towns of Italy.

Vespasian: emperor 69–79. His parsimony was legendary.

accusers: the implication is that, if the legislation on extravagance had been carried, there would have been a widening of the scope for informers.

term: the tribunician authority is a privilege rather than a title, but its frequent occurrence after the emperor's name in coins and inscriptions, in the form usually of *trib. pot.* (*tribunicia potestas*), plus the year of the award, creates the impression of a title. Augustus received it in June 23 BC and in 18 and 13 conferred it on Agrippa, who held it until his death in 12 BC. Tiberius in fact did not receive the authority until 6 BC. It was only after the death of Gaius Caesar and Tiberius' adoption in AD 4 that the term was renewed.

'dictator': in the *Res Gestae*, Augustus states that he declined the dictatorship and permanent consulships.

125 *at the age*: Drusus was born on 7 October in either 14 or 13 BC.

mutinies: in Pannonia in AD 14.

wars: in Illyricum and Germany, AD 17–19.

triumph: celebrated on 28 May AD 20.

consul: in AD 15 and 21.

proposing: Silanus' motion was clearly unsuccessful, since the years continued to be marked by the consuls, although in their communications with provinces the emperors used the tribunician year.

Quintus Haterius': see note to p. 12; he was by this time about 85 years old.

Servius Maluginensis, the flamen of Jupiter: consul in AD 10 (see 4.16); there were fifteen flamens in Rome, devoted to specific cults. The most important was the *Flamen Dialis*, responsible for the worship of Jupiter. He was subjected to a wide range of taboos.

allotted: since Africa was reserved for Blaesus, there would not have been an actual lot.

plebiscites: these would have the status of laws. Presumably the flamen had in the past been detained in Rome by his duties, and legislation had not been deemed necessary.

Cornelius Merula's suicide: he committed suicide in 87 BC on the return of Marius and Cinna to the city, and seventy-five years had elapsed before Augustus appointed a flamen to replace him.

supreme pontiffs: from 12 BC until the fourth century the office of *Pontifex Maximus* was held by the emperor. Tiberius assumed the office on 10 March AD 15.

126 *provinces*: the measures applied only to the senatorial provinces. The deputations mentioned in chapter 61 and in 4.14 are from Asia, Cyprus, and Crete.

Temples . . . capital crimes: it has been observed that the issue of asylum offered by certain temples and sacred precincts in the Greek world was as much a matter of politics as of religion. The rights of asylum implied a degree of autonomy, which became a major issue as Roman power began to spread throughout the East and the pressure for recognition of ancient rights became intense.

127 *Amazons*: according to Pausanias (7.2.7), Pindar ascribed to them the founding of the temple of Diana at Ephesus.

Macedonians: in 334 BC Alexander the Great gained control of Ephesus and extended the boundary of the asylum. His example was followed by a number of others, including Antonius. Because of the abuses, Augustus curtailed it.

Lucius Scipio: Lucius Cornelius Scipio Asiagenes defeated Antiochus the Great in 190/89 BC.

Lucius Sulla: Lucius Cornelius Sulla defeated Mithridates in 87/6 BC.

Parthian assault: the reference is to the joint invasion of Quintus Labienus and Pacorus, son of the Persian king Orodes, in 40 BC.

127 *Perpenna's*: he defeated and captured Aristonicus of Pergamum in 130 BC.

Isauricus: consul with Caesar in 48 BC and governor of Asia 46–44 BC.

128 *Aesculapius*: the cult of this healing god (Greek Asclepios) was brought to the important city of Pergamum from Epidaurus.

critical illness: by careful diet and daily consumption of wine Livia had enjoyed a robust health. This is her first recorded illness; she was now in her eighties.

statue: the inscription recording the dedication of the effigy in the theatre of Marcellus has survived. It is dated to 23 April AD 22. It confirms that Livia's name stood ahead of Tiberius' and, more remarkably, that the dedication was made to the deified Augustus: *patri* (father). Livia had been adopted by Augustus in his will.

septemvirs: a board of seven officials responsible primarily for arranging banquets during games.

Augustal fraternity: the body established in AD 14 on the death of Augustus and charged with the worship of two deified men, Julius Caesar and Augustus.

Fetials: this body of twenty priests had become largely obsolete and had a totally formal role in declaring war and concluding treaties.

129 *lower-ranking senators*: Tacitus uses a term, *pedarii*, that was obscure and archaic in his own age. It may refer to those senators who had not yet obtained curule office (Tacitus was perhaps overlooking the small number who had not progressed beyond the curule aedileship).

Gaius Silanus: consul in AD 10, Gaius Junius Silanus had apparently succeeded Marcus Lepidus as proconsul of Asia. Already accused of extortion in his province, he was additionally charged with *maiestas*.

Mamercus Scaurus: see note to p. 12. The grandfather represented as so worthy an ancestor by Tacitus was described by Sallust (*Jugurtha* 15.3) as duplicitous, excessively ambitious, and corrupt.

Junius Otho: Tacitus seems to downplay his talents, since Seneca the Elder (*Contr.* 2.1.33–9) speaks of him as an accomplished speaker and the author of a number of rhetorical works.

Bruttedius Niger: an orator and historical writer, author of an account of Cicero's death (Seneca, *Contr.* 6.20–1). He is thought to have perished in the aftermath of the fall of Sejanus.

Lucius Cotta's: consul in 144, Lucius Aurelius Cotta was accused of extortion in 138 by Scipio Africanus the Younger, he was reputedly acquitted by a jury that wanted to demonstrate that it was not overawed by a great speaker.

Servius Galba's: Servius Sulpicius Galbas was indicted in 149 by the elder Cato for his conduct in Spain; his behaviour there had been savage, but the exact form of the indictment is not known. His acquittal was ascribed to his eloquence, family support, and bribery.

Publius Rutilius': he was a candidate for the consulship in 116 against Marcus Scaurus. After the election, each accused the other of improper electioneering practices (*ambitus*).

130 *Marcus Paconius*: another individual put to death by Tiberius, possibly in the aftermath of Sejanus' fall. According to Suetonius (*Tib.* 61.6), Tiberius imprisoned Paconius and on being reminded later of him by one of his dwarfs ordered his execution.

torture: see note to p. 64.

Volesus Messala: proconsul of Asia in AD 11 or 12, Marcus Valerius Messala Volesus was associated by Seneca (*De Ira* 5) with Phalaris and Hannibal as an archetype of cruelty.

Lucius Piso: his identity is uncertain, possibly the consul of 15 BC (see 6.10) or of 1 BC (see 2.34).

131 *devoid of human habitation*: Pliny (*NH* 8.43) reports a claim in antiquity that Gyarus was deserted because of a plague of mice, but also observes that it was destitute of water.

Torquata: she is recorded in an inscription (*CIL* 6.2127) as having served as a Vestal for sixty-four years.

132 *Equestrian Fortune*: a great temple to Fortune had been vowed in 180 BC and was still visible in the Augustan period, since the architect Vitruvius speaks of seeing it. It must have been demolished by this point in the *Annals*. Antium would be a very suitable location for the dedication, since it housed one of the great imperial villas, and had been a favourite summer residence of Augustus.

Aulus Postumius: his detention occurred in 242 BC, but was not a good precedent, since Postumius had been the flamen of Mars, not of Jupiter.

Lepidus: he appears to have been the grandson of Lucius Aemilius Paullus, consul in 50 BC, who restored the old Basilica Aemilia and founded a splendid new Basilica Pauli, completed and dedicated by his son and restored again by Augustus and others after a fire in 14 BC.

Augustus . . . Balbus: Augustus is recorded as encouraging individuals in such acts of generosity. Suetonius mentions the same three individuals listed here. In 30 BC Titus Statilius Taurus dedicated in the Campus Martius the first amphitheatre built of stone; Lucius Marcius Philippus, consul in 38 BC, dedicated the Temple of Hercules and the Muses; Lucius Cornelius Balbus dedicated in 13 BC a theatre on the Campus Martius near the river.

Pompey's theatre: see 6.45; it seems that only the *scaena* was damaged. The refurbishment was finally dedicated by Caligula.

133 *Spartacus*: he organized a breakout of gladiators from the school at Capua and initiated the famous slave war of 73–71 BC. He defeated the armies of both consuls of 72.

Sertorius: he organized a rebellion in Spain from 80 to 73 BC.

133 *Mithridates*: the reference is to the wars of 83–81 and 74–63 BC.

134 *Augustus*: he did not in fact allow such acclamations after 27 BC.

Asinius Saloninus: one of the sons of Asinius Gallus (see note to p. 8) and of Vipsania, the former wife of Tiberius. He bore the name Saloninus to commemorate the capture of Salonae in Dalmatia by his grandfather Pollio in 39 BC; it was intended that he would marry a daughter of Germanicus.

Ateius Capito . . . Antistius Labeo: they were famous in the history of Roman jurisprudence as the founders of two opposing schools, the Sabiniani (Capito) and Proculiani (Labeo).

outspokenness: Labeo chose to support the ex-triumvir Lepidus, who was exiled, and defended his choice with vigour (Suetonius, *Aug.* 54; Dio 54.15.7).

servility: it is said that he noted that, if a word used by Tiberius did not exist in Latin, it soon would.

Junia: the widow of Gaius Cassius, one of the assassins of Caesar. Instead of naming her ancestors, Tacitus lists the family connections that would evoke her connections with the old republic. She was over 90 at the time of her death. She was the daughter of Servilia and Decimus Junius Silanus. Servilia had previously been married to Marcus Junius Brutus. Hence Marcus Brutus, the other leading assassin of Caesar, born from the first marriage, was her half-brother.

battle of Philippi: 42 BC.

135 *ancestral busts*: *imagines*, funeral masks of famous ancestors, were kept in the home and paraded at funerals. It is known that effigies of Brutus and Cassius were preserved in households and even in Pliny's time were accorded a special reverence. At this period it was clearly thought to be imprudent to show them in public.

Manlii: the son of Titus Manlius Torquatus, consul 165, was adopted by Decimus Junius Silanus. The relationship with the Quinctii is unknown.

BOOK FOUR

136 *praetorian cohorts*: when Tiberius first became emperor, Sejanus shared the command of the guard with his father. On the appointment of the father as prefect of Egypt in AD 15, Sejanus assumed sole command.

Apicius: a famous wealthy gourmet. Seneca (*Ad Helviam* 10) states that he committed suicide when he discovered that he was down to his last million sesterces.

concentrating . . . the city: Suetonius (*Aug.* 49.1) states that Augustus never allowed more than three cohorts of the praetorians inside the city, and even then they did not have a permanent base. The new base was built adjacent to the walls of Rome between the Colline and Viminal gates.

137 *theatres*: Tacitus has already recorded that a statue of Sejanus was decreed for the theatre of Pompey (see 3.72).

legionary headquarters: the *principia* of the legionary base was considered a sacred place, where the legionary standards were housed. Suetonius (*Tib.* 48.2) notes that only the legions in Syria refused to allow images of Sejanus to be carried among their standards.

grandchildren: Germanicus' oldest son, Nero, was born in AD 6, Drusus was born a year later, and Gaius Caligula in 12. Drusus, son of Tiberius, had twin sons, of whom Tiberius Gemellus survived into the next reign.

struck: the aggressive and impetuous side of Drusus' nature is often commented on by the literary sources.

Livilla: she had first been married to Gaius Caesar. Her supposed role in the death of her second husband Drusus would be revealed after Sejanus' fall by his estranged wife, Apicata, and Livilla was put to death, either by Tiberius or by her own mother.

small-town: the taunt is meant to draw attention to Sejanus' humble social origins and lack of senatorial ancestors.

children: the eldest, Aelius Gallus, died with his father; the other two died subsequently (see 5.9).

138 *sympathetic*: the sources speak of the relationship between Drusus and Germanicus as harmonious.

troop-levies: such conscriptions were largely limited to the provinces, and to those provinces that were Romanized. Voluntary enlistment was difficult when times were bad, as after the defeat of Varus in AD 9, when freedmen had been allowed to volunteer and slaves had been freed to make up the numbers.

armed forces: Tacitus is comparing the situation under Tiberius with that under Trajan, when areas like Britain, Mauretania, Dacia, and Mesopotamia had been brought under Roman dominion.

Two fleets: they were commanded by prefects, normally equestrian but sometimes freedmen.

Juba: he was married to Selene, daughter of Antonius and Cleopatra. He had recently been succeeded by his son Ptolemy, who in AD 40 would be put to death by Caligula.

protected . . . our great power: presumably Tacitus wrote this after 116 and Trajan's conquest of Parthia.

Rhoemetalces: the son of Rhescuporis, murderer of the elder Cotys. He shared Thrace nominally with Cotys' sons (see 3.38).

139 *old Latium*: this refers to those towns already with Latin rights before they received full citizenship in 90 BC as a result of the Social War.

in the Senate: in other words the emperor would not try such cases in camera.

companies: of *publicani*.

139 *His own affairs*: the procurators who administered the emperor's private *fiscus* were originally private agents, just as in the estates of private citizens; by Claudius' time at least they had evolved into officers of the state.

provincials: Tiberius had a generally excellent record in continuing Augustus' policy of correcting abuses in the provinces. He extended the term of governors of proven ability and was firm in dealing with bad officials.

140 *share grandsons*: this would come about through the planned marriage of Sejanus' daughter to a son of Claudius.

ordinary seats: the consuls normally sat on their curule chairs, which were raised up on a platform; they might, however, on some occasions sit with the rest of the senators. As a sign of mourning, they would sit with the lower magistracies (see Dio 56.31.3).

Augusta's extreme old age . . . declining years: Livia was 80 or 81 at the time (her birth occurred in 59 or 58 BC). Tiberius was 65.

141 *Aeneas*: the role of the Trojan hero Aeneas as the founder of the Julian line was emphasized in Virgil's *Aeneid*. He was so depicted also on the Ara Pacis.

142 *really progressed*: Tacitus' faith in his sources does not carry conviction, as Apicata can hardly be seen as a disinterested witness.

Agrippina's failure to conceal her ambition: her obstinacy and temper did nothing to allay Tiberius' suspicions about her ambitions for her sons.

accelerated the family's destruction: a surprising claim, since Agrippina and her second son Drusus did not die until AD 33.

143 *virtue*: Agrippina did not remarry, but she did request Tiberius' permission to do so (see 4.53).

Augusta's . . . hatred: this is a frequently repeated claim by Tacitus, although it is not clear what Livia's motives could have been. Agrippina's children were, after all, her grandchildren.

Postumus: unknown, although there was a person of that name who was prefect of Egypt in AD 47.

Mutilia Prisca: she may well have been the wife of the consul of AD 29, Fufius Geminus (see 5.1).

Vibius Serenus: he was one of the accusers of Libo Drusus in AD 16 (see 2.30).

public violence: this offence, which consisted in the beating of a Roman citizen who appealed to the emperor, was, under a law of 8 BC, punishable by exile, usually to a place of the accuser's choice. The specification of the place of exile (Amorgos) was considered an added element of severity.

Carsidius Sacerdos: praetor in 27, he would be exiled in 37 as an associate to Albucilla, then convicted of treason.

Gaius Gracchus: perhaps the accuser at 6.38. His father Sempronius had been exiled as one of Julia's lovers. After fourteen years of exile Sempronius was put to death by soldiers.

Aelius Lamia: consul in AD 3, governor of Africa in 15/16 or 16/17.

his ill-starred family: he was the descendant of Tiberius and Gaius Gracchus, the celebrated tribunes.

144 *on King Mithridates' orders . . . of Asia*: Appian (*Mithridates* 23) records that Mithridates' troops did violate many of the sanctuaries. He targeted equestrians, as belonging to the class who had brought such suffering on local communities. The massacres occurred in 88 BC.

actors: problems with the licentious conduct of actors were one of the recurring themes of Roman history, especially after Augustus had accorded them a number of privileges.

Oscan show: Atellan farces, named after the Oscan town of Atella, were bawdy performances that blended obscenity and political satire.

Lucilius Longus: consul in AD 7, but otherwise of no apparent consequence and barely meriting a state funeral.

state funeral: a funeral at public expense, called a 'censorian funeral' by Tacitus, possibly because at one time such occasions had been contracted by the censors.

Forum of Augustus: the imperial forum opened by Augustus in 2 BC contained the statues of famous Romans.

Lucilius Capito: this is an interesting case in that Capito was a procurator of Tiberius, in charge of the imperial possessions in the senatorial province of Asia, and technically his private agent. By allowing the case to be tried by the Senate, Tiberius contributed to the procuratorship becoming a public office.

Nero: the son of Germanicus. The situation is ironic in that he will die a victim of Tiberius.

145 *confarreatio*: this was the main form of old-fashioned marriage *in manum* (lit., into the hand), where the wife passed into the jurisdiction of the husband, a procedure that was largely in abeyance by Tiberius' day. The name comes from the cake consumed at the ceremony in the presence of the supreme pontiff (*Pontifex Maximus*), the *Flamen Dialis*, and at least ten witnesses. It was necessary for the wife to satisfy the requirements, since she had official duties.

parental: it must be assumed that the parents objected to the loss of this authority.

law: technically a resolution of the Senate had the force of law only once it had been passed by the popular assembly, although this was something of a formality by this time.

take her seat among the Vestals: women normally occupied upper seats in the theatre; Vestals alone had the privilege of watching performances from the more desirable lower seats. Livia's privilege set a precedent for other imperial women, including Antonia and Messalina.

145 *prayers*: prayers for the safety of the state were offered on 1 January. A different set of prayers for the emperor's safety was offered on 3 January.

146 *Agrippina's party*: whether there was an actual 'Agrippina party' is much disputed, but there may at least have been some tensions between the Julian and Claudian sides of the family.

loyal: the mutinies had been fomented among the troops of Lower Germany.

wife: it will be remembered that the issue of wives' conduct in the provinces had been raised by Caecina Severus (3.33–4).

father's quarrels: the command against the rebellion of Sacrovir had been awarded to Silius in preference to the father of the consul Visellius Varro (3.43).

harm: Tiberius uses the formula of the old ultimate decree of the Senate (*senatus consultum ultimum*), used first against Gaius Gracchus, whereby the consuls received near dictatorial powers during a crisis. It had last been employed in 40 BC.

147 *estate*: generally, suicide before conviction saved an estate, although there were many exceptions.

children: their son Gaius Silius would become infamous as the lover of Messalina.

Messalinus Cotta: consul in 20. Tacitus elsewhere (5.3, 6.5) sees him as a flunkey supporting Tiberius, in contrast to the more independently minded senators.

decree: the decree remained in force until the third century (Ulpian 1.16.4.2).

Calpurnius Piso: he had defended his brother during the trial that followed Germanicus' death (3.11). Tiberius was very dismayed by his decision to leave Rome (2.34).

148 *sword*: citizens were prohibited by law from carrying arms in Rome. Even the praetorians were not fully armed.

Plautius Silvanus: son of the consul of 2 BC who had received the triumphal insignia for his campaigns in Illyricum. Aulus Plautius, consul in AD 29 and conqueror of Britain, was almost certainly his brother.

149 *earlier commanders*: Furius Camillus (AD 17–18), Lucius Apronius (AD 18–21), and Quintus Junius Blaesus (AD 21–2).

Ninth Legion: since the legion was still in Africa in Tacitus' survey of the empire, it was probably moved back to Pannonia in AD 23.

Publius Dolabella: see note to p. 119. He was admired by Velleius, and his effectiveness in his command seems to bear out Velleius' judgement. He was not, however, highly regarded by Tacitus, who seems to have viewed him as excessively servile.

Musulamians: they are described as rebelling, and so must be one of those groups who accepted terms at the end of Junius Blaesus' term.

150 *Blaesus*: he lost his life in the aftermath of the fall of Sejanus, which would seem to confirm Tacitus' suggestion of closeness between the men (see 5.7).

toga: the triumphal toga displayed gold stars on a purple background. Scipio Africanus reportedly gave the same gifts and a curule chair to Masinissa (Livy 30.15.11).

151 *agricultural slaves*: the reference is to the bands of armed herdsmen maintained by the large estates of southern Italy.

supervisor of the pasture-lands: little is known about the quaestorian provinces of Italy. According to Dio (55.4.4), they were instituted by Augustus, but might be much older. The most familiar was the *provincia Ostiensis*, with responsibility for the corn-supply.

Vibius Serenus: the father had been an accuser of Libo Drusus (2.30), and was himself banished to Amorgos in AD 23 (see 4.13). This is the first mention of the son, who will later prosecute Fonteius Capito (4.36).

sent to Gaul: from Baetica, which had been Serenus' province, during the rebellion of Sacrovir.

Gnaeus Lentulus and Seius Tubero: Lentulus is probably the consul for 14 BC (see note to p. 18). Seius Tubero had served with Germanicus in Germany (see note to p. 59).

embarrassment: Dio (57.24.8) reported that Lentulus laughed when he heard the charges and Tiberius declared that his own life was unbearable if Lentulus hated him also.

152 *his slaves*: normally slaves could not testify against their masters, with the exception, in the republic, of cases involving incest or conspiracy. *Maiestas* had clearly been added to the list. In the case of Libo Drusus (2.30), his slaves were first sold to obviate the problem.

rock: the Tarpeian rock (see note to p. 65).

parricides: the punishment involved being beaten, sewn into a bag with various animals, then hurled into the Tiber.

unrewarded: the other accusers of Libo had been awarded extraordinary praetorships. Serenus must have already been praetor or was praetor-designate, since he was proconsul in Baetica about 22. His complaint seems to be that he did not receive comparable recognition.

traditional punishment: the punishment was to be pinned by the neck and then scourged to death.

153 *Publius Suillius*: the prosecution may have been part of Sejanus' campaign against Agrippina and her sons (see also 11.1–6, 13.42–3).

Catus Firmius: his conduct as an informer had already been apparent during the trial of Libo Drusus, and he was particularly despised by Tacitus (see 2.27). As a result of his reward in the Libo trial, he attained praetorian rank and hence became a member of the Senate.

154 *Carthaginian*: clearly a reference to Livy. That said, Tacitus himself notes in the next chapter that Livy's patron Augustus thought that Livy was biased towards Pompey in his account of the struggles between the latter and Caesar.

Cremutius Cordus: he wrote a history of the civil wars which formed the basis of the charges described here. He was no friend of Tiberius' regime, and on hearing of the erection of statues to Sejanus in the theatre of Pompey, he commented that it was the kiss of death for the theatre (Seneca, *In Marciam* 22.4). Dio (57.22.2) adds that he was charged also with attacking the Senate and the people and for not showing Augustus exceptional respect.

155 *treason law*: Augustus changed the law to include those who wrote defamatory texts.

Brutus and Cassius: during this period Brutus and Cassius were clearly becoming heroes for the Stoics, as men who stood up against tyranny.

Titus Livius: although he drew on the patronage of Augustus and Maecenas, Livy spoke his mind, and the elder Seneca calls him totally outspoken (*Suasoriae* 6.22).

Scipio: father-in-law of Pompey; he committed suicide after the battle of Thapsus in 46 BC.

Afranius: loyal supporter of Pompey, his legate in Spain. He died at the battle of Thapsus.

Asinius Pollio: consul of 40 BC, father of Tiberius' *bête noire* Asinius Gallus. His history ran from the 'first triumvirate' of 60 BC.

Messalla Corvinus: see note to p. 7. He was second in command to Brutus and Cassius at Philippi and switched his loyalty to Augustus afterwards. More famous as an orator than as a writer, he composed a history that began with the death of Caesar.

Marcus Cicero: in 46 BC Marcus Tullius Cicero composed a book on Cato Uticensis, in which he expressed his disenchantment with Caesar.

Bibaculus: Furius Bibaculus was ranked with Catullus and Horace by Quintilian (*Institutio Oratoria* 10.1.196).

Catullus: perhaps more famous for his love poetry, Gaius Valerius Catullus also wrote scurrilous poems about Julius Caesar's sex-life.

seventy years ago: round figures for the more precise 66; the battle was in 42 BC.

statues: Augustus did in fact preserve one in Milan (Mediolanum) (Plutarchs, *Comparison of Dion with Brutus* 5). It is known that the statues were preserved in private homes.

156 *survived*: Seneca (*In Marciam* 1.3) reports that his daughter Marcia was responsible for preserving his works. They were published, along with other banned works, under Caligula.

Drusus: the son of Germanicus.

Sextus Marius: he was executed in AD 33 for incest, although Tacitus says that the real reason was Tiberius' jealousy of his wealth (see 6.19).

Cyzicus: Dio (57.24.6) records that among the reasons that Cyzicus lost its freedom was the failure to complete a temple to Augustus.

Fonteius Capito: consul in AD 12. His governorship of Asia cannot be dated securely, but he may have taken office in 22, when Maluginensis was disqualified.

Pergamum: the city was given permission to build a temple in 29 BC.

158 *knights*: Suetonius (*Aug.* 63.2) confirms that after Agrippa's death Augustus considered many possible candidates for marriage to Julia, and even contemplated candidates from the equestrian order.

159 *father's friends*: Tiberius is thinking of such equestrians as Maecenas, Sallustius Crispus, and Proculeius, men of considerable influence, but not to be compared with the prefect of the guard.

Gaius Proculeius: a close friend of Augustus, he was sent as his emissary to Antonius and Cleopatra after the battle of Actium.

Marcus Agrippa: see note to p. 4; he was of humble origins, coming from a non-senatorial family. Some members of the nobility refused to attend his funeral because of his modest status.

the moment is granted me: Dio (58.7.5) mentions a betrothal between Sejanus and an unnamed member of the imperial family. Tiberius may have in mind political rather than personal promotion, perhaps the consulship and *tribunicia potestas*, to which Sejanus still aspired in AD 31.

soldiers' hands: letters were carried to Rome by *speculatores*, mounted special units of the praetorian guard, and thus under the command of Sejanus.

160 *Votienus Montanus*: a well-known orator, from Narbonese Gaul. He reputedly had a habit of repeating himself.

Aemilius: presumably a praetorian, set up for the purpose by Sejanus (possibly the Aemilius mentioned at 2.11).

Varius Ligus: otherwise unknown.

Lentulus Gaetulicus: brother of the consul of the current year, Cornelius Cossus, he was later legate of Upper Germany, 29–39 (see 6.30).

Julian law: the penalty under the law of 18 BC was relegation of both parties to separate islands and the partial loss of property. Exile would involve loss of citizenship and total loss of property. Augustus had similarly imposed an excessive penalty on his daughter Julia.

Apidius Merula: otherwise unknown.

Augustus: the oath to the *acta* ('measures') of Augustus was introduced in 29 BC; it was taken by Tiberius on his accession and observed afterwards on 1 January of each year. Tiberius refused to allow a similar oath to be sworn to his own *acta* during his lifetime (see note to p. 45).

160 *Philip of Macedon*: Philip II, the father of Alexander the Great. He invaded Sparta after the battle of Chaeronea in 338 BC.

King Antigonus: Antigonus III occupied Sparta in 222 BC.

161 *Mummius*: most famous for his destruction of Corinth in 146 BC.

arbiters: an inscription at Olympia shows that the arbitration was carried out in 135 BC with a clear decision in favour of the Messenians (584 votes to 16).

Atidius Geminus: unknown, probably an early Augustan governor.

The people of Segesta . . . family member: the city of Erycus (Eryx) was destroyed during the First Punic War and its territory seems to have passed to Segesta, along with its shrine of Venus. Both claimed a Trojan origin and Virgil (*Aeneid* 5.759) linked them to Aeneas, and hence to the Julii, who were relatives of Tiberius since his adoption by Augustus. Tiberius also had his own close ties with Sicily where he had spent part of his childhood during his father's exile.

Publius Rutilius: condemned for extortion 93/2 BC, reputedly through the jealousy of equestrians who made up the jury panel. In exile he received the citizenship of the city of Smyrna.

Vulcacius Moschus: an orator of Pergamum. A familiar figure in the works of Seneca the Elder, exiled to Marseilles (Massilia) after a conviction for poisoning.

Lucius Domitius: consul in 16 BC, grandfather of the future emperor Nero (see note to p. 39).

great fortune: Suetonius (*Tib.* 49) claims that Tiberius drove Lentulus to suicide for his money.

his father: Lucius' father Gnaeus, consul in 32 BC, was originally caught up in the conspiracy against Caesar. He commanded a republican fleet for a time before surrendering to Antonius. He switched loyalty to Octavian in 32 BC. Shakespeare's Enobarbus in *Antony and Cleopatra* is based on Gnaeus.

His grandfather: Lucius' grandfather, also Lucius, a republican, consul in 54 BC, was killed after Pharsalus (48 BC).

younger Antonia: Tacitus is in error here. The younger Antonia married Drusus; the elder married Domitius.

Elbe: Domitius crossed the Elbe when legate in Illyricum. Dio records that he erected a statue of Augustus on the east bank.

Lucius Antonius: the grandson of Marcus Antonius.

Massilia: Marseilles was one of the main centres of Greek culture in the West. Agricola testified to the scholarly atmosphere of the place (Tacitus, *Agr.* 4.3).

Octavii: Iullus Antonius was the son of Marcus Antonius and Fulvia, but had been brought up in Rome by Augustus' sister Octavia. Moreover,

Lucius' mother, the elder Marcella, was the daughter of Octavia. Hence it would be appropriate for Lucius to be placed in the family tomb of the Octavii.

Lucius Piso: the identification of this Lucius Piso is far from certain. He was possibly the son of the Piso mentioned at 4.21. Tiberius is said to have appointed Lucius Arruntius as legate of Nearer Spain but detained him in Rome (6.27). Lucius may have been standing in for him with praetorian rank.

162 *conscription*: it appears from this passage that Rome had abandoned the tradition that client kingdoms would provide occasional military support to a more systematic form of recruitment.

Pomponius Labeo: he is described by Dio (58.24.3) as serving for eight years as governor of Moesia. Technically, Sabinus was legate and Labeo's position may have been as his lieutenant, analogous perhaps to Lucius Piso in Spain (see 4.45). He committed suicide in 34 (see 6.29).

165 *wall-javelins*: *pila muralia* were pointed stakes inserted as a defensive line along the perimeter of a marching camp.

Claudia Pulchra: daughter of Marcella, the daughter of Augustus' sister Octavia, and Marcus Valerius Messala Barbatus Appianus, consul in 12 BC; she was thus second cousin to Agrippina. She had been married to the ill-fated Quinctilius Varus.

Domitius Afer: consul in 29, by reputation the greatest orator of his day. He earned the hatred of Caligula and saved his own skin by yielding to the emperor in the area of oratorical skill. He died in 59 (see 14.19).

166 *sacrificing to his father*: this would have been appropriate for Tiberius as a priest of the deified Augustus.

Greek verse: it is a striking indication of the acquaintance with Hellenism in the imperial house that Tiberius was able to quote a line of Greek, and that Agrippina was presumably able to recognize it.

young enough: she would have been about 40 at the time.

marriage: Agrippina does not state her intended choice of husband but it may have been Asinius Gallus, later denounced by Tiberius as her lover.

journals: Tacitus rarely identifies his sources. He presumably does so here because his source is one that has been ignored by other historians. In fact, only one other citation is known to have come from the younger Agrippina's memoirs, the information in Pliny the Elder (*NH* 7.46) that her son Nero was born by a breach birth.

father-in-law: Tiberius, by virtue of his adoption of Germanicus.

167 *Perses . . . monarchs*: in the war against Perses (171–168 BC), the cities were ruled by Eumenes II of Pergamum (197–160 BC), a supporter of Rome. Eumenes was succeeded by his brother Attalus II (220–138 BC), who was succeeded in turn by Attalus III (170–133 BC). This last ruler bequeathed his kingdom to Rome. Aristonicus, natural son of Eumenes II,

opposed the bequest and fought to oppose it in 131–129 BC (see 12.62). Chief among the 'other monarchs' would have been Pharnaces, Mithridates, and the Parthians.

167 *Sardis*: this city had suffered heavily in the earthquake of AD 17 (see 2.47), but must have recovered by now.

168 *wars abroad*: Smyrna had contributed ships in the war against Antiochus (191–188 BC).

Italy: the reference is to the Social War of 91–88 BC.

Marcus Porcius: i.e. Cato the Elder, consul in 195 BC.

Lucius Sulla: Smyrna helped Sulla during the First Mithridatic War, in 85 BC.

Vibius Marsus: see 2.74; consul in AD 17, a friend of Germanicus, he was accused of *maiestas* in 37 (see 6.47).

a supernumerary legate: Dio (53.14.17) says that a proconsul of consular rank had three such legates. A similar appointment was made in AD 17 to assist the proconsul of Asia after the earthquake.

Nola: Augustus died in his father's house at Nola, and Dio (56.46.3) reports that the house was then turned into a shrine.

historians: among modern scholars, as apparently among ancient historians, there is much debate about Tiberius' motives for leaving Rome permanently. The decision is likely to have been prompted by an accumulation of many factors, including the obsequiousness of the Senate, the irritation with his mother, and his distaste for the insincerities of Rome.

169 *sharing his rule*: the will of Augustus, by which Livia became a Julian and received the title of Augusta, created an ambiguous role for her, although there can not have been any question of a formal sharing of power.

entourage: despite claims recorded by Tacitus and others that Tiberius went to Capri to indulge his lusts, his retinue was made up of sober and scholarly companions. Cocceius Nerva, consul in AD 21 or 22 and grandfather of the later emperor, was the leading jurist of his day. He was the only consular to accompany Tiberius when he finally left Rome. Curtius Atticus was spoken of by Ovid (*Ex P.* 2.11) as a man of literary tastes. He fell victim to Sejanus (see 6.10).

Greeks: Suetonius (*Tib.* 56, 70) speaks of Tiberius finding pleasure in the company of Greek scholars, with whom he would discuss literary questions.

return to the city: he came to the mainland on a number of occasions and even reached the outskirts of Rome, but could not bring himself to enter.

170 *his wife*: Nero was married to Julia, daughter of Drusus, son of Tiberius, and Livilla.

Drusus: Nero's brother Drusus seems to have been quite different from him, and Sejanus was able to exploit the antipathy that he apparently felt towards an older brother who would have taken precedence over him.

Dio (58.3.8) adds that Sejanus seduced Drusus' wife Aemilia Lepida and through her built up evidence against him.

Asinius Agrippa: consul in this year (see 4.34), he was the son of Asinius Gallus and Tiberius' former wife Vipsania. His grandfathers were Marcus Agrippa and the distinguished man of letters, Asinius Pollio.

Quintus Haterius: see note to p. 12. Tiberius seems to have held him in some contempt.

171 *Fifty thousand people*: Suetonius (*Tib.* 40) says that 20,000 actually died. Given the capacity of an amphitheatre, these figures should be treated with the utmost caution.

172 *fire*: the danger of fires in Rome was notorious, and led to the formation of a fire service, the *vigiles*, in AD 6.

Augustan Hill: the scheme seems to have fallen through since the renaming did not take place, and it was hardly likely that Tiberius would have accepted it.

Claudia Quinta: Suetonius (*Tib.* 2.3) reports, among the great exploits of Tiberius' ancestors, Claudia's refloating in 204 BC of the ship that bore Cybele, the Magna Mater ('Great Mother', the 'Mother of the Gods') to Italy. In recognition of this service the Senate ordered that a statue of Claudia be placed in the portico of the temple of the Magna Mater when it was dedicated in 191 BC (Livy 29.14.2). The statue was spared in two fires, in 111 BC and AD 3 (Val. Max. 1.11).

Querquetulanus: a form of this name, which refers to oak trees, is found in both Varro and Pliny, but Tacitus is the only source to assign it to the hill.

Tarquinius Priscus: the first Etruscan king; his traditional dates are 616–579.

disagreement on his identity: the legends are highly confused. Claudius refers to the story in the original speech on the introduction of the Gauls to the Senate, as preserved in the inscription in Lyons (but omitted in Tacitus' account, 11.24). Claudius' version has Caeles an ally of another Etruscan, Mastarna, or of Servius Tullius, making that king an Etruscan also.

173 *Quinctilius Varus*: son of the Varus who had suffered the disaster in AD 9. The younger Varus was at one point engaged to one of Germanicus' daughters. He was related to the imperial house through his mother, Claudia Pulchra.

Publius Dolabella: see notes to pp. 119 and 149; he came from a powerful republican patrician family, and in the eyes of Tacitus this made his sycophantic conduct all the more reprehensible.

related: Dolabella's mother Quinctilia was the sister of Varus' father.

to await the emperor: the absence of the emperor created legal and constitutional problems. The system envisaged his presence in the Senate, presiding and influencing the debate.

Mt Vesuvius' eruptions: the great eruption took place in AD 79.

173 *twelve villas*: it has been argued that they were named after the twelve gods, the Villa Iovis (Villa of Jupiter) being the best known. It is unlikely that Tiberius was responsible for the construction of all twelve, or of any one of them, given his distaste for expensive buildings.

174 *advising them*: Suetonius (*Tib.* 53.2) states that these two schemes, of going to the army in Germany and of seeking sanctuary at the statue of Augustus, were specifically charged in the trial of Agrippina and Nero.

Titius Sabinus: the attack on him had begun eight years earlier (see 4.18) and presumably the evidence had been accumulated in the meantime. He is otherwise unknown.

175 *tension and panic*: it is difficult to understand why there should have been such a state of alarm, given that the actions supposedly all took place in secret.

no delay: it seems that the case ignored the rule of a delay of nine full days between sentence and execution that was put in place after the death of Clutorius Priscus in AD 21 (see 3.51).

176 *to whose children Agrippina was aunt*: Asinius Gallus was married to Agrippina's half-sister, Vipsania; Tacitus uses family links deliberately. Here they show the delicate relationship between Asinius and Tiberius.

Julia: see 3.24. She was the daughter of Julia the Elder, hence granddaughter of Augustus. She married Lucius Aemilius Paullus, consul AD 1, who was executed for conspiracy. Suetonius (*Aug.* 64–5) makes her offence immorality, and records that her lover Decimus Junius Silanus was allowed to return to Rome in AD 20, although not permitted to pursue a career. The whole episode is murkier even than the scandal that brought down her mother. Julia's son Marcus Lepidus married Caligula's sister Drusilla (he would be executed for conspiracy in AD 39).

Augusta: the role of Livia here is surprising and may be a better indication of her attitude to the Julian family than the highly charged narrative of Tacitus seems to imply. It should be noted also that Agrippina and her family were considered 'protected' while Livia was alive (5.3).

178 *altar*: such monuments imply honour and commemoration rather than worship.

Agrippina: the oldest of Germanicus' daughters. Born in what would become Cologne, she would prove to be a woman of considerable spirit and ambition, and plays a major role in the later books of the *Annals*. She was the mother of the future emperor Nero.

Gnaeus Domitius: consul in 32, and son of the consul of 16 BC (see note to p. 39); he came from a distinguished and ancient family but was described by Suetonius (*Nero* 5) as detestable in every aspect of his life. His mother commented on his laziness and lack of ambition.

BOOK FIVE

179 *Julia Augusta*: Dio (58.2.1) states that Livia had lived for eighty-six years at the time of her death in 29. Pliny's claim (*NH* 14.60) that she was only 82 cannot be correct, since it would make her 11 or 12 when Tiberius was born, in 42 BC.

the Claudian family: her father was born a Claudian but became a Livian through adoption, probably by Livius Drusus, celebrated plebeian tribune of 91 BC.

Tiberius Nero: Livia's first husband was, like her, a Claudian and hence a kinsman (the exact relationship is unknown). He had a promising lineage and was for a time considered a possible husband for Cicero's daughter, Tullia. But he was lacking in judgement or drive. He supported Brutus and Cassius after the murder of Caesar, and on their deaths he gave his allegiance to Antonius. In 40 he fled Italy with his family and sought the protection of Sextus Pompeius in Sicily. He was eventually allowed to return to Rome after the general amnesty in 39, and lived in obscurity thereafter.

Perusine War: Perugia was occupied by Lucius Antonius, the brother of Marcus Antonius, in 41 BC, and surrendered to Octavian in 40. Peace was achieved by the Treaty of Misenum in 39 BC.

pregnant: Livia was pregnant with her second son, Drusus, at the time of the marriage. See note to p. 10.

will: the execution of Livia's will had to await the accession of her great-grandson Caligula (Suetonius, *Cal.* 16.3).

divine honours: Livia would eventually be so honoured by Claudius.

Fufius: he and his wife would be compelled to commit suicide (Dio 58.4.5–6).

180 *senatorial proceedings*: the only other mention of senatorial *acta* in Tacitus is at 15.74.

the people: this is one of the rare recorded examples of a popular demonstration actually influencing policy in imperial Rome.

181 *in his hands*: Tiberius had previously been punctilious about leaving major decisions to the Senate. His insistence on dealing with this issue personally is a measure of how affected by it he was.

BOOK SIX

182 *forty-four speeches*: it is generally assumed that these speeches followed the conviction of Livilla for her part in the poisoning of Drusus son of Tiberius; it may well be, however, that they represent the speeches that followed the downfall of Sejanus.

182 *I thought*: although there is no gap in the manuscript this section clearly belongs to a later part of the book than the preceding one. We have no idea who the speaker might be. Clearly it is someone who refuses to renounce his previous close ties to Sejanus.

son-in-law: in AD 25 Sejanus wrote to Tiberius requesting permission to marry Drusus' widow Livilla. The request was refused, but Tiberius did promise that Sejanus would have a link with the imperial family at a later date. This promise was renewed in 31. We are not sure whether the bride was to be Livilla or her daughter Julia, nor can we be sure that the marriage took place, despite the reference to 'son-in-law', which may simply be used presumptively.

Blaesus: see note to p. 13; he had clearly been caught in the downfall of his nephew Sejanus.

Publius Vitellius: see note to p. 43; his links with Sejanus secured his fate, as happened to Blaesus.

Pomponius Secundus: see 11.13, 12.27–8; a multifaceted man, Publius Pomponius Secundus was consul in 44 and a skilled commander in Germany in 50, for which he received the triumphal insignia. But it was as a writer that he was most celebrated, both as a poet and composer of tragedies. He was a friend of Pliny the Elder.

183 *treasury*: here the reference is to the military treasury, founded by Augustus in AD 6 and administered by three ex-praetors.

Aelius Gallus: he is otherwise unknown, but his *nomen* Aelius indicates that he had a family link to Sejanus (Lucius Aelius Sejanus).

sharpener: this was presumably intended to sharpen a reed pen, but a knife could also be used to scrape away text.

remaining children: the phrase suggests that one or even more of Sejanus' children has previously been executed. The account of the horrific deaths of the children is famous and familiar. The events in question are recorded in the Fasti of Ostia, which give us a chronological sequence: 18 October, Sejanus was strangled, 26 October, Apicata, his wife, committed suicide, December, Capito Aelianus and Junilla, the children of Sejanus, were recorded as lying dead on the Gemonian Steps.

a rumour . . . mainland: we discover at 6.23 that Drusus was imprisoned and under close guard on the Palatine. Interesting parallels to this incident are provided by the emergence of a false Agrippa Postumus and a false Nero after their deaths.

184 *Poppaeus Sabinus*: see note to p. 49; the detailed account here, especially the particulars of his journey, of an errand that proved in the end fruitless, is surprising. It could well be that his family connection to Poppaea Sabina (granddaughter), the future wife of Nero, might have provoked Tacitus' interest.

the other sea: the Adriatic.

. . . ended: Tacitus' account is very different from that of Dio (58.25.1), who claims that the false Drusus was arrested and taken to Tiberius. Tacitus rarely explains his historical methodology, and here he insists, unusually, that he carried out his researches as thoroughly as possible.

Regulus: Publius Memmius Regulus became suffect consul on 1 October 31 and was involved in the downfall of Sejanus, in that he presided over the Senate when the emperor's famous long letter was read out on 18 October. We must assume that Tacitus gave a detailed account of his actions in the previous missing section. It seems clear that the Senate was anxious that the issue should not be stirred up now that passions had subsided.

Tiberius . . . coast: Suetonius (*Tib.* 65.2) claims that Tiberius did not in fact leave his villa on Capri for nine months after the fall of Sejanus, while Tacitus here has him on the Campanian coast early in AD 32.

his ancestors' portraits: Tacitus suggests that Tiberius was sexually excited by the fact that some of the young men came from noble families.

sexual activities: compared with the lurid account of Tiberius' sexual excesses in Suetonius (*Tib.* 43–4), Tacitus' description of his indulgences is relatively restrained. *Sellarii* are men who haunt latrines (see Suetonius, *Tib.* 43.1); *spintriae* are young male prostitutes.

185 *difference*: because many of the imperial expenditures came directly from the emperor's private *fiscus*, and the income of that *fiscus* was derived in large part from public sources, the distinction between the state treasury and the emperor's *fiscus* was one that was increasingly difficult to maintain.

Junius Gallio: one of the most distinguished orators of the period, although Tacitus (*Dialogus de Oratoribus* 26.1) criticizes his clattering style (*tinnitus*). He was on close terms with Ovid and a friend of the elder Seneca, whose son he adopted.

service: the praetorians served for sixteen years, four fewer than legionary soldiers.

fourteen rows: see note to p. 92.

186 *the destruction of Gaius Caesar*: details of such a plot were presumably given in the missing part of Book 5.

noted above: at 4.68 and 71 it was revealed that Latiaris was one of the ex-praetors who prosecuted Titius Sabinus, a close friend of Germanicus, and, after his death, of Agrippina.

emperor: it is not clear whether Regulus anticipated this happening in Rome or in Capri (Capreae). In any case his true motive was presumably to delay things.

Sanquinius Maximus: this consulship is undated. He later held a second consulship in 39 and in the same year was city prefect (*praefectus urbi*). He was also governor of Lower Germany under Claudius.

salvation for Regulus . . . destruction for Trio: Regulus lived until 61; Trio committed suicide in 35.

186 *the destruction of illustrious men*: in AD 21, as consul-designate, Haterius had proposed the execution of Clutorius Priscus, a knight.

'a funeral dinner': Livia's birthday was 30 January (as adjusted to the Julian calendar). The funeral dinner (literally, 'nine-day' dinner) was so-called because the ninth day after death saw the end of various funerary rituals and might be marked by a modest feast. The point that Messalinus is presumably trying to make is that a funeral feast was as much as could be hoped for in the case of Livia, because her son had refused deification or any other special honours after her death.

187 *Marcus Lepidus and . . . Lucius Arruntius*: consuls in AD 6. According to Tacitus (1.13), they were among those Augustus considered willing and able to succeed him.

these words: this is the longest verbatim quotation in Tacitus. It is also quoted by Suetonius (*Tib.* 67.1) in virtually identical form. The contexts are quite different. Suetonius gives the quotation as evidence of Tiberius' general concern about his own unpopularity. Tacitus gives it a specific context, the case of Cotta Messalinus.

what the leading man of philosophy used to claim: the reference is to Plato, *Gorgias* 524 E, where the speaker is Socrates. It is unclear whether Socrates or Plato is intended.

authority: Tiberius' order that the charges against Cotta be dropped might have been accompanied by an instruction to the Senate to undertake proceedings against those who had unjustly brought the proceedings against him. This would account for the use of the term 'authority'.

Quintus Servaeus and Minucius Thermus: on Servaeus, see 2.56, 3.13, 19. Minucius is otherwise unknown.

Gaius Cestius: he became consul in 35 (see 6.31).

188 *Marcus Terentius*: the speech of Terentius, a knight who is otherwise unknown, is the longest reported in Book 6. It may be that Tacitus was impressed by his courage and loyalty. Extensive verbatim speeches are usually reserved for senators.

suppliant rags: shabby clothing was often worn by the accused in courts or by suppliants in general as a way of evoking sympathy.

189 *sixteen years*: this figure must presumably refer to the period AD 15–30, with 14 excluded because Tiberius did not succeed until late 14. But Sejanus was still active in 31, and the number is curious.

Satrius and Pomponius: at 4.34 Satrius Secundus is described as a client of Sejanus when he (Satrius) prosecuted Cremutius Cordus. At 6.47 he has become an informer of the plot of Sejanus. It may be this latter action that saved his life. Pomponius is otherwise unknown.

Sextus Vistilius: brother of Vistilia (see 2.85). Tiberius' actions against him are difficult to understand. He apparently offended the emperor because of remarks made against Caligula. But this offence seems identical to one of the charges made against Cotta that Tiberius had quashed. Also,

Vistilius must by now have been over 60, given that he had served with Drusus, who died in 9 BC.

an entire group: the implication is that a large number of people met a fate similar to that of Vistilius. Five names are given, but in fact the prosecutions of all were dropped, three through Tiberius' intervention: (1) (*Gaius*) *Annius Pollio*: consul in AD 21 or 22. (2) (*Lucius Annius*) *Vinicianus*: consul in the latter part of Tiberius' reign and destined to have a prominent role in the final plot against Caligula. He was the son of the Annius Pollio above, and father of the Annius Pollio who conspired against Nero (15.56). (3) *Mamercus* (*Aemilius*) *Scaurus*: consul in AD 21; see 1.13. (4) (*Gaius*) *Appius* (*Junius*) *Silanus*: consul AD 28 (see 4.68), recalled from Spain early under Claudius and shortly afterwards put to death. (5) (*Gaius*) *Calvisius Sabinus*: consul AD 26 (see 4.46), appointed governor of Pannonia after his acquittal. He was recalled by Caligula and committed suicide.

190 *women*: although he mentions 'women' in the plural, Tacitus cites only one case specifically by name, that of Vitia, the mother of Fufius Geminus. It is impossible to tell if he might have been extrapolating from this one example.

Vitia: Dio (58.4.5–6) adds that Fufius' wife also committed suicide by stabbing herself in the Senate House. The account of Fufius' own trial and death would presumably have been in the lost section of Book 5.

Vescularius Flaccus and Julius Marinus: Flaccus had been involved in the prosecution of Libo Drusus in AD 16 (see 2.28). Nothing further is known about Julius Marinus.

the pontiff Lucius Piso: Lucius Calpurnius Piso was consul in 15 BC; it is noteworthy that although he was charged with the security of the city in the absence of the emperor, he was absent from the actions to bring down Sejanus. The section on his father's term as censor is in a part of the *Annals* now lost.

Denter Romulius . . . Tarquinius Superbus: Denter Romulius is otherwise not attested. Livy (1.20.5) claims that Numa Marcius was created pontiff by King Numa (see note to p. 108); there was another tradition (Plutarch, *Numa* 21) that he was the husband of Numa's daughter Pompilia and their son was Ancus Marcius. Spurius Lucretius was a venerable figure of the early republic, father of the Lucretia who was famously defiled by Tarquinius Superbus.

Cilnius Maecenas: twice in the period just before the first settlement in 27 BC Maecenas was left in charge of Rome and Italy by an absent Octavian. Maecenas was an equestrian, and although he fulfilled the duties of city prefect, he could not actually hold the office.

191 *Messala Corvinus*: see 3.34; consul in 31 BC along with Octavian, he achieved distinction as a general (triumph in 27 BC) and also as an orator and literary patron. He was city prefect briefly in 26 BC, but resigned on the grounds that the office was not appropriate for a civilian.

191 *Taurus Statilius*: see note to p. 132. He held office in 16 BC.

a book of the Sibyl: by tradition, the Sibylline Books were brought to Rome during the reign of Tarquinius Priscus. The texts, in Greek verse, were under the stewardship of a board of fifteen, who also were charged with their interpretation. As noted below, the original collection was destroyed by fire in 83 BC and a new official collection was made under Augustus and deposited in the Palatine library.

Quintilianus: consul in AD 38.

Caninius Gallus: consul in 2 BC.

Tiberius sent a letter: a decree of the Senate did not come into force until it was lodged in the state treasury. There was a delay of nine full days between the passing of the decree and its deposition, which would have allowed Tiberius to make his intervention.

the burning . . . Social War: the Capitol was burned in 83 BC during the civil wars that followed the Social War of 91–88. Tacitus' reference here to the 'Social War' is imprecise.

grain: the availability of grain at a reasonable price for the urban masses was one of the chief preoccupations of Roman authorities. In 23, 22, and 6 BC Augustus had been obliged to make large subsidies. Before the end of his reign, a permanent prefect of the grain-supply (*praefectus annonae*) had been appointed. Similar disturbances had occurred under Tiberius, who in AD 19 was obliged to make a financial intervention.

192 *Geminius, Celsus, and Pompeius*: these three are otherwise unknown.

Rubrius Fabatus: nothing is known of him but he was presumably a senator, since only senators were prohibited from leaving Italy.

the choice of husbands . . . Marcus Vinicius: the third sister, Agrippina, mother of the future emperor Nero, had been married in AD 28 to Domitius Ahenobarbus. Drusilla was probably 16 at the time of her marriage, Julia Livilla 15. Both the grooms, Lucius Cassius Longinus and Marcus Vinicius, had originally been supporters of Sejanus, but had later denounced him.

Macro: this is the first mention in the extant *Annals* of Macro, who succeeded Sejanus as prefect of the praetorian guard, after playing a leading role (as prefect of the *vigiles*) in his downfall, an event that would have been covered in the missing section of Book 5. He would be instrumental in securing the succession of Caligula.

193 *Twelve Tables*: Tacitus is the only source to claim that this enactment was found in the early body of laws known as the Twelve Tables, but all the same there was a strong tradition that the legal jurisdiction over debt goes back to the fifth century BC (Livy 2.23.1).

one-twelfth: we are not sure if the period covered is one year, or one month (the usual way of computing debt among the Romans). If one year, the interest would be 100 per cent, if one month 8⅓ per cent. The former seems excessively high, the latter too low.

interest was prohibited altogether: it is hard to believe that no-interest loans could have been made available; nevertheless, a bill prescribing them seems to have been put forward in 342 BC by the tribune Lucius Genucius (Livy 7.42.1).

The senators were alarmed: the majority of usurers would have come from the equestrian class. Clearly senators were also involved to some degree in the practice.

a shortage of ready money: the financial crisis recorded by Tacitus is covered also by Suetonius (*Tib.* 48.1) and Dio (58.21.4–5).

Tiberius brought aid . . . banks: it seems unlikely that Tiberius would have handed over such large sums to private individuals. Dio (58.21.5) suggests that Tiberius gave 100,000 HS to the public treasury, and that the money was to be lent out by senators.

194 *Considius Proculus*: he may be identical to the Considius mentioned at 5.8; the summary justice meted out to him is surprising, given his senatorial rank.

Quintus Pomponius: suffect consul in AD 41; see note to p. 293.

Gnaeus Magnus: i.e. Gnaeus Pompeius, the famous Pompey.

Theophanes of Mytilene: the historian was a friend of Pompey, who granted him Roman citizenship. After his death he received divine honours at Mytilene. He had obtained the status of free city for Mytilene from Pompey, despite its dubious record during the Mithridatic wars.

enormous: Suetonius (*Tib.* 61.4) refers to the same event, claiming that in one day twenty people, including women and children, were dragged down the Gemonian steps and hurled into the Tiber.

195 *Claudia*: Caligula married Junia Claudilla, daughter of Marcus Junius Silanus, consul of AD 15 and close friend of Tiberius (see note to p. 107). Silanus would be forced to commit suicide by his son-in-law in the first year of the reign.

his mother's condemnation or his brothers' ruin: Agrippina was exiled in 29 (14.63), the event presumably covered in the lost portion of Book 5. His brother Nero was put to death in 31; Drusus was starved to death before Caligula's accession.

Passienus: consul in AD 27, a noted wit, and a close associate of Caligula. He was the second husband of Agrippina.

Chaldeans: see note to p. 63.

Thrasyllus: the most celebrated astrologer of the day. The story of Tiberius putting his powers to the test is told also by Suetonius (*Tib.* 14.4) and Dio (55.11.1–3). He returned with Tiberius to Rome from Rhodes and was granted Roman citizenship.

196 *schools*: Tacitus seems to present the position of two schools, that of the Epicureans, who believed in the existence of the gods but denied that they

intervened in human affairs, and an idiosyncratic and selective view of the Stoics.

196 *the prediction of Nero's reign*: the reference is presumably to 14.9, where Agrippina is told by the astrologer that Nero will one day rule and kill his mother. 'Let him kill me, as long as he comes to power' (*occidat, dum imperet*), was her supposed reply.

son: almost certainly Nero's astrologer Tiberius Claudius Balbillus, who may also be the individual of that name who pursued a highly successful political career, leading to the governorship of Egypt.

Asinius Gallus: the details of his arrest in AD 30 are provided in detail by Dio (58.3.1–5) and would doubtless have been covered in the missing section of Book 5.

Drusus' death: his arrest would have been covered among the events of AD 30. The horrific account of his death by starvation appears also in Suetonius (*Tib.* 54.2).

197 *Agrippina*: she died on the anniversary of Sejanus' death, hence 18 October (as recorded in the *Fasti* of Ostia).

198 *moral turpitude*: at 5.3 Tacitus makes the point that Tiberius was unable even to concoct charges of immorality against Agrippina. The accusation is now even less persuasive, given that both she and Asinius Gallus have been under arrest for a number of years.

Plancina: she had enjoyed the protection of Livia, and was presumably protected after Livia's death by her hostility to Agrippina. The implication is that after the latter's death Plancina had no further claim on Tiberius' goodwill.

crimes that were well known: it is not clear whether these are in part or in whole the charges that were laid during the trial of Piso, although Tacitus' characterization of them as 'late in coming' implies that they were the same.

Julia: the marriage of Julia, daughter of Tiberius' son Drusus, to the socially inferior Rubellius Blandus seems anticlimactic, but the importance attached by the Romans to family status should not be underestimated.

Aelius Lamia: see note to p. 143. He had a successful career as governor of Africa and was technically legate of Syria for ten years, but for some reason Tiberius did not allow him to leave Rome during his term of office (see also Arruntius, below). Perhaps the four legions of Syria were seen by Tiberius as a potential threat.

199 *Flaccus Pomponius*: see note to p. 65. Like Lamia, he was a 'new man', but, unlike him, allowed to take up his position in Syria when the latter gave up the legateship to become city prefect. Flaccus seems to have enjoyed Tiberius' confidence; Suetonius (*Tib.* 41.1) describes him as the emperor's drinking buddy.

Arruntius was being held back: Tacitus (*Hist.* 2.65.2) explains that Arruntius was kept in Rome by Tiberius because of fear. How well grounded the suspicions might have been is difficult to ascertain. His influence was mentioned at 6.5.

Marcus Lepidus: see note to p. 12. Tacitus presumably felt that it would be unnecessary to add details of his accomplishments, to which he has made frequent reference already.

Lucius Vitellius: this is the first mention in the *Annals* of this man, who will play a significant role from this point on. He enjoyed a remarkably successful career and held three consulships (subsequent ones are in 43 and 47), and a distinguished term as legate of Syria. He was the father of the later short-lived emperor of the same name.

phoenix: the myth of the phoenix fascinated Greek and Roman writers from the earliest period to the advent of Christianity, when it became the symbol of the Resurrection.

Sesosis: a mythical monarch. Amasis ruled about 570–526, and Ptolemy III, 246–221 BC.

200 *I mentioned above*: see 4.47.

verses: Dio (58.24.3–5) provides more details, claiming that he wrote an *Atreus*, in which he represented Tiberius as the titular subject because of his bloodlust. Tiberius commented that he would make Scaurus an Ajax, and forced him to emulate the Greek hero by committing suicide.

Livilla: the wife of Drusus had by now been dead for two years, so the charges related to long-past events.

201 *Lentulus Gaetulicus*: see 4.42. He was consul in AD 26 and was appointed legate of Upper Germany in 29. He was not an efficient disciplinarian. We do not know which of Sejanus' two sons was intended to become his son-in-law. Also, we do not know to what extent the patronage secured his appointment to Germany; his father-in-law, Lucius Apronius (see next note), legate of Upper Germany, might have played a role. Gaetulicus would be executed by Caligula in 39 for plotting against the emperor.

Lucius Apronius: see note to p. 34. He had served under Germanicus in AD 15, when he won triumphal honours, and was similarly honoured for his services against Tacfarinas in Africa. The date of his appointment to Lower Germany is unknown, but certainly before 28, when he dealt with the revolt of the Frisians.

In the consulship . . . King Artabanus' knowledge: in the next six chapters, Tacitus, for the first time in the *Annals*, abandons his usual annalistic structure, bringing together the events of two years into a single section, not explaining his reason until the beginning of chapter 38. He does so to deal with the complex events in Parthia. Germanicus had established the pro-Roman Zeno/Artaxias on the throne of Armenia. On the latter's death, Artabanus II, king of Parthia, installed his son Arsaces there, ushering in a new period of difficulties between Rome and Parthia. As these chapters reveal, Artabanus was in fact driven out of Parthia, but the Roman nominee Tiridates failed to exploit the opportunity and Artabanus was able to recover his throne.

201 *aged Tiberius*: Suetonius (*Tib.* 66) has Artabanus write a scarcely credible letter to Tiberius, advising him to please his subjects by committing suicide.

202 *thus maintaining his policy . . . intrigue*: Tiberius' strategy was to foment the latent hostilities between Artabanus and the Parthian nobles, to reconcile the Iberian Mithridates to his brother Pharasmenes, to put forward his own champion for the throne of Armenia, and to appoint a vigorous and able governor of Syria.

203 *crime*: i.e. the murder of Arsaces.

Orodes: possibly the son of Artabanus, briefly king of Armenia between 15/16 and 18.

Phrixus: in the myth, he went to Colchis on the back of a golden ram, whose fleece became the object of the quest of Jason.

205 *suovetaurilia*: a sacred rite involving the sacrifice to Mars of a pig, a ram, and a bull.

206 *Dalmatian war*: Tiberius set out to deal with the rebellion of Pannonia and Dalmatia in AD 6. By 9 the rebellion had been suppressed and Tiberius was awarded a triumph.

Fulcinius Trio: consul in 31. Ironically, when first introduced by Tacitus at 2.28 (see note to p. 63), he is a notorious informer, but here his downfall is classed among the disasters of the period and a stain on Tiberius' record.

207 *near the city*: Tiberius' presence in the vicinity of Rome is unexplained. Dio (58.25.2) places him in Antium (Anzio) for the wedding of Caligula in this year (AD 35).

Lucius Aruseius: possibly the Aruseius of 6.7. Presumably more would have been said about him in the missing section of Book 5, and the break in the text here creates added difficulties.

Tigranes: confusingly, Tigranes is a common name for the rulers of Armenia. This individual is particularly obscure.

Gaius Galba: see 3.52. Gaius Sulpicius Galba was consul in AD 22.

the two Blaesi: consuls of 26 and 28, sons of Sejanus' uncle, Quintus Junius Blaesus.

Aemilia Lepida: daughter of the much-admired Marcus Lepidus, whose death is recorded at 6.27. Dio (57.3.8) claims that she was seduced by Sejanus and provided information that he was able to use against her husband Drusus, the son of Germanicus.

Cietae . . . Cappadocia: confusingly, the Cietae did not live in Cappadocia but in Cilicia to the south. Moreover, Archelaus of Cappadocia had been summoned to Rome in AD 17 and had died there. It is possible that a son of the same name had acquired a kingdom in Cilicia and was still reigning there in AD 36.

208 *Tiridates*: Tacitus picks up the narrative from 6.37 where Vitellius had advanced with Tiridates as far as the Euphrates.

provinces: the reference is to the eighteen 'provinces' of Parthia, corresponding roughly to the satrapies of the Persian empire.

209 *the Surena*: the commander-in-chief of the Parthian army, second in importance only to the king. The position seems to have been hereditary.

210 *the Elymaeans*: their exact location is uncertain. Elymais is used of the south-western part of Iran around Susa, but it is hard to see how such a region could support Tiridates from the rear.

Arabs: Tacitus can hardly be alluding to the Arabs of Arabia proper. His reference must be to the Arab kingdom of Osroene (Edesa) in north-western Mesopotamia, ruled by Acbarus (see note to p. 241).

Tiridates: with his retreat to Syria, Tiridates leaves the historical scene. The situation was essentially that of the *status quo ante*. Artabanus was restored to his throne and a Roman nominee ruled Armenia. It remained to confirm the arrangement, which happened when Vitellius and Artabanus met on the banks of the Euphrates. Tacitus, who does not mention the ceremony here, seems to agree with Suetonius (*Cal.* 14.3, *Vit.* 2.4) and Dio (59.27.3) that the pact belongs to the reign of Caligula. But Josephus (*AJ* 18.96) claims that Tiberius oversaw its terms. Perhaps the agreement was reached before the death of Tiberius and its formal confirmation took place in the reign of his successor.

A hundred million sesterces: this is the same sum that Tiberius advanced as a loan during the financial crisis of 33. But on this occasion the grant is an outright gift.

buildings of his own: Suetonius (*Tib.* 47) concurs that Tiberius left no great buildings and that the only two he undertook, the temple of Augustus (see 1.10) and the theatre of Pompey (see note to p. 132), were unfinished at the time of his death.

Publius Petronius: see note to p. 120. He had returned from a six-year governorship of Asia and would be legate of Syria from 37 to possibly 42.

mentioned: see 6.20.

Ennia: Dio (58.28.4) agrees with Tacitus in making Macro a pander while Philo (*Leg.* 6.39–40) places the initiative entirely with his wife Ennia; Suetonius (*Cal.* 12.2) blames Caligula.

211 *Drusus' son*: Tiberius Gemellus, born in AD 19. His twin brother had died in 23. He had entered puberty in the technical sense but had not yet received the *toga virilis* (toga of manhood), which happened after the accession of Caligula (Suetonius, *Cal.* 15.2).

he was leaving a setting sun to look at one that was rising: this was something of a cliché, supposedly said by Pompey to Sulla, when the latter refused him a triumph (Plutarch, *Pompey* 14.4).

211 *'You will kill him, and another will kill you'*: Tiberius' prophecy would be fulfilled. Caligula had Gemellus executed during the first year of his reign and was in turn assassinated in 41.

Albucilla: wife of Satrius Secundus, an ally of Sejanus (see 4.34, 6.8), she seems to be introduced mainly as a link to her three supposed lovers, all of whom were men of considerable distinction: Gnaeus Domitius, father of Nero (see note to p. 178), Vibius Marsus (see note to p. 88), and Lucius Arruntius (see note to p. 8).

records: these are the records of the judicial proceedings held under Macro. It is interesting that the charges were laid before the Senate but the proceedings were conducted by Macro, presumably while on Capri with Tiberius.

212 *Carsidius Sacerdos*: he had been accused in AD 23 of supplying grain to Tacfarinas but was acquitted (see 4.13), and became a praetor in 27. Nothing is then known of his activities up to this point.

Sextus Papinius: because he is described as being from a consular family it is quite possible that he is the son of the consul of 36 (see 6.40).

213 *changes of residence*: Suetonius (*Tib.* 72–3) states that Tiberius went from near Rome to Astura, Circeii, and Misenum, with the intention of returning to Capri from the last, but was detained, by bad weather and his worsening health, at the villa once owned by the notoriously wealthy Lucullus. The villa was a fine one with many historical associations, having once been the home of Marius. It was later owned by the emperor Romulus Augustulus, and supposedly housed the bones of St Severinus.

214 *bedclothes on him*: there were variants to this account. Dio (58.28.3) is fairly close to Tacitus, but gives the main role to Caligula, aided by Macro. Suetonius (*Tib.* 73.2, *Cal.* 12.2) reports several theories, that Caligula poisoned Tiberius, or starved him to death, or smothered or strangled him. Seneca (cited by Suetonius) and Philo (*Leg.* 25), on the other hand, suggest that the death was perfectly natural.

seventy-eighth: Tiberius was born on 16 November 42 BC.

BOOK ELEVEN

215 *. . . for Messalina*: there is a gap in the text after the end of Book 6. Books 7 to 10 are missing, as well as part, perhaps as much as half, of Book 11, covering events from AD 37 to the beginning of 47, thus constituting all of Caligula's reign and about half of Claudius'. The text resumes in midsentence and we soon see that at issue is the downfall of Valerius Asiaticus. He was a wealthy Gaul, from Vienne in Gallia Lugdunensis, who despite his provincial origins went on to hold two consulships. He was a close confidant of the emperor and accompanied him on the expedition against Britain. The chief agent in his downfall was Valeria Messalina, Claudius' third wife. Messalina was determined to kill two

birds with one stone, and simultaneously brought down Poppaea Sabina, mother of Nero's second wife of the same name and reputedly the lover of Messalina's favourite, the pantomime actor Mnester. Messalina claimed that Poppaea and Asiaticus had committed adultery. The accusation was launched by the sinister Publius Suillius, now returned from exile, and orchestrated by Lucius Vitellius, who has already made an appearance in Book 6.

Suillius: a notorious informant, first mentioned at 4.31 (AD 24) as an ex-quaestor of Germanicus, convicted of bribery and later enjoying the friendship of Claudius.

Britannicus: the son of Claudius, born, according to Suetonius (*Claud.* 27.2), twenty days after Claudius came to power.

Gaius Caesar's: Caligula. His assassination would have been covered in the earlier missing books.

Crispinus: first husband of the daughter of Nero's second wife Poppaea Sabina, Rufrius Crispinus was implicated in the conspiracy of Piso in AD 65 and committed suicide the following year (see 16.17).

Poppaea: the wife of Publius Cornelius Scipio, described at 13.45 as the great beauty of her age.

sons: the reputation of Suillius' sons matched their father's. Marcus Suillius Nerullinus (13.43) was accused of extortion; the Suillius Caesoninus mentioned at 11.36 because of his sexual vices is probably also a son.

Scipio: Publius Cornelius Lentulus Scipio could claim distinguished ancestry but also had an accomplished career of his own, as consul in 24 and probably governor of Asia in about 36/7.

216 *Britain*: Asiaticus had presumably participated in the expedition of AD 43.

217 *laws*: Claudius' passion for legal proceedings is confirmed by Suetonius (*Claud.* 14).

Gaius Silius: as consul-designate he was entitled to speak first. He will reappear as the final lover of Messalina (11.12, 27–35).

Cincian law: introduced in 204 BC, this measure, among other things, prohibited the receipt of payment by advocates. It was revived by Augustus in 17 BC, but it had clearly once again fallen into abeyance.

Cossutianus: Cossutianus Capito was another active accuser of the period, a vigorous opponent of the philosopher Thrasea Paetus. He was banished for extortion in Cilicia but restored through the intervention of his father-in-law, Nero's favourite, Tigellinus.

218 *Clodius . . . Curio*: these were strange precedents, no doubt seen as such by Tacitus. Publius Clodius Pulcher, tribune in 58 BC, was the bitter enemy of Cicero, and was killed in a street brawl with Milo. Gaius Scribonius Curio, ally of Clodius and tribune of 50 BC, was bribed to support Caesar during the late 50s, having previously opposed him.

218 *I noted above*: the last mention of Parthian affairs, in Book 6, saw Mithridates established in Armenia and Artabanus restored to the throne of Parthia. Under Caligula, Mithridates was summoned to Rome and arrested, and Armenia fell again under Parthian influence. Events are obscure following the death of Artabanus: Parthia was torn by civil war between his sons Gotarzes and Vardanes (a third brother, Artabanus, had been murdered). Once again Tacitus abandons his annalistic scheme in dealing with the Parthians. In chapters 8–10 he summarizes events from AD 42 to 48, then the narrative breaks off, to resume at 12.10.

three thousand stades: about 350 (modern) miles, an apparently impossible claim.

219 *six years*: the revolt must have begun in AD 36.

220 *Arsacids*: the ruling dynasty of Parthia; it lasted from the middle of the third century BC to about AD 230.

same consulship: Lucius Vitellius and Claudius himself. Their names would have appeared in the missing section.

Secular Games: confusion arose over the appropriate year for these games, since there were two possible cycles, one of 100 years, another of the Etruscan 110 years. Augustus applied the latter, Claudius the former, using the Varronian foundation date of 753 BC as the starting point. Suetonius (*Claud.* 21.2) claims that Claudius deviously recalculated the date although he believed that the Augustan calculation had been correct.

Domitian: Domitian's celebration of the games would have been recounted in the final section of the *Histories*, now lost. For Tacitus' possible responsibilities in the celebration, see the Introduction.

Game of Troy: it was on this occasion celebrated in the Circus games, which had been included in the Secular Games by Augustus in the celebration of 17 BC.

Lucius Domitius: this is the first mention in the extant *Annals* of the future emperor Nero, who had lived with his aunt when his mother Agrippina was exiled by Caligula (see note to p. 266). Nero was presumably reunited with Agrippina on the accession of Claudius, when she was recalled from the exile imposed by Caligula. Their activities after the recall up to this point are uncertain.

221 *Germanicus*: the potency of Germanicus' name had been largely instrumental in securing the accession of his son Caligula, and to some degree that of his brother Claudius.

Junia Silana: (see 13.19) probably the daughter of Marcus Junius Silanus (3.24) and sister of Junia Claudilla, wife of Caligula; her death is recorded at 14.12.

young men: because they were subject to *patria potestas*, sons were not allowed to borrow money without the consent of the head of the house. To get around this, they secured loans that would be repaid (with interest) on the death of the father.

spring water: Claudius constructed two major aqueducts, the Anio Novus and the Aqua Claudia.

new alphabetic letters: Claudius had long had an interest in the shortcomings of the Roman alphabet and wrote a book about it (Suetonius, *Claud.* 41.3).

Cadmus: by tradition, Cadmus brought the Phoenician alphabet to Greece, as related by Herodotus 5.58.

222 *three letters*: Claudius introduced a reversed digamma ⅂ to distinguish the consonantal *v* from the vocalic *u*, and a half H Ⱶ to represent the sound between *u* and *i*; both of these are attested in inscriptions. The third was an antisigma Ɔ to represent ψ.

college of soothsayers: these were the *haruspices*, who practised the Etruscan art of divination. As a result of Claudius' proposal a college of sixty members was established.

one person of royal descent . . . Italicus: he was a Roman citizen, but it was clearly thought that the Cherusci would receive him as though he had been a hostage or a refugee.

Flavus: see 2.9.

224 *Sanquinius*: see note to p. 186. His appointment as legate of Germany would have been covered in the missing books.

Corbulo: this is the first extant reference in the *Annals* to Gnaeus Domitius Corbulo, probably the most distinguished general of the reigns of Claudius and Nero. He was consul in 39, half-brother of the reprobate Suillius (see note to p. 215) and saw service in Germany and as governor of Asia. After sterling work in the East he was summoned by Nero to Greece in 67 and committed suicide to avoid execution.

triremes: these belonged to the Rhine fleet (*Classis Germanica*) established by Drusus, who cut a channel for it from the Rhine to the Zuyder Zee.

Frisian tribe: the revolt of the Frisians in AD 28 is covered at 4.72.

225 *west of the Rhine*: Rome did not again try to occupy the territory east of the lower Rhine.

Curtius Rufus: consul of 43, he is identified by some with Quintus Curtius Rufus, the historian of Alexander the Great; he may, however, have been the historian's father.

financial loss: presumably the reference here is to the wear and tear on the legionaries' clothing, for which they themselves had to pay, without any compensating opportunity for booty.

vision: the same story is told by Pliny the Younger (*Ep.* 7.27.2–3), who adds the information that Curtius would die in Africa while serving as governor (the date is unknown).

226 *Gnaeus Nonius*: otherwise unknown. Claudius was frequently the target of attempted assassinations (Suetonius, *Claud.* 13.1). In the period after his accession he would not even enter the Senate House without an armed guard.

226 *paying their respects*: these refer to the public morning receptions held by the emperor. Claudius had his visitors searched (Suetonius, *Claud.* 35.1).

a gladiatorial show: responsibility for public entertainments fell to the praetors, and the measure of Dolabella would have represented a significant change in procedure.

an age qualification: the formal establishment of minimum ages for the magistracies was enacted in the *Lex Villia Annalis* of 180 BC.

lex curiata: de imperio, a law passed by the curial assembly, the *comitia curiata*, bestowed *imperium* on the consuls and praetors.

Brutus: the first consul of the Roman republic, traditionally in 509 BC.

The first elected quaestors: elected in 447 BC. Tacitus is the only authority to provide this date.

legislation of Sulla: the *Lex Cornelia*, carried in 81 BC, increased the number of quaestors and made them members of the Senate.

227 *Aulus Vitellius*: the son of Claudius' staunchest supporter, Lucius Vitellius, and destined to reign briefly as emperor in 69.

The following two chapters cover one of the most celebrated events of Claudius' reign, the admission of Gallic notables to the Roman Senate. Claudius held the office of censor, which provided him with the opportunity to expand the membership of the Senate. We have an opportunity here to compare Tacitus' account with the public record, since the speech of Claudius in favour of the measure has survived on a bronze tablet at Lyons, discovered there in the sixteenth century (http://www.thelatinlibrary.com/claud.inscr.html). In the tradition of ancient historiography, Tacitus has recast the speech; it is shorter and less rambling than the original.

'Long-haired' Gaul: Claudius had himself been born in Lugdunum (Lyons) in Gallia Lugdunensis, one of the three imperial provinces that made up *Gallia Comata*, translated here as 'Long-haired' Gaul.

citizenship: leading individuals of federate tribes could hold Roman citizenship, but without senatorial rank.

Before the emperor: Tacitus here recounts the debate held in the imperial council, a group of the emperor's close advisers.

Alesia: the scene of the siege in 52 BC of Vercingetorix by Julius Caesar, and of Caesar by the relieving Gallic forces (Caesar, *Bellum Gallicum* 7.68–84).

Capitol: the text is very corrupt here, but the reference is clearly to the capture of Rome and the siege of the Capitol by the Senonians after the battle of the River Allia in 390 BC.

convened the Senate: Claudius had been unable to convince members of his council and accordingly presented his arguments to the Senate, as a *relatio* or formal motion for a vote.

Clausus: see 4.9.

228 *Alps*: Caesar granted citizenship to the Gauls north of the Po in 49 BC.

real peace: the claim is remarkable and seems contrary to historical facts.

settling our legions in colonies: colonies were established throughout the empire to provide for veterans but also as a way of spreading Romanization, largely through intermarriage.

the Balbuses: Lucius Cornelius Balbus from Cadiz received citizenship through Pompey. In 40 BC he became the first foreigner to obtain the consulship, but anomalously, since he remained an equestrian. His nephew of the same name was the first foreign-born Roman to earn a triumph.

the Spartans and the Athenians: Claudius has in mind the relationship between the Spartans and Messenia, and Athens and her confederacy.

Etruscans: there was a tradition that the Etruscans, led by Lars Porsena, occupied Rome after the expulsion of Tarquinius Superbus.

Samnites: the disaster of the Caudine Forks occurred in 321 BC, when Roman troops were compelled by the Samnites to pass under the yoke.

a shorter time than that against the Gauls: 59–50 BC; there had in fact been shorter conquests and in the speech that has survived in the record, Claudius stresses the stubbornness of their resistance.

Aedui: the passage is ambiguous. It is not clear if they were the first among many to receive the privilege on this occasion, or by what process the rights were bestowed (probably by *adlectio*, or special appointment, one of the tasks of the censor). The supposed brotherhood of the Aedui and the Romans was of some antiquity; in his *Gallic War*, Caesar alludes to it having been frequently recognized by the Senate (*Bellum Gallicum* 1.33.2).

treaty: the date is unknown, but they were federate (*foederati*) in the period of the Gracchi (Livy, *Per.* 61).

patricians: it was necessary to maintain the numbers of the patricians, much diminished during the civil wars, since they alone could hold certain religious offices.

'Greater': the hundred greater houses were supposedly established by Romulus, and by tradition the 'Lesser' houses were added by Tarquinius. Only Tacitus ascribes this latter role to Brutus.

229 *Lex Saenia*: in *Res Gestae* 8.1, Augustus refers to increasing the number of patricians during his fifth consulship (29 BC). Saenius was consul in the previous year (30 BC).

census-purification: the formal ceremony (*lustrum*) was conducted by the censors at the end of their term.

the count of the citizens: the Augustan census figures of 28 and 8 BC were 4,063,000 and 4,233,000, indicating a considerable increase in population by Claudius' reign, testimony no doubt to the order and stability brought about by the imperial system in its early days.

229 *an incestuous marriage*: Tacitus is alluding to Claudius' later marriage to his niece Agrippina.

230 *Ostia*: Claudius' presence at Ostia, Rome's port city, may have been connected to issues of the grain-supply.

incredible: Tacitus' admission that the events to be described will seem unbelievable makes his account all the more credible, although the motives of the participants remain baffling.

an actor: Mnester. Tacitus alludes again, a few chapters later, to the affair between Mnester and Messalina (11.36); Dio gives a livelier account, claiming that the adultery was encouraged by Claudius, and that all the bronze coins bearing Caligula's image were melted down to be used by Messalina to make statuettes of Mnester (Dio 60.22.3, 28.3). According to Suetonius (*Cal.* 36), Caligula had earlier been his lover.

231 *Callistus*: he had been a freedman of Caligula, who switched his allegiance to Claudius and was almost certainly involved in Caligula's assassination. He was *a libellis*, in charge of petitions. He was noted for his prodigious wealth.

Narcissus: he was *ab epistulis*, in charge of correspondence, the most powerful and most obstinately loyal of the Claudian freedmen.

Appius: the murder of Appius Junius Silanus occurred in 42 (see the note on 4.91).

Pallas: he had been a slave of Claudius' mother Antonia. He was *a rationibus*, in charge of finances.

Titius, Vettius, and Plautius: lovers of Messalina; Titius Proculus (see 11.35), Vettius Valens (11.31, 35), and Plautius Lateranus (11.36).

Turranius: he had been appointed to the office on the death of Augustus, thirty-four years earlier. He was now in his nineties (Seneca, *De Brevitate Vitae* 20).

Lusius Geta: the praetorian prefect and colleague of Rufrius Crispinus. It was usual for one of the prefects to accompany the emperor on his travels. Lusius would go on to be prefect of Egypt.

232 *Vettius Valens*: mentioned as a lover of Messalina in the above section. He was an eminent physician (Pliny, *NH* 29.1.8).

Vibidia: Vestals had the right of access to the emperor, and were entitled to intervene on behalf of the convicted. Claudius was of course supreme pontiff (*Pontifex Maximus*), which would make a Vestal intervention doubly appropriate.

233 *Largus Caecina*: he had been Claudius' colleague in the consulship of 42, six years earlier.

Silius' father: the condemnation of the elder Silius in AD 24 is recounted at 4.18–20.

Nerones and Drusi: Claudius was a Nero through his paternal grandfather Tiberius Claudius Nero and a Drusus through his grandmother Livia, whose father had been adopted by Livius Drusus.

234 *Suillius Caesoninus*: almost certainly one of the two sons of the delator Publius Suillius Rufus (see 11.2).

Plautius Lateranus: see 11.30; he would return to the Senate in 55 (13.11) and later join the Pisonian conspiracy of 65 against Nero (15.49, 60). His property was confiscated and supposedly given later to the Christian Church, preserving his memory in the name of the Lateran cathedral. His uncle was Aulus Plautius, commander of the expeditions against Britain.

235 *Lepida*: she was the cousin of Agrippina the Younger and great-niece of Augustus. Her first husband was Valerius Messala Barbatus; her second husband, Gaius Appius Junius Silanus, was brought down through the instigation of Messalina, and relations between mother and daughter would not have been especially warm.

It was . . . consequences: the manuscript text of the final sentence of this section is hopelessly corrupt.

BOOK TWELVE

236 *Lollia Paulina*: granddaughter of Marcus Lollius, consul of 21 BC, former wife of Caligula. Her extravagance in jewellery is noted by Pliny (*NH* 9.117).

Aelia Paetina: she had previously been married to Claudius and had borne him a daughter, Antonia.

237 *Gnaeus Ahenobarbus*: see 4.75.

Lucius Silanus: born about 26/7, great-great-grandson of Augustus, Lucius Junius Silanus accompanied Claudius to Britain; he went ahead to Rome to report the victory, and was awarded triumphal honours.

Junia Calvina: a woman of great charm (Seneca, *Apoc.* 8.2), married to Lucius Vitellius, brother of the later emperor.

resign his magistracy: Suetonius (*Claud.* 29.2) reports that Silanus resigned on 29 December.

Eprius Marcellus: consul of 62 and 74, a notorious accuser who amassed great wealth (see 13.33, 16.22, 28, 29).

escorted: the Latin *deducere* (to escort) was often used essentially to mean 'marry', after the practice of accompanying the new bride to the house of her husband.

238 *Palatium*: the reference here is to the imperial residence that stood on and took its name from the Palatine Hill.

mind of a censor: the censors had the task of supervising public morality; Claudius assumed the office in 47 and took his duties seriously. Vitellius acknowledges his special talent for the role, and observes that it was entirely proper that such an individual should have a wife.

at the whim of the Caesars: notoriously, Tiberius Claudius Nero had divorced Livia as a favour to Augustus (see note to p. 10), while within living memory Caligula had obliged the husbands of Livia Orestilla (variously named) and Lollia Paulina to divorce their wives (Suetonius, *Cal.* 24) to make them available for himself.

239 *decree*: the decree allowing marriage between a man and the daughter of his brother (it did not apply to the daughter of his sister) remained in force until the fourth century, when it was possibly abolished by Constantine.

Calvina was banished: she was recalled some ten years later, after the death of Agrippina, and lived into Vespasian's reign.

laws of King Tullus: Tullus Hostilius, Rome's third king, prescribed expiatory rites for Horatius after he killed his sister.

Annaeus Seneca's: this is the first reference in the extant books of the *Annals* to the famous writer and philosopher, who will play a prominent role from now on until his death in 65. He had been exiled to Corsica in 41 on the charge of being the lover of Caligula's sister, Julia Livilla.

Mammius Pollio: as consul-designate he was called upon first to give his opinion on a question, but was not obliged to limit his remarks to that question.

240 *the Parthian representatives*: their mission was referred to at 11.10, and it is to be supposed that the lapse in time is accounted for by their journey.

Augustus . . . a king: on the death of Orodes III in about AD 6, the Parthians requested Rome to provide a king. Augustus sent Vonones, father of Meherdates.

241 *Gaius Cassius*: Gaius Cassius Longinus, consul in 30, appointed governor of Syria in 44. He was an eminent legal scholar and author of several books on civil law. Banished by Nero, he was recalled by Vespasian (see 13.41, 48; 14.42). He was the brother of Lucius Cassius Longinus (see 6.15).

the Cassian family: Gaius Cassius, the assassin of Julius Caesar, had played an important role in defending Syria against a Parthian invasion after the defeat of Crassus at Carrhae in 53 BC.

Acbarus: see note to p. 210.

Carenes: presumably satrap of Mesopotamia.

Adiabeni: located in northern Assyria. Meherdates had clearly advanced a considerable distance.

Izates: he had probably become king early in Claudius' reign. He was a key player in the endless dynastic disputes in Parthia.

final battle: Nineveh (Ninos) was not far from Gaugamela, site of the last battle between Alexander and Darius, in 331 BC.

242 *Vologaeses*: Vologaeses I seems to have been on the throne as early as September 51. He proved to be a powerful opponent, and plays a key role in Tacitus' account of Parthian affairs. He reigned until his death in 79/80.

Mithridates of Bosporus: he is to be distinguished from Mithridates of Armenia (11.8). His kingdom was located in the Crimea and along the north coast of the Black Sea. He had ruled part of it under Caligula, and it was extended by Claudius in 41. He was removed in 46 because of doubts about his loyalty, to be succeeded by his brother Cotys (probably covered by Tacitus in now missing chapters).

Didius: see 12.40, 14.29; consul in AD 39, he was governor of Moesia from 44, and later of Britain (52–7). He had a distinguished career, and won triumphal honours.

244 *Achaemenes*: founder of the Achaemenid Persian dynasty and great-grandfather of Cyrus. The genealogy claimed by Mithridates was highly dubious.

245 *Mithridates . . . taken to Rome*: he remained at Rome until the accession of Galba, when he was put to death as a supposed accomplice of Nymphidius (Plutarch, *Galba* 15).

Junius Cilo: he clearly enjoyed imperial favour; later governor of Bithynia, he was prosecuted for extortion but acquitted through the intervention of Narcissus. He received higher insignia than Aquila, whose role seems to have been more substantial.

Lucius Volusius' sister: Volusia, sister of Lucius Volusius Saturninus, the consul of AD 3 (see 13.30). Lucius died in 56 at the age of 93; inscriptions reveal that he held a number of positions, including that of governor of Dalmatia. He was city prefect at the time of his death (Pliny, *NH* 7.62).

246 *Calpurnia*: 'of great distinction' to distinguish her from the courtesan Calpurnia mentioned at 11.30. She was allowed to return from exile after Agrippina's death (14.12).

Lollia's case: see 12.1; Dio (60.32.4) adds the detail that Lollia's head was brought to Agrippina, who identified it by the teeth.

Cadius Rufus: governor of Bithynia 43–8, he was expelled from the Senate after conviction but later restored by Otho.

Sohaemus: he had been appointed king by Caligula, and presumably died in this year.

Agrippa: 'Herod' Agrippa was given territories by Caligula which were enlarged by Claudius. He had in fact died in 44, some five years earlier than the events described.

pomerium: the consecrated ground constituting the sacred and religious boundary of the city of Rome.

those who extended the empire: the reference is to Claudius' victories in Britain in 43.

Palatine Hill: the *pomerium* of Romulus was drawn along the base of the Palatine Hill.

temple of Consus: the altar of Consus was located between the Palatine and Aventine and uncovered only during certain festivals.

ancient curiae: traditionally the original meeting place of the parishes of the Roman people (*curiae*). It lay somewhere between the Septizonium and the temple of Jupiter Victor.

246 *Titus Tatius*: according to tradition, king of the Sabines.

247 *patricians of the Claudian family*: a distinction is made with the plebeian Claudii Marcelli.

Attus Clausus: see 4.9.

a law was passed: Domitius' father was dead and Domitius was consequently *sui iuris* (not subject to the jurisdiction of a third party); hence a formal law was needed for the adoption.

Augusta: Agrippina was the first woman so honoured while her husband was alive. Livia, and possibly Antonia, had received the title during their own lifetimes.

a colony: the future city of Cologne, founded as Colonia Agrippiniensis at Ara Ubiorum. The colony was very successful, with considerable privileges granted to the town's original inhabitants; it enjoyed a later prosperity that was much resented by other German communities.

248 *Vannius*: see 2.63.

Vibilius: in AD 19 he was responsible for the expulsion of Catualda from his kingdom (2.63). Now he was giving the same treatment to Vannius.

Vangio and Sido: Sido was still in power in AD 69 when he fought on the Flavian side along with Italicus, who had succeeded Vangio.

Palpellius Hister: consul in AD 43.

249 *Britain*: Caligula's planned invasion of Britain and Claudius' actual invasion, and the subsequent advance of the Romans north and westward under the first governor, Aulus Plautius, would have been covered in the lost books of the *Annals*. At this point Tacitus once again violates annalistic principles, as he often does when dealing with military campaigns. Although at 12.25 he introduced the narrative of AD 50, he now goes back to AD 47, and then covers events in Britain up to 54.

Publius Ostorius: Publius Ostorius Scapula was consul in AD 59; he succeeded Aulus Plautius in Britain in 47. He was forced to commit suicide under Nero in 66 (see 14.48).

Trisantona: Trisantona is reconstructed from a very corrupt reading in the manuscripts. As emended, it is taken to refer to the River Trent, although certainty is not possible.

Iceni: they would play an important role in later history when Boudicca, the widow of their king, led a major rebellion.

allied troops: the auxiliaries; the legions were involved in the expansion of Roman territory, and only auxiliaries were available to deal with the unrest.

prize of honour: this refers to the 'civic crown'; see the note to p. 106.

250 *Decangi*: the name is uncertain (the manuscript gives *Cangi*). They were located in North Wales.

legionary camp: at Gloucester.

Camulodunum: Colchester; local resentment over the establishment of this colony fuelled Boudicca's rebellion.

Caratacus: one of the sons of Cunobelinus, an important British king (Shakespeare's Cymbeline), he would presumably have been mentioned in the missing books of the *Annals*, since Dio (60.20.1) speaks of his involvement during the early stages of the invasion. He fled west to Wales after the death of his brother and achieved heroic status (Welsh 'Caradoc').

251 *Caratacus' wife and daughter*: in Britain, as in Germany, it was common for families to accompany warriors to the battlefield.

Cartimandua: she was a steadfast ally of the Romans, and reigned until AD 69. Her name appears in the manuscripts as Cartimandus in the *Annals* and Cartimandua in the *Histories* (with minor variants in both cases); the reading *Cartimandus* may well be correct, but it is by the latter feminized spelling that she has long become familiar.

eight years: presumably AD 51, the year in which an arch was dedicated in Rome to celebrate the victories over the Britons.

252 *forefathers*: she was great-granddaughter of Augustus. In addition she was granddaughter of Drusus and daughter of Germanicus, two men associated in the popular imagination with northern conquests.

Syphax: king of Numidia, paraded in the triumph of Publius Cornelius Scipio Africanus in 201 BC.

Perses: king of Macedonia, paraded in the triumph of Lucius Aemilius Paulus in 167 BC.

253 *Sugambri*: they had been defeated by Tiberius in 8 BC and the remaining elements of the tribe had been moved to the west bank of the Rhine.

Manlius Valens: he survived the defeat and commanded a legion some years later (in 69) and, remarkably, became consul as late as 96.

254 *Venutius . . . already mentioned*: he evidently appeared in the now-missing chapters.

legion: the employment of a legion testifies to the seriousness of the situation.

before his time: Nero had passed his thirteenth birthday. The *toga virilis* was not normally conferred before the fourteenth.

twentieth year: Gaius and Lucius Caesar received the same prerogative. Private citizens could hold the consulship at 32 if they were *nobiles*.

'Prince of the Youth': as elsewhere, Nero here followed the precedent of Gaius and Lucius (see 1.3).

triumphal dress: the *vesta triumphalis* was worn not only by those awarded a triumph but also by senior magistrates on important occasions, and then by the emperor (see 13.8). Caesar was entitled to use it at public events and it was worn by Caligula at the dedication of a temple and by Nero in receiving Tiridates (Dio 44.4.2, 6.1; 59.7.1; 63.3.3). In Nero's case the privilege derived presumably from his proconsular *imperium*.

255 *'Domitius'*: the point of the insult is that by addressing Nero by his old family name, which would have been legally given up when he entered the Claudian family, Britannicus ignores his adoption.

Burrus Afranius: Burrus came from Vasio in Narbonese Gaul and served as procurator, although an inscription from his home town supports Tacitus in speaking of a distinguished military service.

daughter . . . of men: Agrippina was daughter of Germanicus, sister of Caligula, wife of Claudius, and mother of Nero.

Vitellius: this is the last reference in the *Annals* to the familiar Lucius Vitellius, and he presumably died shortly afterwards.

256 *his brothers*: Tiridates and Pacorus, rulers of Media (see 12.50, 15.2).

257 *the Albani*: they appear in 6.33 as the allies of Pharasmanes. Nothing is known of the war alluded to.

Casperius: some years later Corbulo sent Casperius on a mission to Vologaeses (15.5).

Ummidius Quadratus: consul, possibly in AD 40, he succeeded Gaius Cassius as governor of Syria, where he died while still in office, probably in 60.

259 *meeting of his staff*: the staff meeting (*consilium*) would involve the legate and senators and senior military officers (including, one assumes, Casperius, although he is not mentioned). As governor of Syria, Ummidius had jurisdiction over the procurator of Cappadocia.

Helvidius Priscus: the mention of the name without qualification might seem to suggest that he is the famous Stoic who became son-in-law of Thrasea Paetus. But that Helvidius did not apparently acquire the quaestorship until the reign of Nero (*Scholia in Juvenalem* 5.36), while *legati* of legions were normally of at least praetorian rank. It is possible that the Helvidius of this section is a different person and was introduced more fully in one of the missing books.

260 *Tiridates*: he had in the meantime regained Armenia. The last events have jumped forward in time and belong to AD 54. The next section returns to events in Rome in 52. Parthian affairs resume in 13.6.

Furius Scribonianus: nothing more is known of him except that he was the son of Marcus Furius Camillus, who as legate of Dalmatia had joined the unsuccessful conspiracy against Claudius in AD 42. Camillus was survived by his wife, Vibia. Her conduct was much criticized by Arria, the wife of one of the other conspirators, who chose to die along with her husband (Pliny, *Ep.* 3.16.2).

261 *senatorial order*: a similar scrutiny of the senatorial rolls had taken place four years earlier.

It was decided: the *senatus consultum Claudianum* remained in force until the time of Justinian, although the penalties were reduced by subsequent emperors.

Barea Soranus: a distinguished Stoic, Quintus Marcius Barea Soranus was perhaps acting out of character on this occasion and perhaps under pressure from Agrippina. He was put to death in AD 66.

Arcadian: Virgil in *Aeneid* 8 associated Evander, king of the Arcadians and father of Pallas, with the future city of Rome. The connection between the Pallas of antiquity and the freedman of Claudius is a piece of obsequious fiction.

honour: Claudius' words were reflected in the official decree that marked the event (Pliny, *Ep.* 7.29.2, 8.6.4).

Felix: Antonius Felix was the freedman of Claudius' mother Antonia. He was sent as procurator to Judaea, and St Paul was famously tried by him, some time after 52 (Acts 24). He was recalled by Nero and escaped prosecution through his brother's influence.

broke out after: there is a gap in the manuscript at this point. It would probably have contained a reference to Caligula's order that his effigy be placed in the temple in Jerusalem (see Tacitus, *Hist.* 5.9.4).

Ventidius Cumanus: he served in Judaea from 48 to 52.

Galileans . . . Samaritans: Tacitus' account of these events differs markedly from that of Josephus, who does not refer to any division between the two procurators (*AJ* 20.5.3, 6.1). It may be that Tacitus has confused events and that Felix was on the staff of Ummidius while Cumanus was procurator.

262 *Antiochus*: Antiochus IV Epiphanes was created king of Commagene by Caligula, then possibly dismissed by him. He was apparently restored by Claudius and given part of Cilicia in addition. He supported Vespasian but was removed in AD 72, on suspicion of collaboration with the Parthians.

the Fucine lake: located in the Apennines, east of Rome, this was the third-largest lake in Italy. With no natural outlet it frequently overflowed, and plans to drain it were mooted by Julius Caesar, and finally brought about by Claudius. The undertaking took eleven years, involving a tunnel beneath Monte Salviana that in places had to be hewn through solid limestone. The project needed constant maintenance and further work under Trajan and Hadrian. The lake was permanently drained in the nineteenth century.

263 *Narcissus*: Dio (60.33.5) reports that he diverted funds for the project, then deliberately caused the collapse to cover up his misbehaviour.

sixteen: in January 53 Nero had in fact just passed his fifteenth birthday and was in his sixteenth year.

Octavia: after Nero's adoption by Claudius, Octavia became his sister, and he had to be adopted by another family before he was legally allowed to marry her.

Rhodians: they originally won their freedom by serving Rome in the Mithridatic and Macedonian wars. They lost it in AD 44 for crucifying Roman citizens (Dio 60.24.4).

264 *Statilius Taurus*: consul in AD 44, son of the consul of the same name of AD 11 and close associate of Augustus.

Tarquitius Priscus: despite his expulsion at this time from the Senate, he reappears as governor of Bithynia, and must presumably have been readmitted to the Senate, probably under Nero, in whose reign he was convicted of extortion (see 14.46).

judgements made by his procurators . . . himself: this passage is one of the most discussed of all the *Annals*. The difficulty is that we are not sure which procurators are at issue here. The title could refer to a wide range of offices from the governor of a small district (from Claudius on, the term was preferred to the previous *praefectus*) to the steward of one of the emperor's private domains. Under Claudius, these private procurators assumed more of a public role and were accordingly granted jurisdiction in disputes.

Egypt: from the outset of the imperial period, Egypt had special status. Although a major province, it was governed by an equestrian with the rank of prefect.

class struggle: there had been intense competition between the senatorial and equestrian orders for control of the courts from 122 to 80 BC.

Sempronian proposals . . . Servilian laws: the Sempronian proposals refer to the bills of Gaius Gracchus in 122 BC, the Servilian laws to the measures of Servilius Glaucia in 106.

Gaius Oppius and Cornelius Balbus: these were Caesar's close friends and financial agents in Rome when he was away in Gaul. They represented him in his dealings with Pompey.

the Matii, the Vedii: Gaius Matius is well known for a frank and exemplary letter written to Cicero after the murder of Caesar (*Ad Familiares* 11.28). He is coupled here with Publius Vedius Pollio, who had a dark reputation for extravagance and cruelty.

265 *Xenophon*: inscriptions reveal that Gaius Stertinius Xenophon pursued a highly successful military career in addition to gaining a reputation as one of the most renowned doctors of the time (see 12.67).

those same islanders' services: the Coans had remained faithful to Rome in the wars against Antiochus the Great (ended 189 BC) and Perses (ended 168 BC) and had protected Roman citizens during the depredations of Mithridates in 88 BC (see 4.14).

the Macedonian king: Andriscus, in 148 BC. He claimed to be the son of Perses.

Aristonicus: he had claimed the kingdom of Pergamum after it was bequeathed to Rome (see 4.55).

Antonius: Marcus Antonius Creticus, the father of the famous triumvir, who was given a command against the pirates in 74 BC and died in 71.

the Greeks founded Byzantium: it was founded in 657 BC, probably by Megareans. Chalcedon was founded seventeen years earlier.

inferior: Chalcedon was established on the eastern shore of the Bosporus, while Byzantium was located on the western.

266 *wars in Thrace and the Bosporus*: it may be that the Byzantines are referring to the events covered in 4.46–51; for the Bosporan wars, see 12.15–21.

younger Antonia: Tacitus is in error here. Domitia was the daughter of the elder Antonia (for similar confusion, see note to p. 161).

Nero: Domitia had taken in Nero at the age of 3 after the death of his father and the exile of Agrippina (Suetonius, *Nero* 6).

267 . . . *nothing to fear*: the meaning of this passage is far from clear, and the translation is based on the following interpretation of Woodman: if Nero came to power, Narcissus would have the same grounds for accusing Agrippina as he had for accusing Messalina, namely, ambition for power, and would accordingly have to be silenced by Agrippina. If Britannicus succeeded, he, as the new emperor, would owe nothing to Narcissus, and might put him to death as the man who brought about his mother's death.

Britannicus: in Suetonius (*Claud.* 43), it is Claudius who makes the display of affection to Britannicus. Tacitus might have preferred a version which showed a freedman rather than Claudius taking action.

Locusta: she would supposedly be called into service again to abet the murder of Britannicus (see 13.15). She was put to death by Galba (Dio 64.3.4).

Halotus: he survived Nero, and was appointed to an important procuratorship by Galba (Suetonius, *Galba* 15).

268 *reward*: Xenophon and his brother Quintus Stertinus between them left an estate of thirty million sesterces (Pliny, *NH* 29.18).

blocked with guards: the parallels between the deaths of Augustus and of Claudius are striking and it is difficult not to suspect that the tradition about Agrippina influenced the accounts of Livia, who also reputedly blocked the roads with guards (see 1.5).

father's generous distributions: Claudius had promised each praetorian 15,000 sesterces.

BOOK THIRTEEN

270 *The first death*: the language is reminiscent of the opening of Tiberius' reign and the announcement of the death of Agrippa Postumus (1.6).

Junius Silanus: consul in AD 46, criticized by Dio (61.6.5) for his avarice in governing Asia.

mature age: Silanus was 40.

great-great-grandson: Silanus was the grandson of the younger Julia.

270 *Publius Celer*: he was later indicted for misconduct in Asia; his case was postponed until he died of natural causes (see 13.33).

Helius: he was later left in charge of Italy during Nero's absence in Greece. He was put to death by Galba.

related above: see 12.57, 65.

271 *lictors*: these were presumably assigned to her in connection with her priesthood.

priesthood: Livia had similarly been granted a priesthood in the cult of the deified Augustus.

deification: Claudius' temple was begun by Agrippina, but not completed until the time of Vespasian.

cultural pursuits: Suetonius (*Claud.* 41) enumerates Claudius' literary achievements, including a history and an eight-volume autobiography.

Caesar: Cicero claims Atticus said that Caesar had no match among Latin orators (*Brutus* 72, 252).

his coming principate: the format laid out by Nero with its careful division of powers and responsibilities is very close to that prescribed by Augustus.

272 *payment or gifts*: Claudius had earlier fixed the fee that pleaders could command (see 11.7) and the relationship of the Neronian law to Claudius' measure is unclear.

quaestors-designate: Domitian (Suetonius, *Domitian* 4) is said to have reimposed this obligation, but it had perhaps never in practice disappeared. The *Life of Lucan* (anonymous, possibly by Suetonius) claims that the poet, when quaestor, arranged to put on a show 'according to established tradition'.

so that Agrippina could be present . . . her hearing: Nero would later claim (14.11) that she tried to enter the actual chamber.

Gnaeus Pompey: born in 106 BC, he received his first command in 84, when he was actually 23, but had already served under his father in 87.

273 *Caesar Octavianus in his nineteenth*: in 44 BC. In the *Res Gestae* (1.1), Augustus refers to assuming military command at the age of 18.

Agrippa and Antiochus: Marcus Julius Agrippa was the son of Julius 'Herod' Agrippa (see note to p. 246). Originally granted Chalcis by Claudius, his territories had subsequently been enlarged by both Claudius and Nero. For Antiochus IV of Commagene, see note to p. 262.

Aristobulus: the son of Herod of Chalcis, whose kingdom he subsequently acquired. After his reign Armenia seems to have been incorporated into the empire by Vespasian.

Sohaemus: Josephus (*AJ* 20.8.4) states that he was made king of Emesa in Syria in this year (AD 54). He was later a supporter of Vespasian.

triumphal dress: see note to p. 254.

274 *Arrius Varus*: almost certainly to be identified with the distinguished later supporter of Vespasian.

imperial fasces: these were the fasces borne by the twelve lictors assigned to Augustus in 19 BC and retained by his successors. They were wreathed with laurels for victories won under his auspices.

Gnaeus Domitius: he had been dead some fifteen years.

Roman knight: trials in the Senate did not exclusively involve juries of peers; there are several instances of knights being tried in the Senate.

consulship: Claudius had assumed the consulship at the beginning of his reign and Nero followed his example.

275 *Acte*: she came from Asia, survived Nero, and was one of the loyal women who buried his remains (Suetonius, *Nero* 50).

Marcus Otho: the future emperor. Suetonius (*Otho* 2) indicates that he was now 23 years old.

a consular family: Marcus Otho's father, Lucius Otho, was consul in AD 33.

Annaeus Serenus: he was a close younger friend of Seneca, prefect of the *vigiles*; he died along with some of his officers through eating poisonous mushrooms at a banquet (Seneca, *Ep.* 63.14; Pliny, *NH* 22.96).

276 *resignation oath*: on resigning office, a higher magistrate took an oath that he had done nothing against the law.

fourteenth year: the birthday would be an important one, since at that age Britannicus would adopt the *toga virilis*.

277 *the festal days of Saturn*: the Saturnalia were celebrated in Nero's day from 17 to 23 December, a period of licensed merry-making and possibly the precedent for the Christmas festivities.

previously tested: Suetonius (*Nero* 33) reports that he tried it first on a kid, which survived for five hours, then, after improvements, on a pig.

other young nobles: Suetonius (*Titus* 2) claims that the future emperor Titus was among them, and became ill through eating the poison.

278 *Campus Martius*: in the Mausoleum of Augustus.

Claudian bloodline: he was the last male born into the family. Nero was a Claudian by adoption.

the established practice of their ancestors: there was an ancient Roman custom of burial by night. It survived into the imperial period in the case of those whose family could not afford lavish ceremonies or who had died prematurely.

279 *the military watch*: the praetorians attached to her quarters on the Palatine.

Germans: see 1.24.

morning-callers: presumably those who followed the traditional ritual of greeting Nero each morning took the opportunity to visit her.

noted above: see 11.12.

279 *Sextius Africanus*: consul in AD 59, a descendant of Titus Sextius, legate of Nero in Gaul.

280 *Rubellius Plautus*: son of Rubellius Blandus and Julia, granddaughter of Tiberius; he was later exiled and put to death (14.22, 59).

Domitia: sister of Domitia Lepida (see note to p. 235) and Nero's father Gnaeus Domitius Ahenobarbus. Crispus Passienus had divorced her to marry Agrippina. Suetonius (*Nero* 34) and Dio (61.17.1) claim that Nero later had her poisoned to get possession of her property.

Paris: see 13.27; Nero put him to death in AD 67 as a professional rival (Suetonius, *Nero* 54; Dio 63.18).

Fabius Rusticus: a protégé of Seneca the Younger, much admired by Quintilian (10.1.104) and regarded by Tacitus (*Agr.* 10) as the most eloquent of the moderns as Livy was of the ancients (see 14.2, 15.61). He appears along with Tacitus and Pliny in the will of a wealthy Spaniard, Dasumius, drawn up in AD 108. He published a history in 83/4, of which little is known.

Caecina Tuscus: Suetonius (*Nero* 34) and Dio (63.18.1) say that he was the son of Nero's nurse and afterwards became prefect of Egypt, and was banished in the last year of Nero's reign for using his master's bath.

Plinius: Pliny the Elder wrote a history of the later Julio-Claudian period (see 15.53). The history was mentioned by Pliny the Younger (*Ep.* 3.5.6) and by the elder Pliny himself (*NH*, Preface 20).

Cluvius: he had been a consul and assumed the role of Nero's herald in the theatre (Suetonius, *Nero* 21; Dio 63.14.3). He was a historian, but the scope of his history is uncertain; all of Tacitus' specific references to him relate to the reign of Nero.

she was to refute them: Agrippina's refutations come under three broad headings. She begins by questioning the credibility of Silana and Domitia. Then she asks if there is any evidence that she has tried to win support either among soldiers in Rome, or governors in the provinces or even among members of the imperial household. Finally she points out that if Britannicus were to reign she could hardly expect the same tolerance for her occasional indiscretions that she might hope from a son.

281 *her Baiae estate*: according to Dio (61.17.2), it was the prospect of acquiring her estates at Baiae and at Ravenna that led Nero to put Domitia to death.

grain-supply: the office of prefect of the grain-supply (*praefectus annonae*) was an important one, often leading to the praetorian prefecture. Faenius became involved in the conspiracy of Piso, where he did not acquit himself well (see 15.68).

Arruntius Stella: otherwise unknown. He may have been the father or grandfather of the poet Lucius Arruntius Stella of Padua (Patavium).

Claudius Balbillus: he may well have been the son of the astrologer Thrasyllus. Seneca (*QN* 4.2.13) speaks of his refined literary tastes.

Publius Anteius: he is identified in an inscription as legate of Dalmatia in 51 and must at one point have held the consulship. He seems to have been involved in some sort of shady trafficking in property that had legally been confiscated by the state but not collected. The precise nature of his operations is unclear. He took his own life in AD 61 (see 16.14).

kept back: Tiberius had similarly postponed the departure of legates after appointment. Anteius is identified later as an intimate of Agrippina and his loyalty may have been suspect for that reason.

282 *Cornelius Sulla*: he was consul in AD 52; see 12.52. He had close family links to the imperial family through Antonia the Elder and Octavia, sister of Augustus, and was married to Claudius' daughter; see 15.53.

joined the judges in expressing his opinion: Burrus was not a senator, and he must be assumed to be sitting as an assessor in a case that the princeps is holding in private.

games: a cohort of the praetorians was normally charged with keeping order at the games. The next chapter shows that the experiment of removing them was not a success.

283 *a member of the senatorial order*: Montanus would have the right to the senatorial toga either through inheritance or through adlection by the emperor.

a violent attack: Suetonius (*Nero* 26) and Dio (61.9.3) say that Montanus was defending his wife from an attack.

recourse: there is no known law granting such power, although Dio (56.13.7) refers generally to measures taken by Augustus to acknowledge the rights of patrons regarding freedmen. Such powers of relegation without the authority of a magistrate would seem to be a relic of 'paternal authority' (*patria potestas*), with the freedman being regarded as part of the family.

Campanian coast: the most desirable part of Italy, lying 107 Roman miles from Rome. Such a place of exile would hardly constitute a hardship.

284 *tribes*: freedmen seem to have shared in the corn-dole since the republic (Dio 39.24.1) and were probably enrolled in tribes for that reason.

cohorts conscripted in the city: i.e. the *vigiles*, the city fire service.

equestrians: under Tiberius, the privileges of knighthood were limited to the freeborn of three generations, but the rule had been much relaxed.

senators: the Vitellian brothers were all senior senators, yet sons of an equestrian who was probably the son of a freedman (Suetonius, *Vit.* 2.1); Pliny (*Ep.* 3.14.1) mentions a contemporary case of the praetorship being held by the son of a freedman.

formal act: a distinction is drawn between formal manumission, either in an appropriate public ceremony or by enrolment in the census of citizens, and the more private emancipation through a verbal statement in front of a witness or in a will.

284 *chain of servitude*: informally manumitted slaves were subject to a number of disabilities, such as the right to make a will, but had certain Latin rights, with the status of 'Junian Latins'.

freeborn: the legal compendium known as the *Digest* (12.4.3) preserves this case, and records that Paris bought his freedom, and, after the later determination that he was freeborn, successfully claimed to recover from Domitia the sum paid.

Antistius: praetor in AD 62, when he was exiled and almost executed for libel (see 14.48–9; 16.14, 21). He was exiled a second time in 70 (Tacitus, *Hist.* 4.44.3).

the authority of praetors and consuls: the issue at stake seems to have been the habit of tribunes intervening in a case before the praetors or consuls and transferring jurisdiction to themselves.

bring in from Italy: the force of this rule is unclear; perhaps consuls and praetors were given exclusive rights to determine when a civil case could be transferred to the court in Rome.

Lucius Piso: grandson of the notorious Gnaeus Piso (see note to p. 12) and son of Lucius (previously Gnaeus) Calpurnius Piso (see 3.17, 4.62). He was consul in AD 57.

in their own homes: the tribune's home was open to those who wished to invoke his assistance, but his intervention had to take place in public.

public records: registration of fines at the *aerarium* had to take place before the sentence could be imposed.

285 *the power of the aediles*: magistrates had a general coercive power to distrain and to levy fines.

Helvidius Priscus: since he is now tribune he can hardly be the legionary legate from five years previously (see note to p. 259).

Obultronius Sabinus: put to death by Galba in AD 69 (Tacitus, *Hist.* 1.37.3).

prefects: as imperial officials they would not be subject to the intervention of the tribunes.

various forms: during the republic the treasury had been under the quaestors, until 45 BC, when it was placed, possibly as a temporary measure, in the hands of the aediles. Augustus gave jurisdiction to two men of praetorian rank, with the title of prefects, appointed by the Senate.

Nero selected: Nero did not revert to the Augustan system of leaving the choice to the Senate.

timbers: Tacitus refers snidely to previous historical accounts, perhaps including that of Pliny, who refers to the enormous larch beam worked into the amphitheatre (*NH* 16.200) and may have included it also in his general history. Suetonius (*Nero* 12) mentions that the amphitheatre was built of wood, and completed in a year.

286 *four per cent sale-tax*: a duty of 4 per cent was imposed on the purchase of slaves by Augustus in AD 7. Dio (55.31.4), who seems to say it was 2 per cent (the manuscript text is disputed), says that it was used to pay for the fire service (*vigiles*).

oppressing their subjects: the sentiment is that the lavish shows were funded by embezzlement in the provinces and so were themselves a source of corruption.

decree of the Senate: the decree is mentioned by the Jurists; it also extended responsibility for the murder of a wife to the household of the husband and vice versa, while those sold in the meantime were reclaimed and the price had to be made good by the seller.

ovation: Aulus Plautius' ovation was held when he returned from Britain in AD 47 (Dio 60.30.2) and Claudius is said to have paid him the special honour of riding in the procession at his side (Suetonius, *Claud.* 24). Tacitus presumably covered the event in the missing books.

foreign superstition: this is a general term, but there was a later belief that Pomponia was a Christian, based in part on Christian inscriptions referring to a Pomponius Graecinus and Pomponius Bassus.

Julia: she was the granddaughter of Pomponia, the daughter of Atticus, which suggests a possible relationship to Pomponia Graecina. Her death was presumably recorded in the missing section of Book 11.

287 *found guilty*: he was expelled from the Senate but restored later through the influence of Tigellinus, his father-in-law.

a few old men: it is hard to believe that people still living could remember the consulship of Augustus and Corvinus (31 BC). Perhaps the claim should be taken loosely to mean that people would remember Corvinus, who lived some forty years after his consulship.

Aurelius Cotta: probably the son or grandson of Cotta Messalinus; see note to p. 65.

Haterius Antoninus: consul in 53.

Lucullus and Pompey: the reference is to successes against Tigranes I in the Third Mithridatic War (74/3–63 BC).

Syria: the legions in question were Legio III Gallica and VI Ferrata.

288 *Germany*: no legion from Germany is known to have taken part in Corbulo's campaign. Legio VI Scythica was sent from Moesia, not Germany. It is possible that a legion was sent from Germany to make up the strength of Legio X, from which a detachment was sent to Corbulo.

under canvas: up to this point Tacitus has dealt with the preliminaries of the campaign. Without any transition the army is encamped in northern Armenia ready to move in the next campaigning season. The chronology of the campaigns is uncertain. Tacitus seems to put all the events covered in 13.34–41 in AD 57–8, and when he resumes the narrative at 14.23 the year is seemingly AD 60. Thus it is not certain where the campaign of AD 59 belongs.

288 *outside the rampart*: Polybius (6.38.3) notes that this punishment was levied in his own time (second century BC). Frontinus (*Strategemata* 4.2.3, 7.2) speaks of Corbulo's strict discipline.

289 *Pharasmanes*: see note to p. 202; Radamistus had fled to him after escaping from Armenia.

a Roman debacle: he has in mind the defeats of Crassus and Antonius.

290 *Cornelius Flaccus, and . . . Insteius Capito*: Cornelius, who must have been a legionary legate, is otherwise unknown. Insteius is presumably the centurion mentioned in 13.9.

292 *prodigy*: an eclipse of 30 April AD 59 is mentioned by Pliny (*NH* 2.180) as having been seen by Corbulo in Armenia (see 14.12), but the Tacitean description here does not suit an eclipse.

293 *Quintus Pomponius*: consul at the time of Caligula's assassination, he almost lost his life for calling for the restoration of the republic (Josephus, *AJ* 19.4.5). His gesture presumably gave Suillius the grounds to make a charge against him, forcing him to join the rebellion of Camillus Scribonianus.

Sabina Poppaea . . . Valerius Asiaticus: see note to p. 215.

Lusius Saturninus: he is listed as a consular victim of Claudius by Seneca (*Apoc.* 13.5).

Cornelius Lupus: he is another victim mentioned by Seneca (*Apoc.* 13.5). He was proconsul of Crete and Cyrene under Tiberius, and was consul in AD 42.

294 *his son and granddaughter*: the son would be Marcus Suillius Nerullinus, consul in 50 (see note to p. 215), the granddaughter probably the daughter of another son, Caesonius.

295 *murder law*: the *Lex Cornelia* of Sulla imposed the penalty of deportation and loss of property, for which death was later substituted under certain circumstances. This case was celebrated—the *Life of Lucan* (see note to p. 272) says that the poet wrote specimen speeches for both the prosecution and defence. Octavius Sagitta tried to obtain a remission of the sentence twelve years later (Tacitus, *Hist.* 4.44).

his friendship with Sejanus: none of the accounts of Sejanus mentions friendship with Titus Ollius.

a son: Suetonius (*Nero* 35) claims that Nero ordered the son's slaves to murder him while fishing. There is also a tradition that Nero stabbed him ([Seneca], *Octavia* 744–7).

marriage: Tacitus in the earlier *Histories* (1.13) follows a different version found also in Suetonius (*Otho* 3), Plutarch (*Galba* 19.106), and Dio (61.11.2) that Nero had already begun his affair while Poppaea was married to her first husband Crispinus, and that her marriage to Otho was

merely a front to facilitate Nero's meeting with her, a situation complicated when Otho fell in love with her, as a consequence of which he was
exiled. Tacitus may here be correcting his earlier view with a more plausible scenario.

296 *Lusitania*: this province was normally governed by a man of praetorian
rank, but Otho had held nothing higher than the quaestorship, and was at
this time only 26.

civil war: Otho stayed in his office for ten years (58–68) and led the way
in placing his support behind Galba.

Cornelius Sulla: see 12.52, 13.23.

297 *sent to the Senate*: Nero had confirmed the authority of the Senate over the
Italian communities (see 13.4).

town council: in Italy these usually consisted of 100 local citizens, who
tended to be substantial property-holders.

brothers Scribonius: Rufus and Proculus; for a while they were at the same
time governors of Upper and Lower Germany respectively. Nero summoned them to Greece in 67 and compelled them to commit suicide (Dio
63.17.2).

prescribed number of gladiatorial shows: in Rome, Augustus had laid down
the rule in 22 BC that there should be no more than two public gladiatorial shows in any year, and that they should involve no more than 120
gladiators. This number was further reduced by Tiberius, although
relaxed by Caligula. The numbers prescribed for Italy are not known.

Thrasea Paetus: this is the first allusion in the extant *Annals* to the famous
Stoic victim of Nero. Consul in 56, he was a native of Padua and husband
of the daughter of the famous pair, Caecina Paetus and Arria (see note to
p. 260). The *Annals* break off in the account of his suicide.

298 *port-duties*: the *portoria* were import levies imposed at the frontiers of the
empire and also of provinces or groupings of provinces. Here they are
made to stand for the whole class of indirect taxes. Nero remarkably
seems to be contemplating a Bismarckian free-trade area within the
empire. The consequence would not have been totally benign. Since 167
BC Italy had been exempt from direct taxes and abolition of indirect taxes
would have obliged the rest of the empire to shoulder the entire financial
burden of its operation.

'fortieth' and 'fiftieth': nothing further is known of these 2.5 per cent and
2 per cent taxes, presumably two fictitious levies imposed by the *publicani*.

Sulpicius Camerinus: consul in AD 46, he was put to death, along with his
son, by the freedman Helius during Nero's absence in Greece.

Pompeius Silvanus: consul in 45 and at one point governor of Dalmatia.

299 *To that point . . . Germany*: the last treatment of events in Germany belongs
to AD 50 (12.28). The events covered here must have begun before 58 and
the account stretches over several years.

299 *Paulinus Pompeius and Lucius Vetus*: commanders of Lower and Upper Germany respectively. Paulinus (see also 15.18) was consul possibly in AD 54, and was the father or brother of Pompeia Paulina, wife of Seneca. Lucius Antistius Vetus (see 13.11) was consul in 55.

sixty-three years earlier: Drusus died in 9 BC. Vetus may have been sent to Germany in 55 and have been replaced in Rome by a suffect consul.

Dubius Avitus: he served as legate of Aquitania, and held the consulship in AD 56.

300 *some people . . . senators' seats*: Suetonius (*Claud.* 25.4) tells the same story but relates it to the Claudian period, and identifies the ambassadors as Parthians and Armenians. The privilege of a seat among the senators had been granted to the Massilians from an early period. Augustus forbade access of foreign ambassadors into the orchestra (Suetonius, *Aug.* 44.1), a prohibition that seems to have been lifted.

Cheruscan uprising: this was the rebellion of Arminius that led to the Varian disaster in AD 9. Tiberius commanded in Germany for two years after that, and Germanicus in AD 13–16.

small portion of the plain: Boiocalus' words here are bitter and ironic. He is suggesting that the area to be taken by the Romans for their animals was enormous, and that they would happily use land to graze their animals while the people starved.

Usipi: these may be identical to the Usipetes (see 1.51).

301 *Curtilius Mancia*: he seems to have succeeded Lucius Vetus after the latter had served for only one year.

burning trees: Tacitus may have misunderstood a process described by Pliny (*NH* 31.73), where evaporation was accelerated by burning wood.

302 *Ruminal tree*: the fig tree under which, traditionally, the she-wolf had suckled Romulus and Remus. It was located originally in the Lupercal on the Palatine and was translated miraculously by Attus Navius, augur of Tarquinius Priscus, to the Comitium, opposite the Senate House (Pliny, *NH* 15.77).

BOOK FOURTEEN

303 *the fiendish act*: the abrupt announcement of the plan to murder Agrippina comes as something of a surprise. She has been absent from the *Annals* since 13.21.

her triumph-celebrating forebears: in fact, only Poppaea's maternal grandfather, Poppaeus Sabinus, had been granted triumphal insignia, for victories in Thrace under Tiberius.

reveal the insults . . . arrogance and greed: the logic seems to be that as long as Poppaea was in competition with Agrippina Nero would regard her attacks against his mother as simply intended to undermine her position.

Otho: she had been married first to Rufrius Crispinus, by whom she had a son (see 11.1, 13.45). After her divorce she married Otho.

304 *Marcus Lepidus*: Marcus Aemilius Lepidus had been the husband of Agrippina's sister Drusilla, and was executed by Caligula in 39 for alleged involvement in the conspiracy of Gnaeus Lentulus Gaetulicus.

Misenum: at 4.5 it is revealed that there were two fleets off Italy, at Ravenna and Misenum, and one off Gaul at Forum Iulii (Fréjus).

tutor: probably in the sense of accompanying Nero to his classes. He had clearly prospered in the emperor's service; command of the fleet at Misenum was an important position.

Quinquatrus: the fifth day after the Ides, a festival of Minerva, celebrated 19–23 March.

at Baiae: the topography of Tacitus' account of Agrippina's final days is hopelessly confused and has eluded explanation.

305 *Crepereius Gallus*: an equestrian from the Roman colony of Antioch.

Acerronia: sister of Gnaeus Acerronius Proculus, proconsul of Achaea some time after AD 44.

306 *sealed up*: Acerronia's possessions and papers would be put under seal so that nothing could be removed pending the execution of the will.

loyalty: the revelation of the loyalty of the guard to Agrippina is hardly unexpected, given that she had ensured that the middle ranks be recruited from her supporters.

307 *a centurion of the marines*: in the Roman fleet a *trierarchus* had naval command. The *centurio classicus* commanded the marine soldiers on board.

308 *dining couch*: adding insult to injury, Agrippina was cremated on a dining-room couch instead of the traditional funeral bier.

Chaldeans: the astrologer who made the prediction was the son of Thrasyllus (6.22).

309 *joint rule*: this would have been constitutionally impossible for a woman in Rome, and Nero is clearly trading on the resentment felt about Agrippina's patent desire for indirect power.

bursting into the Curia: a considerable exaggeration. Agrippina had sought only to listen to meetings of the Senate (13.5).

deputations: on Agrippina's attempt to meet the Armenian deputation, see 13.5.

Seneca: for Seneca's help in writing Nero's speeches, see 13.3, 11.

public prayers: *supplicationes* were originally days of fasting in times of distress. Images of the gods were placed on a couch and a table with food was set up before it.

unfit for public business: *dies nefasti* were those on which the praetor could not pronounce judgement in the law courts. Her birthday was 6 November.

310 *tribes*: the divisions of the Roman people as instituted by King Servius. He established four city and twenty-six rural tribes. Their number was later raised to thirty-five.

Capitol: the victorious general would mount the Capitol during a triumph, a tradition contributing to the irony of the present situation.

Horse-racing: chariot-racing had long been a popular form of entertainment in Rome, but the charioteers were normally professionals, in contrast to the Greek tradition, in which chariot-racing was an admired aristocratic activity.

311 *Vatican valley*: Pliny (*NH* 36.74) says that Caligula had already begun to construct a circus there.

on the stage: there was a social stigma attached to the acting profession in Rome, despite the distinction of a small number of individual actors, such as the Roscius defended by Cicero. Actors were held in high regard by the Greeks.

'Juvenalian Games': the first trimming of a young man's beard had traditionally been the occasion for a private family celebration. Nero made it the basis for a public festival. After Nero, chariot-races and animal shows replaced the theatrical performances.

the actor's art, whether Greek or Roman: in Greece there were adaptations of scenes from Greek tragedy, performed solo, with musical accompaniment (Suetonius, *Nero* 21). Roman practice was probably recitations from the Latin tragedies.

'Naval Pond': Augustus constructed a lake on the far side of the Tiber to stage a mock naval battle (*RG* 23).

'Augustiani': the claque at imperial performances; their disorderly conduct caused much trouble (see 13.25, 28; Suetonius, *Nero* 20.3).

312 *men . . . proficiency in composition*: these included the epic poet Lucan, who soon showed up Nero to the extent that he was barred from any more public recitals.

Nuceria and Pompeii: Pompeii was settled after the Social War in 89 BC, Nuceria under Augustus.

I noted above: Livineius is not mentioned in the extant chapters of Tacitus, and his expulsion from the Senate must have appeared in one of the lost books.

Senate: the Senate had retained responsibility for Italy under the empire with the consuls acting as its agents. Nero promised on his accession to maintain that tradition (see 13.4).

associations: *collegia* could include any association, ranging from political clubs to burial societies, and they were often the centres of public unrest. Julius Caesar banned all but the ancient *collegia*, but it is likely that many were set up under the guise of burial associations.

Pedius Blaesus: he was restored by Otho ten years later.

Cyrene: the city housed a temple to Aesculapius the god of healing, with an attached medical school.

Acilius Strabo: consul in 71.

Apion: he was the last king of Cyrene, dying in 96 BC and bequeathing his kingdom to Rome.

313 *Marcus Servilius*: consul AD 35, a famous advocate and historian, much admired by Quintilian. He may have been one of Tacitus' sources for the reign of Tiberius.

Quinquennial Games: these were intended to be held at the end of each *lustrum*, or five-year period. Called the *Neronia* (Suetonius, *Nero* 12.3), they combined three types of contest: chariot-races, gymnastics, and music.

on their feet: Plautus (*Aulularia* 719, *Poenulus* 1224) refers to a seated audience, and the practice presumably predates him.

a praetor presided over them: during the republic, public games were staged by the aediles. Augustus shifted responsibility to the praetors.

decuries: the list of jurymen was divided into classes called *decuriae*, originally a group of ten, although that meaning was gradually lost. Augustus established four decuries of judges; Caligula added a fifth. The word should not be confused with the quite distinct term 'decurion', a local town official.

314 *Etruria*: Livy (7.2) reports that when Rome was afflicted by a plague in 365 BC, Etruscan actors were brought to the city to perform in order to appease the divine anger.

annexation of Achaea and Asia: Greece (Achaea) was incorporated by Rome after the defeat of the Achaean League and the destruction of Corinth in 146 BC. Asia was organized from the kingdom bequeathed to Rome by Attalus III, who died in 133.

personal wealth: magistrates had been personally responsible for putting on games, and this had led to much corruption during the republic, when recompense was sought from the provinces that the magistrate later administered.

pantomimi: they performed through dance and gesture, without spoken parts, and usually performed scenes from tragedy. Mimes generally performed scenes from low life with much recourse to buffoonery. Tacitus tends to use the two terms interchangeably. They were expelled in AD 56 (see 13.25).

sacred competitions: the *Neronia* are ranked as the equal of Greek contests held at religious festivals in honour of a god.

comet: Seneca (*QN* 7.17.2) mentions this comet and reports that it took away the bad reputation of comets.

Rubellius Plautus: see note to p. 280; Tacitus seems to suggest that his ancestors were inclined towards Stoicism.

315 *Marcian water*: the water of the Aqua Marcia aqueduct was of the highest quality, praised by Pliny (*NH* 31.41, 36.121) and Frontinus (*De Aquis* 91), which makes Nero's behaviour all the more outrageous. The aqueduct was constructed by Lucius Marcius Rex in 144–140 BC, and restored and expanded by Agrippa and Augustus.

After the destruction of Artaxata: Tacitus resumes his narrative from 13.41. This section covers the campaigns of AD 59–60.

316 *foreign blood*: Corbulo did not expend any Roman lives in the battle.

317 *Red Sea*: this generally can mean the modern Red Sea or the shore of the Persian Gulf. The modern Red Sea can be ruled out here. It is hard to see that there could be a route between the shore of the Persian Gulf and the Caspian that did not cross through Parthian territory, and it has been argued that an allusion to the Caspian is required here.

Tiridates: the brother of Vologaeses and the Parthian candidate for the throne of Armenia.

control: this should not be taken to suggest annexation, but rather a temporary military occupation.

Tigranes: he was the nephew of Tigranes IV, great-grandson of Herod the Great, and great-grandson (Tacitus is casual in referring to him as grandson) of Archelaus, last king of Cappadocia (see note to p. 202).

Pharasmanes: see note to p. 71.

Polemo: Polemo II; see note to p. 79.

Antiochus: Antiochus IV; see note to p. 262.

Puteoli: a colony of Romans had been established at Puteoli as early as 194 BC, and Augustus settled new colonists there. It has been argued that the colonists then existed as a separate community and that colonial status was now given to the rest of the inhabitants.

different maniples: the custom of settling veterans from the same legion together had perhaps been abandoned in Italy because they might pose a threat if their former commander chose to rebel.

318 *three extra candidates*: Augustus had on one occasion been presented with four extra candidates and he had allowed all to hold the office. Nero solved a similar problem by moving three directly to legionary commands (by this time legionary legates had normally already held the praetorship).

civil courts: these are the ordinary praetors' courts. Nero's measure discouraged frivolous appeals by requiring that one-third of the amount at dispute in the case had to be placed on deposit.

Vibius Secundus: otherwise unknown. His brother, Vibius Crispus, was consul possibly in AD 61, and in 74 and 83.

Mauretania: the former kingdom had been divided into two provinces by Claudius.

as I noted above: at 12.40.

Veranius: he probably succeeded Didius in 58, but died in office within the year.

Paulinus Suetonius: first mentioned here by Tacitus, but we know from other sources that he had already been governor of Mauretania. He probably held the consulship before going to Britain but his tenure has not survived in the record. He certainly held a consulship in AD 66.

Druids: these had been known to the Romans since Caesar's campaigns in Gaul.

319 *slaves*: these would presumably have been on the staff of the imperial procurator, who would have had responsibility for collecting taxes.

Claudius: the temple was supposedly decreed during his lifetime (Seneca, *Apoc.* 8).

whole fortunes: the reference might be to unspecified charges exacted from the population by the priests. It is perhaps more likely that the hardships were suffered by the priests themselves, since priesthoods in the Roman world did impose heavy financial burdens on the holders.

320 *Thames estuary*: Colchester is in fact quite distant from the Thames estuary.

Catus Decianus: known only from this passage. From as early as the reign of Augustus (notably in Judaea after Herod's death) procurators had taken temporary command of troops.

Petillius Cerialis: this is the first mention of the distinguished commander who fought for Vespasian (to whom he was related) in the civil war, suppressed the revolt of Civilis and became governor of Britain. He was consul in AD 70 and 74.

Ninth Legion: the Ninth would probably have been based at Lincoln.

Londinium: the earliest historical reference to London, which became an important commercial centre from the beginning of the Roman presence in Britain. It was an open town without defences or garrison.

the sacrifice of a single town: London was unfortified, and Suetonius lacked the troops to enable him to meet the Britons in the open.

321 *the Fourteenth Legion*: based at Wroxeter (near Shrewsbury). The Twentieth was based at Gloucester.

location: the site of Boudicca's last battle has been the subject of much antiquarian debate, with rival locations ranging from the outskirts of Prestatyn to King's Cross Station (Platform 9). The most likely spot is near Mancetter, on Watling Street, in the Midlands.

322 *some reports*: Tacitus may have drawn upon his father-in-law, Agricola, who served on this campaign. The figure could also have been recorded in the memoirs of Suetonius Paulinus.

323 *Poenius Postumus*: as prefect of the camp he would have been in temporary command in the absence of the legate. He is otherwise unknown.

323 *Julius Classicianus*: the increasingly public role of the procurator within imperial provinces made it inevitable that there would be occasional tensions between him and the governor. Classicianus' tombstone is preserved in the British Museum.

Polyclitus: nothing is known of the previous history of this individual, but his rapacity is noted in the *Histories* (1.37.8, 2.95.4). He was left in charge at Rome, along with Helius, when Nero made his trip to Greece.

324 *'peace'*: it is likely that Suetonius was replaced because of his repressive policies, and that Tacitus' sneer against Petronius is unjustified.

Domitius Balbus: otherwise unknown, and no other Domitius seems to have the *cognomen* Balbus.

Antonius Primus: he later recovered his senatorial rank and was placed in command of a legion in Pannonia by Galba. He played a significant role in Vespasian's victory. He is mentioned frequently in Tacitus' *Histories*.

Asinius Marcellus: consul in AD 54; see 12.64.

Asinius Pollio: see note to p. 8.

Cornelian law: one of the laws passed under Sulla in 81 BC to prevent the falsification of wills.

city prefect: the exact scope of his jurisdiction in the Neronian period is not clear, but he would presumably not have been bound by administrative procedure that would have slowed down action in the praetorian courts.

Pedanius Secundus: consul of AD 43. The city prefect always held consular rank.

325 *Gaius Cassius*: see 12.12.

the senatorial decree: this is presumably not the decree of AD 57, which simply extended an already established penalty; see 13.32.

326 *every tenth man . . . with the club*: decimation; see note to p. 105.

Cingonius Varro: consul-designate in AD 68 (Tacitus, *Hist.* 1.6); he was put to death by Galba as an accomplice of Nymphidius.

Quintus Volusius: see 13.25.

Trebellius Maximus: consul, possibly in AD 56. He was governor of Britain in 63–9, for which he is scorned by Tacitus, and still alive in 72, when his name appears in the list of Arval brethren.

Memmius Regulus': see note to p. 184.

327 *oil*: this was provided free of charge in Greek gymnasia.

I have already mentioned: see 13.28.

Tigellinus: this is the first mention in the extant *Annals* of Ofonius Tigellinus. He had modest origins, the son of an exiled Agrigentine. He was brought up in the homes of Lucius Domitius, husband of Agrippina, and Marcus Vinicius, husband of her sister Livilla, was suspected of adultery with both, and exiled in AD 39, living afterwards as a fisherman in Greece. He inherited a fortune, returned to Rome, probably in 41, and bred racehorses, which presumably provides his connection with Nero, with whom he formed a close bond. He became praetorian prefect after the death of Burrus and was ultimately put to death by Otho.

tribune: by virtue of his *tribunicia potestas* Nero could exercise the constitutional powers of the tribune, one of which was the power of veto.

traditional manner: see note to p. 65.

permitted the division: it was the prerogative of the presiding consul to refuse to put any motion to the Senate if he disapproved of it.

328 *Aulus Vitellius*: the future emperor, consul in AD 48 (see 11.23).

Fabricius Veiento: the son (perhaps adopted) of Didius Gallus, governor of Britain, he was three times consul under the Flavians, and gained a reputation as an informer under Domitian. He was highly regarded by Nerva.

'Codicils': it was not uncommon for individuals to vent their spleen against their enemies in supplements to their wills, and it seems that Fabricius' libels took the form of satires of such attacks.

trafficking in imperial privileges: Veiento was accused of receiving money from third parties to enlist his aid in influencing the emperor in their favour.

Burrus: Tacitus is the only source to cast doubt on the claim that Nero poisoned Burrus (see Suetonius, *Nero* 35.5, Dio 62.13.3).

329 *fourteenth year*: he had been appointed tutor to Nero in AD 49, and Claudius had died in 54.

330 *great-great-grandfather*: his grandfather Germanicus had been adopted by Tiberius, and Tiberius by Augustus.

granted Marcus Agrippa retirement: Agrippa at one point withdrew from public life, no doubt largely out of pique over the advancement of Marcellus, and based himself at Mytilene.

Gaius Maecenas: he may have retired because of his brother's involvement in a conspiracy (Suetonius, *Aug.* 66) or because of Augustus' involvement with his wife, Terentia (Dio 54.19.3).

glittering decorations: i.e. his distinguished ancestors.

far-flung investments?: Seneca supposedly had major investments in Britain and his recall of a large loan caused much distress (Dio 62.2.1).

beneath your greatness: Seneca argues that the envy felt towards himself does not affect the emperor.

331 *Vitellius*: Nero seems to be saying that Seneca should assume that Nero would be as generous as Claudius had been in his treatment of Vitellius, and that Nero should be able to expect Seneca to serve him as Vitellius had served Claudius.

Volusius' long-lasting thrift: see note to p. 245; at 13.30 he was said to have gained a fortune honourably.

332 *Faenius Rufus*': curiously, Rufus is not referred to again until AD 65 (see 15.50).

Plautus: for Rubellius Plautus, see 13.19.

Sulla: for Faustus Cornelius Sulla Felix, see 12.52, 13.47.

conflict of interest: Burrus owed his initial appointment to Agrippina (see 12.42). In 55 Agrippina was accused of plotting to make Plautus emperor and it was Burrus who had prevailed on Nero to give her a hearing.

name of the dictator: it seems unlikely that the name of the dictator Sulla, who held office in 82/1 BC, carried much weight a century and a half later.

Drusus as a grandfather: Rubellius Plautus was the son of Rubellius Blandus and Julia, daughter of Drusus, the son of Tiberius.

Stoics: this is the first reference by Tacitus to the notion that Stoicism could be a source of opposition to the emperor. Many of his opponents were indeed Stoics, but it is unlikely that there was a formal Stoic resistance.

333 *ahead of the centurion*: the reference is cryptic, but we discover in the next chapter that the centurion had been sent to execute him.

Lucius Antistius: consul in AD 55; see 13.11. He would be put to death in 65, along with Plautus' widow, Pollitta.

Coeranus and Musonius: apart from a brief mention in Pliny the Elder, Coeranus is otherwise unknown. Gaius Musonius Rufus was a famous equestrian Stoic, friend of Pliny the Younger and teacher of Epictetus. He was exiled on suspicion of involvement in the Pisonian conspiracy (15.71) and returned to Rome after Nero's death (Pliny, *Ep.* 3.11.5).

'*Why, Nero* <. . .>': some of the text is missing, but the joke can be recovered from Dio 62.14.1, where Nero comments that he had not realized that Plautus had such a big nose.

her father's name: Octavia was the biological daughter of Claudius; Nero could claim to be a Claudian only by adoption.

334 *recalled*: there is almost certainly an error in the text as transmitted in the manuscript, since it states that Nero recalled Octavia. This is contradicted in the next chapter where Octavia is still in Campania and Poppaea fears a change of heart on Nero's part. The emendation making such information a rumour is accepted here. It provides a basis for Poppaea's concern.

336 *Agrippina's banishment by Tiberius*: the elder Agrippina, the wife of Germanicus, was similarly banished to Pandateria.

Julia: Julia Livilla, daughter of Germanicus, was banished in AD 41 for suspicion of adultery with Seneca (see note to p. 239). The implication here is that she was also sent to Pandateria.

strength of age: in fact, Julia Livilla was only 23 at the time of her banishment.

wedding day: see 12.58.

maidservant: Acte.

twentieth year: this is a mistake. She was born on 13 February AD 41, and was thus older than Britannicus.

sister: technically, Octavia had been adopted by another family to make her marriage to Nero possible; thus she was not strictly his sister.

the Germanici: Octavia refers to Drusus, brother of Tiberius, and to his son Germanicus, who inherited his posthumous *cognomen*.

337 *Doryphorus*: he held the post of *a libellis*, probably as successor to Callistus.

Gaius Piso: he gave his name to a famous conspiracy against Nero in AD 65, and Seneca was associated with him (15.60). The text suggests that he had not yet initiated his conspiracy and it is not clear why an association with him should have aroused suspicion.

BOOK FIFTEEN

338 *Meanwhile*: the account of eastern affairs is resumed from 14.26, where it had been carried down to the end of AD 60. Tacitus describes the final settlement with Parthia in some detail because of its historical significance. The military and diplomatic events are very complex.

a foreigner: Tigranes did have a connection with the royal house of Parthia, but it was remote and offset by his years in Rome (see 14.26).

unbroken: the treaty of friendship signed in 20 BC had never been formally broken.

Monobazus: hereditary king of Adiabene. According to Dio (62.20–3), he took part in the siege of Tigranocerta and gave hostages to Corbulo after the agreement with Tiridates.

a council meeting: it is not clear what the composition of the meeting would have been. It is perhaps influenced by the idea of the princeps' council.

same father: Vologaeses' mother was a Greek concubine.

Pacorus: Vologaeses' brother, first mentioned here, ruler of Atropatene.

339 *Verulanus Severus*: see 14.26; he would later be consul, probably in AD 66.

Vettius Bolanus: consul AD 66, governor of Britain 69–71, proconsul of Asia about 78–80.

340 *the province*: this must presumably be Syria, although it had not actually been invaded.

341 *Caesennius Paetus*: see 14.29. In spite of his disastrous handling of the Armenian campaign he went on to serve as legate of Syria under Vespasian in AD 70–2.

Funisulanus Vettonianus . . . Calavius Sabinus: Funisulanus is recorded in inscriptions pursuing a successful military career under Domitian. Calavius is unknown.

343 *Arsamosata*: presumably near Paetus' headquarters, the winter quarters of Legio VI, some fifty miles from Melitene on the River Arsanius. Dio (62.21.1) says that the camp was at Rhandeia.

344 *Caudium and Numantia*: in 321 BC Roman soldiers were trapped by the Samnites in the pass of the Caudine Forks and forced to go beneath the yoke; spears were held in an archway and defeated troops were obliged to march under it in a humiliating display of submission (Livy 3.28). In 137 BC the Romans under Hostilius Mancinus surrendered at Numantia in Spain.

346 *no Roman would enter Armenia*: Dio (62.21.1) claims that Paetus promised that Nero would give Armenia to Tiridates.

forty miles: a daily march of forty miles would be remarkable, double the normal rate.

to Syria: Corbulo seems to have feared that the Parthians would launch a cavalry invasion of Syria.

347 *trophies*: setting up a pile of captured arms as a victory memorial was customary.

Lucius Piso . . . Paulinus: Lucius Piso was consul with Nero in AD 57 (see note to p. 284); Ducenius Geminus was consul at an unknown date and city prefect under Galba; for Pompeius Paulinus, see the note to p. 299.

public revenues: strictly speaking the *vectigalia* were indirect taxes, such as harbour dues, but the word seems to be used here generally of all income entering the state treasury from taxation.

annual gift: emperors regularly made gifts from their personal *fiscus* (which drew its revenues from sources that might arguably have been considered public). The reference to an annual grant is unusual and not easily explained.

were allotted praetorships: the praetors were elected generally as praetors, but the specific offices to be held were assigned by lot. Even in the drawing of the lots, men who had fathered children were given an advantage.

348 *Julian laws*: these laws, of 18 and 8 BC, barred a man from office if convicted of bribery of juries or electors, and required a candidate for office to deposit money as a guarantee against corruption.

Calpurnian resolutions: Lucius Calpurnius Piso Frugi, when tribune in 149 BC, introduced the first permanent court to try cases of extortion in the provinces.

349 *formal motion*: a member of the Senate had the right to speak outside the business at hand on any motion that was deemed to be in the public interest. But it was at the discretion of the presiding consul to decide whether that motion should be formally put before the house.

gymnasium: see 14.47 for its dedication.

earthquake: this preceded the major eruption that destroyed Pompeii in AD 79. Seneca (*QN* 6.1) refers to the same event under the year 62 rather than 63. The correct date is uncertain.

Vestal Virgin: there may have been only six of them, a small enough number to make the death of any one worth mentioning.

daughter: she was born on 21 January. This was the first time that the title of Augusta was granted to an infant.

rite of Actium: to celebrate his victory at Actium, Augustus had founded Nicopolis and instituted quinquennial games there. This was appropriate in a Greek city, but Nero was to extend the practice to Italy.

350 *his priesthood*: Pliny (*NH* 30.16–17) claims that Tiridates was a Magian, who refused to travel by water, although he later did overcome his scruples to come to Rome (Dio 63.7).

the leading men: a body of leading citizens with no constitutional position, who constituted the friends of the princeps.

Gaius Cestius: consul in 42, he became legate of Syria in 65.

Marius Celsus: consul in 69.

Tetrarchs: originally the ruler of one-quarter of a country, at this period generally the ruler of a small state in the East.

351 *Pompey*: the *Lex Gabinia* of 67 BC conferred on Pompey power *equal* to that of the proconsuls.

Lucius Lucullus: he had advanced on Tigranocerta in 69 BC; his journey is vaguely described by Plutarch (*Lucullus* 24.2–4).

352 *prefectures*: Pliny (*NH* 6.27) indicates that Armenia was divided into 120 *praefecturae*.

Tiberius Alexander: an Alexandrian Jew, nephew of Philo of Alexandria, procurator of Judaea under Claudius (Josephus, *AJ* 20.100), and later prefect of Egypt. He renounced Judaism and assisted Vespasian in his bid for the principate, and supported Titus in the Jewish War.

Vinicianus Annius: he may well have been the son-in-law of Corbulo. His father (see 6.9; Dio 60.15), brother (see 15.56) and he (Suetonius, *Nero* 36.1) all seem to have been involved in conspiracies.

353 *watch*: the night was divided into four watches, with the leading centurion responsible for their observation.

surrender his sword: it was not normal to enter the presence of the emperor while armed.

Latin rights: the chief effect of these rights was to confer citizenship on anyone who had held office in a town that held them.

the seating of the Roman knights: Livy (1.35.8) reports on special seating areas for knights and senators in the Circus from Rome's earliest period and Dio (55.22.4) suggests that the *equites* sat separately in the Circus from the time of Augustus. Possibly before Nero they sat in groups and it was only later that seats were actually reserved for them; on the 'fourteen rows' in the theatre (see 6.3 and note to p. 92).

353 *Roscian law*: this law in 67 BC reserved the fourteen rows behind the senators in the orchestra of the theatre. But it was limited to the theatre and did not address the seating of the Circus.

354 *Juvenalian Games*: see note to p. 311.

Neapolis: although located in Italy, Naples was founded by Greeks and retained much of its Greek inheritance. The theatrical performances followed the Greek pattern, not the Roman.

Torquatus Silanus: Decimus Junius Torquatus Silanus was consul in AD 53; see 12.58. He died in 65, according to Dio (27.27.2).

355 *Agrippa's lake*: this was a reservoir that stored water for Agrippa's Baths (Ovid, *Ex P.* 1.8.38; Frontinus, *De Aquis* 2.84).

356 *raging fires*: Rome had been subject to continuous fires from the time of the first recorded one after the sack of the city by the Gauls in 390 BC. The crowded nature of the city, with multi-storey buildings containing much flammable material, made fires inevitable.

357 *at Antium*: the fact that Nero was not in Rome at the time of the fire is an argument against his being responsible for it.

building of his . . . the gardens of Maecenas: Augustus took up residence on the Palatine Hill, and established it as the location for later emperors (hence the English 'palace'). Maecenas bequeathed his gardens on the Esquiline to Augustus. Nero built a residence in the valley between the two, the so-called *domus transitoria*, which would be rebuilt as the Golden House.

rumour: Suetonius (*Nero* 38.2) and Dio (62.18.1) treat the story of the performance as a fact.

five days: Suetonius (*Nero* 38) says that the fire lasted six days and seven nights. An inscription (*CIL* 6.826) mentions nine days. The second outbreak might have lasted for three days.

named after him: Suetonius (*Nero* 55) says that the name was to be 'Neropolis'.

fourteen districts: in 7 BC Augustus reorganized the city of Rome and divided it into fourteen districts, identified by numbers.

a few ruined and charred vestiges of buildings were all that remained: this is clearly an exaggeration. The Capitol (see 15.44) and the Forum, to judge from the subsequent references to the intact Curia, which was located there (16.27), seem to have been more or less undamaged, and the Circus was functioning again in the following year (see 15.53).

358 *the Senones . . . the city*: the Gauls burned Rome on 19 July 390 BC.

years, months, and days: from 390 BC to AD 64 is 454 years, or 418 years + 418 months + 418 days.

a palace: the Golden House, covering the Palatine and Esquiline and the area between them, a luxury country-house-type residence, with extravagant works of art and clever mechanical devices. It was never completed.

Lake Avernus: in 37 BC Agrippa had joined this to the Bay of Naples to provide a safe harbour. A canal connecting it to Rome would have been an enormous undertaking.

height limits: attempts by Augustus to limit the height of buildings seem to have been unsuccessful, to judge from complaints on the matter in the time of Tiberius (Seneca, *Contr.* 2.9).

359 *rock from Gabii or Alba*: much of the stone used at Rome came from Gabii on the Praeneste road and Marino on the Alban lake.

Sibylline Books: see note to p. 191.

ritual feasts: *sellisternia* involved the propitiation of the goddesses at formal banquets set before their images. Gods reclined (in *lectisternia*); the goddesses were seated.

shameful offences: charges of cannibalism and infanticide are familiar from writers of the second century AD, and this passage suggests that the belief that such practices were common among Christians had taken a firm hold as early as the Neronian period.

Christians: the manuscripts originally read *Chrestiani* and were corrected to *Christiani* by a later hand. *Chrestiani* may possibly be the form by which early Christians were known, perhaps through confusion with the Greek *chrestos*, 'worthy' or 'good'.

the procurator Pontius Pilatus: the rank of procurator for equestrian governors of small provinces was a Claudian innovation, and here Tacitus is being anachronistic. We know from an inscription that Pilate governed as prefect.

360 *those who confessed . . . because they were arsonists*: Tacitus says that, on the evidence of those who confessed, others were arrested, more because of who they were than because they were arsonists. The very strong implication is that the first group, unlike the second, did in fact confess to arson, although some commentators argue that they confessed to being Christians. The fire may have been accidental, but some Christians might have thought it was the destruction by fire that was expected to mark the second coming (as promised in the Book of Revelation) and might consequently have helped it along. They could have been the ones adding to the flames on the grounds that they were 'under orders' (see 15.38).

Acratus and Secundus Carrinas: little else is known of Acratus (see 16.23). Carrinas is probably the son of a rhetorician executed by Caligula (Dio 59.20.6).

361 *gladiators*: gladiators were trained in schools, both state and private. The establishment at Praeneste was presumably an imperial institution, to judge from the military guard.

Spartacus: see note to p. 133.

a stable peace: the conflict with Parthia had come to an end and the temple of Janus was soon to be closed.

361 *comet*: Tacitus mentions only one other comet of Nero's reign (see note to p. 314), following the exile of Rubellius Plautus.

Gaius Piso: exiled by Caligula (Dio 59.8.7), Gaius Calpurnius Piso was recalled by Claudius, under whom he held a consulship (date unknown). He was the object of a contemporary panegyric (the *Laus Pisonis*).

362 *Annaeus Lucanus*: the poet Lucan, author of *De Bello Civili* on the civil conflict between Caesar and Pompey; nephew of Seneca. He was 26 when forced to commit suicide.

Claudius Senecio: he has been earlier identified as a henchman of Nero (see 13.12); the others on the list are known only from this passage.

Faenius Rufus: see 13.22, 14.51. In AD 62, he was appointed joint prefect of the praetorians with Tigellinus.

363 *Volusius Proculus*: he was not actually mentioned in the account of Agrippina's murder but it was organized by his commander at Misenum, who presumably had a number of subordinate assistants.

364 *detested abode*: the allusion is clearly to the Golden House (see 15.42), but it can not yet have been ready for occupation and in fact Nero at the time was living elsewhere (see 15.55).

Lucius Silanus: he was the son of Marcus Silanus (the 'golden sheep', see 13.1) and nephew of Decimus Silanus (see 15.35), and thus the only living male descendant of Augustus other than Nero.

Gaius Cassius: the famous legal scholar (see note to p. 241), Gaius Cassius Longinus was uncle of Lucius Silanus through Cassius' marriage to Junia Lepida.

Ceres: the festival of Ceres was held 12–19 April. Games were held in the Circus Maximus on the last day.

365 *Salus . . . Ferentinum*: the text is uncertain here, but it seems that Tacitus was referring to a single temple but was not sure about the deity's name. The town is almost certainly Ferentinum in Etruria.

another marriage: Tacitus suggests cryptically that Piso intended to marry Antonia should the conspiracy be successful and should he be appointed as successor.

betrayal: Plutarch (*Moralia* 6.505) gives a variant explanation that the conspiracy was betrayed by a careless comment from an indiscreet conspirator.

366 *Gardens of Servilius*: their precise location is uncertain, but Nero went there on a later occasion (Suetonius, *Nero* 47.1) when contemplating flight to Ostia; thus they must presumably have lain in that direction.

Epaphroditus: he was *a libellis* to Nero and later assisted his suicide, and was executed for so doing by Domitian (Suetonius, *Domitian* 14.4).

367 *Annaeus Seneca*: his possible role in the conspiracy is uncertain. Dio (62.24.1) presents him as a ringleader. Tacitus leaves the question of his involvement open.

Glitius Gallus: he was perhaps connected to Corbulo through the latter's mother, first married to a Publius Glitius Gallus.

Annius Pollio: probably the son of the Annius Vinicianus mentioned at 6.9, and hence brother of Vinicianus Annius (15.28).

Germans: Batavians, who, from Augustus to Galba, made up the personal bodyguard of the imperial family.

369 *Pompeia Paulina*: she was probably the sister of Pompeius Paulinus, legate of Upper Germany in AD 56 (see note to p. 299) and daughter of an identically named equestrian from Arles (Pliny, *NH* 33.143).

371 *a long work*: given the time constraints, it seems unlikely that Seneca could have composed at any great length. The work has not survived. It may have been destroyed by Nero.

Statius Annaeus: otherwise unknown, but his name suggests that he was a client of Seneca, probably his former slave.

Athens: the allusion is to the famous death of Socrates.

372 *of his own accord*: presumably Scaevinus is urging Faenius to take the initiative and confess before he is accused.

373 *Statilia Messalina*: reputedly rich, clever, and beautiful, the granddaughter of Titus Statilius Taurus (see note to p. 132); she became Nero's third wife. She had reputedly been married four times previously.

374 *poem*: *carmen* here probably refers to part of a poem. The reference may be to *De Bello Civili* 3.635–46, involving a sea-fight in which one of the participants is wounded by a grappling iron and bleeds to death.

Pompeius . . . Domitius: these men were presumably tribunes of the praetorian guard, but no other information on them is available.

Novius Priscus: consul of AD 78.

Glitius Gallus . . . Egnatia Maximilla: their place of exile was Andros, where an inscription records them as patrons and benefactors.

375 *Rufrius Crispinus*: he had once been praetorian prefect, removed by Agrippina (11.1, 12.42). He was exiled to Sardinia.

Verginius Flavus: a teacher of rhetoric mentioned by Quintilian (*Institutio Oratoria* 7.4.40).

Caesennius Maximus: philosopher and friend of Seneca (Seneca, *Ep.* 87.2).

grain-rations: soldiers had payment for rations deducted from their pay. The grant of free rations represented a de facto pay-increase.

Petronius Turpilianus: he had been consul in 61 and afterwards governor of Britain (see 14.29, 39).

Cocceius Nerva: the future emperor. At this time he would have been about 33.

Nymphidius Sabinus: he played an important role in the events of 68. After Nero's death he was put to death by the soldiers of Galba, who claimed that he was plotting to make himself emperor. Plutarch (*Galba* 9) says that Caligula was a boy when Nymphidius was born and that his father was actually a gladiator.

376 *Junius Gallio*: born Annaeus Novatus, he was adopted by Junius Gallio (see 6.3). Consul in 55, he had earlier refused, when governor of Achaea in 51/2, to listen to the charges of the Jews against Paul (Acts 18: 12–16). He was forced into suicide in 66. His accuser Clemens is otherwise unknown.

Julius Vindex: Vindex, governor of Lugdunensis, initiated a major rebellion against Nero in 68, which was crushed by Verginius Rufus.

records of the Senate: the notion of a consul-designate proposing the worship of a living emperor in Rome is remarkable and it may be because of this that Tacitus uniquely cites his own scrutiny of the *acta senatus*.

Anicius Cerialis: he committed suicide in the following year (AD 66).

BOOK SIXTEEN

377 *Quinquennial Games*: see note to p. 313. Suetonius (*Nero* 21.1) claimed that although Nero got the year right, he moved the day forward.

378 *a poem*: Dio (62.29) reports that the poem was part of his Trojan epic.

he entered the theatre again: after first performing as a poet, Nero returned to the theatre to perform as a lyre-player. Suetonius (*Vit.* 4) reports that Nero left the theatre and came back only in response to a popular demand, conveyed to him through Vitellius, to return to perform on the lyre.

379 *Vespasian*: Titus Flavius Vespasianus, the future emperor. Apart from an allusion to his frugality (see 3.55), there is no other reference to Vespasian in the extant *Annals*, but he would presumably have appeared in the missing section on Britain and the Jewish rebellion (after the extant Book 16). Suetonius (*Vesp.* 4.4) and Dio (66.11.2) both tell this story, Suetonius adding that he was effectively banished frowm the centre of activity until his appointment to handle the Jewish rebellion.

the normal Roman practice: Pliny (*NH* 7.187) in fact states that cremation was not an old Roman custom but an expedient adopted to dispose of corpses after wars and that it only later made its way to Rome.

the Mausoleum of the Julii: the Mausoleum of Augustus, in the Campus Martius (see note to p. 278).

state funeral: Pliny (*NH* 12.83) claims that more spices were burned at Poppaea's funeral than the annual produce of Arabia.

the bust of Gaius Cassius: see notes to pp. 135 and 155; mere private possession of the busts of Brutus and Cassius was not in fact illegal, and their birthdays were celebrated by people with republican sympathies (Juvenal 5.36).

380 *Calpurnius Fabatus*: he survived until the time of Pliny the Younger, who married his granddaughter Calpurnia and wrote to him on a number of occasions.

Lucius Vetus: Lucius Antistius Vetus, consul in 55 at the same time as Nero (see 13.11), supporter of Rubellius Plautus (see 14.48). His daughter Pollitta is called Antistia at 14.22.

381 *on equal terms*: on principle, freedmen were prohibited from bringing criminal charges against their patrons and could be punished for doing so.

a principal heir: Suetonius (*Nero* 32.2) reports that Nero enacted legislation that the estates of those who had omitted the emperor should go to the emperor's private *fiscus* and that even the lawyers who had written up such wills should be punished.

382 *amongst the couriers of the tribunes*: an interesting piece of evidence that not only the magistrates but also their assistants were assigned reserved seats in the theatre.

Maius . . . Germanicus: Nero himself bore those names, and it is unnecessary to see here an honour intended for his adoptive father and his maternal grandfather.

disaster in Lugdunum: Seneca (*Ep*. 91.14) reports that Lugdunum was burnt down in the hundredth year since its foundation as a colony, that is, in AD 58, and Nero's gesture may belong to some seven years after the event.

I have already mentioned: see 14.48–9.

383 *nobody would witness Anteius' will*: Roman law required that a will be witnessed by seven individuals, all Roman citizens.

384 *In this case*: Tacitus' train of thought in this section is far from clear.

prefect of the praetorian guard: he had been removed through the intercession of Agrippina (see 12.42).

consular insignia: he appears to have been the first praetorian prefect to have been so honoured, although at 11.4 he is recorded as having received the lesser praetorian insignia.

calling in the debts: Lucan was known to be wealthy (Juvenal 7.79) and it appears that his estate was not confiscated after his death.

forged: the reasoning is not totally clear, but Tacitus seems to be saying that it was believed that Nero had forged this part of the will to justify one death and to bring about another.

385 *Not long afterwards . . . Gaius Caesar*: Dio (59.25.5^b) has a different version, claiming that in AD 40 Nicius (*sic*) Cerialis and his son Sextus Papinius were arrested and tortured and that the son turned informant. Note also that Seneca (*De ira* 3.18.3) says that Papinius was tortured on a whim, not through a judicial process.

'arbiter of good taste': the phrase *arbiter elegantiae* should not be taken as an official title but rather perhaps a humorous self-reference. It is largely on the basis of this passage that this Petronius has been identified with the Petronius who composed the *Satyricon*, which some have associated with the 'depravities' mentioned in the next chapter.

386 *as I have noted*: see 14.12.

divine honours were decreed to Poppaea: Tacitus does not mention the apotheosis in his account of Poppaea's funeral (16.6). She is identified as DIVA (goddess) on Neronian coinage, and Dio (63.26.5) mentions that Nero consecrated a temple to her.

Capito Cossutianus: Tacitus earlier recorded the accusations made against him by the Cilicians (see 13.33), but without mentioning any role by Thrasea.

the customary oath: the oath to maintain the acts of the princeps was taken in 1 January of each year.

prayer-offerings: prayers for the well-being of the state were taken on 1 January, and for the well-being of the princeps on 3 January of each year.

387 *attended diligently*: under the republic, senators were fined for non-attendance. Enforcement had become lax, though restored by Augustus and Claudius. It appears that it had been allowed to lapse again under Nero (see also 16.27).

Gaius Julius Caesar and Marcus Cato: Cato of Utica led the republican opposition against Caesar.

stiff and gloomy: the morose airs of the Stoics were notorious. Suetonius (*Nero* 37.1) makes Thrasea's gloomy expression the only charge against him.

the acts of the deified Augustus and Julius: it is perhaps to be expected that the acts of Tiberius and Caligula were not included in the oath (Dio 59.9.1, Suetonius, *Claud.* 11), but the omission of Claudius is surprising.

Tubero and Favonius: Cicero represents Quintus Aelius Tubero, opponent of the Gracchus brothers, as austere to the point of rudeness (*Brutus* 31.117, *Pro Murena* 36.75). Marcus Favonius, an admirer of Cato of Utica, had a similar reputation.

the rivals . . . flourish: the fall of Gaius Cassius was described at 16.7–9. He is assumed to represent the famous Cassius of the late republic, and Thrasea is thus depicted as emulating Marcus and Decimus Brutus.

Barea Soranus: see note to p. 261. He was consul in 52, but the date of his governorship of Asia is not known.

the harbour of Ephesus: notoriously prone to silting up because of the mud deposits of the River Cayster.

388 *Tiridates*: he journeyed from Parthia with a large retinue and met Nero in Naples, to be accompanied from there to Rome.

king-like: no irony need be intended. Tacitus' reference is to the arbitrary behaviour of an eastern king.

389 *Rusticus Arulenus*: Tacitus records (*Agr.* 2.2) that Lucius Junius Rusticus Arulenus was put to death under Domitian for his biography of Thrasea, and that the books were burned. Pliny (*Ep.* 1.14.2) thought highly of him and was a friend of his brother.

futile: the tribune's veto could be overridden by the tribunician authority of the princeps.

civilians, their swords not concealed: ordinary citizens were strictly prohibited from bearing arms (see 4.21, 11.22). On this occasion they even displayed them openly.

Curia: the Curia could mean whatever building the Senate happened to use for their session. Here it almost certainly refers to the official location, the Curia Iulia built by Augustus. It seems to have survived the great fire, since it is recorded as having burned down in the time of Titus.

quaestor: the emperor seems to have had two personal quaestors, paralleling the quaestors who served proconsuls in the provinces. Their duties, beyond bringing imperial messages to the Senate, are obscure, but in this case the task was to read out the emperor's speech. Tacitus probably held this office (see the Introduction).

Helvidius Priscus: this is the first certain mention of the famous Stoic in the extant *Annals*, unless he is the person of that name at 12.49 and 13.28 (see notes to pp. 259 and 285). He was married to Thrasea's daughter Fannia. Following his exile (see 16.33), he became praetor and was banished a second time (and executed) under Vespasian. There is a detailed account of him at Tacitus, *Hist.* 4.5.

Paconius Agrippinus: another distinguished Stoic, possibly the son of the Marcus Paconius who may have been brought down after the fall of Sejanus (see note to p. 130). His modest demeanour at the time of his trial was acclaimed in antiquity.

390 *Curtius Montanus*: although required to retire from public life (see 16.33), he played a prominent role in the Senate after the accession of Vespasian.

worldwide peace: on the termination of military action in Armenia, Nero closed the temple of Janus, a symbol of peace throughout the empire (Suetonius, *Nero* 13.2).

father: the action of his father Marcus Paconius is not recorded and may have appeared in the missing section of Book 5. Suetonius (*Tib.* 61.6) reports that Tiberius imprisoned him and forgot about him, but on being reminded put him to death.

391 *consuls' tribunal*: consuls presided over trials in the Senate and their curule chairs were set up in a prominent place, at either side of the princeps.

altar: it has been suggested that the Senate was meeting in the temple of Venus (see 16.27), but it may be that an altar of Victory was attached to the Curia.

Publius Egnatius': Dio (62.26.2) reports that he was well rewarded for his role in these events. He did however pay later, when in 70 he was exiled (see Tacitus, *Hist.* 4.10, 40; 40.4).

the Stoic sect: we know from Juvenal (3.117) that he was educated at a famous school of philosophy at Tarsus, said to have surpassed even Athens and Alexandria.

392 *Cassius Asclepiodotus*: Dio (62.26.2) informs us that he returned from exile under Galba.

392 *five million sesterces*: the smallest sum mentioned exceeds the minimum senatorial census, and the rewards paid to the accusers would almost certainly have exceeded the one-fourth of the property of the condemned to which they were entitled by law.

quaestor: each consul had attached to him a quaestor, who would be the appropriate person to convey the sentence to the accused, since the consul presided at the trial.

Demetrius: he was much admired by Seneca, exiled by Vespasian (Suetonius, *Vesp.* 13; Dio 66.13.3). The Cynics in many ways were the precursors to the Stoics and had been somewhat eclipsed by them, but were starting to regain some of their ground.

Arria's: her mother had volunteered to die along with her husband Caecina Paetus, involved in the rebellion of Scribonianus in 42. The younger Arria lived and later, under Domitian, went into exile along with her daughter, both returning under Nerva.

393 *young man!*: it is not clear whether these words were addressed to the quaestor (the minimum age was 25) or Helvidius. The latter, however, seems to have been a plebeian tribune ten years earlier (see note to p. 285) and he must now have been at least 37.

GLOSSARY OF ROMAN TERMS

aedile magistrate between the ranks of quaestor and praetor; his duties generally related to city administration

assemblies groupings of the Roman citizens convened to carry out specific tasks. There were four main assemblies: (*a*) the centuriate assembly (*comitia centuriata*), organized in 'centuries' according to wealth, convened to elect senior magistrates and to pass legislation; (*b*) the curiate assembly (*comitia curiata*) based originally on the thirty *curiae* or parishes; (*c*) the tribal assembly (*comitia tributa*), representing the thirty-five Roman 'tribes', convened to elect junior magistrates and to pass limited legislation; and (*d*) the plebeian council (*concilium plebis*), convened to elect tribunes of the plebs and plebeian aediles, and to pass *plebiscita*, which were binding on the whole state

augur a member of one of the four priestly colleges with expertise in divination based on the characteristics and behaviour of birds

augury of safety an obscure ritual involving a query to the gods whether it was permissible to offer prayers for the safety of the nation. The ritual had been revived by Augustus

auspices strictly speaking, interpretation of the flight of birds, also applied more generally to interpretation of other phenomena; auspices would be taken at the outset of major undertakings

auxiliaries elements of the Roman army made up of non-citizens, distinguished from legionaries, who were citizens

censor magistrate charged with public morality, most importantly in supervising the citizen list and the rolls of the Senate; in the imperial period, the emperors discharged the duties of the censor

centurion the commander of a legionary 'century', consisting originally of 100 men but by the imperial period of 80

civic crown a crown made of oak-leaves awarded for saving the life of a citizen

cognomen the third element of a Roman name

cohort an operational unit of the Roman army, ten to a legion; the term is also used of independent units of the auxiliaries

colony originally a settlement of Roman citizens, usually veterans; later the status could be conferred on other towns as a mark of distinction

consul the senior Roman magistrate, elected in pairs. During the republic, consuls exercised military command. In the imperial period, the consuls appointed at the beginning of the year (*ordinarii*) would routinely step down at some point in the year and their places were taken by substitutes (*suffecti*). The emperor regularly held the consulship

Curia the Senate House in Rome; the word can be applied to the specific official building in the Forum Romanum or to whichever building was used by the Senate at any given time

curule the term was originally applied to a special chair on which certain senior magistrates were allowed to sit; it was eventually applied to the senior magistrates entitled to use it, especially the consuls, praetors and the patrician aediles, and, on occasion, priests (see 2.83)

decurion member of a local senate

denarius silver coin, worth four sesterces

dictator a magistrate elected during the republic in an emergency; he would hold office for six months

equestrian an order originally related to service in the cavalry, whose members are often referred to as 'knights'. It required a property qualification of 400,000 sesterces. Although not eligible for the Roman Senate, members of the order played an important part in the administration of the empire in the imperial period, and held certain key offices, such as the prefectures of Egypt and of the praetorian guard

fasces a bundle of rods binding an axe that symbolized the authority of senior magistrates to impose punishment; they were carried by a lictor during a magistrate's progress, the rank of the magistrate indicated by the number of fasces

fasti official lists of important events in Rome or in other cities, in the form of a calendar; often published on inscribed tablets

Father of the Nation in the republic, this title was conferred first on Cicero for exceptional service to the state. It was awarded to Augustus in 2 BC. He considered it his most significant honour and initially refused it. Tiberius seems never to have accepted the title, although it is found on coins and inscriptions outside Italy; even Caligula delayed accepting it

fire and water from the early period the formal sentence of exile in Rome was defined as an interdiction of fire and water (*aquae et ignis interdictio*)

fiscus the private funds of the emperor, paradoxically derived from sources that were essentially public, and used for public expenditures

flamen member of a specialized priesthood, with responsibility for a specific god. The chief flamens were those of Jupiter (the *Flamen Dialis*), Mars and Quirinus, and flamens were also assigned to the cult of deified emperors

Game of Troy a complicated cavalry manoeuvre, supposedly of great antiquity, performed by young men, described by Virgil in the *Aeneid* (5.545-603). Its popularity under the Julio-Claudians is explained to some degree by the fictitious connection between Iulus (son of the Trojan founder of the Roman people, Aeneas) and Julius Caesar

imagines the funeral masks of distinguished ancestors were kept displayed on house walls; during funerals of a member of the family they were worn by actors who walked in the procession

Imperator during the republic a victorious general would be given the salutation of *Imperator* (Commander) by his troops and awarded a crown of bay-leaves in the field; legionary commanders served as Augustus' legates and the salutations that followed their successes became the prerogative of the emperor

imperium the power to command, vested for a fixed period in magistrates of a certain rank

knight, *see* EQUESTRIAN

legate a flexible term with three main applications: (*a*) an individual delegated to a particular task; (*b*) the officer in charge of a legion; (*c*) the governor of an imperial province

legion the major operational unit of the Roman army, made up of between five and six thousand men, all Roman citizens, commanded by a legate appointed by the emperor; each legion eventually had a hundred and twenty cavalry attached to it

lector attendant who preceded a magistrate and carried the fasces

maiestas, see TREASON LAW

maniple strictly speaking, a military unit made up of two centuries (each of eighty men); Tacitus often uses the term loosely to refer generally to a unit of soldiers

oath of obedience on 1 January of each year, an oath was taken to uphold the acts of the emperor, and of earlier emperors; it eventually became the practice for senior magistrates to take an annual oath to uphold the *acta* of the emperors, an extension in some ways of the republican practice of magistrates taking an oath to uphold the laws

ovation a lesser triumph; the victorious commander would wear myrtle rather than laurel, and enter the city on foot

patrician member of an exclusive branch of the Roman aristocracy that controlled power in the early republic; the rank could only be inherited for most of the republican period, but as the numbers fell new grants of patrician status were made by Julius Caesar and his successors

plebeian tribune magistrate originally elected to protect the plebeians against the patricians; during the republic, the office was important because of the right to veto and to initiate legislation, while the person of the holder was inviolate; in the imperial period the importance declined and the rank became a routine stage between the quaestorship and praetorship

plebs originally, the order of citizens who were not patrician; Tacitus tends to use the term broadly of the common people of Rome, those not in the equestrian or senatorial classes

Pontifex Maximus the senior priest of Rome; from 12 BC the office was held by the emperor

pontiffs members of one of the four priestly colleges of Rome

praenomen the first element in the name of a Roman man, the 'given' name; there was a very limited number of such names

praetor the magistrate second in seniority after the consul. His main task was to preside over the courts. In the early republic praetors governed provinces, and Tacitus is fond of the archaic use of the term (see e.g. 1.74, 2.77, 4.43, 12.60, where it is translated as 'governor'). In the administration of his legal duties the *praetor peregrinus* (literally, the 'foreign' praetor) had responsibility for lawsuits in which one of the parties was a foreigner, as distinct from the *praetor urbanus* (literally, the 'urban' praetor), who dealt with cases involving citizens

praetorian guard the imperial guard, originally made up of nine cohorts, commanded by a prefect or pair of prefects; the term 'praetorian' could also be used of the authority of an ex-praetor

prefect this term means basically 'the person placed in charge', and could have a range of applications, both military and administrative. The more significant military *praefecturae* are prefecture of an auxiliary unit or of the fleet, prefecture of the camp (the holder was second in rank to the legionary legate and had authority over the troops in the legate's absence), and prefecture of the praetorian guard or of the fire service (*vigiles*). The more significant administrative *praefecturae* are the governorship of Egypt or of smaller administrative districts (the latter had the titles of 'procurator' (q.v.) from Claudius on), and the prefecture of the grain supply (*praefectus annonae*). All these *praefecturae* were held by equestrians, but a small number were held by senators, the most important being the ancient republican office of city prefect (*praefectus urbi*). By the late republic the city prefect's duties were largely ritual, but his functions were revived by Augustus, and he was given responsibility for maintaining order in the city and commanding the city police (the *cohortes urbanae*); he was allowed summary justice in dealing with minor criminal cases and gradually assumed responsibility for more serious cases

Prince of the Youth 'leader of the youth', a title first given to Gaius and Lucius Caesar and eventually used for all intended heirs to the principate

proconsul the governor of a public province, chosen by lot

procurator a highly flexible term. It could be used of a private agent or bailiff on an estate. At the other end of the scale, from Claudius on, the term is used of governors of smaller administrative districts, like Judaea. There were also procurators who oversaw financial matters relating to the imperial properties within the provinces, but, in a process that is not too clear, some of them eventually assumed official administrative duties, as 'provincial' procurators, serving in subordinate roles to the governors in both the imperial and public provinces. The position was held by equestrians or freedmen

propraetor the governor of a province with the rank of praetor; legates (governors) of even major imperial provinces held this rank, so as to be outranked by the consular authority of the emperor

province originally, the term referred to the sphere of competence of a magistrate, but it came to have a more geographical character, designating individual overseas territories governed by Rome. Following the Augustan settlement provinces were of two types: (*a*) 'imperial', in the less-settled part of the empire, housing elements of the Roman army, with governors appointed directly by the emperor; governors were usually of the senatorial class, and bore the title of legate, but some smaller districts were governed by equestrians with the rank of procurator from Claudius on (the title of prefect is usual earlier); Egypt was a major imperial province in its own class, governed by an equestrian prefect; (*b*) 'public', in the more stable areas, with rare exceptions not housing troops; public provinces were governed by proconsuls, men of the senatorial class elected by lot. These latter provinces are sometimes misleadingly referred to as 'senatorial'

publicani a company of men in each province who collected state revenues for a profit, and often proved ruthless in exacting the maximum return; they are the 'publicans' of the New Testament

quaestor the lowest of the major magistracies, granting the holder membership of the Senate; their duties were mainly financial, although two were elected annually as quaestors of the emperor

quindecimvir a member of a board of fifteen, one of the four priestly colleges; their main responsibility was the consultation of the Sibylline Books and the organization of the Secular Games; Tacitus held the office (11.11)

relegation a limited form of banishment that entailed the loss of property but not of citizen rights

Secular Games celebrated in Rome for three days and nights to mark the end of one era (*saeculum*) and the beginning of another; they were held on 21 April, the traditional birthday of the city

Senate the senior governing body of the Roman state, made up of ex-magistrates of the rank of quaestor and above, or of other individuals deemed worthy by the censor or by the emperor. In the Augustan period, the number was approximately six hundred, each with a census rating of one million sesterces. The term is used also for governing bodies outside of Rome. Resolutions of the Senate (*consulta*) did not yet in the Julio-Claudian period have the force of law, but technically had to be enacted by the popular assembly

sesterce (sestertius) the highest-value base-metal Roman coin, made of an alloy of zinc and copper; used by the Romans as the basic unit to express monetary values, with the symbol HS. Monetary equivalence is a dubious concept, but it might be noted that the annual pay of a legionary 'private' in the Julio-Claudian period was 900 HS

Sibylline Books sacred works containing oracular verses, supposedly sold to Tarquinius Priscus by one of the Sibyls, prophetic priestesses who delivered their prophecies in a state of ecstasy

sortition the taking of lots; governors of senatorial provinces were normally chosen by lot, although the process was not totally random; the key provinces of Africa and Asia were assigned by a lot taken only among senior senators

toga the traditional public garb of respectable Roman men, made of fine white wool. Young boys wore the *toga praetexta*, distinguished by a purple border. At about the age of 14, they put it aside in favour of a plain white version, the *toga virilis*, in a ceremony that marked the transition to manhood. The wearing of the *toga praetexta* was resumed by those entering into curule magistracies

tortoise formation a tactic in which the shields were linked into a kind of protective shell above the heads of the soldiers

treason law the laws against treason (*maiestas*) were the main source of fear and resentment under the principate. Under the republic, they seem initially to have been aimed against incompetence rather than criminality. By the time of Sulla they were used to restrain ambitious generals. From Augustus on, they offered protection against verbal abuse and slander (although such protection existed under the republic, if never invoked), with the corollary that an insult to the emperor or his family was an insult to the state; also, penalties grew increasingly severe; later in Tiberius' reign, banishment or the death penalty were not uncommon

treasury the state treasury, housed in the temple of Saturn on the Capitoline Hill, a repository for senatorial documents; the term is used also of the 'military' treasury established by Augustus to fund the pensions of veterans

tribune (military) an officer, six to a legion, acting as adjutants to the legate; five were equestrians, professional soldiers serving long-term; one would be a young man from a senatorial family, for whom the office was a stage in a public career

tribunician authority emperors did not assume the actual office of tribune of the plebs, but were granted the tribunes' authority (*tribunicia potestas*) and their sacrosanctity; this authority was, in many ways, the constitutional foundation of the imperial position, and emperors dated their accession from the time of its bestowal

triumph the procession led by a victorious commander through the streets of the city of Rome up to the Temple of Jupiter on the Capitoline Hill; the procession would be accompanied by war booty and prisoners of war. The triumph conferred enormous prestige on the celebrant and in the imperial period was restricted to members of the imperial family

triumphal honours/insignia (*ornamenta triumphalia*) legates of the emperor could not celebrate personal triumphs and their victories were recognized by the right to wear the garb of the *triumphator*

triumvir the term is most commonly used of the three members of the triumvirate, the pact of Marcus Antonius, Aemilius Lepidus, and Octavian concluded in 43 BC

vexillarii soldiers belonging to a *vexillatio* or subdivision of a legion

vigiles members of a fire service organized by Augustus for Rome in AD 6; the service consisted of seven cohorts, commanded by an equestrian prefect; occasionally the *vigiles* were called upon for broader duties related to law and order

vows a reciprocal arrangement in Roman religion, whereby the individual promised certain offerings to the gods on the understanding that the gods would first provide a service

GLOSSARY OF PEOPLES AND PLACES

For clarity and simplicity some geographical names, such as Iraq and Georgia, are used anachronistically. General architectural and topographical sites that are qualified by a specific name are indexed under that name (with the exception of 'Forum'). For instance, 'theatre of Pompey' is indexed under 'Pompey, theatre of'.

Achaea Roman province comprising much of Greece
Actium promontory on the west coast of Greece, scene of a famous naval battle in 31 BC
Adiabene region in the west of Iraq
Adrana the River Eder
Aedui a people from the area between the Loire and the Saône, with their capital at Autun
Aegeae (1) town in western Asia Minor; (2) town in southern Asia Minor; the latter is referred to at 13.9
Aegium coastal town in the northern Peloponnese
Aequi a people living to the east of Rome
Africa Roman province, comprising roughly modern Tunisia and northern Libya
Alba Longa ancient city south-east of Rome
Albani tribe in Georgia
Alexandria the famous foundation of Alexander the Great in Egypt, a city of major importance in the Julio-Claudian period
Aliso outpost on the River Lippe in Germany
Amanus mountain range in the south of Asia Minor
Amisia the River Ems
Amorgos island in the Aegean
Ampsivarii a northern Germanic people between the Ems and the Weser
Amynclan Sea region off the coast of Campania
Ancona town on the east coast of Italy
Anemurium town on the south coast of Asia Minor
Andecavi a people of Gaul in the area of Anjou
Angrivarii a people in the area of the Weser
Anthemusias town of ancient Mesopotamia
Antioch capital of the province of Syria, in southern Asia Minor
Antium Anzio, city on the west coast of Italy
Aorsi a people east of the Sea of Azov
Apamea city on the River Maeander in western Asia Minor

Aphrodisias important city on the south-west coast of Asia Minor

Apollonis town in western Asia Minor

Apulia Puglia, a region of southern Italy

Aquitania, *see* LONG-HAIRED GAUL

Arabia the land mass between the Red Sea and the Persian Gulf

Ara Maxima altar near the north-west of the Circus, traditionally built by Evander after Hercules had killed the cattle-stealer Cacus

Arar the River Saône

Araxes the Aras, a major river flowing through Asia Minor, Iran, Armenia, and Azerbaijan and entering the Caspian

Arcadia central mountainous region of the Peloponnese

Arduenna the Ardennes region of Belgium and France

Arii the people of Aria, a region in north-west Afghanistan and eastern Iran

Armenia country occupying the plateau east of the Euphrates, once a separate kingdom of Urartu, then incorporated into the Persian empire and a source of continuous struggle between Rome and Parthia

Armenia Minor country to the west of the Euphrates and Armenia proper, between Pontus and Cappadocia, in north-east Asia Minor

Arnus the River Arno in Tuscany

Arsamosata city near the Euphrates in Armenia

Arsanias river in north-east Asia Minor

Artaxata the capital of Armenia, located on the River Araxes

Artemita Parthian town some thirty miles north-east of Baghdad

Asia Roman province, located in the western area of Asia Minor

Atropatene the name of Azerbaijan from the time of Alexander the Great until the Arab conquest of Iran, after which Arabs modified the name to Azerbaijan

Augustodunum Autun, city in central France

Augustus, Mausoleum of the enormous tomb built by Augustus at the north end of the Campus Martius

Augustus, temple of located somewhere between the Capitoline and Palatine hills; not completed until the reign of Caligula

Auzea forested area in Algeria

Avernus, Lake small lake formed in a volcanic crater near Cumae in south-central Italy

Bactria region roughly equivalent to Afghanistan, between the Oxus and the Hindu Kush

Baetica part of a province originally called Further Spain, created as a senatorial province by Augustus

Baiae fashionable resort on the Bay of Naples

Balearic Islands group of islands, the major being Majorca and Minorca, part of the province of Hispania Tarraconensis

Barium Bari, Adriatic port of southern Italy

Bastarnae a people of uncertain origin, perhaps Germano-Celtic, in the Danube delta area

Batavians a people located between the Rhine and the Waal

Belgae a people of north-east Gaul, in the area north of the Seine and Marne

Belgica, *see* LONG-HAIRED GAUL

Beneventum hill-town in Campania, north of Naples

Bithynia province in Asia Minor, on the south coast of the Black Sea

Bononia Bologna, founded as a colony in 189 BC

Bovillae town on the Appian Way, ten miles from Rome, traditionally founded by Iulus, son of Aeneas and founder of the Julian *gens*

Brigantes powerful tribe in the north of Britain

Bructeri a people of north-west Germany, from the area of the River Lippe

Brundisium Brindisi, seaport on the southern Adriatic coast of Italy

Byzantium the ancient predecessor of Constantinople (later Istanbul)

Cadra hill in Rough Cilicia

Caesian forest region probably between the rivers Lippe and Ruhr

Calabria region of Italy, in ancient times essentially the 'heel'

Cales colony founded in 334 BC, in Campania

Camerium settlement in Latium

Campania highly salubrious area of southern Italy much favoured by wealthy Romans

Campus Martius an open area in the north-west of Rome originally left open, but built on in the late republic and even more so in the imperial period; the traditional place of assembly for the election of consuls and praetors

Camulodunum near Colchester, tribal capital of the Trinovantes and first capital of Roman Britannia

Canninefates Germanic tribe in Holland at the Rhine delta

Canopus city about ten miles east of Alexandria, highly important before the founding of the latter; it gave its name to the western branch of the Nile

Capitoline Hill or **Capitol** one of the seven hills of Rome, arguably the most historical and significant, housing the temple of Capitoline Jupiter

Cappadocia region in eastern Asia Minor, annexed by Rome in AD 17

Capreae Capri, island in the Gulf of Naples that became imperial property in 29 BC

Capua city of Campania, north of Naples

Carmania part of the Achaemenid empire, stretching north from the Persian Gulf

Carthage ancient city in North Africa, capital of an empire hostile to Rome, later the capital of the Roman province of Africa

Celenderis port and fortress in Isauria in southern Asia Minor

Cenchreus river near Ephesus in north-west Asia Minor

Cercina one of the Kerkenna islands off the coast of Tunisia

Chalcedon town on the east side of the Bosporus

Chamavi a people living east of the Batavians in the area of the Issel

Cherusci the tribe of Arminius, occupying the area of the middle Weser; after the death of Arminius they were torn by internal faction and lost their significance

Chatti a people to the south of the Cherusci, in the area of the upper Weser, Rome's most powerful German enemy in the Julio-Claudian period

Chauci a powerful tribe in the area of the lower Weser by the North Sea, much admired by Tacitus

Cibyra town in Caria in south-west Asia Minor

Cietae a people from the wild area of western Cilicia

Cilicia region of southern Asia Minor, in the regions of Mts. Taurus and Amanus

Cinithii a people of North Africa

Circus generic name often used specifically of the Circus Maximus between the Palatine, Aventine, and Caelian hills

Cirta town in Numidia

Clanis the River Chiana in Tuscany

Coelaletae a Thracian people in the southern region of Bulgaria

Colchians the people of Colchis, a district on the east of the Black Sea, south of the Caucasus

Colonia Agrippinensis Cologne, colony founded under Claudius

Colophon city of Asia Minor some twenty miles south of Smyrna; nearby was the village of Claros with its famous oracle of Apollo

Comitium the traditional location for the popular assemblies in Rome, next to the Curia

Commagene territory to the west of the Euphrates, bound by Syria, Cilicia, and Cappadocia

Corcyra Corfu, island in the Ionian Sea

Corinth city on the isthmus that joins the Peloponnese to mainland Greece; destroyed by the Romans in 146 BC and refounded as a colony in 44 BC

Corma tributary of the Tigris

Cos island in the Aegean, housing one of the great cult centres of Asclepius

Cosa town on the coast of Tuscany

Crete island combined with Cyrenaica in 27 BC to form a senatorial province

Ctesiphon the ancient capital of the Parthian empire, located on the Tigris some twenty miles south-east of Baghdad

Cumae old Greek settlement on the coast of Campania, famous for its oracle of the Sibyl

Curia the official Senate House in Rome, to the north of the Forum Romanum

Cusus river of Slovakia

Cyme city on the west coast of Asia Minor, about twenty-five miles north of Smyrna

Cyrenaica region that extended from the eastern boundary of Africa to the frontier of Egypt; joined with Crete as a province after 27 BC

Cythnus large island of the Cyclades, south of Ceos

Cyrene Greek city in North Africa, capital of Cyrenaica

Cyrrus city in the province of Syria, about sixty miles north of Antioch

Cyzicus city of Mysia on the southern coast of the Sea of Marmara

Dahae a Scythian people inhabiting the area between the Caspian Sea and the Oxus

Dalmatia region of the eastern Adriatic; subdued by Octavian, it became part of the province of Illyricum and later a separate province bearing its own name

Dandaridae a Sarmatian people between the Caspian and the Sea of Azov

Davara hill in Cappadocia

Decangi a British people of uncertain name (the MS gives *Cangi*); located in North Wales

Delos small island in the Aegean, an important cult centre and traditional birthplace of Apollo

Delphi ancient sanctuary of Apollo in the hills above the Gulf of Corinth

Denthaliatis fertile strip of land at the foot of Mt. Taygetos, an area of dispute between Sparta and Messene

Diana Limnatis, temple of the temple of Diana of the Lakes lay on the upper length of the Nedon on the border between the Spartans and the Messenians

Dii a people of southern Bulgaria

Donusa the most northerly of the Cycladic islands, east of Naxos

Ecbatana city of Iran, the location of the main mint of the Parthians

Edessa capital city of the kingdom of Osroëne in the upper Euphrates region

Elephantine island in the Nile near Aswan

Elymaeans inhabitants of Elam on the northern shore of the Persian Gulf, bordered on the west by the Tigris

Ephesus the major city of the province of Asia, once located on the west coast at the mouth of the Cayster

Erindes unidentified river in northern Iran

Erycus, Eryx mountain in north-west Sicily

Erythrae town on the west coast of Asia Minor, opposite the island of Chios

Ethiopia broad term used of the region south of Egypt

Etruria region in north-west Italy, comprising Tuscany and part of Umbria, the home of the Etruscans

Euboea large island in the Aegean, lying off the coast of mainland Greece

Euphrates the more westerly of the two rivers of Mesopotamia, the longest in western Asia

Fidenae a Sabine settlement about five miles from Rome on the Via Salaria; an insignificant town by the Julio-Claudian period

Flaminian Way the Via Flaminia, a road from Rome to Ariminum (Rimini), constructed by Gaius Flaminius in 220 BC

Flevum stronghold on the North Sea coast, perhaps Velsen

Flora, temple of located near the Circus Maximus (to be distinguished from another temple of Flora on the Quirinal)

Florentia Florence, an insignificant town until the late empire

Formiae town in Campania on the Appian Way

Fors Fortuna, temple of one of several temples of this ancient cult figure in Rome, in the Forum Boarium and elsewhere; the allusion in Tacitus is to a temple dedicated on the right bank of the Tiber in the Gardens of Caesar

Forum Julii Fréjus, a colony and important naval station on the Aurelian Way

Forum the main public area of a town; when used without qualification in the context of Rome it refers to the Forum Romanum, the main public square of Rome to the east of the Capitol

Forum Augusti vast precinct, north of the Forum Romanum and almost at right angles to it

Forum Boarium the ancient cattle market of Rome, bound by the Capitoline, Palatine, and Aventine hills

Forum Holitorium the vegetable market, between the Tiber and the Capitoline Hill, occupied largely by the theatre of Marcellus

Forum Iulium or **Caesaris** north-east of the Forum Romanum, the area surrounded by a colonnade; dedicated by Julius Caesar in 46 BC

Frentani an ancient people on the east coast of central Italy, thought by Strabo to be Samnites

Frisians a people occupying the North Sea coast in what is now modern Friesland, as well as much of the adjoining territory in the coastal area between the Yssel and the Ems

Fucine lake lake of central Italy, drained in the nineteenth century

Fundi Volscian town in Campania, on the Appian Way, noted for its fine wines and villas

Gabii ancient Latin city, some twelve miles east of Rome

Galatia region in central Anatolia, incorporated as a Roman province in 25 BC with its capital at Ancyra (Ankara)

Galilee region of northern Palestine

Garamantes a people in the area of south-west Libya

Gemonian Steps stairs leading from the jail towards the Capitol, on which the bodies of executed criminals were displayed

Germania the Roman military zones in German territory consisted of Lower Germany on the north Rhine, its administrative centre at Cologne, and Upper Germany on the south Rhine, its centre Mainz

Getae a Thracian people in the area of the lower Danube

Gorneae fortress in Armenia

Gotones a people on the east bank of the lower Vistula, later known as the Goths

Gyarus one of the islands of the Cyclades, a common destination for the banished

Hadrumetum Sousse, ancient Phoenician colony in Tunisia; it became very prosperous in the Roman imperial period

Haemus, Mt. the ancient name for the Balkans

Halicarnassus Bodrum, coastal town of Caria in south-west Asia Minor; once noted for its splendour, it was insignificant by the Roman period

Halus town in Parthia

Heliopolis important religious centre in Egypt, about five miles north-east of Cairo

Heniochi a people of the Caucasus

Hercules, temple of there were several temples of Hercules in Rome; Tacitus' reference (15.41) is probably to that of Hercules Victor in the Forum Boarium

Hercynia there is considerable inconsistency in the ancient sources about the location of this region, which lay somewhere between the Rhine and the Carpathians

Hermunduri an ancient Germanic people in the area around Thuringia and northern Bavaria

Hibernia Ireland

Hierocaesaria city of western Asia Minor, north of Smyrna

Hispania Tarraconensis the region encompassed much of the Mediterranean coast of Spain along with the central plateau and the north coast; it became an imperial province under Augustus

Homonadenses a people in the area around southern Galatia and western Cilicia

Hypaepa ancient city of Lydia on the southern slope of the Tmolus

Hyrcania area south of the Caspian, bounded on the east by the Oxus

Iazyges a nomadic tribe from central Asia who migrated to the Ukraine and Moldavia

Iberi a people in the region between the Caucasus range and Armenia

Iceni a people located in Norfolk and Suffolk with their capital at Venta Icenorum, near Norwich

Idistaviso there has been much speculation about the identity of this place in Germany but the topography of Germanicus' campaigns is too obscure to allow a solution

Ilium alternative name for Troy, used particularly for the Roman town

Illyricum confusingly, Illyricum is sometimes used of the province of that name (later Dalmatia), sometimes used more loosely of the Danube area including Pannonia, which became a separate province in about AD 9

Insubrians a people of Gallia Transpadana, around Milan

Interamna town in Umbria on the Flaminian Way

Ituraeans an Arab people in the area north of Damascus, with their capital at Chalcis

Janus, temple of a famous temple of Janus Geminus was located in the Forum Romanum; Tacitus' allusion (2.49) is to a less familiar one in the Forum Holitorium

Julius Caesar, Gardens of located on the right bank of the Tiber to the south-west of the city; these gardens were bequeathed by Caesar to the Roman people

Jupiter Capitolinus, temple of the most significant temple in Rome, located on the Capitoline Hill

Jupiter Stator, temple of the location is uncertain but the general consensus is that it was near the Arch of Titus on the northern slope of the Palatine Hill; the temple was vowed by Romulus if Jupiter would stay the flight of the Romans from the Sabines

Langobardi a people who lived north of the Cherusci, concentrated on the west side of the lower Elbe

Lanuvium ancient Latin city in the Alban Hills

Laodicea (ad Lycum) major city of Phrygia in Asia Minor on a hill overlooking the River Lycus; referred to at 4.55, 14.27

Laodicea (Maritima) coastal town of Asia Minor, opposite northern Cyprus; referred to at 2.80

Latium area of western Italy in the region of Rome, home of the original Latin people

Legerda (if correctly read at 14.25), fortress near the north Tigris, possibly Lidjia on the upper slopes of the Taurus

Lepcitani inhabitants of one of two different towns on the coast of North Africa, Leptis Magna in Libya or Leptis Minor in Tunisia

Lesbos large island just off the north-west coast of Asia Minor

Leucophryne the name apparently derives from an older town on the site of the later Magnesia on the River Maeander; the temple on the site was renowned for its size and beauty

Liber, Libera, and Ceres, temple of located on the slope of the Aventine Hill, near the western end of the Circus Maximus

Libya the Greek name for non-Egyptian North Africa

Ligurians inhabitants of an area in north-western Italy

Limnae a town in the Peloponnese on the boundaries between Laconia and Messenia

Liris river originating in the Apennines, close to the Fucine lake

Long-haired Gaul *Gallia comata*, region of Gaul consisting of the three imperial provinces of Aquitania, Lugdunensis, and Belgica, distinguished from the Romanized senatorial province of Narbonensis

Lucania mountainous region of southern Italy

Lucrine lake this was located in Campania, separated from the sea by a narrow strip of land, and formed into a harbour by Agrippa

Lucullus, Gardens of this magnificent estate was created by Lucius Licinius Lucullus, consul 74 BC; he was notorious for his wealth and extravagance

Lugdunensis, *see* LONG-HAIRED GAUL

Lugdunum Lyons, major city and capital of the province of Gallia Lugdunensis, the birthplace of Claudius

Lugii confederation of tribes, probably Germanic, in the general region of eastern Germany

Luna, temple of located on the Aventine; it may be identical with the temple of Diana on the Aventine, founded by Servius Tullius

Lupia the River Lippe in northern Germany

Lusitania imperial province in Spain organized by Augustus in 27 BC, comprising Portugal and part of western Spain

Lycia region of southern Anatolia, united with Pamphylia in AD 43 to form the province of Lycia

Lydia territory of western Asia Minor, once an independent kingdom with its capital at Sardis; under the Romans it was part of the province of Asia

Macedonia old Balkan kingdom, annexed as a province in 146 BC

Maecenas, Gardens of located on the Esquiline Hill; they became imperial property on Maecenas' death

Magnesia (on Maeander) city a little to the north of the Maeander on a tributary stream; it played a leading role in working with the Romans to defeat Antiochus in 190 BC, and alone in Asia held out against Mithridates in 88 BC; 3.62 presumably refers to this town

Magnesia (on Sipylus) city of western Asia Minor in the Hermus valley; this is the city referred to at 2.47

Marcellus, theatre of located on the southern edge of the Campus Martius

Marcian aqueduct constructed by the praetor Lucius Marcius Rex in 149 BC, it brought Rome its best drinking water, from the Sabine hills

Marcomani a people located in the upper Elbe and Danube regions

Mardi a people in the area of Lake Van, seen by some as ancestors of the modern Kurds

Maritime Alps a small Alpine province formed by Augustus in 14 BC

Mars Ultor, temple of the temple of Mars the Avenger, built by Augustus in the Forum Augusti to commemorate the vengeance wreaked on the assassins of Caesar; dedicated in 2 BC, it became the location for victory insignia

Marsi a people living south of the River Lippe in Germany (to be distinguished from the Marsi of central Italy)

Marus the River Morava

Massilia Marseilles, Greek city on the Mediterranean coast that maintained its Hellenic character after absorption by Rome

Mattiaci a Germanic people from the area of Wiesbaden

Mattium unidentified settlement of the Chatti, probably in the region north of the Rhine and Main, in the area of Wiesbaden and Homburg

Mauretania the northern coastal area of the African continent, stretching from the Roman province of Africa to the Atlantic, incorporated into two provinces by Claudius

Mauri broad term for the people of the western strip of the coast of North Africa

Medes a people akin to the Persians, inhabiting Media, a mountainous area south-west of the Caspian

Melitene capital of the small Hittite kingdom of Malatya in the eastern Taurus

Messenia the south-west region of the Peloponnese

Miletus city of Asia Minor at the mouth of the Maeander; it housed a major temple of Apollo Didymaeus within its territory

Misenum town near Baiae on the north side of the Bay of Naples

Moesia region on the lower Danube, in the area of Serbia and Bulgaria, incorporated as a province some time between Augustus and Claudius

Mona Anglesey; the name Mona is preserved in the Welsh name for the island, Môn

Mosa the River Meuse

Moschi a people located in north-west Armenia; they may be the Meshech of Ezekiel 27: 13, 38: 3

Mosella the River Moselle

Mosteni people of Lydia, in Asia Minor; coin evidence suggests that they were located close to Magnesia on Sipylus

Mulvian Bridge this was located on the Flaminian Way, two miles outside Rome

Musulamians a people of North Africa

Mutina Modena, city on the south side of the Po valley, the scene of a major battle in 44 BC

Myrina city of Mysia in western Asia Minor

Mytilene the main city of Lesbos

Nabataeans a people of the region of north-west Arabia; their chief city was Petra

Nar the River Nera, a tributary of the Tiber, flowing through Umbria

Narnia town of Umbria, settled on a hill overlooking the River Nera

Nauportus town on the Ljubljanica river in Slovenia

Naxos the largest and most fertile of the Cycladic islands

Neapolis Naples, the main city of Campania, founded by Greeks; it kept much of its Greek character during the Roman period

Nemetes a Germanic people living in the region of the Rhine between the Palatinate and the Bodensee

Nicephorium Al Raqqa, city founded by Alexander the Great on the Euphrates

Nicephorius river of Armenia on which Tigranocerta stood, probably a major tributary of the Tigris

Nicopolis colony founded by Augustus on the north side of the Ambracian Gulf, opposite Actium

Ninos the famous city of Nineveh, on the River Tigris

Nisibis ancient Mesopotamian city in south-east Asia Minor, often fought over by Rome and Parthia

Nola city of Campania, close to Naples

Noricum Roman province, formed soon after 16 BC, along the Danube, from the Inn to modern Vienna, between Raetia and Pannonia

Nuceria town of Campania at the foot of Mt. Albino

Numa, palace of the traditional palace of Numa Pompilius, second king of Rome, later the official residence of the *Pontifex Maximus*; given to the Vestals by Augustus

Numantia fortress on the Douro in Spain, centre of Celtiberian resistance to Rome, rebuilt by Augustus

Numidia region in North Africa comprising eastern Algeria and northern Tunisia, incorporated into the province of Africa

Odrysae a Thracian people in the area of southern Bulgaria

Ordovices a people from the centre and north of Wales

Ortygia familiar poetic name for Delos

Osroëne Assyrian kingdom in the area of the upper Euphrates, enjoying considerable independence from the years of 132 BC to AD 244; its capital was Edessa

Ostia the port of Rome at the mouth of the Tiber

Pagyda unidentified river in North Africa

Palatine Hill one of Rome's seven hills, with rich historical associations; the word 'palace' derives from the imperial residence erected on it

Panda unidentified river in the region north of the Black Sea

Pandateria island off the Campanian coast, much employed as a place of exile

Pannonia a Danube province, roughly the equivalent of modern Hungary, originally part of Illyricum but becoming a separate province about the time of the suppression of a major revolt in AD 6

Paphos city located on the west coast of Cyprus, a famous cult centre of Aphrodite

Parthia a kingdom that at its height comprised modern Iran and surrounding territories as far east as Pakistan; the arch-enemy of the Romans

Patavium Padua, in the time of Augustus the wealthiest city of northern Italy

Paulus, Basilica of a structure built on the northern side of the Forum Romanum, begun by Lucius Aemilius Paulus in 55 BC

Pergamum major city of Mysia in Asia Minor, bequeathed to Rome in 133 BC by its last king, Attalus III

Perinthus ancient town settled by the Samians on the north shore of the Sea of Marmara

Perusia Perugia, city perhaps of Etruscan origin, brutally besieged during the conflict between Octavian and Mark Antony

Pharsalus hill-town in Thessaly, the scene of the final great battle between Caesar and Pompey in 48 BC

Philadelphia city of Lydia in Asia Minor, in the valley of the Cogamus; it suffered considerably from earthquakes

Philippi city in eastern Macedonia, the site of the final battles fought by Octavian and Antony against Brutus and Cassius in 42 BC

Philippopolis city on the River Maritsa in southern Bulgaria

Picenum region on the east-central coast of Italy

Placentia Latin colony settled at the juncture of the Po and Trebia rivers on the Aemilian Way in northern Italy

Planasia small island near Elba off the Tuscan coast, used as a place of imprisonment

Pompey, theatre of Rome's first permanent theatre, built in 55 BC near the Campus Martius by Pompey from the wealth that he had amassed during his eastern campaign; restored by Augustus

Pomptine marshes malarial marshes behind Cape Circeo, not successfully drained until the 1930s

Pontus the Black Sea; also the kingdom, later Roman province, along its southern shore

Praeneste Palestrina, town located on a spur of the Apennines just over twenty miles from Rome; a notable villa resort and the location of an enormous temple of Fortuna Primigenia

Propontis the Sea of Marmara, linking the Aegean and the Black Sea

Puteoli port of Campania; it became a major trade centre and the entry point for much of Rome's grain

Pyramus one of the great rivers of Asia Minor; it flowed through a narrow valley of Mt. Taurus to Cilicia and the sea

Quadi a powerful people in the area of modern Moravia and upper Hungary; a formidable foe of Marcus Aurelius

Raetia an Alpine province embracing parts of modern Switzerland, Bavaria, and the Austrian Tyrol

Ravenna important port on the Adriatic coast of northern Italy; made the base of the northern fleet by Augustus

Reate Sabine hill-town in central Italy; birthplace of Vespasian

Rhegium Greek colony founded about 720 BC in the 'toe' of Italy; it retained its Greek character and its prosperity through the imperial period

Rostra the speaker's platform at the north-west corner of the Forum, named after the prows (*rostra*) from enemy ships captured at the battle of Antium in 338 BC which originally decorated it

Sabines an ancient people who inhabited the Apennine region north-east of Rome; in frequent conflict with Rome during their early history, by the late republic they had become thoroughly Romanized

Sabrina the River Severn, rising in mid-Wales and flowing south into the Bristol Channel

Salamis the principal Greek city on the island of Cyprus

Sallust, Gardens of located in the valley between the Quirinal and Pincian hills in Rome; laid out by Sallust the historian, and inherited by his adopted son, from whom it is likely that they passed to Tiberius

Samaritans people of Samaria, the mountainous region of Palestine between Galilee and Judaea

Samnites a warlike people of the southern Apennine region, hostile to Rome for most of the period of the republic

Samos island off the western coast of Asia Minor, housing one of the most celebrated buildings of antiquity, a temple of Juno

Samothrace island in the north-east Aegean, home of the mystery cult of the Cabiri

Sanbulos mountain range in Iran, not positively identified

Santoni a tribe in western Gaul, in the region of Saintes

Sardis capital of the old kingdom of Lydia, incorporated into the province of Asia

Sarmatians a nomadic tribe in two branches, the Roxolani and the Scythians; they migrated to the Danube estuary and over the Carpathians into the plain between the mid-Danube and the Theiss

Saturn, temple of located north of the Sacred Way between the Rostra and the Basilica Julia

Scythia ill-defined region occupied by nomads in modern Russia, Ukraine, and Kazakhstan

Segesta city in north-west Sicily, claiming descent from Troy

Seleucia on Tigris city founded by Seleucus I on the bank of the Tigris opposite the Parthian city of Ctesiphon shortly before 300 BC; it became a centre of some importance

Seleucia Pieria city on the mouth of the Orontes; the usual port of embarkation for Antioch

Semnones a Germanic people from the region between the Elbe and the Oder

Senones a Gallic people from the region of the Seine valley

Sequani a Gallic people from the region of the upper Saône

Seriphos an island in the western Cyclades

Servilius, Gardens of location uncertain; possibly in the south-west of Rome

Silures a people of south Wales; under the leadership of Caratacus they were fierce opponents of Rome

Simbruine lakes lakes formed in the Sabine hills by the River Anio

Sindes unidentified river, possibly the Tejen in Turkmenistan

Sinuessa coastal city located between Naples and Terracina

Siraci a Sarmatian people from between the Caspian and the Sea of Azov

Smyrna Izmir, ancient city on the west coast of Asia Minor at the mouth of the Hermus; refounded on a slightly different site by Alexander, in the Roman period it became one of the most important cities of Asia

Soza unknown town in the area north of the Black Sea

Spartans inhabitants of the city-state of Sparta, which occupied the central projection of the southern Peloponnese

Statilius Taurus, Gardens of located on the Esquiline

Stratonicea city in the valley of the River Caicus in Lydia in Asia Minor

Sublaqueum Subiaco, town in Latium on the River Anio

Suebi a large Germanic group made of several tribes, most significantly the Marcomani, Quadi, and Semnones

Sugambri a German people in the area of the rivers Ruhr and Lippe; in 8 BC Tiberius forcibly settled them on the west bank of the Rhine

Surrentum Sorrento, a coastal town of Campania overlooking the Bay of Naples

Syene Aswan, a trading town on the right bank of the Nile just below the First Cataract

Tanais the River Don

Tarentum ancient city in the south of Italy; once a major seaport, it fell into decay in the late republic

Tarpeian Rock a steep part of the Capitoline from which condemned prisoners were thrown

Tarracina coastal town, located at the edge of the Volscian Hills, in a site commanding the Pomptine marshes

Tarraco capital of Hispania Tarraconensis on the south-east coast of Spain. It received colonial status under Julius Caesar or Augustus and became the first city of Roman Spain

Taunus mountain range in Hessen, Germany

Tauri a people on the south coast of the Crimea

Tauronites a people probably from the Antitaurus region, west of Lake Van

Taurus mountain range in southern Asia Minor

Teleboans inhabitants of a group of islands lying off the coast of Acarnania in north-western Greece

Temnus town in Aeolia in Asia Minor, near the River Hermus

Tencteri a Germanic people located on the east bank of the Rhine

Tenos island of the Cyclades; it was small but housed a celebrated temple of Poseidon

Termestines the people of Termes, a town on the River Douro in Numantia in Hispania Tarraconensis

Teutoburg Forest the site of the Varian disaster in AD 9; thought to be in the area of Kalkreise

Thala town of North Africa, not securely identified

Thebes the old capital of Egypt, a popular tourist site in the Roman period

Thermae bay of the Aegean in north-east Greece

Thessaly area of northern Greece absorbed by the Romans into the province of Macedonia

Thrace region of the Balkans; it became a Roman province in AD 46

Thubursicum small unidentified town in North Africa

Thurii Greek colony founded in the fifth century BC in Bruttium, on the site of the city of Sybaris; it fell into decay in the late-republican period

Tibur Tivoli, town about twenty miles from Rome, famed for its beauty and fine villas

Ticinum Pavia, city of northern Italy on the River Ticino

Tigranocerta city founded in Armenia by Tigranes I, replacing Artaxata as the capital

Tigris the more easterly of the two rivers of Mesopotamia, rising in Armenia

Tmolus mountain range in Lydia in Asia Minor

Torone city of Chalcidice in north-east Greece

Tralles city on the River Meander on the border of Lydia and Caria in Asia Minor

Trapezus Trebizond, trading city on the southern shore of the Black Sea, growing in importance in the early imperial period

Treveri a Gallic tribe with a strong Germanic element, in the Moselle area, with their capital at Trier (Augusta Treverorum); often rebellious, they were apparently pro-Roman during the Tiberian period

Trimetus one of the Tremiti islands off the Adriatic coast of southern Italy, used for political internment in modern as well as ancient times

Trinovantes a people to the south of the Iceni, in Suffolk and Essex, with their capital at Camulodunum

Trisantona the River Trent

Tubantes a Germanic people on the right bank of the north Rhine

Turoni a people of north-west Gaul in the region of Touraine

Tusculum hill-town of Latium some fifteen miles south-east of Rome; a fashionable resort town

Tyre Phoenician city in south Lebanon; a major port and centre of the dye industry, it retained its importance in the Roman imperial period

Ubii a tribe friendly to Rome; resettled from the east to the west bank of the Rhine by Agrippa; their capital was the site of the later Cologne

Umbria mountainous region of central Italy

Usipetes a Germanic people from the region of the north Rhine

Uspe unidentified town to the north of the Black Sea

Vahalis the River Waal

Vangiones a Germanic people from the area of Worms

Vatican district on the west bank of the Tiber, approximating to the modern precinct of St Peter's

Velinus, Lake a small lake fed by the River Velino in the Sabine area

Veneti a tribe of Gallia Transpadana in the area around Padua; they received citizenship from Caesar in 49 BC

Venus Genetrix, temple of located in the centre of the Forum Iulium

Verulamium St Albans, a city of some importance in the early Roman period of Britain

Vesta, temple of circular temple, containing Vesta's sacred flame, built in the Forum Romanum in the third century BC

Vetera Roman military site near Xanten, at the juncture of the Rhine and Lippe

Vienne capital of the Allobroges, an important city of Narbonese Gaul

Vindelici the dominant people of the south Germanic–north Danube region, defeated by Tiberius in 15 BC; Vindelicia was eventually incorporated into the province of Raetia

Visurgis the River Weser in north Germany

Volandum unknown, but must have been south of the Araxes and west of Tigranocerta in Armenia

Vulsci a people of central Italy

Vulsinii Bolsena, town in Etruria

Zeugma town of Commagene; built by Seleucus Nicator to control the crossing of the Euphrates into northern Mesopotamia

INDEX

The text is indexed by book and chapter numbers, the Introduction by page numbers

American Literature

British and Irish Literature

Children's Literature

Classics and Ancient Literature

Colonial Literature

Eastern Literature

European Literature

Gothic Literature

History

Medieval Literature

Oxford English Drama

Poetry

Philosophy

Politics

Religion

The Oxford Shakespeare

A complete list of Oxford World's Classics, including Authors in Context, Oxford English Drama, and the Oxford Shakespeare, is available in the UK from the Marketing Services Department, Oxford University Press, Great Clarendon Street, Oxford OX2 6DP, or visit the website at www.oup.com/uk/worldsclassics.

In the USA, visit www.oup.com/us/owc for a complete title list.

Oxford World's Classics are available from all good bookshops. In case of difficulty, customers in the UK should contact Oxford University Press Bookshop, 116 High Street, Oxford OX1 4BR.